FROM BLACKOUT TO BUNGALOWS...

From Blackout
to Bungalows...

WWII Home Front Wiltshire

&

the Austerity Years 1939–55

JULIE DAVIS

First published in 2016 by
The Hobnob Press, 30c Deverill Road Trading Estate, Sutton Veny,
Warminster BA12 7BZ
www.hobnobpress.co.uk

British Library Cataloguing in Publication Data
A catalogue record for this book is available from the British Library

ISBN 978-1-906978-38-9

Typeset in Adobe Garamond Pro 10.5/12.5pt. Typesetting and origination by John Chandler
Printed by Lightning Source

The cover illustration incorporates Imperial War Museum image H22171, 'Covenanter tanks pass through the village of Stockton in Wiltshire, 7 August 1942', and is reproduced by kind permission of the Imperial War Museum.

Contents

TO GEMMA AND ABI
FOR THEIR NEVERENDING SUPPORT
AND ENCOURAGEMENT
AND TO JIM

Preface

FROM BLACKOUT TO BUNGALOWS is the culmination of an attempt to discover how the reality of Total War during WWII affected the lives of Britain's civilians in rural areas, studying the county of Wiltshire as a case in point. How did the day-to-day lives of local residents change; what were the challenges they really faced, and were the changes that took place only transitory in nature, or did they have long-term repercussions?

The study of events at a local level through the actions of Local Government and those in the communities they served give the ability to delve much deeper into the social history of the Second World War. The chapters have been arranged into topics focusing on the many and varied new arrivals to the county: evacuees, war workers, the military, Land Girls, members of the Pioneer Corps and Prisoners of War. They also chart the additional work which rural-dwelling civilians undertook, the problems they faced and how they were able to continue their journey through the war years. But difficulties during WWII did not end abruptly when victory arrived; there were more challenges yet to face. The issues at both a national level and in a Wiltshire context are charted up to the year 1955, a fitting conclusion after the full elimination of rationing in 1954. It must be noted, however, that in a few instances more recent material has been quoted which particularly highlight the issues involved. Each chapter contains information relating to wartime and the post-war period before concluding with Chapter 12 which looks at general issues in the post-war period and also at specific concerns such as the housing shortage.

In recent years social historians such as Asa Briggs[1] have wanted to see 'individuals, not masses,' but every individual resides within a local community and is affected by it. Material held at regional archives is perfectly placed to fulfil this role, providing us with a different view of Britain in wartime, one of local endeavour and the particular difficulties faced by those trying to maintain stability in a time of turmoil. The focus of research at a local level has been via the Wiltshire & Swindon History Centre; both its Archive and Local Studies Library. The sheer variety of Local Authority material held in the Archive at the Wiltshire and Swindon History Centre is astounding, covering departments set up in wartime such as the Invasion and Civil Defence Committee and also long-standing departments such as that of Education and the County Surveyor. Resources include maps, plans, publicity material and Government reports, circulars and memoranda, photographs, school log books, and the material of organisations such as the Women's Institute. There is also a vast amount of correspondence from central Government, industry, the military and from individuals themselves which in many cases (such as the 1938 planned evacuation scheme) can help to enhance and clarify material from central Government, available from sources such as The National Archives. This fascinating and under utilised resource charts the experiences of Wiltshire people throughout WWII and beyond. The Local Studies Library is a rich resource for published and unpublished memoirs and local history research, printed recollections and oral history, alongside local newspapers. But it is not only regional archives which can help to paint a picture of life in wartime. Local museum collections are also a useful resource in the hunt for knowledge and understanding.

It must be remembered that the material discovered at the Wiltshire and Swindon History Centre is not a full representation of the reality of life during the years 1939–1955; it never could be. The real experiences remain with those individuals who lived through them, and an archive is never a complete collection of material which was created during that time. In Wiltshire, the survival rate of material differs greatly for individual districts within the county, and the effects such as paper shortages and later incidents or processes have had an affect on the survival of documents. It would also be unfair to suggest that this book can accurately provide a full picture of the whole of the county – the amount of material which exists is just too great. The aim therefore has been to provide where possible the most pertinent examples and to provide a general and, so far as possible, representative picture of the events and themes which occurred. However, a picture of Wiltshire during WWII has emerged, giving us a glimpse of what it was like to live in the county during the years 1939–1955.

Wherever possible the examples utilised are Wiltshire based, and those which are not have been described by county as well as by place. The reference WSA has been used for material located at the Wiltshire and Swindon History Centre Archives. The WSHC reference denotes the material held by the Local Studies Library at the Wiltshire and Swindon History Centre, including the Wiltshire Historic Photograph and Print Collection, denoted by a number prefixed with a 'P'.

The author wishes to extend her thanks to all those who have kindly donated material for this publication in the form of photographs and/or memories of the time, either personally themselves or via members of their family or friends, past and present; these have been greatly appreciated. It must also be stated that this book would not have been possible without the painstaking research conducted over many years by many writers, from academics through to local historians and individuals, each of whom has been quoted and/or recorded and referenced as a source, and to whom thanks are due. Thanks must also be given to colleagues at the Wiltshire & Swindon History Centre, especially the Production Team who made all material quickly and easily accessible. Special thanks also go to the author's proof-reader Janis Packham, whose dedication was impeccable.

1
Introduction

A Prelude to War

NEVILLE CHAMBERLAIN BECAME Prime Minister of Britain in May 1937 at the age of 70. In the early 1930s Hitler had risen to power and Mussolini had, as Angus Calder puts it, 'assaulted' Abyssinia. The Spanish Civil war had begun by 1936. Fascism and Nazism were on the rise in Europe, and Chamberlain's stance was to be what he called a 'general scheme of appeasement' with Calder noting that Communist Russia was also on Chamberlain's mind. Members of both the Tory and Labour parties were divided and confused, and the League of Nations (created after World War One) with its idea of 'collective security' was now doomed to failure, although 11.5 million people in Britain voted in a peace ballot in the summer of 1935 (instigated by League supporters) with ten to one in favour of the collective security policy.[1]

Hitler annexed Austria in spring 1938 and Chamberlain flew to meet him on 15 September, sparking what was to become known as the 'Munich Crisis'. By 22 September Hitler had become unhappy at the slow stance both Britain and France were taking regarding Czechoslovakia and Chamberlain went once more to meet him. On 28 September Chamberlain was addressing Parliament when he was handed a note: another invitation to meet Hitler. Calder notes that 'the Czechs were briskly sold out' and the Munich Crisis concluded on 30 September with the signing of the Munich Agreement. Chamberlain flew home with a piece of paper, said to prove that Hitler 'renounced all war-like intentions against Great Britain'. Calder notes the mood of the people: shame, fear... and unease.[2] A treaty of alliance was signed with Poland on 25 August 1939 but on 1 September German troops were moving in[3] although immediately after the war and, in fact, in more recent times, there have been those who have felt that Hitler was not to blame for instigating the Second World War. The British Prime Minister Chamberlain, the US President Roosevelt and the Russian leader Stalin were all purported by various individuals to be instigators in their own right, alongside a situation which began much earlier with the role of the League of Nations after WWI. Some particularly look to Chamberlain's guarantee to Poland and Churchill's refusal to accept a peace offer after 10 May 1940. Others accuse Roosevelt of a planned strategy of war in the Pacific and of intense personal feelings against Hitler.[3 4 5 6 7 8 9]

It was on 3 September 1939 that Prime Minister Neville Chamberlain declared that Britain was at war with Germany. The *Wiltshire Gazette* reported in its 7 September 1939 edition that the 'fateful' announcement had been given at 11.15am. Chamberlain had broadcast from the Chamber Room at No. 10 Downing Street with his fateful message to the people:

> This morning the British Ambassador in Berlin handed the German Government a final note stating that, unless we heard from them by 11 o'clock that they were prepared at once to withdraw their troops from Poland, a state of war would exist between us.
>
> I have to tell you now that no such undertaking has been received, and that consequently this country is at war with Germany.

King George VI broadcast his own message to the people at 6pm that evening from his study at Buckingham Palace.

> In this grave hour, perhaps the most fateful in our history, I send to every household of my people, both at home and overseas, this message spoken with the same depth of feeling for each one of you as if I were able to cross your threshold and speak to you myself…

A copy of his message was to be sent to every household in the country for people to keep as 'a permanent record'.

At Freshford on the Somerset/Wiltshire border, the author Fay Inchfawn noted that: 'Peace had gone from us, so it seemed – suddenly and imperceptibly. We had not realised we had lost the precious thing which had made our blessedness. None of us were free – as we had once known freedom. We were all of us restricted in one way or another – but this was a trivial matter compared with the new realization of the uncertainty of life.'[10]

The *Wiltshire Times* on 9 September 1939 printed a poem by a Trowbridge resident, Mrs Lily Cairns, who was reflecting on the tumultuous events which had taken place:

> The Gentleman of England,
> You know who I mean,
> Perhaps you've never met him,
> But in pictures often seen.
> He carries an umbrella,
> He's straight, and he is fine,
> No humbug about this gentleman,
> Sign on the dotted line.

He loves both peace and freedom,
His country he adores;
Before we pass along the line,
Just look at him and pause.
To think that last September,
He worked both day and night,
To keep the peace in foreign lands,
And thus avert the fight.
But Hitler would not have it so,
He cannot play the game;
His promises broke like pie crusts,
'Tis war, more war, then fame!
But is it fame I ask you,
To slaughter all our men;
Hitler, wake up, before too late,
Our victory, your loss, what then?
You will stand before your maker,
Not knowing what to say:
"Thou shalt not kill, vengeance is Mine",
That's what the Lord will say.
Be more like our English Gent.,
Chamberlain is his name;
Look to God, and pray for peace,
You will not pray in vain.

The Reverend W.B. Church wrote in Trowbridge's *Holy Trinity Parish Magazine*, October 1939:

The worst has happened and we are at war again. But yet it is not the worst; a worse thing would be to let Poland down and to dishonour our pledged word to come to their assistance.... Momentous days are ahead of us and we shall all live from hand to mouth and from day to day, trusting in God who will vindicate right...

2

The Unexpected Guests

Evacuation

THE GOVERNMENT HAD been considering the necessity of evacuating children long before war had been declared; the Committee of Imperial Defence established a sub committee which reported in 1934 that three million people should be evacuated from London in the event of war.[1] There were many who remembered the WWI Zeppelin and Gotha raids on London, and recent events such as the Spanish Civil War showed the danger that could be wrought via air attack.[2] The Ministry of Health (MOH) and Department of Education (DOE) were to work together; the Ministry of Health in charge of day to day operations with the Board of Education to take on organisational responsibility, although Niko Gärtner feels that London County Council (LCC) was 'crucial for both the design and execution of the Evacuation Scheme'. The weakness of the two Government departments, 'be it overblown bureaucracy at the MOH or the DOE's lack of authority with politicians and population' meant that LCC had no choice but to get involved.[3] The knowledge that Germany was increasing its production of aircraft led to the formation of more specific plans and a report of July 1938 under the chairmanship of John Anderson,[4] but it was his future replacement Herbert Morrison at LCC who pushed forward London's Air Raid Protection (ARP) plans onto the national agenda. He acted as a Local Authority representative against the Home Office on the finance of ARP between 1935 and 1937, persuading the Government to subsidise 85% of the total cost[5] and the recommendations of LCC's working paper *Evacuation of the Child Population of London – An Appreciation* was incorporated into Anderson's report.[6] The LCC report noted that the greatest difficulties would be found in moving the children by the only viable option – the railways – and the difficulty in persuading parents that they should send their children away. It was estimated that 500,000 children from the LCC area and 270,000 children from the surrounding counties would need to be relocated. The role of teachers was highlighted as a requirement for gaining the co-operation of parents. As for other considerations: camps to accommodate the children were seen as too costly and would incur problems with catering, supervision and medical services.[7] The Anderson Report was to become the 'most authoritative document' as it provided both the legislative and legal framework.[8]

As a result of the Munich Crisis in 1938 there was a rush to complete the plans for an evacuation. A meeting was held on 15 September 1938 between the Education Officers' Department and the Heads of Secondary Schools, Junior Technical Schools and Elementary Schools to engage the help of teachers.[9] The Government sent memoranda stating that Local Authorities at the 'unspecified destination within the specified distance range – from Kent to Peterborough – were in charge of billeting'. Parents were to be informed that their children would only be sent 20-30 miles from the capital; 50 at most.[10] But it appears that the Government were planning to send London's children much further afield. Wiltshire's Local Authority files show that Wiltshire County Council representatives were invited to a meeting at the Home Office on 16 September 1938 to discuss plans for evacuating children from Central London in time of war with Sir John Anderson in attendance. A list of those who were asked to attend also included representatives from Bedfordshire, Berkshire, Buckinghamshire, Cambridgeshire, the Isle of Ely, Essex, Hampshire, Hertfordshire, Huntingdonshire, Kent, Northamptonshire (and Peterborough), Suffolk, Surrey and Sussex.[11] At the meeting the representatives were briefed that a draft scheme had been prepared, whereby non-essential persons would be sent to their areas via certain rail heads, the distribution carried out by the Ministry of Transport. The Government were to use compulsory powers to billet in private houses.[12] On the same day Circular 1742 was issued, asking the country's Local Housing Authorities to provide a return of housing accommodation, to include all classes of houses and to include 'the amount of such accommodation in excess of a standard per house of 1 person per habitable room, a child for this purpose being treated as a whole unit.' The purpose was to give the Government an idea of the 'broad picture of available accommodation in a particular district.' The circular was marked as very urgent and confidential.[13] Wiltshire County Council were doing their best, arranging a meeting for the following week to ascertain, amongst other things, the names of Local Authority employees over the age of 26 who could act as billetors. The Clerk advised that 'the whole matter seems to be one where secrecy is necessary.' One concern discussed at the meeting was that although spare accommodation could be found, there was no spare furniture or bedding available.[14] The Government must have been considering this problem, as in September 1938 the Master Mattress Company Limited were writing to Wiltshire County Council regarding their special emergency mattresses which were 'now being produced in large quantities to the instructions of His Majesty's Office of Works and also the Middlesex County Council'.[15] By December 1938 the Home Office was issuing guidance regarding mattresses which had been purchased 'in connection with the proposed evacuation of schoolchildren from London during the recent crisis' and which were not now required.[16]

A list of the areas available for 'refugees' in the county was drawn up as of 26 September 1938: Cricklade, Wootton Bassett and Highworth (8,900); Malmesbury

(5,600); Chippenham and Calne (10,400); Melksham and part of Bradford on Avon (3,450); Trowbridge and Bradford on Avon (8,550); Marlborough (3,050); Pewsey (2,750); Devizes (7,100); Westbury and part of Warminster (4,050); Warminster, Westbury, Mere and Tisbury (5,850); Salisbury, Wilton, Amesbury and Tisbury (12,000) (total of 71,700) and the location of the railhead for each area was provided. Swindon was excluded due to its vulnerability. Interestingly the figures had been revised downwards, perhaps in line with the Local Authorities' own estimates. For instance Pewsey's final figure was nearly half that listed in the initial area listing. For Devizes the figure was similar although their own estimate was 5,055. The initial figure allocated to Salisbury was a massive 26,600.[17]

These, as Angus Calder notes, 'hastily concocted' plans were published on 29 September 1938 in order for two million people to be evacuated[18] on 30 September.[19] Priority groups including nursery children and those with a physical disability were moved on 27 and 29 September,[20] and also some children attending private schools,[21] but as the Munich Agreement was signed on 30 September the mass evacuation did not take place.[22] Disabled children had returned to London by 6 October 1938.[23]

The Government began asking for feedback from those authorities which had been involved in the scheme. In Wiltshire suggestions were raised, including that children should stay in large houses with their teachers.[24] The issue of forced secrecy was found to have caused problems and misunderstandings, and the disorganisation at the top was apparent, with a letter from Wiltshire County Council on 16 September 1938 mentioning that the Home Office was in a 'very panicky condition' regarding the evacuation of civilians.[25] The Council wrote to the Home Office on 30 September 1938 stating that the number of evacuees due to arrive in the county far exceeded that which Wiltshire's Local Authorities could have dealt with.[26] Although a telegram was received on 29 September 1938 cancelling the evacuation, one Westbury resident distinctly remembers receiving a mother and son 'on the Government Scheme' in 1938 and Local Authorities such as Calne and Chippenham Rural District Council reported in their feedback to the Government that: 'It was found that some refugees had arrived on their own initiative though not in any large numbers.' In Marlborough '[q]uite a small number of Refugees arrived on their own, but they either went to Hotels or took empty flats'.[27] It is interesting to note that this was not the first time Wiltshire had received evacuees as during WWI Belgian refugees arrived in the county.[28] Private evacuation from London also took place during the First World War with Wiltshire's school admission registers and log books recording the event, such as the Swindon Great Western Railway (later College Street Girls) School Log Book. The 28 September 1917 entry states: 'Girls are being frequently admitted from the London area where air raids are frequent recently. They have come for the period of the war.'[29] Wiltshire residents were also caring for other types of evacuee during WWII. The renowned etcher Robin Tanner and his wife Heather had worked hard to bring a German Jew to live with them in Kington Langley after they discovered their plight through publications such as the *New Statesman* and the Quakers' publication, *The Friend*.[30] After much red tape and frustration, which Heather described in her joint book with Dieti, published after the war as 'inconceivable, amounting to cruelty'.[31] Dieti finally arrived on 3 April 1939[32] and had to register with the Police[33] who then kept an eye on him by riding past the gate of their house, asking 'Still got yer alien?'[34] worked first as a farmhand,[35] after the war becoming a teacher at Hawthorn near Corsham, a pre-fabricated school set up for the children of volunteer workers from Europe.[36]

The firm of Chapmans of Trowbridge Ltd. had already been enquiring about the mattresses they had produced for the evacuees. The mattresses were made with a special filling which was not suitable for their regular business and at present they were being stored rolled up which was bad for the mattresses. The firm had worked hard to produce as many mattresses as they could. They had held off for 24 hours as requested by telephone at the time of the Crisis, but felt that: 'We had, however, put the whole of our Department on this work to do what we could, and it is only reasonable that you take what we have got made.' Wilkinson and Riddell of Bristol, Masters of Chippenham and J. Sawtell and Co. from Holt had also made mattresses, the latter like Chapmans to be invoiced at 17s. per mattress. '100 mattresses were ordered and 50 were made and material cut for 100... As it was a national emergency, this firm do not wish to press for payment.'[37] An account from the London Metropolitan Archives states it was not common knowledge that in September 1938 there had been a 'short-range' plan to evacuate schoolchildren from London, but the system was used as the basis of the 1939 organisation for travel arrangements.[38]

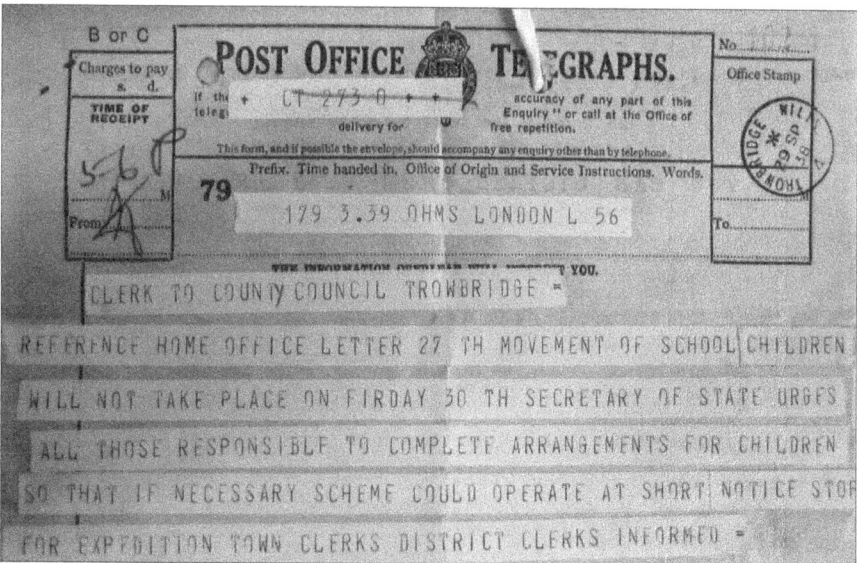

Telegram received 29 September 1938 cancelling the Government planned evacuation (WSA F2/850/1)

In January 1939 an Evacuation Branch was set up within the newly formed Evacuation Planning Division at the Ministry of Health. Gärtner notes that the reception areas were devised as being 'nearly all the area from Bristol to the Wash, with organisation built on the transport possibilities'. The capacity of the railways would be pivotal[39] and they had been put under the jurisdiction of the Ministry of Transport in September 1938.[40] The organisation of the reception areas, which Gärtner states had been a problem in the first evacuation attempt[41] was also critical, and the winter of 1938-9 saw reception areas surveying their localities for accommodation.[42]

A survey had already been undertaken by Wiltshire's Women's Voluntary Service (WVS) branches for the distribution of evacuees, discovering who had spare rooms and to obtain gifts or loans of blankets and mattresses to help those taking evacuees.[43] The number of items available was disappointingly few. The Government had put in orders for both camp beds and blankets with the rate of delivery restricted by the rate of production by the manufacturers. Many of Wiltshire's Local Authorities, such as Pewsey Rural District Council and Cricklade and Wootton Bassett Rural District Council were forced to purchase their own. Calne and Chippenham Rural District Council also purchased 2,000 blankets and Bradford on Avon Urban District Council purchased 600 at the cost of £167.[44] It was not only bedding; furniture was in short supply too.[45] Sometimes people would arrange to bring their furniture with them, but for those who had been bombed out of their homes, looters would quickly try to salvage goods. The homeowners themselves or friends and relatives had to be quick to compile a mental inventory to ensure that little was taken.[46] If anything was salvageable, it was a real trial attempting to get it moved to a new home in a reception area. Evacuees could borrow items on loan from the Local Authority in their reception district, such as one family who were evacuated to a farm in Bromham. The list contained:

> 5 Pallets, 15 blankets, 2 armchairs, 1 kettle, 1 10' frying pan, 3 pudding basins, 1 baking tin, 5 cups, 3 saucers, 4 dinner plates, 3 dessert plates, 1 tea pot, 1 tin washing bowl, 1 broom handle, 1 broom head, 2 kitchen tables, 1 scrubbing brush, 1 large and 1 small chamber, 1 bucket, 1 dustbin with cover, 1 small shovel, 5 knives, 5 forks, 3 dessert spoons, 4 tea spoons and 17 yards of blackout material.[47]

By the end of September a local ratepayer was wondering what would happen to goods such as blankets when the evacuees returned home.[48] At a Trowbridge Council meeting in December 1939 it was stated that the reception of evacuees had cost £400 and as many as 50% had now left the town. It was hoped to recover the cost by applying for Government grants, although the Chairman noted: 'Government departments are funny folks to deal with... We must recover as much as we can, and what we can't recover we shall have to put up with'.[49] However, Wiltshire County Council was proudly reporting in June 1941 that it

One of many Registers of Accommodation for Wiltshire undertaken for evacuation purposes, this one for Mere and Tisbury Rural District Council (WSA G9/220/1)

was third on the list of highest percentages for retaining evacuees at 76% behind Somerset and Surrey with the average being 56%.[50]

A set of information leaflets for the public, published in July 1939 as part of the Civil Defence preparations, began with leaflet No. 1, entitled *Some things you should know if war should come.* It mentioned evacuation, stating that arrangements had been made by the Government for the voluntary evacuation of certain parts of London. Those parents affected would have had or would soon be given instructions on what to do. Parents were encouraged to '[t]ry to decide whether you wish your children to go under the Government Evacuation Scheme and let your Local Authority know: if you propose to make private arrangements to send your children away do not leave them to the last moment.' Leaflet No. 3, *Evacuation Why and How?* went into more detail, explaining who would be arriving in reception areas: schoolchildren, expectant mothers, children under 5, the blind, and why.

> There are still a number of people who ask 'What is the need for all this business about evacuation? Surely if war comes it would be better for families to stick together and not go breaking up their homes?'
>
> It is quite easy to understand this feeling, because it is difficult for us in this country to realise what war in these days might mean. If we are involved in war, our big cities might be subjected to determined attacks from the air-at any rate in the early stages-and although our defences are strong and are rapidly growing stronger, some bombers would undoubtedly get through.
>
> We must see to it then that the enemy does not secure his chief objects-

the creation of anything like panic, or the crippling dislocation of our civil life. *One of the first measures we can take to prevent this is the removal of the children from the more dangerous areas.*'[51]

By August 1939 Swindon was this time included in the Evacuation Plan, told to expect 15,000 evacuees,[52] although in September it was reported in the *Wiltshire News* that Wiltshire was to receive 15,000 evacuees in total.[53] Those in Swindon who had not yet volunteered but had room would be compulsorily billeted.[54] In August 1939 Calne was expecting *c.* 1,000 children and 100 blind persons, with an additional 300-400 evacuees arriving who had made private arrangements in the town.[55] The Town Clerk, also acting as the Food Executive Officer, was considering the impact of their arrival. 'In the event of War breaking out we expect the arrival in Calne of about 1000 evacuees, of whom some fifty percent will be children. The dairymen of the town should be prepared therefore, to extend their purchases of milk for retail sale so that they may be in a position to serve 1000 more customers.'[56] Private evacuation also occurred – London institutions arranged to be 'adopted' by a rural school or use alumni or parent connections for their move to rural surroundings.[57] The Bath Girls' High School moved to the rural setting of Longleat House for the duration of the war, its premises having been requisitioned by the Admiralty.[58] The Woolwich Polytechnic School of Art and the Hammersmith School of Building relocated to Trowbridge during the war, and were regularly contacting Trowbridge's Chief Billeting Officer requesting billets for prospective pupils, such as two boys from Woking in May 1941.[59] The Fitzmaurice Grammar School in Bradford on Avon was due to take in evacuees from Secondary Schools in Bristol. The Clerk of the Urban District Council was extremely concerned over the numbers of children allocated in August 1941 as 'I do not think it would be possible to accommodate anything like 300 children in this District at the present time.'[60] It appears that businesses could also evacuate their staff privately, with one lady remembering her family being re-housed to a rural community through the bank where her father worked.[61] One local firm had arranged for all of their London Office staff and families (numbering 300) to be transferred to Trowbridge during the 1938 crisis. Trowbridge Urban District Council had been canvassing for billets for them.[62] Private evacuation could cause problems, however. One lady from Swindon had her niece from Fulham staying with her on holiday in September 1939 when the evacuation began. The niece stayed on as a private evacuee with her parents paying for her keep, but this proved impossible when her father lost his job. They were told to go to the Local Authority in Fulham so that they could get the niece set up as an official evacuee, but the issue needed to be sorted out in Swindon, and '[m]y wife has been to the evacuation office twice, and they will not even look at the letter from Fulham and say they can do nothing. As far as I am concerned, I suppose I am in a position to keep the child without asking for help, but the parents are not and are too proud to keep her here without paying. So it seems another little victim of the War will go home to the Danger Zone...'.[63] By August

1941 Military Billeting Notices were hampering the evacuation of children to Castle Combe where the Chief Billeting Officer in Chippenham had been advised that 'the householders proposing to take the children have had further Military billeting notices served on them, this barring the admission of the six children…' The restrictions meant that the London County Council partially sighted school was at present only operating at half strength. The Clerk was working to release the billets on behalf of the children.[64] In May 1941 one mother decided to quit Kent for Salisbury with her child under private arrangements. 'My mother and I arrived at Salisbury station in the early afternoon. My uncle was there to meet us. I had not been to Salisbury before. The streets looked bleak and unfamiliar. There were no men about. The occasional army lorry passed, but there were no cars. Sandbags stood at important doorways. Some shops had criss-crossed tape to prevent flying glass if a bomb fell.'[65]

The first three days of September 1939 saw almost 1.5 million official evacuees and about 2 million private evacuees relocating to rural areas.[66] During the time of the 'Phoney War' from September 1939 to May 1940 many householders in Salisbury took in evacuees but there were many more evacuees than billets. A letter dated September 1939 from the Town Clerk, Salisbury, to the Ministry of Health related the difficulties in placing evacuees from the Portsmouth slums in billets. All 'working class' types of billets had been filled, many workers were lodged in the city, along with soldiers and friends and relations in private arrangements; accommodation was limited.[67] One of these evacuees was aged 10 but had only been told that she was going on an outing. She and her sister were two of the last to be chosen, 'no one seemed to want two sisters.' Their new host parents were from Bemerton and were seen by the girls to be very old. They had no children of their own and 'did not have much of an idea of what children were like.' Both girls slept in the same bed, the elder covering up the hole in the wall which the younger girl had picked out.[68] Interestingly, the term 'phoney' was begun by the Americans and later adopted by the British. It covered the period of the war which ended in April 1940. At the time it was referred to by the British as the 'Bore War', the 'funny war' or as Chamberlain put it, 'this strange war'.[69]

Other Local Authorities in Wiltshire were also experiencing problems in September 1939 and felt the County Council should call a conference to discuss the various difficulties. A letter was written to the Secretary, Minister of Health, to raise the issue.[70] Swindon, after being left off the list of reception areas in the 1938 scheme, was included in 1939 but there was a desperate need for accommodation. An appeal was sent out to householders not yet taking evacuees with the Council appealing to every resident's national unity. 'The care of evacuee school children particularly is a service of first-rate national importance, affecting as it does the coming generation. I wish to urge householders most strongly to respond to this appeal by sending their names and addresses to me at the Civic Offices, Swindon, as quickly as possible.'[71]

The writer and broadcaster A. G. Street wrote of his house in South Wiltshire:

To-day in addition to its native population the rural scene is filled with soldiers, airmen, evacuated women and children, and Government servants galore. For instance, at the moment my own house has somehow found room for a mother and three little children, two billeted Officers, and also a Government Official. The last mentioned now occupies my study, drat him, but his conversation in the evenings almost makes up for this.[72]

In Freshford on the Somerset/Wiltshire border the Billeting Officer came around soon after Poland was invaded on 1 September 1939, before war was announced. The evacuees were expected to arrive 'at teatime on the Sunday afternoon'.[73] The writer Fay Inchfawn was told to make room for two mothers and two children. They decided to forego the use of their much loved pantry: 'I could scarcely bear to contemplate giving up all these conveniences, yet this seemed to us a lesser evil than having to share our own kitchen with two entirely unknown quantities.' Another villager was extremely house-proud and Fay knew how tortuous it would be for her having strangers in her midst. She tried to reassure her, but: 'She hurried away at a run to pack up some of her treasures and to make up beds for the invaders.'[74] Whilst waiting for their two mothers to arrive Fay later wrote: 'Silence and solitude – the two things which have been most precious, and most helpful – must now, I know very well, be mine no longer. Frankly, I *did not like it*. Soon there would be strange feet upon the stairs, and unaccustomed noises about the house...' She realised that she was actually more afraid of her own reaction than of them; her unwillingness to share her privacy and the selfishness of wanting freedom in her own house. She wanted to help her country but at the same time secretly hoped her lodgers would be 'refined, grateful and agreeable (but not presuming) people.'[75] The evacuees duly arrived, and the locals noticed that they looked downtrodden, aimlessly wandering along the country lanes, voicing their distress at the lack of shops or cinema. One resolutely declared that she 'did not want to see another green tree as long as she lived.' The food was too expensive compared to home and there were no fried-fish shops. They preferred food from a tin with no cooking and minimal washing up involved. They had 'strange hair,' were loud and sharp witted with an odd sounding accent. 'It was not easy for the Village to feel any sympathy with such an outlook' and the village soon heard of a poor elderly widow who was looking after a brother and sister. 'They keeps asking me for biscuits which I haven't got, and for tinned milk which I don't hold with. I've brought up eight,' [she] said... tearfully, 'and made 'em eat what was on the plates, but these have got me beat, Man, and there it is.'[76]

The Women's Voluntary Service (WVS) issued a leaflet to help householders through any difficulties in September 1939. *A Healthy Child is a Happy Child* advised a regular routine with 11 to 12 hours sleep and a rest during the day for young children. To help to prevent illness, householders were to feed the children plenty of fresh vegetables and fluids with pasteurised milk. Frequent baths were advocated and regular changes of clothing. Care of the head was mentioned. 'Children may have been subjected to infection on the journey. Heads should be combed with a small tooth-comb for three days. All heads should be washed weekly and inspected daily.'[77] The use of books to help children adjust to an unfamiliar environment, especially in long, dark winter evenings was brought up in the Board of Education Circular 1493, December 1939. They were working to secure adequate supplies of books for general reading via the Public Library Service, transferring books and increasing stock in reception areas.[78]

The villagers of Freshford tried to help, receiving the newcomers at the Village Hall. They discovered more about them: 'the pitiful little suitcases... which contained badly washed and shrunken underwear sadly in need of mending; of pretty and engaging mites who were quickly pounced upon by foster mothers; of belligerent and none too clean little persons who were with difficulty provided billets.'[79]

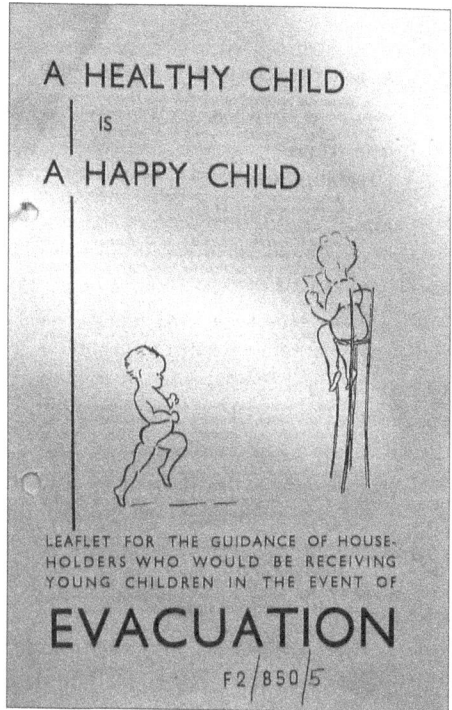

WVS leaflet for the guidance of householders receiving young children in the event of evacuation (WSA F2/850/5)

Frances Partridge wrote in her diary at Ham Spray House in Ham on 14 September 1939: 'Mrs. Hill on the telephone again! "I've just heard that twenty refugees are arriving in half an hour. Could you have some more?"... I drove down to the village and waited. Then the bus came lumbering in, and children ran out to gape and stare. One very small child thudded along screeching out 'VACU-EES! VACU-EES!' As soon as they got out it was clear they were neither children nor docksiders, but respectable-looking middle-aged women and a few children, who stood like sheep beside the bus looking infinitely apathetic. 'Who'll take these?' 'How many are you?' 'Oh well, I can have these two but no more,' and the piteous cry, 'But we're *together*.' It was terrible. I felt we were like sharp-nosed housewives haggling over fillets of fish.'[80] Some evacuees from East Ham arrived in Wroughton and the Wroughton History Group note that they

> ... waited apprehensively to be chosen and the local people sorted through the children rather like a cattle market to see if anyone was to their liking. We were chosen by Mr. & Mrs. Izzard...The Izzards had no children of their own which was a great disappointment to them. So it was like a miracle for them to have two boys given to them for the duration of the war.'[81]

At Steeple Ashton they were preparing to receive their contingent of evacuees. The arrival time came and went… unfortunately the schoolchildren had been sent to Westbury Upon Trym, Bristol, rather than Westbury Station in Wiltshire where they were due to be picked up. Instead, it was mothers and babies who arrived at Westbury Station. Betty Smith reports that by 11 o'clock at night there was 'a heart rending scene – there were babies asleep on cushions on the floor, tired, worried and bewildered mothers were sitting around drinking tea, while [one lady] and her helpers, with [the local] Nurse… re-arranged the accommodation. Some prospective foster-mothers were less willing to take mothers and babies. They didn't have suitable accommodation.[82] One evacuee from Notting Hill, evacuated to Castle Combe, remembered that the villagers did not know what to do with so many children. 'They had expected twenty and here were almost a hundred.' The Billeting Officer struggled to find a home for this evacuee and his siblings and the evacuee 'confess[ed], given the incidents of the day [he felt] abandoned.'[83] One Cricklade resident, only a small child himself at the time, vividly remembers another young evacuee who had said goodbye to his mother at Paddington Station '… he stood in the courtyard holding his teddy bear, crying. I was only little myself, but I felt for him.'[84]

Two boys evacuated with the West Kensington Central School to Melksham wrote letters home, telling their parents how they were faring. Arriving

The arrival of evacuees at Trowbridge Railway Station, September 1939, reproduced by kind permission of Mike Marshman (WSHC P55102)

at Melksham Station from London Paddington on 2 September 1939 they had with them their suitcases, gas masks, and an issue of chocolates in bags handed out before the journey. They were taken around door to door visiting potential foster parents to see if they would take them in:

> 3 September 1939
> I had quite a pleasant journey, although we were a bit crowded in the tube as you saw at the station. Then at Ealing Broadway, we changed to the GWR which took us right here, without a single stop (except of course signals). When we arrived at Melksham, we went to the school buildings and waited there to be put into our billets. While we were waiting we had tea, milk, or water as we chose. [85]

The *Wiltshire Times* was announcing on 8 September 1939 that the local population felt they had done their bit to help: 'Trowbridge has done her share'. The paper's 9 September 1939 edition stated that '[t]he effect of this influx of population has been to bring about a complete change in the general appearance of the public places of the town – the streets, the Park, the shops, and the public buildings – and nothing less than a revolution in the domestic lives of practically the whole population.' The letter of Peggy Pickford from Warminster to her sister Elizabeth Martin in Australia on 20 September 1939 goes some way to sum up the feeling in the reception areas.

> The wireless, of course, was full of 'Evacuation' and kept on praising everybody and everything up to the skies, but funnily enough they never mentioned (nor did the newspapers) the most praiseworthy people of all – the receivers of the children. They praised the children, the teachers, the organisers, the railways, the receiving officers and again the children, but never a word of the wretched women who had, at twelve hours notice, to provide accommodation, beds, blankets and food. [86]

The local Welfare Committees began to advise householders of their duties; full board, lodging and all care necessary to give the child a home. The allowance in 1939 was five shillings per adult and three shillings per accompanying child per week. It was also stated that the cost did not cover clothes or boots, for which the child's parents should pay. [87] The WVS fielded complaints from householders that they were faced with providing evacuees with boots and clothes when they themselves were on low incomes. It was felt unfair that certain standards were expected for evacuated children but not their own. [88] Of the 31,000 children registered for evacuation from Newcastle, 4,000 had inadequate footwear and 6,500 inadequate clothing. [89] An appeal for clothes and shoes was broadcast by the Ministry of Health on 8 September 1939. [90] The *Wiltshire Times* reported in its 4 November 1939 edition that in Trowbridge, the London County Council Headmaster soon realised that the children would inevitably have an inadequate supply of clothes due to the limited amount of luggage they could bring with them. He noted that '... very valuable help was at once organised from the Co-operative Hall and Head Teachers with the school party wish to express their most grateful thanks to all those ladies who worked so indefatigably to supply the urgent need.' A clothing inspection of the unaccompanied evacuees took place at Ivy Lane School in Chippenham in January 1941: 'records were being kept.'[91] Some parents tried to do their best. 'Mum tried to keep us nicely clothed...' '[she] didn't manage to come to see us very often as it was rather a long way, but they did write and send us parcels. Mostly new clothes and sweets.'[92] Circular 1907 from the Ministry of Health tried to allay fears in November 1940. 'The Minister is aware that many householders throughout the country have been extremely generous in providing children in need with clothing at their own expense and he is deeply appreciative of their kindness. He is anxious, however, that householders should not be put to this form of expense, and he certainly would not wish that they should feel that it is expected of them.' The cost should be borne by the parents, and the Minister had 'no doubt that most parents will readily recognise this responsibility,' but that the need should be brought to their attention by teachers, helpers and householders keeping in regular contact. 'The teachers will, from their daily contact with the children, be in a position to judge how far these efforts are successful and what proportion of children there are who remain unprovided with essential garments.'[93] The Government set the maximum contribution for parents at 6s. but only an average of 2s. 3d. was collected initially. One quarter of parents (those whose pay was too low) did not have to contribute at all.[94]

The *Wiltshire Times* was reporting in its 25 November 1939 edition that the Trowbridge Unitary Council was in full agreement with householders that the 8s. 6d. weekly allowance for evacuees was inadequate and was causing them hardship. It was resolved that the amount should be increased to 10s. and a letter was written to the local MP to that effect. Host families were expected to pay for health treatment for the evacuees in their care and then be reimbursed from the parents. A resident of Edington was writing to the Warminster and Westbury Rural District Council about an evacuee brought to her who had been suffering from toothache for two nights. '... so I took her to the dentist in Trowbridge and had it taken out she had an absess [*sic*] under it so had to have gas so he charged 5/- and 1/11 fares. Can you get this for me as the child had to have it done. She could not be allowed to suffer like that.'[95] If the parents were unable to contribute, 'there would be no objection to the amount not recoverable being shown as a charge on the Evacuation Account. The cost will rank for reimbursement by the Exchequer, subject to review at audit.'[96] It is not possible to know when the host would finally have received reimbursement ...

The *Wiltshire Gazette* printed an article in its 14 September 1939 edition, reporting on the need for a Social Service for evacuated children.

The presence in such large numbers of evacuated children in our reception areas raises the important question of their social welfare. They had been transferred

Edington
hr Westbury
Wilts

Dear Sir

I am sending you a reciept I have had from the Dentist when I took Eileen Weeks an Evacuee as she came to me suffering from Acute Toothache I was told by the Billeting Officers here to put in my claim to you also 1/11 return fare's to Trowbridge.

Yours truly

Letter from Warminster and Westbury Rural District Council, October 1944, regarding the issue of payment for health treatment (WSA G12/225/1)

to continue their lives for what may be an appreciable period under conditions entirely different from those to which they have been accustomed and where the arrangements for looking after their social welfare are, therefore, comparatively speaking, non-existent.

The article suggested that it should be the Ministry of Health, Board of Education and the County Local Authorities that should be brought together in reception areas to consider the issue, and to 'see that plans are ready and in operation before the dark days of winter bring new difficulties.' It appears that on the ground at least, little was done practically to help, except with the provision of a little funding. The rest was left up to the willingness of local volunteers. But in Wiltshire local communities did work hard to put on entertainment for the evacuees, especially at Christmas. The Trowbridge Urban District Council reported that £25 was raised locally via voluntary subscriptions. The money was combined with £9 from London County Council (LCC) and a Christmas party was given for 180 evacuees in December 1939. The children were to receive a tea, a toy, and the gift of a scarf each. There would also be a mobile cinema showing from Messrs Fry and Sons Ltd. of Bristol. The Women's Voluntary Service organised a party for evacuated adults for early in the New Year.[97] The *Wiltshire News* reported many such children's Christmas parties in its 5 January 1940 edition, such as one at Calne Town Hall with three large Christmas trees donated by the Marchioness of Lansdowne at Bowood and a coach provided to take the evacuees back to their billets. The Welfare Committee for Evacuees arranged the party with help from an LCC grant. The Welfare Committee's Chairman also played the part of Father Christmas. At Box the Billeting Officers helped provide 'goodies' for the children. Evacuees from Heywood were taken to see a special performance at the Vista Cinema in Westbury in January 1940.[98] A letter was sent in June 1940 from the acting Secretary of LCC's Christmas Tree Fund to Swindon's Town Clerk saying how impressed they had been by enthusiasm and resolve displayed to ensure the children had a good time.[99] The Regional Offices of the Ministry of Health in Bristol were issuing a second Christmas Toy Appeal in 1944 with a letter sent to the Town Clerk of Trowbridge. Their first appeal saw workers in the Regional Offices of Government Departments give 1,700 toys to needy children in Public Assistance Homes and other Residential Institutions. This year they were hoping to do even better. 'This year, in the knowledge that the good results of last year, still only touched the fringe of the problem, we are going all out for a much bigger total – with the minimum aim of providing at least one toy for each child in all institutions in the Region…' To do this they would need the help of the National Fire Service and Civil Defence Service with working parties and local appeals. The Women's Institute was also being approached.[100]

Host parents were also worried at the thought of keeping the children entertained in the long winter evenings. The *Wiltshire Times* edition of 25 November 1939 was printing advice given by *Parents* magazine. 'Until one knows one's new family, it is advisable to get the children to talk as much as possible. Try to get familiar with the atmosphere they have been accustomed to at home.' The pantomime *Aladdin* was organised by an adult evacuee from Shepherd's Bush (now residing in Lacock in December 1939) to help relieve the boredom of blackout evenings. Blackout curtains were fitted at Stratton St. Margaret School so that it could be used in the evenings as a play centre by the evacuees.[101]

There was much confusion over the administration of the Evacuation Scheme, both within Local Councils and amongst the public. In September 1939 one lady in Swindon had put her name down to volunteer to take evacuees but had not heard anything. A neighbour told her that she should have been sent a card to put in her window to show that she was taking in an evacuee; she hadn't received one and was wondering if she had been overlooked.[102] The cards were meant to show that householders were undertaking a vital service for the war effort.

> It has been represented to the Minster [of Health] that while volunteers for many forms of National Service were entitled to wear a badge or uniform, those undertaking to receive and care for children were without any tangible proof of their readiness to serve, although this form of service might well make such demands on their time and energy as to preclude them from volunteering for any other work. The object of the window card is to remedy this deficiency.[103]

It is suggested that the 'panic' which ensued regarding evacuation in September 1939 was also due to an ongoing power struggle which led to mismanagement. The Board of Education lacked initiative and was happy to be only a small partner in the organisational structure. Gärtner feels that the Ministry of Health, although responsible for the scheme, was 'too timid to produce any serious policy'.[104] As early as 1940 many assumed that the Evacuation Scheme was about to collapse with thousands of children returning to London each week. The Scheme had cost £20 million and the Fabian Society felt that some of the requests made of parents, such as the levy to contribute towards clothing, were damaging. The scheme was becoming 'widely unpopular'.[105] It was true that evacuees came and went. School Log Books report many children arriving, leaving, and more arriving, all in response to the bombs that were falling in their home towns and cities, such as the children admitted to Yatton Keynell from Bath in May 1942 after the Baedeker bombing raid on the nights of 25-27 April.[106] Autumn 1939 saw the evacuees in Freshford arriving and departing. The village had struggled to cope with the resignations of cooks, 'harassed' housewives and busy streets, but the villagers realised it had been hard for the evacuees too. Fay Inchfawn was wondering why the situation had been so difficult; there had been good intentions and 'real sacrifice' made. She came to the conclusion that it was because 'nothing in the least sensational happened. There was no sudden air attack upon London. There were no breath-taking fearsome odours of peardrops or geraniums to justify the troublesomeness of carrying gas-masks… there was, on the part of the evacuees, a determined trek towards home.'[107] The lack of air attacks after war was declared and the unhappiness of some city dwellers who were transported to rural locations led to a 'trickle-back'; by January 1940 *c*. 700,000 evacuees had returned home.[108]

The Government-run evacuation plan was reviewed and redesigned more than once before the war was over, but Gärtner notes that the civilian wartime population would never wholeheartedly 'embrace the scheme after the disappointment of the Phoney War'.[109] Other reasons for the return of evacuees included missing family, concerns over the care given by foster parents and financial strain.[110]

It was soon realised by the Ministers in Whitehall that in future, evacuation should not include mothers as their conduct and behaviour in the reception areas had been cited as one of its failures, although this approach needed to be altered with the onset of the V1 and V2 bombardment.[111] A letter from the Director of Education at Swindon Borough Council ran along similar lines in December 1939… 'Our general experience in these cases is, however, that trouble and difficulties arise with the householders on whom unaccompanied children are billeted owing to the interference and fussiness of the mothers. We have had many cases of children being happy and contented in good billets until the mother has transferred into the town, after which trouble has begun.'[112] A lady from East Tytherton was writing to the *Wiltshire Gazette*, published in the 21 September 1939 issue regarding her ideas to help stop the exodus of mothers with young children returning to London. She noted that the majority of those who returned had been billeted in 'individual units.' Those who had been staying together in large or unoccupied houses had tended to remain; even more so when a superintendent had been appointed. She felt that a scheme to house mothers and their children as groups in unoccupied properties should be considered if or when another mass evacuation became necessary.

A report by Bradford on Avon Urban District Council noted great dissatisfaction on the part of householders regarding women with children and expectant mothers.[113] Women's Institute members said they could find little sympathy with women who could not sew or cook and who wanted to go out all the time.[114] Wiltshire's Federation of Women's Institutes Executive Committee decided to ask all Institutes situated in villages who had received evacuees to take part in an Evacuation Survey of December 1939, organised by the National Federation of Women's Institutes. The covering letter stated that

[t]he earlier reports as to the condition and habits of a small section of evacuees were of a distressing kind, but it is now being said that such reports were greatly exaggerated. Your committee feels that it would be a constructive piece of work if the Institutes can give an accurate picture of the condition of the mothers and children when they arrived in the villages. If this is done while the events are still clear in our minds it will be of great value to the authorities who are responsible for the social conditions and health education of the community. Such a survey would not be undertaken in a spirit of grievance but as a definite contribution to the welfare of our fellow citizens.' The survey instructions advised that pains should be taken not to cause offence to any remaining evacuees and noted that: 'In a small village it will be possible to obtain most of the information at the Institute monthly meeting, unless evacuees are present at it.

Any happy experiences gained or interesting facts 'throwing light on the children's home diet' were to be included.[115] The survey results from the Landford WI were as follows:

13 women and 35 children from Wimbledon.

Of the 13 women 3 had trained their children well, 3 fairly well, 3 had not tried to do so but were grateful for help and instruction. 4 lacked all desire to do so and allowed the children to run wild.

About half the children were definitely troublesome, but in all but a few cases the 'hostesses' were of opinion that had they been unaccompanied they would in a short time have become reasonably obedient.

There were no cases of head lice. Only three families were really dirty, and one of these had skin disease. Only 4 of the 'hostesses' did not complain of bedwetting, which in several cases was very serious.

Almost all the children were well clothed and fed, but quite half the women were amazed to see their hostesses taking trouble over their cooking and being economical, repeatedly stating that they preferred food from tins and the fish-and-chip shop.

Four women wrote to thank their hostesses or to send Christmas greetings. Most of them regarded their visit as a free holiday and soon returned home because the country was too dull. None now remain in the village.[116]

Mr Walter Elliot from the Ministry of Health gave a broadcast on 15 February 1940 regarding the Government's latest plans for evacuation, stating that they had learnt from their experiences in 1939. 'Our evacuation plans for 1940 are simple. In the first place, we shall not, in general try to move adults at all. In the second place, we are drawing up plans in advance for the children, but we shall not move them at all, in any area, until air warfare is developing in such a way as to actually threaten our civilian population.' He also wanted to keep the hosts in the reception areas on board. 'We want to assure the hosts in reception areas, those who have given hospitality to children, that they have done, and are doing, a national

Letter from Swindon Borough Council's Director of Education, 1 December 1939, regarding the 'fussiness of mothers' (WSA G24/225/1)

service second to none.'[117] He also announced measures to increase the billeting allowance from 8s. 6d. to 10s. 6d. for children over 14 years old and to extend the billeting allowance for private arrangements, giving similar terms to both, and to ensure meals at school canteens did not require coupons from the children's ration books.[118] The Ministry of Health's Memo. EV. 8 entitled *Government Evacuation Scheme* in 1940 admitted that the 1939 scheme had resulted in less than 50% of parents being willing to evacuate their children. The Government was, however, holding 'firmly to the view that this danger of air attack is not removed, though the moment of its impact is not calculable. They are therefore still of the opinion that the removal of children from the large cities is a substantial advantage to the national prosecution of the war...' To help stop the continual drift of evacuees back to their homes, the Government was making arrangements for cheap fares to enable parents to visit their children more frequently,[119] although it was aware that frequent visits could hamper the children settling down and cause an increase in the number of evacuees returning home with their visitors. Visitors could also put pressure on householders who would then have to provide hospitality. They had, however, made provision for one day return tickets on trains running on Sundays at a reduced fare.[120] In June 1941 the Minister of Health sent a handwritten plea to parents, stating he was sorry to hear that they were bringing their children back.

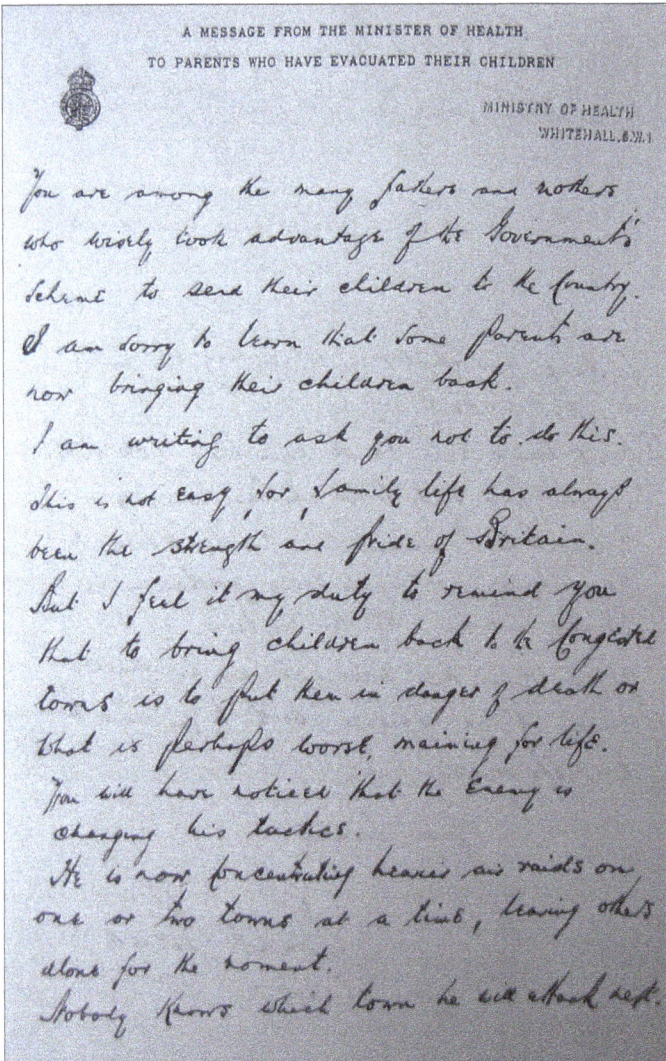

A MESSAGE FROM THE MINISTER OF HEALTH
TO PARENTS WHO HAVE EVACUATED THEIR CHILDREN

MINISTRY OF HEALTH
WHITEHALL, S.W.1

Letter to the parents of evacuated children by Ernest Brown, Minster of Health (WSA F2/850/10)

'... I feel it is my duty to remind you that to bring children back... is to put them in danger of death or what is perhaps worse, maiming for life... Remember that in April over 600 children under sixteen were killed and over 500 seriously injured in air raids...'[121]

A number of County Conferences were arranged by the Government to discuss the 1940 Evacuation Scheme (Plan IV). In Wiltshire a meeting was convened between Wiltshire's Billeting Authorities and others such as the Great Western Railway (GWR) and London County Council at the request of the Minister of Health, taking place on 4 March 1940. The Clerk of Wiltshire County

Council advised that the maximum number of evacuees expected to be sent to the county had been received, and that the number could not be altered. He was aware that many Local Authorities were extremely concerned as to how they would accommodate the additional evacuees in view of the number of military units in the locality requiring billets. Full compulsory powers would have to be used by Billeting Officers which was 'unpleasant,' but necessary. The use of compulsion by Billeting Officers needed to be stressed 'over and over again.' 'It is unfortunate to have to issue a legal notice to friend or neighbour that he has to take this or that child and it does not help for the reception of the child. This has to be prepared and if necessary you will have to use your compulsory powers.'[122] Plans would be required for emergency hostels to take in children suffering from skin diseases, and it was stressed that the children would be medically examined before travel, and if not, the Authority would be advised of the situation so that they could be examined before billeting. The children would arrive by train over six days: Day One, 900 due into Trowbridge; Day Two, 800 to Devizes; Day Four, 800 to Wootton Bassett; Day Five, 700 to Melksham, 200 to Chippenham, 600 to Westbury, 100 to Warminster; Day Six, 300 to Marlborough, 600 to Malmesbury, 200 to Pewsey, 300 to Devizes, all with the Great Western Railway Company. 500 were due to arrive in Salisbury with the Southern Railway Company and all children were to be dispersed from the railheads. The London County Council representative hoped that representatives in Wiltshire would ask them for help more often, and work with them a little more closely than had been the case the first time around.[123]

There were those, however, who had retained their evacuees from September 1939. Memo EV. 6 in November 1939 was looking at the redistribution of evacuees in reception areas. There were some who were looking after evacuees but were less capable than volunteers who had not yet been called upon, and some householders were hoping to be temporarily relieved of their charges.[124] It can be said that by the early months of 1940 some Wiltshire householders were feeling the strain. A lady from Swindon had been looking after two boys and needed 'a rest from the extra work and responsibility entailed.' She felt that it was now 'the turn of someone else to bear this responsibility which I have willingly undertaken for five months.'[125] The hosts of Swindon were by February 1940 holding a public meeting on the issue of billeting. As billeting had now become compulsory in the town, 'this meeting is of the opinion that the only fair method of its application is on a rota basis of the available billets in the town and requests the Local Authority to take steps for the drawing up of such a rota from the available information collected at the census taken last year.' They requested that the Town Council receive a deputation to discuss the issue further. There were many local inhabitants who didn't feel able to take in evacuees because they were elderly or ill and the Local Authorities in Wiltshire appear to have been sympathetic. Householders receiving children took a great deal on, probably more than they initially realised, when they took in evacuees. A letter was sent from Whitehall to the Mayors in reception areas, March 1940, asking for the names of householders so that the Queen could write them a personal message in 'recognition of the exceptional difficulties and responsibilities of their work, the length of time over which and the manner in which it has been carried out' when sheltering evacuated children.[126]

In November 1939 a Government circular pointed out the advantages of offering the evacuees communal lunch time meals.

> It will undoubtedly save much labour in the performance of their own household duties if arrangements can be made in the receiving district which will relieve them of the responsibility of providing a meal for the children in the middle of the day ie. if the children are absent from home after breakfast till tea time.

The Ministry of Health was in favour of such meals, writing to reception areas in November 1939 about the pioneering work being done by some Local Authorities and wanting to 'secure the speedy development of such extension in those areas where its operation [would] be beneficial.'[127]

Evacuees arrived under Plan IV June 1940, the Government having set up an Assistance Scheme. Free travel vouchers and billeting certificates were available to those who knew someone who would take them in.[128] A man from Essex was desperate to move his family to Wiltshire, writing to the Clerk of the County Council in June 1940. 'Please help me, I can still feel the quick beating of the children's hearts from the bombs dropping under ½ a mile from our house last Tuesday…'[129] but the 'blitz' itself began in London on the night of 7 September 1940. The Government had drawn up a list of areas which could be evacuated but this proved to be highly controversial. Plymouth had been subjected to heavy raids but although many requests were made to put the city on the list of evacuation areas, the Government refused until after the heaviest raids in March and April 1941.[130] The Government had been looking at a Plan III but it did not become operational; they relied instead on Plan IV in June 1940 when the military situation began to worsen, but it only encompassed those children who had already been registered,[131] and would be put into operation after one clear day's notice of the Government's decision. An announcement would be broadcast by radio when the order for evacuation was given. Each child would have a Party Number, noted on armlets, labels etc. which would be quoted in correspondence from reception areas. The number would also be placed on a label which would be worn loosely around the child's neck, tucked under their upper garment, which would also contain their name and home address. Another would be fixed to their luggage. When the children were settled into their accommodation it was the task of the leader of their party to find a Post Office which would act as a reception point for correspondence. Notices would then be posted for parents at their home school. The children would also send a postcard home as soon as possible after they had settled in; the official post cards to be collected from Post Offices and distributed by the Party Leaders who would then supervise correct addressing.[132] On 13-18 June 1940 103,000 children were transported to rural areas, each party being medically checked before travel.[133]

One of many slips contained within the records of Trowbridge Urban District Council at the Wiltshire and Swindon History Centre, used to record the details of every officially evacuated child in the 1940 Plan IV Scheme (WSA G15/225/21)

Plan IV was superseded by Plan V, the 'trickle' evacuation which became operational on 6 July 1940 and which catered for those who had not already registered. This plan was closed in November 1942. Plan VI was meant to replace it but it never got off the ground; instead when the Blitz was at its height Plan V was extended to cover homeless women and children. This soon became Plan VII.[134] Plan VIII was begun in 1943 when a scheme was being put into place if evacuation had to be instigated again. The V Bombs of June 1944 began the process with evacuation taking place between 5 and 8 September 1944 at the request of the Government,[135] again bringing evacuees to Wiltshire. This became the second great evacuation from the capital.[136] During the period of January to March 1944 more bombs had been dropped in Britain than in the whole of the previous year, 90% of which fell on London. There was great criticism that the evacuation had not begun earlier but the railways were busy transporting troops and materials to build the Normandy bridgehead and so Government Evacuation did not begin until July.[137]

It has been suggested that the upper and middle classes did not take as large a part in homing the evacuees as the ordinary populace.[138] Billeting Officers could often come from the middle class themselves and could be sympathetic towards their peers. In the third year of evacuation, a Senior Officer in the Ministry of Health, situated in a larger reception area, reported that 'the real hard core' of billeting problems remained with the upper middle classes. Angus Calder notes just how often the larger houses were spared.[139] In Wiltshire many large houses were requisitioned by the military but Billeting Officers did have

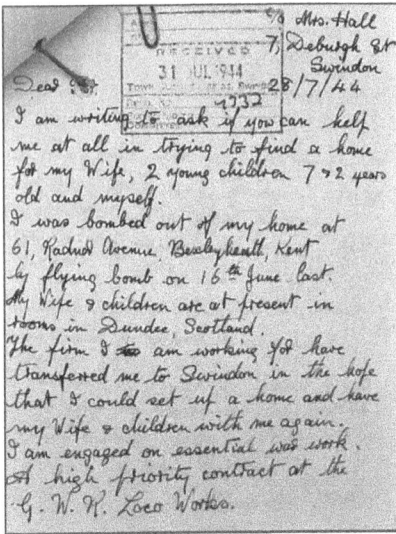

Letter from a man hoping to get his family transferred to Swindon after his house in Kent was bombed by a V rocket (WSA G24/225/6)

problems with wealthier property owners. A Billeting Officer at Bradford on Avon served a Billeting Notice on a large house to accommodate an expectant mother, since she was of 'a very superior type.' He later discovered that the lady had been moved on to the Maternity Home as she was told she could not stay at the House. He felt that the occupier had infringed the Defence Regulations by failing to comply with the Billeting Notice and also felt that:

if the Occupier of a better-class type of house can be so easily relieved of the obligation to provide accommodation as required by a Billeting Notice, what will be the position of Occupiers of smaller houses who do not desire Evacuees and who may do the same thing? It seems to me that the present difficulties will be increased, and that it will only to possible to Billet upon people who are willing to carry out their obligations, which will mean that certain sections of the community will be unduly imposed upon, and that the authority of the Billeting Officers will count for nothing.[140]

It was the Billeting Officer's job to meet the evacuees when they arrived, bringing with them the Survey Books which had been used to mark down the houses where billets were available. They were to 'do all in [their] power to establish a friendly understanding between householders and those billeted upon them.'[141] At Freshford on the Somerset/Wiltshire border, the author Fay Inchfawn was noting that it was not an easy thing to be a Billeting Officer.

… I view with veneration the people who undertake this difficult task. I think that out of all of them [one in particular] must be given the palm for showing tact, self-giving, and sheer goodness of heart when confronted with strange and harassing circumstances. No one knows better than he the curious dilemmas which may quite suddenly arise when persons totally unknown to one another have to live under the same roof, and often in the same rooms.[142]

In Bradford on Avon the Billeting Officer was having trouble finding billets for women with children and expectant mothers. 200 letters had been sent out asking for billets for expectant mothers near the Maternity Home at Berryfield House. Accommodation was found for only 15 and compulsory powers had to be used. '[N]umerous complaints' were raised but the Billeting Officer worked hard to 'adjust matters, by re-distribution of Evacuees, with a view to satisfying the complaints of all parties concerned.' The Billeting Officer reported that experience had shown that voluntary co-operation on the part of householders was necessary for the successful billeting of women accompanied by children, and that using compulsory powers to billet expectant mothers was 'doomed to failure.'[143] Other problems noted by Billeting Officers included householders who '…have deliberately left their homes and remained away during the period of Billeting, in an attempt to avoid having to provide accommodation,' but on other occasions householders had made ready their homes to accommodate expectant mothers, only to find that they did not arrive. 'The result ha[d] been that the Occupiers to whom notice ha[d] been given ha[d] been very resentful at being put to unnecessary trouble.'[144] It appears that Billeting Officers were also being asked to look for savings. Under the heading *Recovery of Billeting Costs* the Chief Billeting Officer for Trowbridge Urban District Council listed refunds paid weekly into his office, evacuees who had de-billeted themselves rather than state their means, and others who were de-billeted because they were working in Trowbridge. 'Reckoning the first 6 months of this year my work in this Department is saving the Government a sum equivalent to the rate of £1,963 per annum.'[145] By May 1943 he was notifying the Civil Defence Committee of his resignation. 'I have given seven days' careful thought to this matter and it is transparently clear to me that the Urban District Council will not support me in the task I have to perform, neither will they give me any credit for the work I have done during the past eight and a half months.'[146]

By spring 1940 Wiltshire was becoming full to the brim. The overcrowding led to outbreaks of spotted fever, measles and scarlet fever. There were also worries that rural water supplies would be overstretched, especially if there was a dry summer. The Clerk of Warminster Urban District Council who was also working as the Chief Billeting Officer, noted the sewage disposal difficulties. 'Despite all our efforts at re-organisation, it has been difficult to cope with a very sudden increase of the population from something like 5,500 to over 7,000, and every addition to the number will worsen matters.'[147] Both Pewsey Rural District Council and Calne and Chippenham Rural District Council felt that they could not accept any more evacuees. They were accommodating troops and were already using

> Hudds Mill Farm,
> Edington,
> Nr. Westbury,
> Wilts.
>
> Sir,
>
> Just a line to ask you if you could help me and my family to get a house in Westbury, I am liveing in a condeme House that is not fit for pigs to live in when it rains we get wet through I have to go to work which is 7 miles there is no bus or trains to get there so I have had to go in digs which is to much as I go to send home.   I am a London woman I was bomb out at West Ham at prince regent Lane Custom House £16. I have been to the blitsde office. Mr. Wever he nows the place and say I did not ought to bother as we have been very ill as we have on water only a brook and the cows and horse they drink and stand and do things in it so I would be so glad if you could do something for me
>
> Your Oblig

Letter from a lady living in a condemned house in Edington 'not fit for pigs to live in'. She had been bombed out of her home in West Ham (WSA G12/225/1)

condemned houses.[148] The *Wiltshire Times* was reporting a meeting of the Trowbridge Urban Council in its 4 November 1939 edition. Council Members were discussing how to go about evicting London evacuees from a condemned house.

In Malmesbury during March 1940 the Billeting Officer reported that more children would be arriving in their area; a proposed quota of 400 had been given. It was suggested a list be made of all those householders willing to take the children. In April Malmesbury Rural District Council reported that the response to the appeal had been disappointing with less than 100 families willing to accommodate evacuees, and some of those were already billetors. The argument was made again, as per the year

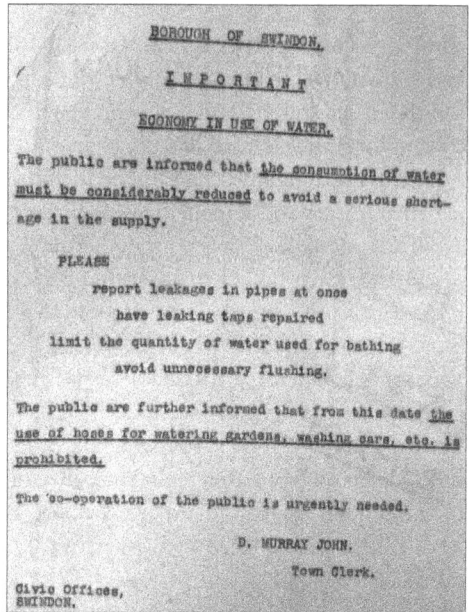

Public announcement by the Borough of Swindon regarding water shortages (WSA G24/225/12)

before, for camps to be constructed, but the Ministry's reply stated that although it had constructed 31 camps for evacuees, none were planned for Wiltshire.[149] Marlborough reported that troops had arrived as well as evacuees. Although anxious to co-operate they were not able to accept any additional cases.[150]

A letter from the Marlborough Borough Town Clerk on 28 September 1940 detailed the additional strain being placed on Wiltshire's housing and services: 'Since the arrival of evacuees from Bexhill we are being continually asked to provide accommodation for stragglers from London. The provision of this has entailed the use of all Condemned Houses and the point has been reached when no further accommodation is available.'[151] Wilton was also struggling to find room for the Bexhill evacuees due to the military presence in the town and the numbers of clerical and military staff also requiring billets.[152] A meeting was arranged by the Government to discuss the forthcoming Plan IV evacuation in 1940. When asked why certain areas of the county had received relatively few evacuees compared to others in the new Plan, the answer by the Ministry of Health Inspector is surprising. It was not based on the greatest availability of accommodation or school places, but: 'These figures were set up at Whitehall and they are based on the number who took the greatest number on the previous evacuation.' Whitehall had been alerted regarding the situation but the Town Clerk of Devizes had been given the reply that the numbers still stood '… it was the policy of the Ministry.'[153]

Swindon was placed under a Lodgings Restrictions Order in 1940 due to the chronic lack of billets. From then on anyone who wished to gain accommodation in Swindon needed to apply. Applications were arriving at the rate of 40/50 per day in 1941.[154] In Trowbridge a 'Closing Order' was being considered in May 1941 for all evacuees except war workers. The Council was 'somewhat apprehensive of the result of such an Order' and was requesting further information on the effect it might have on visits or shelter for the relatives of Trowbridge residents.[155] The town's Lodgings Restrictions Order came into effect on 1 May 1943.[156] Westbury's Chief Billeting Officer was considering attending a conference in August 1944 to 'stop an influx of evacuees in Westbury.' They had been arriving at a rate of 45 per week since his last report.[157] For Swindon with its Lodgings Restrictions Order, Plan VIII was causing difficulties and some applications by evacuees had to be refused. Appeals were heard, such as those in January 1945 by people coming from the 'flying bomb' area.[158]

Letter from the Chief Billeting Officer of Westbury regarding the conference on evacuation, 3 August 1944 (WSA G12/225/1)

A different type of evacuee received a decidedly warm welcome even when space was limited, although perhaps understandably. The military were seen as doing an essential job, and Swindon residents were praised for their help with the British Expeditionary Force (BEF), temporarily accommodated in the town after the Dunkirk evacuation of 1940.[159] In the summer of 1940 some Warminster residents came out of … 'the Minster after Matins one Sunday… and there were 50 exhausted Frenchmen, dressed in fisherman's jerseys, their legs covered in tar. They had had a terrible ordeal and had been standing in the sea for hours, if not days, waiting to be rescued. The Vicar asked everyone to take them home and about 6 or 8 came with us. My mother dressed them in my late grandfather's clothes and they stayed for a few days, until other accommodation could be found. I remember them playing tennis wearing my grandfather's stiff shirts!' It was also noted that despite the language barrier, the Frenchman 'made a big impact on the ladies of Warminster'…![160] In 1944 Trowbridge had to find space for 'Bolero' billeting on the lead up to D-Day, on this occasion for medical staff. They were having such difficulty finding billets for the women which 'had to be of a much higher standard than even the men officers' that the arrival of the nurses had to be delayed by almost a week, but with the help of the Women's' Voluntary Service '[c]o-operation between Police, British Army, U.S. Army and Civil billeting authority was perfect… The attitude of the householders changed almost overnight and they had nothing but praise for the men's behaviour.'[161]

It was factory workers and clerical staff who were not welcomed with open arms. With the war-time necessity of 'secrets cost lives' and 'keeping mum', the local population had no idea what their lodgers were doing to help the war effort. Many felt that these incomers had an easy time of it, especially the male workers.[162] There were many rumours of men escaping the war and retiring to 'funkholes' in the country.[163] In June 1941 the Trowbridge Urban District Council's Chief Billeting Officer had been charged with billeting 200 employees engaged by G. N. Haden and Sons Ltd., and also for billeting the war workers of Messrs. Parnell of Yate, Bristol, who were 'now being dispersed to Atworth'.[164] On 8 July 1941 he was submitting his monthly report to the Civil Defence Committee, noting that there were within the town 585 unaccompanied children, 870 adults with children, 41 teachers, 6 helpers, 44 evacuees living in condemned houses, 80 evacuees at the Adcroft Hostel, 10 children at Conigre House, 51 blind people and 595 war workers (including their dependants); a total of 2,282 persons.[165]

The experiences of evacuees were as many and varied as the evacuees themselves. Initially the Salisbury City Clerk was worried about the care some evacuees would receive. He felt that although the working classes showed a willingness to house evacuees, the motivation was purely financial and that they would not care properly for the children.[166] As the years have gone by, testimonies by evacuees now show that his prediction unfortunately proved true for some.[167] Some had harrowing experiences in Wiltshire, such as two sisters evacuated from London who ended up with a farm labourer and his wife:

> They resented us very much, and we had to sleep on boxes out in the washhouse with the dogs. We were fed there too, pigs' trotters, no green vegetables or fruit. I remember drinking lots of water in the evening to try to fill my stomach – we were hungry all the time.

When we grew out of our dresses we had to wear sacks with holes cut out for head and arms. There was no warmth in them and the rough edges made us very sore, as you can imagine.

Finally my sister contracted pneumonia and some people realised the conditions in which we were living. The vicar found another home for us. There at least we had better food, though we had ours in the kitchen, not with the rest of the family. We had dresses too, but there was a lot of cold and hard work to be done after school every day and at weekends. However, when we were taken back to London to live in our sister's flat (our parents were killed in the Blitz) we were very neglected and unhappy, and finally we were allowed to return to Wiltshire; we were glad to come, in spite of the hard work and discipline still put on us. We both married Wiltshire men and brought up our families here.[168]

Children from Wanstead High School were evacuated to Chippenham. The High School put them under a curfew at night 'but as my billet parents went to whist drives several evenings a week, I had to stay out of the house until they came home. As I dare not be seen out of the doors after curfew, I used to sit in the shed in the garden until they returned. After a year in this house I was 'rescued' by another couple who lived further along the road and knew I was unhappy. I then stayed with them and they were extremely kind to me.'[169]

Evacuees from Wormwood Scrubs remember their arrival at Devizes station. They were greeted by a line of schoolchildren who called out: 'We don't want you. Go home.'[170] Some of the boys in Swindon were talking of the imminent arrival of the evacuees. 'There'll be 'vacuees coming, and we'd better be there to see what's going on. We can't have them, running about all over the place, not knowing where to go. We can sort 'em out, those that look like good fighters, they can come up 'ere with us. Those that don't, they can shove off.'[171] One London evacuee found that the village children resented them. They spoke differently, often dressed differently, and went to their own 'evacuee' school. Adjustments were made and integration was achieved, although sometimes after fights![172]

James Hinton cites work which denounces the middle class elements of society such as members of the WVS as using stereotypes to distance themselves from the lower classes.[173] A stereotypical attitude was certainly true of the Diocesan Inspector attending Chippenham Ivy Lane School who included in his report: 'It was gratifying to note that although a number of evacuees have come to the school, a high moral tone has been maintained.'[174] An account is given in the Bemerton Parish Magazine of how the evacuees were settling in, and is perhaps a little superior in tone.

The misfits were speedily adjusted, and the children made welcome in all cases. Indeed they are being fathered and mothered by our good people in a most generous spirit and treated as if they were their own children; and if they are not learning in school hours as much as we would like, on account of undug trench shelters and provision of classroom difficulties, they are learning ways of friendliness, civility, good manners and religions which are far better.[175]

Maureen Duffy, a London resident privately evacuated to Trowbridge with her mother did not feel at all welcome. She later wrote a novel about her wartime experiences. 'I think I hated [Trowbridge] from the beginning. I was different from these people. I knew it and they knew it. Later on, rationalising, I said the place had all the worst characteristics of town and country. The people seemed to me slow and thick, in speech and in the head. My accent marked me out at once as a vaccy. I gloried in it. I cherished and cosseted my cockney ways. I wouldn't have become a moonraker, a swede. Once they refused to serve my mother in the fish-and-chip shop because she was a 'bloody Londoner'. 'And who's winning the war for you?' my mother replied. 'The bloody Londoners. You don't know there's a war on down here', and she marched out, all five feet and one and a half inches rigid with fury. That's how our private war was declared. In their turn, of course, the [Trowbridge people] distrusted the vaccies with their quick ways and sharp, pinched faces. They said they were all dirty, had fleas, were sewn into their clothes for the winter, that they were light-fingered and only out for what they could get out of you. Oh, an endless list of complaints. I reckon they'd've been nicer to the enemy…' She felt that most of those who hosted evacuees did so with a 'thwarted missionary spirit'. Her billetor was determined to reform her so-called lying and thieving ways.[176] The Chippenham doctor Joan Hickson wrote in her diary about the evacuees from Bath, Somerset who came to stay with them on 27 April 1942, and the reaction of her children, home from boarding school and who were '… not too keen on turning out of their rooms, but tolerably pleasant. Didn't see why it should be they to turn out, but they were occupying one large room each (spare room and nursery) which were the obvious ones in which to accommodate refugees.' She also noted of her children three days later:

> They have been so appallingly adolescent all the time, touchy and inclined to take offence at anything said to them or any criticism or request to do anything. Don't see why they should or why the beastly old war should spoil things for them. I can remember feeling like it myself in the last war so ought to be sympathetic. But a perpetual state of busyness and fatigue drives me to chronic irritability, and though they understand the cause of it and would cope occasionally, it is naturally difficult for them to do so permanently, so it is a vicious circle.

A doctor from Aylesbury wrote to the *British Medical Journal* regarding the evacuees.

> We have learnt by very uncomfortable contact how the other half of the world lives, and we have seen that the other half appreciates us as little as we appreciate them. Town mothers arriving into the country were seen as not grateful, and

the rising tide of country resentment was said to match the objections of the unwilling guests.[178]

In June 1942 Joan Hickson was talking of her long-term patients with a new found fondness, and was already wondering over the post-war world. 'These old original patients produce a spontaneous but warm feeling of friendliness when I see them, quite a different feeling from that felt for the hoards of newcomers, though these are of all sorts, some nice and some horrid. Would we still have this feeling under a State Medical Service I wonder, and if not would it matter to medicine? A very difficult question.'[179]

One case which illustrates some of the complexities and difficulties facing evacuees is that of a lady and her two children who had been evacuated when they were bombed out of their London home. By February 1945 they were living at a remote cottage near Roundway. The lady's husband was very worried as her letters showed that she appeared 'very anxious and depressed' and felt she could not 'stand the loneliness and difficulties of her present billet much longer.' The Council had not been able to carry out the necessary repairs to her London house and so she could not return. By June 1946 her sister-in-law had moved in to the cottage; she had two children, one of whom was an illegitimate child her husband had refused to acknowledge or pay an allowance for (the evacuee's husband therefore had to support both families). The evacuee's husband was still in the Forces and was once again worried about his wife; her sister-in-law had been told she must find a job, leaving the evacuee mother looking after all the children in a 'very lonely place' which he felt she would not be able to cope with. The evacuee's husband did not want to turn his sister out but was worried he would soon be getting himself into debt supporting them all.[180] The stress felt by those evacuees who found it hard to adapt, and the worry this caused their next of kin must have been a heavy burden to bear. Many evacuees missed home and some did not like where they were billeted. The pressure children were under when they were away from home was noted by one evacuee's father who was writing to Swindon Borough Council from his home in Essex. He had been receiving letters from his 13 year old son asking to be brought home, and showing that

> he is getting very homesick... Although, as much as I would like to have him home, I quite realise the danger of doing such a rash deed. His mother is evacuated at Swindon with the youngest child of my family, and my other children are at Bradford on Avon, Wilts. If he could be transferred to his mother, or to his brothers and sisters, I believe he would be in quite a different frame of mind... I have nothing against his billets but just that the boy wants to be with someone of his family. He is a big boy and I know that he misses us more than the younger children would...So if you could do something to relieve my boy of this homesick feeling and relieve his mother from worry... I and my wife would be grateful.[181]

Others went missing, such as a boy from Edmonton, London. The *Wiltshire Times* reported the case in its 9 September 1939 edition, providing a description and his home address in London. He was probably riding his bicycle. The evacuees escaping from their bombed out homes must have been traumatised by their experiences; people they had known may well have died or been injured and their homes and possessions lay in tatters.[182] The stress that children suffered as a result of moving away from home could result in behaviour changes, but could also manifest itself in other ways, such as bedwetting. The Women's Voluntary Service's leaflet *A Healthy Child is a Happy Child* advised householders to '[r]emember that the younger children especially will be feeling homesick, frightened and thoroughly upset and over-excited for several days.' Householders were not to force the children to eat or to offer alternatives. Suggestions were made regarding how to cope with bed wetting; try to get them up at 10pm, do not scold or punish, and to seek advice from the District Nurse if the problem persisted. A supply of mackintosh overlays for the beds of young children had been ordered by the Government and would be available via Local Authorities.

> Be patient! Give them as much affection and sense of security as possible. Do all you can to gain their confidence. A sense of security will be given by a regular life. See that they have plenty of occupation and play. Discuss nothing in front of the children that has frightened them or may frighten them in the future. Do not discuss the child's health or conduct in its presence...[183]

It must also be noted that those children who remained in Britain's bombed cities witnessed the true horror of total war firsthand, leaving their own psychological scars.[184]

At school, some evacuees were kept together;[185] others were placed in mixed classes.[186] Teachers had to cope with working in buildings which had not been designed as schools as many schools in reception areas were not big enough to accommodate the new influx of pupils. There was also the issue of dealing with behavioural problems that could arise from children being separated from their families and placed in an unfamiliar environment.[187] One evacuee who went to stay with her grandparents at Bratton aged six remembers the yearning to have familiar things around her.

> Every time I was helped to write a letter [home] I begged for them to send my precious tricycle which was mouldering in the air raid shelter. It was a cry from the heart that I wanted all the things back round me that made life tolerable. Visits from the parents were not frequent enough and then there was the awful moment, as the short stay ended, when there had to be a tearful parting on Westbury Station. In the end my Darling Mother struggled down with the tricycle. Oh Joy![188]

Evacuees, not unlike local children, did get into trouble but the profiles of these evacuee cases were prominently positioned in the newspaper, such as 'Evacuees in trouble: Theft of Torches' in the *Wiltshire Times*, 4 November 1939 about four boys aged 13-15 staying in Melksham. The householder of one boy said that he was a good boy at heart but had caused her a lot of trouble; the other foster parents gave their evacuees good character references. The statement of the Chairman of Magistrates reveals the extent to which he sympathised with the possible underlying causes for their behaviour; the break up of their families and their departure from

Parents arriving at Trowbridge Station on 23 December 1939 to visit their children who had been evacuated to Trowbridge and the surrounding area (WSA 1772/1/308/1 B/W)

home. 'This is a very serious matter. You cannot come down into the country and think you can do just as you like. We are anxious not to mar your careers but because we appear lenient to-day that will not apply if there should be any future cases.' By May 1940 the evacuees were being seen to cause a disturbance in Malmesbury during out of school hours and some residents wanted a Recreation Centre established to 'keep these visitors off the streets. As they play around the War Memorial they cause an absolute uproar, causing distress to numbers of aged and invalid residents of the locality. The trouble is especially bad on Sunday evenings.'[189]

The problem of absenteeism from school was highlighted at a Wiltshire General Education Committee meeting in August 1944. It was noted that there had been too many children absent from school and recommendations were presented for prosecuting. 'Children could not be educated unless they went to school, and were in these days often kept away from school for trivial reasons.' The Head of a Malmesbury School wrote in the School Log Book in November 1940:

> The standard of attendance has fallen badly. So many absences are now unavoidable that there is no surprise at broken attendance and it no longer causes comment. Children who always made a point of regular attendance now do not care.
>
> The standard of behaviour is rougher probably as a result of the war and more boys get involved with the police.
>
> Without a doubt the war is having a disastrous effect on education.'[191]

Difficulties with the London Teachers' 'Lack of Assistance' was discussed at a meeting of the Calne and Chippenham Rural District Council, reported in the *Wiltshire Gazette* on 19 October 1939. The teachers were not helping to care for the evacuees outside school hours, and an 'experiment' had been started by the Hon. Mrs Methuen of Corsham Court to help the issue, but it required the help of volunteers. 'There was general regret that the London teachers had not done what they might in looking after the children. 'The lack of assistance on the part of these teachers is what we meet everywhere,' said one speaker…' A report had been sent to the Ministry and it was added that '… some of the children were practically impossible. Others did damage in the houses, and they could not allow householders to suffer from damage done by the children.' A Malmesbury Head wrote in his log book in November 1940:

> The continual changing of teachers, the lack of materials, and the continual alterations in time (including holidays) is having a serious effect which is now beginning to show quite clearly. The visiting teachers do not show the same interest in the school or in the pupils as the old staff did and as a result they get less response from the children.[192]

A Surrey resident had great sympathy for the evacuated teachers of Chippenham in October 1939, condemned by Corsham's Lord Methuen in a *Daily Express* article. He felt it was disheartening that they were treated as outcasts and stated they had come voluntarily, incurring the expenses of keeping their London homes and paying additional lodging fees (the Government paid the first 5s.). A teacher from Paddington School offered to take some of the 'difficult' evacuees on in a house but it needed furniture, bedding and crockery. The Billeting Officer of Corsham stated: 'This seems to us here to be a truly public-spirited act on the part of the school teachers and we in turn are anxious to help the effort on.' Appeals were made for funds.[194]

On 17 September 1941 the head of Ivy Lane School in Chippenham was busy filling in forms for 300 evacuees connected with the school which 'necessitated a considerable amount of clerical work.' By October he was describing how it was impossible for him to take a class even for a day on account of matters of organisation such as parents' interviews and 'manifold enquiries officially.' That month nine to ten columns of an official form had been completed in respect of 320 evacuees. 'The amount of clerical work connected with this school is unknown except in the case of the head teacher.' More work was forthcoming later that month when he received instructions that 'immigrants receiving 'Billeting Allowances' will rank as evacuees. Others will be regarded as Wiltshire children and will need to be re-registered.' Their names would have to be transferred. One weekend in March 1942 saw the Head Teacher making 'prodigious efforts as a result of working Saturday and Sunday.' Over 100 record forms regarding the exams were then sent to the County Office.[195]

During WWI many schools had resorted to a 'double shift' form of education with the children being taught on a part-time basis due to a lack of staff. During WWII teachers made a huge effort to avoid the problem occurring again[196] but Wiltshire's School Log Books report an increasing strain due to teacher absences through illness or taking leave when supply teachers were at a premium, as in May 1942 when two teachers were absent, taking time off when their husbands were on leave. The school was 'upset and disorganised completely.' 'County Office expects us to "carry on" during the temporary absences of teachers.'[197] There were also teacher absences due to the additional Civil Defence responsibilities that they had taken on. On 3 June 1942 one teacher from the County School in Bromham was required to attend a day course in Trowbridge 'in connection with the work of the Emergency Rest Centre'. On 10 July 1942 the Head Mistress and an Assistant had to attend a Civil Defence Meeting in Devizes in connection with the Rest Centre and had no option but to close the school for the afternoon. It was not a one-off occurrence.[198]

It appears that the Ministry of Education began a re-organisation of schools *c.* 1941 which was causing difficulties for the Milk Marketing Board when distributing milk as part of the Schools Milk Scheme. They were requesting that schools provide the former name and new name of the school along with their address and registered number to ensure that rebate claims were not delayed.[199] One evacuee in Minety found that her local contemporaries were further behind in their studies than the London children. She found it quite frustrating to be taught things that she already knew.[200] As previously noted, the Government was also found to take no interest in the number of school places available when looking at billeting children in an area. In Wiltshire '... in some cases the numbers of children far exceeded the number of places and in other districts was far below the number of school places vacant.'[201] It would have been hard for the receiving Local Authorities to plan effectively with no details being given regarding the ages of the children. It would be even harder in those villages where maximum capacity had been reached and where there were no other schools nearby. In a meeting between all of Wiltshire's Local Authorities, held to discuss the planned 1940 Evacuation Scheme, the Clerk of Wilshire County Council stressed the point that co-operation between Billeting and the Education Authorities would be difficult but very important. 'The main point is the safety of the children and I am afraid education must come second.'[202] By early 1940 London County Council and Portsmouth City Council recognised that many children were not being taught at all in their cities. Schools were being used for other purposes and there were fewer teachers because many were still with their charges in the reception areas.[203] What Robert Mackay finds surprising, however, is that in 1945 the number of children successfully taking public examinations increased, and that the School Certificate and Higher School Certificate pass rates had remained unaltered at *c.* 77%. Although the standard of education an individual child received could vary greatly, the results were a testament to the dedication and hard work of teachers and administrators during the war,[204] but due to the evacuees education became a 'burning political issue' for reform.[205]

Evacuated children were often unused to rural ways of life; fresh milk from the farm (many children had only seen it in bottles and did not associate it with cows) and collecting eggs from the hens. Helping with haymaking was also required. A life outdoors in the countryside was a novelty.[206] A trip was organised to enable some six and seven year old Trowbridge evacuees to visit a local dairy farm to learn about the country, hoping to 'bridge the gap between town and country folk,' as was reported in the *Wiltshire Times* on 30 September 1939. It was said that the highlight of the afternoon was receiving apples from the farmer's wife. The children wrote to say thank you, one on the back of a strip of wallpaper (due to the paper shortages), saying 'Dear Mr. Stone. Thank you for the apples. Thank you for letting us watch you milk the cows, thank you for letting us see the milk being cooled. Thank you for letting us see Sister (the cat).' Rural housing could appear primitive with no indoor toilets, water supply or electricity.[207] One London evacuee was very pleased with her bedroom at a house in Broughton Gifford. 'I was given a pretty little bedroom in which was a very large brass bedstead. I cannot remember ever being cold in that gorgeous bed, even in the most severe weather when water froze in the jug, and frost patterned the windows.' She does remember being terrified by the trip to the toilet, 100 yards from the house down a dark and muddy path. She would never go there at night on her own.[208] In Minety some of the evacuees were shocked when they discovered the toilet was to be found at the bottom of the garden. The shock turned to fear when they discovered they would have to take a candle with them in the dark.[209] In many places washing facilities were either limited or were having so much strain put on them that Local Authorities such as Calne provided facilities for clothes washing for those who could not get them at their billets. The proposed Welfare Centre would also be used as a day centre for adults, a nursery for children and temporary sleeping accommodation for those evacuees who arrived late at night. It would also include the means to obtain a hot bath. The Centre was seen by the Billeting Officer as an 'essential and pressing need'.[210]

Calder notes that if seen in a positive light, town children had their horizons widened whilst country children discovered new ideas and ambitions.[211] The local children of Minety found that they were more reserved and shy than their London guests who '… sang and danced with gusto' at the organised dances and pantomimes. The locals learnt new expressions such as 'Cor blimey' and 'Stone a flipping crow,' although their parents often did not approve![212] The Wroughton History Group note that some evacuees from East Ham were amazed that '[w]hen we went to bed we saw from the window that they had some chickens in a pen in the back garden. This was a real novelty for us and it was promised that we could collect eggs the next day. Suddenly I realised that living in the country was going to be a whole new experience. I had never before seen chickens running around.'[213] Malcolm Martin, evacuated from London to Hilperton and Staverton, later recalled that:

> For a youth at a time when one's interest starts to expand beyond home and school towards a greater realisation that there was a big and interesting world out there, evacuation could not have had better timing. This early experience

to natural history resulted in it becoming a big part of my life… For that alone I have warm memories of the Wiltshire countryside.' Malcolm's foster parents taught him how to swim, took cycling trips to the Westbury white horse, and 'proudly attended school concerts as any true parents could… In short treated me as one of them, a novel distinction from my earlier days in London.'[214]

Malcolm Martin with other evacuees at Staverton, reproduced by his kind permission (WSHC P53721)

In Malmesbury it was said that 'many evacuated children in the rural area were found to be unclean'.[215] An *Open Discussion* regarding war workers, voluntary lodgings and compulsory billeting found in Swindon Borough's Wartime Correspondence files noted that the principal cause of difficulty when taking evacuees were: late hours, drunkenness, dirty habits (including soiled bedding), verminous condition, scabies.[216] At a meeting between Wiltshire's Local Authorities and other organisations, organised by the Ministry of Health to discuss the proposed 1940 Evacuation Scheme, the Town Clerk of Devizes talked frankly to his London County Council counterpart.

I am glad to hear that the L.C.C. is represented here today, I am not going to blame them at all, but when the children came down, we put these children in the houses of the people who volunteered to take them, they were very glad when they went back or other billets were found for them. It is absolutely impossible to get people to take children now, in view of the experience of the people who have had them. I hope you will forgive me, it is easy to say what should have been done, but we are faced with what actually happened. This is the position of Devizes today, we have not any volunteers… I do feel that nothing short of compulsory billeting will meet the situation… even for exchange; people who have had children for four or five months and with absolutely good intentions want the next door neighbour to have them but they will not do it… I tell you quite frankly, we cannot billet, unless we open the door and push the children in like leaflets. … I am speaking of the worst cases, the children who foul the beds, with the best intentions in the world the people will not put up with it.

The Clerk of Devizes Rural District Council corroborated the experiences of the Town Clerk, and that due to children who were unsuitable for billeting being sent into homes, the voluntary scheme had been 'killed'.[217] Advice given to parents by London County Council for Plan IV included information about health and cleanliness.

After evacuation had taken place last September complaints were made by householders in the receiving areas that some of the children were not clean. You will wish to be sure that this cannot be said about your own child and to do everything possible to make sure that he goes away with clean clothes, clean hair and a clean body… Every mother will wish her child to arrive at his new home in a state in which he will be gladly welcomed…

The parents' local council had set up treatment centres and bathing stations; parents would receive an invitation to present their children for an initial medical inspection. They were urged to attend.[218] The *British Medical Journal* published a letter from Dr Kerr. 'I do not think it is using language any too strong to say that in many cases the scum of a town has been poured into a clean countryside with a most callous disregard to the consequences and apparently without the most elementary safeguards for the public health.'[219]

But this time of disgust also brought with it a desire for change as the *British Medical Journal* commented: 'eventually good will result if this wartime experience draws attention to the persistence of verminous conditions in the homes of the poor as a social scandal!'[220] The issue was raised in Parliament.[221] After pressure from the National Federation of Women's Institutes and National Union of Townswomen's Guilds, the National Council of Social Service (NCSS) convened a conference in September 1939 to consider problems arising from the evacuation.[222] The *Our Towns* Report, published in April 1943 and which almost sold out of its first edition run of 5,000 copies, gave an overview of the evacuation and the debate this had raised, and what could be done in terms of the education of families, environment and nutrition, but it also brought about the term 'problem families'.[223]

The health of the evacuees was noticed in Wiltshire. Children with 'dirty habits' were sent to Marlborough children's convalescent home for treatment and there 'were no further complaints' when they were returned to the district.[224] A report of the Trowbridge District Joint Hospital Board at Warminster in the *Wiltshire Times*, 21 October 1939, stated that many patients in the isolation hospital were evacuees. Interestingly, many of the cases would not usually be treated in hospital but this was necessary because of the conditions of some of the houses in which the children were being evacuated to. '…it was absolutely necessary' and a clinic was being set up. It was resolved that more medical attention should be given to every evacuee before they left home. A newly arrived evacuee was excluded from attending school in Ashton Keynes with impetigo in September 1941,[225] but it must be noted that the poor state of some children was not just visible in the case of evacuees. The *Salisbury and Winchester Journal*, 16 June 1944, was reporting a case in Shrewton where the children of a local family were found to be very dirty and in a verminous condition. 'Where the children slept was appalling. There were no sheets or proper pillows, just a few blankets and dirty mattresses which were infested with fleas…' A *Wiltshire Times* article of 3 June 1944 relayed the 'disgraceful' case of two Melksham mothers who were sent to gaol over the neglect of their children. The Medical Officer stated: 'In my thirty years of practice, including 24 years as a Medical Officer of Health, and including what I have seen in the slums of London, I have never struck anything so disgraceful as this.' The children were meant to be being looked after by the eldest, aged 14. She had arrived home with an American soldier and was now also being looked after by the authorities. It was discovered the women had been away in London for four days and nights. The location of children in a poor condition was not only restricted to Britain's cities.

The blind people arriving in Trowbridge were housed together at the Hollywood Country Club. It was reported in the *Wiltshire Times* on 30 September 1939 that they were 'wonderfully happy, and [were] enjoying the change of life immensely.' The Girl Guides came to help them sew buttons onto their clothes, although some of the blind were keen knitters themselves, helping to knit comforts for the troops.[226] A letter from a local blind lady who had worked in Registered Schools for the Blind disagreed with the policy of housing the blind in Institutions, feeing they could be better cared for individually by householders,[227] but the Clerk of Calne Borough Council urged the need in September 1939 to 'remove blind persons billeted in private houses in Calne.… Some of them are sick and diseased and some are mentally weak or deficient. When, under pressure, we consented to find places for blind people, it was understood that the only defect would be blindness, and many people came forward to house them. It has been a great shock to those people to find that they are now forced to take people who are quite Institutional cases.'[228] In August 1939 the Swindon branch of the Wilts County Association for the Care of the Blind relayed that they would not be able to act to aid the billeting of blind evacuees… '[M]y Committee cannot hold themselves responsible for such an extensive scheme in addition to its normal obligations to our 95 registered blind.'[229] Urchfont Manor was loaned to London County Council for use as a Hospital School for evacuated children with tuberculosis[230] and Lady Laurie (Vice-President of St. Thomas' Babies Hospital) allowed the use of her home, The Manor, Cricklade, as a diabetic hospital for babies under 2 years with the converted wing holding about a dozen cots. The staff brought their equipment with them from London and Norland nurses were billeted in the village.[231] The elderly, infirm and vulnerable also had to be evacuated from the South East. Roundway Hospital received 220 evacuee patients from Hampshire in 1939, and 67 from Surrey and Hampshire in 1941 with patient numbers reaching an all time peak of 1,510 in 1943.[232] Elderly evacuees living in Salisbury were admitted into the Salisbury Institution for short periods and some remained after peace had been declared.[233]

Some of Wiltshire's Communal Care Homes became synonymous with good care. The Medical Officer of the Warminster and Westbury Rural District Council was so impressed with the care being given to children at the Heytesbury Hostel he wrote a letter to the Chairman and Members of the Rural District Council sending his praise and congratulations in December 1942.

> The Medical Officers of the Ministry of Health who have visited, have expressed their admiration at the way the Hostel has been run... [The Matron] and her daily Domestic Help have unstintingly devoted their time and energy to making the Hostel a success, and I feel that the greatest possible praise is due to them for their nurturing and selfless devotion to the welfare of the children. Not only have the children benefited greatly in physical health, but I have been constantly delighted to notice how happy they are when living there.... [the Matron has been] instilling a homely atmosphere which in itself must have been a very difficult job, and which is so essential for the mental development of a growing child. Discipline has been excellent and freedom from infection remarkable.... It has always been a constant source of satisfaction and pride to me that I should have been told by Ministry of Health Doctors that our Hostel is 'One in a thousand'.[234]

A hostel for evacuees was opened in 1940 just outside Bradford on Avon, able to cater for 65 'undesirable' children and becoming known as the 'awkward evacuees home'. Jack Mock records the experience of one of the evacuees sent there. 'At Conigar House there were 30 to 40 of us and it was run by a dear old lady... the home was strict but fair, more important, we all felt secure and loved... I still treasure my time at Conigar House and in fact I was heartbroken when I had to leave.[235]

In 1938 plans had been made to evacuate those under 5s who were without parents or whose mothers were unable to accompany them. The Women's Voluntary Service (WVS) began working with Child Welfare Organisations and started training helpers in 1939 to work as Assistants for the Local Authorities who were tasked with caring for the children. Country houses were used for the purpose, providing residential nurseries with the aid of the American Red Cross. Each unit usually cared for around 40-50 children.[236] When the children reached five they were moved into billets to release spaces.[237] *Picture Post* reported in 1940 that since the Blitz began the WVS had been evacuating 100-200 under 5s a week and the demand for residential nursery places was still growing.[238] By March

APPENDIX A.

Menus.

	Breakfast	Dinner	Tea	Supper
1st Day	Fried potatoes Milk or milky tea Bread and jam	Mixed Vegetable Hotpot Baked bread pudding	Milky tea Bread,butter or margarine Cheese	Cocoa Bread,butter or margarine
2nd Day	Porridge,milk & sugar or treacle Bread,butter or margarine Milk or milky tea	Roast beef or mutton Potatoes Greens Raw fruit	Brawn or fish paste Watercress or lettuce Milky tea	Cocoa Bread,butter or margarine
3rd Day	Porridge,milk & sugar or treacle Bread,butter or margarine Milk or milky tea	Savoury Mince Boiled beetroot Boiled potatoes Fig pudding Custard	Cheese & potato pie Bread,margarine or butter Milky tea	Cocoa Bread,butter or margarine
4th Day	Bacon & fried bread Milk or milky tea	Thick Vegetable Soup Chocolate rice pudding	Scrambled eggs & oatmeal on toast Bread,margarine or butter Milky tea	Cocoa Bread,butter or margarine
5th Day	Porridge,milk & sugar or treacle Bread,butter or margarine Milk or milky tea	Baked fish & tomatoes or peas Fruit charlotte	Cheese & watercress Milky tea Bread,margarine or butter	Cocoa Bread butter or margarine
6th Day	Fried potatoes Bread and jam Milk or milky tea	Liver & Onion stew Treacle or jam tart	Kippers or herrings or herring roes fresh or canned Bread,butter or margarine Milky tea	Cocoa Bread,butter or margarine
7th Day	Porridge,milk & sugar or treacle Milk or milky tea	Cheese & carrot salad Steamed jam pudding	Potatoes in their jackets & margarine Bread,butter or margarine Milky tea	Cocoa Bread,butter or margarine
8th Day	Porridge,milk & sugar or treacle Bread,butter or margarine Milk or milky tea	Sausages Mashed potatoes Tomatoes or greens Milk pudding & dried fruit	Cheese dreams Bread,butter or margarine Milky tea	Cocoa Bread,butter or margarine

Suggested 8 day menu for evacuees contained in a Ministry of Health Circular, 21 May 1940
(WSA F2/850/7)

1940 unaccompanied children aged under five were being viewed as a priority. There were only a few nurseries operating at this time and so places were reserved for selected applicants, but more places were needed, especially as mothers were required for war work. The number of nurseries had reached 190 by March 1941. These were able to offer 6,000 places and by the end of 1942 this figure had increased to 13,000.[239] One lady returned to the village of Little Durnford at the end of the war.

The house at Durnford happily escaped the ravages of enemy action and was merely exposed to forty or so 'under fives' from East London. Rooms where my mother had felt she could not properly house a married couple ... were crowded with a dozen or so little beds... The dining-room lost its atmosphere of leisure and became a factory where forty little mouths were filled three times a day… Most visitors, however well intentioned, were kept at a safe distance from the motley crew by little noses that the country damp, the cotton and paper shortage, and an already overworked staff combined to keep in a most unattractive condition of moistness' but, 'the children seem to have endeared themselves to everyone concerned.' 'It was a pleasure to see them grow so plump and rosy,' say the cottage people, 'and since they left it has been so quiet.'[240]

Requisitioning

CALDER NOTES THAT war had brought with it to rural areas an influx of soldiers, evacuees and Land Girls, overburdening the already inadequate housing,[241] and with the need for additional housing stock, came the need for requisitioning. At Freshford on the Somerset/Wiltshire border, the author Fay Inchfawn wrote of the time when her house was inspected for requisitioning. 'My heart made a sudden leap upwards in my throat! See the house! *Our* house! I knew only too well what that might mean. The big houses around had nearly all been visited, and the occupants told to hold themselves in readiness to quit …' After the man from the Office of Works and Buildings had viewed the house, he asked if they wanted to leave. 'I suppose you have nowhere to go?' He then noted that the house was in fact much smaller than expected and that it was unlikely it would be needed.[242] Houses such as Cowbridge near Malmesbury, taken over by EKCO to be used for engineering, had a brick extension built in the 1940s. 'Like so many country houses taken over as an emergency during the war years, it suffered and has continued to do so…'[243] Householders could appeal against forced billeting, but not when it involved the lodging of military personnel.[244] In Swindon a letter was produced to give to householders asked to billet US troops, asking for their co-operation and a cordial welcome. They were handed to householders by the Police, along with an Army circular giving details of the arrangements; a *fait accompli*![245]

Hosts could also ask to appeal to a tribunal if they felt they were being treated unfairly or being abused by evacuees.[246] The Billeting Officer had to make 'every endeavour' to find willing householders, but if this is not possible, they needed to use their compulsory powers 'leaving the question of an appeal to be dealt with subsequently'.[247] October 1939 saw 17 appeal cases in Devizes; 5 were upheld, 2 were rejected, 4 were withdrawn and 6 were outstanding. In Salisbury there were 53; 33 upheld, 9 rejected, 6 outstanding and 5 withdrawn.[248] Melksham's October 1939 appeals included an application by one householder who had taken in two boys but one would just not settle. It was felt '… she had done everything possible to make the two boys comfortable with the accommodation…' The boy in question was moved. Another householder was having difficulty with her evacuee, a boy who '… was quite unmanageable, and when spoken to became very abusive and insulting.' The Clerk of the Tribunal requested that the boy's headmaster be approached to take the matter in hand, and the householder was told that the matter was being dealt with. Another householder was having difficulties with a mother and her children, the mother coming in late at night and the children climbing over the furniture with some of her possessions being broken. The result of the tribunal was a letter written by the Clerk to the billetee asking her to do everything possible by '… confirming the rules of the household, and by exercising proper control over her children'.[249] Other Authorities such as Malmesbury, Highworth and Pewsey saw no appeals.[250] The process of billeting and requisitioning involved a great deal of work on the part of Local Authorities, and in February 1943 the Ministry of Health was trying to make life easier by changing the requirements for expiry dates of requisitioned properties. A new system was proposed whereby every property would expire on the same date so that 'it [would] be necessary to make only one general application for renewal, covering all premises held for the Ministry of Health purposes; and it [would] also provide a suitable opportunity for the periodical review of need and the extent of use.'[251]

As soon as the war ended Local Authorities began receiving requests for compensation for damage caused by evacuees. This was reported in local newspapers, such as the Billeting Officer's report at the meeting of the Warminster and Westbury Rural District Council in 1945, reported in the 21 September edition of the *Warminster Journal* and which listed both the claimants and the amount they were claiming. One lady from Kingston Deverill had taken in a family from Newcastle. She had found them to be destructive and badly behaved. She was told by the Billeting Officer to go to Court about it and was writing to a solicitor for help. She thought that 'evacuees should not be allowed to abuse benefits, the Government ha[d] placed at their disposal.' They had damaged furniture and taken items away with them upon their return.[252]

The owner of Bishopstrow House took in evacuees for which he had been receiving 17s. per week. The evacuees had left by September 1945 and his claim for repair in respect of 'damage, decoration etc.' came to £89. The builder had prepared a specification and Warminster and Westbury Rural District Council were prepared to offer the owner £25 in settlement, subject to authorisation by the Ministry of Health.[253] It was often very difficult for the Council to estimate properly the cost of the damage reported to have been done by evacuees, as the Warminster and Westbury Billeting Officer's report of April 1941 shows. '… to assess the value of the damage is extremely difficult, as there is no proof as to the condition of the articles at the time the evacuees went in.'[254] In other situations the owners of properties wanted them back but the evacuees either did not want to return home, or had no home to return to. Westbury's Chief Billeting Officer was writing to the Warminster and Westbury Rural District Council in July 1945 about a house which contained evacuees. 'I understand that the husband of the evacuee is working in the district and desires to remain in Codford… As far as obtaining their removal is concerned I do not see any immediate prospect as there are so many similar cases.' The Government itself was putting a stop to derequisitioning in July 1945 due to the housing shortage. Warminster and Westbury Rural District Council were writing to one owner at this time regarding the issue. 'So far as de-requisitioning is concerned, as Executive Officer of the Local Authority I have no power to do this, on the contrary my instructions from the Ministry of Health are that immediately a requisitioned premises is vacated they are to be informed and on no account is a property to be released.'[255]

Trowbridge's Chief Billeting Officer was having concerns over the return of bedding in June 1945. It appears that householders were being asked to return bedding which had been lent to the evacuees, but which in some cases had been put into storage and was now moth-eaten. In other cases the evacuees had been bombed out and would still have no bedding if it was returned; often the sheets had just worn out over the intervening years. 'Are we expected in cases like this (and we usually know the cases personally) to make things unpleasant for householders who have done a grand job by looking after evacuees for years and had everything worn out [that] can be worn out, without any hope of replacement by purchasing at the shops? People say "We are quite prepared to pay for them, if the Government think we should, but we can't return them."' He felt that in the circumstances these types of items should be written off.[256] The Chief Billeting Officer in Westbury appears to have been very weary and frustrated with the system in August 1944. He was asked to attend a conference on evacuation but felt that: 'The conferences and meetings which I have attended during the past three and half years have made decisions or recommendations none of which have ever been carried out.'[257]

Problems also arose when demobbed servicemen returned and moved into the property that their evacuated families had been allotted. A house owner wrote to the Executive Officer of the Warminster and Westbury Rural District Council in July 1945, pleading to have her property derequisitioned. She realised that the husband of the evacuated family staying at her property was to be demobbed soon and that he was a 'most objectionable man' and she did not wish him to live 'rent free… with electric lights provided for him.' If she could get her property back she would be able to evict him. This was not to be the case, however, as the Executive Officer could not release any properties on Ministry of Health instructions, but he was hoping that 'two small cottages at Chitterne may become available.'[258] After requisitioning, property owners could remain in their property with their lodgers or move out with friends or relatives. Sometimes the properties that were requisitioned were already empty; their owners having more than one property or the owners had moved out already due to one reason or another.

The Government made arrangements for the return of evacuees to London in April 1945[259] but did not close down the Evacuation Scheme for mothers and children until 1948,[260] often due to the impossibility of returning families to bombed-out properties.[261] A special train was arranged to return the evacuees in North Wiltshire home to London on 24 June 1945, leaving from Little Somerford station with 52 children and 9 adults, picking up a further 106 in Wootton Bassett and 126 in Swindon; others left under their own steam during the summer of 1945.[262] In July 1945 there were still 76,000 evacuees living in billets throughout the country because their homes were destroyed or were unfit to return to[263] and in Wiltshire the Billeting Officer was worried about those children who had no families to welcome them home. 'I have now received instructions with regard to the return of the evacuated children from our school and hostel at Trowbridge. A point has arisen in connection with the homeless ones and I am suggesting that arrangements be made for them to continue at the hostel until a final decision has been made concerning their future.' He wanted to know if the Ministry of Health was prepared to accept responsibility for maintaining the hostel.[264] One of the Welfare Officers at Wiltshire County Council had been looking into the issue as early as 24 February 1944 at the request of the Ministry of Health.[265] Devizes Rural District Council was putting together a list of vacant accommodation in July 1945 at the request of the Regional Ministry of Health in Bristol. This would also include a schedule of evacuee families who were at present unable to return home as their houses had been destroyed or rendered uninhabitable. It was also necessary to report that some of these families did not wish to remain in the area; the accommodation which had been provided for them was 'not satisfactory, and in which children should not remain'.[266] Some evacuees remained in Wiltshire in 1946 and beyond, leaving only when their billeting allowance was withdrawn.[267] Two children who had been evacuated to Malmesbury were later employed by the firm EKCO which had relocated to the Malmesbury district from Southend on Sea.[268] The company remained at its site after the war. 'During the time of separation the army organised lorries to bring parents from London about once a month to visit the children and return them home in the evening. Later, as things worsened in London, many parents came to join the children, intending to return as soon as possible. Warminster was considered too quiet a place to live. However, it was not long before people grew to love the countryside and the town and stayed here to make Warminster their permanent home.'[269]

Evacuation had a significant impact on plans for war reconstruction, attitudes to state intervention and ideas about poverty, social class and the welfare state; John Welshman states that it opened the eyes of many to the poverty of the urban poor. It is now felt that evacuation revealed the hidden side of rural poverty too.[270] Niko Gärtner feels that although the popular perception of evacuation was that it exposed the condition of the urban poor, surely it was well evident beforehand. Writers had been commenting on urban poverty for over a century already. He feels that perhaps poverty should be viewed as those at the time perceived it – as a failure, pitting class against class and showing how little Civil Servants knew of other classes and communities. Gärtner goes further and suggests that the post-war welfare changes were due possibly to a 'new solidarity and gratefulness in the overall policy decisions', but which were also 'tools to maintain political control over a newly confident part of the population'.[271] But what can be seen is that the medical welfare of children was overhauled; the School Medical Service of the 1930s was reassessed, leading to policy changes in the 1944 Education Act, with the Board of Education's Report following the Beveridge Act stating that evacuation had shown 'how real and formidable the giants of Want, Ignorance and Squalor, and how sadly they are hindering, in town and country alike, the well being of the rising generation'.[272] The child psychologist John Bowlby studied children evacuated to residential nurseries and found that those who had 'affectionless character' had suffered a long separation from their mothers. His theories on the mental health of children were sent to the World Heath Organisation and were published by Penguin in 1953. They then became intertwined with the idea of 'problem families' and with a range of social issues, affecting Government policy on the family in the 1950s and extended disapproving attitudes towards working mothers too.[273]

The war turned 'a settled society into one of refugees', with families separated for long periods and children being separated from their families during their most formative years.[274] The war left a long-lasting emotional impact and, for some, emotional problems as adults.[275] Some children found it difficult to settle back into their pre-war lives. Parents had now become strangers with a different style

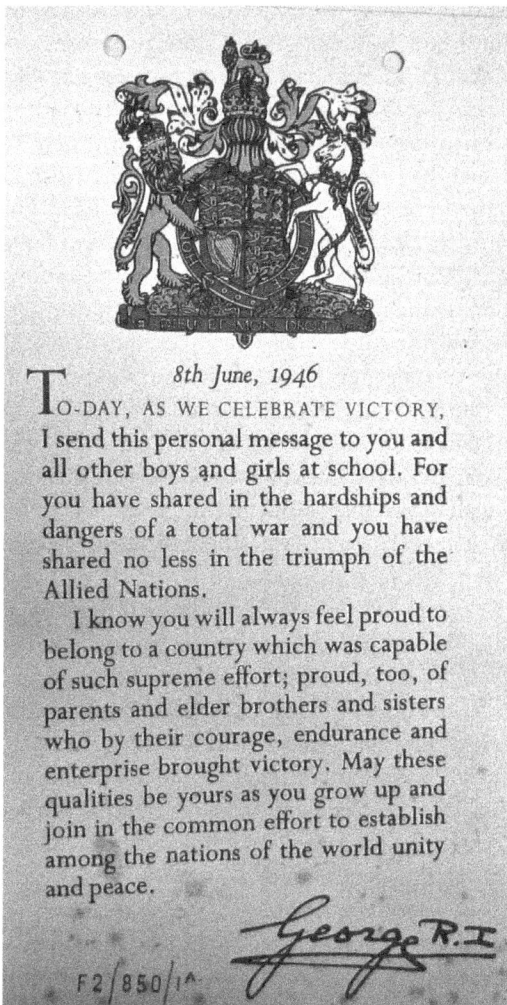

8th June, 1946

To-day, as we celebrate victory, I send this personal message to you and all other boys and girls at school. For you have shared in the hardships and dangers of a total war and you have shared no less in the triumph of the Allied Nations.

I know you will always feel proud to belong to a country which was capable of such supreme effort; proud, too, of parents and elder brothers and sisters who by their courage, endurance and enterprise brought victory. May these qualities be yours as you grow up and join in the common effort to establish among the nations of the world unity and peace.

George R.I

F2/850/1^

Message from the King to the country's children on 8 June 1946 (WSA F2/850/1) (A)

of parenting to that of their foster parents; other children had become orphaned. The Ministry of Health produced a leaflet to help teachers, social workers and nurses in charge of visiting families with former evacuees to check on the progress of reintegration. [276] By the end of the war 3.5 million evacuees,[277] up to 10% of the population of Britain,[278] had been placed in billets throughout the country in a scheme that was to become the largest single movement of a civilian population ever to take place.[279] Many workers who were billeted in Wiltshire communities remained there long after peace was declared and in many cases, settled in the county for good.

Some relationships made during the period of evacuation lasted a lifetime, for others the memories were bitter. What is certain is that the lives of evacuees and those of the Wiltshire people who received them had been forever altered by their presence. Two London sisters evacuated to Warminster finally moved on. They said goodbye to the other members of the family they had been billeted with, but their foster mother carried on cleaning the kitchen range and did not say goodbye. 'It did seem funny at the time, but I can understand it now as she must have felt very sad at our leaving after being there almost two years, and although we were happy enough of course there is no place like your own home and parents. I'd always thought I didn't like it there, but now I know how difficult it must have been to take in two strange little girls and be a mother to them and if all goes well, which it really did for us, what a wrench it must be when they leave. We never saw any of them again.'[280]

In Freshford:

> When the village was almost deserted again, when the little houses and big houses had only their own families to shelter, there was a distinct feeling of relief. But there was something else as well – the Village felt a disposition to recall the good points of the departed guests.
>
> It had been a time of revelation and heart–searching. The Government had asked a really hard thing. It is not easy to share one's own fireside indefinitely with anybody, but those who were least able – so it seemed – were the ones most willing to show the true Samaritan spirit. In that season of testing our village, so easily moved to compassion and also impatience, learned lessons which could not have been learned in any other way.[281]

3
The Friendly Invasion

Enlisting

AT THE START of the war Army service strength was at 400,000 with an equal number of territorial personnel. The Military Training Act of May 1939 brought in conscription for men aged 20-21 who had to undertake six months training.[1] One barracks used for this purpose was in Devizes.[2] After the outbreak of war, the National Service (Armed Forces) Act was passed, which encompassed men between the ages of 18 and 41,[3] other than those exempted on medical grounds or who were engaged in reserved occupations. Registration began sequentially by age, starting on 21 October 1939,[4] and it was only by June 1941 that it reached those men aged 40. By 31 December 1939, 1.5 million men were in the military services and 43,000 women had joined the WRNS (Women's Royal Naval Service, popularly called the Wrens), ATS (Auxiliary Transport Service), WAAFs (Women's Auxiliary Air Force) and Nursing Services.[5] The WRNS and the WRAF (Women's Royal Air Force) services created during WWI had been disbanded in 1919[6] and 1920[7] with the WRNS being re-formed in April 1939[8] and the WAAF being established in the same year.[9] The Women's Auxiliary Army Corps (WAAC) had also been disbanded after WWI. It re-emerged as the ATS.[10] By July 1941 there was a shortage in the workforce of 300,000 in

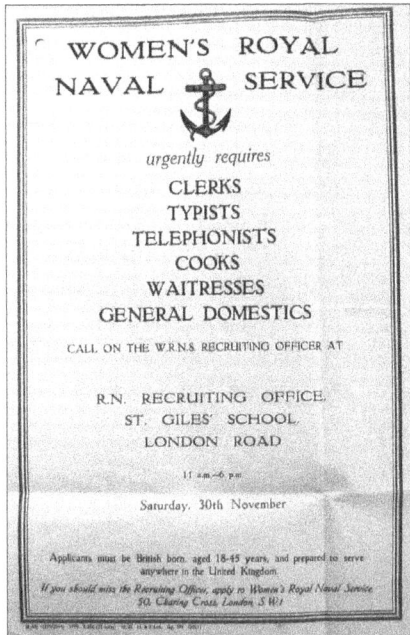

WOMEN'S ROYAL
NAVAL SERVICE

urgently requires

CLERKS
TYPISTS
TELEPHONISTS
COOKS
WAITRESSES
GENERAL DOMESTICS

CALL ON THE W.R.N.S. RECRUITING OFFICER AT

R.N. RECRUITING OFFICE,
ST. GILES' SCHOOL,
LONDON ROAD

11 a.m.–6 p.m.

Saturday, 30th November

Applicants must be British born, aged 18-45 years, and prepared to serve anywhere in the United Kingdom.
If you should miss the Recruiting Officer, apply to Women's Royal Naval Service 50, Charing Cross, London S.W.1

Poster to Join the WRNS (WSA G24/225/29)

Enrolment of Women in the ATS at Trowbridge, 1939 (WSHC P14865)

industry and in the forces. The only way to solve the problem was an extension of the male call up to cover the ages 18-51 and, with no other alternative, the conscription of women.[11] The National Service Act (No. 2) which became law on 18 December 1941 included unmarried women between the ages of 20-30 years, with military service jobs being clerical or culinary in nature.[12]

Twenty-two in every 1,000 of those called up in the first age group claimed the right of conscientious objection, allowable on pacifist or political grounds.[13] The Central Board of Conscientious Objectors (CBCO) provided advice via local Advisory Bureaux, correspondence and publications. They also made representations to Government on behalf of conscientious objectors.[14] The resident of Ham Spray House who had become a Major with Military Cross and Bar in WWI, emerged as a pacifist as the result of serving as an Infantry Officer. He presented a statement to the Appeal Tribunal for Conscientious Objectors in 1943 in which he stated '... but I claim the right to refuse to take a lesson in murder, which is what military service would be for me.

I do not object at all to civil defence, as I regard my neighbours and fellow-countrymen as companions in a common misfortune, but I consider that at present I am of far more real use to the community producing and distributing food than waiting about for emergencies that have so far not arisen in the remote part of Wiltshire where I live.'[15] He found that the locals were decidedly cool towards him and his family after learning they were pacifists.[16] A minority were granted unconditional exemption; others were given exemption but were required to work on the land.[17] A camp, known to locals as the 'non-combatant camp'[18] was set up at Codford and housed such men. The locals understood that they were in the 'Pioneer Corps', and worked as 'jacks of all trades'.[19] 'They used to come down the Milk Bar as well see, and they used to stand back from the others, the regular

REFUSED TO FIRE WATCH

Prison For Jehovah Witness

A Jehovah's Witness who failed to perform fire watch duty allotted to him, between 4 and 5 August, was sent to prison for two months by the Salisbury City magistrates on Monday. Defendant was Ernest Bishop Wootton, New Street, Salisbury.

It was stated that defendant was directed to do fire duty at the Infirmary under the Order, and did such duty until 16 July. Subsequently, he failed to report for duty, and returned a direction to do duty, to the fire guard office.

P.S. Salmon interviewed defendant, who told him he was a Jehovah's Witness, and therefore must be apart from the controversies of the world. He added that he was not a pacifist, and was willing to do duty in New Street and to take the training.

Defendant, in the witness-box, said that he had made a covenant to obey God's laws, and could not place himself under the command or direction of any earthly organisation. He was willing to do and had already done, fire watching on a voluntary basis.

The Mayor (Councillor G. A. Berry), in sentencing defendant, said that the regulations must be obeyed.

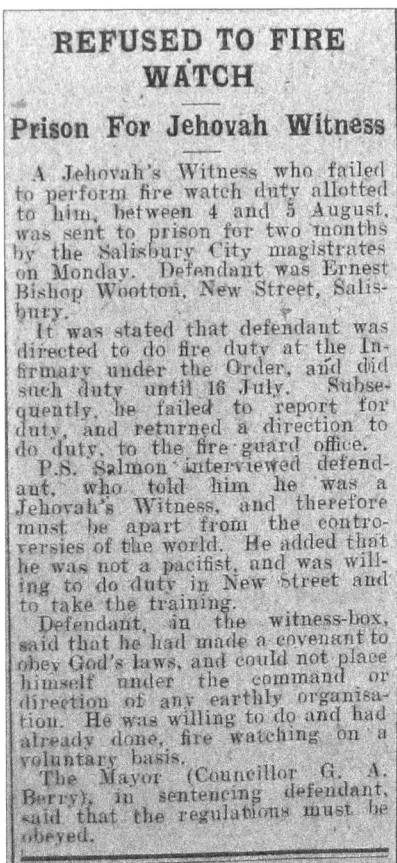

Article in the Wiltshire Gazette, 27 August 1942 'Refused to Fire Watch: Prison for Jehovah Witness' (WSHC Microform Collection)

soldiers, "cause they didn't get on too well."[20] A plan of No. 4 SRD Camp for Pioneers and POWs shows that the camp included libraries, a workshop, canteen and recreation room and a NAAFI, along with a guard room and detention hut.[21] In February 1943 there was opposition to the proposal of establishing a hostel in Malmesbury to house conscientious objectors who would work on the land. Charles Vernon states that 'George Sisum told the Malmesbury National Farmers Union [that] farmers "would prefer to be short of labour rather than employ conscientious objectors. (Hear, hear). If they had the hostel they certainly did not want conscientious objectors in it."[22] The farming Christian Cotswold Bruderhof community had established itself in Ashton Keynes after being expelled from Frankfurt by Hitler in 1936. New converts joined them from places such as Lichtenstein in 1938. Those from the community who came before the Tribunal appear to have been given unconditional exemption from military service. The Cotswold Bruderhof moved from Ashton Keynes to Paraguay at the end of 1940. Men in Malmesbury also appeared before the Tribunal. One such was a schoolmaster who had adopted the Society of Friends' strict attitude to military service and who had joined the Peace Pledge Union in 1935. He was exempted if he continued to do school or humanitarian work. A clerk who had wanted to become a Minister in the Presbyterian Church of Wales did not pass the scrutiny of the board and was transferred to the military register for non-combatant service. A storekeeper's clerk applied for exemption on the grounds that 'he held the same views as the Watchtower Bible and Tract Society for 14 years...' The Tribunal panel felt that he did not show much knowledge of the teaching of Jehovah's Witnesses. He was retained on the register of conscientious objectors and had to work on the land.[23]

In the summer of 1939, the Vicar of St. Paul's Church in Swindon was 'active and vocal for the pacifist cause' but attracted little attention. A Pastor, more vociferous in his views, roused more opposition.[24]

Military Personnel

SALISBURY PLAIN HAD been permanently used by the military since the late 19th century[25] with sites such as Sutton Veny, Codford and Longbridge Deverill being built for troops in WWI. The locals on the Plain had seen Australians, New Zealanders and Canadians in their vicinity a generation before.[26] The Plain was fully utilised throughout WWII, extended by the use of hutted camps and with so many men from different countries trained or assembled there for forthcoming campaigns it became known as 'The United Nations'.[27] The *Warminster Journal* was reporting that a new barracks had been built in Warminster in its 30 September 1938 edition. At the opening it was reported that the day was 'a memorable one for Warminster, marking a stage in their history, when from being a quiet rural town they became a military centre.' The Number 103 Officer Cadet Training Unit, newly formed in 1942, was set up at Perham Down[28] and an Auxiliary Territorial Services Camp was established at Tidworth, with over 1,000 women under canvas.[29] They were attached to garrisons and camps all over the Salisbury Plain area.[30] The Auxiliary Territorial Service also trained at Devizes Barracks in 1941 for the Artillery Radar School, drilled by a sergeant of the Coldstream Guards. He felt that training the girls was 'very much beneath his dignity' and didn't look good with his peers. 'I don't intend being made a laughing stock of by a bunch of – girls, so watch it!' At the end of the course he 'had the grace to say he had never had a squad of men who had learned more quickly or become smarter than we had, and he was proud of us.'[31] The Auxiliary Territorial Service also trained at Chiseldon Camp in a catering section[32] and at Hannington Hall where they worked as radio operators, passing on intelligence reports as part of Churchill's 'Secret Army', the Auxunits.[33]

The job of the Air Transport Auxiliary (ATA) was to deliver new or repaired aircraft from factories to airfields all over the country. It was formed in 1939 to enable more RAF pilots to move to combat duty, but initially even experienced female pilots were ignored.[34] Of the men of the ATA, some were old, some unfit. The service gained the alternative title 'Ancient and Tattered Airmen'.[35] Editor of *The Aeroplane*, Mr Grey, was vociferous: 'The menace is the woman who thinks she ought to be flying a high-speed bomber when she really has not the intelligence to scrub the floor of a hospital properly...' He noted that there were men like that too but '[t]he combination is perhaps even more common amongst women than men. And is one of the commonest causes of crashes, in aeroplanes and other ways.'[36] Upavon trained the first Air Transport Auxillary pilots. Of the women training at the Central Flying School, the youngest, Joan Hughes, was just 17.[37] The highest profile member of the ATA was Amy Johnson, who had been lost in January 1941 over the Thames Estuary.[38] She had delivered planes to Wiltshire airfields during her stint as an ATA pilot and had stayed at The Phoenix pub in Pewsey.[39] Another well known ATA pilot Lettice Curtis recalled her time at Upavon in her autobiography. She had been found rooms at the village, not far from the airfield, and they lunched at the WAAF Officer's mess onsite. The course involved remembering the information given by the course instructors regarding all sorts of technical equipment ranging from retractable undercarriages to the instruments in the various aircraft. 'We all found the CFS course pretty harassing.'[40] The number of female ATA pilots had reached over 100 by the end of the war and Kate Adie reports that many had found the work had been 'at times, frightening and rather isolated... a wonderful achievement, but not a jolly in the blue beyond'.[41]

Another pioneering job was detailed to those WAAFs who'd joined as nursing orderlies. Some voluntarily undertook the task of becoming trained in ambulance duties and a small group soon found themselves being trained for travel to France just after the D-Day landings. They were to become 'Flying Nightingales', travelling to the continent and caring for the casualties who were flown back, on the way out sitting amongst bombs with their medical panniers.[42] Edna Birbeck was one such volunteer and after training was posted to Blakehill Farm near Cricklade in February 1944, attached to 233 Squadron. Edna was on the first flight of its kind to leave Britain; the first to fly into a combat zone to evacuate the wounded. They returned, to be met by 42 press correspondents from British, Canadian and American newspapers. 233 Squadron evacuated 1,092 stretcher cases and 467 sitting wounded with Edna flying 60 casualty operations, and 'despite the severity of the injuries none of her patients ever died on any of her flights'. Edna remembered that the men always wanted to hear when they were over the coast. She would let them know and would say: 'It won't be long before you're home,' 'and they'd cheer'.[43]

Edna Birbeck at work in 233 Squadron's Dakota Aircraft, having returned with the first ever flight casualties on 13 June 1944, courtesy of Cricklade Museum (WSHC P32733)

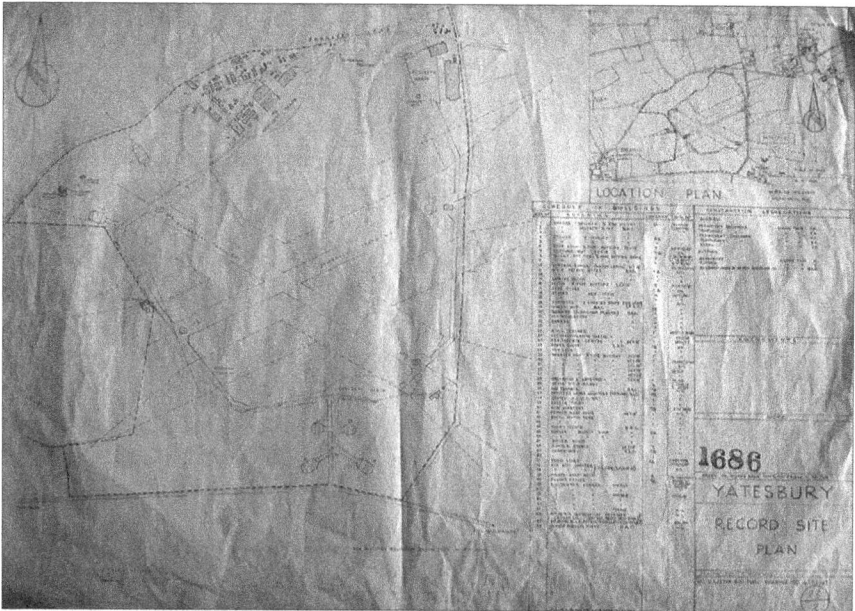

Plan of RAF Yatesbury, 1945. The NAAFI, YMCA, and 'Maccalm' Club were also situated on the site (WSA G3/701/17PC)

Another WAAF, trained as a cook and butcher, and later becoming a batwoman, found herself at RAF Yatesbury, No. 2 Radio School. There were four large wings at the site, all with catering facilities. The work at No. 3 Wing was hard and included a long day, but she found it very rewarding. She was allowed one half day off a week, with a 48 hour pass once a month, and seven days leave every three months, the latter two having to be taken off base. 'I often went to a Youth Hostel for the 48 hours. At that time Marlborough Youth Hostel was in the old town mill...' [44] RAF personnel could also go to Calne, which had a Forces Canteen, open all day and into the evenings. Marlborough, Chippenham, Devizes and Swindon were out of bounds for these sorts of trips, but '... many an airman or woman was invited to the homes of the people of Calne, making friendships which lasted many years after.'[45] At Christmas much merriment would be caused by a tradition that:

> ... the bands would lead a column of airmen and women through the huts. If you were not up and ready to join on to the crocodile, the bed was picked up and deposited firmly outside, whatever the weather... During the war very few went home, so we all joined in any celebrations.' She did not know how the Christmas fayre was spirited up. Unlike a civilian Christmas: 'The puddings and mincemeat were made on the unit, apples and carrots helped the dried fruit out. Nothing seemed to be short, as the menu had a full plate, turkey, stuffing, bread sauce – in fact the lot, and the big puddings were brought in flaming... Nuts, cigarettes and a bottle of beer appeared, crackers and paper hats. The

dining room was decorated with greenery, and the tree had decorations, usually made by the 'girls'.

There was a NAAFI, YMCA 'or Maccalm Club' on site as well as a cinema, for which a trip cost fourpence. There were also military bands, dance bands and ENSA shows. One on-site group played Gilbert and Sullivan Operas, and another put on plays.[46]

The unit was in a bleak position, however. 'We used to get snowed in and nothing could get up the hill, before the hill was lowered… One year, I think it was 1943, we had snow, deep snow for about six weeks, and everything was frozen hard. That year it was so cold that to have extra warmth people were going to bed in their greatcoats. We were not allowed to use the water for baths, as a lot of the pipes froze.'[47] RAF Compton Bassett was used as a radio and signals school.[48] Its No. 3 Radio School opened in June 1940 for the purpose of training Airmen and Wireless Operators (Ground). Early trainees arrived from the recruits centre, Blackpool. In early 1942 Airwomen were posted there for training as Wireless Operators.[49]

The first Wireless Operator (Ground) Course at No. 3 R.S, Compton Bassett, June 1940 (WSA G18/991/1)

Subterranean Stores

TUNNEL QUARRY, MONKTON Farleigh and Eastlays Ridge were collectively known as the Central Ammunition Depot (CAD).[50] As war broke out, stockpiles of ammunition had been stored at Central Ammunition Depots, including those at Corsham, but as output increased these stores reached saturation point. It was not unusual to see ammunition stored alongside country roads or in adjacent fields at Savernake. In July 1940 Savernake was chosen as an ammunition dump, consisting of mature woodland which provided concealment and the possibility to absorb explosive impacts. [51] A member of the Timber Corps working in Savernake Forest described the US presence there. 'Beneath corrugated-iron shelters and scattered over a wide area, large US Army munitions dumps were concealed, guarded by soldiers standing like statues against the silvery trunks of the beeches lining the Avenue on every side; perfectly camouflaged in their grey-green uniforms, they delighted in leaping out from behind the trees to startle and challenge us.'[52] Tented accommodation was erected on Marlborough Common to house the workers but the weather of September to December 1940 was atrocious; high winds and torrential rain blew some tents down.[53] Savernake was the seat of Lord Ailesbury. The increase in military personnel was causing concerns for his lordship's deer population which was reducing as quickly as military cartridges were going missing![54] CAD at Corsham reached its height towards the end of 1943 when over 1,200 RAOC Officers and men, 400 pioneers and 300 civilians were working at the site.[55] The Lend-Lease agreement with the US meant that arms, vehicles, and even batteries for torches could then be imported, the materials to be used until it was time for their return or destruction. The formal title of the agreement showed its purpose: 'An Act to Further Promote the Defence of the United States'. It was enacted on 11 March 1941.[56]

The Admiralty had been opposed to the underground storage of ammunition but for a short while occupied three small quarries in Bradford-on-Avon,[57] with Bethel Quarry being used to store depth charges, although without the detonators.[58] A shortage of suitable storage space meant that ammunition was being kept in railway trucks at the dockside. The Admiralty tried to obtain space at the Corsham site but found that very little 'subterranean real estate remained'. They grabbed Pickwick and, after a bitter battle with the RAF, took possession of Elm Park, also acquiring Monks Park, all in Corsham.[59][60] When much of the Admiralty's Fleet Air Arm warehouse storage capacity was destroyed in Coventry during 1940 a search for surface storage was unsuccessful. They approached the Ministry of Works to find out if they could take one of the Corsham quarries requisitioned on behalf of the Ministry of Aircraft Production. They were able to make use of the ten acre Copenacre Quarry, completing the conversion in July 1942. The stores at Bradford were among those moved to Copenacre and their former owners, the Agaric Mushroom Company, were free to return.[61] A *Daily Mail* article described the Copenacre site on 23 November 1943:

> An underground city which has taken thousands of men 7 years to construct, house Britain's biggest ammunition dump. Details are secret, but it can be said that the stocks are of an incredible size.
>
> This bomb proof city has barracks, offices, a telephone exchange, electric lifts, and an air conditioning plant big enough to provide power and lights for such a city above ground.

There are 14 miles of conveyor belts for carrying shells from the main entrances to the storage sites.

The nerve centre of this vast arsenal, the telephone exchange, is staffed by the ATS. One of them, Lance Corporal Edna Bullin, whose home is in Doncaster, has been working there for 2 years and likes it. 'You forget there is an outside world' she said.

The labour force was drawn from all over England, mostly from the distressed areas of South Wales, Durham, Northumberland and Cumberland...[62] There was even an underground lake for drinking water.[63] The Tunnel Quarry site was prepared in the 1950s to become the Central Government War Headquarters, to include the relocation of the Prime Minister,[64] often referred to as Burlington. They were to be one of a network of Regional Seats of Government in the advent of a Cold War nuclear attack.[65]

The Georgian house called 'Lynchetts' in Bradford on Avon was requisitioned by the Navy in February 1941. It was here that the Government Chronometer and Watch Testing Unit rated, engraved, repaired and serviced watches and chronometers used by the Navy and Fleet Air Arm. They also restored Harrison's famous 17th and 18th century inventions. The chronometers are now housed at the National Maritime Museum, Greenwhich.[66]

The RAF held two small quarries at Chilmark, acquired in 1936 to hold bombs.[67]

Wiltshire Airfields

THE MAJORITY OF Wiltshire's RAF bases were built either just before or during WWII. Of those established before the war, Upavon, Netheravon, Old Sarum, Porton Down and Yatesbury were part of the 'powerhouse' of early aviation,[68] established between 1912 and 1916. High Post was built in the early 1930s. Those established during WWII include Blakehill Farm,[69] Castle Combe,[70] Lyneham,[71] Colerne[72] and Ramsbury.[73] Some, like Wroughton, began being built just after the Munich Crisis in 1938.[74] RAF Rudloe Manor, based below ground at Browns Hill Quarry, was the Command Centre for No. 10 Group HQ, Fighter Command, and took care of the air defence for the south west.[75] 125ha of land at Blakehill became one of many temporary airfields constructed during WWII;[76] the airfield became operational in 1944. Those working at the station soon numbered about twice the population of nearby Cricklade.[77] It must have turned a sleepy rural town into a bustling, busy area. There were also subsidiary sites where the airstrips were used on occasions, helping to free up congestion, such as Everleigh, Manningford, Oatlands Hill, Shrewton, and Wanborough.[78]

Decoy sites were set up to protect the main airfields, such as at Allington to protect Hullavington. 'Starfish' (Special fire) sites were designed to allow fires to be ignited and controlled remotely, and also protected main sites such as at Monkton Farleigh for Box Bridge.[79] It appears that these defences were needed.

Aerial view of Netheravon Airfield, taken during the war (WSHC P19475)

The Luftwaffe had taken an aerial photograph of the Alton Barnes airfield on 3 December 1940. It was discovered in the possession of a captured German Officer in Lubeck in August 1945.[80] Decoy sites were positioned around the village of Minety due to the high number of airfields that could be found in the area. The site was bombed on Good Friday 1941. 'In the early hours of the morning at least one Minety family was woken up by a great explosion, followed by many more which made the house shake. This was followed by the noise of tiles sliding down off the roof. They stayed in their beds, hearts pounding, listening.' The bombs landed in a line, hitting the decoy strip which was sited between Minety and Ashton Keynes. One Minety resident recalled much later that 'the farmers and others living near the airfield, had to agree, without any option, to this danger, in the hope of saving someone else's life. They carried on with their lives and work, knowing what could happen, but then, this sums up the spirit of the British nation those days.'[81]

Many of Wiltshire's airfields saw different nationalities training and it was at RAF Colerne that they practiced advanced flying after having completed the Empire Air Training Scheme. The aim was to acclimatise overseas pilots to the congested northern European skies.[82] At RAF Hullavington the Empire Central Flying School was established in April 1942, its job to standardise flying training procedures between the RAF and Dominion air forces. Before this RAF Hullavington had trained pilots coming out of the Empire Air Training Scheme. Nationalities included Canadians, Dutch, Indians and the Poles[83] who flew from Colerne.[84] After completing their Empire Flying Training Scheme, the newly formed No. 427 Squadron was based at RAF Blakehill and consisted of the Royal Canadian Air Force's first transport unit, nicknamed 'Pickfords' after the removal company![85] Polish Airmen and test pilots lodged in houses in Wilton. Joan Hide recalls that the test pilots 'would breeze in and out like a breath of fresh air, they were noisy and full of fun'. Other Polish lodgers were quieter and more subdued, one showing her photographs of his wife and children in Poland who he'd had no contact with since joining the air force.[86]

Military Hospitals

WITH THE MILITARY came military hospitals such as those at Everleigh Manor,[87] Lydiard Park[88] and Tidworth Military Hospital,[89] the latter two both American. RAF Hospitals were established at Melksham and Wroughton, the former being a temporary convalescence hospital and the latter to become a permanent establishment.[90] The Royal Army Medical Corps moved into Tottenham House on 5 October 1939.[91] In Britford the doctors and nurses from the US hospital used to visit local farms to see the spring lambing. 'They often had supper with us, and liked nothing better than my father's draught cider from our apple orchards... with crusty bread, cheddar cheese and raw onions.'[92] A hospital was also built by the US as the 130th Station Hospital, becoming operational from 3 June 1944 when it became a transit hospital for the Air Evacuation Programme[93] similar to the British Army's at Wroughton.[94] The 130th had started off in Wiltshire at Burderop Park near Swindon between January and April 1944. This hospital also became a transit hospital in the Air Evacuation Programme, receiving its first patients on 19 June 1944 who numbered 445, with most patients being evacuated within a day or two by train or ambulance. 'Too much cannot be said about the efficient manner in which our entire available personnel, administrative and professional, Officers, nurses, Red Cross workers and enlisted men, including litter bearers, took up the huge task suddenly thrown upon them of caring for the thousands of wounded soldiers being sent here from Europe by air.'[95] The site was already being used by the War Department in 1943 when they were bickering over the cost of water charges compared to those of the Air Ministry, stating that the site was classed as a 'duration of War hospital.' Burderop hospital had in fact been newly built in 1942 and was thought at that time to require 50,000 to 60,000 gallons of water per day. Chiseldon Camp was also under the control of the War Department at this time.[96] The staff of the US 130th moved on from Burderop to Pinkney Park near Sherston from April until May 1944 with billets found for them in Swindon.[97]

Intense periods of fighting on the Continent brought with it increased numbers of casualties arriving at the camps. At Wroughton an eyewitness recalled seeing 'a continuous stream of ambulances on Brimble Hill between Wroughton and Chiseldon at the time of the Battle of St. Lo in Normandy.'[98] D-Day casualties were brought in to Wroughton RAF Hospital from Lyneham, still covered in mud.[99] Wingfield House received wounded soldiers of many nationalities and regiments following the D-Day invasion. The house had been a Red Cross Hospital in the First World War and held lot of memories for the older residents of the village.[100]

Military ambulances lined up at Charlton Park House, August 1944 (WSHC P6063)

At Lydiard Park staff were racing to get supplies unloaded, telephones connected and floors laid in the tents to be used as wards. 'Few could sleep on the night before D-Day for the ceaseless drone of aircraft overhead as the planes made their way towards the Normandy coast'. They were to be the casualty station for the 101st Airborne Division and treating 438 patients by the end of June 1944. Many patients could later be found at the Sun Inn (at Lydiard Millicent), taking light refreshment in their pyjamas and dressing gowns.[101] The male staff (enlisted men and Officers) of the 130th Station Hospital were quartered in large nissen huts at Burderop Park, the site as a whole containing 126 buildings. The nurses were given a brick building away from the main hospital. The male staff stayed in tents whilst at Pinkney Park with outside toilets and a wash block. At Chiseldon the male staff again had tented accommodation but also had mess halls in hutment type buildings. The nurses were quartered in apartment type buildings.[102] At Chiseldon the staff had to landscape, remodel and set up yet another hospital, but within a month it was ready for use.[103]

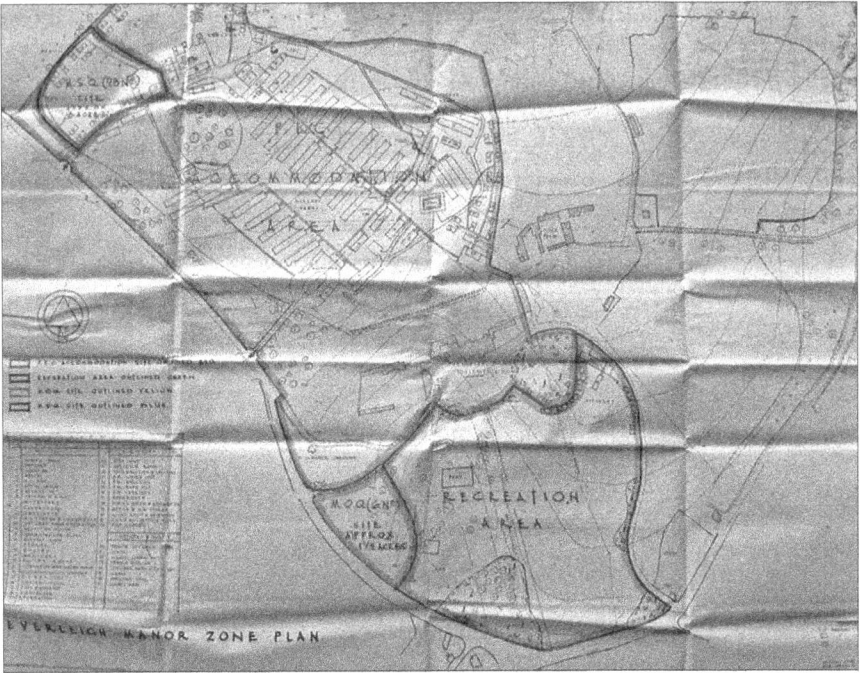

Plan of Everleigh Manor 750 Bed Hospital, October 1942 (WSA G5/132/61)

A Military Training Ground . . .

THE NUMBER OF military sites springing up in Wiltshire was colossal. During the war Wiltshire's towns and villages would be visited by many different military personnel. Buildings would be requisitioned for their use and their presence would invariably affect the lives of those around them.[104] Military camps, even those on the remote Salisbury Plain, were sometimes situated near to the civilian population, making them susceptible to German attack. Bombs were often aimed at military sites but ended up missing their targets and falling near local villages.[105] Military camps also created a great deal of noise and disruption. Military training exercises and manoeuvres were often accompanied by live ammunition and explosives, such as those conducted by the US 101st Airborne Division, 506 Parachute Infantry Regiment, 'Easy Company' around Ramsbury.[106] Training involved digging foxholes in the surrounding countryside and being 'attacked' by Sherman tanks. 'They roared up the hill at us like primeval monsters.' Who knows what the locals made of that, but the village farmers were certainly not impressed to find that barbed wire fences had been cut, leaving their cattle wandering all over the locality. Stephen E. Ambrose reports that '[t]he next morning a contingent of Wiltshire farmers confronted Colonel Strayer'.[107] By early 1944 tank battalions exercised with infantry, engineers and artillery on land to the west of Chitterne.[108] The American GIs were also known to fire live rounds over public roads, and some even drove a jeep up Silbury Hill.[109] A farmer from Alderbury was also having trouble with straying cattle. The military had been using his fields and knocked a gate with a lorry, making it useless. His cattle were now straying onto the main road. He had suggested that 'if two strands of barbed wire and stakes were supplied, he would erect a fence... to overcome the difficulty.' Presumably he was having trouble sourcing the materials himself.[110]

A five year old girl from Chiseldon remembered being very shocked when witnessing parachute training in action '... hundreds of men suddenly came out of the sky... It was quite frightening and I did not like it one bit.'[111] The were many air crashes due to the large number of RAF bases in the county. An RAF Oxford twin engined trainer crashed into a farmhouse in Minety, destroying part of the house and killing two crew members. The farmer's wife had been in the kitchen at the time, and the aircraft struck '... with a terrible crash, the kitchen door burst open and the pilot shot through, coming to rest in [a] sitting position against the far wall. Poor Mrs Webb asked him if he was alright but there was no answer. He was dead... Mrs Webb was very frightened and distressed by the incident.'[112] Children used to watch the bombers at RAF Keevil towing Horsa and Hamilcars and Wacos. On one occasion a glider went out of control, causing the Abermarle it was towing to spin to the ground with fatal results. The 'watching youngsters were horrified.'[113] The Station was involved in Operation Mallard, commencing on D-Day. Thirty-three Stirling aircraft towed Horsa gliders for the 2nd Ox & Bucks Light Infantry to reinforce troops on Operation Tonga. One of the Stirlings failed to return to base, crashing into the sea with no survivors.[114] British paratroopers, the 6th Airborne Division, were to use the gliders on D-Day.[115] They were based for a time on Salisbury Plain, establishing themselves at Tilshead in early 1942.[116] They trained in glider flying elsewhere, finding the Horsas to be larger than expected, like 'a big black crow,' but they were impressed; the seats were also large and positioned side by side and visibility was 'excellent.' Instruments were similar to an ordinary aircraft except for the rev counter and temperature gauge, and there was even telephone communication with the bomber pilot via a wire.[117]

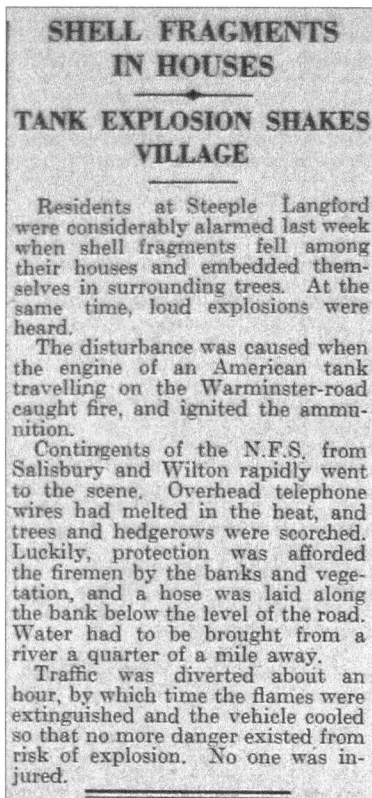

SHELL FRAGMENTS IN HOUSES

TANK EXPLOSION SHAKES VILLAGE

Residents at Steeple Langford were considerably alarmed last week when shell fragments fell among their houses and embedded themselves in surrounding trees. At the same time, loud explosions were heard.

The disturbance was caused when the engine of an American tank travelling on the Warminster-road caught fire, and ignited the ammunition.

Contingents of the N.F.S. from Salisbury and Wilton rapidly went to the scene. Overhead telephone wires had melted in the heat, and trees and hedgerows were scorched. Luckily, protection was afforded the firemen by the banks and vegetation, and a hose was laid along the bank below the level of the road. Water had to be brought from a river a quarter of a mile away.

Traffic was diverted about an hour, by which time the flames were extinguished and the vehicle cooled so that no more danger existed from risk of explosion. No one was injured.

A US Tank explodes at Steeple Langford. The National Fire Service attended the scene, Salisbury Journal, 23 June 1944 (WSHC Microform Collection)

Ammunition depots were high risk. At Savernake on 7 July 1945 an explosion and flames could be seen coming from an ammunition hut beside the Durley Road, 200 yards away from a farm. The blast blew the doors of a barn open one and a half miles away. Nearly every building at the nearby farm was destroyed or seriously damaged and livestock were killed. Sheep in one of the nearby fields were thrown several hundred yards through the air by the shockwave and the stained glass window at nearby St. Katherine's Church was destroyed; its north wall severely weakened. The school was also badly damaged and five civilians were injured.[118] At the beginning of June 1941 a conference was held at Savernake, depot personnel meeting representatives from the Marlborough Police and the local Air Raid Precaution Officer. The issue of the kind of warning to give the local population in the event of a gas spillage was discussed. The civilians learnt that Savernake would be receiving more chemical weapons; little had they known that there had been existing ones on the site for a year.[119] A further explosion at Savernake in 1946 caused considerable unrest amongst the local population and demands were made to close the Savernake CAD. A petition was organised but went unheeded; ammunition continued to arrive. Joan Hide notes that the children living near Larkhill went to search for incendiary cases after a huge fire at the camp. '[T]he smell of sulphur impregnated our clothes and it's a smell that [was] not easy to forget.'[120]

US troops were training around the village of Imber on the Salisbury Plain and although an exclusion zone had been set up, there were concerns for public safety. The villagers were told of their impending eviction at a meeting held on 4 November 1943. Those present included members of the military, farmers whose land was affected, representatives from the War Department, the Ministry of Agriculture and the Wiltshire and Berkshire War Agricultural Executive Committees. The meeting began with the farmers being told that they were not the only ones being affected. Large areas of land in Yorkshire, East Anglia and Devon were also being taken. Sir Hugh Elles, Chairman, stated that the area under question had already been reduced and that it was felt that farming in some capacity would still continue 'as much as it can.' General Sir Charles Lloyd noted: 'I am sure you appreciate that the training of soldiers is absolutely essential for the war effort... the training of a soldier in these times of strife is absolutely vital. There is nobody here, I am quite certain, who would wish to see one more life lost in this war than is absolutely necessary, but in order to train these men we must have land... These areas have been very carefully selected...' He went further: 'I am afraid that the farms close around Imber will probably have to cease... and we may also, I think, have to curtail activities in the areas of that neighbourhood hitherto regarded as danger areas.' Sir Hugh continued by sending his sympathies to the farmers, stating that he realised '[i]n war, I think, many very irritating things happen. They happen to you and they happen to me... Think of those who have lost their lives, who may have been Prisoners of War in Japan over the last three years, those who have been bombed out of their farms completely, and I think if one looks at things a little bit in that light one perhaps is more inclined to suffer a little bit more gladly...' On behalf of the US Army Brigadier General

Hickey spoke. '... Our Army recognises full well what a tremendous additional burden our presence here has placed upon you. We are also fully aware of how acute the food situation throughout the world is...' He continued by saying that the US had hesitated because of this, but to train their large number of armoured units '... we have to have your ground...' Richard Stratton, Chairman of the Wiltshire War Agricultural Executive Committee realised the grief that would be involved for those who would be dispossessed from their homes, but that 'we will be Englishmen and rise above those difficulties...' He had been concerned over the matter of compensation but after a preliminary meeting that morning had been won over. 'I was told that we shall be well and handsomely – perhaps I should not say handsomely – anyway, well compensated...' A question and answer session followed the speakers with one question being: 'Is it likely that these areas will be held for the duration of the war or a limited period?' The answer: 'Nobody knows. I should think it very likely to go on for many months and it all depends on where the war is.' To conclude, Sir Hugh expressed 'his admiration for the way in which the farmers had received the proposals.'[121] The farmers were given until 17 December to quit their homes, but compensation forms show that residents may well have given up their properties as early as 14 November 1943 (stated as the date they were relinquished). The Land Agent for Southern Command then visited Imber to inspect the properties in view of the compensation requests. Letters found in the Defence Land Agent files at the Wiltshire & Swindon History Centre archives show that the military were quibbling over items in the claims. In January 1944 a Captain informed one Imber resident that 'I can agree to your claim of 10/- for stock and crop of garden, but when I made my inspection I did not see the poultry house nor the two coils of wire for which you claim a total of £2 10s. 0d. I hope that there will be an opportunity to go into the area again one day in the near future, and should such an opportunity occur, I will take advantage of it to inspect these two items.' He had, however, discovered the handbag that had been left at the cottage and was in the process of returning it to its owner. It appears that as the people of Imber had to leave in such a hurry, or that the process of leaving was in itself a rather tumultuous and emotional event, other items had also been left behind. Another lady had left her irons by accident. They were in the oven and 'would you please find any way in getting them for me as I am

Letter from an Imber resident asking for compensation for a shed and vegetables he had planted (WSA L7/310/2)

in need of them.' For one resident of Imber the situation was even graver than most. A letter received by the Land Agent from the Legal Advice Bureau of the 4th Wilts stated that a Private, currently residing with his 12 month old daughter in Imber, would soon have to leave. His daughter was being treated for enlarged muscles at the Salisbury Infirmary where she was well known by the specialist, but he had been unable to find any suitable premises for them in Salisbury. The letter concluded: 'I feel sure, when you understand the position, you will do all in your power to help him...'[122]

This remote rural community accepted the loss of their homes and way of life as Henry Buckton notes, with 'great sadness'... Farmers found it necessary to sell their livestock at greatly reduced prices. At the end of the war the community was 'scattered across the county with relatives or in entirely new homes... destined to remain exiles.'[123] On 26 January 1961 the *Wiltshire Gazette & Herald* was reporting the 'Restore Imber' call of 1,200 pilgrims, demonstrating to raise awareness of the issue. One speaker recalled that after the Americans had left the buildings were in a reasonable condition. Even 13 years ago they remained 'not nearly so damaged.' By 1961 the village looked very different. 'Only the shells of door-less, window-less houses remained.' The loss was still felt deeply even as late as the 1980s when the Association for the Restoration of Imber was still active[124] and many visitors look around the site when the military opens it to the pubic. One evacuee staying at Bratton remembered Imber before it was taken over:

'My memory of the area, before 'take over', was going up to Bell's Farm to pick mushrooms. It was one of those magical days, when you think the grown-ups are going to perform some tedious task and then suddenly everyway you turn there are these shining white bumps nestling in the lush green grass, just waiting to be gathered into baskets. Mr Bell's farm was one to be requisitioned.

After the area was taken over, the peace of the surrounding villages reverberated to the sound of gunfire. Sometimes it was distant and we could hear the discharge, the whistle of the shell making its trajectory and the thud as it hit its target or not. Other times it was so loud and seemed so dangerously close that, as a little girl of ten, who had just been re-evacuated from London and scary doodle-bugs I was so terrified by the bangs and thuds that I crept into Granny's bed and clung to her shaking until dawn.'[125]

The requisition of Blakehill Farm near Cricklade by the Air Ministry occasioned the loss of over 30 fields owned or rented by many different farmers.[126] Rumours had started much earlier but the first official news was in November 1942 when: 'Two Officers walked across [the] holding... An Official called and shewed us the map.' The County Land Agent told the tenant that '[i]f they take half your holding it is going to be very awkward but I am afraid it is very difficult to do anything about it.' In April 1943 the tenant was reporting 'the Ministry has now passed its plans for the Aerodrome. The foreman informed me they will be starting on our frontage any day.' He had also been asked by the Ministry to make an exchange of fields, but he was worried about the cows as the exchange would restrict access for moving hay. He asked the County Land Agent that if he was approached by the Ministry, would he also explain to them that if they took the whole place, at least the tenant would 'know where we are.' He was also worried about lots of contractors crossing his fields… 'it has been a worry to keep stopping them every night and day.' He was planning to produce some signs which he hoped would help. Tenants whose land was to be requisitioned were still liable to the Council for all the rent, having to recover the amount for the requisitioned land from the appropriate Ministry.[127] At another part of the site, King's Barn Farm: 'We had to get off in four days… We were allocated a Council house at The Leigh, and moved out that same day because a sale of all our livestock, farm implements, machinery, tractors etc. had to take place within five working days.' All 35 cows and 20 young cattle were sold. A friend recalled: 'I'll never forget how he stood there with tears in his eyes. All his life he'd worked to build up that herd, and now the whole lot was going!' The only compensation the farmer received was from the farm sale. He never got the land or home back, which was knocked down.[128] The US troops were aware of their impact on the landscape, one GI later writing: 'While on manoeuvres with our tanks in the surrounding area I am sure we tore up a lot of the farm land but I think the farmers were compensated for it.' He had been stationed at Codford for nine months and later reminisced: 'I didn't get to know anyone in Codford while I was there but I wish sometimes I had. I have often wondered what the people of Codford thought of all the soldiers being so close and if they resented it.'[129]

Construction and Disruption

SUDDENLY, QUIET RURAL areas were full of noise, the roads busy with trucks needed to bring in the goods and additional personnel to build the sites, equip them and keep them running.[130] The County Surveyor had assessed the situation in May 1940 regarding the plans for the new Sutton Veny hutted camp '…there will doubtless be a number of matters with regard to the piping of ditches across access roads, opening of roads for water supply and other trenches.'[131] The new permanent RAF stations cost around £750,000 each, usually consisting of grass runways, hangars, operational buildings and accommodation, taking around seven months to complete.[132] At Keevil airfield women helped to build the runway. They also helped maintain them by sweeping them clean.[133] One was a 'titled' lady; the story made the national press.[134] With the unprecedented amount of military traffic using rural roads, damage was occurring which endangered the public. At RAF Ramsbury, the damage began when construction started in 1941. Trees were felled, hedgerows bulldozed and living accommodation built in the wooded area. Further damage occurred in 1942 by military constructional traffic[135] when a new road was being constructed on the south side of the aerodrome.[136] In Dinton, one resident remembered when the firm W.C. French arrived to construct new buildings for the RAF. They '… descended on the village with lots of lorries and masses of equipment.'[137] There were also worries that the damage caused by US construction lorries would contaminate the local cress beds in the Dinton area.[138]

At the end of August 1942 Wiltshire's County Surveyor received a letter from the Commanding Officer at Savernake warning of increased movements of lorries over the next months on unclassified roads in the area. He asked that a white line be painted on certain routes to avoid accidents.[139] A Divisional Surveyor recorded the traffic over routes from Dinton and the US Camp between 8.30am and 4pm daily in December 1943, discovering that 16 British vehicles and 285 US vehicles passed through.[140] In September 1944 the USAAF Commander at Dinton discussed with the County Surveyor the state of verges bulldozed by their troops, leading to the filling of roadside ditches. The County Surveyor authorised for costs up to £9,716 for damage caused by the USAAF.[141] British civilians took exception to what they saw as the GIs ready access to military vehicles for pleasure[142] and there were certainly complaints regarding speeding offences by US vehicles.[143] A Minety resident noted how different the driving style of the Americans was '... more flamboyant than our own troops and I don't mean just left hand drive. They would almost lie in the seat with a leg outside, a cigar in their mouths, the chinstrap of their helmets undone... they seemed relaxed...'[144] On 21 October 1943 the 101st US Airborne Division established a parachute jump school in Chilton Foliat which helped prepare men such as Padres and Doctors who did not as yet have any jump experience.[145] Local residents reported the 101st making many 'tailgate' jumps in the country lanes around Aldbourne with the jumps made from the back of trucks.[146] On Brick Hill near Warminster, locals discovered an abandoned American jeep. 'Father called in at the American Military Police office at Wilson & Kennards [in Warminster] and asked them if any of their jeeps were missing, as he had one in one of his cornfields. They said, quite unconcerned, that they had so many of the damn things that a dozen could be missing and they wouldn't know.' They did, however, go with the farmer to collect the jeep. 'I remember seeing father sat up in this jeep, holding on to his hat as they drove away at speed in true American style!'[147]

The *Salisbury Journal* was reporting on 7 January 1944 about US soldiers charged with manslaughter when a local man on a bicycle had been killed by a US jeep travelling on the wrong side of the road. A Police Officer had seen 'a jeep taken from the Market Square into Castle-street without lights.' Two more Police Officers then saw a jeep in Castle Street and stated it was 'travelling at 50 m.p.h. towards Amesbury, and cross[ing] to the wrong side of the road.'

The arrival of soldiers to Freshford on the Wiltshire/Somerset border in the winter of 1939 'was marked by a great clattering and rumbling of lorries, full of merry-faced lads in battle-dress going full speed ahead down the precipitous roadway, which abounds in concealed turnings and cantankerous corners and for a great part of the way has no footpath.'[148] In May 1944 the Honorary Secretary of Landford WI was writing to the Commanding Officer of Southern Command asking if anything could be done regarding the road through the village and near the school. Signs had been erected asking military traffic to drive slowly '... but the American drivers pay no attention to them... the Committee of the Institute would be most grateful if the Military Police could draw the attention of the

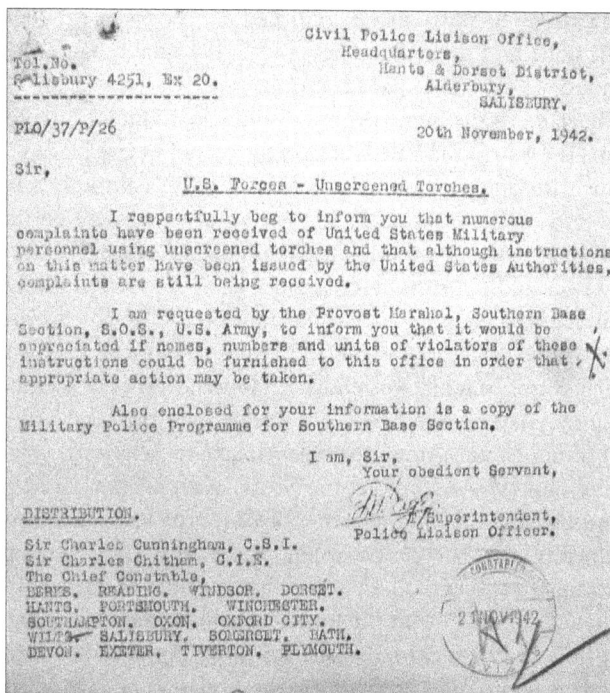

Letter dated 20 November 1942 from the Superintendent Police Liaison Officer, Alderbury, regarding the numerous complaints made about the unscreened torches of US troops (WSA F5/530/6)

American drivers to the great danger to local pedestrians, and especially to the children going to and from school, which daily arises from their excessive speed.'[149] The issue of US drivers ignoring traffic signals was discussed at the staff conference at Wiltshire Constabulary's Devizes HQ in February 1944.

> … that there was a growing tendency on the behalf of drivers of both single U.S. vehicles, and those in convoy, to ignore traffic lights, and that the practice was very dangerous to other road users and had already resulted in several serious accidents causing personal injuries, in some cases fatal.
>
> This Headquarters is anxious that traffic lights shall be observed, and will take disciplinary action against drivers who do not comply.[150]

It appears that effective British policing of the US forces was not that straightforward. In Cricklade: 'The Yanks would continually drive up the High Street with big lorries, going flat out, around that corner into Calcutt Street on their way down to Southampton to pick up supplies. Frustrated by this Sergeant Hand would stand in the middle of the road up there in an attempt to control the traffic, and they'd do anything to tease him… purposely hemmed him in with two fifteen hundredweight trucks on either side all the way up, and wouldn't let him out! The next day the lorry drivers returned…' They gave the sergeant a box containing gin, wine and other liquor of 'very good quality' and wished him a Happy Christmas.[151]

As has been seen, the increased use of military traffic on small rural roads led to accidents. The wall of the Vale Hotel on the corner in Cricklade was knocked down by a tank with one person injured. They also 'hit Auntie Ev's house when a tank crashed into it. The front door, and everything else, were pushed so far in that the front room she was so proud of collapsed inside'. Aunt Eve was helped out of the window by a soldier. 'Although of course she <u>was</u> worried it might happen again, she'd still have all the soldiers in for a cup of tea!' The Town Clock was also knocked down. It was partly reconstructed in 1946 using steel from Morrison air raid shelters.[152] US troops took over Draycot House at Draycot Cerne, having to make many journeys across the lovely old bridge over the lake. The bridge got damaged, and although the Americans left money to help with its restoration, it was never the same.[153] At Codford the Scots Guards '… were always having complaints that the Milk Bar, on the corner of Chitterne Road, had been knocked down by yet another tank. It was close to the road… and it was a standing joke in the Brigade headquarters 'Oh God, they've done it again!" At its height, there were up to 200 tanks at Codford[154] with the Americans doing their fair share of damage too. 'Hardly a building on a corner wasn't run into' by the GIs.[155] Hindon's war memorial stood near the road crossing at The Square, and was knocked down by a runaway tank. It '… careered across the road junction, knocked down the

A tank stuck in one of Wiltshire's country lanes at Knook during WWII, taken by the Wiltshire County Council's Environment Department (WSA F4/843/8)

memorial, maybe four trees and a water standpipe, finally coming to rest against another tree'. Much later, there was a tendency to blame the US troops but witness accounts at the time stated it was the Irish Guards who were responsible. The Americans, though, were the ones to sit on the remains of the memorial and whistle at the girls![156]

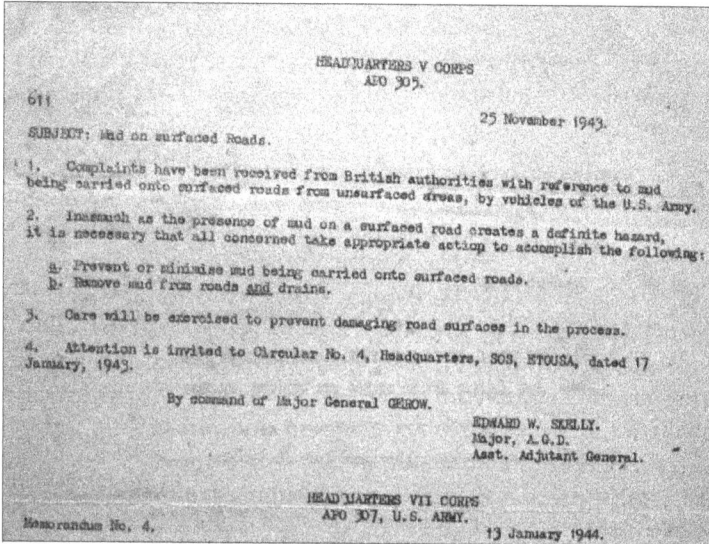

US Army Memorandum, 25 November 1943, relaying complaints regarding mud on the road (WSA F5/530/6)

The Women's Land Army (WLA) travelling Supervisors used motorbikes to get around from one location to another to check on the gangs in their areas and they were very vulnerable in the wake of military traffic. In Wiltshire two came across US lorries travelling at high speed whilst they were travelling down a narrow lane in single file:

'Coming round a sharp bend we met a convoy of American lorries… I drove my bike up the nearside bank, while Phyl tried to race to the other side of the road as the Yanks were taking up all the lane. The front lorry hit the back of Phyl's bike, and she was flung headlong into a deep ditch. Not a single lorry in the convoy stopped, so apparently drivers were too high up to see our bikes. How relieved I was, on reaching her, to hear a flow of impolite language issuing from the ditch, and to see Phyl well covered in runny mud but recovering amazingly well from the shock.'[157] Richard Meakin recalls that a lady was killed walking under a bridge at Minety and the local Police Officer 'worked night and day to find the killer and pretty well took on the whole American army during his investigations.'[158]

However it appears that in Longbridge Deverill it was the ducks that got their own back. Forty of them would cross the road between a farm and their pond every day at 10.30am and 4.30pm. The military convoys would be held up waiting for them to cross. Needless, to say, there were often feathered casualties left behind.[159] By April 1944 there were *c.* 104,000 US vehicles in Britain.[160]

Public complaints also arose about the state of the roads. A letter from Lt. Colonel Assistant Director of Claims at Milford Manor, Salisbury, in March 1944 to the County Surveyor emphasised that US station commanders were responsible for the removal of mud on highways caused by US vehicles.[161] The first winter after the US arrived at Tidworth the roads around the village become a sea of mud as jeeps and trucks 'tore around the village churning up the ill-prepared roads'. 'The British were mortified at the appearance of this once immaculate 'model' British garrison'.[162] At Codford the Scots Guards in their Churchill tanks 'were up and down the street all day long, learning to drive, and there was mud nearly a foot deep in that street. Well, they used to call it Codford-on-the-mud... It was like walking through a swamp. Terrible.'[163] It is interesting to note that Codford had been 'in the mud' once before. The *Wiltshire News* was remembering the term in its 29 September edition of 1939. The question 'Where is Codford-on-the-mud?' had been asked many a time during the Great War. Wiltshire's County Surveyor was drawing the attention of the Divisional Surveyor to the 'large quantity of water' flowing on Hungerdown Lane, Chippenham, from the US Camp which was situated between the Pheasant pub and Sheldon Road. 'I understand that this matter was raised at the time the Camp was constructed, but no action appears to have been taken, with the result that during the recent wet weather considerable annoyance was caused, particularly to the children passing along the road to and from school at Frogwell.'[164]

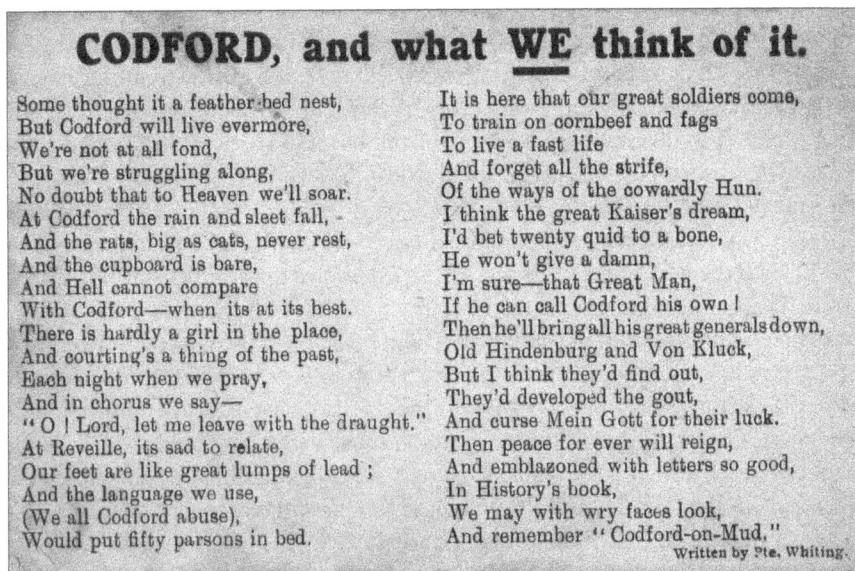

CODFORD, and what WE think of it.

Some thought it a feather-bed nest,
But Codford will live evermore,
We're not at all fond,
But we're struggling along,
No doubt that to Heaven we'll soar.
At Codford the rain and sleet fall, -
And the rats, big as cats, never rest,
And the cupboard is bare,
And Hell cannot compare
With Codford—when its at its best.
There is hardly a girl in the place,
And courting's a thing of the past,
Each night when we pray,
And in chorus we say—
"O ! Lord, let me leave with the draught."
At Reveille, its sad to relate,
Our feet are like great lumps of lead ;
And the language we use,
(We all Codford abuse),
Would put fifty parsons in bed.

It is here that our great soldiers come,
To train on cornbeef and fags
To live a fast life
And forget all the strife,
Of the ways of the cowardly Hun.
I think the great Kaiser's dream,
I'd bet twenty quid to a bone,
He won't give a damn,
I'm sure—that Great Man,
If he can call Codford his own !
Then he'll bring all his great generals down,
Old Hindenburg and Von Kluck,
But I think they'd find out,
They'd developed the gout,
And curse Mein Gott for their luck.
Then peace for ever will reign,
And emblazoned with letters so good,
In History's book,
We may with wry faces look,
And remember " Codford-on-Mud."

Written by Pte. Whiting.

Postcard of a printed poem by Private Whiting which mentions 'Codford in the mud' and the Kaiser during WWI (WSHC P54077)

The village of Ludgershall had changed little over the years but now it was filled with military vehicles and over-run with American soldiers. The entire area adjacent to the railway from Ludgershall to Tidworth was filled with every sort of military vehicle from 1943-45.[165] Reportedly at Wilton: 'On other nights, a convoy of tanks and military lorries passe[d] through the lane. These convoys can truly be said to make night hideous, and it is quite impossible to sleep while they go by. Between me and the road are a lawn, a shrubbery, a high wall, but these cannot deaden the noise of the convoy; and the din of battle made by totalitarian war even penetrates, night after night, into this remote and peaceful park.'[166]

As early as January 1940 the County Surveyor was sending a report to the Superintending Engineer at the Ministry of Works Directorate, describing road damage and giving locations. By June 1940 he was reporting that damage had been taking place at Wootton Bassett, Lyneham, Colerne and Wroughton. In March 1941 the Clerk of Wiltshire County Council was writing to the Ministry of Transport, complaining that the damage was making the roads impassable for farmers whose work was essential for the war effort. In June 1942 a letter from the Colonel of the Salisbury Plain District to a Military Liaison Officer stated that if extensive damage were to take place they would be worried about danger to the public and claims arising from it. It was noted that the County Council could not close the public highway and allow the public to use it at their own risk, but the military authorities could.[167] When the army moved into the area around Minety they closed the road to the town of Malmesbury. 'A longer route was available to traffic wishing to travel to the town. This meant an extra three or so miles on the journey by travelling via Hankerton, joining the B4040 in Charlton.' The B4040 was closed in 1943, as was Minety Common. The roads were controlled by armed sentries who had a sentry box, manned night and day.[168]

In May 1942 a conference was held at Wiltshire County Council's headquarters in Trowbridge regarding damage to roads by tanks. The County Surveyor drew attention to the dangerous condition of roads; a shortage of labour meant it was hard to fix the problem. The Bridges and Roads Committee also considered the problem, particularly with a view to Operation Bolero in 1944 when the military also felt it would be necessary to close roads.[169] By May 1944 Reilly, a surveyor in Market Place, Warminster, wrote to the County Surveyor intonating that he was 'getting a little bit annoyed and fed up' to see the amount of damage done to the main road and footpaths on almost a daily basis by military traffic. It was getting worse, leaving footpaths in a dangerous condition for pedestrians. The following month the Town Surveyor in the Urban Council Offices, Warminster, wrote to the County Surveyor in the same vein, stating that it was tanks doing the damage. In fact nothing was done as the County Surveyor felt in 1945 that military traffic would remain a problem for the foreseeable future. There were endless letters to and fro regarding the issue and September 1947 found a claim for injuries by a pedestrian. By December 1947 the paving was in such a bad state, pleas were sent, this time by the County Surveyor, for work to begin immediately. It finally began in 1948.[170]

Dear Sir,

Footpaths.

I am getting a little bit annoyed and fed up to the amount of damage being done to the main road footpaths by the Military Traffic practically daily, which is getting worse, and leaving the footpaths in a dangerous condition for the pedestrians.

Could you kindly inspect these footpaths with me by appointment, and give me your suggestion as to the repairs, and would you in your opinion, think it would be advisable to take the matter up with the Ministry or War Dept. who might make some definate instruction or care while that traffic is passing through the town to avoid getting on the footpath especially at the turning points.. I cannot keep pace with the temporary repairs owing to other work on hand at the present time, and with the trouble of getting materials and labour. On hearing from you, I will put this matter before my next Committee.

Thanking you for an early reply.

Yours faithfully,

Surveyor.

County Surveyor,
County Hall,
Trowbridge.

Letter from Warminster's Town Surveyor to the County Surveyor regarding the state of footpaths, 25 May 1944 (WSA F4/550/35)

Some locals found the volume of vehicles now using their country roads to have a silver lining. A lady whose tea shop was situated on the A346 from Marlborough to Burbage found trade markedly increased when it became the road which linked the military camps around Swindon with those on Salisbury Plain. Her shop became popular with troops buying sandwiches and cigarettes.[171] The private traders in Bulford Barracks must have improved their trade with an enlarged garrison. Traders included an ironmonger and hardware merchant, hairdresser, tobacconist, café and general store, newsagent, tailor's shop, greengrocer's shop, drapers, milliners and outfitters, boot and shoe maker, motor cycle accessories dealer, motor garage and repair shop.[172] The arrival of the military at the hunt kennels at Culverhay in Cricklade helped boost trade at a little shop nearby. The owner '…vowed she'd buy a fur coat one day with her extra takings!'[173] In Devizes, the influx of troops increased trade, making it a 'livelier and more prosperous place'. The restaurant trade was boosted by Canadians, GIs and American nurses.[174] Dorothy Devenish wrote of the changes to Salisbury that took place during the war. The city was '… washed over by successive waves of soldiers. It was like one long market-day… In the inns and places of entertainment, even on the pavements, the citizens were jostled and all but obliterated by a sea of khaki.'[175] Officers frequented the Polly Tea Rooms in Marlborough for 'weak coffee and tasteless but filling wartime cakes, a life-saver after driving through icy mist off the Downs.'[176] Locals, such as those in Codford, also made money taking in washing for the troops.[177] At Chiseldon, '… socks and handkerchiefs were washed and ironed for one penny per pair. Underclothes cost tuppence, shorts thruppence each, with an extra sixpence if they required their shirts and jackets tailored to fit.' Often the men would come for their washing when it was half dry, as they had to fly out on an early mission. Many were never to be seen again but often 'a small gift would be left at the camp, to be delivered to the lady, by way of a thank-you.'[178] For Wiltshire's indigenous population, British troops were just another addition to their locality; to be offered hospitality for the role they were playing to win the war. In Bemerton one family took in a Welsh airman and developed such a close relationship that they travelled to Wales to spend a week with his family.[179] The

Scots Guards Armoured Division were stationed at Codford from 1941-43 and proved very popular with local residents.[180] Every Sunday, one of the Battalions would attend Codford Church, announcing their arrival by their march behind the Brigade drums and fifes.[181] The 2nd (Armoured) Battallion of the Irish Guards were stationed in Fonthill Park; Nissen huts for the men at the top of the park and the tanks at the bottom. Their time there from September 1941 to the autumn of 1942 appears to have been a happy one, as one Irish Guardsman recalled.

> We were very happy at Fonhill Gifford... The Camp... had been built by refugees from Germany. They gave concerts, and among them we discovered an Austrian tailor who had represented Meyer and Mortimer in Vienna. He did a roaring trade in service dress jackets and trousers. From these people we first heard of the horrors of concentration camps – which we were to witness later at Sandbostel.[182]

As with other arrivals, their accents may have often seemed strange, and their way of communicating may have been slightly different, but they understood the difficulties faced by their fellow citizens. Foreign troops which were stationed or passed through the county during the war years could not possibly have the same home-grown knowledge of their British counterparts.

On Foreign Soil

COMMONWEALTH TROOPS IN the form of Canadians, Australians, New Zealanders and Indians had been stationed in Britain and in Wiltshire around Salisbury Plain since 1940, such as The Mule Company of the Royal Indian Army Service Corps which was camped in the sports ground and in the woods at Bulford.[183] Australian troops had been invited into people's homes in Chiseldon for debates and to attend the local church,[184] but the overwhelming 'friendly invasion' began in January 1942. By the end of the war almost three million US servicemen had visited British shores, their numbers peaking at 228,000 in the spring and summer of 1942.[185] It was felt that US and British supply services should not cross and thereby avoid confusion and congestion. It was decided that US troops would be predominantly stationed in the western half of the country,[186] although with the massive build up of US troops in 1944 US Stations could be found in counties as far afield as Staffordshire, Lancashire, Ayrshire and Northern Ireland.[187] Airfields such as Ramsbury were taken over by the US military, where an army camp was also positioned nearby. Here a small number of RAF personnel stayed on to act as liaison and keep the airfield open. One stationed at Ramsbury felt that: 'The Americans were very generous and I can remember being given cartons of cigarettes.' Here cultural differences told, as although the British were pleased to accept the superior US rations, they did not like having to eat their main meal and desert on one sectioned tray. A compromise was reached and the British were allowed two trays, as long as they washed up themselves![188] RAF Zeals was allocated for American use in July 1943 to support the large numbers of US military units expected soon.[189] One US soldier recalled: 'We enjoyed visits with the English families in our vicinity, became more acquainted with the pubs, red telephone boxes, narrow roads and country lanes, the mostly two-story buses [*sic*] and the chilly, rainy and foggy atmosphere common to England.'[190]

When the US troops arrived en masse, the whole of Salisbury Plain was given over for their use.[191] At Chiseldon in the north of the county, the departing British troops told their counterparts: 'Well done, son. Look after the splendid camp of ours. It's your responsibility now.' 'The GI looked round in horror at the waste of elderly grey asbestos huts abandoned to him...'[192] US troops took over or built sites at Warminster, Sutton Veny, Codford, Longbridge Deverill, Fonthill Bishop, East Knoyle, Upton Lovell, Downton, Charlton Park, Sherston, Heytesbury, Hindon, Trowbridge, Salisbury, Stonehenge, Dinton, Chippenham, Westbury and Mere[193][194][195] to name but a few. Tented camps also became a feature at Marlborough, Charlton, Lydiard Millicent, Bishopstrow, Langley Burrell and Draycot Cerne.[196] The 355th Engineer General Service Regiment contained the first American personnel to be stationed in the Malmesbury area at Charlton Park, working on many construction projects in the county such as expansions at Chippenham, Calne, Bidddestone, a summer camp at Grittleton Park and a parachute 'dry bidg.' [*sic*] at Chilton Foliat. The command tried to create a favourable impression of the American soldier to the English people, contacting the Mayor and Constabulary for their views regarding whether they wanted Military Police, curfews and entertainment. 'The people at first, as typical of a small community in England, stayed apart and aloof from the troops.' But the Mayor made plans with the Commanding Officer for a 'Thanks Giving Day'. After the trial period of a week or so, invitations 'arrived daily for the troops to attend parties, dinners and participation in the town's social activities' and 'On Thanksgiving the Mayor, in full regalia, formally welcomed the unit and gave a dinner and dance for the entire command, [the evening] climaxed with his reading of a letter he had sent to our Commanding General, European Theater of Operations, concerning the exemplary behaviour of members of the command. The Regiment heartily enjoyed its stay at Malmesbury...'[197] The Americans used Fugglestone Church for their own celebrations 'which are quite different from ours.' A Bemerton parish magazine article stated: 'Generally speaking Americans will appreciate a more demonstrative welcome than would be expected, or even desired, by British soldiers.'[198]

E. Company of the 506th Regiment, 101st Airborne Division recalled that the people in the village of Aldbourne were 'conservative, set in their ways, apprehensive about all these young Yanks in their midst. The danger of friction was great but the army put together an excellent orientation program that worked well'. Ambrose notes that the men were told to 'save their hell-raising for Swindon'![199] The G, H, and HQ Companies of the 3rd Batallion of the 506th Parachute Infantry Regiment were based at a camp in Loves Lane, Ramsbury. The buildings in this camp were not Nissen huts, but tar paper shacks.[200] 'A' Company of the 506th were billeted in Hightown Stables, Aldbourne,[201] considered by many of the troops to be, as Matthew Pellett notes, 'the best of the best', with others billeted in a purpose built army camp that is now the football pitch.[202] After WWII the stables eventually fell into disrepair. They were dismantled and shipped to the Currahee Military Museum in Toccoa, Georgia, to be reconstructed there in 2005.[203]

Many country houses were requisitioned for the war effort, with British and US troops moving in; a trying time for their owners. Lydiard House was requisitioned in 1941 and a sympathetic friend wrote to the owner Lord Bolingbroke. 'Dear Lord Bolingbroke, Thank you for your kind letter received today. I can quite understand what it must have been for you having to turn out of your beautiful place, how awful all this is. I am so sorry about it... I am greatly surprised and indeed sorry to know you are turned out by the military – what will they do next, no-one can tell. If this frightful war would end what a blessing it would be.'[204] At Tottenham House in Savernake the Marquis of Ailesbury and his daughter continued to live in the upper level of the house with the US Company's HQ and Officers' living quarters downstairs.[205] Wingfield House was one of those requisitioned and homes in the village were used as billets for soldiers. 'Life before the war in the quiet hamlet of Wingfield was carefree.... then we were plunged into disruption by the war and the Army who had been billeted in the manor house.'[206]

Major concerns for the British Government were relations between the British and US troops, and those between the US troops and British civilian women.[207] US troops were well paid and had noticeably superior clothes and equipment. Malcolm Martin, evacuated to Hilperton, remembers how the image of the US soldier was impressed upon Trowbridge residents during a flag parade in the town with 'the quietness of their rubber soled boots compared with the clatter of hob nailed Tommies'.[208] When American soldiers arrived at Fugglestone '... we all thought they looked even smarter with their jackets open to show collared shirts and ties. Our army did allow our boys to wear collars and ties so I offered to make them collars by using cloth cut from the tail of their shirts. They were so grateful.'[209] The British soldier received one third of a GI's disposable income. The pay of Canadian and Australian troops was also higher but in the Canadian case that which was made available to them was equivalent to the British,[210] although one WAAF said of the Canadians: 'They have more money than the English. For example 'my' Canadian took me for a night out. We visited two pubs. Had four drinks in each (rum and lime, 2/4 each). Finished it off with a double whiskey each.'[211] Peggy Pickford from Warminster was writing to her sister Elizabeth Martin in Australia on 5 November 1941, noting that her husband's cousin from Canada was visiting them whilst on leave. 'He kept saying how "behind the times" we seem over here (plumbing and central heating etc.) which wasn't very tactful... he seemed very nice really, it was just thoughtless speaking.' He talked about some Canadians finding the remote locations they were stationed in very lonely and that thirty of the men had married local girls. He was asked if he had ever considered this himself. His reply had been; "Lord, no," but that he'd had plenty of proposals. One girl had asked him to marry her when he hadn't even spent the whole evening in her company! Peggy goes on to say that 'I suppose it is the money the girls want. A Canadian soldier's wife's marriage allowance is fifty dollars a month or about £3 a week!... They have rather a good system. If a man is not married, they deduct the money just the same and he gets it in a lump sum when he leaves the Army. I think it is a good idea, because then they are all the same for "spending money" as it were, and the bachelors will have a jolly good start when they want to get married.'[212] Churchill asked if the US could use the Canadian system but they refused, although this may have been the reason why the British did concede to a flat rate 20% pay rise for British troops in August 1942.[213]

The wives of British servicemen had difficulties managing on service pay and also had to cope with running a house, and more likely than not, working too. They also had to cope with the emotional aspect of having their loved ones on active service. One Malmesbury wife remarked:

> I had such a disappointment this weekend. My husband was to have forty-eight hours' leave, and then on Friday night I got a wire to say he couldn't come. Oh, I could have cried my eyes out. I'd been getting all worked up for it – you know. I'd bought myself a new pair of stockings, and I'[d] sat up every evening to finish my cardigan, and I'd just finished it when the wire came. Its blue – a sort of powder blue, that's his favourite colour on me. I couldn't put it on.... I'd got it planned I was going to put it on when he came home, I just hadn't any heart for it. Just pushed it away in my drawer as if it was one of my old things, I never even held it up to see how it looked.[214]

The first thing the US soldier noticed on arrival was the compactness of the country. Everything from fields to infrastructure was very small. The GIs associated 'big' with 'great' and wondered how Britain could be called Great Britain 'when you can fly to the coast in a couple of hours?'[215] E Company of the 506th Regiment, 101st Airborne Division arrived at Ogbourne St. George Station en route from Liverpool for their nine month stay in Aldbourne. They saw what they described as 'fairybrook' cottages with thatched roofs, cobblestone lanes and a village green like those 'on a Hollywood movie set'.[216] The average GI took a little while to settle into their new environment. 'A lot of their customs are a little funny at first but they are friendly people and since the language they use is nearly 'English', as we know it, it's pretty nice. Driving on the 'wrong' side of the road is really quite an experience. You want to stop the car and get out to run every time you see a car coming towards you at more than two miles-per-hour. They call a battery an accumulator, a truck a lorry, a railroad car a truck, radio tubes are valves and a flash light is a torch.'[217]

The British opinion of Americans was discovered by the Home Intelligence Division of the Ministry of Information and Mass Observation in their surveys and reports. In 1942 the general opinion about the American 'character' included friendliness, generosity, candour, virility, openness, but also boastfulness, ostentation, materialism and greed. The older members of the British upper class tended to be the most critical and there was a general lack of positive admiration for American achievements or institutions, alongside a worry about the loosening of British morals. For the majority of young people, however, the story was very different. American fashion, slang and music were a source of fascination, 'epitomised in the movies'.[218]

It appears that in the months leading up to July 1942, US soldiers did not fully understand how scarce supplies were in Britain. Reports were coming in to Whitehall that they were buying up any goods which did not require ration coupons: combs, razor blades, watches, torch batteries, blankets etc., and they did not realise how meagre the British diet was. They were also 'drinking pubs dry (of warm beer they disliked), emptying fish and chip shops and going to exclusive restaurants that no British private could afford'.[219] George Orwell reported in January 1943: 'There is widespread anti-American feeling among the working class, thanks to the presence of US soldiers and I believe, very bitter anti-British feeling amongst them. GIs are always boasting and get paid much more.' He noted the general opinion was that the only US soldiers with decent manners were the 'negroes'.[220] By August 1942 US troops were given the pamphlet *A Short Guide to Great Britain* which included a warning about bragging and to 'never criticise the King or Queen'. There were also on-board lectures warning against excessive drinking of beer due to shortages and to be discreet when spending money.[221]

During WWII crime was on the increase, and this could also involve military personnel. If it involved foreign troops, it could prove particularly difficult. The Wiltshire Housing Officer was wondering what to do with arrested US troops in 1942 and detectives at a South West District Conference were discussing what to do with American sheets in civilian hands.[222] There appears to have been friction between local Police Authorities and the US military with the Police becoming worried about a number of interviews taking place by US Investigating Officers with civilians without a British Police Officer present. A letter in December 1942 from the Home Office communicated that the British Police felt there was a delay by the US forces in involving them in respect of civilian witnesses, as was their duty set out under Circular 72, 9 September 1941.[223]

In 1942 the British offered to welcome the GI's with a hospitality scheme but the Ministry of Information declared that the British '[c]ame forward with premature offers of hospitality which the Americans were not ready and not organised to accept and this undoubtedly led to disappointment and a feeling of frustration'.[224] The American Red Cross was criticised for banning British and Allied personnel from its clubs, except when they were a guest of a GI, proudly wanting to create a purely American atmosphere with 'a little touch of home abroad'.[225] Tedworth House at Tidworth became an American Red Cross Club, run by helpers from the Volunteer Aid Detachment (VAD), a part of the British Army,[226] and locals.[227] Eleanor Roosevelt, the wife of Brigadier General Mark Theodore Roosevelt Junior, son of the US president, had volunteered for overseas service with the American Red Cross. She ended up at Tedworth with her husband who had established a headquarters at the barracks. She quickly set up a canteen for US troops and 'in primitive conditions began cooking 30 dozen hamburgers a night in two small frying pans and making over 80 gallons of coffee. Dishes were washed in fire buckets...' It was said the club was '[l]ike a cross between Bedlam and the Ritz'. By September 1942 Tedworth House became popular with British servicewomen and local girls. It was reported that the Hokey Cokey was introduced to Britain there in 1943 before becoming 'the rage'. [228] Many of the girls who worked in the clubs were recruited locally, such as those in the Devizes club, situated on The Green. [229]

The *Salisbury Journal* reported on 30 June 1944 that it was the Navy, Army and Air Force Institutes (NAAFI) who served to help provide provisions for British troops, 'financially self-supporting and all its available profits [were] used for the benefit of the Forces.' Some civilian NAAFI workers lived on the camp, as did those in camps around Cricklade, working from 7am until midnight serving food in a canteen on the base and also visiting those working on the bases with a NAAFI wagon. 'You worked late, and you got up early, but I must say I did enjoy the war, and we girls had some good laughs!' [230] A large NAAFI was situated at RAF Blakehill. A cup of tea was charged at 1d. and 'rock buns' were also 1d. Lyons fruit pies and sandwiches (known as 'wads') were 2d. per item. [231] On 30 June 1944 an advert in the *Salisbury Journal* announced it was 'D' Day for NAAFI: 'zero hour for the greatest

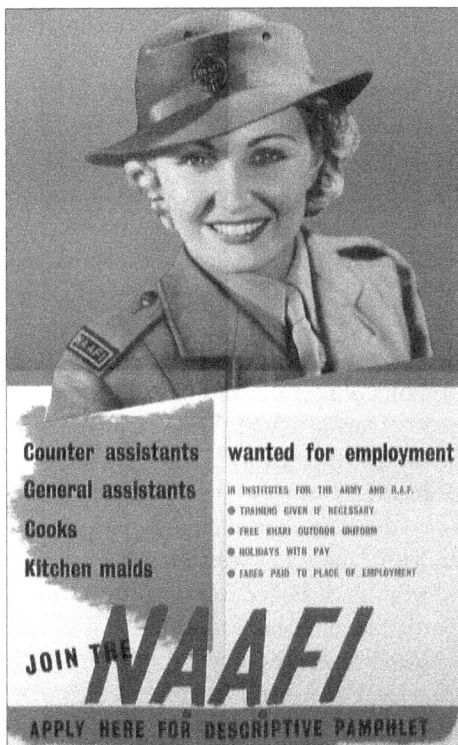

Recruitment Poster for the NAAFI (WSA G24/225/29)

canteen 'exercise' in history. In these decisive weeks, NAAFI will march close upon the heels of Britain's invasion army, pledged to serve the fighting men, whenever they pause for rest and refreshment.' NAAFI had already travelled to Crete, Greece, North Africa, Sicily, Salerno, Anzio, but these would be 'dwarfed' beside the challenge of the Second Front. The *Wiltshire Times* announced on 15 July 1944 that 'For weeks prior to the invasion thousands of Naafi girls were voluntarily 'imprisoned' in the invasion camps in order that Naafi – the only canteen service operating in the sealed areas – should be available for the fighting men.'

The NAAFI girls often felt they were forgotten. 'You know how little the NAAFI girls were thought of... we always felt we were the poor relations of the services, as we did not come under orders of the armed forces...' They worked long hours but had fewer 'perks' than their counterparts. Kate Adie reports that even their uniforms were seen as 'something worn by Little Orphan Annie'. They got no medals for their war duties, even though they were based on military sites, sharing the same risks as other service personnel. 'Running shops and canteens, cooking and organising recreational activities, producing the "ever more welcome, even stranger tea."'[232]

In Wiltshire the locals did try to organise facilities for US troops. By 1944 funds had become available to help the British 'Welcome Clubs' which were run by the Women's Voluntary Service. Correspondence in the Swindon Borough Clerk's Correspondence Files at the Wiltshire & Swindon History Centre tells of the WVS' 'experimental scheme' in December 1943, to 'encourage British Centres, run by civilians for their service friends'. It suggested that a Committee of elder and respected local people, who knew most of the community between them, were to pick the British members. It was also noted that '.... Old fashioned party games have been particularly successful.' Suggested games included darts, cards, draughts, chess and dominoes. A Junior Committee comprised of local girls, Service women, members of the Women's Land Army and Americans from the local stations who were to run the entertainments. A grant of £30 would be made available to set up the scheme.[233] In Swindon during March 1944, the Ministry of Labour and the National Service Employment Exchange held conferences with shop stewards and factory men over the welfare of women and girls outside the factory, asking if a British Restaurant could be opened up in the evenings. It was noted that the US Red Cross and US Army Police felt that café accommodation was inadequate and the Council's General Purposes Committee took up the case.[234] In Malmesbury the Mass Observation writer and factory worker Celia Fremlin noted: 'At every corner there are knots of soldiers, just standing. Some are smoking, some not even doing that; others are strolling languidly up and down outside the Y.M.C.A.'[235] with nothing to do. The unanimous view was of 'the dangers of troops and young women war workers walking about the streets, and the great need of suitable premises, under appropriate supervision, where proper social intercourse could take place.' After an experimental first month, it was found that in Swindon there was definitely a need to 'establish a club...mixing forces and civilians is a difficult but necessary contribution to social stability.'[236] Finding facilities was a real problem, however. A letter from the Deputy Regional Controller, Board of Trade to the Swindon Town Clerk in May 1944 made it clear. 'I need hardly say that a lot of the people who are chasing around looking for space are really not authorised to do so.' The Swindon Town Clerk was unhappy that the Americans were looking at the public library for use by American nurses, feeling that the library was serving an important wartime need and impracticable suggestions were being offered up by US Officers.[237] In Calne, the pressure for accommodation meant that the Service Canteen being held in the Methodist schoolroom was under threat. The Methodist Trust felt that the work being done there presently was vitally important for the moral and social welfare of thousands of young men in the district and catering for them was the wish of the authorities. The *Wiltshire Times* reported on 25 November 1939 that many of the townspeople were asking about the provision of a canteen and recreation room for the troops. The vicar felt that it was a matter for the town to discuss.

> There were, as they knew, he continued, many soldiers who came into the town and it was very desirable that they should have somewhere to go – somewhere they could find recreation and refreshment if need be… it was the concern of many people that they saw a large number of men in the evenings with nothing to do. It was said they could go to the cinema, but many of the young men who were just lately recruited had only a very little amount of pay and they could not afford to go to the cinema very often.

In Trowbridge the need was just as great four and a half years later when the suggestion of snack bars was raised. It was stated that at present the troops could not even get a cup of tea.[238]

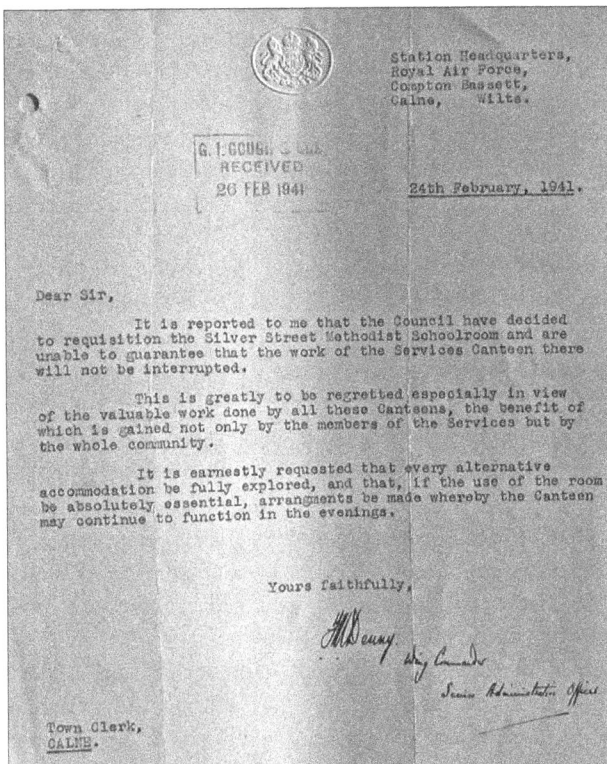

Letter dated 24 February 1941 from the Senior Administrator at RAF Compton Bassett regarding the potential loss of Calne's Services Canteen (WSA G18/225/6)

French Soldiers in Warminster During WWII, reproduced by kind permission of Ivan Clark (WSHC P53986)

Swindon's Welcome Club was proving popular with servicemen in November 1944 and they were conducting themselves 'very well indeed'. It was the male civilians attending who were more of a problem. Most were under 20 and 'potentially dangerous,' due to 'hooliganism and destruction' and they needed to be kept under supervision.[239] In Devizes, cinema showings were given on Sunday evenings to keep troops off the streets, a move which caused some local disapproval.[240]

It was reported on 23 June 1944 in the *Salisbury Journal* that a centre for troops had been built jointly by the US and Britain. The British Army made the site available and the US Army Engineers put up the building. It was to be called an 'Allied Forces Centre' and could seat 200 for lectures, concerts and film shows. It had a library, writing room and a discussions room. Planned activities included 'dramatic, musical, photographic and drawing circles' and meetings of groups who had shared professional and occupational interests.

Wiltshire's inhabitants appeared keen to learn about their new American neighbours. There were lectures held in villages such as Urchfont[241] and a second lecture was held on the subject of 'world politics' at The Deanery, Salisbury, in October 1942 after the first, also on America, proved so popular.[242]

Relations between GIs and local girls had been so close there was national concern that some girls felt it was their passport to the 'American Dream'.[243] The 'goodtime girls' were also more than ready to make the most of a GI's pay and prostitutes plied their trade. Some arrived in Codford from Bristol to entertain both GIs and POWs. They were often accidentally discovered by locals and were given the name 'Haystack Annies' after the location of their liaisons.[244] This term was also used in Great Cheverell, for the hostess of a house of ill repute, traced by the Americans as the source of venereal infection. This 'Haystack Annie', as her clients called her, was charged with allowing children to live in a disorderly house and was sentenced to six months in Holloway.[245] The renowned American anthropologist and author Margaret Mead had been asked to turn her expertise to the issue of British and American relations. She felt that the culture of 'dating' was very different. In the US it was expected that girls would play 'hard to get', but that British girls would often take everything at face value. Whilst the US soldiers expected to get their advances turned down the British girls, unused to the American way of spoiling a girl and acting flamboyantly, tried to please. Teenage girls were the most susceptible and therefore the most vulnerable, many working away from home or having become an evacuee with no parental constraints.[246] Home Office Circular 202/1944, sent to Wiltshire's Chief Constable in July 1944, was considering the question of how to improve the conduct between members of the forces and the civilian population. 'Such conduct is not, of course, confined to members of the U.S. Forces, but the present circular is concerned primarily with the position of Police vis-à-vis the United States troops who are not subject to the jurisdiction of the British criminal courts...' It went on to state that the Police could not censor morals or behaviour and could not intervene unless the complaint breeched criminal law, even if it gave 'offence on grounds of good taste or manners.' If the girl was seen to be of 'tender years' and needed protection, the Police could intervene if the situation was seen to be of threatening or moral danger to her, but the preferred option would be to warn her parents or guardian that she could be brought before the court with an Order under Section 62 of the Children and Young Persons Act, 1934. It noted that the most common complaints against GIs were indiscretion in public areas such as public squares, air raid shelters or the gardens of dwelling houses... 'and that they force[d] their attentions on respectable girls or women by pestering them on the streets or even by making their way into private houses' but that the majority of US forces observed a proper code of conduct and it could often be the case that it was the British women themselves who made the advancements, along with a 'genuine misunderstanding of British habits and social relations.' Even so, everything possible needed to be done 'to check conduct which afford[ed] grounds for complaint.' The US authorities were anxious that the good reputation of their troops should not be prejudiced by the misbehaviour of a few.[247] One teenager from Chippenham stated that it was 'almost de rigueur for a local girl to have a GI boyfriend'.[248] A good way to meet one was to strike up a conversation in the cinema queue. 'Queuing was an ideal way to strike up an acquaintance and sever it if necessary as one reached the top of the line.'[249] The Ministry of Labour and National Service in Swindon were so concerned for the welfare of women and young girls that they hoped an expert on sex education would undertake some talks in the factory canteen over the issue.[250] On 9 June 1944 the *Salisbury Journal* reported the case of two girls who were found in an American Camp. They were charged with being found on War Department land after staying at the camp overnight and being found by an Officer the next morning. The *Wiltshire Times* published the following month on 1 July the case of a girl who was reported as having a 'mania for coloured soldiers' and was being sentenced to two years hard labour for being in unlawful possession of American

Army property. She was aged 20 and had already been placed under the care of a Probation Officer as being 'a juvenile exposed to moral danger,' having been sent to an 'approved school for a similar offence… In 1943 she had given birth to a coloured child.' The National Council of Women had been expressing concern about young girls hanging around military establishments. They wanted more women Police Officers to deal with women and girls whose behaviour was deemed 'questionable'.[251] But it was not just the US troops who were wooing the British female population… In June 1940 varying divisions were camped hurriedly at Tidworth. 'Belgian soldiers rub shoulders with French sailors – marines and British Expeditionary Force jostle on the roads; the Frenchmen got down to it quickly and have collared all the prettiest girls…'[252]

By 1942 the Army Morale Committee began to voice the anxieties of those British soldiers posted overseas for over two years who were worried about the behaviour of their loved ones back home, thought to be a major cause of low morale. Worry over the fidelity of wives and sweethearts became an 'epidemic' with the size of the US contingent preparing for D-Day.[253] The build up to Operation Bolero began at the end of 1943 and Ministry of Information felt that '[t]hese American soldiers are going to be a great trouble until the fighting starts'. Joint British/US military and civilian liaison divisions were set up to smooth relations, but caused a great deal of infighting at meetings.[254] It was even rumoured that the invasion was welcomed by British soldiers serving in the Middle East as it removed the GIs from the country.[255] The *Wiltshire Times* printed a *Letter to the Editor* in its 23 October 1943 edition, sent by some British servicemen:

If Girls Want Decent Husbands

Sir: There is something that the boys in our hut have got so upset about, that we have all made up our minds to make a stand for it. In our hut there are 17 of us not married, and when the time comes we want to marry decent English girls.

Well, Sir, the girls seem to be demoralised, and to take no notice of self-respect and decent behaviour that is part of what we are fighting for. Everywhere we see girls being embraced by strangers as they walk along with them, talking loud slang without respect, and being familiar and greedy, and being mauled about and letting themselves be put to public disgrace.

Well, Sir, we have made up our minds to shew public disapproval of these girls whenever we see such things, and also we will shew contempt and never have anything to do with any girl who has lowered herself like this in war-time. If girls want decent English husbands, the girls will have to act decently.

An English Girl's Lament
Dear old England's not the same,
We dreaded invasion – well, it came,
But no, it's not the beastly Hun
The bloody, damned Yankee Army's come.

You see them in the trams and bus,
there isn't room for all of us,
We walk to let them have our seats,
Then get run over by their jeeps.
They['re] mean about our lukewarm beer,
and say it's like running water here,
But after drinking one or more,
You find them lying on the floor,
And you should see them try to dance,
They get a partner, start to prance,
when you're half dead they stop and smile,
'How's about it, Honey Chile?'.
You'll see them try to jitterbug,
They twist and turn and pull and hug,
It's enough to make a monkey jealous,
The Yanks are civilized – so they tell us.
The Yankee Officers make us smile,
with their light pants you can see a mile,
We wonder if they are mice or men,
Decide their values, so avoid their den.
In admiration we would stare,
at all the ribbons that they wear.
And think of deeds both bold and daring,
Which won the medals they are wearing.
The green ribbon alone denotes,
They crossed the Atlantic – brave men – in boats.
We speak to them, they just look hazy,
They think we're mad, we think they're crazy.
Yet to our Allies we must be nice,
We love them as the cats love mice.
They laugh at us for drinking tea,
Yet funnier sight you'll never see,
Than a gum chewing Yank with a dumb-looking face,
He'll raise a laugh most any place.
They say they can shoot – yes, and fight,
Sure they can fight, but when they're tight,
We must admit their shooting is fine,
Of course they can shoot, but what a line.
They tell us we have teeth like pearls,
they like our hair the way it curls,
'Your eyes would dim the brightest star,
You're the competition for Miss Lamar.'
You are their life, their love, their all,
and for no other would they fall.

'And love you till death do us part,
and if you leave me dear, you'll break my heart.
And then they leave, you're broken-hearted,
The camp has moved, your love departed,
You wait for mail that does not come,
then realise you're awful dumb.
In a different town, a different place,
It's a different girl, a different face.
'I love you, sweetheart, please be mine',
It's the same old Yank with the same old line.

Author unknown, enclosed with a letter from a GI based in Wiltshire to his wife, 10/9/44[256]

Close contact between troops of many nations and local communities inevitably caused friction. One Land Girl working at a farm in Codford remembers that the local Milk Bar was '… always lively. The troops used to queue for food and cups of tea at a penny each. It was quite a meeting place.'[257] US troops stationed at Tidworth ventured across to Bulford to attend dances. This led to numerous fist-fights, normally over girls or regimental rivalry, particularly between British and US paratroopers. It did not take long before the Americans were banned from attending the dances.[258] Social forays to village pubs or at dances could also cause a different kind of disturbance. In Freshford on the Wiltshire/Somerset border: 'The lads who came home late at night came singing from the station, causing sighs, and otherwise, from the Village which was already in bed and trying to snatch at those precious hours before midnight…'[259]

The Home Office feared racial friction could occur over black GIs and tried to cluster black units where there was already a British black presence, but friction did not usually occur between black GIs and the local populace. Eisenhower wrote in September 1942 that the population was 'devoid of racial consciousness. They know nothing at all about the conventions and habits of polite society that have been developed in the U.S. in order to preserve segregation…' 'To most English people, including the village girls – even those of perfectly fine character – the negro soldier is just another man, rather fascinating because he is unique in their experience, a jolly good fellow and with money to spend…'[260] To affect this policy of segregation there must have been co-operation by the British forces and Police; the issue was hotly debated by Churchill's Government, more so in 1942 than any other aspect of the American 'occupation'. A letter dated 4 September 1942 from the Home Office to Wiltshire's Chief Constable reveals the British Government's position regarding black troops at that time.

It is not the policy of His Majesty's Government that any discrimination as regards the treatment of coloured troops should be made by the British authorities…' 'If the American Service authorities decide to put certain places out of bounds for their coloured troops, such prohibition can be effected only by means of an Order issued by the appropriate American Army and Naval authorities. The Police themselves should not make themselves in any way responsible for the enforcement of such orders.

Eisenhower's staff became aware of the letter and moved to counter it, saying that they did not 'make restrictions on the basis of colour'.[261] By December 1943 joint US/British Police patrols were taking place in Trowbridge and Devizes where US Military Police were stationed. There were also coloured US Police on duty in Trowbridge, found to be 'very effective'. 'In fact there ha[d] not been a single incident during the Christmas.'[262]

At Savernake a sizeable proportion of the US presence was black although they were never allowed to mix socially with white troops. Rotating passes ensured that they never met. In Marlborough dances for the black GIs were held on a Monday and for the white troops on a Friday. 'A lot of girls said 'oh no, we're not going on Monday', but my sister and I and two or three other girls said 'poor devils they've got to have some amusement, we're going!' The other girls joined in, but the Friday dances were always more popular. I can still remember dancing with a black soldier who was six feet tall – I was about 5'6' – and he would bend over me and hum in my ear, he always made a beeline for me at the dances. We found the blacks to be far more polite. If you were walking along the street and they were coming towards you they would say 'get off the sidewalk and let the lady go past.'[263] Many black GIs spent their leisure time in Bradford on Avon and an old man from the town noted: 'I like them Yanks, but oo be they white chaps they'm brought along wee em?'[264] At the Three Horseshoes in Burbage the black GIs drank at the back of the pub, in a small area known as the 'tea room', entertaining the locals with jazz on the piano. The white soldiers used the main bar.[265] Black GIs from Lydiard Park often joined services at the local church, their choir and organist giving renderings of the 'Negro Spirituals'.[266] The Officer commanding the Southern Base Section of the Services of Supply of the US Army was very anxious to

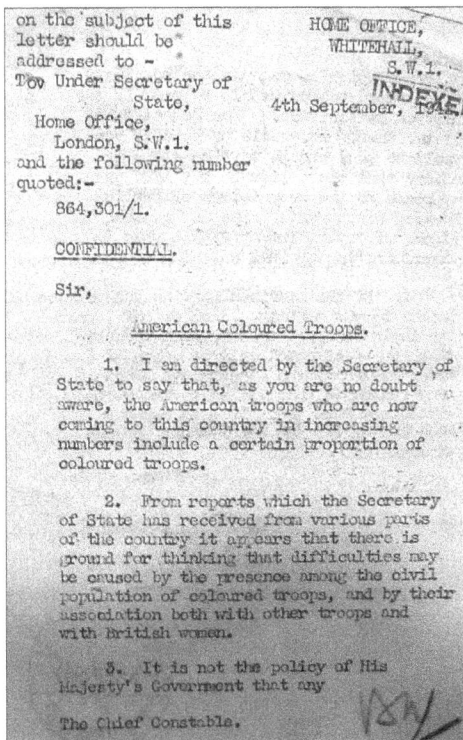

Letter to Wiltshire's Chief Constable, 4 September 1942, regarding black American troops (WSA F5/530/6)

be kept informed regarding local public feeling towards US troops in July 1943, 'especially coloured troops, so that he may know what is going on, and take at any early stage any action which he may deem necessary.'[267] The Swindon Borough Wartime Correspondence files show that it was necessary for US troops to be billeted in private houses by the end of 1943. It was stated that coloured troops were not to be billeted in any private house.[268]

Many American soldiers felt unhappy with the way children begged for sweets and the low morals of some British women.[269] For some children, getting money from GIs became a game, with the phrase 'Got a penny, mister?' being well used. The money they were given helped them go to the cinema or was used for other treats, as one evacuee in Trowbridge recalled.[270] 'We saw that Davis boy again last night, outside the Lamb [in Trowbridge], begging off the Americans'... 'It's disgraceful, kids out begging in the street, and goodness knows what Gladys gets up to, out with the Yanks every night. Before we know where we are the'll be another bundle on the way. It's no good me telling her, she takes not a scrap of notice, but let me hear either Billy or Arthur have been out cadging off the Americans and I'll give them the pasting of their lives.'[271] In Cricklade the Americans were mainly remembered for throwing sweets and cigarette packets to children from railway carriages or lorries as they moved through. The soldiers knew that the children collected the cigarette cards.[272] At Whiteparish, the Americans would throw bars of chocolate into a child's pram as they passed.[273] The children at Heywood School were given a talk about not accepting sweets from Americans,[274] probably not abided by, but some boys from Langley Burrell found that because they never asked for gum they were usually given some. 'We hated hearing children call out 'Give us some gum, chum'.'[275] The US soldiers and local boys often became friendly. In Codford '... as the weeks went by, we became very friendly with the American soldiers, they were only young men and away from home. In their spare time they came to visit us and talked about America and how they lived',[276] although the village was also finding it difficult to cope with so many troops stationed nearby. One member of the Women's Land Army, working at a farm at Codford, would catch the bus home to Salisbury on her days off, '... but with so many troops at Codford it was a fight to get on the bus. If lucky, one could jump on before it stopped. We nearly always had to stand or sit on the stairs.'[277]

By November 1943 it was realised that the overriding feeling of the American soldier was that he was only interested in when he could get home. Only 2% of American troops were accepting hospitality and most visited pubs to seek a diversion from being in a country they didn't necessarily like or want to be in.[278] The troops had been forced to be there and their thoughts, perhaps understandably, were of going to war and what it would bring. Many admitted their feelings for Britain would have been different had they chosen to visit its shores.[279] Eisenhower, though, had always supported the objective of getting Americans into British homes to create a positive relationship between GIs and the locals, and it was discovered that enforced billeting was successful. A survey of US mail from Normandy in July 1944 showed that one quarter of letters were addressed to British homes.[280] A local Hilperton family regularly invited a GI to Sunday lunch, having met him through their Chapel, and maintained contact after the war was over. Their descendents still keep in touch to this day.[281] In Bratton, one resident 'came home with a black American serviceman, who he had found walking along the road from Westbury. He was entertained by my Granny to tea on the lawn.' It was also noted that as these troops were stationed nearby, a few babies of mixed race were left behind. In both cases no one appeared to comment about it and the children grew up and married locally.[282] A house in Devizes became an 'open house' for US servicemen stationed in the town who came for coffee and a chat. The local children enjoyed their company and the sweets they brought with them.[283] In Warminster, one family used to invite about eight soldiers to supper on Sunday evenings: '… my mother would play the piano while they sang.'[284] Troops working at Savernake got evening and weekend passes into Marlborough and the surrounding villages. Football matches were held between the military units and Marlborough Town Football Club.[285] One Chippenham resident felt sorry for a GI and invited him to his home. He loaned him a bicycle so that he could go cycling with the family because he was so homesick.[286] The first GIs to be stationed in Codford were '… mostly from the country places, quiet towns, homesteads and farms. Softly spoken, happy, kindly natured men, who missed their homes and loved to sit in the houses of the village people, smoke their endless American cigarettes and cigars, and just talk of their pops and moms. Delightful companions…'[287] In May 1941 Sybil Eccles in Chute invited two Free French men to tea. They were in the British Army and stationed at Tidworth. 'More than once [one] wandered off by himself and we watched him standing alone at the edge of the garden staring out over the fields… I feel frantically sorry for them with their khaki – their rusty borrowed bicycles and their borrowed names – it must be a nightmare of anonymity – bewilderment and distress…'[288]

It is interesting to note that little is mentioned in local newspapers about the GIs during their stay in Wiltshire. In 1942-3 the British press had been practicing 'almost complete censorship' on any stories about friction with the GIs'.[289] A few 'good news' stories were to be found, such as a ceremony reported in the 7 January edition of the *Salisbury Journal* to give an American Flag to Salisbury Cathedral, timed to coincide with President Roosevelt's National Day of Prayer. Colonel Thrasher spoke: 'You are a brave, generous people…and we are entrusting you with this flag knowing it will be in safe hands.' It was also reported in the *Wiltshire Gazette* on 23 December 1942 that US soldiers had given a party at the Bishops Cannings schoolhouse. The children 'as a consequence … have been made loyal admirers of the States for life.' "Nice guys, these Yanks; can't beat'em" whispered Jonnie 'and his words were echoed by all the 115 children who sang, danced, played games and chewed sweets.' The hospital staff at the 130th US Station Hospital at Chiseldon made dolls for the children at Christmas 1944. They also held a party at the site, freely giving rations and ice cream; American films were shown at the camp. A report dated 13 January 1945 stated that it was done '[t]o increase our Anglo-American relation policy.'[290] The Americans brought new foods with them too. One Longbridge Deverill resident remembered tasting cranberry sauce for the first time at a Christmas party given for the children.[291]

One harrowing story was reported in the local newspapers, however; the murder of a local girl in Marlborough on 28 September 1943 by a black American GI. The soldier was Private Davis, in 'C' Company of the 248th Quartermaster Battalion, Services of Supply, stationed at Savernake. The Private had no alibi and blood had been discovered on his clothes. He admitted the crime and was executed on 14 December 1943 in HM Prison, Shepton Mallet, Somerset.[292]

George Orwell surmised that this void in discussion in both print and on the air would store up problems for the future[293] but it is not certain whether this has been proved to be correct, except perhaps in the case of sexual conduct and illegitimate births of wartime and the immediate post-war years. The social stigma surrounding illegitimacy and problems caused by the birth of children where the husband was not the father affected some families greatly during the immediate post war period and beyond. The United States did try to aid the British in the case of affiliation and wife maintenance by being prepared to arrange for the delivery of a court order when the defendant had been posted overseas before the postal delivery took place. Two copies of the order were required, along with a covering letter applying for the issue of Family Allowance. If the summons had not yet been served when the overseas posting took place then nothing could be done whilst the father was overseas.[294] After the war Tidworth and Perham Down became transit camps for those women departing for the U.S. – 640 GI brides and their 176 babies were processed.[295] The brides were housed at Jellalabad and Delhi Barracks at Tidworth with German POWs put to service as their batmen.[296]

D-Day

D-DAY WAS PARTLY planned at Wilton House[297] as it was the HQ of Southern Command, and a 'vital centre of operations' for logistical preparations.[298] Many of Wiltshire's RAF stations were the sites of glider practice leading up to D-Day[299] and Bulford was used for training the British 6th Airborne Division; they were also to use gliders for their part in D-Day at Pegasus Bridge. Tape was used to lay out a river and canal, with bridges on top, all to exact specifications to simulate the original in France.[300] For about a month beforehand the military started stockpiling along the country lanes around Cricklade, with British and US troops stationed on guard duty.[301] In Donhead St. Mary telephone posts were demolished by tanks on the lead up to D-Day. Lots of vehicles could be seen parked at night all around a farmer's fields to prevent them being seen by air.[302] There was '[c]ontinual movement of convoys bumper to bumper going past our house [in Marlborough] and up through the forest... The movement of vehicles went on all night long, it never ceased... It continued all the next day as well.' And at Postern Hill... 'Convoy after convoy of vehicles loaded with troops and equipment passed our house heading south towards the coast. As darkness fell the vehicles would often park up-their crews spending the night in 'pup' tents pitched beneath the trees.' [303] Parts of England were now so packed with men and material that the troops joked that if the invasion of North Western Europe did not come soon, England would tilt and sink beneath the weight of preparations.[304] It is said that at Ramsbury army camp an American soldier, just before D-Day, decorated what had been their canteen with crayons including a life-size drawing of an American soldier lying down resting his head on his helmet. Many such cases occurred, as at nearby RAF Membury which lies in both Berkshire and Wiltshire. Some pieces were removed to be conserved[305]

If Wiltshire's roads had not been busy enough, military traffic increased exponentially on the run up to D-Day. Ammunition was continually taken from the US army supply depot in Savernake. 'In the months before D-Day we shipped ammo by night from the forest to Army camps and sea ports in Southern England.'[306] Old Sarum Airfield was the site where hundreds of vehicles were modified for D-Day so that they could be driven ashore for the beach landings. The airfield and surrounding fields were used for the storage and preparation of vehicles. The Supply and Transport Column was also formed at Old Sarum at this time. Known as 'Silcock's Travelling Circus', its task was to equip and supply the Allied Forces from D-Day onwards. The unit worked with thousands of tons of equipment, operating in danger areas in Europe.[307] Included in the D-Day preparations were the widening of the Bath to Southampton Road southwards from Warminster and to the Salisbury to Bournemouth road south of Salisbury. Bridges along the route were widened too. It enabled troops to be transported to the coast as quickly as possible but it also permanently improved the roads for locals.[308] Troops were carried to the south coast on Wiltshire's roads before their departure for the French coast, which eventually took place after some delay on 6 June 1944.[309] Airborne divisions flew from Wiltshire airfields. In Cricklade the locals saw Dakotas setting off from RAF Blakehill and Gloucestershire's nearby RAF Down Ampney with gliders behind them. It was late in the day but still light because of double summer time. 'They took off within minutes of each other from all these air bases, and then circled in a certain way until they formed a massive armada.'[310] In Swindon some residents heard '[t]he sound of aircraft flying overhead, and judging by the increasing volume of noise they were passing over in large numbers... the sound continued to grow in intensity, we went into the garden to investigate, only to find that most neighbours had the same idea... Bert from next door [informed] us that something big was building, and it could be the start of the long awaited invasion... we could see aircraft towing gliders... There was no doubting the general excitement, and Bert was convinced the invasion had begun, and advised us all to listen to the next radio bulletin.'[311]

Stephen E. Ambrose reports that: 'On the last day of May, [Easy] Company marched down to trucks lined up on the Hungerford Road. Half the people of Aldbourne, and nearly all the unmarried girls, were there to wave goodbye. There were many tears'.[312] In Bemerton, one girl 'was asleep in bed, when my Mother woke me to a thundering roar and carried me to a north-facing window, where the sky was full of wave after wave of what must have been hundreds of aeroplanes

US Soldier Stationed at Westbury during WWII, reproduced by kind permission of Ivan Clark (WSHC P53382)

flying towards the coast. We watched for a long time, and then she told me that I should always remember this night, and I always have.'[313]

King George V's D-Day speech was broadcast on 6 June. He wanted to 'Call my people to prayer and dedication' and asked for a vigil of prayer as a 'great crusade sets forth'.[314] At Ham Spray House, the Partridge family drew up chairs in front of the wireless to listen to the nine o'clock news, after which the King's Speech came on. 'I could hardly draw a deep breath throughout the broadcast, and looked at the tossing trees outside the window with a sudden stab of realization that our fate now hangs in the balance, as individuals and as a nation. And this, here and now, is what we have expected and waited for with such a horrible mixture of dread and longing, for months.'[315]

By 30 September 1944 there were under 700,000 soldiers remaining in Britain, less than half the D-Day peak of over 1.3 million. But between October 1944 and April 1945 an unexpected 300,000 men arrived when the D-Day plans went slower than expected. Camps in the Chippenham area were hastily re-appropriated. As a consequence of this, Wiltshire remained the most densely occupied county through the winter of 1944-5,[316] and US troops remained for a great many months after. The Canadians took over RAF Down Ampney in Gloucestershire in the autumn of 1945. These troops visited Cricklade, but the locals found the atmosphere was different. '… [T]he war was over, and everyone wanted to get back home.' The last US personnel left Tidworth in 1946.[317] Unfortunately, as also occurred with British troops, US troops left damaged property behind them. In Lydiard Millicent some American soldiers broke into the Church and Lydiard House, causing a lot of damage. A staircase was damaged, the church walls were chalked on and the communion wine taken. The incident was reported to the commanding Officer who forced every soldier to go to church the following Sunday. The camp Chaplain spoke and the service was 'almost a service of repentance'. [318] An architect from the Ministry of Works surveyed the property in September 1943. The house had been requisitioned twice, and then surrendered almost immediately as being unfit for occupation. He had also heard the story and it seemed that the facts had 'become exaggerated'. 'Approximately 150 Americans forced entry, possibly in search of souvenirs – damage confined to smashing some door furniture, pulling off pieces of wallpaper (probably damp and hanging loose) and removal of small items such as wooden knobs from the handrail.'[319] It is interesting to note that Fontainville House in Westbury was also used by US troops, falling into a state of disrepair by 1947. It was later knocked down.[320]

Fontainville House c. 1946, reproduced by kind permission of Ivan Clark (WSHC P53988)

When the military camps finally became deserted what would happen to the goods they left behind? The US authorities did not want the locals taking them and many were destroyed before departure. The Americans denied it and the British authorities couldn't quite believe it.[321] The Acting Inspector of Constabulary, 7th Region, relayed information to Wiltshire's Chief Constable regarding US goods left behind. The US Commandant wanted to be made aware of any goods that were left:

> ... this is sometimes unavoidable owing to short warning of the move. He is doing what he can to prevent this kind of thing but does not always know in

sufficient time to prevent stores being left behind, or in time to clear up what is left.

He is, however, very anxious to avoid material, stores etc. being wasted or left about and would be very grateful if, should the Police become aware of such leavings, he could be informed of it as early as possible...'[322]

Any surviving goods were quickly taken by the locals, as can be seen the day after the 4th Armoured Division left Chippenham in July 1944. Three cartloads of wood, chairs, a table, a 'rare' fifty pound bag of white flour and part of a crate of tomatoes were salvaged.[323] The GIs themselves were often generous, as at Longbridge Deverill when some departing soldiers gave the local boys their new bicycles.[324]

Children thought the abandoned camps made great play areas. Some boys from Corsham explored the abandoned US servicemen's barracks. '... bits and pieces had been left, including live ammunition lying around for small boys to find.' The boys decided to build a raft, and then one boy discovered a grenade and threw it at the construction. '... causing a very large explosion, and the hasty exit of the boys!'[325] Many of the RAF stations were put to 'Care and Maintenance', although a few such as Colerne, Lyneham and Hullavington remained and became a working part of the Wiltshire community. RAF Lyneham was used as the base for the military funeral repatriations of British troops, local people lining the street of Wootton Bassett to honour those Servicemen and women who had lost their lives overseas. As a tribute to their dedication, the town was granted royal patronage and given the title 'Royal Wootton Bassett' in 2011. There was great sadness at the closure of RAF Lyneham in 2012; the base had opened as a product of WWII and had since become a valued part of the local community. The familiar sight of its Hercules transport aircraft over the North Wiltshire skies had finally come to an end.

After the war many of the newly vacated camps were taken over by squatters for housing, with others being used by the Council for educational purposes. One Polish teenager, Janusz Konarejk, had taken part in the Warsaw Uprising of 1944. He was taken prisoner and interned in a German POW camp. After being liberated by the Americans he ended up in Italy with some other teenagers and fellow Polish POWs who had been teachers. They decided to start a school, and arrived at Chiseldon Camp in the autumn of 1946 with the Secondary School of the Polish 5th Infantry Division from Codford. Their section was 'right in the north-east corner, in front of the well established 'English camp''. The school was transferred to Norfolk in November 1947.[326] Knook Camp was used to house the Polish Corps until they were demobbed; some remained behind.[327]

The British Army would continue to retain much of its size and presence in and around Salisbury Plain, maintaining an army of conscripts for National Service.[328] The military wanted to keep at least some of the land they had requisitioned, such as that at Sutton Veny. The War Department had invested large sums on roads, services, parade grounds etc. and also wanted to build married quarters if they took over the site permanently. Their argument was that returning it to agricultural land was reported to be very expensive and the existence of the site had already resulted in an improved water supply and a better bus service for the village. The Army realised that the attitude of the local Planning Authority was generally to oppose any proposal by Service Departments to acquire further land 'in view of the very considerable acreage in Wiltshire already controlled by such Departments.' The Local Authority felt there were problems with the site; it was positioned either side of a road and from a safety point of view '[t]he erection of permanent barracks and married quarters would have a considerable effect on the existing village, and it was felt that the social, recreational and educational facilities, other than those provided by the Army, would be inadequate.' They presumed the number of troops training on Salisbury Plain would increase and the roads would not be adequate for additional military traffic, as had often been the case during the war.[329] Corsham Parish Council was very keen to get back access to the town's public footpaths which had been closed by the military and which had still not been re-opened in the immediate post-war period. Agreement had been reached on some, but not all.[330] In the post-war period National Service became compulsory. Devizes was used as one of the training centres, with a recruit of the 1950s noting that the train from Paddington was packed with others just like him.[331] The recruits had to undertake ten weeks of training at the Centre with their day starting at 0600 hours.[332] They were allowed out of camp and into the town for the first time after three weeks. The people of Devizes, as during the war, would come across the now familiar site of servicemen 'look[ing] around at the shops... [going to] the cinema and then end[ing] up in a fish and chip shop before returning to camp.'[333]

The stay of troops in Wiltshire meant that civilians underwent sweeping changes to their everyday lives, but these same troops also gave civilians a feeling of hope.[334] The British journalist Kingsley Martin said in January 1944 that the American presence in Britain was 'one of the greatest

MARLBOROUGH, Wilts

on the main Bath Road with numerous Bus Services and Station on G.W.R.

CATALOGUE OF SALE

OF

HUTS and BUILDINGS

forming part of the Hospital Camp situate on Marlborough Common

WHICH

Hooper, Pinniger & Co.

are instructed by the Corporation of Marlborough to offer for SALE by AUCTION on the site

ON

WEDNESDAY, 30th APRIL, 1947

commencing at 2.30 p.m.

Catalogues (price 3d.), may be obtained of the Auctioneers, Marlborough and Devizes (Telephone: Marlborough 41).

County Paper, MARLBOROUGH

Sales Particular for Marlborough Common Camp, 20 December 1947 (WSA G22/132/17)

social experiments of the war'.[335] David Reynolds states that many troops did not spend long in Britain and did not have time to make lasting contact with the local population, but it appears that in Wiltshire some did, and the British got a sense of the US colour bar in action. The feeling in 1944 was that America was less democratic than had been the case two years before.[336] In turn, some GIs gained a sense of what it was like to be a British civilian during those six years of war. On 16 September 1944 a GI stationed at Tidworth wrote to his wife that the blackout was officially over.

> It is a big day for the English. Just think, children here four or five years old have never seen a lighted city or village. Thank goodness [our daughter] has a place to grow up where things are normal and they hardly know there is a war going on. Sometimes the going gets tough, you get mighty disgusted and wonder why you have to come way over here away from the ones you love and your home to fight on foreign soil. Then you stop and think if we weren't over here and hadn't been, maybe our families would be going through the same thing that these people have and you realize that it is well worth leaving home to fight for.[337]

The US presence in Britain was to have a long lasting effect on the country. In July 1948 the first B29s arrived in East Anglia bringing atomic bombs with them. The base was to herald a permanent US nuclear presence in Britain, an unprecedented step. The US General who brought the bombers over commented: 'Never before in history… has one first-class Power gone into another first-class power's country without an agreement. We were just told to come over and 'we shall be pleased to have you'.[338]

It would later become known that Wiltshire's military sites were the base of important work which aided the success of Britain's war effort. On 5 September 1939 the Chemical Research Department moved from Grosvenor Gardens, London, to Porton, but due to liaison difficulties with other Government departments it was moved back to the Adelphi in London, leaving the records and intelligence branches at Porton. The Chemical Defence Experimental Station at Porton expanded considerably in the early months of the war with an influx of scientists and technologists from the universities and industry.[339] Protective clothing for all three forces was developed at Porton, which aided the health of the troops by preventing lice. Also studied on site were burns treatments, the effects of underwater explosions, air purification in submarines, the development of air crew gas masks and fume hazards.[340] It appears that Agatha Christie may have alluded to Porton in one of her books which was published during the war, when a refugee was seen working at a 'chemical research laboratory… on the problem of immunising certain gases and in general decontamination experiments.'[341] The staff at Boscombe Down worked on the Bouncing Bomb, developing the Tallboy and Grand Slam among others. Staff from Boscombe tested the first jet aircraft, the Meteor, but the first jet aircraft to appear at the site was the Spider Crab in

April 1944, due to become Britain's first true jet fighter with its engines modified to fit into its airframe. [342] RAF Colerne with its Gloster Meteor jet engines brought down V1s[343] and RAF Keevil was one site which dropped supplies to the Special Operations Executive (SOE) agents working in Europe.[344] RAF Lyneham established and maintained a transport route between Britain and the Atlantic, the Far East and North Africa. The station transported Churchill to the Casablanca Conference in January 1943 to meet Roosevelt and Stalin in a VIP fitted out Liberator called 'Commando'.[345] RAF Netheravon repatriated liberated Prisoners of War in February 1945.[346] And of course, we must not forget that there were also those Wiltshire men and women who were away from home in the Forces, serving their country in battle or through auxiliary work.

A poem by former Trowbridge man William Brocklehurst was printed in the *Wiltshire Times* on 5 February 1944 for flag day, celebrating the achievements of the Wiltshire Yeomanry in North Africa:

> *The Charge of the Royal Wiltshire Yeomanry*
> We've read of Balaclava,
> And the famous Light Brigade,
> But the great charge of forty-two
> Nigh puts it in the shade.
> Those Crimean heroes, gallant men,
> With swords and horses fought
> And hacked their way through Russian hordes,
> A victory dearly bought.
> We've heard the official story –
> It almost takes our breath –
> How Trowbridge lads on mounts of steel
> Charged in the vale of death.
> Through the dust and smoke of battle
> The Royal Wiltshires went,
> With all the vim and all the dash
> Of foxhounds on the scent.
> Tank engines screamed. The German guns
> Appeared to sound much louder,
> But not a Wiltshire lad that day,
> But didn't feel the prouder.
> The epic feet of British arms
> Was told but yesterday,
> And every husband, father, son,
> From Wiltshire in the fray.
> They dashed upon the maddened Huns,
> And crushed them in their tracks,
> Amid the thundering, milling crowd,
> Although the Huns were 'Cracks.'

These lads from Wiltshire came from vale,
From city, town and hamlet,
From cottage, farmstead and dairy,
Each meant to do his bit.
With names scrawled on their tanks
The 'Castle' and 'the Crown,'
The 'Lion White,' 'the Bear Hotel,'
Their mounts went screaming down.
This band of British Yeomanry,
The oldest in the land,
All Wiltshire sons and fathers;
A gallant, noble band.
And so we will at dawn to-day,
In memory of those tanks,
Hoist up the Yeoman's glorious flag
To give these laddies thanks.
We won't forget the work you did
In nineteen-forty-two;
For the charge at Tel-el-Aquaqqir,
All allied thanks are due.
So raise the standard, yes and sing;
Ye Wiltshire lad and lassies;
A charge so grand, their work shall stand,
No other deed surpasses.
With lads like this who know not fear,
Old England is secure;
We raise our hats to Wiltshire boys,
Who made this victory sure.

For those who remained at home; as with other 'arrivals' in the county during the Second World War, many relationships were made, some to be broken. Others would, just perhaps, last the test of time.

4
Wartime Workers

Home Front Occupations

THE MUNICH CRISIS of 1938 brought with it a wave of applications from workers to join the services and Civil Defence units; the Government was aware that it needed to control this movement. In November a *Schedule of Reserved Occupations* was published, closely followed in January 1939 by a handbook sent to every household in the country to help direct people to the correct services and check the flow of volunteering by skilled workers, so as not to adversely affect war production. It listed a variety of full-time and part-time war work.[1] The explanatory notes for the May 1939 revised edition stated that its purpose was to 'ensure that skilled workpeople who would be required in time of war for the maintenance of necessary production or essential services are not accepted for service (other than service in their trade capacity) in the Auxiliary Forces or the Civil Defence Services which, while only part-time in peace would become whole-time in war.' The occupations included in the schedule fell into three classes:-

'those of direct importance in time of war, such as the medical profession, the Mercantile Marine and the Police Forces;

those which are of importance for the production of munitions, or for providing commodities or services necessary for the maintenance of the life of the community, such as skilled engineering, shipbuilding, coal-mining, transport, food production, gas, water and electricity occupations;

occupations in which the workpeople possess skills which could be used in time of war in industries essential to the war effort but different from the industries in which they are occupied in peace-time. For example watch and clock makers could be employed on certain types of scientific instrument making.'

The schedule goes on to state that it did not restrict service in the armed forces or in the Air Raid Precaution services at the volunteer's workplace. Some occupations on the list were also subject to conditions regarding the age of the worker and there was a separate list at the end for the occupations of women.[2] The schedule of reserved occupations was wound down between 1941 and 1942.[3]

Men up to the age of 46 had been required to register by the end of 1941 and were invited to an interview at a local labour exchange if they were not yet doing essential work. Most workers were open minded and moved into the war work which was suggested to them, but not all, as this example in the 6 November 1943 edition of the *Wiltshire Times* shows. One man from Bradenstoke near Chippenham had refused to go into the work he was directed to by the Ministry of Labour and National Service, claiming that he was 'physically incapable' of taking up the work. He had been classed at a medical category of Grade C3, unfit for military service but capable of fulfilling work of 'national importance' as an alternative. The National Service Officer was reported to have taken 'exceptional trouble and care to do what was possible to find work in the locality.' The man was convicted of the offence but appealed successfully against the conviction as the appeals court felt a fine would have been more appropriate.

The Essential Work Order (EWO), put into place in March 1941, had the power to declare work done in any establishment to be essential. If one was put into place, the employer could not dismiss any workers and the employees could not leave without permission.[4] Appeal was possible through local boards. It was not popular with workers, but the Minister of Labour Ernest Bevin used it as little as possible and ensured that affected workers received adequate wages, working conditions and welfare.[5] The EWO was quickly utilised for engineering and aircraft work, the railways and the building industry, amongst others. The Board of Trade published in March 1941 a new policy for civilian industry. Labour would be released by concentrating work in 'nucleus' factories which would also find additional space for the war industry and protect labour.[6] By July 1941 it was obvious that the manpower shortage was getting worse. Call-up was extended; down to age 18 and up to age 51. The block reservations were replaced by individual deferments for each key worker. Everyone from the age of 18 to 60 would now be obliged to do some kind of 'national service' duty to free up those who were able to undertake other essential tasks. The newspapers began calling for 'the indiscriminate transfer of young men into the armed forces' and the receipt of a notorious relic of WWI, the white feather, caused at least two deaths of young workers by suicide. The Government introduced a badge to identify those men who were exempt from military service on medical grounds[7] although a Trowbridge man, a reporter for the *Wiltshire Times*, found that the silver lapel badge was not understood. He was attending an opening ceremony when '...a Land Girl, who was travelling on a float of some kind, pointed her finger at me and shouted in a loud voice: 'Why aren't you in the Forces?''[8]

Wages in the aircraft industry had always been much higher than those in engineering at large and in wartime they continued to rise, where bonuses could be up to 581% of the regional standard being paid. Some factories were paying £4 10s. a day, more than an agricultural labourer or railwayman could earn in a week, and it was even possible for women to take home £3 a day, but most of these firms were based in the Midlands. Skilled male workers had now become an important commodity, but they could be transferred to lower paid work at any time unless they were constantly employed on important jobs.[9] Bevin's biographer later noted that it was coal that 'came closest to defeating' the Minister of Labour,[10] with his attempts to boost the workforce at the coal face failing in June 1941 and then going downhill again in the first part of 1942.[11] From the end of 1943 one in ten young men called up was chosen by ballot to be a 'Bevin Boy', working in the mines to increase coal production. It was considered a fate worse than the forces.[12]

The Government needed war workers and those that were available were in high demand. In the summer of 1942 Bevin suspended the call up for building workers if they transferred to Government contracts,[13] but as early as

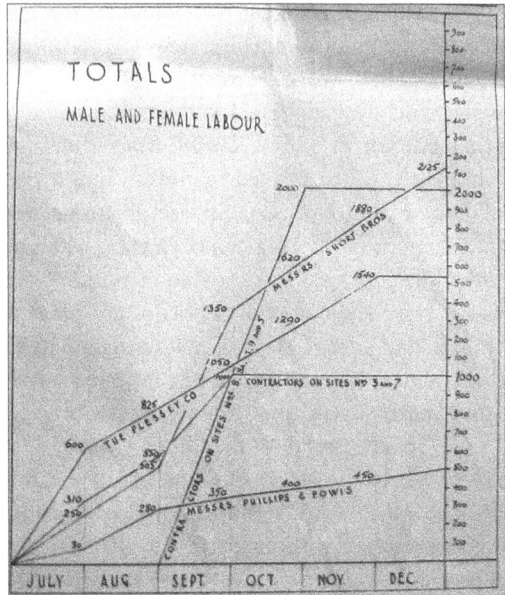

Section of a chart dated 14 August 1940 by the Ministry of Production: Monthly Labour Intake Requirements for Swindon Companies, Male and Female, by the Plessy Co., Messrs. Short Bros., Messrs. Phillips & Powis, Boots & Co., Trollope & Collis. All were rising exponentially (WSA G24/225/35)

February 1941 the Director of Squires and Sons Ltd., a Wiltshire based Building and Public Works Contractor was complaining that since work had begun on a large number of Government contracts such as aerodromes, their staff were being poached. The Government contractors were offering higher wages.[14] By May 1942 Wiltshire's County Surveyor was reporting problems with the Council's roadmen, working in close proximity to the Ministry of Transport agency gangs who were getting higher wages.[15] M. M. Postan reports that the poaching of workers had begun as early as 1939, leading to a high and very irregular turnover of skilled labour.[16]

A report by William Beveridge in December 1940 showed that there were great shortages of unskilled labour but more men were needed for the services and they would have to come from the munitions industries. The Government would have no option but to recruit women and deploy men from non-munitions work to the munitions industry. 750,000 women were needed for non-munitions work and over one million for munitions factories. The emphasis of the Ministry of Labour policy was for a large proportion of married women and mothers to take up work.[17] Lloyd George had not resorted to conscription for women during WWI, instead making a pact with the suffragette movement to encourage women to volunteer for munitions work. The 'Munitionettes' had been working in Britain's war factories over the course of the Great War and by 1918 approximately 1.5 million women had replaced men.[18] In the Second World War the Government had initially tried a call for volunteers with the Registration for Employment Order, introduced in March 1941,[19] but although by August two million women had registered, only one quarter had been interviewed and only 87,000 of these had gone into war factory work. The Ministry was not able to cope with the large number of volunteers and those eager to do their bit were left, as Peter Lewis puts it, 'furious and frustrated'.[20] A wartime social survey found that 97% of women agreed emphatically that women should undertake war work,[21] but some felt that factory work would be monotonous and dirty, and others thought they would be unable to work and see to their domestic responsibilities.[22] Many husbands were also not keen on the idea[23] and numbers were lower than anticipated. The Government then felt it had no choice but to conscript and introduced the National Service Act (No. 2) in December 1941.[24] The women of Melksham were responding to an appeal in December, one hundred and fifty attending a meeting held by Avon Rubber at Melksham House to discuss plans to employ women in part-time work. Those who volunteered 'would be capable of earning one shilling per hour'.[25]

Only single women in their 20s were conscripted to industry and the services, able to be posted anywhere in the country. Married women were not legally obliged to enter work unless they were childless and aged 20-30. Women with children aged below 14 were exempt, as were those whose household responsibilities were felt to be too great to justify the compulsion to war work, but they were encouraged to enter into work voluntarily. After April 1941 if they were aged between 18 and 45 they had to register at a labour exchange. Later the upper age limit was extended to 51, causing an outcry in Parliament but less so from the women themselves.[26] There were 18.5 million workers in British industry and the armed forces in 1939, growing to slightly over 22 million at the peak of British war production in 1943[27] when full employment had been reached. At this time 7.3 million women were in paid employment; half a million in the armed services; one and a half million in essential industries. Over three million were married and one million had children under the age of fourteen,[28] but only 41% of wives without children or with children over 14 years undertook paid work during the war compared to 80% of single women. Middle-class wives often signed up for voluntary work rather than paid work.[29]

The conscription of women was considered to be one of the most controversial and drastic actions of the war[30] and male counterparts often felt threatened. Newly arrived women at the GWR works in Swindon discovered that no provision had been made for them. Their first job was to trim the tops of 'quite heavy shells' and place them on a belt made of rollers; hard work on their hands. They asked the foreman for gloves and he duly promised they would arrive. 'During our first week all the girls had joined the NUR so after asking continually, we all stopped work, much to the men in the shop's dismay. They said we would not get the gloves, but we did, having stopped work only one afternoon.'

A rest room was provided solely for the women; the men continued to eat at their lathes. 'They were very envious of our rest room, but we told them they would have it after the war. They said never! And as far as I know they never did.' This female worker spent four years in the 'Western' and became shop steward.[31] The company made an assortment of munitions during the war, from bombs, through to midget submarine superstructures, to massive mountings for cross-Channel guns.[32] Women took the place of skilled mechanics at the Royal Electrical and Mechanical Engineers (REME) workshops in Warminster, replacing engines on tanks. 'They [took] a little longer than the men... but their work [was] perfect.'[33]

Into Battle!

No Commandos in this battle, no roar of cannon or rumble of tank. Just ordinary men and women—drivers, conductors, passengers, and those familiar buses that are the vital link between home and work. All working together under difficult conditions.

WILTS & DORSET
MOTOR SERVICES LIMITED

Advert for the Wilts and Dorset Bus Company in the Salisbury Journal, 23 June 1944, men and women 'working together under difficult conditions' (WSHC Microform Collection)

The arrival of the first woman into the installations section of an aircraft factory in 1941 was commented on by her male counterparts who looked at the feminine (and at first awkward) way she used the equipment. They made fun of her behind her back but treated her extremely politely to her face. Angus Calder notes that the woman turned out to be highly competent at her job.[34] At Enfield Precision Engineering working from Westwood Quarry, 70% of the workforce were women. 'Some turned out to be brilliant machinists and fitters. Work was highly specialised and technical...'[35] At EKCO near Malmesbury one local girl from the nearby village of Little Somerford had been recruited to the offices. She was struggling to understand the industry jargon and the strong accent of her boss, and had been so unhappy that she had asked for a transfer to the assembly line. What followed was an apologetic letter, along with a gift and a little more understanding.[36] The Amalgamated Engineering Union (AEU) president remarked in 1943: 'The system which allows women to be brought into industry as 'cheap labour' and uses them with the double object of exploiting them and undermining the men's rates has left its scars on us all.'[37] In 1942 Clement Attlee, Churchill's deputy, stated: 'The work women are performing in munitions factories has to be seen to be believed. Precision engineering jobs which a few years ago would have made a skilled turner's hair stand on end, are being performed with dead accuracy by girls who have had no industrial experience.'[38] By the end of 1945 there were 8,500,000 men and women waiting to be released from the war factories.[39]

The subject of equal pay for women was raised by female MPs and mass rallies were held. In 1942 a resolution was moved for equal compensation at a meeting of the Conservative Association[40] but in 1943 a debate was held in the Commons where Sir Francis Fremantle spoke. 'This war has given us a wrong turn. There is a great temptation because women have discovered means of making money and buying better off than is compatible with family life... The women's movement has become an anti-population movement, very largely because there is a wrong division of the males and females shares in national life.'[41] The average earnings for women industrial workers rose during the war but they still remained substantially lower than the men's. The new female workers trained in basic engineering and directed to the Air Ministry Maintenance Unit at RAF Wroughton were shocked at the conditions they would have to work in. 'We were the first women ever sent to work on the aircraft and it was obvious nobody wanted us and didn't know what to do with us. There were no facilities for women, or rest rooms... A shock awaited us as we entered the canteen. The rough facilities and the unpleasant odour that always pervaded the place appalled us...On hearing how low our wages were to be we were all very worried that we wouldn't have enough to pay for our lodgings and we gathered in the pub in the village near the aerodrome to discuss it. After a couple of glasses of cider and full of Dutch courage we decided to go back to the Swindon Labour Exchange en masse to protest. Our little mutiny soon fizzled out, as we got short shrift there, being threatened with dire consequences if we didn't go where we were directed.'[42] A Gallup poll of 1941 found that public opinion was in favour of equal pay with 68% supporting it. The Woman Power Committee and other feminist groups established an Equal Pay Campaign Committee in January 1944, focusing on equal pay for the 'common classes' of the Civil Defence. Members of the cabinet prevented a bill going through but support for equal pay continued to trouble them. They appointed a Royal Commission to investigate, thereby effectively halting the reform movement. The Commission reported in 1946 by which time the pressure for reform had evaporated. [43]

The Government reluctantly removed the Marriage Bar for employees for the duration of the war. In education there was opposition by the Board of Education and it was not until 1942 that the board issued a recommendation to Local Education Authorities that the marriage bar would be suspended. By October 1945 there were over 33,000 married women working as teachers. It was the National Union of Women Teachers who raised the issue of a permanent abolition of the Bar, meeting with the president of the Board of Education in 1942 and at the Government's National Conference of Women in 1943. The Women Power Commission (WPC) actively took on the cause in late 1943 and the National Council of Women was also involved in lobbying. With the rise in the school leaving age to be considered, Butler accepted the need for the elimination of a Marriage Bar in the teaching profession. [44] After this success, the WPC drove for an elimination of the Bar for the Civil Service but Hugh Dalton, the Minister responsible, finally decided to retain the Bar with modification. Other Cabinet Members found the position illogical in view of the labour shortage but interestingly, of several firms surveyed in 1946 concerning their future plans for the bar, only Boots Pure Drug Co. Ltd. had decided to end it. The four main railway companies, Unilever, Imperial Chemical Industries, the Bank of England, Rowntree and Co., and Cadbury Brothers Ltd. were all planning for its restoration. [45]

The National Service (No. 2) Act made the same provision of rights for Conscientious Objectors in civilian work as it did in the Forces, but the Registration for Employment Orders did not. [46] Those war workers who felt unable to consider war work on these grounds, women amongst them, had no choice. [47] A total of 911 women were granted the status of Conscientious Objector after a tribunal hearing, but many more identified themselves as Conscientious Objectors without state approval. [48] The Peace Pledge Union encouraged women to follow their consciences [49] and women who felt this way were often aggrieved that they were denied the opportunity to have their stance publicly recognised. [50] The same could probably be said of the men.

Memorandum from the General Manager, Passenger Transport Department in Swindon to the Town Clerk, 3 June, 1940, stating that a Conscientious Objector had decided to take service with the RAMC or another non-combatant force (WSA G24/225/29)

A New Way of Life

FOR THOSE WORKERS recruited into war work, a new way of life ensued.
Munitions workers found the shift patterns difficult as by 1940 they often had
to finish late on one shift and didn't have much time to go home before the next.[51]
One war factory worker in Wiltshire worked 6am to 9pm shifts and only saw her
children when they were asleep. She eventually gave up the work as she felt they
would forget she was their mother.[52] Ernest Bevin the Minister of Labour stepped
in and introduced a compulsory maximum 60 hour week, first for women and
then for men. This did not apply to aircraft production, under the command of
Lord Beaverbrook, who continued with the 7 day working week.[53] Carol Harris
notes that the munitions factories under Bevin brought in 'some of the most
advanced manufacturing practices to maximise production' working three shift
days instead of the old 12 hour shift pattern. They proved very successful.[55] The
Avon Rubber factory in Melksham opened 'work centres' in 1942 to help women
work 'as many hours as they could spare'.[55]

Wiltshire villagers found that with the coming of the war, part of their
population was transported daily by bus to full-time or part-time work[56] in the
newly established factories nearby, although bus services were being reduced.
There were fewer drivers, fewer bus parts being manufactured, less petrol and
rubber... getting to work could be, as Robert MacKay reports, 'wearying and
time- consuming'. By 1943 posters were asking: 'Is your journey really necessary'.[57]

The lives of a group of wartime workers in the county were vividly recorded
by the Mass Observation worker Celia Fremlin, sent to the EKCO factory near
Malmesbury to work as an unskilled hand in the machine shop. *War Factory* was
published in October 1943 and lauded by the press as the 'first coherent and
serious study of a wartime industrial community lodged in the middle of the
countryside.' It was, however, the observation and subjective analysis of just one
individual,[58] usually from the middle class.[59] Celia began work at the factory in
February 1942 to aid the Factory Manager who was concerned about the low
level of morale among the women workers.[60] The site of the factory had originally
been chosen to match the geographical area for an estimated 250 employees but
the factory expanded and the number of employees became out of proportion to
the size of the local population.[61] Celia reported that some of the girls, even when
they lived locally at home, felt cut off from their families due to the shifts they
worked.[62] One worker was quoted as saying she sometimes envied the girls in their
billets. She realised that it was 'miserable' for them never seeing their family, but
she felt that even though she was living at home she never did either. When she
got home they were going to bed and in the morning she left too early to see her
mother. 'I might just as well be living in lodgings, really I might.'[63] Some EKCO
workers also found it hard to get household jobs done, some getting home at nine
o'clock and feeling so exhausted they had to go straight to bed with no time for

'mending'. Although they didn't want to, they had to rely very much on their mothers. One worker would get back from work at 9pm to find the wireless on, her father asleep in the chair and her mother exhausted after getting up at 5.30am each morning. She felt her family slipping away from her as she never saw her little brother any more. Only about 10% of these EKCO workers felt able to go out most evenings 'at any cost', and usually to a dance.[64]

Factory workers also found it difficult to have a social life simply because they were living in a rural area. 'There's nothing to do in this dump' was heard again and again by Celia Fremlin, and she noted that this was also true of soldiers and Ministry employees. Celia felt that incomers didn't want to adapt to their life in rural Malmesbury as they knew the move was only temporary.[65] EKCO did have a Sports and Social Club, who in October 1940 organised a successful dance at the Town Hall which around 250 attended,[66] and a Social Centre was opened in Malmesbury in July 1941 thanks to the company. 'For many years the need for some place where workers could assemble and enjoy a little social recreation has been recognised, and attempts have been made to fill the want... it is a pleasure to record that at long last, and thanks – in the main – to the enthusiasm of the head of the largest local employers, such facilities are now available.' [67] The Club, however, was designed as an attempt to integrate the employees with the locals, and in this it wasn't overly successful.[68]

The experiences of war workers in the county could vary greatly. Those working at the underground war factories situated around Corsham who were lodging in hostels found that the site was fully equipped, the restaurant having 'all the trappings of a four star restaurant'.[69] On the menu were a full English breakfast[70] and roast potatoes, sprouts, roast pork, chicken and greens, not seen for a very long time by a man who started work there in 1943.[71] The women from the Birmingham Small Arms Factory, now underground at the Hawthorn site, could be seen working at their equipment, singing to their hearts content at the music being relayed throughout the factory area.[72] They were making *Hispano* aircraft cannons for the Ministry of Aircraft Production (MAP) and *Oerlikon* anti-aircraft guns for the Admiralty. Bristol Aeroplane Company (BAC) employees, also at Hawthorn, were turning out *Centaurus* aero-engines.[73] There were sixteen hostels on the site, occupied by single men and women and accommodating around 800 people. The purpose built 'plush' cinema showed the latest releases from Britain and the US, along with a purpose built ballroom large enough for the visiting big bands to play in, including many of the best known famous acts[74] such as Glen Miller, a month before he went missing.[75] There was also one bar on site.[76] The majority of workers were aged between 18 and 35, and for many it appears to have been a time for working hard, but also for having fun.[77]

One worker at the Hawthorn site, sent there by the General Post Office (GPO) from Bristol to work on telephone cables, was lodging at the Thorny Pits Hostel. He described it as having a large communal dining hall within the main complex along with a theatre cum dance floor, rest room and shops. Nearby were the male and female accommodation blocks, each block having washing facilities,

Workers relaxing in the Hostel Canteen, Enfield Precision Engineering Factory, Westwood, WWII (WSHC P43369)

bathrooms, showers etc. and also central heating.[78] The Corsham Hostels were run by the National Service Hostels Corporation Ltd., an agency of the Ministry of Labour.[79] The Lypiatt Hostel in Corsham was used as accommodation for workers at the Bristol Aeroplane Company (BAC) as well as Land Girls[80] and staff working from RAF Rudloe Manor.

Thorny Pits was the site of some contention in the post-war years and demonstrative of the social friction caused by the influx of war workers and the changes that came with them. Lady Fuller of Neston Park near Corsham (who later went on to win a seat in the County Council election in 1955)[82] wrote to the Council when a plan to use Thorny Pits as a Borstal Institution was put forward in 1959. 'I am very much against this and I hope everything will be done to refuse permission. My main reason is that for the past 15 years this area has had the most unsatisfactory people in it who have given much trouble and caused the local people much annoyance and disquiet. It would not be fair to turn this area into a permanent site for undesirable families.'[83] Thorny Pits had also been used as a voluntary camp for agricultural workers on holiday in the summer of 1945.[84]

The war brought with it the use of trousers by female workers for a variety of jobs. Vera Lynn recalled people noting that '[m]ilk girls, window cleaners, drivers, railway workers, bus conductors – all are dressed for the job. If war goes on much longer it may be a sign of eccentricity for young women to wear a skirt.'[85] On 1 November 1941 *Picture Post* was asking 'Should women wear trousers?' It was noted that trouser wearing began as a functional requirement; many wartime jobs would not be possible in a skirt, but 'the trouser fashion grew'..., and the question became not so much who, but when, where and how? *Vogue* was looking at trousers (called slacks) in April 1939 and calling them masculine in their tailoring, although women were putting their own stamp on them in terms of colour choice and accessories[86] but by December 1939 they were critical: 'We deplore the crop of young women who take war as an excuse for... parading about in slacks...'. Trousers became popular even with older women during the war. They were practical[87] and could help cover up a lack of stockings! Clothing manufacturers had realised the potential of this massive new market, especially with many workers not owning a proper kit for work. *Vogue* introduced its Knit series No. 9, *War Jumpers and Woolies for War Workers*, which ranged from a smart twin sweater set, to weekend waistcoats... to a warm tailored jacket; 12 designs for 7d. On the front cover was a sketch of a woman fixing a car.[88]

Conscription sent young women far from home into unfamiliar places and strange trades. Many gained wages and an independence they'd never dreamt of and an escape from ill paid domestic service or shop work,[89] but many could also feel very alone and insecure in their new environment.

Nursery Provision

WITH MOTHERS NOW entering the workforce, the demand for nurseries was voiced at the Women's Parliament during 1942, getting press coverage.[90] Bevin was keen to introduce nursery provision and employers suggested there was a need, but there were problems at a local level.[91] A system was put into place whereby a Ministry of Labour (MOL) Official would claim to get a 'feel' for demand from women's enquiries to Employment Exchanges, from comments by those employing women and by local voluntary bodies such as the Citizen's Advice Bureau (CAB), the Co-operative Women's Guild and Women's Voluntary Service (WVS).[92] When a MOL Divisional Controller (renamed Regional Controller in 1941) claimed that there was a need for a nursery, the local Medical Officer of Health made enquiries regarding demand and reported back to the Ministry of Health. If they agreed, the Medical Officer would then engage with the Local Authority over nursery provision.[93] The Local Authorities appear to have placed more reliance on a Medical Officer's evidence and Penny Summerfield notes that 'it didn't take long for the MOL officials to become convinced that the Medical Officers were thoroughly biased against nurseries'.[94] It could be that fears of epidemics caused medical concern,[95] and it appears that the movement of people during the Second World War caused outbreaks in Wiltshire; a Swindon nursery suffered outbreaks of measles and dysentery in April 1943[96] and schools also reported outbreaks of illness.[97] It has yet to be seen if the rates of outbreaks were higher than in previous years. Research into infant mortality in the early 20th century has shown that infant losses were fewer amongst mothers who worked outside the home due to the better nutrition and sanitation that their wages could buy. The Chief Medical Officer's *Report for the War Years* showed that epidemics had

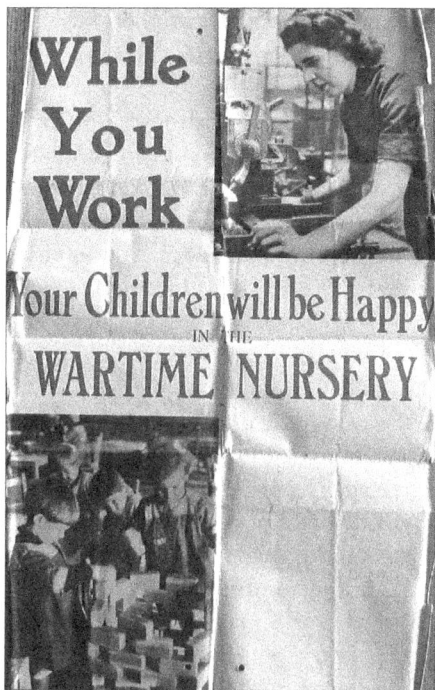

Wartime Poster 'While You Work your Children will be Happy in the Wartime Nursery' (WSA G24/225/3)

not been commonplace, and there had been evidence to suggest that nursery children were physically and socially better equipped than non-nursery children, which Summerfield feels suggests excessive caution by some Medical Officers in wartime.[98]

The Clerk's Correspondence files in the records of Swindon Borough Council at the Wiltshire and Swindon History Centre give us a glimpse of the way war-time nurseries were set up. In 1940 the Honorary Secretary of the Sick Benefit and Benevolent Society of the Garrards Engineering and Manufacturing Co. wrote to the Town Clerk, asking if the Council was considering the establishment of a crèche. They had been having difficulties in finding accommodation for one unmarried mother 'as the main objection appears to be, not to having the mother and child, but to having to look after the child whilst the mother is away at work.' In response the Clerk wrote to Medical Officer of Health, wanting observations. The Council had in fact received a standard letter from the Ministry of Health in Whitehall dated 18 June 1940 regarding the provision of day nurseries for munitions workers, stating that:

> … it is desirable for immediate arrangements to be made in the case of your Council for the provision of one or more Day Nurseries for the young children of women so employed. Arrangements of this nature are required in order to facilitate the recruitment of the large number of additional women workers urgently needed, without jeopardising the well-being of the children. The Minister of Labour has represented that it is of paramount importance that the fullest possible use should be made of the reserve of female labour which exists in any area within daily travelling distance of important war factories. Such recruitment will, however, be seriously hampered if women with young children are deterred from coming forward because of the lack of adequate arrangements for the care of their children. The Minister, will, therefore, be obliged if the Council will take this matter into their consideration at the earliest possible moment and formulate proposals for submission to this Department.[99]

In February 1941 the Clerk received a letter from a Swindon solicitor, respectfully requesting to make further enquiries regarding nursery provision. The Inspector of the NSPCC had drawn his attention to the issue. '... even in peace time, to the necessity for a crèche in Swindon.' He had looked into how to set up a crèche via the Ministry of Health and was updating the Council on the steps involved! It appears that a Swindon Councillor had begun looking into the situation as the Medical Officer of Health had duly received a letter from him regarding the establishment of a crèche in Swindon in March 1941. The Ministry of Labour was right to be concerned, however; the Medical Officer felt that as Garrards was the first request of its kind, there was not enough demand at present, but Short Bros. Aeronautical Engineers had sent the Medical Officer a list of women workers with children under 14, just to be helpful.[100]

By May 1941 the Ministry of Labour were stating that the need for female workers in the Swindon district was likely to become acute and they would be encouraging mothers with children under the age of two to enter into war work. At this time the Regional Welfare Officer wanted to arrange a conference on the subject but by September the Town Clerk was reporting conflicting requests made to Officers of his Council: 'that having regard to the number of conflicting verbal requests made to officers of my Council by officials of Government Departments regarding the establishment of day nurseries, my Council are unable to take any action until they have officially in writing from the Ministry of Health the appropriate authority dealing with day nurseries, a clear indication of what is required in Swindon in this connection, having regard to local circumstances.' Representatives from the Ministry of Labour, the Ministry of Health, the Education Service and the Local Authority had met and felt that 'there was no evidence at the moment indicating the need for Day nurseries and that if the Ministry of Health desired an experimental Day nursery to be started, they should give a clear lead on this point.'[101]

In July 1941 a representative of the Ministry of Aircraft Production together with the Manager of Plessey in Swindon raised the 'urgent' matter of a day nursery at the factory. The Council agreed with some reluctance, and by August 1941 a Ministry of Health Officer had visited the factory and was disapproving of the proposal, suggesting that a 'central nursery' should be established. On 23 August there was a '[v]erbal request from the Ministry of Health to [the] Local Authority to select one of the halls (unspecified) which were, it was understood, being released by the military for welfare work in Swindon.' The Town Clerk was reiterating his request for a clear official lead. A letter dated September 1941 from the Senior Regional Officer at the Ministry of Health in Bristol reveals that: 'It is not possible at this stage to give any reliable estimate of the ultimate requirements of Swindon. Experience has, however, indicated that the demand is stimulated by the establishment of full-time Day Nurseries and that women with young children are often prepared to register for employment in war factories if accommodation is available for their children.'[102] A conference in December 1941 reached the conclusion that the establishment of wartime nurseries needed to be undertaken as soon as possible and that local factories would probably have to be approached at a future date to ensure that the working hours of the women fitted in with nursery hours. A letter was received from the Swindon branch of the Clerical and Administrative Workers' Union on 31 December 1941 requesting that facilities in the form of crèches be made before married women entered the industry through conscription.[103]

Letter from a Lady in Berkshire anxious to do war work and move to Swindon, but could not get any information on Day Nurseries. She had been told by the Billeting Officer that she could not get accommodation until she was actually in war employment (WSA G24/225/51)

An article in the *Wiltshire Gazette* on 23 December 1943 also suggested the recruitment of war workers would be aided if women could be assured that their children would be cared for before and after school and in the school holidays. The manager of the Trowbridge Employment Exchange had approached the Teacher's Advisory Committee on the matter, wanting to raise the point that there was an urgent need of additional women workers for the war effort. It was reported that in Trowbridge the Ministry of Labour had practically exhausted all possibility of whole-time employment, and wanted to recruit women half or part-time, who had domestic duties at home and also children. It was not likely that such an appeal would attract many women unless some provision could be made for the children from the time their parents went to, and returned from, work. '...the teachers of the district concerned should be asked to meet and consider what arrangements could be made.' They were found to be willing to co-operate.

Nurseries in Swindon were finally opened in 1942, with the Upham Road and Broad Street establishments opening in May. The local press notice was advertising the opening of the nurseries, but there were restrictions. 'They are intended to aid mothers with young children to volunteer for service in the war time factories. Except in cases of special hardship or special recommendation, children will not be received under twelve months old.' Opening hours were 7am to 7.30pm, Monday to Friday and up until 1.30pm on Saturdays. They were not open on Sundays. The cost would be 1s. daily and 9d. for a Saturday. The Medical Officer reported on the progress of one of the nurseries in April 1943, noting that both the Ministry of Health and the Maternity & Child Welfare Committee had expressed concern over the large ratio of trained staff to children, but the Medical Officer felt that it would be a mistake to lower the quality of the nursing staff. There appears to have been problems getting mothers to use the Swindon nurseries. A letter dated July 1943 was sent from the local Welfare Officer, Ministry of Labour and National Service to the Town Clerk about a forthcoming nursery publicity campaign, and a local conference took place in August regarding how to popularise wartime nurseries. Suggestions at this time included direction signs, leaflets in wage packets and conducted tours.[104] Sybil Eccles, wife of David Eccles the Government's principal Economic Adviser, and resident of Chute, had been tasked with setting up a wartime nursery in her area. In March 1942 she noted: 'Tomorrow I go off for my week in London. I have a full programme and shall spend each day in a different War-Time Nursery – picking the brains of their leaders. 'National Nurseries' Mr Bevin wants to call them'... but 'It seems that the Mothers of England still prefer 'the neighbour' to 'the Nursery'.'[105] By May she was 'sitting in a borrowed car outside a local factory – all day I've been on tour – propaganding for the War Time Nursery – country women are not so well acquainted with Social Services as their metropolitan sisters. They look doubtful when the Nursery is suggested and one can read the thoughts revolving in their heads: 'I reckon I'll still leave Pat with Flo.' So I have to make speeches to them pointing out the good food and extra milk that Pat will have at the Nursery to build her up for the war's fourth winter – and sometimes I'm the victor and sometimes I leave defeated.'[106]

Miss Smeiton, Assistant Secretary at the Factory and Welfare Department, Ministry of Labour, had considerable influence on the nursery policy and her views were quoted in the Chief Medical Officer's *Report for the War Years*. Her views were utilised by the Ministry of Health to develop a policy which established chid minding as taking precedence over nursery provision. The policy was protested against by Bevin and the labour movement but it was too little, too late. Two schemes were set up; the Registered Daily Guardian Scheme in February 1941 where the Local Authority paid the registered guardian 6*d.* a day per child and the mother paid 6d. Both premises and persons had to meet certain standards, and were to be used as a temporary substitute for nurseries. The 'Volunteer Housewife' scheme was announced in December 1941. It encouraged private arrangements and promoted the policy that nurseries were to be seen as a last resort when all else failed. Mothers were to make all the arrangements but if they were unable to do so, the Local Authority would 'make introductions' between mothers and potential child minders. Summerfield notes that women were told that they 'must between them carry out the two tasks of looking after the children and working in the factories. Those who cannot go to the factory will help those who can… In this way there will be a real partnership in the war effort.'[107] In Freshford on the Wiltshire/Somerset border the writer Fay Inchfawn was remarking that grandmothers had now suddenly became invaluable. They were no longer looked on as fussy and interfering, but as useful babysitters and housekeepers who also did the shopping.[108] Correspondence between the Ministry of Health's Regional Office in Bristol and the Swindon Town Clerk in November 1941 reveals that day nurseries were last on their list of childcare provision, although it was noted that the issue of nurseries was urgent:

'After consultation between this Ministry, the Ministry of Labour and the Supply and Production Departments, it has been decided that immediate provision must be made for the care of young children, to enable married women with children to meet the needs of the war factories. Such provision will be along the lines of encouraging private arrangements with relatives or friends; or of arrangements with other householders made through the co-operation of the Local Authority.

As far as nurseries are concerned, it has been decided that it is necessary at once to establish four wartime nurseries in Swindon and the Departments concerned have been informed that arrangements will be made in this respect.' The Ministry did, however, understand that there was 'an acute shortage of suitable available buildings', and had taken steps to order some prefab huts for erection on suitable sites.[109]

This pressure of 'self-help' entered Government policy when women were under mounting pressure to enter work. It became the main form of childcare provision. In 1943, *c.* 59,000 children of women war workers were in nurseries, 5,000 with Registered Daily Guardians and 159,000 cared for under private minding arrangements. The opening hours of nurseries were not always run concurrently with working hours, and were probably less flexible, but Mass Observation's published book *People in Production* contained only negative comments about child minders, with both positive and negative feedback for nurseries. It was often felt to be the case that minders were unreliable, tended to lose interest and would not care for the children properly.[110]

Contained within Wiltshire Council's Wartime Committee files is a booklet issued jointly by the Board of Education and the Ministry of Health in October 1942 entitled *Not yet five: Children over two in War-Time Nurseries*. It talked of the continued growth of war-time nurseries with the purpose of the booklet being to 'explain in an unofficial way, with a minimum of technicalities, what War-Time Nurseries do for the children' and to enlighten the public regarding what went on inside, hoping to encourage girls and women aged sixteen and over to take up nursery work. The booklet stated: 'You will realise that these nurseries, by releasing mothers for war work, form a vital part of the national effort. The Government realise this too, and they are backing a widespread scheme to set up War-time Nurseries where they are most needed.' The aim of the nursery was to provide the children with a sense of security from the attitude of the staff and the 'orderly arrangement' of toys and equipment. One section was devoted to cleanliness through washing, dressing, the care of hair and the use of the toilet, the emphasis being placed on children learning to care for themselves, with specific reference to evacuees. 'The habit of going to the lavatory at regular times is an important piece of training which all nurseries give. It is one which in the past has often been neglected at home, with results which caused some dismay when children were first billeted in reception areas under the Government Evacuation Scheme.' There was also a large section regarding the different forms of play, emphasising the fact that as much time as possible would be spent outdoors.[111] On 18 August 1942 the Chippenham doctor Joan Hickson noted in her diary a conversation between herself and the superintendent of a local nursery school. 'She says being run by the Ministry of Health, everything is done for the physical health of the children, but nothing for their mental health and development.'[112] Swindon Borough Council was trying to stay informed regarding the issue of nursery provision and the welfare of the children in their district. Contained within the Clerk's Correspondence files is a typed extract taken from *Time & Tide's* issue of 20 February 1943, entitled *The Nursery School Idea* which gave the view that Local Authorities must provide nurseries and that the scheme was not as good as a permanent policy. 'The Day Nurseries, though admirable as a wartime measure are not ideal as a permanent policy...' They wanted the Education Department to take on the role.[113]

The success of Melksham's Day Nursery was reported in the 24 July 1943 edition of the *Wiltshire Times*. A recent visitor to the nursery observed that there were '30 children all well cared for and looked after. The nursery was a great success, and was proving a great social service.' Not everyone was singing the praises of wartime nurseries, however. The owner of The Priory in Malmesbury had been aggrieved that a nursery had been erected on his requisitioned land and in full view of his house. He felt that the building of the nursery had been 'a planning example of uncontrolled officialdom... complete disregard was shewn that the structure would be a blot on the landscape.' He also pointed out that the nursery had been built to accommodate 40 children but that in the end it was used for 80.[114] A bug-bear for him maybe, but the nursery was proving a success. It had opened in March 1943 and, presumably much to the owner's dismay, was also made good use of in the autumn of 1946, when squatters took residence.[115]

A Ministry of Labour memo of 1941 reported that Medical Officers greatly preferred it if women with young children remained at home. They did not feel much inclined to persuade Councils to incur their share of the cost. The MOL became exasperated by 1942 by claims that nurseries were not wanted; in 1945 the Ministry of Health withdrew funding. The reluctance of Local Authorities to foot the bill meant that many closed.[116] There was still a need for nursery provision in Swindon in the immediate post-war period. A member of the Ministry of Aircraft Production Tenants' Association had, on 18 January 1946, 'received a deputation of married women', complaining that the remaining nurseries in their area 'cannot or will not accommodate their children.' It had meant that some of them had been unable to work.[117]

The Women Power Committee tried to forestall the closure of nurseries after the war. At their meeting in April 1945 they agreed to write to the Ministry of Health urging them to delay action.[118] In 1946 the eminent paediatrician James Spence in a lecture called The *Purpose of the Family* emphasised the welfare of children, arguing that the family unit had come under 'unprecedented pressure' during the war and wanting to save the family unit by 'preserving the art of motherhood'.[119] An article by Denise Riley entitled *War in the Nursery* held the view that children who were deprived of their mother's care were psychologically damaged, posing a threat to 'social stability', a view which lent its weight to the closure of wartime nurseries and shaped public opinion regarding the role of the working mother.[120] In Swindon, the pleas of those working mothers who could not get places at local nurseries were answered by the Medical Officer of Health in a Memorandum to the Town Clerk on 22 January 1946. He stated that the reduction of staff, especially that of fully trained staff due to sickness and other reasons, had 'made it impossible to provide for all the children requiring care, and the future of nurseries is, at the moment, under consideration. Unless staff is available it may be necessary to close the nursery.'[121] A letter sent by the Ministry of Health to the Clerk of Wiltshire County Council in August 1945 showed it was already looking to reduce the opening hours of nurseries. 'Although in paragraph 7(b) of Circular 2388, it was suggested that war-time nurseries would normally open for periods up to 12 hours or more per day, it is thought that in some districts the needs of the women workers can now be met by shorter hours.'[122] A number of letters were discovered in the Wartime Committee files of Wiltshire County Council protesting against the closure of wartime nurseries. The Town Clerk of Devizes felt in March 1946 that the proposed closure was premature. '... the British Rola Co... are likely to remain in the town for some considerable time to come and are in urgent need of further female employees.' The Committee felt that the closing of the nursery was 'somewhat premature, as it is the only place in the Borough where married women, desirous of working, and in many cases compelled to work, can safely leave their children.' The Town Clerk of Chippenham in March 1946 reported on the last meeting of the Council in which a resolution was passed: 'That in view of the Prime Minister's recent appeal to women to return to, or remain in industry in order to assist the production drive, this Council urges the County Council to reconsider the closing of the Chippenham Day Nursery, as many of the women likely to be available could not possibly assist in the drive unless they have

Ladies and Gentlemen,

FUTURE OF THE WAR-TIME NURSERIES

As mentioned to the Maternity and Child Welfare Committee, a census was taken of mothers with children in the three nurseries, and it appears that there will be between 50 and 60 children, from the age of 1 to 4 years, requiring further care, especially in view of the fact that the Education Committee are not able, because of shortage of staff, to provide more nursery classes at the moment.

The Circular 221/45, issued jointly by the Ministry of Education and Ministry of Health, deals with nursery provision for children under five years. It admits that it may be necessary to continue to look after the younger children under two, but considers the children from two to five should be under the care of the Education Committee. It also considers the proper place for a child under two is with its mother at home. The 100 per cent grant will also be reduced by half, after the 1st April 1946, and finally the Education Committee and Health Committee are expected to propound their scheme for the care of children under five by the end of February.

It is suggested and agreed by the Joint Health and Education Committee, that the number of nurseries be reduced to two by the closure of Upham Road. This would mean saving in the rent of Upham Road and also the return of requisitioned premises. In any case, I am unable to provide staff for three nurses. We are then left with Broad Street and Pinehurst Nurseries, and a scheme of selection of the persons requiring the use of the nurseries will have to be made.

The Education Committee are not in a position to undertake the running of the nurseries owing to shortage of staff, and I would suggest that it be undertaken by the Maternity and Child Welfare Committee, at least, for the time being.

Nurseries are extremely expensive and I feel that the Committee should consider the possibility of raising the fee for mothers who can afford to pay up to 1/6d. per day, to include, breakfast, dinner, tea, and care of the child. There would be cases who could not afford the full fee and if the scheme is approved I would like especially to deal with this.

It is further considered that in view of the shortage of nurses, including assistants for the nurseries, that training of a pre-nursing character should be provided and the nurseries could be utilized for part of this training. The general scheme would be for girls between the age of 14 and 18, to have the opportunity to take this training, the aim of which would be to prepare them for the nursery nurses examination. The theoretical training would be (a) technical, and (b) general education. The practical side of the training would be provided at the Nurseries, Clinics, Nursery Classes, Public Health Office, Maternity Home, 81 Bath Road and Common Hill (In some cases, they would be resident). Although the bulk of the theoretical training would fall upon the education staff, it is hoped that most of the technical training could be undertaken by the Health Visitors and the Medical Officers.

I would like to arrange a pre-nursing course, that is, train the young girls so that they could take the preliminary examination for entry to a hospital; for general nursing training I am, however, doubtful whether the General Nursing Council would accept these arrangements, but I would like to try and make this arrangement. As to the future of the girls – those who enter the course already possessing their school leaving certificate could go on for nursing

The Medical Officers of Health writing to the Chairman and members of the Health and Welfare Committee in Swindon, 22 January 1946, stating their position on the future of the war-time nurseries in Swindon, in conjunction with the policy of the Ministry of Education and Ministry of Health (WSA G24/225/51)

suitable accommodation for their children during working hours.' The Women's Co-operative Guilds of Corsham and Calne were also unhappy about the closures, the Corsham Guild '… seeing that there [were] many women still doing essential work. Unless something is done in the immediate future, it may cause a slowing down of production at this critical period…' and considering the 1945 election win by Labour's Clement Attlee, the nursery issue appears to have been so serious that local Labour Parties railed against the decision. The Chippenham Divisional Labour Party passed a resolution '[t]hat this meeting learns with considerable concern and disquiet of the closing or proposed closing of the Day Nurseries at Boxfield, Calne, Corsham, and Chippenham, and beseeches the Public Health Committee of the Wilts. County Council to reconsider its decision. Apart from the individual cases of hardship to working mothers already sending their children to these Nurseries, there is also the question of the return of women to work to help in the production drive. Unless Day Nurseries are provided it is obvious that mothers of young children will be unable to return to the work in which they became so proficient during the war years, when the National emergency was little more pressing than it is to day.' The Corsham Local Labour Party was even more vehement. It 'deplore[d] the decision of the Wilts County Council to close the Day Nurseries, and appeal[ed] to the Council for a reversion of that totally unwarranted and unjustifiable verdict. On behalf of the working class mothers of this area we demand the continuation and extension of this service, based on the grounds of justice, humanity, and necessity.'[123] By December 1947 only 879 wartime nurseries remained open country-wide.[124] The Ministry of Labour and National Service advised the Town Clerk of Swindon that the Registered Daily Guardian Scheme was due to continue until 31 March 1946 'for the benefit of mothers in employment.'[125] In September 1946 the number of women in work was 5.8 million compared to the war-time peak of 7.2 million[126] and by early 1947 the Government continued to put pressure on young married women to return to work due to the labour shortage. The editor and columnist of *Woman* magazine expressed the difficulties of the 'stressed and exhausted' housewife, calling on 'husbands, industry and the Government to offer practical help to make it more realistic for married women, especially mothers, to return to work'. The 1948 film *The Red Shoes* epitomised the dilemma faced by women who were forced to choose between a career and their husbands.[127]

Working Women

WORKING IN 1940s Britain meant little time to spare for that essential but incredibly difficult household chore: shopping. A Wartime Social Survey found that 32% of married women workers gave shopping difficulties as the main disadvantage of work and the findings were confirmed by Mass Observation.[128] Approximately half of working women were responsible for the household shopping, but shops resolutely stuck to peace-time opening hours.[129] The Ministry of Labour tried to develop a wartime shopping policy in 1941, working in conjunction with the Ministry of Food on projects such as factory canteens, British Restaurants (communal places where civilians could buy inexpensive meals) and school meals, but figures suggest it only made a small difference regarding the need to shop.[130] The Ministry of Labour also pressed for retailers to change their opening hours but the Ministry of Food did not want to get involved in 'official regulations' and held the view that shopkeepers would not find later opening hours acceptable or workable;

with wartime restrictions they would have little to sell late in the day. The Ministry of Food felt that industry should change, not retailers.[131]

Leave was granted at the employer's discretion, with many employers saying the time had to be made up, such as working on a Sunday instead of a Saturday. It had been realised that productivity suffered less when an employer controlled absence in the case of domestic responsibilities, but many firms would only grant leave under certain circumstances, for example the size of a family. There were no allowances made for men or other family members to share the burden of shopping, although Penny Summerfield suggests that men would have helped if they had been given the chance.[132] It was often alleged that women used shopping problems as an excuse to get time off, and they were even accused as being the cause of the queues. They were told that it should be easy for them to arrange for a neighbour or friend to make their purchases for them, and they should form a 'shopping league'.[133] Celia Fremlin, the Mass Observation worker at EKCO, noted that

HOME AND HEALTH

WAR-TIME shopping is difficult. No leisurely shopping with time to choose this and that. Time and patience are saved when you shop at Timothy Whites & Taylors, for under one roof you can buy everything for health and home.

In times of sickness, you will find in our drug department efficient and helpful service always available. You will also still find such well-known winter remedies as Lobelline for coughs and colds and Maltogen the tonic food for all ages. National Health prescriptions are dispensed by fully-qualified chemists. Looking ahead, we may see extended State health schemes inaugurated and Timothy Whites & Taylors are ready and equipped to give full co-operation in any scheme of the future for the benefit of public health. Stocks of your favourite remedies are still well-maintained at all our branches.

Timothy Whites & Taylors LTD

CHEMISTS & HOUSEHOLD STORES

OVER 900 BRANCHES

Advert for Timothy Whites & Taylors Ltd., Chemists and Household Stores in the Salisbury Journal, promoting the fact that they understood the difficulties of wartime shopping, 11 February 1944 (WSHC Microform Collection)

female factory workers bought practically no household goods whatsoever, even when they were married and living at home. She felt the reason was that due to wartime working they were unable to look after their homes themselves. The person who was now doing that job for them would be the one to do the weekly shop. She was quite derisive in her attitude, going so far as to say that '[i]n fact those shopping lists provide a perfect illustration of the point made earlier – that this type of factory work fosters an attitude of carefree irresponsibility to every aspect of daily life.'[134] However, Celia also noted how tired many workers were and how little time they had for household chores. The Chippenham doctor Joan Hickson was a little more sympathetic when writing in her diary of a tour around the underground factories at Corsham on 18 February 1943. She went

> ostensibly to see what working conditions were like, really because we were interested, though we do constantly get asked for certificates not to work underground… the general layout, lighting, air-conditioning and spaciousness was pretty marvellous… However I decided I would not choose to work in a munitions factory if I had to change jobs. The noise was pretty bad and although conditions were about as perfect as possible the girls all looked white and tired under their make-up… I felt I could sympathise with them wanting to spend [all their money] on fur coats and luxurious living after standing eight or more hours putting one thing through one machine all day.[135]

The WVS was involved in discussions with the Ministry of Labour over shopping leagues but their leadership felt it could not be classed as Civil Defence work and that as an organisation they should not be involved. Mass Observation reported that for most women it was difficult to ask for help. 'It's a problem, all this shopping. You can't get anyone to do it, it's too big a thing to ask when it takes so long.'[136]

Family life during wartime must have been difficult, especially when both parents were absent due to wartime commitments. The head teacher of Ivy Lane School in Chippenham cited the case of one girl in June 1942 who had missed 30 days of schooling since Easter without her parents knowing. Her father was employed by the Oxo Company and her mother was on war work at the hospital. He noted that a new School Attendance Officer had been appointed, rather than blaming the parents.[137]

The wartime emphasis on working women did not lead to their role permanently changing; collective childcare provision was not taken seriously during wartime, and taken away in the immediate post-war years; changes in retail practices which may have helped working women were resisted. Summerfield's view is that 'the stake of professional and business interests in the continuity of women's central position in the home was too great to risk change, even in wartime.'[138]

Wiltshire Industry

WILTSHIRE HAD REMAINED predominantly agricultural before 1939, but even so there were established industries in the county. Devizes and Trowbridge had well known breweries, Wilton was the home of carpet making[139] and the GWR works in Swindon had been well established since the 1840s.[140] Salisbury had become well known for motors, established by Scout Motors until 1921, renowned for their quality and reliability.[141] The engineering firm Westinghouse had been situated in Chippenham since the 19th century and Devizes was also home to a tobacco and snuff works.[142] Other industries included the Avon rubber factory at Melksham, Harris's meat factory at Calne, Spencer Moulton & Co. at Bradford on Avon, and Nestlés milk factory in Chippenham,[143] to name but a few.

Some local firms found themselves taking on additional work during wartime, such as Harris's of Calne. John Whiles notes that '[w]hen the bombing of London increased, the Sainsbury factory was in danger. The whole of the pie produce was manufactured at Harris's Calne factory. Many of their workers were employed in the pie department.'[144] Other factories turned their hand to munitions, such as the Salisbury factory which turned from building Scout cars and motor coaches to making shells and employing many local women.[145] Firms such as John Wallis Titt, the Warminster Iron Works producer of wind engines for the agricultural industry, had been established in the county since 1876, but had a resurgence during wartime due to the heightened importance of the agricultural industry. By the post-war period it was the second largest employer in the town after the Royal Electrical and Mechanical Engineers (REME) workshops.[146] The town's silk factory had also turned its hand to making parachute silk.[147]

But new wartime industries were also making their mark on the county. A flax factory was established on the London Road in Devizes for wartime work where the flax was, as the Devizes Local History Group describe, 'stripped from the stalks, bundled and then sent to another factory to be made into webbing'. Many local girls[148] (and men such as one Bromham resident who been classed as unfit for the forces) were directed to work there. The Ministry of Supply requisitioned all of the Bath and Portland Stone quarries in December 1940, except Monks Park which had already been taken by the Admiralty. It came as a big surprise with no warning and no terms discussed. The Managing Director

tried to find out whether we should be allowed to do the clearing but could get no reply on that point. As you can imagine we are left rather high and dry, but I suppose we shall hear something this week... Meantime of course it is somewhat difficult to know what to do with the men as I do not want to disperse them knowing how difficult it will be to get them back again, but with all the quarries requisitioned it leaves very little work to which we can put them.

To this day in some parts of Spring Quarry, Copenacre and Hayes Wood mine at Limpley Stoke, the tools remain untouched awaiting the quarrymen's return.[149]

Shadow Factories were set up under a Government scheme, begun back in 1936 and designed to promote expansion. They were built completely from public funds and were fully owned by the Government who also equipped them and paid for new extensions.[150] Shadow Factories were also planned by the Government as a means of rearmament for the mass production of weapons which would be needed in time of war. Christiaan van Schaardenburgh describes the term Shadow Factory as 'duplicated facilities under the direct control of the parent company, as well as distributed facilities managed by other companies with appropriate skills'.[151] By 1945, there were 265 Shadow Factories, alternatively known as agency factories; 159 controlled by the Ministry of Supply, 87 under the Ministry of Aircraft Production (MAP) and 19 under the Admiralty.[152] An example is the Air Ministry's factory at South Marston near Swindon which remained in place after the war.[153] Trowbridge became the site of MAP Spitfire production factories at Bradley Road and Hilperton Road, and the town's garages were also used, such as Fore Street Garage, Rutland Garage and Curries Garage with associated workshops in Devizes and Westbury. The town was chosen due to its being within a 70 mile radius of the Vickers-Supermarine works in Hampshire; it was also near an aerodrome.[154] The garages in the town proved insufficient and so three extra premises were built with the main site being situated at the glove factory. The components made their way to Keevil Airfield for assembly and flight-testing.[155] There was also a factory at Southwick, near Trowbridge, whose employees worked from eight in the morning until eight in the evening. One female worker recalled that: 'We done a bit of everything. When we went to Southwick first, we were making wings for Spitfires. We had the ribs and we made the whole wing.'[156] Vickers-Supermarine chose Salisbury as another of its dispersed production network, requisitioning Anna Valley Motors and building new premises in Castle Road, with the city eventually holding eight sites, including Wessex Garages, with accommodation and covering at W.H. Smith's.[157] The Government had been encouraging this kind of subcontracting to increase capacity, but it reached 'riotous proportions' and motor dealers like the Wilts. and Dorset Motor Co. and Anna Valley Motors in Salisbury[158] could do very well on the production of components. By 1943, 42% of construction and assembly work was subcontracted, but these subcontractors did not often take advice from MAP and their products were commonly, as Angus Calder notes, 'unsatisfactory in regard to quality, delivery or price'. It could also be the case, however, that these 'daughter' firms were neglected by their much larger parent companies.[159] The Ministry of Aircraft Production's plan to disperse factories to lots of smaller units led to bottlenecks in the supply of raw materials, mostly due to poor planning rather than an actual shortage.[160] Cripps' shake up of MAP took place in March 1943 when he, as Calder puts it, 'rudely nationalised' Shorts due to its inefficient management and removed its Board of Directors.[161] MAP swapped production of Shorts' Stirling bomber to South Marston in August 1940; the fuselages were already being constructed at Blunsdon.[162] In fact the firm were also well known by Swindon Borough Council, the firm's staff having been in trouble over their complaints regarding the town's Lodgings Restriction Order.[163] By 1943 the Air Ministry saw the need for more Spitfires. Vickers-Supermarine took over the Shorts and Phillips & Powys sites in April.[164] The Wiltshire & Swindon History Centre holds a photograph album of the progress of constructing the MAP factory at West Harnham during 1941-2; Wellworthy Piston Rings Ltd were relocated to the site.

Spitfire factory in Southwick near Trowbridge (WSHC P41436)

The Bristol Aeroplane Company (BAC) at Filton had been attacked by the Luftwaffe in September 1940 and in reply their aircraft plant requisitioned four quarries: Spring Quarry, Westwood, Monks Park and Limpley Stoke. BAC began to get cold feet and eventually took only one part of Spring Quarry near Corsham to produce its engines. The rest were occupied by companies producing gun turrets and undercarriage assemblies for bombers. The Royal Enfield Company of Redditch, well known as motorcycle manufacturers, were persuaded to open a factory at Westwood Quarry.[165] The quarry was converted by Irish labourers and the factory was adjacent to the storage area for the Victoria and Albert Museum.[166] The Enfield workers produced missile control mechanisms for the Bristol Bloodhound Rocket, hydraulic equipment for the Bofors anti-aircraft guns for use against the V1 rockets and equipment for the increased accuracy of anti-aircraft radar controlled predictors. One worker recalled: 'The factory itself was a marvellous place. It was ninety-eight feet underground with brick pillars every few yards. Although it was a large, open area you couldn't say that it was one big workshop because it wasn't a regular shape, you would see a row of machines then you would go round a pillar and here would be another row of machines round the corner. Walls and ceiling had been whitewashed and everywhere was spotlessly clean.' The workers bought themselves a bib and brace overall as they were not provided with industrial clothing. They worked 60 hours a week, 8am to 6pm, six days, with one Saturday afternoon off a month.[167]

EKCO Radio of Southend on Sea was approached by the Air Ministry to participate in the production of airborne radar equipment. They bought Cowbridge House near Malmesbury and converted the outbuildings into factory premises with staff using a hostel three miles away and also billets in the town.[168] They soon expanded exponentially and were having to billet workers in a 20 mile radius of Malmesbury, bussing them in on a daily basis. Local women were also employed and the percentage of the local population of workers compared to imported employees over a 5 mile radius was over 35%.[169] The Corsham underground sites were so large that, as in Malmesbury, workers were being bussed in from the local area. In 1942 'the undertaking at Corsham is very large... is situated in open country...when this place is in full production...many will no doubt have to be recruited from surrounding towns.'[170] The site, its project code name 'Hawthorn', had so many entrances when it was being constructed, it is said that worries over security led to a squad of Metropolitan Police Officers being drafted in to guard them.[171] Margaret Dobson reports that when it became operational,

> [t]here were men billeted in Bradford [on Avon] and for 30 miles around as far as Salisbury... We were brought in every day and had to be taken back afterwards. I'd go outside my house just after 7 and get on one of those coaches. Before we got halfway to Corsham we would be in a convoy with coaches coming in from all directions. The worst part was when we got to the Bath to Melksham Road, they'd be in a queue bumper to bumper coming up from Bath. There was no right of way then for anyone coming from the right, so we had trouble trying to dodge into this continual column. There were thousands and thousands of us there... There were rows and rows of great long huts for checking in and checking out with every so far a little window with someone checking.' Metal and chemical industries were the Government's highest priority during WWII; it was their products which would win the war. In Wilton it was obvious where you worked according to the colour of your skin. 'Most people during those days had skin stained orange from working with flares, green from camouflage paint or white from the whiting works![173]

Celia Fremlin concluded that the low morale of women workers was due to the horrendously long working hours and the nature of the work which was repetitive and tedious; the importance of the work was also unknown to them at the time. Unfortunately the Manager did not agree and stuck to his feelings that propaganda was the cause.[174] The work at EKCO was in fact highly valuable to the war effort, one of its 'greatest triumphs' being the development of the AI Mark VIII, an interceptor set used in night fighting aircraft, using a synthetic rubber tank supplied by Moulton's of Bradford-on-Avon.[175] Avon Rubber at Melksham was another local manufacturer that had turned its hand to war work, developing new techniques when their natural source of rubber from Malaya and Indonesia became unavailable. Gas masks were made at the site and their newly developed bonding of rubber tyres to steel for tank wheels was a development which they shared with other companies to 'aid the war effort'. Their mainstay was tyres, but they also produced a total of 20 million gas masks and 6,000 tons of 'general rubber goods' for the Government and 'essential services of the country'. They produced a private exhibition of the products that passed through their factory 'to give some idea of the results of their work'.[176] The Westinghouse works in Chippenham appear to have thought of employee morale in 1943. They had realised that 'very few of our employees knew the whole story of our War effort'.[177] Their war work had included metal rectifiers for use on aircraft, in tanks, in signalling and communications. By the end of the war 115,000,000 had been made. Transformers and other non-electrical equipment were also produced, such as soluble plug devices, gun sights and shock absorbers for bombers.[178] Avon Rubber wanted to praise the efforts of its wartime employees at the Victory Carnival Parade in May 1946 which was raising funds for the town's *Welcome Home Fund* for returning servicemen. Its prize winning float declared: 'Avon workers did their full share – victory moved on rubber.'[179]

Moulton's already had in place great expertise for getting the most out of rubber and synthetics. This knowledge was also to become of great value to the war effort. One Moulton's employee worked on 'Special Developments' as part of the reserved occupation allocation. He tackled the problem of birds getting into a plane's engine. 'We developed a little guard which was made of piano wire and had rubber surrounding it and which was very strong... [We'd have] a call from Bristol Aeroplanes, could they do something about some important part on a plane... I'd do my best to sort it out. I were pretty good at it. Rubber's a funny material, but over the years, if you spend a long time... you build up a picture of what you can do and I used to love it.' One employee had this to say of her time at the factory. 'We had to work hard, sometimes seven days a week. There were many good times with laughter and singing which could be heard throughout the factory. A real family feeling which helped to get us through the war time problems. We felt we were 'doing our bit' for the war effort.' At the Melksham site they were working on 'highly secret' work with gas masks. 'My job was the inspection of gas masks. Then 12 of us were put in a room on our own... We were working on inflatable rubber boats that had been made in the factory. We had to make sure there were no bubbles on the canvas that had been put on the boats which had to pass our inspection before they could go out. So we were the last ones to touch them. We didn't know at the time but those boats were for the D-Day invasion on 6 June 1944...'[180] The war also brought with it a plethora of new Government Departments which fed down to county level. The numbers of women civil servants more than doubled during the wartime period.[181]

The war saw the closure of some factories, such as two of Warminster's gloving factories and its bacon factory. They re-opened after the war. Other businesses moved into the county after the war, making use of wartime buildings which had since become vacant. Avalon, maker of soles and heels for the shoe firm Clarks, moved into the old corrugated huts in Warminster in 1955. They had previously been used by the Ministry of Food for storage.[182] In 1947 there were plans for establishing temporary office buildings for the Ministries of National Insurance and Inland Revenue at a site in Lowden, Chippenham. There would be no objections if it the plans were approved by the Planning Authority.[183]

Infrastructure

THERE WERE WATER shortages in wartime, especially when the military, industry, agriculture and householders needed supplies.[184] In 1944 the Town Clerk at Swindon issued a notice to the Swindon public asking them to limit their water use.[185] The siting of the EKCO factory at Cowbridge, Malmesbury, meant increased demand for water, taking water pressure away from local houses. The Factory Manager received a very irate call from a local resident complaining about the interference with her bathing routine. She was reminded that 'There [was] a war on!'[186] A correspondent was reporting in the *Wiltshire Times*, 19 August 1944 that the water had failed again. 'It was like old times again at Corsham last week-end, when the water supply failed without notice, and some people were without its use for no less than 36 hours. Those householders who have a pump were kept busy supplying their less fortunate neighbours.'

Military sites were also causing problems. It appears that the Local Authorities also had to foot the bill for certain parts of water provision to military establishments. In February 1943 the Town Clerk of Swindon Borough Council was noting: 'the Corporation have expended a sum of over £12,000 in laying a ring main around the Town in order to make it possible to give a bulk supply to one large aerodrome and various military camps in the immediate vicinity.'[187] In turn, the War Department were bickering over the costs of their water charges compared to those of the Air Ministry, having previously (in July 1942) extended Chiseldon Camp with no prior warning. The Borough Surveyor was warning of a possible curtailment of usage and in a memo sent the same month: 'I do know it is going to prove an extremely difficult matter to keep the whole of the Old Town of Swindon provided with water from Ogbourne...'[188]

The movement of people due to newly created or relocated war industry meant that extra pressures were placed on rural England. According to Angus Calder, the 'social ulcer' of overcrowded industrial conurbations had now spread to smaller towns entering the war industry. The 'sleepy' town of Chippenham had become 'a town in the throes of the managerial revolution... a pallid population working long hours at an armament manufacturer'.[189] Glynn and Booth[190] feel that the Government handled the tight wartime labour market with great success, but Nick McCamley notes that there were issues regarding local accommodation and transporting people to work,[191] and in Wiltshire, it is no exaggeration to say that the influx was huge.

```
The O.E.,
Salisbury Plain District,
BULFORD, WILTS.


Dear Sir,

            I have to confirm the telephonic conversation
you had with the Deputy Borough Surveyor yesterday regarding
the extension of the Chiseldon Camp, and it is to be regretted
that this Department should have been presented with an
accomplished fact without prior consultation having taken
place between the Military Authorities and this Corporation.

            Ogbourne Pumping Station and the Overtown
reservoir, having to meet an increased demand of 50,000 gallons
per day, will, under conditions of drought, considerably embarrass
the water supply in this area.

            Notification of this increased demand is part-
icularly disturbing just as negotiations have been completed
by me for a supply of water to a proposed establishment in the
neighbourhood.   However, the extension has been made without
the sanction of the Corporation and the Military Authorities
must, therefore, realise that they must face the probability
of a considerable curtailment of water under conditions of
drought.

            It is to be hoped that no further extension
will be made without prior consultation with this Departmen

                    Yours faithfully,


                                Borough Surveyor,
```

Swindon's Borough Surveyor warning of possible water shortages, 21 July 1942 (WSA G24/225/11)

It wasn't just factory workers; construction workers arrived in the county too. Thousands of men were drafted in from the 'distressed areas' of South Wales, Durham, Northumberland and Cumberland and put to work on constructing the underground factories in and around Corsham.[192] These workers were found billets in the surrounding towns and villages and bussed into work by the Bath Tramways Company. The men also brought their families with them. The work was very desirable; there was accident benefit, paid holidays and also sickness and injury benefit, none of which were available at collieries such as those in Somerset. Councillor Steynor of the Bath Public Assistance Committee in Somerset noted 'the very debatable policy of the Government for dealing with the 'Industrial black-spot' problem, which is unashamedly the repatriation of the unfortunate inhabitants of such areas to those more prosperous.' He felt that these workers and their families would be loathe to leave, 'preferring our equitable climate, natural attractions, unique voluntary social services and cultural entertainment facilities.'[192] In Cricklade, Irish workmen were drafted in to construct nearby runways. They lodged in the town, adding to the pressure alongside evacuees. 'Some came to stay with us, just at the drop of a hat.'[193] By the end of March

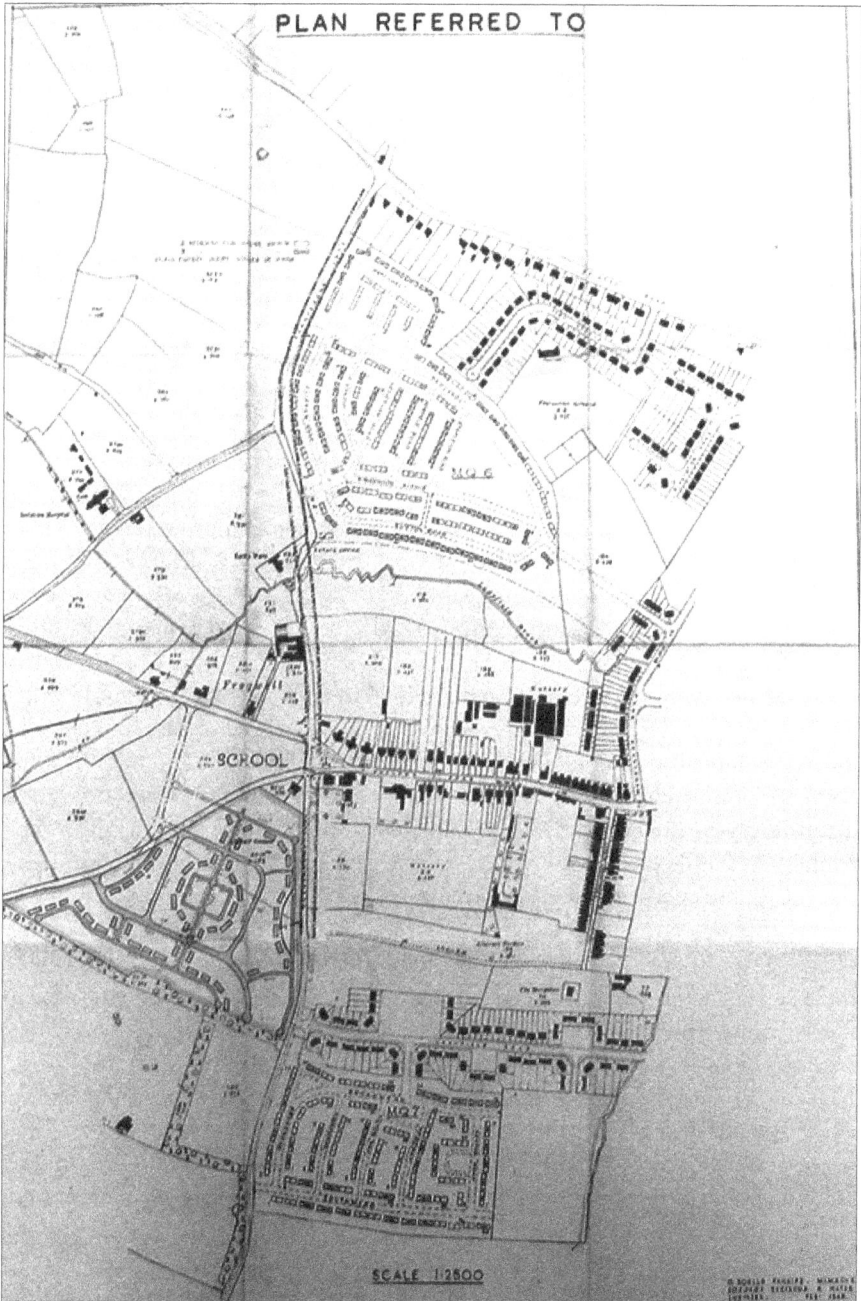

Plan of a new estate drawn by the Borough Surveyor, scale 1:2500, February 1943. One of two sites off Hungerdown Lane, Chippenham (WSA F4/760/474)

1942, 3,000 hostel places were available in Corsham but of those, 2,000 were currently being used to house construction workers. The Clerk told the Council, 'It is almost impossible to give you an adequate picture of the present situation at Corsham. It must be seen to be believed...'[194] Married employees working at the underground factory in Corsham for the Bristol Aircraft Company could not all be accommodated and so initially many had to find lodgings in Chippenham, Bradford on Avon and Trowbridge.[195] It is interesting to note that prefabs were built off Hungerdown Lane in Chippenham during the war for Ministry of Aircraft Production employees.[196] A plan of the estate dated 1943 indicates the road names: Redland, Patchway, Clifton Close, Stapleton Road, Horfield Road, Kingswood Avenue, Broadmead, Fishponds, Filton Way ... denoting their connection with Bristol through BAC and its work at Corsham.[197] The prefabs are long gone, but some of the original road names have survived.

Re-location

TWENTY THOUSAND CIVIL Servants were among the first to be evacuated out of London, but they were so critical of the move it was recommended that further evacuations be suspended. The main complaints were about poor accommodation, and the disruption to private and social lives. Concessions involved assistance with transferring families to the reception areas. However, the evacuation of Government staff continued and was accelerated to ensure that there was sufficient accommodation in London for war work.[198] The War Office had relocated many of its staff to the Empire Hotel in Bath, Somerset. Ironically, they had to be moved as a precautionary measure to the Town Hall at Bradford on Avon during the city's Baedeker raid in 1942.[199] Even in rural Freshford on the Wiltshire/ Somerset border a house was taken over by a London Building Society, housing a 'band of gay-hearted happy young people with something metropolitan in their clothes, and in their manners' which, after a period of inquiry and doubtfulness, the village 'took these newcomers to their hearts.'[200]

This was not always to be the case, as is vividly described in the writings of the Mass Observation worker Celia Fremlin. For the residents of Malmesbury, these 'brisk, town bred men' had no connection with the locality and what is more, 'came almost simultaneously with the wartime invasion of evacuees, ministry officials, soldiers, etc., etc., that has been the lot of most country towns. No wonder that the local population ha[d] barely yet woken from the state of dazed bewilderment into which it was stunned by the avalanche of events. Their peaceful old-world town [was] gone; and in its place [was] something resembling a London railway terminus, with its endless comings and goings of strangers from all parts of the country; with its atmosphere of irritable bustle, impersonal pushing and hurrying.'[201] It appears it was hard going recruiting local workers for the local, newly arrived, EKCO factory. Hostility was directed at them because their activities were the least understood. Conversations were overheard: 'They ought to be shot, some of those fellows up there. They've got nothing to do, and they're

just sitting tight there because they're frightened they'll have to join the army…'
'It makes me sick to see those great lumps of men hiding away up there while our
boys do the fighting. The cowardly swine!' The women workers were also the topic
of conversation. 'Mrs H. is supposed to be working in the factory, but I've seen
her wandering about the streets at eleven in the morning. She's the dodger type; I
wouldn't trust that woman further than I could throw a bull by the tail.'[202] These
misunderstandings made employment there unpopular, with the belief that the
company could be making radiograms for the black market or providing 'sham'
employment for the sons of the rich and famous, but the higher wages did look
attractive to some local girls. They would otherwise have been looking at a career
in domestic service, but this in turn did not endear them to the local gentry who
were finding it difficult to hold onto staff. One mother was worried about her 17
year old daughter getting three times her old wage; how would she make the most
of this newfound income?[203]

The newcomers moaned and grumbled about their billets which the locals
took as an insult to themselves and to their town, but the locals did not realise
that it partly came from a sense of upheaval and bewilderment that was equal to
their own.[204] Friction between the newcomers and the locals didn't end there. The
cinema queue was a contentious issue: 'We didn't ought to have to wait like this.
They ought to let us get in first, we've lived here all our lives, and let they others
wait. Pushing in front like they do, and I don't suppose they knew there was such
a place as [Malmesbury] six weeks ago.' The factory girls weren't worried about
pushing in, wanting to eat their fish and chips first. 'You can't really eat them
when you're pushing in, can you?'[205] Fish and cosmetics were in high demand, as
were cigarettes and beer. The situation came to a head at the Old Bell when the
proprietor put up a sign which read 'Employees of E.K. Cole are not welcome
in this Bar.' When asked by the Chairman of EKCO in Southend to remove it,
he did, but Browning reports that it was the trigger for the company to ask for a
Mass Observation worker to visit.[206] Celia's work is corroborated by the memoirs
of Charles Exton, a worker at the EKCO factory during the war who remembered
the hostility and suspicion of the locals who were busy wondering why a company
from Southend on Sea should move there. They felt that maybe the workers had
paid large sums of money to avoid conscription. He recalled that many a time the
locals had sold the last cigarette or pulled the last pint of beer and so couldn't serve
them… until it magically reappeared again for the next local![207]

The problems encountered around billets stemmed in the main from issues
over food, privacy, coming in at night and the difficulties of having friends over.
The lodgers often felt they were not getting their full share of rations.[208] One Civil
Servant evacuated to nearby Bath, Somerset, denounced his hosts as 'despicable,
money-grabbing billetors'. He complained that he and a colleague had to 'eat,
sleep and live in a dimly lit room where dust accumulate[d] undisturbed. We had
to buy our own coal and light our own fire'. They also felt that they were growing
thinner and thought the billetor was utilising part of their ration allowance.[209] On
12 June 1941 the Director of A. T. Rowley (London) Ltd. was writing to the Clerk

of Wiltshire County Council about the 'manner in which our men are treated by the people at Winterbourne Bassett.' One of their workmen had returned to London after paying 30s. per week with an additional charge for washing and '[said] he was practically starved, being given no meat, tea, sugar etc.' His word had been corroborated by three other workmen. 'It seems scandalous to us that men should be sent by the Ministry of Labour to work in County Districts far from their homes to be treated in this disgusting manner by the local inhabitants and we shall be glad to have your views on the matter.'[210]The lack of meat during the week and the disappearance of an egg became a bone of contention in one Malmesbury billet. The quality and contents of meals were also looked on dubiously by some.[211]

Celia recorded the run of conversation in one Malmesbury billet where the lodgers were moaning about paying thirty shillings for sharing a sitting room with 'all these discomforts.' They wanted to know what was happening with their points as one felt they'd seen nothing of them. One of the lodgers mentioned that they had had prunes, but that they were off points. The reply was derisive. 'Prunes? I wouldn't eat muck like that if I ever had a decent meal here, but you have to have something to fill you up.' It was felt that the landlady even fed her chickens off them.[212]

Some of the workers struggled with the tradition in many households of having a main meal at lunchtime and a light supper in the evening; their work schedule meant they could easily miss the meal or have to eat it in a rush.[213] It was noted at an Open Discussion held by the Ministry of Health with representatives from Swindon and Cheltenham that the opening of British Restaurants was a great help. 'They have opened specially for evening meals at 6 p.m. and buses conveying workers home stop there. Many housewives are more willing to offer bed and breakfast when they know the man can get his other main meals out.'[214] EKCO's Works Manager had stated his positive attitude towards British Restaurants; that they would be advantageous toward workers and could ease the food problems of those providing billets, but he found that the Local Authority was reluctant to open a restaurant in Malmesbury in 1943 and 'steadfastly refuse to make a move'.[215] The issue of a British Restaurant in Malmesbury was proving highly contentious. The Ministry of Health felt that one was necessary and the Ministry of Labour representative in the town agreed, but the Town Councillors' argument was that a restaurant would be unfair on local people. The workers would be able to get additional rations when they were already able to get 'two pennyworth of meat three times a day'. The local restaurateurs reported that they were already finding it difficult to source food, but they could meet extra demand if necessary, and this was deemed an acceptable way forward. The statement about the two pennyworth of meat started a furore, with the EKCO's workers' representative refuting the claim as untrue; that statements of this nature would only cause friction. He noted that the restaurant would be open to 'all comers'. The issue was put forward again in August 1943 when a petition was raised, containing 1,000 signatures. The need for a British Restaurant in the town was felt by EKCO's Production and Shop Stewards Committee to be 'one of the most pressing needs of the moment'. The town's Councillors were obviously unmoved, as a British Restaurant was never opened.[216]

The EKCO workers were also billeted in a hostel, which in itself caused issues. Grumbling and bickering, backbiting and feuds... Celia Fremlin reported that the quality of the hostel was lost on those lodging there due to the ill-tempered environment which was rife.[217]

The Open Discussion held by the Ministry of Health was in fact a course for Billeting Officers. It focused on war workers: *Voluntary Lodgers v. Compulsory Billeting* and it was noted that '... the workers themselves dislike the idea of being put where they were not wanted. No man works well if he is unhappy in his lodgings; therefore it is the duty of the Billeting Officer to produce welcoming homes with a friendly atmosphere.' The Chairman concluded that the experiences of Swindon and Cheltenham showed that the Ministry's view was correct in thinking that voluntary lodgings were always preferable to compulsory billets (which should be used with discretion). It was also noted: 'It is quite evident that, if a billeting authority relies solely upon spontaneous voluntary offers in response to a merely general appeal it cannot expect much success. The only way to convert public opinion to the realisation that it is a National duty to sacrifice the privacy and comfort of the home circle is by means of a campaign which has the features of a crusade... The real essential... is willing co-operation by the main body of the town's residents, in the realisation that the use of existing accommodation is a privilege that must be shared with others in just the same way as other resources are pooled for the benefit of the Nation.'[218]

Swindon was placed under a Lodgings Restrictions order in 1940 as the housing shortage was so acute in the town. The object of the Order was to '... reserve accommodation for persons engaged on work of essential national importance. The Government and the Town Council trust that every householder who is in a position to do so will be willing to provide lodging for a war worker. If you are able to accommodate someone who has to come to Swindon for some important work you will perform a very valuable piece of national service. The Town Council has the power to billet war workers on householders compulsorily, but it is hoped that it will seldom be necessary to exercise it and that most of the incoming workpeople will be able to find accommodation by voluntary arrangement.' By the summer of 1944 the Town Clerk was stating that 'Swindon [was] closed. Consent granted only to relatives of householders.'[219] Trowbridge was also placed under such an order, coming into effect on 1 May 1943.[220]

The Swindon Borough Clerk was replying to the Deputy Clerk in Plymouth regarding accommodation in the town in August 1941. He noted that Swindon and the surrounding district was very full 'with various classes of people who have come to live here.' It appeared that those who could buy property could bypass the system. 'A loop hole is that any person can buy a house and reside in it himself with his family.' Delays often occurred in the application process and one case in Swindon brought up an issue regarding billeting notices being issued for the occupation of a whole house and the 'flouting' of the Order by the military and

A Lodgings Restriction Order application form for Swindon (WSA G24/225/6)

the Police. A letter regarding the case was sent to the Secretary at the Ministry of Health in April 1941 for clarification, as the Clerk felt that: 'If this incident is left unchallenged, a substantial loophole in the Order is created.'[221]

By December 1941 it had become clear that those Old Age Pensioners doing their duty and taking in lodgers were losing out. The Chief Billeting Officer in Swindon was continually receiving questions from OAPs losing part of their supplementary pension when they took in lodgers. He reported that one lady had lost 13s. 0d. per week supplementary pension owing to taking in war workers and another had had her supplementary pension stopped because she was taking in two workmen rather than one. '… she was told to get rid of her lodgers, yet she has two bedrooms to let and is a very good billet.' He noted that '… these elderly people are willing and able to undertake this useful National Service and in my opinion their patriotic effort ought not to be discouraged in this way.' The 'part played [by the elderly] to house workmen has not been fully appreciated and they should not be penalised.'[222]

Hutment sites were being established across the county and in Swindon many were for the use of MAP workers and their families. The Swindon Borough Clerk was concerned over this rapid development, writing to the Estate Surveyor in Bristol in July 1941 that although he wanted to further the national effort he was concerned at the proposals and wanted to safeguard town planning and housing standards. He was worried that the buildings would turn into slums.[223] One initial concern in January 1941 was the cost to the Council regarding the liability of surplus houses after the war. Upon corresponding with the Regional Offices of the Ministry of Health it was discovered that the Government would offer no guarantees and the Town Clerk replied: 'My Council ultimately stated that without more precise financial assistance than that offered by the Ministry they could not proceed.' A letter was sent to the Ministry of Health at Whitehall requesting a deputation and a meeting took place on 17 February 1941 where the Swindon delegation '…stressed that they were anxious to do what was their duty as a housing authority in the present circumstances, but that the responsibilities which they undertook must be limited by the financial resources of the town; further it seemed only reasonable that if factories for war time purposes were moved to Swindon, then the Government must have some responsibility in solving the housing problem.' They suggested a Government subsidy so that wartime houses could be let at the present rent of 13/- per week and stressed that if the Ministry could not make an offer which suited the circumstances of the town, '… the Council were faced with the two alternatives of doing nothing or assuming a burden too heavy for the town and one which seemed unfair in the circumstances.' The outcome was that accommodation would have to be provided in hostels or camps built by the Production Departments.[224]

Factories such as Messrs. Phillips & Powys Ltd. at South Marston were trying to build houses for their employees by May 1941 but were unable to do so due to a shortage of construction workers. The building contractors reported that '… the Ministry of Labour came down on us last week and practically cleaned us out of all the labour we had, whereas we want at least double the number of men which they took from us.' They had since received a visit from officials of the Ministry of Health and Air Ministry, relaying the urgency of the need to provide houses for aircraft workers, and had explained the position to them. They urged Messrs. Phillips & Powys Ltd. to bring as much pressure as they could to bear on the various Government departments to help get the additional workers that were required.[225] The county's roadmen were also in short supply in July 1940 when the Divisional Surveyor at Malmesbury asked for some to be released at once at Malmesbury for urgent defence work at the nearby EKCO factory.[226] Contractors were so short of staff they were willing to employ anyone who was prepared to work for them, one foreman in the Trowbridge area offering a local reporter £5 a week, double his current pay. He had arrived to find out more about the story of a titled lady driving a tractor as part of a team constructing a runway in the Trowbridge area. The story proved so sensational that it was soon reported in the national press.[227] The Ministry of Aircraft Production finally managed to build their bungalows at the end of 1941 and 820 were erected, the families moving in as of January 1942. Hostels were also provided for single men and women, consisting of accommodation for 220 women and 288 men, together with a sick bay, dining hall, recreation room and stores, opened in July 1942. The erection of these properties necessitated finding additional lodgings for one thousand construction workers.[228] Government ministries also erected married quarters, such as those found in Corsham. They contained medical and catering facilities, a welfare centre, and sometimes even shops, a cinema and a church.[229] Some hostels were used to house workers temporarily until lodgings could be found for them, as in the case of one which opened up in the same building as the British Restaurant in Maxwell Street, Swindon, in 1941 with accommodation for *c.* 120 men on two tier wooden bunks.[230]

Constructing new industrial premises brought with it road closures, such as those at the Air Ministry's Shadow Factory at South Marston, run by Phillips & Powys Aircraft Ltd. and which required a road closure *c.* 1940.[231] The South Marston Factory produced over 900 aircraft during the course of the war.[232]

By 1952 it was reported that many of the firms which located to Wiltshire in wartime appeared reluctant to leave, and the manufacture of aircraft components was still taking place in Salisbury, Trowbridge and Swindon.[233] Some factories found that they could not leave. The level of interference by central Government is apparent from correspondence found in Local Government records in Wiltshire. In 1949 Vickers-Armstrong were not allowed to reopen their Southampton factory which had been bombed; the company had no choice but to expand their operation in North Wiltshire instead.[234]

They bought the South Marston site from MAP which became their Aircraft Section.[235] In Trowbridge, the wartime shadow factory of Vickers Armstrong still remained post-war. It had brought with it an 'influx of fresh residents, many of whom have stayed in the town'.[236] Vickers reduced output in Salisbury after the war but did retain their Castle Road premises until at least 1947.[237] Their factory

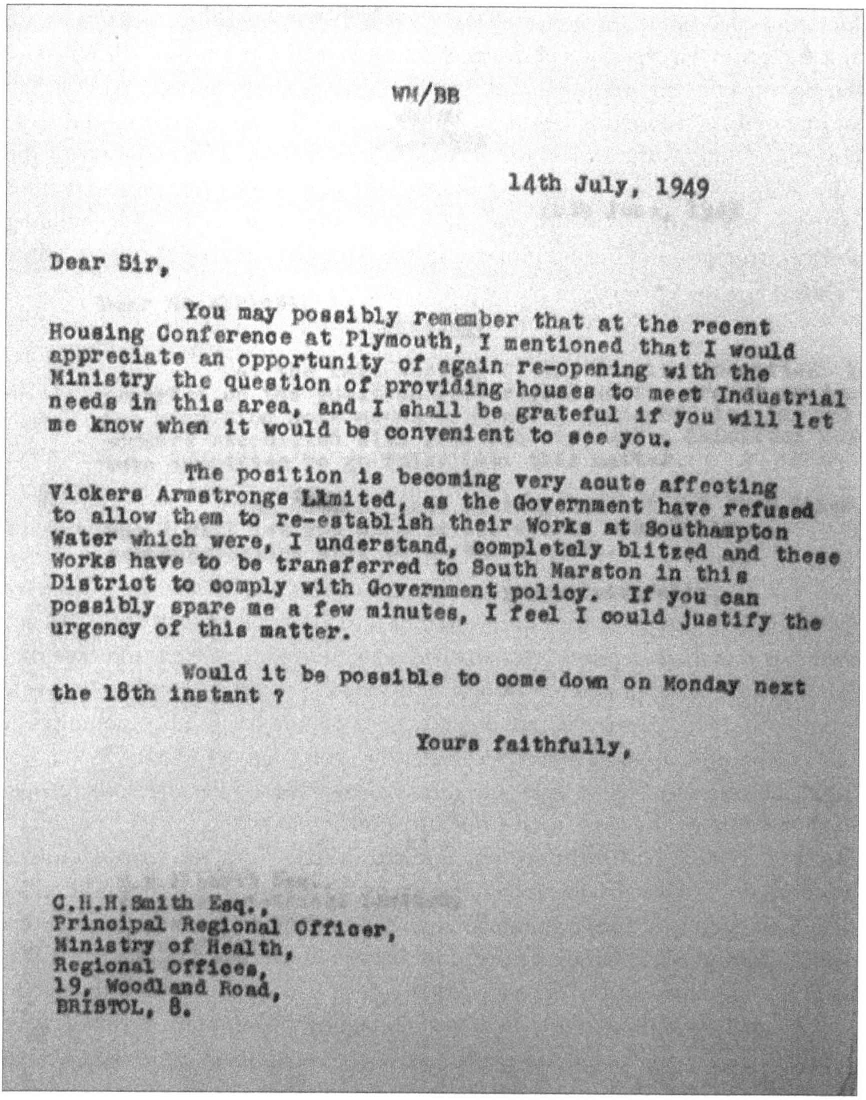

WM/BB

14th July, 1949

Dear Sir,

You may possibly remember that at the recent
Housing Conference at Plymouth, I mentioned that I would
appreciate an opportunity of again re-opening with the
Ministry the question of providing houses to meet Industrial
needs in this area, and I shall be grateful if you will let
me know when it would be convenient to see you.

The position is becoming very acute affecting
Vickers Armstrongs Limited, as the Government have refused
to allow them to re-establish their Works at Southampton
Water which were, I understand, completely blitzed and these
Works have to be transferred to South Marston in this
District to comply with Government policy. If you can
possibly spare me a few minutes, I feel I could justify the
urgency of this matter.

Would it be possible to come down on Monday next
the 18th instant ?

Yours faithfully,

C.H.H.Smith Esq.,
Principal Regional Officer,
Ministry of Health,
Regional Offices,
19, Woodland Road,
BRISTOL, 8.

Letter dated 14 July 1949. Vickers-Armstrong could not re-open their Southampton factory
(WSA G6/132/12)

at Trowbridge closed in 1958.[238] Enfield Engineering reverted back to commercial
work after the war and remained at Westwood into the 1960s and beyond. Their
factory at Bradford on Avon was making mowers post-war.[239] Avon Rubber at
Melksham found that the post-war years brought with them a period of rapid
growth.[240]

These factories still required female workers, bringing new job opportunities
that were not present before the war.[241] Summerfield has shown that the majority
of married and single women wished to remain in employment after the war[242] and

McCamley has noted the increase of workers in North Wiltshire during wartime and the continued expansion post-war. Workers were brought into North Wiltshire during wartime and certainly in the Swindon and Corsham district, many stayed and more were required. Clerical jobs increased in Warminster during the post-war period due to the expansion of local Government and the creation of the West Wilts. Water Board. The job opportunities were mainly for women. A third of those Warminster residents working in the town were employed in building and construction on housing projects, in the Army base and at the old wartime camps.[243]

In 1952 H. E. Bracey compared the 1949 population estimates of the county to the previous 1931 census and discovered that the total population of Wiltshire was due to increase by 40,000, not including the family of service personnel, in fewer than 20 years. In the 20 years before 1931 the increase was 12,000. He felt that the increase was a consequence of the industrial development in a number of towns which remained after the war, and of expansion of the War Department in several rural areas.[244] As might be expected, planning greatly affected the siting of industry in North Wiltshire, and these plans were begun pre-war. Some Councils found it difficult to stop the expansion that wartime brought. Military establishments had sprung up in this part of the county which still remain today. Swindon was the exception; planners had wanted expansion here and Swindon Borough Council appeared to welcome it, feeling in 1946 that Swindon was a one industry and one class town and 'urgently need a more balanced community'. It was felt that this could be done by a greater diversification of industry.[245]

Understandably, it was only after the war was over that local people became aware of the work local firms had been undertaking for the war effort. Messrs. Colborne of Trowbridge was featured in the 31 August 1946 edition of the *Wiltshire Times* as having been 'On Urgent War Work.' The veil was lifted on their manufacture of bank indicators for aircraft instruments and the making of a course-plotting clock, alongside the production fine parts (which before the war had been imported for Switzerland) and which had made the most of their skills as watchmakers and jewellers. They were joined by many more 'technical work experts.' Their work '… played a vital part in the anti-U-boat campaigns, and in the actions fought off the Norwegian coast.'

Post-War Employment

FOR WOMEN, JOBS in industry had often expanded their horizons and boosted their self confidence and aspirations, but Mass Observation also reported in March 1944 that many were tired of the daily grind, often bored and weary from war work.[246] Glynn and Booth note that many argue that women's wages were substantially lower than those of men during the war.[247] A study by Gazeley using monthly reports of changes in wage rates derived from Ministry of Labour reports found that there was actually widespread levelling during the course of the war, but for women this relative equality did not last. By 1945 in the manufacturing sector, the differences between men and women in terms of skill and pay were more even than in pre-war Britain.[248] Some women did continue in paid work; a photograph on the cover of the GWR's magazine showed in 1946 that 16,000 women were still 'carrying on' in the company,[249] but for many the economic and social position of women in the post-war world would be to return home and, according to Sean Glynn and Alan Booth, to 'reinforce the traditional position of women in society'.[250] The pressure on women after marriage to remain primarily to supply domestic labour and provide a caring role was established in 1945 when Beveridge assumed that women would leave the labour market upon marriage; key parts of the Social Security System were designed to reflect this view.[251] The findings of wartime studies of employed women are mixed, with one showing that only 25% unequivocally wanted to remain in paid employment after the war; those mostly in professional and administrative posts.[252] Surveys conducted during 1944-5 by the Amalgamated Engineering Union found that of the 68% of women surveyed, three quarters of those who had entered during the war wanted to remain. This included 77% of married women who had not been in paid work in 1939 and 86% of those over 40. The Government's own 1943 Social Survey found that only 20% of women workers were determined to give up work altogether, as against 55% who were resolved to stay on. It found that married women with children were the keenest, wanting the additional income and also the company of others.[253] The post-war housing shortage brought with it higher rents[254] which could put pressure on a household income, and there was a desire for a higher standard of living and those 'extras' for the family that an additional income could bring.[255] A 1951 survey conducted by the sociologist Margot Jeffreys found that for some, the desire for a 'middle class way of life' led to the desire to remain in employment.[256] By 1951 women were making up 32% of the workforce in Britain and the number of women working in part-time posts had increased rapidly, much more so than in any other OECD country.[257] MacKay points out, however, that 85% of women doing paid work during the war had already been in paid employment before the war began, and that between 1939 and 1942 the number of women workers in civilian occupations increased from 4.8 million to 6.7 million, falling to 6.2 million by June 1945.[258]

Women were aware that their WWI counterparts had been dismissed from their jobs en masse and wanted to prevent this happening after the Second World War was over. In February 1942 the Woman Power Committee began to consider the question. They met the Deputy Prime Minister Clement Attlee in March 1943, requesting '(1) a declaration of the Government's policy on the position of women in the post-war world, (2) recognition of the right of women to a place in the machinery involved in planning reconstruction, and (3) the creation of a representative committee of women to advise on matters affecting women in the way that the employers' organisations were consulted on industrial matters'. Attlee's reply was that there were an adequate number of women being appointed to committees already. The TUC Women's Advisory Committee insisted that as a result of their participation in war work women had 'an equal right to employment after the war'. They called on the Government to accept its responsibility and ensure that all those employed on war work were 'assured of employment after the war'. By 1944 the Government felt that in the post-war years there would be a shortage of workers, rather than a shortage of jobs. Therefore, if women had to leave their job when their male counterpart returned, opportunities would be available for them. By January 1947, 58% of the women employed in the engineering industry in 1943 had been made redundant. In engineering women were paid more than those women in jobs which were considered to be 'women's work' and employers were under pressure from the AEU to remove women from men's jobs; their policy was to actively promote, as Harold Smith puts it, 'a clear demarcation between men's and women's' work'.[259] Robert Mackay states the case of one girl who had enjoyed working with machinery so much that she wanted to become an apprentice and progress. The response was clear. 'This of course is not possible on account of Union agreements. There's a feeling among the men at the moment women must be in the factory solely because of the war but that really women's place is in the home.'[260] One Trowbridge lady volunteered for the ATS and found after the war that she had no job to come back to. 'If you waited to be called up they kept your job for you, but because I'd volunteered I didn't have a job at County Hall to come back to... Jobs were scarce with all the men coming back as well.'[261]

Chippenham's Westinghouse Brake and Signal's brochure *Engineering as a Career*, 1946, stated the company's wartime record and policy of 'progressive development.' It also stated: 'It is realised, however, that if the position is to be maintained in the difficult years of the post-war period, a regular intake of trained personnel is essential, and the apprenticeship scheme described herein is designed to take care of this need.' What is also noticeable is the absence of any references to female apprentices, using only the term 'boys'; the idea appears not to have been given any consideration.[262]

Those mothers who worked were often condemned for their frivolity.[263] Dr John Bowlby's report for the World Health Organisation *Childcare and the Growth of Love* and excerpted by Penguin in 1953, theorised that children were harmed by separation from their mother. The theory gained supporters but the research had in fact been based on children who had been completely separated from their parents and housed in institutions as wartime evacuees; the dissimilarities were ignored. One expert of the day, Dr Ronald MacKeith, claimed that putting a young child in nursery 'may cause more lasting and irreparable damage to the child even than under-feeding it through poverty'. In his 1958 pamphlet *Can I Leave my Baby?* he argued that to leave a baby with anyone except its father or a close relative would cause severe damage. Delinquency became associated with a mother's absence, even if only for a short time. The Government sure-footedly followed this line of argument in the face of conflicting data.[264]

Undertaking part-time work was rare before the Second World War, but rose rapidly in the post-war world, quadrupling in the 1950s and 60s. Almost all were married women. Child-care was cheaper and easier to arrange on a part-time basis as the Government had restricted the number of nursery places available and also raised the cost.[265] Summerfield notes that the rise in part-time work for women in the post-war years was not surprising. It was attractive to employers who saved on bonuses, insurance and pensions. Another consequence was that it also reinforced the idea that women were 'inferior workers, working to supplement a male income, not as breadwinners in their own right'. To the industry and the unions this justified the case for lower wages for women.[266] Job opportunities for women had widened, but at the cost of financial downgrading.[267]

It is widely understood that the Government managed the movement of people and the wartime labour market effectively during the course of the war, but it is less clear if this labour was utilised as effectively in the production process.[268] Correlli Barnett has argued that the use of small, poorly equipped production units in aircraft production, coupled with poor technical education and shortages of production engineers severely restricted productivity,[269] but this theory in which he emphasised the potential of the unions and business to work with Government to direct resources has been criticised.[270] The war industry slowly began to release workers towards the end of 1944 and a drive to produce consumer goods for export began.[271] Ernest Bevin's work to raise wages, introduce staff canteens, sick rooms etc. meant that it would not be as easy to treat industrial workers as badly as it had been in pre war years.[272] It must be acknowledged, however, that disruption, delay and dislocation due to total war and the dilution and lack of skilled labour could not match productivity.[273]

The period of reconstructive planning from 1943-5 has been regarded as the best opportunity to face the fundamental problems of British industry and increase competitiveness but the chance was lost. No long term goals were set and there was little investment in new machinery, even though the Government was well aware of British industrial weakness.[274]

If the wartime industries of Britain were found wanting when it came to production processes, the sterling effort of the country's wartime workers and the difficulties they faced should not be forgotten. *Manpower*, produced by the Ministry of Labour, National Service and Ministry of Information in 1944 stated:

'We could never have survived at all if we had not mobilised our manpower, if the people had not been willing, and, indeed, eager, to grant the Government vast new compulsory powers, and if the Government had not been willing to accept so grand a responsibility...'[275]

5
Toil in the Fields

1930s Farming

BY THE EARLY 1930s, most of the food consumed in Britain was being cheaply imported,[1] with quotas having been negotiated and supplies from the colonies rising by nearly 50% between 1932 and 1939.[2] Britain was receiving into port 68 million tons a year with 22 million tons being made up of food.[3] By 1939, 70% of all food consumed in Britain was imported[4] and with technological advances in refrigeration came the import of meat alongside cereals.[5] In England, farm workers had been drifting away from agriculture[6] with a loss of 10,000 a year between the wars.[7] The Wiltshire writer and broadcaster Arthur George Street from Ditchampton noted: 'This trouble is not one which can be cured completely by farm wages being raised to the town level; for, money rewards apart, monotonous and laborious manual work of all kinds has become very distasteful to the modern generation… In spite of the increasing use of machinery farm work means a lot of manual work which cannot be dodged.'[8] Less than 4% of the British population worked on the land by 1938 and the acreage of arable land had reduced to two thirds of its 1801 level.[9] Low prices for agricultural goods resulted in this contraction of land up until the 1930s.[10]

In 1938 A. G. Street was reporting that farmers were sick of the 'doles, sops, and subsidies, and all the other special political treatment which their industry receives, and threaten to vote against the Government unless farming is treated on all fours with other industries of equal size and importance.' Farmers were currently in receipt of Government subsidies but were being forced to pay out more than they received in the form of tariffs on their purchases from town businesses. Street felt that one Wiltshire farmer had hit the nail on the head when he relayed a situation he had found himself in: The average milk-producer in Wiltshire kept an eighteen cow dairy herd and paid yearly tariffs on purchases to help other industries to the value of one cow. Their annual share of farming subsidies etc. only came to the value of a milk bucket. 'And I don't want their bloody bucket,' he shouted. 'It's an insult. I can buy all the buckets I require. But

I do want my cow back.'[11] Farmers of the inter-war period felt unable to take control of their problems to help themselves, and had to be more concerned with economic survival rather than raising output.[12] It had become more cost effective to import animal foodstuffs and keep livestock than to manage grassland effectively. This inter-war period saw the Minister of Agriculture feeling that '... It is ceasing to be farming at all and is becoming a matter of processing raw materials.' It was often the case that to farm well meant to lose money.[13]

However, the Agriculture Act of 1931 had transformed the agricultural sector.[14] It enabled the introduction of the Marketing Act of 1931 and the beginning of an organised practice of marketing produce. Marketing boards were set up, organising the sale of milk, hops and potatoes, and proved 'quite successful.'[15] By 1939 almost 40% of agricultural holdings had registered with the board as milk producers.[16] The North Wiltshire farmer L.J. Manners noted that farming was at a 'very low ebb' before the introduction of the Milk Marketing Board.[17] The Government only took a real interest in the lucrative crop of sugar beet at this time, sponsoring farms in East Anglia.[18] Manners felt that '[a]griculture was the poor relation until the country became involved in war. Then when imports were being cut off or sunk to the bottom of the sea it was realised too late that it had been allowed to fall into decay.'[19] Large tracts of land had become derelict and subsidies were helping milk production, but overall farming remained a depressed industry.[20] Street saw farmers complaining that they did not enjoy as high a standard of living as townsfolk, and that these very same townspeople were complaining that farming 'does not pay'; it was slow to adopt modern methods and was living in the past whilst town industries had progressed 'by leaps and bounds'. Street felt this view of farming was unfair, and that although progress in farming had been slower than that of industry over the last quarter of a century, it was in

The Hosier Milking Bail in Wiltshire (WSHC P41826)

fact thousands of years ahead, with industry yet to catch up.[21] One innovation had come into being; the Hosier milk production system, designed by A. J. Hosier, a farmer from Wexcombe in Wiltshire. For outdoor use, its introduction meant that cows could be kept outside in the winter. It provided a low cost, economically viable option, if a controversial one.[22] John Martin feels that farmers in the 1930s should not be criticised for their slow uptake of mechanisation. The operating costs of tractors were only low when using them for heavy work like ploughing, and over large areas. Many farms were small with already high overheads and also small fields which prohibited the use of combine harvesters.[23]

Wartime Changes

PLANS TO ACCELERATE agriculture to meet the demands of wartime had begun in the spring of 1938[24] but the intensification of these activities brought no real changes to the Ministry of Agriculture and Fisheries, except to move them into the territories of labour supply, price control and the control of agricultural operations.[25] William Morrison had been in charge at the Ministry of Agriculture but had been effectively demoted in April 1938, moved on to the Ministry of Food. Kevin Manton has noted that as Minister of Agriculture he had 'notably failed to prepare agriculture for war, arguing, like many others in Government, that war was not inevitable.'[26] The Ministry of Agriculture's stock of training films amounted to only 20 in 1938, many of which were outdated. It was the local press and radio which helped spread the much needed modern agricultural knowledge through publications like *Farmer's Weekly* and *Farmer and Stockbreeder.*[27] Morrison did formulate proposals for increasing soil productivity and the Land Fertility Committee was set up, offering farmers an assistance programme. They also emphasised the need to make it easier to clear minor watercourses, to introduce grants for drainage work to increase the tillage area and to produce plans to slow the pace of animal disease,[28] but the Government policy of the 1930s did not mobilise the industry; instead it only assisted a depressed one.[29] The ideas of the Land Fertility Committee were formalised by the 1937 Agriculture Act[30] and the work of the Milk Marketing Board had paved the way for the Ministry of Agriculture to set up wider controls in agricultural production as they had done to improve efficiency in marketing and distribution.[31]

There had been huge price rises in the cost of food towards the end of WWI and to stop a repeat if another war was to break out, the Committee of Imperial Defence recommended in 1933 that there be a 'peacetime creation' of an organisation to co-ordinate food control. These recommendations would be slow in coming, being approved by the Committee in May 1934 and accepted by the Board of Trade in 1935. A Food (Defence Plans) Sub-Committee was formed in March 1936 for planning and co-coordinating a rationing system in the event of war, but even then the Government was criticised for acting too slowly. Unsuccessful attempts were made in December 1936 and February and July 1938 to get the Government to begin stockpiling, but it was not until 1938 that the Essential Commodities (Reserves) Act was put into place; too little, too late.[32] Another lesson learnt from the Great War was that the responsibility for food control should be split between the Ministry of Food (distribution) and the Ministry of Agriculture (production). The Minister of Agriculture promised that '[t]here [would] be no farming from Whitehall this time. Instead both farmers' and allotment holders' efforts [were] being organised locally by committees of practical men who [knew] what [could] and [could not] be done in [their] town and village.'[33] During WWI there had been a reluctance amongst some landowners to adhere to the ploughing up campaign. The Government felt that additional greater powers would be needed, and at a local level if lessons were to be learned.[34] After war was declared, the Government decided to increase the country's arable land by over two million acres. Wiltshire's share would be 40,000 acres, about 10% of its existing grassland area.[35]

At first farmers were unsure what would happen to home production when a call-up took place. They expected it would wait until after the 1941 harvest, and guessed that the men who would be taken would be aged 20-30. Some farmers felt that all skilled farmworkers should remain in their jobs, whatever their age as 'it takes ten times longer to turn a novice into a passable farm worker than to turn the rawest recruit into a useful fighting man',[36] but the majority realised that Britain would need fighting men more than farming efficiency. Street, with great insight, felt that: 'Farmers should remember that our townsfolk, the same people who will have suffered most, both physically and financially, from enemy bombing during the war, are the people who will decide the agricultural policy of this country during the early years of peace. In my view an agriculture that has made no contribution of man-power to the services will receive and should receive little consideration at their hands.' Farmers sadly said goodbye to their workers, such as Street himself, who did as he'd been asked and 'wrangle[d] a vacancy for him into the Tank Corps. As a skilled tractor driver that was obviously the right place for him.'[37] By the end of 1942 all farmhands over 18 were called up.[38]

Yet another product of WWI was resurrected; the County War Agricultural Executive Committees (CWAECs). These 61 committees represented the Ministry to the farmers. The Chairman and Executive Officers of these committees had been designated in advance. When war was declared they established themselves and became operational very quickly. Their powers were imposed under the Cultivation of Lands Order and their recommendations to farmers had to be acted upon.[39] They were to oversee the Government's plan to put additional acres under plough,[40] known as the 'battle for wheat'.[41] A. G. Street noted in October 1939 that in his part of Wiltshire, as elsewhere in rural England, '... British farmers can be divided into five classes. One, those who are ploughing up grassland; two, those who are cultivating and sowing ploughed-up grassland; three, those who are talking about their intention to plough-up some grassland; four, those who are toiling and worrying on the local committees responsible for getting a certain acreage of grassland ploughed; and five, those who are objecting to any suggestions that they should plough up any of their grassland.'[42] By April 1940 the first target had been completed, with farmers ploughing by lamplight seven days a week, having been given special permission by the ARP authorities.[43] The farmer and member of the Wiltshire CWAEC Charles Whatley was reporting in *Country Life's* 20 April 1940 edition that: 'It is really amazing how little opposition there has been to this programme,' but was also reporting the abnormally cold weather conditions following the Christmas of 1939 which had put a temporary halt to the planned addition of 40,000 additional acres due to be put under plough in 1940. Other obstacles included labour shortages and competition for land by the army and air force.[44] By 1942, when imports were at their lowest, a further 3.5 million acres had been ploughed. Farmers went on to exceed their target for the year of 1942-3, producing a bumper harvest in 1943.[45] At Wilton it was noted that: 'It was a little short of a miracle that the harvest of 1942, worked by emergency staffs, and temporary staffs, and amateur staffs, should have been a "record" one... We have had the greatest harvest within the memory of man. And more.'[46] The Wiltshire National Farmer's Union's *Record* was noting in its August 1942 edition that '[i]n view of the demand on shipping for the transport of troops and war material, the Minister of Agriculture has told the Wiltshire War Agricultural Committee that they must find another 25,000-30,000 acres of grassland for the plough, and that the acreage of wheat in this country for the 1943 harvest must show an increase of 25 per cent, over the 1942 harvest. This means that we must plough a larger proportion of our better and heavier grass land. To make good the loss occasioned by the ploughing, our remaining grass land must be frequently dressed with Sulphate of Ammonia, so that two fields shall grow as much as three did formerly.'[47] It is interesting to note, however, that the cereal varieties in Britain hadn't changed since they were introduced in WWI.[48] In November 1942 Wiltshire National Farmer's Union's *Record* was setting out the Minister of Agriculture's expectation for Wiltshire for the 1944 harvest. '... to plough another 30,000 acres of grassland for the 1944 harvest and to keep up our stock and milk output. This can be done by sowing temporary grasses and clovers, by growing roots and kale, and by using Sulphate of Ammonia not only on your temporary grasses but on your permanent pastures.'[49] In November 1942 Charles Whatley who farmed at Burderop near Wroughton noted that the ploughing policy could 'be called success beyond expectation... But casting back to the autumn of 1939 it will be remembered that not a few men were very sceptical about these new orders to plough up land; perhaps the greatest fear of all being that of wireworm. Too many could recall the ravages caused by this pest during the first World War, when field after field was marked out as being a failure in all efforts to grow a cereal crop and in the end these fields were allowed to fall back to weeds and rubbish.' Government help meant that farmers could also improve drainage[51] and by 1944 Wiltshire's County Wartime Agricultural Committee's Chief Executive Officer W. T. Price was reporting that '[d]itching [was] the main activity and 150 water supplies [were] installed on farms.'[52] Forest in Wiltshire was also cut down to be put under plough.[53] The Ministry of Agriculture and Fisheries was promoting 'Better tillage for maximum crops' in the *Wiltshire Gazette*, 18 February 1943,

All out
for the
1943
Harvest

This is the most critical year in our history. Hitler still aims to sink our ships—to starve us out. You are fighting the "Battle of the Fields" to defeat him. Every possible ship that might bring us food must now carry tanks and planes and guns. Every extra acre of tillage crops you can grow in 1943 will help to release ships and bring the day of victory nearer.

★ THE NATION
   MUST HAVE BREAD
   — grow all the wheat and barley you possibly can

★ THE NATION
   MUST HAVE POTATOES
   — we can never have too many. They are your country's "iron rations"—an insurance against hunger and defeat.

★ THE NATION
   MUST HAVE MILK
   — it is vital for young children. Grow the crops needed to keep your herd in full production, especially next winter

These crops are vital. To make sure that the Nation gets enough of them we must plough up more grassland and increase the tillage area. Any of your grassland that is not essential to maintain your dairy herd—any seeds area that can go into the tillage pool—must grow these war-winning crops.

Play your part
in the
food production battle

ISSUED BY THE MINISTRY OF AGRICULTURE AND FISHERIES

through good cultivation, making time for ploughing and preparing the seed bed thoroughly.

The ploughing of grassland would inevitably have an impact on livestock, and the total destruction of the livestock industry would bring the traditional mixed farming culture to an end as well as jeopardize milk production.[54] In fact Wiltshire had seen an earlier attempt to cultivate crops on a large scale at Knighton Manor, Broad Chalke, in the early 1930s when Dr T. Croft Neville from London and Mr Scott, an Australian who had been stationed on Salisbury Plain in WWI, levelled three miles of hedges and made good over 150 acres of underproductive gorse-covered land to make 'a real mechanised farm, entirely self-contained...' The farm was transformed from mixed to purely arable, and in a good year such as 1938, it yielded up to sixteen sacks to the acre of wheat. The farmers had also experimented with treating their fields with nitrogenous substances, gaining a yield increase of over 30%.[55]

By 1943-4 there were more cows than before the war, but beef, veal, mutton and lamb were all below pre-war levels. Pig and poultry stocks were decimated.[56] In Wiltshire it was considered important to increase the number of sheep as it was essential to the fertility of the land. Price, the Chief Executive Officer of the County War Agricultural Executive Committee, also wanted to look into the use of commercial egg production on the farm with 'folded poultry units'.[57] The

The Ministry of Agriculture and Fisheries, encouraging farmers to play their part in the food production battle by going 'All out for the 1943 Harvest'. Printed in the 7 January 1943 edition of the Wiltshire Gazette (WSHC Microform Collection)

number of milking machines rose by 60% between 1942 and 1946. In 1943-4 the total area for crops had increased by 5,750,000 acres compared to the 1939 level. It must also be noted that this increase came at a time when land was being requisitioned for wartime activities such as aerodromes, camps and factories.[58] The military's need for land was frustrating Wiltshire's CWAEC. In an article for *Country Life*, 20 April 1940, the CWAEC member Charles Whatley was noting the military's presence in the county and the effect it was having on agriculture:

> The invasion of billeted troops in the county is a very disturbing factor... the most disturbing factor of all is the invasion of camp and aerodrome contractors; they seem to be lodged in every area of the county, and they do not hesitate to take men by motor lorry from every village. The poor farmer has not a hope of competing in wages... the labour difficulty is a very serious matter, but I am sure our farmers are meeting the situation bravely... One would have thought

EVERY FARM — A BETTER FARM

PLAN FOR PROTEIN FOR NEXT WINTER'S MILK

Milk is still Priority No. 1—especially winter milk. The output marketed so far this winter has been greater than ever before, despite difficulties. Have YOU played your part in this great performance? Winter milk demands protein. On many dairy farms protein is now very short. Act now, so that YOUR cows won't go short next winter.

● PEAS AND BEANS
are in a class by themselves for balancing up home-grown oats. Sow separately, if possible, or mixed with oats. Get in early — ½ acre mixed crop or ¼ acre each oats and legume per cow.

● KALE
—Grow enough to last into the new year —⅛th acre per cow. Kale + oat straw = hay. Sow early.

● SWEDES, MANGOLDS AND TURNIPS
¼ acre per cow is enough.

● GRASS
¼ acre per cow of new ley should be enough for grazing — the same for hay. 9 lb. good seeds hay produces a gallon of milk; so does 20 lb. good quality silage.

PLAN FOR A BALANCED WINTER RATION FOR YOUR HERD

If in doubt, consult your County War Committee

Maximising milk production included planning in advance, and adverts in newspapers such as the Salisbury Journal, 25 February 1944, promoted action sooner rather than later (WSHC Microform Collection)

that as Wiltshire has some 100,000 acres of land occupied by the Service departments, the county would be spared any further call for land on which to train the fighting Forces. The question is often asked: 'Why is it the Service departments, in selecting new sites for camps, aerodromes and landing grounds, will chose the best and most productive land?

He was also asking if the Labour Exchanges were operating effectively as the published unemployment figures stood at 27,555 in Great Britain in agriculture.[59]

This greatly enhanced acreage of ploughed land inevitably led to additional crop planting, which in many cases was very different from that which had been traditionally grown. Flax was one of the many crops imported before the war; only 4,000 acres were home-grown in 1939. There were anxieties that Britain would not have the capacity to grow enough to fulfil the need of the armed forces to make products such as canvas for parachutes and tents. Targets were set but many farmers were reluctant, not sure that it would be a worthwhile enterprise. Many did not have the expertise or equipment to feel they would be able to grow it successfully. It was also very labour intensive to harvest and would need to be done at the same time as potatoes, difficult when labour was limited. The majority of farmers had no choice but to grow the crops their CWAEC decided were best suited for their farm and each county had a quota to meet.[60] In Wiltshire flax had been re-introduced as a crop and the acreage had been sufficient to maintain a new factory which had been built in Devizes[61] for the Ministry of Supply.[62] The intake in 1943 was 6,000 tons of flax.[63] The playing field at the top of Whaddon, near Trowbridge, was covered with flax.[64] '... there were all these chequered colours [in the fields], and blue too because they grew a lot of flax.'[65] In Wiltshire flax production appears to have been successful. Scrub clearings in Savernake Forest, once home to grazing deer and rabbits, were transformed into '450a... producing excellent crops of cereals, flax and potatoes'.[66] The Mere Women's Land Army gang had managed to clear 45 acres of flax and were quickly working through the next 36 acres during one week. The farmer was 'well satisfied with their efforts.'[67] At Upavon a favourite job of some of the women and girls employed in the corn and flax fields was weeding. 'The flax fields were a pretty sight, like carpets of blue. When the flax was harvested it went to the local flax factory for processing into linseed oil etc. It was all very hard work and we suffered from stiff backs due to all the bending.'[68] With many farmers growing crops for the first time, advice was published for help to cope with diseases and pests. The May 1942 edition of the Wiltshire National Farmer's Union's *Record* was advising keeping a careful watch on flax crops for signs of attack by leatherjackets. To overcome the problem, the bran 'Paris Green' would need to be applied. If a flax field became infested with Charlock it would need to be sprayed. 'A careful watch should be kept on the crop to note any signs of disease or insect attack. Contact should be made with the entomologists and mycologists appointed in each area to investigate...'[69]

The *Wiltshire Times* was reporting on a successful enterprise at Westwood cross-roads on 22 July 1944:

[A] very handsome field of flax which is now under harvesting treatment by a number of very energetic maidens of the Land Army, and operations have been watched with much interest by those many people who take their walks in this direction.

Little more than a year ago this was a plantation of fir trees, and when the owner objected to the direction of the Wiltshire War Agricultural Committee that he should reclaim the land and put it under plough, the Committee requisitioned the field. Their action was criticised in some quarters on the grounds that it was a pity to spoil a rather prettily wooded area, and also that the crops which would be obtained from such land could hardly be worth while. The result shews how wrong were the critics, and that the land has produced material which is of much value to the War effort...

Country Life reported in its 3 November 1944 edition that flax was needed to produce canvas for tents and aeroplanes, and for parachutes in 'very large quantity,' increasing from 93,000 tonnes in 1943 to 124,000 in 1944; the better quality flax being used for netting. The article featured photographs of workers at Flax Mill, Devizes, owned by English Flax Limited. The mill took water from the Kennet & Avon Canal, bringing workers in from outlying villages by bus, and operating a 24 hour shift system.[70] At the factory which had been opened specifically for the war effort, the flax was stripped from the stalks, bundled and sent to another factory to be made into webbing for parachute harnesses.[71] In 1944 the Ministry of Agriculture was declaring that the expanded flax industry was one of the 'outstanding achievements' of the war.[72] An article by W. E. Barber in *Country Life*'s 3 November 1944 edition was considering the fact that like many wartime industries, flax was backed by Government finance. How would it fare in the post-war period? After the war it was realised that the Devizes flax factory had never applied to regularise its existence, the manager of the company stating that it had always been Crown property. By 1951 it was being seen as more of a nuisance than a necessity, the County Planning Officer writing that it was important that the future of this 'obnoxious industry' be settled as soon as possible.[73]

Sugar had been on the minds of the Government for some time; the Sugar Beet Act of 1925 had been intended to secure home grown supplies in the event of any import blockade. It was one of the few agricultural interwar interventions that had led to an increase in acreage of the crop. The 1923 acreage of *c.* 17,000 had reached 335,000 by 1938. This meant that by September 1939 Britain was well on its way towards sustaining the nation's 12oz weekly personal sugar ration.[74] Wiltshire had demonstrated that it had both the soil and climate to grow a 'heavy yield' of sugar beet, but its distance from the production factories limited its acreage in the county.[75]

However, the Wiltshire National Farmer's Union's *Record* was introducing a new crop in April 1942. 'Wiltshire will be growing during the coming year a promising acreage of peas – edible for drying.' It had been noted at the recent

Horticultural Conference held in Trowbridge that it looked less likely that peas would be rationed the following year due to Wiltshire farmers 'growing this highly important crop; they will do so with the interest which a new crop always stimulates.' Crouch & Sons of Teffont Magna had already been successfully growing 'considerable acreages' for several years, and were sharing their knowledge to help other Wiltshire farmers do the same.[76]

W. T. Price, the Chief Executive Officer of Wiltshire's CWAEC, noted that before the war Malmesbury Common contained '500 acres of heavy, clay land... partially derelict, falling down to weedy pasture and scrub...' but was now 'carrying good crops, mainly beans, wheat and leys, while straw is fed back to cattle in straw yards.'[77] It appears that that the greyhound track in Salisbury was dug up for agriculture during the war, and no unlicensed greyhound tracks could be found in the city by 1947.[78] The Marlborough Downs near Beckhampton were ploughed up for barley with the help of US Army Engineers. At 160a it was purported to be the largest field in England under a single crop.[79] To complete this feat, mechanisation was essential and the Government had in place a contract with Ford which would meet demand. The number of tractors had risen from 56,000 in 1939 to 203,000 in January 1946[80] meaning that by 1946 the number of farmers owning a tractor had quadrupled (in 1939 the number was one in six).[81] Wiltshire had already been pioneering agricultural mechanisation; one of the first combine harvesters in the country came to a Wiltshire farm. It was towed by a crawler tractor and driven by a farmer who had been a tank driver in WWI. Published in a book by Sir Daniel Hall in 1939 was an essay which looked at the costs of running a tractor compared to horses. At the end of the essay a question was posed – would the running costs of a tractor make it an economically viable proposition? An answer was not even attempted as the effectiveness and versatility of the tractor was not seen to be fully proven at that time.[82] In April 1940 Wiltshire's CWAEC had listed 1,487 tractors working in the county.[83] By March 1941 the farmer at Draycot House was feeling that tractors should be hired from depots when the war came to an end to enable them to meet 'world competition'.[84] Whatley, a Wiltshire CWAEC member and farmer at Burderop near Wroughton later noted: 'Farmers began to see that modern machinery could tackle problems which hitherto seemed insoluble. Clay soils which baffled the horse plough in days gone by responded to the caterpillar tractor pulling a modern plough...'[85] In June 1942 the Ministry of Agriculture and Fisheries was writing to Richard Stratton, Chairman of the Wiltshire War Agricultural Executive Committee about the demands that were likely to be made for the following year. The spring crops were in review. 'Wheat and other crops for human consumption... must have priority over the requirements of livestock except for those of the dairy herd'. They realised the programme would involve a heavy 'call' on tractor power and they were doing their best to obtain tractors from the U.S.[86] The Ministry of Agriculture was allowed to buy and store between 3,000 and 5,000 tractors and the only viable option was to ask the Ford Motor Co. to fulfil the order, but there were problems with the Fordson tractors. Being 10 years out of date, they were notoriously awkward to work and used 60% more fuel than other makes.[87] If farmers needed help to keep their unreliable tractors fully functional, they could look no further than their local Ford dealer. H. C. Preater Ltd. of Swindon who was advertising his services in the *Herald and Advertiser* on 15 October 1943. 'Keep your tractors fighting fit…The Fordson tractor is the farmer's greatest asset…' In Wiltshire, Charles Whatley was reporting in April 1940 that combine harvesters were already at work in some parts of the county with more to follow.[88] Price noted in his report *War-time Farming in Wiltshire*, 1944 (printed in the Ministry of Agriculture Journal) that the average size of Wiltshire's holdings was greater than any other county. Many were over 300 acres and some farms in the chalk region to the south reached 600-800 acres. This meant that mechanisation was an easier prospect and it was developed 'to a high degree.'[89] Mr Crouch had proved this at Manor Farm, Teffont, in 1931, one of the first to use the newly imported combine harvester.[90] From 1940-1945 there was a rapid increase in the mechanisation and state control of agriculture. Street noted there had been a 'national admission that half the Battle of the Atlantic was being fought and won on the fields of farming Britain.'[91] The speed and intensity of modernisation during the war might well have taken decades in peacetime.[92]

Fertilizers were being advocated by the CWAECs as being very favourable, and their scarcity due to rationing restrictions helped convince farmers they were worth investing in. As Angus Calder notes: 'Agricultural science had put its foot in the door'.[93] They were imported from countries as far afield as Canada, Russia, Palestine and the US. Chemical companies were jumping on the bandwagon, as an advert in the 25 February 1944 edition of *Salisbury Journal* shows with ICI appraising farmers of the fact that: 'There can be no fertility without lime, which is constantly being lost from the soil in drainage water… The need for lime is a question of degree. Potatoes are one of the few crops that grow well on a fairly acid soil while sugar beet, barley beans and red-clover love lime.' The article goes on to explain other ways in which lime improves the land and how it was 'vital to animals.' It concluded by stating that 'more than half of the farm land in Great Britain would benefit by discriminate dressings of lime. There is plenty of scope for improving fertility.' Farmers doubled their use of nitrogen and phosphate fertilizers during the war and also significantly increased their use of potash and lime.[94] In Wiltshire, Aberystwyth grass was being used for re-seeding grassland to maintain soil fertility.[95]

The 1943 harvest in Wiltshire hit an all time record and by 1944 a further 30,000 acres were under the plough. Price relayed that it was achieved by the 'raising of the general level of farming, by the introduction of improved methods of cultivation, the scientific use of fertilisers and the use of improved strains of crops.' New farming techniques also got the most out of the land all year round. 'Emphasis has been laid on the need for adequate and well-planned water furrows on those heavy lands that are sown with winter corn.'[96] The county of Wiltshire had concentrated its efforts on milk and bread, also trying to make every farm self supporting as the Ministry's policy stated. The harvest of 1943 had compared very

favourably to that of 1939:-
- acreage of bread-corn (wheat, barley, rye) up by 2.5 times
- potato acreage increased sixfold[97]

1943 produced a bumper crop of wheat, and the country's potato production had risen by an amazing 87%. This was not the best of news, however, as the Government had encouraged over production and although potatoes were now plentiful, British civilians did not want to replace bread with potatoes. The success of the 1943 crop was mostly due to extending the utilisation of land for crops and the climate that year had been agreeable. The labour input and acreage had increased, but there had been little improvement in yield; the land had not become more productive.[98]

During the war Wiltshire was one of many counties making silage. Charles Whatley noted that: 'Ensilage making was never very popular before the war, perhaps because the science to make it good and therefore valuable was little known. To make it as our fathers of old did it, involved a lot of hard work, generally ending in a stinking mass which no one liked handling and in the end hauled out as manure. However, in the war days it again came to the fore. Better tackle for cutting and carting, movable silos in which to store the young and succulent grass, this scientific way of making it proved it to be a valuable product for producing milk.'[99] Street reported that he had turned to making his first batch of silage in the autumn of 1939. He realised that most farmers disliked making silage as 'a sinful waste of good stuff' which they felt their cows definitely would not eat, but which they did 'with relish!'[100]

During the war, the pay of arable farmers jumped, by 1942 reaching an increase of 207%. Many felt that this increase reflected the fact that farmers were doing more than a little too well in their new position of importance, and had been as Calder notes, 'coddled by the state' before the war. But whilst farmers' wages were rising, guaranteed prices for their products was causing discontent. In 1942 there were complaints when a wartime price review failed to cover a pay increase for farm workers, and more protests when it happened again the following year.[101] The *Wiltshire Times* was reporting in its 29 July 1944 edition that the Codford Branch of the Agricultural Workers' Union had passed the following resolution. 'That this branch gives full support to the workers' representatives on the Central Agricultural Wages Board in their claim for a national minimum wage for £4 10s. per week, and urges the Board to fix this new rate without delay in order to raise the agricultural worker to the level of the town worker.' The Government made concessions whilst reassuring the critics that guaranteed prices would remain until the summer of 1948[102] and continued its policy of price subsidies to keep the cost of living steady, with additional measures used such as grants to influence food production.[103] By September 1945 the issue of wages was being brought up at a meeting of the National Union of Agriculture and Allied Workers Local Committee (Devizes) to ask that 'representations of the wages board be asked to press for £4 10s. per week and all Bank Holidays with pay, also double time for Sunday, & Saturday afternoons & time and a half for overtime from Mon: Friday.'[104]

At the outbreak of war the average wage for a farm worker was less than half the average wage for unskilled labour in other occupations.[105] By 1940 many farm workers were lured into higher paid construction jobs and a Restriction on Engagements Order was needed to keep farm workers on the land. Unfortunately it was too slow in coming, and those who had wanted to go had already left. The agricultural wages board established a national minimum wage to try to tempt workers back, but despite rises they were still lower than in the industrial sector.[106] Lady Denman battled to get a minimum wage of 28 shillings a week for the Women's Land Army (WLA). There was never any doubt that equal pay would not be achieved. It was inconceivable at that time when it was perceived that a girl could not work as hard as a man. Many girls had to take a pay cut when they joined the Land Army and could often struggle to find the payment for their billets. With Lady Denman's hard work and perseverance wages did increase. '… she should be paid a weekly wage of not less than 32s. if she is 18 or over for a working week of up to 48 hours, with a minimum overtime rate of 8d. per hour…' Members of the Women's Timber Corps were paid 45 shillings a week at this time as it was regarded as skilled work. Pay rates rose again in 1943, rising to 40s 6d increasing to 45s after a month. The male rate also increased to 63s and by 1944 the rate for WLA members had become 48s.[107]

Wartime Agricultural Control

A. G. STREET saw the need for the control of farming, both during and after the war. He felt it would take the enjoyment out of farming but was necessary. 'The day is gone for ever when the self-interest of any individual can be allowed to farm one foot of the land of his own country, no matter whether that individual be landlord, farmer, or farm worker, speculative builder, town trespasser or any other.'[108] Farmers were told what to grow, how to sell it and for how much. In the eyes of the Government they were 'trustees for the nation' and the land that they farmed needed to be 'at the full disposal of the Government to be used in the way that is best for the war effort.' The Ministry of Information claimed that the CWAECs were arguably the 'most successful example of decentralization and the most democratic use of 'control' this war has produced'.[109] The War Agricultural Committees (CWAECs) were set up in 1936 at a county level.[110] They were made up of eight to ten men, including an agricultural trade unionist, and later a representative of the Women's' Land Army. These members, appointed by the Minister, would issue responsibility to the District Committees which consisted of four to seven local residents.[111] It appears that even Parish Councils came under the control of the War Ags. The Bromham Parish Council Minute Book in November 1939 included correspondence from the Wiltshire War Agricultural Executive Committee who had recently inspected their allotments. They were ordered to get all waste land under cultivation. There was also correspondence regarding the ploughing of grassland in July 1943.[112] The Government's system of using a small number of Civil Servants attending daily Committees and taking current attitudes back to their departments developed a corporate thought which was more instantaneous than minuted decisions. The decisions and targets were then transmitted downwards via the War Ags.,[113] but the advice from the CWAECs could often lack both a quality and understanding of local conditions.[114] Although the system looked to be run at a local level, John Martin feels this was not true in practice as most of the power was held by the main CWAECs and their Chief Executive Officers[115] who conducted an administrative role, offering technical advice and giving out sanctions.[116] The majority of farmers and representatives on the District Committees had virtually no way of directly influencing the Ministry of Agriculture.[117] In Wiltshire, the Chairman of the CWAEC was Richard Stratton, a farmer from Kingston Deverill who had appeared in *Farmer's Weekly* and the *Successful Farming* series of 1937. His Chief Executive Officer W. T. Price had been Wiltshire County Council's County Organiser before the war.[118] Charles Whatley, a member of the Wiltshire War Agricultural Executive Committee noted in April 1940 that: 'Like other counties, we have our Executive Committee, but their task has been much lightened by the fact that local knowledge is scheduling the land to be broken up. This wise provision in the national campaign has saved unsuitable land from the plough and avoided the mistakes inevitable in too centralised organisations.'[119]

Committee members visited their allotted *c.* 50 farms regularly to give instruction or advice. All worked in a voluntary capacity and were resident in the county they worked in. Each had the power to dispossess a farmer of their land if they did not adhere to the directions given to them. They could also allocate farm labour, machinery, fertilizer and feeding stuffs. This system worked successfully in the main, with quotas for principal crops worked out by County, District, and at Parish Committee level.[120] The receptiveness of the farming community could sometimes be found wanting, however. Many remembered 'The Great Betrayal' and were suspicious of Government intervention.[121] The Great Betrayal occurred soon after the end of WWI. The Government had been set to guarantee prices for corn for the next five years in the Agriculture Act 1920, but instead decided to repeal the legislation in 1921 to relieve the Exchequer of the cost. The four-year notice clause put into the Agriculture Act was abandoned.[122] In the early days of WWII Peter Ginn notes that '[t]ales of ministry men requesting farmers to grow alien crops unsuited to the soil without providing them with the equipment and the know-how to do so were common, and it is clear that in places this most unlikely of relationships struggled in its early days,' but communication did improve.[123] A newspaper article in the *Wiltshire Times*, 21 October 1939, reveals that making sense of these orders could be a way to promote agricultural publications, focusing on a farmer's concerns. 'Not the least of the farmers' war-time difficulties is the interpretation of the many emergency orders which continue to come 'like a snowstorm from Whitehall.' There are penalties for disregarding orders, and in legal matters ignorance is no excuse… No paper is so well qualified to help in these matters as 'The Farmer and Stock-Breeder…'" In Wiltshire, Price was noting in *c.* 1944 that '[i]n many instances before a suitable system of alternate husbandry can be introduced the installation of an adequate water supply and a considerable amount of fencing will be necessary.'[124]

In May 1940[125] the Committees were also asked by the Government to compile in 1941-3 what can be described as a 20th century Domesday Book; a National Farm Survey with every farm being visited and notes taken on soil type, the state of the buildings etc. and more.[126] The aim was to inform the Government of the current situation to improve efficiency where possible.[127] The survey would include three aims:

the completion of a 'Primary Farm Record' for each farm, with information on the conditions of tenure, occupation, natural state and fertility of the farm, adequacy of its equipment, water and electricity supplies, and the management of it.

A census to be completed on 4 June 1941 giving crop acreages, livestock numbers, information on rent and occupancy.

Plan of the farm to include its extent and field boundaries.[128]

Farms were graded A, B, or C 'according to merit.' Only one farm out of 20 got a C grading, meaning they were achieving only 60% of maximum production on their land.[129] The Survey also included a section on how likely the farmer was to embrace any changes, adopt new technologies and support the Ministry in its aims.[130] For those farmers who received a C rating, they would be either overwhelmed with offers to help, or dispossessed of their land. The Farmers' Rights Association (FRA) was set up after the sad case of the Hampshire farmer Walden, who barricaded himself into his farmhouse and shot police officers who were attempting to break in. He in turn was shot down and killed.[131] The National Farmer's Union called Hampshire's policy 'vindictive', dispossessing many farmers.[132] The FRA reported cases of real or apparent corruption by CWAEC members, and the fact that the only form of appeal was to the CWAEC itself was an issue.[133] During WWI farmers had the right to use the Law Courts to address their grievances toward the local committees, but this was not to be the case in WWII.[134] The Farmers' Rights Association did raise the issue of the legal position when dispossessing farmers but the organisation was only a small one, and was not taken seriously. There may have been many farmers who quit their farms voluntarily rather than face dispossession.[135]

The National Farm Survey records are kept at The National Archives, Kew. Wiltshire County Council had been conducting farm inspections since 1938, using notebooks to report on each farm. By 1940 details included the name of the farm, the owner and tenant, a description of all buildings and stock and the inspector's evaluation. These evaluations ranged from glowing, as at the Draycot [Cerne] Estate in May 1941. 'An energetic young tenant who is 'driving' his holding, using a lot of artificial manure to advantage. Every ground has been improved since he moved in two years ago' to the damning, as at a farm near Lyneham in November 1940. 'Not the best of holding nor the best of tenants. There is an undue proportion of lands which are not in the best order... the land is foul with couch... the buildings are rather untidy and the holding is rather worse off for buildings both in quality

& equipment than those adjoining. The house is awkward & the larder useless; one bedroom has plain brick walling! Poor looking cattle. The wife has the money & the man has no interest or pride in the holding.'[136] It is unclear whether these Wiltshire surveys formed the basis for the National Farm Surveys, but the 'primary survey' of 1941 included a visit to the farm and an interview with the farmer.[137]

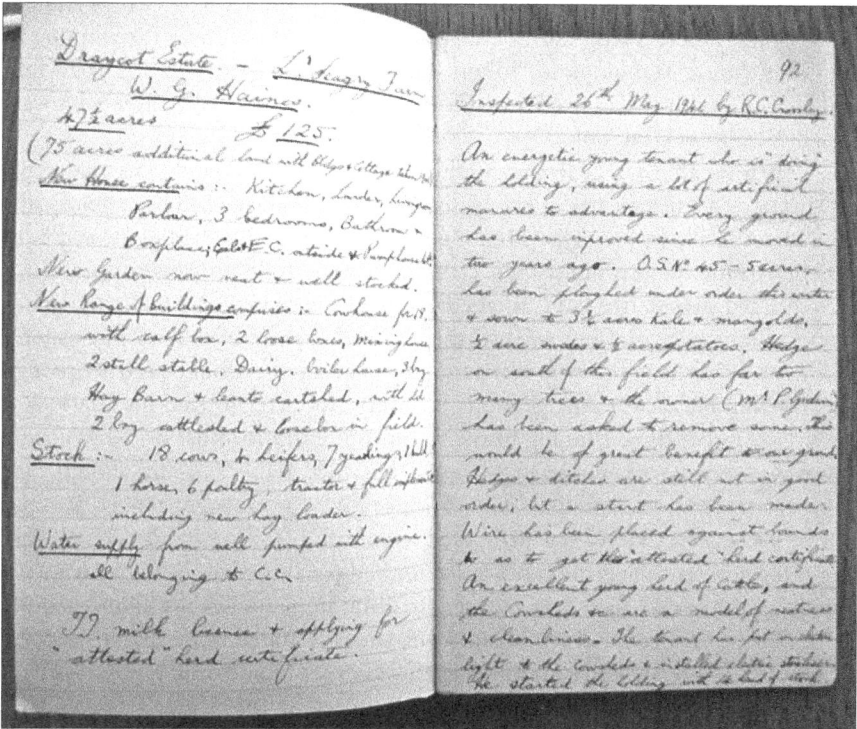

Entry in the Farm Inspection Book: North Western District for a farm in Lower Seagry, inspected 26 May 1941 (WSA F9/150/4)

The Farmers' Rights Association felt that 'standards of assessment varied considerably between one county and another;' they were also subjective, dependent on the view of Committee members. It appears that the National Farm Survey self-fulfilled the view that small farms were not efficient, figures pointing to a strong correlation between the size of holding and the grade allocated.[138] Charles Vernon states that many farmers disagreed with the demands of the Wiltshire War Agricultural Executive Committee and that Malmesbury farmers' cases were heard in the town in June 1940 for failure to cultivate land. One farmer's defence was that he would have had to 'sell a proportion of his young stock which would not aid the country, also the land was heavy and the season too far advanced.' Another said that he did not have enough labour and it was too late for planting. All were found guilty, being fined £2 each. The Malmesbury branch of the NFU was criticising the Wiltshire War Agricultural Executive Committee in May 1941 after they had given a farmer only six days notice to quit his holding due to it being under-productive. The farmer's landlord had never complained about his tenant during his 35 year tenure; the Committee had refused him a hearing.[139] CWAECs were accused of being corrupt, with cases of innocent farmers being turned out of farms so that the friends or relatives of CWAEC members could move in and avoid conscription.[140] The 1946 court case between the farmers George Odlum and George Hudson (the wartime Minister of Agriculture) over the running of Manor Farm at Manningford Bohun during the war illustrated the behaviour of CWAECs with their unequal treatment of farmers, especially those who were progressive in their outlook.[141]

Before the war George Odlum was nationally and internationally acclaimed as a dairy farmer.[142] His pedigree herd of Friesians had been genetically bred scientifically by genotype to produce high yields and he had pioneered both genetic selection and produced a successful strategy to limit disease to produce a rare certified disease free herd. By the late 1930s his cows were producing 2,000-3,000 gallons per year compared to the national average of only *c.* 400 gallons. Odlum realised that the new wartime policy meant he would need to plough up an additional acre of forage crops for every two acres to feed his livestock if he wished to continue running his herd, but not every member of the Wiltshire CWAEC agreed with his strategy. Some felt that arable farming should take priority over livestock, and that Odlum's innovative way of silage producing would not be successful. Odlum was hampered with both his silage and forage schemes being forbidden. Facing the prospect of limited feed supplies for his herd[143] (the supply of imported feed was reduced to minimum levels),[144] Odlum had no choice but to reduce the size of his herd in 1940, although ironically in 1942 the Wiltshire CWAEC would be producing an Order for him to milk more cows than he would then hold.[145] Odlum sold the farm in 1942[146] to George Hudson, who would set a precedent and become the first Agriculture Minister to run a farm of his own and who is known to have co-ordinated organisation and publicity in his Department to ensure that farmers utilised as much land as possible for food production.[147] Wiltshire's CWAEC were much more lenient with Hudson than they had been with his predecessor,[148] and during a tour of Manor Farm, organised and conducted by Wiltshire's Chief Executive Officer W. T. Price for the benefit of journalists and the BBC, it was stated that Hudson had much improved the farm which had been in a 'very poor condition but is now showing excellent crops.' George Odlum was outraged by this libellous allegation and through his solicitor began legal proceedings to clear his name. Price had made the statement, but it was the Wiltshire CWAECs Chairman Richard Stratton who took responsibility,[149] with the Ministry of Agriculture picking up the bill. The judge vindicated Odlum; Hudson had received special treatment from Wiltshire's CWAEC which included the ability to increase his area of forage even though the policy was out of kilter at both a national and local level. Odlum was awarded £500 damages, a much larger sum than was usually awarded and which reflected the 'seriousness of the accusations.'[150] It is interesting to note that the judge was not able to see the results of the National Farm Survey as they were classed as 'confidential state documents,' but which would have revealed Odlum's farm receiving an A grade.[151] Stratton resigned not long after the verdict was announced but Price remained untarnished with the Minister of Agriculture Tom Williams's continued trust in his integrity. He continued to present lectures for the BBC. The impact on Hudson's long-term career was also short-lived and he continued his farming interests in Wiltshire.[152]

The National Farm Survey was regarded as possibly the most innovative of the Government's measures to improve agricultural output[153] and interestingly a survey of this type had been considered before the war, but was decided against as being too 'Socialist or Germanic'.[154] Wartime agricultural control was absolute.[155]

Rural Conditions

PROPERTY WAS AT a premium in wartime Britain,[156] including that for agricultural workers, already often burdened with primitive housing conditions.[157] The Government had given special permission to build 2,000 new agricultural cottages in 1943, but in fact only 600 were built.[158] A letter sent by the Rural District Councils' Association to the Bradford & Melksham Rural District Council relayed the detail of the issue on 4 February 1943:

> Agricultural Housing
> Following a question put by Sir Percy Hurd, M.P., President of the Association, in the House of Commons to the Minister of Health today, you will be receiving a communication from the Minister on the policy adopted by the Government to meet the urgent need of more houses for agricultural workers...
>
> The matter is of extreme urgency and you will appreciate that upon the manner in which individual rural district councils perform their task, the competence of such councils in the future structure of Local Government may be judged...[159]

In Wiltshire the Local Authorities were trying to act. A survey carried out by Wiltshire's CWAEC highlighted the lack of sufficient housing for workers. This housing was necessary to implement the Ministry's proposals.[160] The Clerk of Bradford & Melksham Rural District Council was writing to one of its tenants on 1 March 1943, giving him notice to quit his tenancy on 3 April. 'The Minister of Health has decided that the needs of war-time food production call for the urgent erection of a number of houses, and my Council have been requested to build some of them.' The Council had decided to use sites it already owned, including one at Bradford Road, Winsley, which the tenant was currently renting. 'My Council regret having to upset your tenancy this way, but you will see that they have no option in the matter.'[161] The Wiltshire Branch of the Rural District Councils' Association was giving advice on how and where the properties should be located: to build in blocks of four for economy of labour and ease of sewerage etc. (the County Executive Committee had requested blocks of two); to remember that the supply of timber would be limited; it was most important that the houses be sited near a main water supply, even if this meant they would have to be built away from the farm itself; an electric supply would be desirable and easy access to village shops, school, church etc. should be considered.[162] On 27 October 1943 Malmesbury Rural District Council had decided on the rent it would charge on the eight new 'parlour type houses' that were being built at Burton Hill, Charlton, Foxley and Minety, setting the amount at 10/- per week exclusive of rates. A newspaper advertisement was inviting applications via a CWAEC form and by February 1944 the council was receiving applicants for the houses: their age, agricultural occupation, the number of children they had (if applicable) and details of their employer. The Wiltshire CWAEC was also nominating tenants. Included in the paperwork were details of the 37 agricultural workers who were currently residing in council houses in villages throughout the locality.[163] By 29 October 1945 the Wiltshire Federation of Women's Institutes had made a resolution '[t]hat this meeting urges the County Council to press for an extension of the grant available under the Rural Workers' Housing Act, so as to enable more Rural cottages to be re-conditioned.'[164]

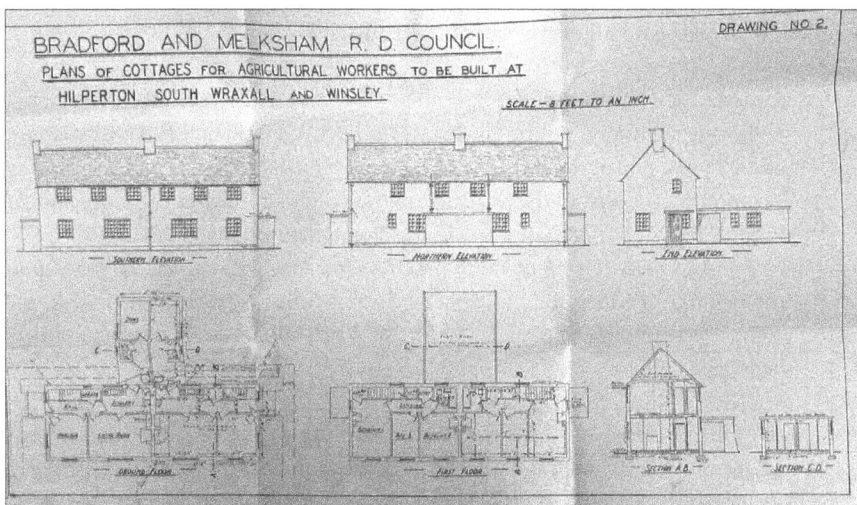

Architectural Plans for proposed agricultural workers' cottages in Hilperton, South Wraxall and Winsley, scale 8ft to 1' c. 1943 (WSA G2/132/37)

Rural water supplies were often inadequate. A report of November 1941 found in the Bradford & Melksham Rural District Council Clerk's Correspondence files shows the water supply to Monkton Farleigh was not satisfactory for the main portion of the village. The council had been asked to erect houses for agricultural workers but was unable to do so because of the poor water supply.[165]

Foot and mouth disease reared its ugly head in Wiltshire during the war. An early outbreak in January 1939 had caused restricted movement of livestock and it happened again in November 1940, lasting longer because of illegal movement.[166]

An evacuee, Malcolm Martin, remembers how it ravished the Staverton area. There were 'fires of cattle carcasses, burial pits and the need to sterilize shoes.'[167] In Freshford on the Somerset/Wiltshire border it came closer and closer for the first time in 25 years. A whole herd was slaughtered and the smell of disinfectant filled the air.[168] Local people felt for the farmers; it took great time and effort to establish and maintain a herd of cows and they knew how much they meant.[169] Foot and mouth had broken out in Biddestone again in December 1942. The Chippenham doctor Joan Hickson was noting in her diary entry that it was 'in a farm that had it before and ha[d] evidently been allowed to restock too quickly. Many curses because Xmas markets and other movement of animals have been stopped. I thought Devizes looked less crowded than usual but didn't realise why till later.'[170] In September 1942 foot and mouth cases were occurring in Chippenham, Swindon and Trowbridge, affecting cattle, sheep, pigs and even one goat. It was being reported on 25 September 1942 in the Minutes of Wiltshire Council's Diseases of Animals Sub-Committee that the recent outbreak in West Wiltshire and North Somerset had been reaching 'serious proportions,' not helped by the delay in obtaining mechanical excavators and additional labour for the burial of carcasses, causing delays of up to a week. The farmers had been highly appreciative of the help received from the Ministry of Agriculture's Veterinary Inspectors and the Police. It was not just foot and mouth that was affecting livestock in the 1940s; cases of swine fever and anthrax were also being reported.[171]

Extensive damage done by military traffic to unclassified roads made them impassable for farmers, limiting the productive working of farms. In March 1941 Wiltshire County Council's Clerk was writing to the Secretary of Transport about the issue.[172] Many anti-tank ditches were cut. They were V shaped and zigzag in style, often up to 9ft deep and 18ft wide. The ditches hampered agricultural workings, disrupting agricultural life in Bemerton. They had commonly been filled in before the end of the war.[173] The Warminster Branch of the NFU were discussing damage done by the military in 1943, and advising that it should be reported immediately by notifying the authorities at Seend Green House, Melksham. This also included damage to land that had been requisitioned. One farmer was already making a claim in 1944 against the US Army regarding one of his farm workers who had been knocked off his bicycle. The Home Guard were also causing problems for one farmer near Warminster in July 1944 when gas was used during an exercise. It caused 'great inconvenience and illness to persons and livestock…' After a discussion at the Warminster NFU Branch August meeting the farmer was advised to send in a claim for damages.[174]

Lend a Hand on the Land

MORE WORKERS WERE needed on the land and some old hands came back to aid the war effort. A. G. Street remarked in his diary on 20 September 1939: 'What a satisfactory job ploughing is! … I have not personally ploughed a furrow since 1928, but I find that I have not forgotten my old skill.'[175] By March

1940 agricultural workers had been reduced with over 30,000 men increasing the ranks of the army and 15-20,000 to other occupations such as labourers constructing camps and factories.[176] Retired farm workers were brought back into service, such as the old age pensioner with his scythe that Street required to help cut an area of barley that the tractor could not reach. He proudly announced whilst completing the job: 'Whenever there be a job on thease varm wot none o' yer machines ner none o' yer young men kin tackle, 'tis I got to do it. An' wots more, I can.'[177] The Land Girls discovered at Fyfield that '[t]here was an old, old man who used to stand and say, "By four o'clock this afternoon it'll be raining" and we learned to recognise the signs ourselves.'[178] A Restriction Order had already been put into place in June 1940 due to a shortage of workers[179] and in 1941 agricultural work came under an Essential Work Order which put an end to the movement of agricultural workers to alternative occupations.[180] This Order was used to turn unemployed agricultural workers into CWAEC employees which would effectively prevent them from leaving their employment[181] but many more workers were now needed to increase production. By 1940 it was already estimated that there was a shortfall of 50,000 agricultural workers.[182]

Wartime labour shortages in the agricultural sector took their toll. The *Wiltshire Times* was reporting as early as 7 September 1939 that soldiers were needed to help with the harvest. They needed volunteers as 'necessary staff ha[d] been depleted through military service.' Soldiers were helping to bring in a harvest near Warminster. 'We had some help to gather in the corn. They brought three army lorries with them to load the corn on to.'[183] Evacuees were among those children called upon to help with the harvest and longer holidays were used to enable this to happen. Niko Gärtner feels that in this way the war 'was used to undermine and sabotage school attendance... turning a blind eye on abuses of the Children and Young Persons Act.'[184] However, A. G. Street noted that at the National Union of Agricultural Workers Biennial Conference in Bournemouth in the early 1940s there was complete agreement to do all that was possible to increase food production, viewing food to be one of the 'major munitions' but that there was opposition over the proposal to employ school-aged under 14s on the land, the reason being worry over the slipping of educational rights for children. '[T]he farm worker is opposed to any attempt to take from his children the smallest amount of educational rights for which his long-suffering fathers and grandfathers and great-grandfathers fought so hard and long.' It was felt that the new regulations must be tight enough to prevent exploitation. Street, attending the conference, felt that '...this year's cropping and harvesting boils down to this. With a lot of machinery a few skilled experts have planted the crops, but the weight of the produce to be harvested will need many more hands.' Children would be needed to help; for each potato that was planted, around a dozen would need to be harvested.[185] By September 1941 the Deputy Director of Education in Wiltshire was reminding Heads of secondary schools that: 'Local Education Authorities have been asked by the Board of Education to give every possible facility in releasing children of over 14 years of age to help in gathering the harvest. It has been suggested that local farmers should get into touch with heads in regard to this.'[186] On 30 March 1944 Swindon's Education Committee was holding a meeting regarding the employment of schoolchildren in agriculture. It was decided that the children should assist with summer harvest work in accordance with the Board of Education's Administrative Memorandum 52. It was reported that 'On Wednesday 13th September a telephone message was received by the Director from the Chief Labour Officer, Wilts. War Agricultural Executive Committee at Trowbridge asking for school parties to assist in potato-picking at Clench Common, Marlborough. Owing to the general late harvest it was impossible to cope with the work without extra labour. Seventy-five acres of potatoes were urgently needed for current consumption and the W.W.A.E.C. were prepared to provide transport for parties of school children in the event of their being willing to help. A party of 35-40 children was needed for approximately 3 hours each morning and another party for the same period each afternoon.' With the agreement of the parents a Scheme was put into place the following Monday. Ten schools sent working parties over the coming five weeks, each party being accompanied by a teacher. It was reported that the work was carried out 'smoothly'. It was also noted that due to local bye-laws governing the employment of children, only boys aged 13 years or over could join a party, and even then only those boys who had the correct clothes and boots could take part. 'It was made quite clear that regular school attendance would have to be maintained. No school party worked more than three half-days in any one week.' The rate paid by the Wiltshire CWAEC to under 14s was 5d. per hour but this was negotiated up to 6d. plus an extra 6d. to cover travelling time. It was noted that each boy received 2s. for his three hours work. As well as Clench Common, the boys also worked at Clench Farm, Marlborough, Manor Farm, Broad Hinton and Penhill Farm, Blunsdon with the approximate weight of potatoes harvested reaching 320 tons. It was noted that '[e]veryone concerned, W.W.A.E.C. officials and farmers, teaching staff and boys, entered into the scheme whole-heartedly; and if the enthusiasm of the latter waned a little towards the end of the period it was largely the fault of the weather.'[187]

Wiltshire County Council's Education Department was putting into place personal accident insurance for children working on farms, highlighted after the case of Camkin v Bishop, the father of a Warwickshire boy suing the school's Head Teacher for damages over personal injuries he felt were caused by the negligence of said Head Teacher. A report of the Court of Appeal was given in *The Times* on 4 July 1941 and '[t]he question raised by the case was the nature and degree of the responsibility of the headmaster of a school in respect of boys who were permitted to help a farmer on a half-holiday or in their free time.' The Head Teacher of Bishop Wordsworth's School in Salisbury reported to the Wiltshire War Agricultural Executive Committee about an accident which had occurred during the potato harvest in September 1941 in which a boy had broken his arm. The school had insurance but the company was quibbling. 'I think the Insurance Company with which I insured will, on compassionate grounds, fork out the amount [of medical expenses] I am asking for, but they are arguing that legally they need not do so, since the boy was able to return to school at the beginning of the school term and is thus only entitled to compensation for the fortnight between the time of the accident and the commencement of the school term. One may take the medical expenses of this boy as being on the minimum scale, since treatment has been given by the Salisbury Infirmary. I think that on principle, if one asks parents to allow their sons to engage on this sort of work of national importance it must be assured that medical expenses, which apparently may have to be incurred in the case of accident, must not fall on the parents, and that the present scheme does not ensure.' The Bishop Wordsworth's School had been looking into the problem of insurance since the summer of 1940 and by November 1941 the Headmaster was giving evidence on the issue before a Regional Committee of the Ministry of Agriculture.[188]

The 1941 harvest was delayed by bad weather and the fact that a much larger area had been put to crop. Head Teachers had a dilemma. The Head of Wandsworth School, whose children had been evacuated to Chippenham, noted in a letter to the County Education Officer: 'We are arranging to continue the Harvest Camp at Aldbourne at least for a further week. As you will understand, it is not easy to spare the staff and the boys concerned are mainly those who have important examinations at the end of the year and consequently it is not easy for them to give up a lot of time during the term. However, if it is necessary and possible to continue after the week we will do what we can.' The Bishop Wordsworth's School's Head wrote to the Deputy Director of Education. 'It seems unlikely… farmers will be able to get in their harvest before term time starts on September 12th, and will be seriously handicapped if no school boy is available after that date. To secure the Nation's food supply seems to be more important than school arrangements or academic work…'[189] A two week potato harvesting holiday became a regular September occurrence in Wiltshire schools. The children of Stratton St. Margaret were doing their duty in 1941;[190] in September 1942 the children of Kington St. Michael were just some of many who were helping farmers pick potatoes,[191] the Ashton Keynes Head Teacher stating it was by order of the Local Education Authority[192] and Leigh schoolchildren were also taking part in 1943.[193] Also in 1943 the Wiltshire Council Emergency Committee was approving the use of a holiday camp for Wiltshire's evacuees for the summer months.[194] The Kington St. Michael Head Teacher noted in the school's log book that the children were requested again in 1944.[194] Farmers sang the praises of British children throughout the land and, although the move to work children on the land was controversial, Peter Ginn feels that 'without such, it is doubtful whether the one million acres of potatoes grown annually between 1941 and 1944 would have been planted, let alone harvested.'[194] The schoolchildren working on Harvest Camps were allowed an additional cheese ration, but problems had occurred in the 1940 harvest in Wiltshire for some children engaged in harvest work which was not entitled 'Harvest Camp' and who did not receive the extra ration.[195] In August 1942 the Chairman of the Wiltshire War Agricultural Executive Committee

Richard Stratton was announcing that the Meat Pie Scheme had been set up for agricultural workers, along with residents in Rural District areas. Interested parties were asked to enquire at the local bakers or village shop.[196] The National Farmer's Union had also been considering the rations of agricultural workers, with representatives of the NFU and the Workers' Unions discussing the issue with Lord Woolton on 2 September 1942. Lord Woolton had been sympathetic and was looking at extending British Restaurants and the Meat Pie Scheme.[197]

Land Clubs were formed to help with additional labour on the land. The North Wiltshire farmer and member of Wiltshire's CWAEC Charles Whatley reported that: 'Another feature of supplementary labour, a most useful one, has been the Country-Town land club. In this movement Salisbury stands out foremost with a membership of 3,000.' Mr. A. J. Garnett had organised the Salisbury club. Whatley described him as 'a man who has devoted much time to this national effort… It was no light task, entailing time they could ill afford and patience beyond measure.'[198]

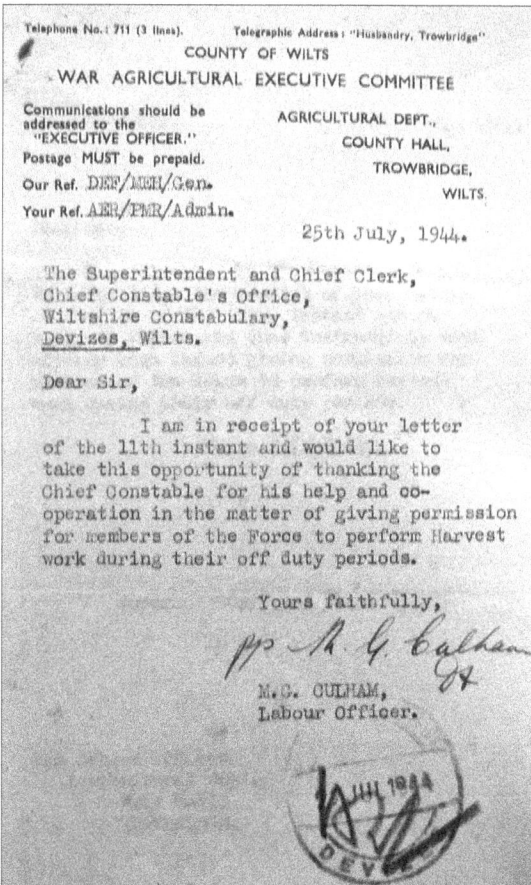

Camps had been used for urban children and the pupils of public schools since 1940[199] and use was also made of military personnel stationed in the area. The *Wiltshire Gazette* was reporting on 7 September 1939 that serving soldiers were volunteering to help with the harvest, the War Office agreeing with the Ministry of Agriculture that a certain number of soldiers could be released due to the 'vital importance of securing this year's harvest with the least possible delay,' so many farm workers having already been called up for military service. Soldiers also assisted farmers with the harvest in the Savernake area in 1941[200] including US GIs after their arrival at the nearby military site.[201] Local Police Officers[202]

Letter from the Wiltshire War Agricultural Executive Committee re. helping with the harvest, 25 July 1944 (WSA F5/540/7)

and local school children also helped. Included in the October 1942 issue of the Wiltshire National Farmer's Union's *Record* was a thank you to those who helped with the harvest. 'We have grown a very good crop of corn and after a struggle most of it is safely gathered in. Great credit is due to our farmers and their regular staff of men and women who have been working on this crop for the last twelve months. We should like to thank the Southern and American Commands and their men for the help they have so ungrudgingly given to get in the corn. We should also wish to thank the village women, the Women's Land Army, school boys and girls, and all other volunteers for their help.'[203] Wiltshire's CWAEC Labour Officer was extremely grateful to the Superintendent of the Wiltshire Constabulary for 'giving permission for members of the Force to perform Harvest work during their off duty periods' in July 1944.[204] Army Pioneers (conscientious objectors) worked on the land themselves as well as taking charge of POWs. In 1941, 200 of them were hard at work, improving drainage across the county to aid agriculture.[205] No. 4 SRD Camp near Swindon housed Pioneers and POWs. The camp included libraries, a workshop, canteen and recreation room and a NAAFI, along with a guard room and detention hut.[206]

Plan of No. 4 SRD Pioneer and POW Camp, scale 1:500, 1945 (WSA G24/719/4)

Farm holidays were encouraged as a cheap way of taking a break whilst aiding the war effort. There were also weekend clubs, whose members cycled out on a Saturday afternoon, returning home on a Sunday evening.[207] WLA Forewomen drove the volunteer holiday workers to the farms, along with Italian prisoners from POW camps such as the one in Chippenham.[208] The Minister of Agriculture Hudson made a public appeal for help with the 1943 harvest,[209] which saw 3,000 additional workers in Wiltshire, mostly from the volunteer harvest camps, of which there were 86 in the County.[210]

The 17 June 1944 edition of the *Wiltshire Times* was announcing the forthcoming Volunteer Agricultural Camps. 'After all what could be more enjoyable or patriotic at this period of the War, when holidays at seaside and other resorts are almost out of the question than a week or longer on a farm in the sunshine and fresh air, and with the knowledge that one is helping ones' country in this great campaign, and also helping to provide the large stock of foodstuffs which will be needed to feed millions of liberated European peoples?' The inclusive charge for board at a hostel was 28s. per week and wages were 2s. per hour. The work was to include potato lifting, root singling, hoeing, weeding of crops, flax pulling etc. The 1944 season saw 70 Wiltshire camps with 2,500 workers participating.[211] The *Wiltshire Times'* 17 June 1944 edition reported that the camp at Sutton Veny included dormitories which were 'exceptionally neat and tidy [in] the stout canvas tents in which many of the workers prefer[red] to sleep. Shower baths [were] provided in the adjoining building.' Evening entertainment at the camp included treasure hunts, dances and competitions. Volunteers were asked to bring their own towels, soap, feeding utensils and old clothing. In all, 1,000 camps were set up all over the country. Volunteers spent two weeks at their camp in exchange for an officially set rate of pay. A volunteer harvest camp was run at a farm in Donhead St. Mary, the farm buildings needing to be turned into adequate accommodation for 20-40 adults who were giving their holiday time to work on the land. In 48 hours the Women's Land Army (WLA) had to transform a barn and large shed into male and female dormitories, pig pens as wash and shower rooms, and a further barn as a dining room and kitchen. There were floors and walls to scrub, 'and then to erect the camp beds and put four folded blankets and a pillow on each bed.' Then there was shopping and the ordering of supplies. By the following evening the workers felt 'we had done at least a week's work in twenty-four hours.' There was so much to do that the volunteers themselves pitched in to make the camp more comfortable when they arrived. Entertainment for the campers usually consisted of a trip to the local pub with a chance to meet the locals. 'Some of the campers were adept at arranging good home-spun entertainment in the camp, revealing quite a lot of unsuspected talent.' The 'holiday makers' were warned that the local Wiltshire cider was pretty potent stuff. Anne Hall noted that 'On one occasion a group of students ignored the warning to go easy on the cider… they were chasing each other round the back of the lorry [which was to take them back to camp] wielding reaping hooks. The Vicar had warned me they had rather too much cider and had helped to load them into the lorry…'[212] Another Volunteer Agricultural Camp called Ladbrook was set up at Corsham in July 1944, situated off the Lacock Road out of Corsham. The camp consisted of old Nissen huts which had been used by an army searchlight party. The main meals at this camp were to be provided by the school catering service.[213] Camp Supervisors had to work long hours, often up at 4.30am to be ready for farmers' calls for labour. Anne Hall noted that they would 'have to get parties of friends sorted out to work together on the jobs they preferred. I would have to get them to the lorry at the time it was going to the area in which they were to work, and I would have to do at least three trips to get all the campers to work. I would have to sort out the parties at breakfast when all would be assembled and hope to get something to eat when they were at work... There were reports to write on campers and work, and entertainments to arrange for the evenings...' One Wiltshire Camp Supervisor was often driving volunteers to Bath in the evening, to the cinema in Chippenham, or to a dance or pub which might even have some beer. It was a long working day. The campers, however were 'always full of energy, and really enjoyed the informal camp life and were in no hurry to leave.' Farmers were generally appreciative of the 'novices' and thankful for 'the way these good people gave holiday time to try to help.' Volunteers who came to work at the Corsham camp included a Persian, a Chinese student and a Russian international lawyer![214] At Malmesbury Common workers came from a Jewish Youth Movement Colony known as 'The Habonium'.[215] Most of the holiday camps closed early in October each year when they were dismantled.[216]

Posters announcing 'Lend a hand on the land... at a farming holiday camp' were produced by the Minister of Agriculture and Fisheries in 1943,[217] but the Government began its national Lend a Hand on the Land campaign a little later, *c.* 1945, its aim to attract people from urban areas to work in rural areas during their holidays. The campaign continued into the post-war period, running alongside the 'Holidays at Home' campaign.[218]

Queen Mary inspecting the harvest camp at Twatley near Malmesbury (WSA F2/860/5)

The Women's Land Army

THE ISSUE OF women becoming farm workers had been raised during a meeting at the Ministry of Agriculture in April 1938, looking at farming labour in the event of war. The meeting resulted in an agreement to 'set up a Women's Branch of the Ministry under the Directorship of a woman' and Lady Denman, a pioneer of the Women's Institute, was thought to be an ideal candidate. In fact Lady Denman had also assisted in setting up the Land Army during the First World War and was, according to Nicola Tyrer, a 'ready-made networker'.[219] She set about planning with gusto, but her requests for interviews were ignored by the Minister of Agriculture and the Treasury who were 'extraordinarily complacent'. By April 1939 she had reached the limit of her patience due to the 'bumbling incompetence and sheer discourtesy of the officials with whom she was supposed to be in partnership' and she announced her ultimatum; that she would resign if she could not appoint her own headquarters staff. The threat had the desired effect. Local Education Authorities and farmers were now waiting to train the women, administrative staff were being put into place and a recruiting campaign began. The campaign was successful and by September 1939 17,000 had enrolled with 1,000 trained and being sent into employment. However, Lady Denman and her staff were finding it extremely difficult to find places of employment for their volunteers. The agricultural trade unions were prejudiced and also worried that women would prove a source of cheap labour, hampering their campaign for better wages. Agricultural workers were certain that women would not be up to the task. '... They cannot lay drains, they cannot cart or spread chalk, or spread dung and load it... In fact they cannot do any heavy work on the farm, and there is not a great deal of light work; the idea of substituting women for men on the farm is absurd.' The Government's lack of a positive campaign to counteract that of the farming press was a source of great frustration considering the recruitment drive had been a success. This first winter was at first wet and then hard, and the girls had no uniforms as yet but they refused to give in to the elements, keeping their feet warm by stuffing their gumboots with hay. The tipping point came in June 1940 when two radio broadcasts were made to farmers telling them to approach the Labour Exchange or their local CWAEC for additional labour but did not mention the Women's Land Army (WLA) at all. Lady Denman wrote to the new Minister of Agriculture Hudson explaining that it would give farmers the impression that the Ministry 'does not consider the Land Army seriously as a source of labour ....' Hudson appears to have understood the issue and it proved to be pivotal to the later success of the Land Army.[220]

The WLA was a one-rank force with Lancashire supplying the most recruits at 25,000. Many were drawn to the Land Army by the thought of freedom and open air[221] or to 'keep this land alive'.[222] Many of the Land Army organisers felt that the recruitment posters were dishonest, glamourising the work which was in fact a tough job in difficult conditions. The entrance age was 17, although some found a way around this.[223] Land Girls were paid directly by their employers and so could move on at any time. Tyrer reports it was impressed on them that: 'Every volunteer should remember that money has been spent on her equipment and training to make her a specialist for a vital job. She should not, therefore, *ever drop out*. She must feel that *she* is feeding the nation. If she drops out, someone may starve. The Land Army must have a motto – 'Stick to it'.[224] The WLA did not get the same medical provision as those in the services. They had to register with a local doctor and insure themselves against injury with a civilian scheme. They were also banned from Service and YMCA canteens. Their badges were made out of bakelite from the summer of 1942 even though brass continued to be used for all other uniforms.[225]

By mid 1941 members of the WLA had reached 20,000. After conscription was introduced its ranks swelled to a peak of over 80,000.[226] Joining became so popular that in August 1943 the Government stopped further recruitment to encourage women into the less popular types of work.[227] This came at the time when farmers finally saw the girls' worth; the food shortage due to shipping losses in spring 1942 revealed that the women could in fact far exceed expectations.[228] Thinking ahead, the ban on recruiting in 1943 was later lifted as the Government realised that it would take time for servicemen to return to the land and the POWs would be repatriated when war was over,[229] but by the first half of 1948 there were still thousands of German POWs left in the country.[230]

One Land Girl from Yorkshire who came to work at Fyfield near Marlborough remarked: 'We just didn't want to go into the ATS or into factories, we'd rather go on the land and you had to do something when you got to be 21. So rather than wait and be sent into something you didn't want, we became land girls.'[231] 'I came to Wiltshire in 1942 as a Land Army girl. I had previously worked in a bank in London and my only knowledge of the countryside had been the annual Girl Guide camp... I was sent to a training centre at Lockeridge, near Marlborough... We did a month's training on the farms... We learned to milk cows, to drive a tractor and to help with the harvest. Most of us had never milked a cow before and our hands ached terribly at first but we got used to it.'[232]

By 4 November 1939 the *Wiltshire Times* was reporting that:

> 133 members of the Women's Land Army have been placed in work on the farms in Wiltshire, a very large number of these members being Wiltshire girls, although a certain number have been placed from other counties. The girls are all eager and good workers, and their employers, the farmers, show by their letters that they are well satisfied with the work of the Wiltshire members of the Women's Land Army.
>
> The demand for the services of the Women's Land Army is steady and growing...

Farmers were asked to give the Committee notice of their 'impending requirements.'

WLA Reps. were the link between the Land Girls and the County Office, visiting every month to ensure the standard of living was good and to check on the emotional welfare of the girls. They also helped introduce the girls to the Women's Institute and Young Farmers' Club, and encouraged them to improve and extend their agricultural knowledge.[233] The Annual Report of the National Federation of

Young Farmers' Clubs in 1942 reported the formation of clubs 'for the purpose of giving training to girls who may enter the Women's Land Army.' It also noted that, after the setback of 1941 'imposed by war conditions,' 1942 was looking more promising, with an increase in the number of clubs formed, an announcement by the Government of 'greatly increased' support for the Federation, and 'a grand response by the clubs to calls made on them to play their part in the agricultural effort that is helping to win the war.'[234] Badges were awarded after certain periods of service and a girl could be promoted to Forewoman, going out to work with their 'gangs' to complete pre-arranged jobs for which farmers applied to the CWAEC.[235] Anne Hall found the Forewoman of the Salisbury WLA to be authoritative and a little brisk, but also very helpful, giving information and advice about the new role of Forewoman for which she was in training. Anne began working with the Winterbourne Stoke gangleader, an Estonian by the name of Aino Trumees, a Russian citizen. The gangs worked long hours and the work was back breaking. 'By 3 o'clock not only was my back groaning, but blisters were threatening on my hands…' Anne recalled that her landlady's 'kindness and concern' kept her going. By the end of June 1943 she was spending her time in the Salisbury area working on 'threshing many a very dirty rick of beans, or corn, pulling acres of flax, repaired cornfields on the plains damaged by army tanks taking the wrong routes.'[236] It appears that Anne turned out to be a very capable Forewoman, dealing with her team at Mere who had been complaining about the standard of food at their hostel and being 'not properly fed.' She was asked to 'tackle a larger and troublesome gang in the north of the County.'[238] This gang proved to be the Corsham gang from the Lypiatt Hostel, who had already seen off more than one of their previous Forewomen. They had become known as a 'tiresome gang' of poor workers. Mrs Methuen of Corsham Court (the local Rep.) and Lady Catherine McNeil the WLA County Organiser were to take action after hearing her report and recommendations. 'Though there were troublemakers and slackers in the gang, many of the girls were co-operative and good workers' but unfortunately their reputation preceded them and this made work on one nearby estate unpleasant, even though 'the girls worked satisfactorily in difficult conditions, they could not do anything right for him.' After changes had been made to the team, the girls were found to be hard workers but the farmers were upset by their bad tempered attitude and quarrelling, possibly understandable as the girls were very tired. It can be said that one farmer's attitude did have an effect on the girls and their attitude to work, however. A farmer at Lower Stanton thanked the Corsham gang and gave them all a 5s. tip which 'was exactly the encouragement they needed and deserved and it transformed their attitude to work.' By the time the Corsham gang worked on the fields at Langley Burrell, the farmer and tractor driver were 'amazed at the girls' speed and thoroughness.' The farmer was so impressed he called the CWAEC but was annoyed by their response. '[T]hey all laughed and thought he was being sarcastic'! The Chippenham Labour Officer came to see for himself and agreed that the girls were doing an excellent job.[239] Another farmer at Grittleton also approached the CWAEC to say how pleased he was with the girls. They had worked well and kept at the job until 6.30pm so that it could be finished. As with the previous farmer, he was greeted with a disbelief which annoyed him. 'Praise then followed the gang's hard work at many farms, pulling mangolds in very hard weather. I was proud of the way they worked without any grumbling, despite the hard work and uncomfortable conditions.'[240]

At the beginning of the war most girls were billeted on farms and many experienced a lack of facilities which often came with rural housing, along with an isolation they were unused to[241] but in Codford the villagers felt that the girls soon adapted well to rural life with its lack of modern conveniences.[242] Some girls lived on billets near the farm but even if the facilities were better, there could be difficulties. Some farmers underfed and overworked their Land Girls to such a degree that they lost stones in weight, becoming ill and exhausted.[243] One Land Girl had thought she would be able to stay in Lancashire to work after training, but as no place could be found for her there, she was assigned to a farm near Purton Stoke with an elderly couple who were unused to strangers. '[She] found her new life on this dairy farm very different from what she'd expected, and very primitive at that. The agricultural college had been equipped for modern farming methods – certainly not an enormous dung heap in the middle of the yard!' She was expected to milk the cows by lamplight if there was no moon to see by. She also had to gather potatoes, clean and pack them which was hard work on her hands until her mother sent her some lanolin. 'I also did muck spreading, covering a huge field with a prong (pitchfork) on my own – a very tedious task!' The long hours and hard work in cold and wet conditions meant that her health deteriorated and she was sent home with serious kidney problems. She returned to another farm in the area which already had a Land Girl stationed at it. She recalls that '… they were great days; I wouldn't have missed the experience for anything.'[244] Some girls who lodged with a farmer could find themselves being given inferior food and some lived under strict rules and regulations regarding the times they went to bed, talking after 'lights out' or when they came in at night.[245] One girl in Wiltshire did not get a hot meal for three months as her landlady 'preferred the blandishments of the pub to cooking'.[246] 'We had rations given to us every fortnight… Our landlady could get twice the ration that others had and we earned two guineas a week but we had to give her one guinea.'[247] The US troops stationed in Upavon would share their rations with the Land Girls who were pulling flax. 'Amongst these [rations] were sachets of instant coffee – something we had never seen before – and we went home that day anxious to try our our new drink.'[248] Some farmers would sack girls every winter and employ more the following spring to save money.[249] Land girls often felt inferior, both towards women in other services and to civilians.[250]

Complaints to the County Offices became commonplace and to remedy the situation hostels were introduced. 696 buildings throughout the country had been converted by 1944, each housing 30-40 in all; one third of the total number of land girls. These girls were less likely to become lonely or depressed and food was plentiful.[251] The Corsham hostel consisted of single storey huts in blocks, occupied by many Irish workers employed at the underground aircraft factory at

Hawthorn and working on shifts. The adjoining camp consisted of Royal Marine troops. There was an entertainment hall and buffet room on the site which hosted dances, ENSA or CEMA events and showed films. There was also a sick-bay with a nursing sister.[252] The Eden Vale site at Wesbury was the location of one Land Army Hostel near allotments and Eden Vale House;[253] the area had also been the site of a POW Camp.[331]

For the Land Girls the work was hard, the hours were long and the time off minimal (seven days official leave compared to 28 days for the military). The pay was less than the official minimum of 48 shillings.[254] Their basic working week was 48 hours long in winter and 50 hours in summer. Additional hours such as up to 11pm in double summer time (introduced during the war and moving the clocks two hours in advance of GMT over the summer period)[255] was classed as overtime.[256] The Mere WLA gang agreed to work late until 8.30pm all week to enable the farmer's men to 'press on with the corn harvest' in 1943.[257] Others noted: 'We started work at seven in the morning and worked until dusk. In the summertime, of course, we had to work very late.'[258] The double daylight saving time appears to have had an effect on the whole of the civilian population. The Chippenham doctor Joan Hickson's Good Friday diary entry, 1944 noted:

> Double daylight saving started last Sunday and we can never get used to it for weeks. The second hour seems the last straw and as if we are getting up in the middle of the night.'[259] Peggy Pickford from Warminster (whose husband was a farm worker) was writing to her sister Elizabeth Martin in Australia on 28 November 1940. 'This carrying on of Summer-time all through the Winter is an awful fraud. Do you know that we sometimes have to have lamps on until nearly 9 a.m., and yet the farm workers leave their work at 5 p.m. in daylight, and it is light sometimes until about 6 p.m. The poor wretches who get up at 4.30 a.m. to milk have to struggle with shaded lanterns and (more-or-less) blacked out cow-sheds for more than four hours and then go home in daylight! It seems to me just a trick to make people who work in offices get up an hour earlier so they can go home by daylight. But surely they could arrange their office hours to suit themselves without making everyone else fall in too? After all, Agriculture is the largest industry in Britain (or is it second to coal-mining?) but nobody ever dreams of planning a day to suit the farm labourer.[260]

The Agricultural Wages (Regulation) Acts 1924 and 1940, Holidays with Pay Act 1938, and Regulations 23 of the Defence (Agriculture and Fisheries) Regulations 1939 (Wiltshire), to take effect from December 1943 stated that:

> 6. Where an employer retains a whole-time worker in his regular employment for a period of three months or more the following directions in regard to holidays and holiday remuneration shall have effect.
>
> Upon completion of 3, 6, 9 or 12 consecutive months of the employment by any date in the period 1st January to 31st December in any

year, commencing with the year 1943 (hereinafter referred to as the 'holiday year') the worker shall be allowed holidays of 1, 2, 3 or 4 days respectively.[261]

There were a number of provisional requirements to fulfil such as no more than four days in any holiday year and two or three of such days would be allowed on consecutive days. The Act also stated that Good Friday, Easter Monday, Whit Monday, August Bank Holiday, Christmas Day, Boxing Day and Sundays 'shall not be days on which any such holiday may be allowed.'[262] One Land Girl later recalled that '[y]ou couldn't get home when you'd like to, you had to go home between haymaking and harvesting; you could go home either at Christmas or New Year.'[263] Tireless campaigning ensued over the subject of time off and in July 1944 *Land Girl* magazine announced: 'Once more the Land Army has given a lead in the Agricultural industry. For over a year it has been a Land Army regulation that its members shall have one week's holiday on pay during the working year. Now a new order of the Agricultural Wages Board has made a week's holiday on pay the legal right of every agricultural worker.'[264]

Amazingly, some members of the WLA still had enough energy for a bit of fun when they were able. 'We would go dancing in Fittleton, Netheravon or Enford and on Sunday afternoons to Marlborough to tea dances. There was always plenty of transport. The American army were wonderful to us, they sent us transport but wherever you went you had wardens from the hostel to come with you, you were well watched.'[265] The Land Girls stationed near Tottenham House remembered the dances there and also trips to the cinema in Marlborough. 'There was a weekly bus service on a Saturday afternoon from Burbage to Marlborough, which meant that we could do some shopping and visit the cinema. The bus waited for the cinema to close at 10pm and then brought us back to Burbage – standing room only! Then we had to walk back across the park. We must have been quite fit because we were up at 5am the next morning for milking.'[266] The Mere girls were encouraged by the Pioneer Warden who ran their hostel to form an entertainment committee and plan evening entertainment, whether it be a visit to a local dance, occasional ENSA show, or to a film. The girls were also allowed to invite their soldier friends to the hostel.[267]

The Land Girls' uniform consisted of a green jersey, brown breeches, a brown felt slouch hat and a khaki overcoat[268] in country colours with a 'sporty fashionable feel'[269] that was often mixed with other garments.[270] Women wearing trousers to work was also a new concept. Lady Denman herself helped to design the great coat which had added width in the shoulders to make them both attractive and practical but there were problems equipping girls who joined in the winter[271] and many of the uniforms were ill fitting; not all girls got a full set of kit.[272] When gum boots (Wellington boots) became scarce they became restricted to dairy workers only. Although the Land Girls needed them, they often had to make do without. DIY fixes included patching them up with cycle puncture outfits but they still leaked.[273] In the October 1942 edition of the *Record*, the Wiltshire NFU Branch was announcing clothing coupons for agricultural workers, following an urgent request by the NFU for supplementary clothing. The Board of Trade had announced an additional ten coupon occupational supplement for 'all workers in agriculture, horticulture, forestry and land drainage. Agricultural workers, including working farmers regularly engaged in actual physical labour for not less than 22 hours a week, will receive this supplement.'[274]

In the October 1942 edition of the Wiltshire NFU's *Record* Charles Whatley, Chariman of the Labour Committee, was announcing that the Wiltshire War Agricutural Executive Committee (WWAEC) had decided to organise gangs of Land Girls to help with threshing. A team of four girls would 'follow the [threshing] machines around from farm to farm and thus complete a gang of six, men and girls (including driver and feeder). This extra staff should enable any farmer to make an early start in the morning and also permit him to carry on threshing until a late hour in the evening… These girls will be housed and paid for by the W.W.A.E.C. The head girl will be responsible for booking up the time[s]…' The contractor and farmers were asked to co-operate to make the scheme a success, by contractors 'insisting that the farmers employ the girls when they arrive at the farm with the tackle, and the farmer being patient with the girls by giving them the jobs they can do. Girls have already proved themselves capable of doing any work connected with threshing operations except perhaps the handling of sacks, and I might add the over head work of putting the sheaves on the machine, but surely there will be one chivalrous man around willing to change jobs with the girls and take on when the over head work begins. I have no hesitation in saying that if these few suggestions are put into practice the girls will prove a success and speed up the working hours of many threshing sets.'[275] One by one, the farmers were won over. They discovered that although the girls may have been slower, they were thorough. The men would be watching the clock and 'seeing how quickly they could get the job done.' Many farmers found that productivity had increased. 'This year, with only one man, who is sixty-six years old, and two girls, we have maintained last year's production, and at the present time are producing ten gallons a day more milk than at the same period last year. I think these figures speak for themselves.'[276]

One farmer could not believe what he was seeing at a ploughing competition in 1944. Even though they had such limited experience, the Land Girls were proving to be better than the 'lads,' taking more care and time over the tasks.[277] A Land Army girl came to help a farmer near Warminster cut the corn. 'She drove the tractor and father operated the binder.'[278] Another noted that: 'A lot of people didn't like us because we were here and their boys were not. Except one old lady who used to see us walking to work. She used to come out and say, 'Good marnin' to 'ee, bless 'ee.' It was a long time before we knew what she was saying.'! After a time the Land Girls impressed farmers and locals alike with their dedication, open-mindedness and cheerfulness.[280] [281] They were also on hand to help Wiltshire farmers in time of crisis; at Upper Spray in Ham Land Girls helped to put out a fire in the dairy.[282]

The Mere gang had already heard of the reputation of one farmer as a 'slave driver' who would 'swear at the girls if he thought they were not giving their

Land Girl being filmed on a tractor, courtesy of Wiltshire College Lackham (WSHC P43963)

best all day.' The farmer began by lecturing the Forewoman, who was amused when he came to her later to say he was impressed by their hoeing.[283] Farmers would often employ Land Girls and POWs as a last resort; correspondence to the Wiltshire County Council Surveyor contains testimony to this effect. During the summer of 1943 farmers from Wootton Bassett, Burderop near Wroughton and Dinton were enquiring about the services of Council roadmen who had been redirected to farm work in the past and had proved to be good workers. A letter from the Wiltshire's CWAEC Labour Officer to the County Surveyor on 14 July 1943 stated: 'Roadmen for Agricultural Work. I am receiving a large number of applications from farmers for the services of roadmen…'[284] The County Surveyor asked if they had tried Land Girls or POWs but it appeared the farmers much preferred the roadmen, even if, as some roadmen complained, they were unwilling to do the work. The roadmen themselves were needed for essential jobs such as tar spraying, and could often not be spared.[285]

Some Land Girls were given the job of catching rats and every county had its own team of 'dedicated catchers'.[286] At the beginning of the war Britain's forestry industry had been in decline and timber was being imported for telegraph poles and pit props. Savernake Forest was one of those used for four week training courses, starting in 1940, to select trees for telegraph poles.[287] It wasn't until 1942, however, that the first training camp for what was to become the Women's Timber Corps was set up, starting with the 1,000 girls already working in forestry. The girls became known as 'Lumber Jills.' The WLA uniform was retained for the Corps except for the hat, substituted with a green beret. The badge was a fir tree surmounted by a Royal Crown instead of a wheatsheaf. By the end of 1942 their ranks had risen to 3,900 in England and Wales and 1,000 in Scotland. The Timber Corps managed to acquire an upmarket image and some Land Girls thought their timber counterparts considered themselves superior. Most Timber Corps girls lived in private billets[288] and as with the Land Girls, often had inadequate diets. One 17 year old member of the Timber Corps, billeted in Wroughton,[289] did not get a single hot meal from December to March. The Italian POWs would take pity on them and share a part of their lunch.[290] Members of the WLA and Timber Corps could often find themselves working 'alongside Italian prisoners… and found them charming… they knew we were hungry and used to give us bits of dried fruit from the rations.'[291]

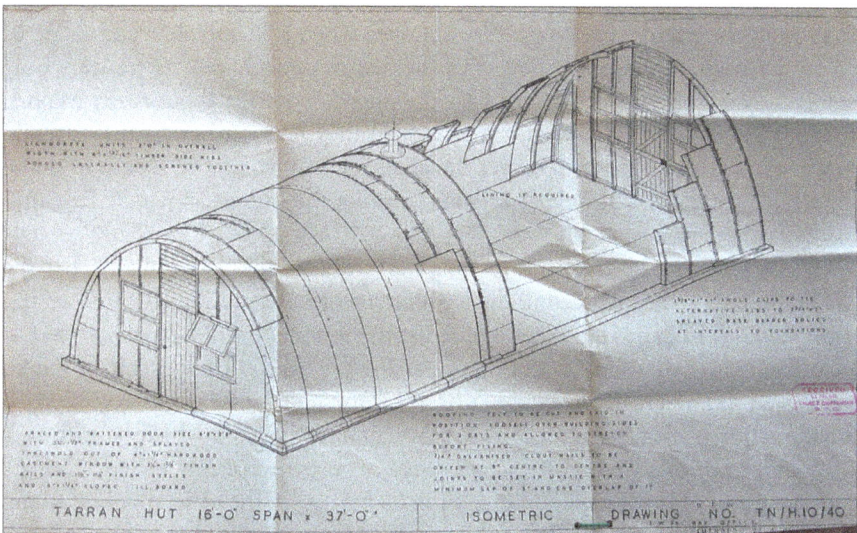

By April 1941 Tarran huts were being planned for a site near Hungerdown Lane in Chippenham for the Home Grown Timber Department to include three small huts for sleeping accommodation and one large hut to include a kitchen, dining room and bathrooms etc. (WSA G3/761/63)

There was a 'palpable rivalry' between the Land Army and the Timber Corps, 'each accusing the other of lack of expertise'.[292] One girl went from selling silk to felling trees, driving trucks and giant caterpillar tractors; working alongside Italian, German, and Austrian prisoners of war, Norwegian whalers and English conscientious objectors in Savernake Forest. To begin with the tasks felt physically daunting. Early every morning in Savernake, two girls, billeted together in Marlborough, had cycled from the town to the sawmill near the Grand Avenue.[293] New Zealand's 14th Forestry Co. also worked at the saw mills in Savernake Forest until 1943[294] and were billeted in the village of Burbage.[295] One Lumber

Jill, working around Wiltshire and Gloucestershire, remembered that her least favourite task was charcoal burning. 'Even the extra soap coupons and 'dirt money' did little to compensate for the penetrating, choking dust when one 'broke' the kiln and bagged up the still warm charcoal, which was needed in large quantities for gas mask filters.'[296]

The girls of the Women's Land Army found that working life was hard but there were compensations. 'The first summer we were here, it was beautiful; Wiltshire took on lovely colours, all gold and white and brown and green. The farmers chopped up the hedges to make the fields bigger.' '... when the local people began to know us, then they grew to like us and we got to like Wiltshire. At first we didn't, we thought it was a dreadful place, nothing like Yorkshire.'[297]

The Land Girls celebrated VE day in Mere, travelling there from their hostel at Southbrook.[298] The Corsham WLA Gang took part in a Victory Parade in Corsham. 'The gang turned out in smart array and in good numbers. Placed well up in the parade, [we] were very annoyed when a Major came and made us go to the back of the procession with the Scouts and Guides, as we were only civilians. It was as well he did not hear the uncivil language about Army Majors. It spoilt the day for the girls and they wished they had not bothered to attend.' However, 'Churchill came to relieve the gloom with a wonderful speech of praise for all in another broadcast that evening, making the little local parade fade into insignificance.'[299]

The Ministry of Agriculture failed to persuade the War Cabinet that the WLA should also be included in the Reinstatement in Civil Employment Act and went so far as to deny them the resettlement grants of up to £150 which were to be offered to Civil Defence and other Auxiliary workers. Lady Denman felt so devastated she resigned. She wrote: 'The WLA is a uniformed service recruited on a national basis by a Government Department and the work which its members have undertaken… is in my view as arduous and exacting as any branch of women's war work and of as great importance to the country…' The general public, along with the Queen, were appalled.[300] On 7 October 1944, members of the North-West Wilts section of the WLA paraded in Malmesbury. It was stated that the Wiltshire Members of the Fund hoped to present Lady Denman with a cheque, due to the 'admirable work' done on their behalf.[301]

Upon leaving the WLA a recruit had to hand in her uniform. She was also denied the right to claim the National Service Medal which even civilians could claim if they had been minimally involved in the war effort.[302] The WLA did not even get a discharge badge and Churchill stuck to the decision even when MPs were protesting in the Commons. Instead the Government decided it would pay £15,000 into the WLA Benevolent Fund and allowed the girls to keep their great coats (if they dyed them blue) and their shoes, but this was felt not to go far enough. Members formed a charter and demonstrated in London, lobbied the Minister of Agriculture and Churchill; some went on strike. The Government did not change its position.[303] The WLA Benevolent Fund was the source of a £100 cheque given to Anne Hall when she left the WLA to enable her to undertake training on a social worker course. References by Lady Methuen of Corsham Court and Lady Catherine McNeil had also helped secure the place. Anne was pleased to receive her message from the Queen when she resigned from the Land Army in 1946. she was also grateful to be able to keep and cherish her black armband with its many six month half diamonds embroidered on it, but felt that the greatest value she placed on the 'wonderful store of memories afforded by those years of rewarding toil. I felt a great debt of gratitude was owed to the many farmers and country dwellers who were so kind to us raw recruits until we became of real use to them. Our efforts were accepted with such good humour and patience that any hardships were well outweighed by enjoyment.'[304] Information on individual members of the WLA can be found at The National Archives and the Imperial War Museum.

By 1945 members had dropped to 54,000 even though they were sorely needed[305] and new recruits were required.[306] The WLA was finally disbanded in 1950. At the time of the Stand Down parade on 21 October WLA numbers had reduced to 8,000.[307] Known as the 'Forgotten Army,' members of the WLA were finally given official recognition of their role in 2007 when they were able to apply for a specially designed badge commemorating their service, 'acknowledging the debt that the country owes to them',[308] but for many it had come too late. The first memorial to be erected to commemorate the Land Girls was unveiled by the Prince of Wales at the Fochabers estate in Moray, Scotland, in 2012.[309]

Prisoners of War

As IN THE Great War,[310] prisoners of war (POWs) were put to work in the fields, and *c.* 40,000 Italian POWs were used during the course of the war.[311] In Wiltshire great use was made of POWs as the supply of labour in agriculture was an ongoing problem. They worked in mobile gangs and 500 individuals were placed as resident workers on farms by 1944. It appeared by this time that this was the system which produced the best output.[312] Wiltshire Council's Constabulary files contain a list of Italian prisoners billeted in the county, giving addresses in Semley, East Knoyle, Chilmark, Broadchalke, Warminster, Mere and Upton Scudamore amongst others.[313] The Italians were amongst the first POWs to arrive, having been captured in the Near East. Many were ill when they arrived and had to be screened and inoculated; the possibility of malaria was a very real one and the British public needed to be protected, but the Government felt that the need for labour was so pressing that they opted for a risk reduction strategy. No camps were to be housed in places deemed susceptible to mosquitoes. Farncombe Down near Baydon was one of the first camps to take prisoners.[314] Some of the Italian POWs had actually had dealings with Wiltshire before they were sent to Britain. After the battle of El Alamein in 1942, trooper W. R. Cabble from the Royal Wiltshire Yeomanry was tasked with looking after the newly captured POWs.

> After several weeks in Sarafand hospital [Red Cross Hospital in Palestine], and my last time in Nathania convalescent barracks, I took charge of 50 Italian

P.O.W's. They were willing and hard working lads, glad their fighting days were over, and although they were on the opposite side, an unusual friendship blossomed. When I told them I was due to leave, they brought their wine ration over to give me a good send off, each one shook hands and gave me a big Italian hug. I can't explain it, but I left with tears running down my face, what a funny world, enemies, yet friends. Before leaving the Depot the R.S.M called me in and thanked me. For once I must have done something right.[315]

As for POWs captured on home soil; the Chief Constable of Wiltshire was briefed in April 1941 that they should be handed over to the nearest military unit before 'disposal' at Command Cage in Swindon. By April 1942 it had become necessary to provide Collecting Centres for the collection and disposal of prisoners.[316] Britain had a serious agricultural labour shortage in 1943 and Italians were the first to be used. If they volunteered they were paid the same rate as the British workers. It was a way to relieve boredom and the cramped conditions in the camps, and they were also given greater privileges. Some farmers were as reluctant to take POWs as they had been to take Land Girls, and stories of thieving and laziness abounded, along with tales of sexual harassment of the Land Girls.[317] The stories certainly became a reality for some, as one WLA member who joined the Timber Corps at the age of 17 soon discovered. She was working to clear some woods near Salisbury and found the Italian POWs to be 'bone idle.' They would try to grope the girls in the back of the lorry on the way home and would lie in wait for them if they needed to go to the toilet in the woods. 'We were only kids. It really wasn't fair. It got so bad we refused to go to work in the lorry with them.'[318] In June 1944 it had been noted by the Commandant of Lodge Farm Camp, Lambourn, Berks that billeted POWs in Wiltshire had been fraternising with women. 'All billeted prisoners are finally warned that if any future cases come to the notice of the Camp Authorities instant disciplinary action will be taken. It is forbidden to:-

Fraternise with women.

Enter places of entertainment – Public House, shops etc.

It is also an offence to ride a bicycle when off duty except for the purpose of attending Mass, and then only when the distance exceeds two miles.'

The police had been notified.[319]

Conversing with the general public was forbidden at first but after August 1944 the rules were relaxed and the POWs could talk freely to anyone they chose.[320] In Wiltshire it was clear by 18 July 1944 that the rules had been relaxed; Wiltshire's Chief Constable was writing to his Superintendent: 'Please see the Officer in charge of the Italian Prisoners of the War Hostel at Devizes and explain to him that I have been informed by letter from the Commandant of the 47th Italian Labour Battalion, Motcombe Park Camp, that under the re-organisation scheme, Co-operators (Ex-Prisoners of War) are allowed to fraternise with the public; provided that they do not indulge in amorous or sexual relations.' In Wiltshire, Italian non co-operators were housed in separate camps, such as at a site in Lyneham, in use

To:-

Ref:- BC/PW/6/6.

Subject:- P.W. Billetees.

It has come to the notice of the Commandant that certain billeted prisoners of war are fraternizing with women.

All billeted prisoners are finally warned that if any future cases come to the notice of the Camp Authorities instant disciplinary action will be taken.

It is forbidden to:-

(i) Fraternize with women.
(ii) Enter places of entertainment - Public Houses, shops etc.
(iii) It is also an offence to ride a bicycle when off duty except for the purpose of attending Mass, and only then when the distance exceeds two miles.

Employers of billeted prisoners of war are reminded that careful supervision can stop any attempted breach of regulations covering the employment of Ps/W.

A copy of this letter has been forwarded to the police authorities who have been asked to immediately inform this Camp of any breach of discipline on the part of Ps/W in their particular locality.

Lambourn, Berks.
25 June 1944.

Lt. Col.,
Commandant,
Lodge Farm Camp.

A V V I S O

SOGGETTO: PRIGIONIERI DI GUERRA NELLE FATTERIE. -

Sono venute a conoscenza che di sono dei Prigionieri in fattorie che fraternizzano con le donne.

Tutti i prigionieri sono avvisati per l'ultima volta che se altri casi vengono a conoscenza alle autorita' del Campo, verranno prese energiche azioni disciplinari. Richiamo l'attenzione dei prigionieri di guerra sui seguenti articoli:-

1. E' vietato fraternizzare con le donne.
2. E' vietato entrare in posti di divertimento, locali pubblici, e negozi.
3. Non e' permesso usare la bicicletta per passeggiare. E' concesso soltanto l'uso della bicicletta per recarsi ad ascoltare la messa quando la chiesa dista piu' di due miglia (Km.3) dal posto di lavoro.

Una copia delle presente disposizioni e' stata mandata alle autorita' di polizia le quali comunicheranno le eventuali infrazioni alle disposizioni di cui sopra, da parte dei prigionieri di guerra in famiglia.

25/6/44.

Il Comandante del Campo 25

Letter from the Commandant of Lodge Farm Camp at Lambourn, Berkshire, to the Wiltshire Constabulary regarding fraternisation with women, sent in English and Italian, 25 June 1944 (WSA F5/530/3)

by March 1945, and another in Lydiard Millicent for 500 non-cooperative men in April 1945, an alternative to their present location at Crowdys Field, Cricklade Road, Swindon.[321] It was designated as Camp No. 160.[322]

Italian POWs were used often at farms in and around Codford. '... many were likeable men and good workers, but they were rather apt to pick up things which did not belong to them. Under the circumstances that could be understood.

It's no fun being a prisoner in an enemy country.'[323] 'They also made rings from the old imperial multi flat-sided three-penny pieces and mugs from small empty bake bean tins. One of the prisoners showed me how to make a whistle from a willow stick and it is something that I have never forgotten.'[324]

Correspondence from the Director of Prisoners of War at the War Office on 22 December 1941 shows that Italian POWs were to be housed in Land Army hostels at various places throughout the country. The hostels were to be used as an experimental trial and it appears that in Wiltshire ten were planned: Greenway Lane, Chippenham; Hyde, Purton; The Castle, Devizes; Patney near Devizes; Arena Road Camp, Tidworth; Fargo Hutted Camp, Larkhill; The Old Rectory, Shipton Bellinger (on the border in Hampshire); Swindon, P/W Cage; Wilton. There were to be conditions attached:

...3. It will be realised that these prisoners must be carefully selected, but in view of the type of prisoner involved this should not be difficult. In no circumstances will members of the Italian Air Force be selected.

No hostel will be occupied by prisoners until ample work is guaranteed by the local Agricultural Officer for the numbers despatched and until Commands are satisfied that accommodation is complete.

The prisoners will work throughout the day without Guards and during black-out hours will be locked in the Hostel, but prisoners required for special employment such as milking, may be let out for this purpose. A Guard of 1 N.C.C. and 9 men is suggested as a maximum. The actual size of the Guard is left to the discretion General Officers Commanding-in-Chief but it must be understood that no addition to the authorised War Establishment of Camps will be allowed for this purpose. Prisoners should be searched occasionally on their return from work. During the day at least one private should be present at the hostel and a larger number should be on duty on rest-days.

The transport allotted to each camp now includes one 3-ton lorry and one 15-cwt. truck. It should therefore be possible for the guard to be taken over as necessary by the truck together with the prisoners rations (sic). The prisoners will be responsible for their own cooking.

The prisoners' requirements from the camp canteen should be taken weekly; they will continue to be paid token money.

It will be realised that the hostel and its immediate surroundings must be kept scrupulously clean by the prisoners.

Prisoners of war reporting sick will be returned for inspection by the Camp Medical Officer when the Guard returns in the morning but, in cases of emergency, a civil medical practitioner can be employed. An Italian medical orderly will be attached to each Hostel to deal with minor injuries.

In the event of invasion arrangements will be made to collect the prisoners and return them immediately to the camp by which they are administered.

On the prisoners' rest-day they will be restricted to the [a]rea within a short distance of the Hostel. Definite landmarks should be arranged so that there may be no doubt. Prisoners will not be allowed to go into houses, shops or public-houses, but local arrangements may be made, where possible, for them to attend mass. Walks may be allowed under escort.

Prisoners are forbidden to post their letters at local post offices. Their correspondence will be dealt with through the camp by which they are administered.

It has been agreed that the accommodation stores (with the exception of bedsteads, stoves and electric fittings) which are at present in the Hostels, and are the property of the Ministry of Works and Buildings will be removed by the Ministry. The bedsteads, stoves and electric fittings will be taken on ledger charge. The buildings will be equipped by Commands to War accommodation schedules of furniture and accommodation stores for hutments. The Ministry of Agriculture are being asked to provide the fuel required for cooking and heating.

You are requested to report on 31st January the extent to which the scheme is operating, whether it is satisfactory, and what special difficulties have been encountered.[325]

The Ministry of Agriculture's hostel at Chippenham was taken over for use as accommodation for 30 Italian POWs in March 1942.[326] Minety had a search light camp which became unused. Extra huts were brought in and barbed wire fences placed around the perimeter. It became a satellite camp under the umbrella of the larger Easton Grey Camp situated nearby,[327] used to house Italian POWs, and then Germans.[328] Easton Grey Camp (No. 89) was of the purpose-built 'standard' type and was used to house workers for light industrial and agricultural use.[329] Other satellite camps included Alderton, Chippenham, Devizes, Ladyfield, Latton, Lyneham, Purton, Nibley (Gloucestershire), Sherston, Thornbury (Gloucestershire) and Westonbirt (Gloucestershire).[330] No. 114 Camp at Eden Vale, Westbury, was also of standard type, situated on a site that was also occupied by housing.[331] Of those POWs billeted on farms in the Minety area, most came from the Easton Grey camp. '... a Camp Officer, a Padre and a barber would visit them about once a month... [the Italians] always seemed to take great care of their looks. My Auntie's daughter..., then a young girl of about fourteen, remembers taking breakfast to the room of one Italian POW who was ill in bed and found him wearing a strange looking hair net!'[332]

Some of those POWs staying with farmers lived in wooden huts, such as one on a farm near Cricklade. 'They lived in a big wooden hut put up in the field across the lane away from the farm. It was quite comfortable, and had beds, a cooker and so on, but it was only big enough for two people.' Another Cricklade resident recalled: 'We were provided with a hut for them to live in, brought out on army lorries by uniformed men.'[333] The POWs came from the Wiltshire camps but were also bussed over the border from Camp 25 at Lodge Farm in Berkshire.[334] The camps had 'affiliated hostels' which included Whiteparish and

Wilton attached to a labour camp in Romsey (Hampshire). Hostels in Purton and Lydiard Millicent were affiliated with Lodge Farm Camp (Berkshire). Eden Vale Camp in Westbury had affiliated hostels in Patney and Frome (Somerset), whilst Easton Grey Camp had affiliated hostels based at Sherston, Ladyfield, Lyenham, Thornbury (Gloucestershire) and Nibley (Gloucestershire). There were 'working companies' at Chiseldon and at Larkhill with a base camp located at Le Marchant, Devizes and a US labour camp in Savernake. There appears to have been a second camp in Westbury; a labour camp.[335]

Italian POWs came to work on a farm in Burbage.

> The Italians soon destroyed our idea of the proper demeanour of a conquered people... Bruno had a passion for babies and endeared himself to the village mums by dashing up to the prams with cries of 'Oh, the beautiful bambino' and embracing mum as well as baby, which added colour and excitement to our drab village street usually rattling with tanks. When Italy surrendered and the Italians went home we were all a little sad and the children cried...'[336] One was a tailor, doing work for the family, but he also drove a tractor, christening it 'my Spitfire'.

He was well known in the village. He promised to return, but when he wrote some time later enquiring after work, there was unfortunately none available to offer him.[337] The POWs working in Cricklade came from the Latton Camp. One local boy remembers how they were used for loading and unloading railway wagons. 'We children often watched these gangs working, but one day we became puzzled by the intense interest an Italian gang were showing in one particular bush, yet also keenly watching us. Eventually a lorry arrived to take them back to their huts for the night. As soon as they'd gone, we decided to investigate, only to discover nothing less than a three-foot-long sword! We came to the conclusion that they must have hidden it in the bush with a view to retrieving it later... We dumped the sword in a pond on the other side of the railway line, making sure we kept well away from the Italians afterwards!'[338]

The POWs could be sent to work on farms, railways, gas works or coal wharves. More Italians were due to arrive in the country in 1944, with a letter from the Ministry of War Transport to the Surveyors of County and Borough Councils on 27 October 1943 announcing their impending arrival. 'The Government hopes that it will be possible to bring a substantial number of Italians, during 1944, to this country to place in employment.' Now that the relationship had changed between the British and Italian Governments, it was assumed that the Italians would be employed in the same ilk as British soldiers rather than as prisoners. 'The skilled men amongst the Italians will be identified and will be available for employment in their trade,' but the majority would only be available for use as labourers.[339] The arrival of more Italians would probably have caused Wiltshire's County Surveyor more than a little consternation; he was already having problems with his current Italian workforce. On 16 September 1943 he was writing to the Divisional Engineer in frustration. 'It seems that since the Italian collapse the guards for these men are disarmed and have even less authority than before, for the prisoners now do little more than stand up and laugh at passers by... [the Chargehand] has on several occasions asked for somebody from the Camp to come out and meet him on the site to see the position and give him some help in increasing the output but this request has never been complied with...' In Wiltshire Italian POWs were being used for work on the Deverill to Mere road, the Heytesbury to Chitterne Road (B390), the Warminster to Shaftesbury Road (at Lords Hill) and at Fonthill Bishop, and also for the restoration of Marlborough roads (Marlborough to Rockley) in June 1944 alongside agricultural work. [340] They continued to have a reputation for incompetence and poor performance in 1944, but this reached crisis point when 1,000 went on strike at harvest time. The farmers were furious; the POWs were put into confinement; the War Office stated that they were not technically the enemy. [341] A letter from the Divisional Surveyor at the Warminster Depot on 8 May 1944 relays the difficulties faced on the ground:

> ... I regret that the position shows no improvement. The conditions today are as follows:-
>
> With the exception of the Italians on the Fonthill job who are a really good gang, the remainder are hopeless. Since the sort-out of last week and the resultant mixing up of the gangs, they appear to have adopted a 'Go Slow' policy, and it is no exaggeration to say that the value of their work does not represent the cost of their Bus Hire.
>
> I particularly request that the Italian Sergeant with Party T.14.B should be removed and not sent out with any of my gangs, as he encourages his men in wasting time holding discussions... [342]

The County Surveyor was writing to the Commandant of the Eden Vale Camp, Westbury, on 9 June 1944 corroborating a complaint made against some Italian POWs '... refusal to work, threatening the Chargehand with a shovel and prisoners wandering off over the Downs.' It appeared that the gang in question had come into contact with another gang on the Mere Downs which was known to consist of 'non-co-operators.' The contact between the two groups had an adverse effect on the previously good workers in the first gang. The Chargehand was finding the situation very difficult and had asked to be relieved of the work, but the shortage of man power meant that he had to remain in his post. Wiltshire's Prisoner of War road improvement programme had been called 'dis-organised' by the Divisional Surveyor of the Westbury Depot in June 1944 when some POWs were suddenly withdrawn from work in the Marlborough area without notice. In August 1944 the County Surveyor was writing to the Divisional Road Engineer at the Ministry of Transport in Bristol regarding payment to the Italian POWs working as roadmen. At present they were paid with grant money, and this was emphasised clearly. '... The amount of work forthcoming from the prisoners is generally so small that they are certainly not worth anything like the roadmen's rate of pay, and I do not think my Council would be a party to employing these men if this rate had to be paid.'[343] By September the County Surveyor had paid a site visit and was writing to the Commandant of the Lambourn Camp, Berkshire, to complain:

> I visited the job on which the above prisoners are employed yesterday and am very dissatisfied with the amount of work being done.
>
> Prior to the prisoners being employed I had seven roadmen and a supervisor on this work. Since the prisoners have been there these roadmen have largely been used to supervise the work of the prisoners, but instead of finding an appreciable speed-up in the amount of work done I found that there has been no increase in the speed of the work which, with the cost of the transport provided for the prisoners, will add to the cost of the job considerably. When I was there most of the prisoners were sitting under the bank and little or no work was being done, and I am informed that this is the state of affairs for most of the day...
>
> I appreciate that the weather during this week has not been favourable, but even allowing for this the output per prisoner is most unsatisfactory.[344]

But, as with the Land Girls, some of those who had benefited from the hard work of individual POWs wished to make their gratitude known. On 17 July 1944 the County Surveyor was writing to the Camp Commandant at Eden Vale Camp, Westbury, about one of the Italian POWs who had been working for him. '... I write to inform you that one of the men in Squad T.6. Ghilardi Ambrosio is continuously engaged as a mason and is giving very satisfactory service. If it were possible to recognise this by an increase in payment, I think such action would be fully justified.'[345] As mentioned by the Director of Prisoners of War, wages were in the form of 'token money' which could be used in the camp canteen.[346]

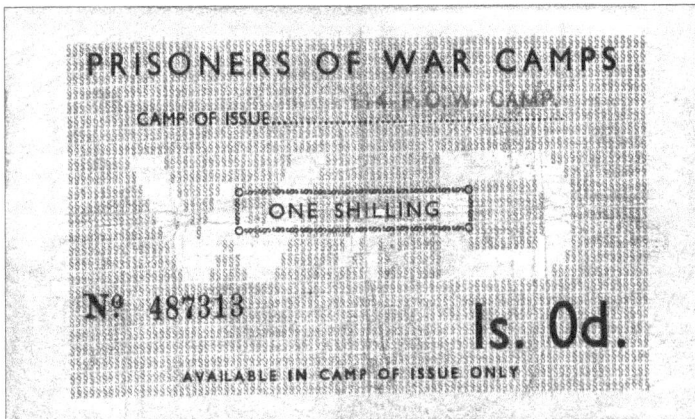

POW token money from Camp No. 114 at Westbury, reproduced by kind permission of Ivan Clark (WSHC P53383)

By 1944 the POWs were able to change part of their weekly wages into sterling for use in local shops. They were able to send two airmail letters a month, use public telephones and visit the cinema. '...some of these young Italians had been prisoners a long time, and it was sad to hear from some that close relatives had died in their absence, or that their wives had left them. Their hope of being allowed home now that Italy had surrendered had not been realised and they were very disheartened.'[347] It is clear by September 1944 in Wiltshire that although the POWs were entitled to go to the cinema, they were being refused admission, such as at the Rex Cinema in Pewsey. 'Complaints have been received from the Commandants of Italian Prisoners of War Camps that Cinema Managers have refused admission to Co-operators. Would you please explain to them that they have permission to attend although as far as the Police are concerned we cannot insist upon individual Managers allowing them to pay and enter. It may be that they are under the impression that these men are attempting to break the Camp rules by attending the pictures.'[348] One Minety farmer took his Italian prisoner on a trip to the Empire Theatre in Swindon for a night out. 'Mario was carefully dressed in some [of the farmer's] clothes, which were a little on the large size and off they went. Although communication was difficult, both had a good night out and no doubt the family received in exchange total co-operation from the happy young man.'[349] Perhaps, considering the lengths they appear to have gone to regarding secrecy, they felt that the trip would be frowned upon by the authorities.

POWs worked on many farms like that at Potterne Wick, clearing out the stream and remaking a farm track. The children, although warned against approaching them, of course did. 'We were fascinated to see them make withy baskets and slippers from rushes...They also made rings from three penny pieces... sold all these things for pocket money.'[350] At a farm near Warminster: '... we also had a batch of Italian prisoners of war to clean out and tidy up the stream which ran down through the centre of the home field... They were always accompanied by a couple of armed soldiers to watch over them... They were a happy lot and seemed glad to be out of the war.'[351] Italian POWs also helped with the school sports at Ham on VE Day.[352] On the ridge near Hindon, POWs of different nationalities worked in the sawmills. The difference in their arrival at the site typified the differences in their culture. When the Italians arrived, they 'drifted up the hill in twos and threes, with the rifle of the British pioneer corporal in charge of them being carried by one of them.' When it was the turn of the Germans, they 'formed themselves up under their own command, and marched up as a squad.'[353]

POWs arrived from the Mediterranean from 1941 and by July 1943 over 37,000 prisoners (mostly Italian) were working on the land. The following year out of necessity this rose to *c.* 74,000, often Germans and Austrians. Due to the Geneva Convention being applied 'with vigour,' the POWs benefited from a shorter working day, were better fed and were given more luxurious transport. They were also provided with 'ludicrous protection from inclement weather,' much to the chagrin of the Land Girls. The issue became so controversial that it became the cause of a Parliamentary debate.[354] This appears to have been the case in Wiltshire too. In November 1943 the Commandant of Eden Vale Camp, Westbury was complaining to the Divisional Road Engineer in Bristol that the POW transport was not available near enough to their site of work. '... it was found the vehicle which had conveyed the P.O.W to work was parked in the village of Chittern, some two miles from the site of the working party. This means that if there is rainfall (which there was on that date) the P.O.W. are without shelter.'[355] The County Surveyor appeared to have the welfare of the POWs at Ogbourne Maizey Camp near Marlborough on his mind in February 1944. He was enquiring with the Royal Engineers Stores in Marlborough for 'a limited supply of hedging or similar leather gloves' for those POWs who were working with block limestone. Some had been complaining of lacerated hands. The prisoners also had time off at Christmas, finishing work at 12.30pm on Christmas Eve to return at 8.30pm on 28 December.[355]

The POWs' arrival could cause consternation and it was known that those arriving at Devizes by train would not get a civil reception. They were marched along an alternative route to get to the camp on the London Road to avoid the Market Place where they would have been shouted at and spat upon[356] although the Chippenham doctor Joan Hickson noted in her diary entry on 15 June 1944 that '... about 1000 prisoners had been marched through [Devizes] a day or two ago, and that they were very arrogant, all doing the Nazi salute, several turning round and putting out their tongues at women on the pavements and some spitting at the Union Jack as they passed. Most of the onlookers just laughed but it did not seem a very tactful way of ingratiating themselves to their captors.'[357] A Home Office Circular dated 28 December 1944 requested that the Police complete a questionnaire regarding the Italian prisoners in their area in respect of complaints received to establish whether the 'recent press reports' were correct. 'As you are aware, considerable publicity has been given recently to complaints about the conduct of Italian Co-operators... The matter is, as you will appreciate, of concern to the Home Office from the point of view of public order... the Home Secretary is anxious to find out how far the incidents reported in the Press and elsewhere are exceptional or exaggerated or are really representative of the general situation.' The reply from the Trowbridge Division stated that no complaints had been received and that behaviour overall had been good. Privileges had only been abused in 'very few instances.' The Warminster Division stated that there had been five minor complaints and these had been dealt with by the Camp Commandant. 'There appears to be no public feeling against these men, and no comments have been made by the public regarding their use of shops and cinemas.'[358] Frances Partridge, resident of Ham Spray house in Ham, wrote of the POWs working on Tidcombe Hill. 'We caught a glimpse of handsome dark and youthful faces, and extravagant rows of white teeth, as they smiled and waved to us. Each had a crimson disc sewn on his back and an armed soldier watching them. As we were describing them to the Guinnesses at tea... [one said;] 'Don't lets be *sentimental* about the Italian prisoners,' which in fact I don't think we were being. They seemed to have no connection with the war, that was one thing that gave our spirits a lift. We talk a good deal about the futility of worry. Well, all I can say is if one can't stop worrying one must just endure it, futile and exhausting though it is…'[359]

In Wiltshire, Hampshire and Berkshire Italians were being withdrawn from their billets in March 1946. Contained within the Wiltshire Constabulary files held at the Wiltshire and Swindon History Centre is a list giving the name and number of the Italian, the name and address of the farmer, a map reference and the date of withdrawal.[360] When the Italians finally began to be repatriated another solution had to be found and this was solved by using German POWs instead.[361] The Wiltshire Constabulary received a message in October 1944 stating:

> It is intended to accommodate German prisoners of war of the non-violent and non-ardent-Nazi type at existing Prisoner-of-War Camps at Easton Grey and Westbury, and to send them out to work in the area in unescorted small groups. They would be escorted to their places of work and escorts would be sent to bring them back to camp. They would not be allowed as much licence as the Italians were. Members of the Luftwaffe or of the Submarine Service would not be among them.
>
> This policy has been definitely adopted, though in the case of Westbury prisoners might not be there for some time to come because of lack of accommodation.
>
> Major W.J.L. Morrison, G.2.I, Headquarters Southern Command (tel. as above) would like to receive as soon as possible the Chief Constable's views as regards public reaction and public order, and would like a reply by telephone.[362]

It appears that the farmers did not have long to wait. At the end of the Wiltshire Constabulary list of withdrawn Italians is a list of German POWs billeted with Wiltshire, Hampshire and Berkshire farmers; also dated March 1946. The list contains the number, surname and first initial of the prisoner, the name and address of the farmer, a map reference and date.[363] The German POWs were less popular than their Italian counterparts. They were often sullen and stone faced but unlike the popular belief that followed the Italians, they were hard working.[364] Their terms of employment were similar but they were given less freedom and were initially used in agriculture and forestry.[365] In May 1945 the Divisional Road Engineer at the Ministry of Transport in Exeter was enquiring how many German POWs Wiltshire's County Surveyor could employ for the restoration and repair of roads by military traffic so that arrangements could be made for their accommodation. The County Surveyor thought it was not possible to prepare and submit estimates for the work, excepting the A345 Marlborough to Ogbourne road which had already been submitted.[366] By January 1946 the Divisional Engineer was advising Wiltshire's County Surveyor that he should soon be expecting the arrival of a 'considerable number' of German prisoners to begin work in March 1946 although he was not able to give an exact date. It was thought that accommodation may present some difficulties and to gauge the situation he was asking the County Surveyor for areas the prisoners could be deployed in, the number required in each area and the probable duration of the work. It appears that the County Surveyor felt that the cart was being put before the horse. '... at the present time I do not know if your Headquarters will approve all or any of these [maintenance programmes], or if they may be let to contract and until I have further details I cannot give you any reply which would be of service.'[367]

It was also intended by February 1945 that German POWs be used in US Army Hospitals at Busigny Fowler Barracks near Tidworth; Erlestoke Park; Perham Down; Charlton Park; Waller Barracks and Prince Maurice Barracks near Devizes; Chiseldon; Burderop Park; Odstock; Everleigh; Longleat; Grimsditch near Salisbury; Lydiard Park near Swindon and Marlborough Common. They were also to be used at US Army depots at Fugglestone Camp, Wilton; Salisbury; Swindon; Westbury; Savernake and Warminster.[368]

The villagers of Burbage were a little more apprehensive over the arrival of their German POWs, who struck a 'somber note.' 'After years of aeroplanes buzzing overhead which might, and sometimes did, drop bombs... toys and sweets in short supply because of the Germans' the children naturally viewed their arrival with some alarm.' They proved to be 'tremendous' workers, however.[369] One German POW, confined at Le Marchant Barracks in Devizes, wrote an account of his life as a prisoner in rhyming German in November or December 1944, shortly after it became a permanent POW camp; also included were illustrations. By December 1944 the camp was filled with 7,500 German and Italian POWs. Each Romney hut could house 300 prisoners. Daily life consisted of a 5-6am start, breakfast at 7am in the mess huts with trusted prisoners to go out to work in nearby farms, the local flax factory or the US military hospital opposite, to return to camp at 5pm for dinner, and lights out at 10pm.[370] The prisoner recorded:

> THE DAY
> The morning roll call now behind you
> And the always happy marriage
> Of white bread, tea and porridge-
> Bed-making is next.
> The blankets are folded up
> Neat and straight.
> Then the large room is swept
> Pretty clean, as is proper,
> To show that even a glance from outside
> Proves that here are soldiers housed.
> When this is done, then you can go,
> You can stay, run or stand about.[371]

For the POWs at Le Marchant Barracks, breakfast included a thin unappetising porridge, two slices of white bread and a mug of tea,[372] interesting in itself as after the 1942 introduction of the intensely disliked 'National Loaf',[373] bread for the civilian population was wholemeal. Meal tokens made from old tin cans were issued three a day per inmate, to be presented at each mealtime to prevent second helpings. The POW's 1944 account stated:

> There one forms double rows,
> And even if it rains again
> You are standing straight without complaint
> And just as pleased is your stomach.
> However, you feel a sudden scare:
> Wherever can your tokens be,
> That guarantee your food for you!?
> You think no further; to lose them
> Means a whole day of starvation.
> You search your pockets... here and there
> Nothing! Bloody hell! The interpreter
> Handed them all out before the roll call.
> I now stand inside the kitchen
> And hand in the breakfast token.
> I am warmly kissed by the kitchen air,
> A sweet aroma reaches my nose.
> Take spoon, plate, reach the head of the queue,
> Hold it out – and receive my ladle full,
> A whole plate of sweet gruel –
> How good I feel with that!
> I see raisins, see two plums...
> Can hardly control my palate...
> Take tea, and notice with delight:
> Two slices of white bread are offered today.[374]

Life could be difficult for POWs in other ways. The Police at Marlborough were advising their CID colleagues in Wiltshire Constabulary that the body of a German POW had been discovered in the River Avon on 8 October 1946. He had left two letters written in German which were being translated and was reported to have been depressed, having received no letters from home recently. The German POWs received extended privileges as from 22 December 1946.[375]

Escapes were known, such as that on 27 February 1945 at Devizes. During the attempt one POW was shot and other escapees were discovered.[376] There had been a previous attempt on Christmas Eve 1944 at Camp No. 23, called Le Marchant Camp, Devizes. The escape was planned in early December and was set to coincide with the Christmas preparations. The plan was to commandeer some lorries whilst the festivities were in full swing. The POWs would take control of a radio station and request that German warships come to pick them up. It is supposed that a guard overheard them and a large scale investigation began. The ringleaders were transferred to Camp 21[377] (Comrie Camp)[378] in Perthshire but before they left fellow prisoners ensured that the leader (who had admitted to the British that a plot had existed) was 'thrashed by his fellows' and a second man, suspected to have betrayed the plot, was given a mock trial and hanged.[379] A letter dated 24 December 1944 from the Lieutenant Colonel, General Staff of the Salisbury Plain and Dorset District to the Commander of Le Marchant Camp, copying in the Chief Constable and 8th US Armoured Division, raised concerns over possible co-ordinated escapes:

'In light of possible co-ordinated escapes from POW Camps during the Xmas period, the following precautions will be put into force during the period Sunday, 24 Dec 44 to Tuesday, 26 Dec 44, both dates inclusive :

Guards will be increased to a maximum.
Inlying picquets to be detailed.
Sentries will be instructed to challenge once and shoot to kill.
PW will be warned accordingly.[380]

Another escape from one of the Devizes POW Camps was described by David Berryman and occurred on 18 November 1944. The POWs found themselves at RAF Yatesbury. One of the prisoners was a glider pilot and thought he could fly a gilder if he could steal one. They waited until the next nightfall and tried to start a glider without success; none would start. They were by then cold, wet, hungry and disillusioned. The following morning they handed themselves in at the Black Horse pub at Cherhill. They were taken away by the guards after a hearty breakfast![381]

Eden Vale POW Camp, Westbury. Reproduced by kind permission of Ivan Clark (WSHC P53991)

POW labour was not always popular with local people who felt that the prisoners were getting larger rations.[382] The prosecution of civilians for obtaining food from POWs also led some to believe that they were getting too much food.[383] The returning British POWs had survived on Red Cross parcels alone and the question was put in the House of Commons; should the British be feeding their POWs so well? The world-wide food shortage post-war solved the issue and reductions were made.[384] In some cases it looked like the POWs were taking jobs away from local men, but the Government had stipulated that no POW should undertake work that could be done by the British workforce. In some cases however, the POWs were better skilled and progress would be delayed if the work was given to the locals.[385] The Government struggled with POW labour post-war, fearing it would arouse the suspicion of utilising cheap labour in local communities.[386] By 1945 *c.* 350,000 POWs had arrived in Britain[387] and numbers reached a peak in 1946 of 402,200 prisoners.[388]

Prisoners of War were still located in Mere in 1945. They made toys for the children such as wooden dolls.[389] By October 1945 the Surveyor of Swindon Borough Council was reporting that a sanction (official permission) was needed to secure POW labour to lay house foundations and to obtain priority for other types of labour required. He was surprised that the Ministry could not give any sanctions at the present time, due to 'technical difficulties which must be overcome.'[390] German prisoners were being brought to 89 Camp[391] at Easton Grey from the USA after the war ended, and by 1946 they were providing one quarter of the agricultural workforce. Most had returned home by the summer of 1948.[392] By the summer of 1946 the number of POWs still in Britain was causing great disquiet. Pressure was placed on the Government by religious leaders and individual MPs. The trade unions were not at all happy. Even the POWs themselves were feeling the tension, 'showing signs of apathy and despondency'. A definitive policy was called for. German POWs were still required as post-war labour was short, but an agreement was reached that they would be returned to Germany by the winter of 1948, to be replaced by Poles and other free foreign labour.[393] The task of repatriating the POWs was begun at the end of 1946,[394] but it was felt to be an agonisingly slow process.[395] Greenway Camp in Chippenham had closed by January 1947 when the Police were being asked to guard the premises against squatters.[396] A survey of rural housing requirements by the Wiltshire County branch of the National Farmer's Union in 1948 stated that in Melksham the additional workers required were mostly POWs. Another Wiltshire farmer was using 'prisoners travelling a distance.'[397] The majority of POW camps continued to be used for their original purpose until 1948. After this date many continued to remain in use as hostels for agricultural workers and some POWs took on this new role rather than return to their native country.[398]

One Minety resident felt that the work of the POWs did 'improve the fields, with ditches, brooks and rivers dug out. Brooks that had flooded in the winter covering fields no longer did so.'[399] Charles Whatley, farming in the Cricklade area noted: 'During the war draining the land went forward with an amazing speed, the impetus for which was given by the Government's subsidy on the one hand and work for P.O.W. on the other... It is no exaggeration to say that no period in history can record so much being done in so little time... The P.O.W. have let out much stagnant water to the sea and let in air and sunshine to many a field.'[400] Sophie Jackson feels that the story of the POWs has been largely ignored, but that it affected many lives. She feels that the British showed a great deal of tolerance toward the POWs compared to other countries. The British were prepared to see the men behind the uniforms and were sometimes able to 'call them friends'.[401] There were clandestine relationships; both marriages and illegitimate children did occur.[402] Official repatriation finally came to an end in 1948.[403]

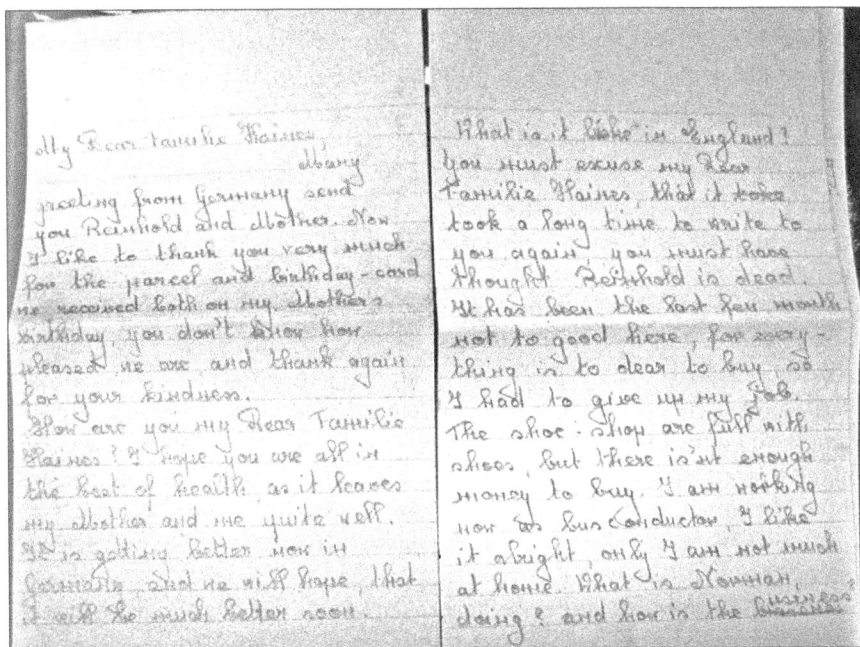

One German prisoner kept in touch with the English housewife he had come to know well after staying with her and her husband in Calne, writing to her on his return to Germany and thanking her for the birthday gift she had sent his mother. Reproduced by kind permission of Norman Haines (WSA 3572/3)

There were opportunities for POWs to continue their studies in Britain and in Camp 23 at Devizes a doctor's training scheme was put into place early in 1945. Those who had been training in medicine before the war were able to continue.[404] There was also a re-education policy after the war, so that the German prisoners could learn about 'the ways of democracy with a programme of lectures on current affairs, recent history and other topics, which the POWs did understand was full of propaganda.'[405] A few of the country's former POW camps remained in use into the 1980s, used to house foreign students.[406]

Agriculture Post-War

A CONFERENCE ON AGRICULTURE held at Bristol University as the war was drawing to a close stated that their regional survey was based on the assumption of a continued high level of agricultural efficiency post-war with no large extension of industry.[407] At County Planning Level it was hoped that all unnecessary wartime camps would be put back to agricultural use.[408] A post-war sub-committee report of the Cricklade and Wootton Bassett Rural District Council looked at rural housing and its effect on agriculture. The water needs of farmers were also considered with estimates of each farmer's daily requirements.[409] With the world food situation being seen as a serious problem in the immediate post-war period, Wiltshire's War Agricultural Executive Committee Statement of February 1946 appealed to all Wiltshire farmers to 'plant as much cereals as possible, particularly spring wheat where conditions are stable. You should bear in mind that the feeding stuffs position for stock will be even more difficult next winter than it was during the war years, and it is most essential that you should take steps to make yourself as self-sufficient in this respect as possible by the growing of roots, dredge corn, etc., and the making of silage from arable crops… The Committee know that farmers will respond to this appeal by doing their utmost to maintain their tillage acreage and by growing the maximum amount of cereals.' The County Agricultural Officer was putting on demonstrations of grass drying and showing a film on silage making, good hay and spring on the farm in 1948.[410] Although fertilizers had been utilised during the war, it was not until the post-war period that farmers really began to make the most of them.[411] Farming had been transformed into a system of applications for artificial fertilizers, herbicides, pesticides alongside selective plant breeding which in turn led to an increase of larger farms and a decrease in the number of farmers in the industry. To become successful, a holding needed to be large and to have adopted the latest scientific methods and machinery.[412] The campaign of ploughing to increase food production continued after the war as mechanical equipment became more powerful. Open downland and heathland came under the plough to change the British landscape permanently. Hedgerows were lost and fields became larger to accommodate bulkier machinery. The use of chemical herbicides and pesticides, introduced in the war years,[413] still remain commonplace. By 1973 mechanization had transformed the production of root crops; only 3% of main crop potatoes were planted by hand compared to between 65 and 70% in 1948.[414]

In October 1942 the National Farmer's Union's *Record* was praising Lord Justice Scott and the support he was giving to British agriculture. Part IV of the Scott Report had set out a Five Year Plan and 'emphasis [was] laid upon the fact that the completion of the parts of the plan which affect the countryside must be contingent upon the laying down by the Government of a definite agricultural plan and food policy.'[415] The Wiltshire Branch of the Council for Protection of Rural England (CPRE) were reporting at their meeting of 10 July 1946 that they had been actively campaigning regarding post-war policy; that the problems they faced were the same as after the last war, but this time in an 'aggravated form.' They felt that the Scott, Barlow and Uthwatt reports had provided foresight, and they had secured substantial amendments in the Requisitioned Land & War Works Acts, but had lost ground in the Forestry and Water Acts, which had been 'rushed through with little debate.' They were anxious to revive the County Branches to act as 'watch-dogs' and had been looking into the case of Imber where the military had requisitioned land and the village for military purposes.[416] Peter Hennessy reports that the 1942 Uthwatt report on Land Use 'led to nowhere and nothing.' If put into place, it would have altered the balance of land ownership substantially, but the new Labour Government of the post-war era relied instead on the Town & Country Planning Act of 1947[417] to protect agricultural land and maintain the rural character of the countryside. The Agricultural Act of 1947 was designed to affect the working of the land; to maximise food production to feed the population, and to keep down food imports. This was accomplished by continuing to guarantee farmer's prices, enabling farmers to modernise thorough grant aid, and access to the Government's Scientific Advisory Service.[418]

The post-war years in Wiltshire saw the beginnings of larger scale poultry farming, with the newly invented broiler houses appearing throughout the county. To help, there was another new invention as R. E. Rogers notes, the automatic 'feeding, watering and cleaning, deep litter houses with thermostatically controlled ventilation'.[419] The Lackham School of Agriculture near Chippenham was established by Wiltshire County Council as the County Farm Institute in October 1950, offering three courses to fifty students. The focus was on dairy farming, farm machinery and crop husbandry.[420]

Charles Orwin had already noted in 1944 that towns had begun to prosper but villages remained unchanged, unable to keep up with the changing standards of society at large and the post-war period saw rural facilities like water supply and sewerage as non existent or simply unable to cope. The changes in rural society had begun in the interwar period with the break up of large estates due to tax reform, but Howard Newby felt that changes to the middle classes led to the dominance of the upper classes diminishing in the post-war period. The social geographers Bradley, Lowe and Wright feel that countryside planning had a major impact on social deprivation in rural areas.[421] Farm labourers continued to endure a system of tied cottages and remained on relatively poor pay compared to other industries with long working hours.[422] Poor housing also remained an issue. By 1947 the Cricklade and Wootton Bassett Rural District Council were reporting that the houses for agricultural workers were due to be ready when the POWs were withdrawn and the importance of agriculture was highlighted. The council was aware of the chronic shortage of housing and the extreme need of some, but the first consideration was to be given to agricultural workers.[423]

The National Farmer's Union (NFU) was worried about the lack of housing in 1947. In an economic survey for housing needs it reported:

1. Problem is to accommodate existing workers in agriculture and to provide accommodation for the 100,000 additional adult male British workers which it is estimated are required in the industry. For these purposes, it is estimated that some 80,000 houses will be required.

2. To this end the allocations to rural districts (and urban districts of a rural character) of building materials, and labour should be increased, without reference to the proportion of population as between town and country, since the accommodation required in the countryside is needed principally in the first instance to attract workers to agriculture. It is feared that if houses are not available in the countryside, workers will tend to take jobs in the towns, where, at any rate, temporary lodging accommodation is more likely to be available meantime.[424]

The Minister of Agriculture had asked for the NFU's help to improve the rural housing position. By April 1947 the NFU was appraising the Clerks of the various Urban District Councils (UDCs) and Rural District Councils (RDCs) in Wiltshire of the issue. 'You are no doubt aware that the acute shortage of housing accommodation for Agricultural workers has been giving the Agricultural industry considerable anxiety for some years. It has been established beyond doubt that one of the principal factors in alleviating the present very acute food position is a more adequate supply of permanent British Agricultural labour. In this connection, the most serious limiting factor is the grossly inadequate housing situation.' At a conference held by the Wiltshire County branch of the NFU in May 1947 at which a number of RDCs and UDCs attended it was stated by the NFU's County Chairman that: 'the present acute world food shortage demanded the maximum production of home grown food. This was largely dependent on the labour force available, and this labour force was being maintained by supplementary labour, the main source, namely, Prisoners of War, were a rapidly diminishing force, and it was absolutely essential, both in the national interest, and that of the Agricultural industry, to encourage permanent additional Agricultural labour…' It was suggested that 'Airey' houses 'should make the maximum reasonable allocation of other houses now being built for the agricultural industry, and that they should make it easy for farmers to secure licences for the reconditioning of existing cottages, many of which were now occupied by prisoners of war who would be returning to Germany.'[425] The 'most serious limiting factor is the grossly inadequate housing situations.'[426] Wiltshire County Council (WCC) appears to have been listening to the NFU, and due to a meeting of the Wiltshire Joint Rural Housing Advisory Committee, it was thirteen days later, on 13 May 1947, that the Wiltshire County Council Clerk was writing about the issue.

1. Housing (Rural Workers) Acts. The Committee passed the following resolutions:-

That the attention of the Ministry of Health be drawn to the number of houses classified in categories III and IV in the Housing Survey already carried out by the Rural District Councils in this County, and that the Ministry be informed that this Committee reiterate their opinion that it is imperative that the Housing (Rural Workers) Acts be re-instated if a programme of reconditioning of houses in rural areas is to be successful.

That copies of this resolution be sent to the County Council Association and the Rural District Councils Association.

2. Airey Pre-Cast Concrete Houses. The Ministry of Health representative informed the Committee that the Government programme already in hand for rural areas is being supplemented in England and Wales by a special scheme for the erection of 20,000 houses of the Airey type, that he understood the allocation of these houses to the South-Western region for the current year would be 1,500, and that there was a scarcity of certain components for these houses.[427]

DEVIZES RURAL DISTRICT COUNCIL.

Summary of Information obtained regarding Agricultural Employees need for housing accommodation.

Parish.	Number of present employees.	Total No. of employees required if houses available.	No. of employees now satisfactorily housed.	No. of houses still required for Agricultural Workers.
Allcannings.	28	34	22	10 or 11
Bromham.	38	49	25	24
Chirton.	12	13	6	4
Erlestoke.	16	16	14	2
Etchilhampton.	10	10	6	4
Great Cheverell.	16	21	15	4
Marden.	20	25	18	7
Poulshot.	17	17	12	8
Roundway.	51	53	49	4
Rowde.	7	7	1	6
Urchfont.	33	37	12	14
Worton.	18	22	13	9
	266	304	193	97

List of houses needed for agricultural workers in the Devizes Rural District area, 1947 (WSA G5/132/27)

By October 1947 the Ministry of Health had understood the need for houses for agricultural workers. The Clerk of Calne and Chippenham RDC was notifying Wiltshire County Council's Director of Education that since the housing programme had been prepared, 'the Ministry of Health have decided that new houses may only be erected where they are mainly required for agricultural workers and miners. As a result enquiries are now being made to establish the agricultural need and it is possible the programme may have to be revised.' The current programme had included school accommodation at Corsham.[428]

In February 1948 the county's Rural District Councils decided to hold a series of conferences to include the entire county's RDCs in response to a recent Parliamentary Question regarding houses for agricultural workers. Their aim was to 'arrange for the speedy compilation and submission of realistic estimates of the urgent needs of new houses...' Returns were also made showing how many people were currently on the waiting list of each RDC, both those already in the county and those from outside who had approached the councils wanting to take up work if a house could be provided.[429] It was noted that estimates for the number of new agricultural workers required in England and Wales in 1948 was '60,000; but of these anything up to 30,000 may be Poles and European Volunteer workers and up to 10,000 German ex-prisoners. Thus the need for British new recruits may not exceed 20,000 (including an increase in the W.L.A.).' If this was to be the case, hostels rather than houses would be needed. 'In view of the programme of restrictions imposed by the limited supply of labour and materials, it is clearly of the utmost importance to estimate, with the greatest possible accuracy, the incidence of the actual needs for housing... It is equally important to strike a proper balance as between the provision of houses needed to improve the living conditions of the existing agricultural population and the provision of houses for new recruits urgently required for the programme of agricultural expansion.'[430] By March 1949 the Clerk of Cricklade and Wootton Bassett RDC was enquiring about accommodation for a family at Lydiard Park Camp as they were currently living in a cottage which was to be converted into a farmhouse. The Agricultural Executive Committee was 'very much pressing for the release of this house' but the council were having problems relocating the family.[431] In October 1949 the Wiltshire County Branch of the NFU was writing to all the county's Rural District Councils over worries that there was to be a 'marked reduction' in the rural housing allocation for 1950. 'You will be aware, no doubt, that the N.F.U. have pledged agriculturists to an Expansion Programme which will require the greatest possible concentration of effort by all concerned to attain. One of the most important factors in the implementation of this programme is the provision of an adequate number of houses for agricultural workers within our County.'[432]

It wasn't only housing that was causing issues for post-war agriculture in Wiltshire. The Chippenham MP David Eccles raised the issue of rural water supplies in a speech to the House of Commons on Wednesday 1 June 1949. There were thousands of acres of land without piped water in and around Salisbury Plain where farmers were finding 'it difficult, if not impossible, to practice modern methods of grass management. The essential improvement, if he has to increase his output, is water for the grazing... water is a prime necessity... on the farm.' Eccles also stated that if a farmer wanted to increase the quality of his milk and livestock he would also require plenty of clean water.[433] In January 1949 it was clear that Wiltshire's farmers were struggling. The Chairman of the Wiltshire Agricultural Executive Committee and the Chairman of the Wiltshire County Branch of the NFU were reporting that there was a 'grave danger' that wheat, potato and tillage acreage would fall below those targets that had been agreed. They appealed to farmers to plough extra grassland for cereal crops; to increase the amount of wheat planted by growing additional acres of spring wheat and to grow approximately the same acreage of potatoes as the previous year. 'It is of the utmost importance both from the national point of view and from that of the farmers that these targets should be achieved.'[434] There was still a shortage of housing for agricultural workers.

Farmers in Wiltshire were also frustrated, understanding the need to utilise as much agricultural land as possible, but often hampered by wartime requisitioning which had led to the forced possession of their land by various Government Ministries for the war effort. After the war the military authorities often wanted to keep their new sites such as that at Sutton Veny. This land was situated on a potentially productive belt of Upper Greensand and was of high agricultural value. The Local Authorities were opposed to it remaining in the hands of the military and talks were progressing regarding its future.[435] A letter of 10 January 1947 from the War Department's Land Agent to the Ministry of Health in Bristol stated that the tenant at Common Farm had been allowed to graze his land. It had been requisitioned during the war for use as a tented campsite. 'He has been paying the Department the sum of £10 per annum.' A letter from the owner of Langley House dated 29 October 1947 found it odd that in one camp the council would pay compensation and in another none. 'I have sometimes wondered if part of the Langley Burrell Camp could be derequisitioned. It seems a pity in these times to let good agricultural land deteriorate.'[436] The Wiltshire Branch of the CPRE had been looking at the question of derequisitioning in July 1946, wanting to lend as much support as possible to the Minister of Town & Country Planning. He 'needs the fullest possible public support and encouragement in his efforts to solve this problem and to secure speedier release of requisitioned land.'[437] The disposal of the wartime camps was the job of the Board of Trade; they did not appear to be taking planning control into consideration. It was also noted that clearing derequisitioned land could prove problematic. It appeared that the Government 'could not face the cost' and that the owners of the land would only receive the 1939 value by way of compensation; not enough to afford the cost either. The Requisitioning Departments did have the power under the Requisitioned Land Act to restore the land 'as far as practicable,' but 'it had been difficult to induce them to do so.'[438] It appears that the law may have been hampering Cricklade and Wootton Bassett RDC from offering an appropriate level of compensation when trying to purchase land from a farmer for a new school in 1955. The farmer's solicitor stated that: 'We wish to make it clear that we do not want anything unreasonable, but consider that present legislation does not give a small farmer... a fair chance.'[439] By 1946 a letter to the Clerk of Devizes RDC shows that one owner is despairing over the state of the meadow attached to their property. 'You will recollect that both last year and the year before I had to draw your attention to the bad state of the field at Lydeway, which you saw fit to requisition from my mother. I was passing the property a few days ago & noticed the Thistles are more numerous than ever & the field is entirely neglected, and must ask you to request the tenant to cut the Thistles forthwith before they seed. This meadow, when you requisitioned it, was an excellent pasture, but is now in a deplorable state & devoid of grass, through the utter neglect of your tenant, who has not the slightest interest in the care of this field. Please give this matter your most urgent attention.' This friction is understandable; frustration on behalf of the owner who did not want to give up the property, towards a tenant who may well have known nothing of farming.[440] In June 1948 some local people were protesting about a proposed speedway site at Blunsdon St. Andrew. One of their arguments was that it was good agricultural land which should be used for food production.[441]

Merton College Oxford owned land in Stratton St. Margaret near the station, renting it for agricultural purposes. The land was requisitioned for a military camp called Kingsdown Camp during the war for which the owner received compensation in the form of agricultural rent for the land. The Bursar at Merton, understanding of the situation during the war, was not so happy by December 1946. The land had passed to the Highworth RDC and the camp there was now occupied by squatters who paid rent. He felt that the both the owner and tenant of the land should receive additional compensation as the tenant of each hut on the camp now paid rent, going so far as to accuse the council of making a profit. In a letter dated July 1947 he accused the squatter's children of trespassing on the farmer's fields and damaging crops. A reply stated that the field had been inspected and that no apparent damage had been done. Farmers were also reporting to the Clerk at Cricklade and Wootton Bassett Rural District Council that people in the new housing estate were throwing rubbish into the fields behind their houses, rendering crops unfit for use as a feeding stuff and unsaleable in March 1949.[442]

A. G. Street felt that by 1943 the war had restored the pride to British farming and its workers.[443] He felt that the industry had become 'nationally recognized as one of Britain's greatest and most successful industries, likely to be as important in peace as it was during war, with the country people engaged in it much better off than their town cousins at every social and financial level.'[444] John Martin feels that the Government control of British agriculture during WWII has been seen as 'an unparalleled success' due to the quick rise and sustainability of the levels of food production which were achieved at a crucial time. The fact that the civilian population were 'neither starved into submission nor subjected to widespread food shortages' meant that it succeeded.[445] In terms of calories, the net output of farm production increased by 91% during the war years[446] but Martin feels that the increase in output of some crops was due to the utilisation of larger areas of land rather an increase in soil productivity. The quality of grain had actually declined, perhaps due to the lack of knowledge of farmers who were being told what they had to grow.[447] The policy of reducing livestock farming and focusing on arable also meant that an increase in output was inevitable.[448] Paul Brassley suggests that farm productivity may have in fact decreased by up to 30% during wartime, but that this was irrelevant as 'the assumption of agriculture's success was in everyone's best interests – it made the farmers heroes and the Government look effective.'[449]

Government controls over agriculture during WWII transformed the way Britain was farmed[450] and Martin feels that it arguably had the greatest significance for the development of agriculture ever seen up to that point.[451] There was an increase in tillage farming and a reduction in livestock production;[452] agriculture became dominated by cash crops such as wheat and potatoes.[453] New legislation led to guaranteed prices for farmers and intervention in the production process,[454] exceeding the successes of WWI.[455] WWII brought large financial gain to many farmers,[456] but it was those who farmed large holdings who gained the most. Smaller concerns, as Martin puts it, 'bore the brunt of wartime transformation' but in turn were not well compensated.[457] The new Labour Government's major legislation was the 1947 Agricultural Act, which aimed to provide a stable agricultural sector so that farmers, farm workers and landlords received a fair return, alongside a system which would further increase food production[458] as rationing would still be needed in the short term. Howard Newby felt that the formulation of agricultural policy in the immediate post-war years did not give any serious consideration to the possible social implications for the countryside despite the encouragement of rapid technical change. The interwar agricultural depression and wartime dependence on maximising food production were both the legacy and foundation for the future.[459] The increase in the number of large farms and the new technologies used meant that the size of the workforce began to decline by 1950[460] but productivity remained high; output in 1950 was almost at 146% of its pre-war level.[461] By the 1960s a repeat of the interwar pattern was occurring with one quarter of a million workers leaving the land.[462]

The legacy of WWII meant that British farming became irrevocably linked with state intervention; a move that would have been unprecedented in peacetime.[463] The Government's policy of maximising food production through intensive farming would have long-term consequences for British wildlife, the rural landscape and its communities[464] in years to come.

6

Doing your Bit...

Civil Defence

THE WWI ZEPPELIN and Gotha raids had shown that Britain was a target for air attack,[1] and the planning of Air Raid Precautions (ARP) had begun as early as the 1920s.[2] However, the ARP policies being put into place during the inter-war years developed slowly and in virtual secrecy. An ARP Department was created at the Home Office in 1935 to serve as a channel between the Government and Local Authorities, focused by the Air Ministry's bleak view of the possible scale of damage which could be wrought by air.[3] It was during the mid 1930s that the term Civil Defence began to be used, explaining the group of services needed to counter the threat of airborne attack.[4] In Wiltshire, the Malmesbury Rural District Council sent two representatives to a conference in Trowbridge to discuss precautions against air raids in January 1936 and Wiltshire County Council set aside £500 for the purpose of organising air raid and gas attack precautions in January 1937. It intended to introduce fifteen training centres throughout the county for specialist training,[5] probably as a result of the first radio broadcast regarding ARP which explained the Government's plans.[6] At a meeting of the Malmesbury Rural District Council in February 1937 it was noted that there was not much enthusiasm for a scheme: 'disappointment was expressed at what appeared to be a somewhat apathetic disposition towards the important matter of air-raid protection on the parts of some villages in the rural area.'[7]

The ARP Act was established on 1 January 1938 with Local Authorities being asked to submit plans which, if approved, were eligible for 60-70% grant funding.[8] By February 1938 the situation in Malmesbury looked more positive; lectures had been given in association with the air-raid precaution scheme. Charles Vernon states that these first-aid lectures 'had not even started in Bristol or Swindon'.[9] However, this general feeling of apathy on the part of the country's civilian population meant that a second radio broadcast was needed in March 1938, appealing for an additional one million volunteers.[10] A public meeting was held in Malmesbury on 3 October 1938 in which the district's Head Warden complained that 'air defence work had been regarded more in the nature of comic turn until its importance had been realised in the Czech crisis of the last few days'. Many at the meeting asked if it was necessary, and that surely the Armed Services would protect the country. It was emphasised how close England was to Germany, and how large an attack could be delivered. Volunteers were needed, particularly women.[11] A public meeting was held at the Corn Exchange in Devizes the following February to explain the Civil Defence system – there was standing room only.[12] In March 1939 the Chairman of the Combined Urban District Council and Rural District Council ARP Committee for the Borough of Malmesbury published a letter in the local newspaper.

> One would have thought that constant appeals from the Government and the recent crisis, with the possibility of further and more serious trouble to come, would have awakened the public conscience and would have helped recruiting... I notice with regret that many inhabitants of the town appear to think they have 'done their bit' for National Defence when they allow the posting of notices in their windows of appeals for other persons to volunteer for the cause, without doing so themselves.' Some had done valuable work with the evacuee census, but: 'On the other hand, it is manifestly unfair, and indeed impossible, that the burden should be borne by a few, when there are so many of both sexes who could spare the time for training, but who appear to treat the matter with complete apathy, and in a few cases, with derision.[13]

The 1 June 1939 edition of the *Wiltshire Gazette* printed a scathing attack by one Devizes Alderman regarding the amount of money which had been spent on the 'foolhardy' exercise of air raid precautions. 'Can anyone tell me why it is being done? Is there anyone here who seriously thinks there is going to be a war?'

By the end of August 1939 the Home Office was writing to all Local Authorities, asking them to complete their preparation and adaptation of buildings for use as First Aid Posts, in 'anticipation of Local War Instruction Telegram', Circulars 59 and 72/1939. The same was to be done for Report and Control Centres, and also ARP depots. However, the Lord Privy Seal did not wish councils to use their powers of requisitioning until they had received instruction to do so.[14] Local Authorities were in charge of appointing an ARP Controller who was to implement policy, working with the Chief Medical Officer, Surveyor, Chief Warden, Police and Fire Brigade. Many of the Controllers were already working for Local Authorities as Town Clerks; others were elected members such as Mayors. From this directive local Control Centres emerged, with the various posts and stations distributed evenly across each area.[15]

At a local level, each parish was required to produce its own plan to put into effect in time of invasion, called a *War Book*. These varied in detail from a list of useful contacts to full action plans; including the details of those chosen to assist when or if the time came. Some contained maps locating strategic buildings and facilities.[16] The Regional Civil Defence Office of the Regional Commissioner

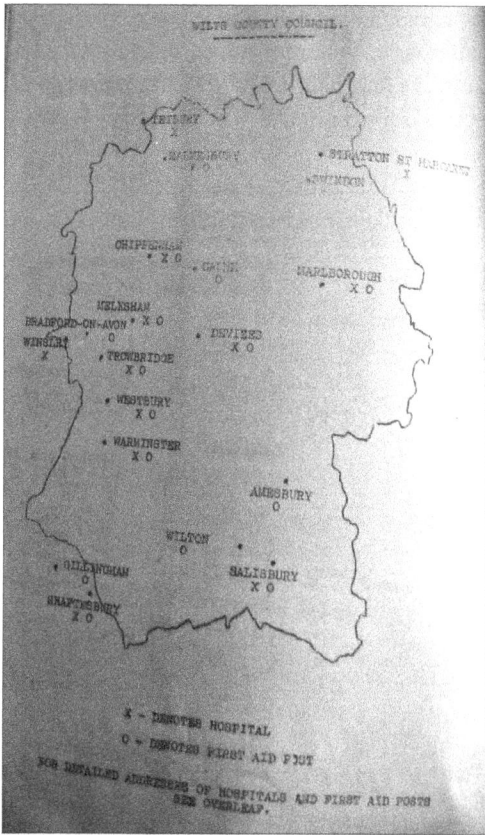

The location of Wiltshire's hospitals and First Aid Posts contained within Trowbridge Urban District Council's County Casualty Service files (WSA G15/225/1)

liaised with local Civil Defence organisations, and in the 1943 Circular it was requesting that the Invasion Committees 'which form a vital part of the civilian organisation for the defence of this country against Invasion' should complete their Civil Defence plans within three months. It was noted that the Committees had 'for some time been working to the standard of the model War Book given in the Regional Memorandum issued with *Consolidated Instructions to Invasion Committees*, and most Committees should have already attained, or at least be within easy reach of that objective.' The items expected to be found in a 'model' War Book were: provision for casualties; emergency feeding arrangements; organisation for emergency labour, tools and transport; supplementary drinking water supplies; additional Rest Centre accommodation; arrangements for supply of messengers.[17] The Deputy Town Clerk of Salisbury City Council was compiling the city's War Book in 1942, in accordance with the booklet *Consolidated Instructions to Invasion Committees*, writing to various organisations and individuals, such as the City Engineer regarding water supplies for domestic purposes.[19] Many of Wiltshire's War Books have survived in the now archived files of Wiltshire County Council, and for Cholderton this included annotated working versions as well as unused copies.[20] The Chippenham Without Parish War Book contained sections on the Home Guard, Police & Military, Wardens, First Aid and Veterinary, Messengers, Fire Guards, National Fire Service, agricultural tools and plants, details of neighbouring Invasion Committees and Control/Report Centres, and the WVS. It gave details of how each unit would be able to help and what their job would be; rendezvous points and addresses of personnel. Doubts were stated as to whether messengers would be able to get through to the Home Guard Military Commander. It was agreed that a second messenger could be sent to the American Commander at Lanhill who had offered his services.[21] The Melksham Urban District Council book covered the subjects of coal gas poisoning and portable resuscitation units, casualty services, Wiltshire County Council mobile canteens and help units, distribution of food, decontamination squads, and Housewives' services. It also detailed how the Home Guard would be deployed.[22]

The Parish War Books hold many similarities to the records of similar preparations in 1803-5 before the Battle of Trafalgar removed the threat of invasion,

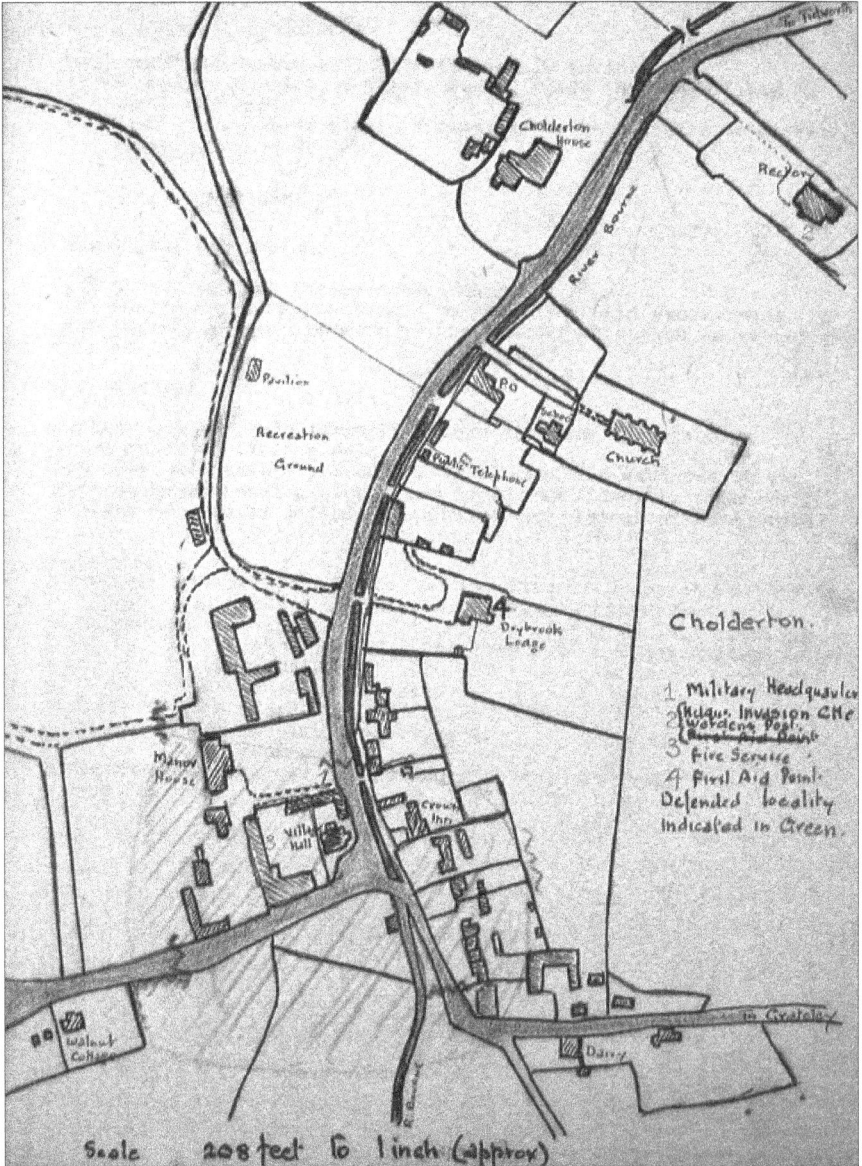

Cholderton's annotated map, included in their Parish War Book (WSA F2/851/3/20)

and the Wanborough book is inscribed with a quotation by Oliver Cromwell some 300 years earlier. 'Well, your danger, is as you have seen. And truly I think it will not, for we are Englishmen.'[23]

In September 1939 the Air Raid Precautions Department became the Ministry of Home Security[24] with the phrase ARP being phased out in 1941 to ensure the unity of ARP with the other Civil Defence services. It was to become known as the all-encompassing term 'Civil Defence'.[25] The Minister of Home Security had close links with the Secretary of State for Home Affairs and some responsibilities, such as fire fighting, were shared. The Ministry of Home Security undertook the regional organisation and co-ordination of defence activities, including the Police and Fire Brigades (where they formed part of Civil Defence), overseeing the ARP organisations run by the Local Authorities, and also for the related roles of research, design, supply and finance. The Home Office still retained its pre-war responsibilities in the case of the Police and Fire Services, and the Ministry of Health in terms of evacuation.[26] There were twelve Regional Commissioners working under the Minister of Home Security who organised the establishment of Regional Headquarters and Regional Control Rooms for Civil Defence. Counties were arranged into divisions with Area Controllers, based at an Area HQ. Every area also had its own Group Controllers, each having a Group HQ.[27]

The 1939 Civil Defence Act had empowered Local Authorities to prepare existing buildings for shelter or other ARP purposes and legally obliged employers to organise ARP services in the workplace.[28] By September 1939 the Government's ARP planning had produced a policy aimed at dealing with any form of air attack. The supply of the domestic air raid shelter, the civilian gas-mask and the stirrup pump for use by the general public at national expense could be regarded as 'revolutionary', but Joseph Meisel feels that if there was a revolution, it was a conservative one.[29] Robert Mackay regards WWII air raid precautions as fragmented, and that the deficiencies in planning should have been foreseen. It appears to have been hard for Local Authorities to learn from each other; instead they muddled through the difficulties by relying on what MacKay calls the 'freely given efforts of public spirited citizens'.[30]

But by 1940 and the fall of Dunkirk, Civil Defence was being viewed by the civilian population as increasingly important. One 12 year old evacuee in Castle Combe was helping to 'prepare Castle Combe against imminent invasion' by creating sand-bagged 'strong-points' at the village's road junctions and in surrounding fields.[31] Sand bagged Warden's Posts began appearing in Purton during the summer.[32]

Wiltshire County Council's Invasion and Civil Defence Committee met regularly during the war years. Representatives attending included those from the district Defence Committees, Women's Voluntary Service, Home Guard, Bath City Council, RAF, the Police Superintendent, Commander of the Salisbury Plain Area, a Military Liaison Officer, the Red Cross, an ARP Officer and the Women's Institute.[33] Topics for discussion ranged from shelters for the public and hospitals, to the release of roadmen for harvest, Food Control Centres and respirator distribution in 1939,[34] to fire watching in corn growing areas, food and yeast distribution, petrol and immobilising vehicles in 1941.[35]

A pamphlet published by Swindon Borough Council was prepared as a permanent record of the extent of Swindon's Civil Defence Organisation 'as it existed at its peak in 1943'. It lists Civil Defence Transport, Civil Defence Ancillary Services-Rest Centres, Emergency Feeding to include British Restaurants, Emergency Centres, Cooking Depots, Mobile Canteens, Women's Voluntary Services (750 personnel) and the Housewives' Service (520 personnel). There was also a Board of Trade Scheme for the erection of Emergency Shopping Booths in case of damage to shops and a National ARP Animals Committee registered vet for Swindon and districts, in charge of arrangements for animal casualties.[36]

Preparations continued for those on the Home Front, and 'doing your bit' for many meant working additional hours on Civil Defence duty, more often than not on top of their daytime work. There was a multitude of organisations established either in the years preceding the war or during wartime itself which were recruiting volunteers.[37]

Air Raid Precautions

AN APPEAL WAS made early in 1937 for volunteers to act as Air Raid Wardens in case of air attack[38] and by mid 1938 200,000 citizens had been recruited.[39] The Air Raid Precautions (ARP) Act of 1937 was designed to 'provide shelter against blast and splinters for people caught in the street during an air raid, and for those whose houses were impractical for refuge'.[40] In early 1938 Wiltshire County Council appointed Mr. D. B. H. Lennox-Boyd from Bedfordshire as Air Raids Officer to prepare the scheme in consultation with the County's Local Authorities. He was aged 30 and had previously been in the Scots Guards. Very quickly he had ascertained that 4,500 volunteers were required. Of these, 3,000 would be Wardens and 1,500 First Aiders.[41] On 25 September 1938 just before the Munich Agreement was signed, the ARP services were mobilised and were enlisting new volunteers.[42] On the front page of the *Warminster Journal*, 30 September 1938, there was a call to arms:

What are you Doing for the ARP?
Urgently Wanted NOW
Air Raid Wardens
First Aid Helpers
Stretcher Bearers
Decontamination Squads
Warminster Needs Your Help
Before it is too Late
Join Now.

Trowbridge's ARP Committee was meeting in October 1938, drafting a Fire Emergency Organisation Scheme. An emergency telephone service would be established at the Magistrates' Room in the Town Hall, Trowbridge, to be manned 24 hours. 244 men and 40 women had volunteered but at present only 26 had been fully trained.[43] By March 1939 it was reported that an extra 6,000 volunteers were needed for the ARP; Salisbury and Swindon had the greatest shortages but Malmesbury the greatest need. The Auxiliary Fire Service (AFS) required 660 more personnel and the Special Police needed 68 (although the regular Police Force was above strength). The Observer Corps were short of 175. In March 1939 Wiltshire Constabulary took on a greater role with regards to ARP, appointing Sergeants in six towns to oversee activities[44] and by May 1939 the 89 Wardens who had enrolled under the command of Wiltshire's Chief Constable took part in a special exercise simulating an aerial attack on an area stretching from Calne through to Devizes and Market Lavington, alongside a practice blackout with RAF planes flying overhead. The *Wiltshire Gazette* reported on 1 June 1939 that the exercise was seen as serving 'a most useful purpose' and many lessons were learnt. It had also been viewed by Home Office officials. However, in July 1939 reports went out that a Wiltshire wide blackout had not been met in Malmesbury. It had been a 'wash-out' rather than a 'black-out' due to a shortfall of male ARP volunteers. As for women: 'We can barely raise one first-aid party for the whole of the borough. We ought to have four. The men we want so urgently are those between 30 and 50. There are plenty of them, but many say they will not join until an emergency arises. This is not the way to be prepared,'[45] but by the autumn of 1939 the acronym ARP had become the most familiar of the day.[46] Full-time ARP workers were being paid £3 5s per week for men and £2 3s. 6d. for women.[47] No overtime was paid to ARP workers who were theoretically meant to work 72 hours per week.[47] In practice most were not paid recruits but unpaid volunteers.[48]

ARP Wardens were at first seen as parasites, as Bette Anderson recalls, 'drawing wages but doing nothing to earn them',[49] with many working class men feeling they were 'no more than lackeys of the police'. Almost immediately after the outbreak of war the press began suggesting that the full-time staff were, as Angus Calder notes, 'overpaid army-dodgers'. On 11 September 1939 the Government began reducing the number of personnel with the result that by December, more than half the full-time workers had either been fired or had quit 'in disgust'.[50] In Swindon, Trevor Cockbill recalls that the 'early endeavours' of the ARP Wardens to prepare the town's residents for total war '... were treated with a mixture of disdain and amusement. There were those who dismissed the A.R.P. training and activities as the doings of 'the usual crowd of officious busybodies,' 'frustrated sergeant-majors' and 'comedians." Some of the town's A.R.P. Wardens complained that their rehearsals were 'watched by groups of people who scoffed at their exertions.'[51]

John Anderson, the Minister for Home Security, issued a Christmas Message in 1939 to Civil Defence workers via Local Authorities:

I desire to express to you my sincere wishes for a Happy Christmas, coupled with my warmest thanks for the work you have done as a member of the Civil Defence Services towards making this country ready to meet air attack.

Your work may not yet have been tested by actual war experience, but those who are responsible for Civil Defence appreciate to the full the sacrifices you have made during the year which will soon be closing.

The New Year will call for more sacrifices, for some patience and for constant readiness, but may it also bring you and yours Good Fortune.

John Anderson.[52]

Unfortunately, as in the case of those in Swindon, the message was received too late to be distributed through local schools and so was not received in time for Christmas.[53]

ARP Wardens

BY JUNE 1940 over 50,000 women througout the country were employed full-time and many more part-time;[54] one in six of the total. Those working full-time oversaw their areas during the day with the part-timers taking on the night shift.[55] The duties of ARP Wardens were to understand the organisation of air raid services in their locality and the means by which they should communicate with them; to help persons in the street after an air raid warning including where to find the nearest shelter; to report the fall of bombs and fires immediately to the fire brigade and if the presence of gas was discovered, to sound the alarm; to survey the extent of bomb damage and make a report as soon as possible; to assist occupants of damaged buildings to find shelter; to guide the Police, Fire Brigade, First Aid parties, Rescue parties etc. on arrival at the scene and render any other assistance required; to help prevent panic and set an example of 'coolness and steadiness' for their neighbours; to fight 'incipient' fires whilst waiting for the fire brigade.[56] Some Wardens were trained as 'Incident Officers', wearing a special badge and a blue covering on their steel helmets. Their job was to set up an incident room near the emergency and organise clear routes up wind of any fires to aid emergency vehicles.[57] ARP members displayed a metal plaque on their front door so that people would know who to turn to in an emergency. Each had a telephone in their house which was not a common occurrence at the time.[58] Warden's Posts were set up, but it appears that in Swindon at least they were not adequately equipped. In October 1943 the Town Clerk had been requesting improved amenities and storage accommodation at various Wardens' Posts in the town. The Minister of Home Security appeared to understand the issues involved as he 'approve[d] in principle...' The Chief Warden had told the Clerk '... I would stress that for practical purposes, the wardens posts in this area are not large enough to provide shelter for wardens under the circumstances of Warning Conditions which at present obtain in the Area of this Authority's Scheme.' Under 'Warning Conditions' the Wardens had to be off their beds but they had no facilities for making refreshments or taking a proper rest; they were having to improvise.[59]

Uniforms trickled through very slowly and, as for the Home Guard, were often inadequate when they arrived, initially with no rank badges. The Government tried to recall them to announce a standard badge. One Malmesbury Warden wrote bitterly that presumably 'the new badges were to be sewn on our pyjamas.' In Malmesbury, 1941, the Head Warden of the Borough felt that:

> [m]any wardens ha[d] no steel helmet, no C.C. respirator and no gumboots. As to uniform, although we may be called on to deal with fires, render first-aid and help in rescue work, it has not so far been considered necessary to issue us with overalls, although the services directly concerned with these tasks have all got them.
>
> Many of us have been in the Wardens' Service for more than three years now, is it surprising that we feel slightly disheartened?'[60]

It was not until May 1941 that the full-timers and regular part-timers received their proper uniform of blue serge with overcoat, berets and boots.[61]

Westbury ARP workers in their berets and great coats, c. 1941, reproduced by kind permission of Ivan Clark (WSHC P53998)

All ARP members had to attend weekly training sessions[62] where training in gas precautions, fire fighting etc. was carried out.[63] In Malmesbury a gas van was due to visit in August 1938. The vans were used for training purposes; ARP workers would not be able to qualify for their badges unless they had entered a gas chamber.[64] A letter was sent in September 1939 from the Co-ordinating Officer,

Trowbridge ARP regarding their request for the Trowbridge Fire Brigade officers to assist with training. Unfortunately the fire brigade didn't have enough time to help.[65] In January 1940 ARP Wardens took part in one of the first air raid exercises in Wiltshire, held at Trowbridge. On 12 January the *Wiltshire News* reported on what appeared to be a highly organised event. 'When the clock struck ten, A.R.P. sirens shrieked out their warning notes and there were remarkable scenes in the streets of Trowbridge... by the Town Bridge at 10.16 a.m. when a 'high explosive bomb' fell there. A big fire was started and the big mills were in danger. This incident brought into action the fire brigade with other A.R.P workers to deal with traffic, gas mains, water mains, casualties etc.

Ambulances dashed to the scene and 'casualties' were put on stretchers and taken off to hospital in vehicles driven by women A.R.P. drivers...' but, '[i]n the midst of this important incident it was a coincidence that about 50 pigs, a small

Details of Civil Defence training in Swindon, including the NFS, WVS, Housewives' Service, ARP Wardens and Fire Guards (WSA G24/225/28)

herd of bullocks and a party of gipsies with ponies arrived there. The drovers and gipsies [*sic*] went on their way while the A.R.P. volunteers did their job'!

There was an ARP practice at Ludgershall in May 1940, a much smaller and locally organised affair. Sybil Eccles from Chute reported in a letter to her husband David, the Government's Principal Economic Adviser:

Two workers 'turned up with the vans. Too funny it was for words. Such squabbles about who did turn up at the 'Rendy Voos' and who didn't. Who gave orders when he shouldn't and who didn't when he should. How disgraceful it was when the fire brigade overshot the mark.

But they're a worthy lot on the whole and determined to do their duty – so if and when the Huns arrive they'll be up and about the business.'[66]

The doctor Joan Hickson wrote in her diary of an 'Invasion Exercise' on 25 July 1942 in Chippenham. 'I don't think we shall be 'playing' unless the casualties become very numerous and rumour has it that the 'Enemy' will not arrive before dawn. I suppose these stunts do some good, though the British public is quite incapable of taking them seriously.'[67] An ARP educational show was held in the Town Hall, Malmesbury, on 24 June 1942[68] and it was also the job of the ARP Warden to warn children of the dangers of incendiary bombs, as one did at Minety in June 1940, included in a talk about air raids.[69]

Control Centres

ARP UNITS IN Wiltshire were based in Salisbury, Swindon, Trowbridge, Bradford on Avon, Devizes, Melksham, Market Lavington, Chippenham, Calne, Corsham, Wootton Bassett, Highworth, Purton, Cricklade, Chiseldon, Marlborough, Ramsbury, Amesbury, Pewsey, Ludgershall, Wilton, Downton, Tisbury, Mere, Warminster, Westbury and Codford. Buildings were requisitioned for use as ARP Control Offices, such as the Town Hall, Devizes, and Control Rooms, such as part of the Town Hall in Chippenham.[70] The Regional Control Rooms included clerical staff, Intelligence and Communications Officers, telephonists, clerks, messengers,[71] Liaison Officers from the Police, Fire Brigade, public utilities and the Home Guard. There was also a District or County Surveyor present, as well as a Gas Identification Officer.[72] Instructions prepared for the guidance of Assistant Controllers and Police Officers on duty at the County Control Centres included details of how to deal with buildings of architectural and historical importance including churches. A list had been prepared by a panel of architects on behalf of the Ministry of Works. Should any of the buildings be damaged by enemy action the 'County District' was to telephone County Control giving particulars of the damage. Instructions for staff at the County Control Centre listed situations such as Ministry of Food convoys, enemy aircraft brought down, damage to electricity, mutual assistance schemes, unexploded bombs, blocked roads and enemy parachutes.[73] Incidents would be plotted on maps and charts at each Control Centre, and the numbers of available parties would also be displayed, the Controller watching the situation as it unfolded. Heads of Service would then send out parties from their Depots. The Control Centre's Controller was also responsible for agreeing the use of Rest Centres and emergency mortuaries, and could ask for reinforcements from a neighbouring area or from the Region if necessary. The Control Room issued reports on local damage to properties and services, casualties etc. which was sent to the Regional HQ and from there to the Minister of Home Security and the Cabinet.[74]

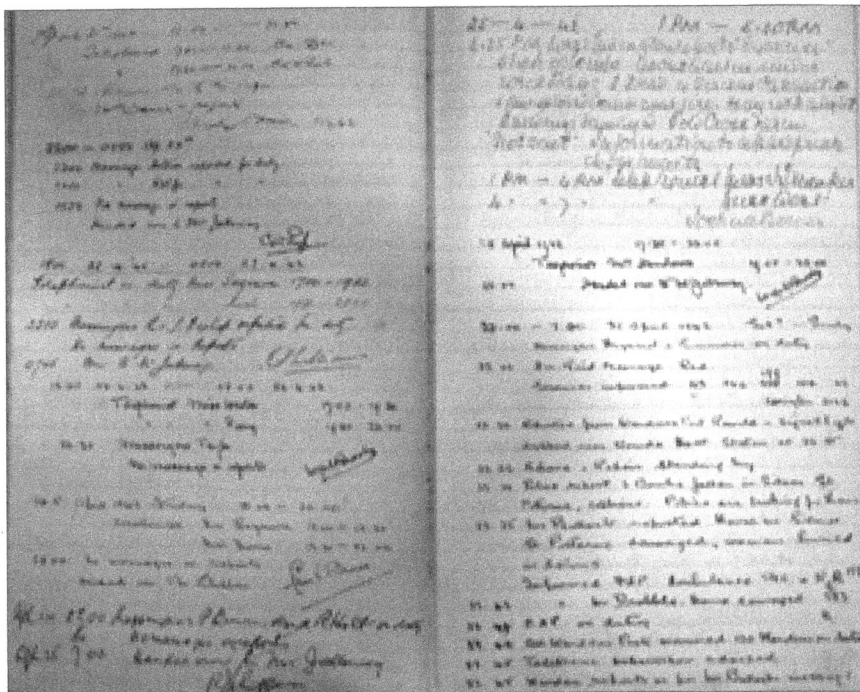

Entries in the Devizes Control Centre Daily Log Book, 21-25 April 1942 detailing messages received (WSA G20/223/3)

In September 1939 the society photographer Cecil Beaton volunteered to serve part-time as a Control Room telephonist in Wilton. He had leased Ashcombe House from 1930 where he rested, wrote, gardened and entertained. He recalled that the 'squad of nine persons foregathered for duty from eleven in the evening until eight in the morning' with their 'Thermos flasks of cocoa and Bovril, biscuits and books.'[25] They were only vaguely briefed when it came to their duties and at the sign of an alarm Beaton felt sure he would get 'hopelessly entangled' with the many wires and plugs at the switchboard. Mr Lush, the Town Clerk, was available in case they needed help and Mr Keating, a retired civil servant, was their 'rather quavering lead.' With him were a couple of gentleman farmers, a lady with her debutante daughter, Lady Pembroke and her butler.[76] The operators dealt with calls regarding bomb damage and crashed German planes, but there were also reports of suspected raids, many of which were false. One telephonist at the Control Room in Devizes gave a caller short shrift when their 'explosions' turned out to be a car backfiring. 'I told them politely but firmly not to trouble the Control with such trivialities

REGISTER of AIR RAIDS and ALARMS.

Melksham Report Centre,
Town Hall,
Melksham.

I. SIGNALS.
a. Air Raid Message   YELLOW.   Received.....................
b. Air Raid Message   PURPLE   ....
c. Air Raid Warning   RED   ....
d. Air Raid Message   WHITE   ....

II. BOMBS.
HIGH EXPLOSIVE. One. .... 50 yds. from Garnbrook Farm House. ATWORTH
INCENDIARY .... approx. 120 .... in Fields. Coke's Brk.
SMOKE.
DELAYED ACTION...
UNEXPLODED ....
POISON GAS ....
Notes
..... Approx. time: 23.05. hrs.
MACHINE GUNNING..
....

III. SERVICES CALLED.
First Aid......................
Fire... 2. Trailers..........
Demolition....................
Decontamination...............
Ambulances....................
Mobile First Aid Post.........
Vet. Services.................
Rescue Party..................
Gas Identification Officer ....
Party for Unexploded Bombs ....,....
Road Repair...................
Utilities.....................

IV. DAMAGE.
a. Utilities.................................
GAS.....................................
ELECTRICITY.............................
WATER...................................
SEWERS..................................
G.P.O.LINES.............................
b. ROADS................................
....
c. BUILDINGS. Garnbrook Farm House. Shattered Windows.
....
d. LIVESTOCK............................
....
CASUALTIES.

	Deaths.			Injured.	
Male	Female	Children	Male	Female	Children

Date 24th Aug. 1940

Form for Registering Air Raids and Alarms at the Melksham Report Centre, Town Hall, Melksham. This entry is for one high explosive and approximately 120 incendiary bombs. Two fire trailers were called to the scene and damage included shattered windows at Garnbrook Farmhouse, 24 August, 1940 (WSA G2/132/1) and that I was busy with a *real* bomb.'⁷⁷ On 2 October 1940 it was reported at the Wiltshire County Council Emergency Committee meeting that the Chippenham ARP Officer was having great difficulty manning the Chippenham Control Centre for 24 hours a day. He was instructed to liaise with the Women's Voluntary Service and Home Guard 'with a view to some arrangements being come to for carrying out this work and also similar work at other Control Centres'.⁷⁸

There were also Report Centres; one for every 100,000 people, although in rural districts which were less densely populated there were instead a series of Report Posts. Mike Brown reports that their function was to 'receive, sift and collate all information', to sort the raw data into an accurate picture of events to enable the Control Centre to respond appropriately.⁷⁹

ARP Duties

IN RURAL AREAS, ARP duties were more routine; enforcing blackout restrictions and ensuring the readiness of all services in case of need. In the Wiltshire countryside ARP wardens played Patience through their night-time fire watching sessions.⁸⁰ The Trowbridge ARP Wardens' log book for the Head Post of West Sector at the boys' High School makes enlightening reading. During March 1941 the continual flight of German bombers passed overhead, noted on 6,7,11,13,14,15,16,18 and 19 March. On the night of 15/16:

> 'The 'Raiders Passed' again at 11.25pm. Wardens foregathering at the Post were very suspicious about this, and speculation was rife as to what further pleasantries were in store. After a time, however, the Wardens manning the Post displayed an inclination to yawn, as being wishful to retire, but the others were very hard to dis-lodge, eventually reluctantly departing about midnight. [Night 18/19:] Rather a cold, raw morning, with a waning half moon lying on its back. A plane (probably enemy) passed over at 4.30am flying from north to south. District was patrolled and contact made with fire watchers in all the streets. Just before 5am a thick mist settled down, obscuring the moon. [Night of 29/30 March:] Great activity in the Bristol direction tonight – flares, gun-flashes and shell burst, also a great red glow rising and falling in the sky. [Sunday 30/31:] A fine clear starlight night, with some activity by our own planes. Later, the drone of planes and the snores of nameless warden merged into the blissful unconsciousness of a pleasant undisturbed night. And so, housewards, in a stinging white frost, about 7am.
>
> [By 8/9 April 1941:] On patrol, conversation languished, but a fire watcher in the Avenue did tender the opinion that the weather was on the change... Fortunately 'Raiders Passed' sounded at 3.44am. Aha! But the night's adventures were not yet finished with. A sweet blissful, dreamless sleep was rudely shattered at 5.10am by the ringing of the 'phone for another Purple Message. Warden... said it ought to be blue, not 'purple' but his remark was received with a pained silence. And then the Siren blared out with another Red Warning, at 5.19! We could hardly believe our ears, but there it was. Out

we turned once more, & patrolled to a vantage point, but found nothing or no-one but one faithful fire-watcher. The sky was now leaden, but not our footsteps as we returned to the Post for at 5.45 came what proved to be the final 'Raiders Passed.'[81]

Air raid warning messages came through the telephone exchange colour coded. *Yellow* meant danger coming nearer, *Red* was danger overhead. *Purple* would be danger passing away and *White*, all clear.[82] On the night of Good Friday, 11/12 April 1941:

> Up to 11.30pm great activity was in evidence in the Bristol direction. AA gunfire was intense; gunflashes flickered incessantly, and the sound of the gunfire itself was much heavier than usual.... A loud report, with accompanying blast was heard at 12.20 and the Siren sounded... Sustained intense activity – probably more than on any other previous night – now followed until about 3.15am. A glow in the sky over the N.W. told its own story.[83]

Miss E. Berrett from Hilperton was a school teacher who also worked as a Fire Watcher. Her diary entry on 5 May 1941 explains how the different Civil Defence teams worked together.

> We were awakened at 12.20 by the whistling of a bomb. Then we heard the shouts of the firewatchers. I put on my firewatcher's helmet & went out. The bomb had fallen in the allotments in Hill Street... The Wardens watched all night & the police took over at 6AM. Several policemen came to look at the crater which was 4' across. The military had a look & decided that it was safe and must have exploded in the earth. The crater has been filled with sand.[84]

Through no fault of their own, many of Wiltshire's ARP Wardens did far more watching than doing, but some did attend emergencies. Twelve ARP Wardens from Devizes travelled to Purley, Surrey, for a week to give their counterparts a rest during the second half of 1944 when the VI and VII bombs were causing destruction in London and the south east. They were later sent a letter of thanks from Purley and the Chief Constable of Wiltshire.[85] At the end of February 1941 Mr O. E. Parsloe from Swindon was awarded the Medal for Gallantry for his actions during an air raid. Vernon records that he was in charge of the rescue and demolition squad who, with a colleague, 'worked for some hours in a tunnel less than 2ft. high to rescue a woman and two children who were buried under a house.'[86]

Fire Services

Auxiliary Fire Service

AS EARLY AS 1932 the Home Office's Fire Advisor was warning that existing fire services would not be able to cope in the event of war and that expansion would be needed.[87] It was the ARP Act of 1937 which required all local Fire Brigades to recruit and train volunteers.[88] In January 1938 the Government began asking Local Authorities to set up an Emergency Fire Brigade organisation which included Auxiliary Fire Stations, and to recruit and train personnel.[89] Malmesbury had created twelve posts for Auxiliary Firemen for training in connection with the preparation of an ARP scheme by June 1938.[90] The Fire Brigades Act of July 1938 enforced the issue and gave Local Authorities two years to assemble their services.[91] In April 1939 the Home Office was reminding Local Authorities of their requirement to 'enter into arrangements with other fire authorities and persons who maintain the fire brigades to secure the provision of assistance by those authorities and persons for the purpose of dealing with fires which cannot adequately be dealt with by the local fire services.' Guidance on the matter had been sent on 20 September 1938[92] and by May 1939 Bath City Council were enquiring whether Devizes Rural District Council (RDC) wished to consider entering into a mutual assistance scheme as per Section 1 (5) of the Fire Brigades Act 1938. Other towns being approached included Bradford on Avon, Corsham, Trowbridge, Melksham, Calne, Westbury, Warminster and Chippenham, as well as locations in Somerset. In the previous month, Devizes RDC had considered the Fire Brigade Act 1938, passing a resolution: '... that this Council protests against the serious burden to be thrown upon the Ratepayers, particularly in rural districts...' Before this, volunteer Fire Brigades had been maintained by contributions from property owners and through insurance companies, but with the new act, all finance had to be raised via the rates 'with advantages to the Companies far in excess of the £60,000 to be paid by them to the Exchequer.' Their resolution was sent to the Home Secretary at Whitehall.[93]

By August 1939 the country was to be divided into Special Fire Brigade Areas. Wiltshire fell into the No. 7 (South Western) Region with Gloucestershire, Dorset (with some exceptions), Somerset, Devon and Cornwall. This area was to be further divided into Emergency Fire Districts. In September the Home Office was sending the Clerk of Salisbury and Wilton RDC a copy of Circular 70/1939, stating that the Minister of Home Security was impressed at the 'speed and efficiency with which the Auxiliary Fire Service was mobilised on receipt of the instructions issued on the 1st instant.' He wished to express his 'high appreciation'. The autumn of 1940 saw the Home Office deciding to defer the call up of members of the part-time Auxiliary Fire Service to military service as their 'services [were] required for the efficient operation of the Emergency Fire Brigade organisation...'[94]

At the advent of the war, the two established Trowbridge Fire Brigades, the Town and Usher's Brewery, joined together to aid the war effort. The Chief Fire Officer '... went around Trowbridge giving advice on how to use the stirrup pump and a bucket of water for incendiary bombs.'[95] The regular fire service in Devizes comprised twelve full-time firemen and four firewomen, forty-one part-time men and eight women, covering the ten pumping stations. Some of the town's residents also had stirrup pumps, advertising the equipment by placing a notice in their

TEL. No.: VICtoria 4433.

*Any communication on the
subject of this letter should be
addressed to :—*

THE UNDER SECRETARY OF STATE,
  HOME OFFICE (FIRE BRIGADES DIVISION),
    CLELAND HOUSE,
      PAGE STREET,
        LONDON, S.W.1.

and the following number quoted :—
  F.B.Gen.166/1

HOME OFFICE,

CLELAND HOUSE,

PAGE STREET,

LONDON, S.W.1.

Telegrams:- Emblaz Sowest London.
13th September, 1939.

Sir,

Message from His Majesty the King to Members
of the Auxiliary Fire Service.
F.B. Circular No. 63/1939.

I am directed by the Secretary of State to say that
he wishes the following message from His Majesty the King to
be conveyed to the members of the Auxiliary Fire Service:-

"NOW THAT THE EMERGENCY HAS COME I WISH TO EXPRESS
TO ALL THE CIVIL DEFENCE VOLUNTEERS MY APPRECIATION OF
THE WAY THEY HAVE RESPONDED TO THE CALL AND OF THE FINE
SPIRIT IN WHICH THEY ARE FACING THE LONG HOURS AND
DISCOMFORT INSEPARABLE FROM THE PERFORMANCE OF THEIR
DUTIES.   THE QUEEN AND I HAVE SEEN FOR OURSELVES SOME-
THING OF YOUR ORGANISATION AND WE HAVE NO DOUBT WHATEVER
THAT THE COURAGE OF THE VOLUNTEERS, COUPLED WITH PATIENCE
DURING TIMES OF INACTION, WILL BE EQUAL TO WHATEVER TASKS
MAY BE IN STORE FOR THEM.   SIGNED – GEORGE R.I."

I am to ask that steps may be taken to communicate
His Majesty's message to all concerned.

I am,

Sir,

Your obedient Servant,

Issued to:-
  The London County Council
  All County Borough and Borough Councils
  All Urban District Councils
  All Rural District Councils.
  Chief Constables
  Chief Officers of Fire Brigades in England and Wales.

*Statement by His Majesty the King to members of the Auxiliary Fire Service, 13 September
1939 (WSA G11/225/12)*

window. The pump was available for householders to help themselves or to aid their
neighbours in an emergency. Every householder was allowed to take a bucketful
of sand for use in their home in case of incendiary bombs.[96] There were ten times
the numbers of full-time Auxiliary Firemen compared to regular Firemen, and

over 100,000 part-timers. Women were recruited as drivers, clerks, telephonists and watch room staff, their duties extending to extinguishing incendiary bombs.[97] In Warminster, the volunteers were trained by Captain Dewey from 1938 and included the first women who staffed the watch room.[98]

The Auxiliary Fire Service (AFS) was not welcomed by the regular Fire Service units who felt their jobs might be threatened.[99] The peacetime service had been underpaid and now Calder reports, 'along came throngs of 'amateurs'', agreeing to work for low wages, and for unspecified hours with no sick leave or holidays, often without a uniform.[100] Mike Brown notes: 'Fifty bob a week army dodgers, they called us'. The volunteers left in droves during the spring and summer of 1940; the routine drills, often during blackout, and with nothing else to do… they joined the services instead.[101] By the end of 1940 the AFS received 12 days annual leave and three weeks sick leave. Those working full-time received £3 5s. a week for men and £2 3s. 6d. for women.[102] The working hours of the firemen were the most standardised of all the Civil Defence services, with 48 hours on and 24 hours off. The part-time auxiliaries did one night on duty, one on call and one free.[103] The AFS teams were issued with pumps, but not the vehicles with which to tow them. Many had to make do by borrowing or purchasing any type of vehicle they could get hold of.[104] In April 1940 the Minister of Home Security was considering Melksham Urban District Council's proposed purchase of vehicles for towing trailer units as unnecessary. Melksham was not regarded as a 'first line' unit but, as two cars had already been obtained for £30 each, the adaptation could be made, but only as cheaply as possible.[105]

Auxiliary Fire Service personnel in uniform outside the First-Aid Depot in Bradford on Avon, reproduced by kind permission of Mike Marshman (WSHC P55100)

As the months passed, the main job of the AFS was often pumping out flooded Anderson shelters.[106] By 1942 in Cricklade, the regular firemen were working during the day with the auxiliaries taking over at night. They practised pumping at the Latton Lido around once a week.[107] Many of those AFS members who were lucky enough to have a uniform did not wear it due to the cutting remarks they received from members of the public regarding their pay.[108] The issue of uniform had been tackled by the Home Office in June 1938 when they issued a list of uniform articles and equipment for both men and women[109] but in Malmesbury, contention was rife over uniform, although the issue was over which companies should procure or produce it. A Town Council meeting in June 1939 had approved the purchase of a uniform and had recommended accepting certain tenders. The question was raised whether local traders had had the opportunity to apply, but others felt that any local tenders would prove more expensive. The town's shopkeepers were unhappy, voicing their protest in a local newspaper.[110]

Receipt for an Auxiliary Fire Service badge (WSA G14/228/3)

By early 1940 the Malmesbury Rural District Council area AFS was proving successful. Forty recruits from the town and surrounding area attended the first drill on a Friday evening. They shared a 'keen interest' in their duties. But, as with other services, there was often the case of a shortage of volunteers.[111] An article in the *Wilshire Gazette* on 27 August 1942 was appealing for recruits for the National Fire Service. 'Women Needed in N.F.S. To Release Men For Fire Fighting.' It had been discovered that fire hydrant sizes differed from one region to another, and the hoses of relieving fire crews from other areas could not be used. The Minister of Home Security Herbert Morrison had to act and on 13 May 1941 the creation of a National Fire Service (NFS) was announced in Parliament. The reorganisation was completed before the autumn and, as Calder points out, 'an efficient organisation was shaped from a chaos of petty interests'.[112] Lane and White feel that '[t]he co-operation of employers and the commitment of the men were, and remain, the major features of its success.'[113]

Some larger companies like Westinghouse in Chippenham already had their own fire team and engine, manned by workers at the factory.[114] In April 1944 the NFS held a demonstration before a crowded audience in Malmesbury with every parish in the Malmesbury district represented. It was attended by a 'very interested audience'.[115] (Vernon, p. 88).

Home Office Circular 154/1940 was inviting Local Authorities to send their Auxiliary Firemen to assist in exchanges of personnel. '... the arrangements which have been made in some cases for exchanging whole-time personnel between heavily bombed areas and other districts have proved very useful in providing, on the one hand, rest for personnel who have been heavily engaged, and, on the other, valuable experience for crews whose home stations have not so far been called upon to deal with air-raid fires on a large scale...' The period of exchange was to be no longer than a week but it could be extended by mutual agreement; the extent of travel was to take up to one day only.[116] The Salisbury AFS met up on Skew Bridge, 'the Green Goddesses all lined up before setting off to Southampton' to help when it was being blitzed.[117] The Warminster National Fire Service was sent to Bristol and Plymouth during the blitzes to aid the beleaguered crews[118] and Civil Defence workers from Purton travelled as far as Coventry and London to offer their aid. A member of the Trowbridge Auxiliary Fire Service was called to do duty in Bristol and was '… almost lost for words on his return to the office in trying to describe the terrible devastation.'[120]

In 1947 Wiltshire's Fire Service was returned to local council care[121] but at least one local council was not happy at the prospect. Calne Town Council was protesting at the measure, its Financial Committee claiming that the estimated cost of running the Fire Service in 1948/9 after the changes was 'alarming.' They wanted the draft scheme modified. It was also felt that the proposals would in no way improve the efficiency or performance '… of the Fire service at Calne [which] has always been of a high standard, and it is considered that this can be maintained at a cost well below the 6d. rate proposed.' It was also felt the scheme was 'unfair and unjust to the smaller authorities financially'.[122] The draft of the Fire Services Act had been sent to the councils of the County Districts for their consideration on 27 November 1947 and a meeting had been arranged at County Hall, Trowbridge, where representatives of the twenty-one District Councils were present. Their main objections were: excessive cost, fire cover unduly high, proportion of Officers and NCOs to Firemen too high, division of the County into three districts both unnecessary and undesirable, the staff ratio at Headquarters too heavy and the smaller authorities subsidising the larger towns. The Fire Brigade Committee had carefully considered the points but '… on further consideration, and with the greatest reluctance, they came to the conclusion that they must adhere to their original scheme.'[123]

Fire Guards

DURING WWII FIRE Watching had been organised as an extension of the Wardens' Service[124] until the Fire Watchers Order was introduced in September 1940. The owners or occupiers of business premises were obliged to ensure that a Fire Watcher was present on the premises at all times, but the system often broke down[125] and was presumably not well enforced. The duty was made compulsory from early 1941[126] after the fire that almost engulfed St. Paul's Cathedral on 29 December 1940,[127] saved by the rapid response of the Fire Watchers, but the majority of buildings in the vicinity did not have anyone to watch over them and were obliterated.[128] The event became known as the 'Second Great Fire of London'.[129] Churchill demanded that something be done and in response the Minister of Home Security Herbert Morrison announced the call which encompassed men aged 16-60[130] and also women aged 20-45 if they worked less than 60 or 55 hours per week respectively.[131] Morrison had suggested that civic duty was being shirked, but the *Daily Mail* had already been calling on the Government to improve the organisation.[132] Employees volunteered to act as Fire

Fighters to protect their companies, such as one Marks & Spencer employee in Swindon. After the store was closed the 17 year old would sit on the roof 'with a stirrup pump, a bucket of sand and a tin hat waiting for the Germans to drop their bombs. I really believed I would be able to stop the store burning down. My bit to help the war!'[133] On 23 August 1940 Miss E. Berrett of Hilperton, a Firewatcher, was noting in her diary: 'Air raid warning lasted from 10.40pm last night until 3.30am this morning. Heard more guns & bombs than ever before. Watched the shells burst in the Bristol direction. During the night we heard bombs fall & today we heard that they fell near Southwick.'[134] Fire Watchers were paid 1s. 6d. in summer and 2s 3d in winter[135] and in August 1941 Fire Watchers and Street Parties (where groups of neighbours had agreed to share the burden and take turns)[136] became known as Fire Guards.[137] The numbers of Fire Guards reached a peak of almost 6 million in 1942 and by April 1943 there was the introduction of the Fire Guard Plan, moving the service under the umbrella of Local Authorities.[138]

CIVIL DEFENCE

FIRE PREVENTION

A PUBLIC MEETING

will be held at the

TOWN HALL

on

MONDAY, 3RD FEBRUARY 1941

at 7.30 p.m.

to discuss measures to be taken for detecting and dealing with incendiary bombs, and the Organisation of parties of Fire Watchers and Fire Bomb Fighters, in connection therewith.

C. J. BARRINGTON
Clerk of the Council.

Poster advertising a public meeting for Civil Defence Fire Prevention in Melksham, February 1941, regarding the organisation of Fire Watchers and Fire Bomb Fighters (WSA G14/225/6)

The Ministry of Home Security issued a news-sheet called *Night Watch* for Fire Watchers. Herbert Morrison wrote: 'If you were not there our country would soon be ravaged by huge destructive fires far beyond the power of the fire service to control.'[139] In 1942 the Fire Guard was given new duties, linking it to the National Fire Service. Alongside spotting incendiary bombs and stifling those wherever possible, Fire Guard leaders also directed the combating of fires in their early stages and decided when to send for the NFS. Once the fires were under control it would be the duty of the Fire Guard to dampen them down and prevent them becoming re-established so that Firemen could attend other emergencies.[140] Many teachers volunteered to become Fire Watchers; at Ivy Lane School in Chippenham the teachers were asked by the School Managers if they would be able to do Fire Watching duty in February 1941. Four members of staff had volunteered by the beginning of April; those who lived closest to the school,[141] and ARP equipment was purchased, consisting of stirrup pumps and ladders. However, at a conference of the Incorporated Association of Headmasters in 1941, guidance was requested regarding the role of school staff in Fire Watching as the Board of Education had not issued any definitive guidance.[142] In Warminster, some 300 Fire Guards were appointed and additional equipment was purchased for their use.[143]

In Freshford on the Somerset/Wiltshire border the writer Fay Inchfawn recalled: 'England now began to fire watch in deadly earnest. Practically everybody – able or otherwise – became members of fire-watching parties. Up and down the country garages and club rooms were used as Fire Posts, but barns and lofts and farm kitchens were more usual in districts like ours, where to lighten the tedium the watchers played chess and darts and draughts and other games.' Those solitary Fire Watchers in private houses often finished off 'odds and ends' when it was quiet. Reading, mending and letter writing were popular occupations. Fay's friend from Salisbury wiled away the hours by producing a magazine for his thirty-strong Fire Post team, called *The Incendiary*. With a certified circulation of four copies it claimed to be 'the journal with the red-hot news' and enlightened its readership with humorous tales regarding the Fire Watcher's duty and routine… 'After signing his name in the book, his next duty is to set up his bed in such a manner that it is in no danger of collapsing under him during the night, and alarming his brother fire watchers. Then he is free to light his pipe – if any - or a cigarette if any – and engage in pleasant converse with his colleagues until it is time to go to sleep. When he wakes he enters his name in the book again, says: 'Cheerio my lucky lads!' and pushes off home, conscious of duty well and truly performed.' *The Incendiary* also contained 'clever' cartoons and contributions from other members of the Post. Fay sent her salutations to the editor and those like him with their ability to go about tedious work with a twinkle in their eyes.[144]

Joan Hickson, the Chippenham doctor, was also a Fire Guard. She reported in her diary in 1942: 'Fire-watchers meeting at 8pm. It is all being reorganised and we have to go on once a week with three people.' The man who took the meeting 'waffled on about who would like to do it with whom, and of course no one would say, but all giggled sheepishly. After half an hour of this we had to ask to be excused as Dr Royal had sent in an accident to the hospital from Castle Combe…'[145] One Red Cross worker was also required to do Fire Guard duty at the swimming pool in Devizes. 'It was not very comfortable sitting in the changing rooms with the blackout in place, because the walls ran with condensation.' She ended up sitting on the carpet one night due to complaints from neighbours of a party being held. It was discovered later that a group of soldiers had climbed over the wall and had been using the swimming pool.[146]

The Fire Watcher's Order issued in September 1940 had initially only applied to large factories, warehouses and yards.[147] Trowbridge appears to have had difficulties with the Fire Prevention (Business Premises) Order in 1942. They were having trouble finding enough personnel for Fire Watching and by October 1943 the Trowbridge Urban Council were discussing the need for the relaxation of the Compulsory Order, asking the Principal Officer for Civil Defence at the Office

Enrolment form for Fire Prevention Duties in the Urban District of Melksham (WSA G14/225/6)

of the Regional Commissioner if this was possible. The reply from Whitehall was non-committal. 'The man-power shortage is, of course, extremely acute everywhere... You will see that the Ministry of Home Security are attempting to find additional personnel for fire watching, and they hope in this way it will be possible to ease the general situation.' The Home Secretary had begun a census of Civil Defence workers in March 1942, concerned over continuing staff shortages,[148] but the Civil Defence Office of the Regional Commissioner was more expansive regarding the issue of allowing some towns to avoid compulsory Fire Watching.

... I notice from the report of the meeting that some of those present expressed the view that compulsory fireguarding was unnecessary, and that the voluntary system was sufficient because everybody concerned would turn out on an alert. This is not the case. An untrained fire guard is likely to be more of a hindrance than a help... Experience of past raids has shown that the present system of obtaining fire guard reinforcements and of calling for N.F.S. assistance is very defective, and for that reason it has been necessary to bring in the Fire Guard Plan. Without compulsion, which ensures that a certain number of trained fire guards with definite duties to perform are on duty each night, it is not possible to carry out the Fire Guard Plan.' He noted that a number of towns in the Region had been allowed to 'deprescribe' as they were not considered to have enough factories and buildings of national importance to make the 'prescription' necessary for 'military reasons.' The stance by Trowbridge had 'caused considerable trouble in the fire guard organisations in the various towns in the county which [were] still prescribed.' By August 1944 the Fire Guard Officer in Trowbridge was notifying the Clerk of the Council that the Regional Commissioner had withdrawn the Fire Guard Orders from the Trowbridge Urban District Council area and that Fire Guard Duty should 'cease immediately'.[149]

Fire watching, though often uneventful, disrupted and reduced sleep for those on guard[150] and it must have been a dull, thankless task. The Government

Register of Enrolment for Fireguard Duties, 1943, Melksham Urban District Council (WSA G14/228/1)

suggested patrols on a street by street basis and in Salisbury one street organised a rota. This worked well, but often the Guards felt 'dog tired'.[151] Tiredness may well have been an issue in Melksham too, as guidelines were drawn up making it clear that at least one Fire Guard had to be awake at all times. 'When there is no "alert" no fire watching need be performed but watchers should be awake, dressed, and ready to take up their duties. When an "alert" is sounded or when there is gunfire, or enemy aeroplanes are about, they must be prepared to detect incendiary bomb attacks. In both cases the rest of the party can remain indoors and may be in bed. The important consideration is that at least one person should be awake during the black-out period, where there is an "alert" or not so that the alarm can be given as required.'[152] In Wiltshire there were many cases of Fire Watching fines being imposed for not attending duty. In Malmesbury, Fire Guards could find it hard to work a full day and then go on duty, some having volunteered with the Home Guard too, and some suffering illness. Most were fined, and those who weren't had to pay costs.[153] The *Wiltshire Times* reported on 7 August 1943 that in Bradford-on-Avon it was ascertained that 'certain fire-watchers in the town were absenting themselves, although signing their names and drawing monetary allowance.' One Fire Guard had been reported as absent from his post at the Western National Omnibus Co. Ltd., Trowbridge, in May 1944. It appears, however, that the ARP Officer may have been a little overzealous in reporting him. It was noted that although the man had known that he could not offer his place to someone else, he had willingly done so, but as it was only his first offence, the case should not really have been placed in the hands of the Fire Guard Authorities.[154]

One anonymous female worker wrote in to the *Salisbury Times*, calling herself 'Women Workers' with her views about the need for more female Fire

Watchers in the City, printed on 18 September 1942. She wondered why women were being targeted as there were many part-time workers and unemployed who could help. '... we find that the majority of posts in Salisbury are being manned, during the evenings, by women already doing full-time work (in addition, in some cases, to household duties).'

By 1942 Fire Watching had become routine[155] and although the Fire Guard did not have much success during the Baedeker Raids of 1942 due to understaffing and a lack of equipment,[156] 75% of the fires in the 'Little Blitz' of 1943 were extinguished by the Fire Guard without the need of the Fire Service to assist.[157] It was easy to evade Fire Guard duty and it was not seen as a worthwhile service to be part of, as although members wore armlets, there was no uniform or, as Calder puts it, 'esprit de corps; it was simply a weight of wasted time – forty-eight hours a month – which was hung around the necks of men and women.'[158] The numbers of Fire Guards declined from September 1944 until their disbandment at the end of the war.[159]

Law and Order

Auxiliary Police Force

BY 1938 IT was realised that the role of the Police would become paramount in wartime, and that numbers would need to increase threefold. This would be undertaken by creating a Police reserve of retired Police Officers, the utilisation of Special Constables and the creation of a third 'war' reserve of full-time Officers, signed up for wartime duty only.[160] The *Wiltshire Gazette* was reporting on 19 October 1939 that Special Constables in the Marlborough and County Police Divisions were receiving their badges. The Mayor was presenting the badges and noted that he 'knew many among the special constables who served in the last war, and it was gratifying to him to realise that they were still ready and willing to do what they could in defence of their country.' The Special Constables were of 'real assistance,' and tribute was given to the full-time regular Constabulary for devoting so much time and effort to their training. By June 1940, the Police, like Firemen, had been frozen in their jobs due to the constant loss of so many staff to the Home Guard and the Services. The following month the Rescue and Stretcher Parties received the same treatment,[161] although the regular Police were later de-reserved up to the age of 30 with the war reservists up to the age of 33, putting additional pressure on the Specials.[162] The Police Force also had its own messenger service, the Police Auxiliary Messenger Service.[163] A Women's Auxiliary Police Force was established, but numbers only ever reached 10,000 and some forces did not employ any women at all.[164] In Cricklade, Special Policewomen were recruited to man the telephones and deal with clerical work[165] and a Policewoman appeared on the streets in Trowbridge.[166]

Policewomen had first been seen on the streets in 1914, recruited as volunteers by the National Council of Women at the request of Scotland Yard, 'keeping the peace and giving warning and advice, especially to young girls'. It wasn't until war broke out again that the appointment of female Police Officers was encouraged by the Home Office due to the social problems which were foreseen. By 1944 they had the same power of arrest as Policemen, having a basic wage of 56s. per week, rising by increment, with uniform and rent-aid.[167] In December 1943 Swindon Policewoman Cox had been helping to check up on dance halls and places of entertainment, working with the British Military Police (both men and women), and the US Military Police. The US were 'whole-heartedly in favour' of these triple patrols.[168] By 7 October 1944 *Picture Post* was asking 'Do we need more Policewomen?' It noted that it had taken a long time for female Police Officers to become an acknowledged part of social life.

Form No. 73 (Unlined).   S.O. No.

WILTSHIRE CONSTABULARY.

From   J. J. Meaney, Superintendent.

Station   Swindon.

Division   Swindon.

To Lieut. Col. Sir Hoël Llewellyn, D.S.O., D.L.,
                    Chief Constable of Wiltshire.

Date   3rd Dec.   19 43

Police Patrolling in company
with American Military Police.

With reference to your instructions dated the 25th November, 1943, I beg to report that joint foot patrols as necessary have been done in this Division.
In connection with the check up of dance halls and places of public entertainment under the National Registration Act Insp. Toop is in charge of this, and visits have been paid by parties of Police consisting of Civil Police, British Military Police, R.A.F. Police, U.S.A. Police, Police Woman Cox and British Women Military Police.
I have quick contact with all Service Police in Swindon and we all keep up a close liason, going to places in the Division outside the Borough of Swindon when necessary by transport.
I have contacted Major Wilbraham, British Provost Corps and he does not favour the regular triple foot or motor patrol.
Lieut. Stockdale, U.S.A. Police, is whole-heartedly in favour of the triple patrols and I think to meet the situation with an increase in the number of foot patrols and the adoption of motor patrols with the U.S.A. Police, with British Military Police coming on special occasions would be the best plan for this Division.

Superintendent.

The Triple Patrol Scheme in Swindon, 1943 (WSA F5/530/6)

The Police liaised not only with other Civil Defence workers, but also with the military, both British and foreign, and dealt with issues such as identity cards and Prisoners of War; requisitioning, which included a 'Central Register of Accommodation'; ration abuses and more. They kept records of crashed aircraft, and had a *Messages in and Out* record book at the County's Police Control Centre.[169]

Police Messages In and Out book (WSA F5/270/2)

Air crashes were to prove difficult to fully record until August 1943 as Officers were not allowed near a crash site if the military had arrived first and mounted a guard. The new instruction meant that they would now be able to approach any scene 'for the purpose of obtaining information concerning details of type, number and nationality and casualties in order to make the necessary report to the R.A.F. Station concerned.'[170] It had also been their job to provide as much assistance as possible to enumerate homeless people when the National Register was undertaken upon the outbreak of war.[171] The Police were to work with the Home Guard, with the task of 'anti-sabotage by means of fixed posts on entrances to quarries and patrols above and below ground' in areas such as Corsham which had a large number of underground facilities, and traffic and road block control if an alarm signal was received; they would be asked to 'man the defences'.[172] Duties also included dealing with those who refused to heed the warnings of the ARP Wardens when enforcing the blackout; a constant 'headache'.[173]

Casualty Services

UNDER THE AIR Raid Precaution Act 1937, all Local Authorities had to submit their scheme for their county's First Aid Posts. For Wiltshire, Swindon and Salisbury were excluded from the County Plan as they had been sanctioned to submit their own.[174] The Casualty Service was placed under the Ministry of Health after 1938 and in each Warden's sector a Doctor was placed on the team, called an ARP Medical Officer or Incident Doctor. The Ministry of Health's local representative, the Medical Officer of Health, was tasked with ensuring the smooth running of emergency mortuaries, food decontamination and gas cleansing.[175] In Bradford on Avon the swimming baths were chosen for use as a First Aid Post. They had access to hot and cold water and could be adapted for cleansing. The maximum number of patients that could be treated at the post was considered to be 92, with the estimated cost of the alterations required being £150.[176] Other sites detailed by the Deputy County Medical Officer and submitted to the Ministry of Health in March 1939 included the swimming baths at Devizes and Westbury; the Pavilion at Calne; the Cottage Hospital, Malmesbury; the Public Assistance Institutions at Chippenham, Amesbury and Warminster (although the latter was not yet decided); Melksham House, Melksham; The Talbot and Wyvern Institute, Wilton. The Council was also planning for mobile First Aid Posts to be used in places such as Stratton St. Margaret.[177] In Devizes, First Aid parties were on duty from 8pm to 6am, at first sleeping in the Town Hall or in their vehicles, using specially supplied blankets. The County Council became concerned that Civil Defence workers were not getting enough rest and this was affecting their daytime work. It was agreed that they would be summoned from their homes by messenger if required.[178]

First Aid and Rescue

AT THE BEGINNING of the war the Rescue and First Aid parties were separate, being combined into a single Civil Defence Rescue Service in May 1942.[179] First Aid parties attended casualties at the scene. At first they were recruited from members of the Red Cross and St. John's Ambulance, but later just needed a first aid certificate.[180] Rescue Parties were trained to rescue survivors from damaged buildings as originally described in an ARP Circular of July 1935. Their initial title was 'rescue, repair and demolition parties' with their role also including shoring up damaged properties. Many members belonged to the building trade, their training drawn around the experiences of those in earthquake zones.[181] Members of the First Aid and Rescue Parties were prevented from leaving their employment in July 1940 due to a 'freezing order' as staff losses were becoming critical but in January 1941 the National Service Act's new conscripts were allowed to choose to work in a First Aid Party and in April compulsion was introduced for the Civil Defence Reserve.[182] In Wiltshire, companies such as Boots Pure Drug Co. Ltd. submitted plans of their air raid shelters with locations to the relevant Local Authority so that Rescue Parties would know how to reach casualties.[183] So typically British, one staple of the First

Aid Post appears to have been tea and sugar. It was required to treat casualties for shock, both feigned during exercises, but also for genuine cases.[184]

Decontamination

THE GOVERNMENT HAD viewed the possibility of poison gas attack as a real threat. All ARP workers received anti-gas training but there were ARP services designed specifically for anti-gas measures.[185] Gas Identification Officers were appointed; part-time volunteers from the sphere of science such as teachers and pharmacists who worked to detect and identify if gas was present.[186] The Decontamination Unit was charged with the decontamination of roads, buildings, vehicles etc. by washing with neutralisation agents such as bleach powder.[187] The Decontamination Squads were based at specialist depots so that their clothing and equipment could be properly cleaned after an incident. The nature of the work, the suits and equipment they used meant that these workers could only operate for a period of three hours out of 24. Cleansing Stations would be used to decontaminate gas victims; first aid posts and hospitals had specially trained staff for this purpose and treatment was to include a shower. Mobile Gas Cleansing Units were also set up using converted vans and lorries. It was the Women's Voluntary Service (WVS) who eventually provided facilities for gas cleansing in most streets, via the Housewives' Service.[188] The equipment listed at a Wiltshire Gas Cleansing Station consisted of brushes, decontamination bins, anti-gas oilskin suits, aprons, gloves and boots, rubber gloves, green 'battledress' suits, and also additional clothing items such as socks and underwear; hand lamps and lanterns, string bags, towels, soap, salt, tins of ointment and rubber over-shoes.[189] There were also Decontamination Squads set up to deal with food contamination, inspecting and destroying foodstuffs where necessary.[190]

British Red Cross

OTHER VOLUNTARY ORGANISATIONS also had a part to play in wartime Casualty Services, their roots having begun much earlier. In 1909 the War Office issued a scheme for the organisation of voluntary aid to the Territorial Forces Medical Service in the event of war. The British Red Cross was given the task and trained personnel in first aid and nursing through County Branches, organising Units called Voluntary Aid Detachments (VADs).[191] When WWII broke out the Red Cross again worked with St. John Ambulance as they had in WWI, once more forming the Joint War Organisation from which VADs played a role (both overseas and at home) as nurses, Welfare Officers, Civil Defence workers and ambulance drivers.[192] During the Second World War there were 15,000 serving VAD members, but as early as January 1936 the British Red Cross in Malmesbury had been thinking of gas attack. Their attendance at anti-gas lectures with the St. John Ambulance Brigade was reported and they submitted themselves for exams on the subject.[193] By November 1938 first-aid lectures were being held for women only at Malmesbury's Town Hall.[194] The Order of St. John and the British Red Cross Society Wiltshire in the Borough of Malmesbury formed a committee to aid the work of the Malmesbury

Hospital Linen League, providing bandages and surgical supplies to the hospital, local regiments and seamen.[195] In Freshford Fay Inchfawn noted that during the lead up to the war, the village 'was becoming casualty-minded, and after much lecturing and bandaging, those in charge decided to organize a 'black-out.'' The Red Cross detachment had already been practising on family members, but this time they would be situated in the Casualty Station in an old stable in the Manor House. The 'village was interested but inclined to jeer at the whole proceeding as a harmless, but rather foolish waste of time'. The room was quite small and lit by three oil lamps with two oil stoves for warmth. The first casualty, 'after a label tied to her waist-band had been consulted, was found to be suffering from compound fracture of the ribs…' Another had 'severe head wounds. Under his cap, to simulate blood-matted hair, protruded a bunch of red shavings from a chocolate box…The room was soon filled with the lamps, stoves, arriving casualties and shut windows.' The only *bona fide* casualty of the evening was the first 'casualty', who had by then begun to feel rather faint. The only remedy to hand was a bottle of water 'labelled 'Sal Volatile'; her bed being moved to the stable yard produced better results.' The next day the story had spread and the village was 'contemptuous of the whole affair' with the events of the 'dead faint' becoming fabricated out of all proportion. It continued to be mentioned whenever the role of the ARP came to the fore in the village.[196]

The Red Cross Women's Detachment in Warminster, VAD number 36, was reported to have 57 members. All gave '… full time service in hospitals, convalescent homes, ambulances, and on trains.' The rest offered their spare time voluntarily at the ARP First Aid Post, many also serving with the local Red Cross Ambulance.[197] A London socialite was commandant of the Cricklade Red Cross. There was a uniform which had to be purchased with their own funds, and first aid classes were run, to which the Red Cross Cadets also had to attend. Young women were strongly encouraged to participate. The branch trained every week and learnt about mustard gas. As part of their training they were required to help out for the day at the Victoria Hospital in Swindon, doing washing for those mothers with newborns. They also bathed evacuees who had been sent to establishments created for those with health issues, such as impetigo.[198] After successfully completing training, certificates were awarded in first aid, home nursing, infant and child welfare, and anti-gas training.[199]

Red Cross workers and helpers in uniform outside a First-Aid Depot in Bradford on Avon, reproduced by kind permission of Mike Marshman (WSHC P55104)

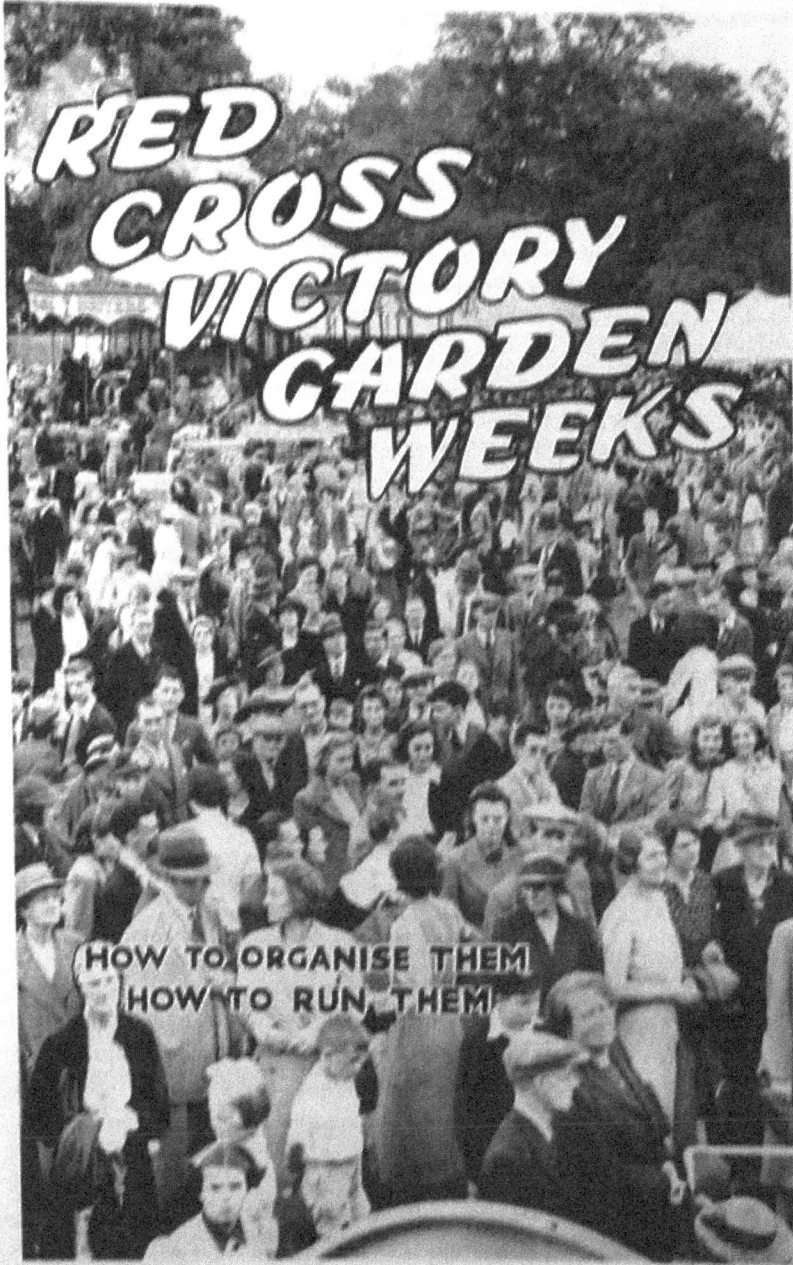

Red Cross' Victory Garden Weeks How to Organise them (WSA G24/225/45)

The Cricklade Red Cross volunteers used their ambulance to help ferry casualties from RAF Blakehill, a Casualty Clearing Station. The ambulance was a converted saloon vehicle. Volunteers received a knock on the door, mainly at night, often around 3am, with an estimated time of arrival. The call was never turned down as it would give the RAF personnel a much needed break. The wounded arriving from France were of all nationalities, including Germans. There were usually about 60 patients to see to; '... the first thing you were given was a box of cigarettes and told to put one in each of the patients' mouths and light it, just to calm them.' 'M' was marked on their foreheads if they needed morphine.[200]

It was reported in the *Wiltshire Times* on 2 December 1939 that 'fine work' was being done at the Trowbridge Red Cross Hospital's supply depot which had opened on 26 October. The 60 or more townswomen were working alongside those from local villages such as Holt, Keevil, West Ashton and Wingfield twice weekly to make hospital bed jackets, chest bandages and other supplies such as socks, shirts, swabs etc. for despatch to military hospitals. It was stated that the Bristol depot was 'now running short, and would be grateful for anything the [Trowbridge workers] could provide.' Clementine S. Churchill of the Duke of Gloucester's Red Cross and the wife of Winston Churchill sent out an appeal on 15 December 1942 to the Swindon branch of the Red Cross, asking for help with fund raising for her 'Aid to Russia' Appeal which was providing 'much needed surgical equipment and medical supplies' for 'our Russian allies.'[201]

Civil Nursing Reserve

THE MINISTER OF Health organised the Civil Nursing Reserve during the war[202] and the Ministry was writing to all County Councils, Urban District Councils and Rural District Councils in June 1940, urging them to give encouragement to those thinking of joining. It was the Local Emergency Organisations which were responsible for recruitment, set up in each County District under the Medical Officer of Health. The Ministry requested that each council 'arrange for all enquirers, whether trained Nurses, Assistant Nurses or women desiring to be trained as Nursing Auxiliaries, to be informed of the address to which they should apply.'[203] Entry into the service was dependent on possession of certificates in home nursing and first aid, along with 80-100 hours of hospital experience. Pay was £4 per week, half of which was deducted for board and lodgings. The service had a uniform which included the insignia 'NA' for Nursing Auxiliaries, leading them to be nicknamed the 'Naughty Annies'.[204] The Civil Nursing Reserve Committee received a great deal of criticism, the press reporting them as having 'intolerable inefficiency'. By February 1940 they were reorganising, appointing a Regional Nursing Officer to each of the 11 Civil Defence Regions with the task of supervising the emergency nursing services of their region, keeping in touch with Medical Officers of Health and Local Emergency Committees.[205] One NA came to work at the Emergency Hospital in Marlborough, formerly a workhouse. Their patients included elderly evacuees from London's chronic-sick hospitals. Each ward consisted of only one trained nurse and the Auxiliary Nurses. In 1943 there were almost 19,000 in the Civil Nursing Reserve.[206]

It was decided at the outset that those VADs who were immobile and who would not be needed in service hospitals would be able to join the Reserve (British Red Cross and St. John's Ambulance), and members of the Red Cross were directed to it. They wore their Red Cross Uniform and had to learn on the job, working long hours and being subjected to many rules and regulations.[207]

Ambulance Services

WOMEN HAD WORKED as Voluntary Aid Detachment Motor Drivers in WWI[208] and had driven ambulances overseas as part of the Scottish Women's Hospitals Unit.[209] [210] The Women's Reserve Ambulance Service (Green Cross Society) operated during the Zeppelin and Gotha raids on London, Evalina Haverfield being appointed as their Commandant in Chief in 1914. The Auxiliary Ambulance Service was set up in 1938 as part of the Government's Civil Defence Service, and began taking female volunteers.[211]

Under the ARP Act of 1937 arrangements had to be made by Local Authorities for the provision of an ambulance service in co-operation with neighbouring services and in co-ordination with voluntary services. In Wiltshire the County Medical Officer made a report and submitted it to the Ministry of Health in March 1939. Vehicles could be earmarked for use as ambulances and the Ministry of Transport would be producing a special form to use for the purpose but it had not been issued as yet. By 17 September 1939 the County's ARP Officer was telling his Districts not to let lorries and other commercial vehicles lie idle, and to take steps at once.[212] The vehicles were initially borrowed and converted, gradually replaced by purpose built ambulances[213] and by May 1939 Wiltshire's County Ambulance Officer had received a list of volunteer ambulance drivers from the WVS.[214] On 15 November 1939 the County Medical Officer had obtained tenders to convert six second hand cars into ambulances, the average cost not to exceed £60. On 16 October 1940 he had placed orders for nine 'converted car ambulances, complete with fire extinguishers, at £75 each.'[215] The volunteers in rural areas such as Wiltshire were taught to map read and drive confidently with minimal lighting and by the summer of 1939 men were also accepted as volunteers. Drivers needed to check and clean their vehicles with the attendants looking after the equipment.[216]

In Bradford on Avon, one of the first lady Ambulance Drivers in the town arranged the transport. 'We didn't have a proper ambulance so we used our Ford V8 shooting brake and I would drive it. We had to put the stretcher on the floor and I think the poor patients must have suffered every bump in the road – it must have been agony. Then they sent us an ambulance, a big old Chrysler which took four stretchers, in two double decks. It was an old wooden thing. It was awful to drive because the accelerator and the clutch were on the opposite side to normal. If you forgot, you wouldn't go in the right direction.'[217] Warminster's Emergency Committee organised the establishment of ambulances in the town with a total of two four-stretcher ambulances and one two-stretcher trailer working full-time, one two-stretcher British Red Cross Society ambulance and one two-stretcher town ambulance working part-time, and one four-stretcher converted van as a reserve.[218] In Devizes, each mobile medical ambulance was manned by a female driver and attendant. There were also cars containing first aid squads of four men, including the driver. There were lectures in first aid and gas warfare which led to exams, and workers also attended exercises and occasional parades such as the Wings for Victory Week. Their uniform consisted of a steel helmet, special respirator, overall and very heavy greatcoat. When the air raid siren sounded all on duty had to report to the bus depot in Station Road, Devizes, and wait for the all clear.[219]

Some of Wiltshire's First Aid teams with their ambulances were sent to aid their exhausted counterparts on the third night of the Bath Baedeker Raid in April 1942. The vehicles converged at the meeting point in Box '...we formed a long convoy of first aid squad cars, ambulances and rescue and demolition lorries. While we were waiting to go into Bath, lorry loads of people were coming out to spend the night in the fields.'[220] Many of the rescue workers must have been distressed at what they saw, such as a man from Trowbridge at the death of two WAAFs in a bombed apartment.[221] The Chippenham doctor Joan Hickson also worked at the Eye Infirmary in Bath and visited the city the morning after the bombing to see if she could help. She recorded in her diary...

> I shall never forget a blitzed town the morning after or regret that I had the experience of seeing it, though it was a good deal worse than I anticipated... glass and debris all over the road with occasional signs of greater damage... Made my way over the endless hoses to the Guildhall and Abbey. A good deal of traffic so had to keep going in a stream... Abbey seems intact except for the windows, but could not look round much owing to traffic jams... Crescent looked shattered – not a window left. Many roofs damaged but standing, very desolate. Several cars outside with people piling in suitcases and obviously evacuating. No one to direct traffic and difficult to turn... Many fires raging, houses completely demolished, pathetic bits of furniture in the road, and people looking oh so tired... Reached the Eye Infirmary eventually after two and a half hours driving. Practically no windows, blood on the steps and devastation all round. Went and found Matron rendering first aid and the waiting hall full of beds with recumbent forms. She said they were all alive but only just, and it had been pretty grim... Dirt, dust, broken glass and mess indescribable. Cooking on open fires.[222]

Joan also wrote of a fellow Chippenham resident at the scene. 'Another Bath story concerns a quite inconspicuous little man from Chippenham, no one we knew or had even heard of. He happened on a heap of rubble that had been a house where he had reason to believe there were people buried. He at once organised a party and started digging. The aimless, sightseeing crowd became a nuisance and would not keep back. Ultimately a special constable appeared and was greeted with joy by the man, who asked him to control the crowd. 'Dunno as I can do that' was the reply, 'dunno as I'm allowed to'.[223]

In Freshford the villagers had seen and heard the attack, and had decided to open the Rest Centre at the National School. Fay Inchfawn noted:

> That Monday morning the scholars very gleefully dispersed, and the schoolrooms were cleared for action. A band of helpers assembled. Oil stoves from a consignment sent by the U.S.A. to every hospital in Britain were commandeered. Mr. Hazeldean supplied bread, cooked meats, margarine, buns and cakes. Piles of sandwiches were cut. Milk, mattresses, easy chairs, blankets and rugs were delivered in procession. A board with the word 'REST' upon it was set up in the school yard, and in the afternoon the victims of the raid began to come in. Two elderly women were first to arrive. They had walked the whole way – five miles – and were dead beat. They stood at the school-house door asking whether they might come in, and could they be given shelter for the night?
>
> After that there was a rush. By train, bus, on lorries and in vans, refugees came to our Rest Centre. They all carried bundles or baggage of some kind, and all made the same enquiry: might they stay all night? Anywhere just to feel safe – on the floor, in a chair, just a roof over them and to be free from fear.
>
> The forty-eight hours which is the usual limit for keeping Rest Centres open was extended to a week. The helpers laboured in shifts and they were kept hard at it. Practically everyone in the Village lent a hand... Workers going back each morning to the Roman City told their intimates of the hospitality to be found in our Village. So each evening the numbers increased, and the affair tended to become quite a happy gathering of fellow townsfolk. There was much chatting, much comparing of notes over the happenings of those two dreadful nights... One would scarcely have thought they could laugh so easily, not so often, but the situation had its humorous side.[224]

Ambulance services which had developed during the war were placed entirely under County Council control following the National Health Service Act of 1946.[225]

Women's Services

Women's Voluntary Service

WOMEN'S SOCIETIES HAD operated to aid the war effort in WWI, such as the Queen Mary's Needlework Guild in Salisbury, whose members had knitted socks and sent parcels of comfort for the troops.[226] In June 1938 the Women's Voluntary Service (WVS) was set up by Lady Reading to help Local Authorities recruit and train women for ARP work.[227] Lady Reading herself visited Trowbridge to see the WVS in action.[228] The Home Office was advising all Local Authorities (including Chief Constables) by letter on 24 June 1938 of the purpose of the newly formed organisation. 'I am directed by the Secretary of State to say, for the information of your Council, that with his approval a Women's Organisation has been created called 'The Women's Voluntary Services for A.R.P.' The primary purpose of the organisation is to assist and co-operate with Local Authorities in the enrolment of women for A.R.P. services and for the expansion of hospital services that would be necessary if an emergency arose.'[229] The Wiltshire branch was formed by the Marchioness of Lansdowne[230] who was providing the County Air Raid Precautions Officer in October 1939 with a list of the county's 'Centre Leaders'.[231] The WVS worked with the Home Office and Local Authorities, earning the slogan 'ladies who never say no' and wore a uniform designed by one of the leading London couturiers, Digby Morton. This uniform made them distinct from other voluntary organisations, marking them as an auxiliary service with members '... proudly wear[ing] the emblem of the Crown upon their badge as a sign that they serve King and Country.'[232] However, WVS volunteers were not issued with a uniform; of those able to wear it the majority were from the middle and upper classes who could afford to buy it. Many compromised by just buying the hat.[233] 32,000 volunteers had enrolled by the end of 1938.[234]

The role of the WVS was extended to include evacuation, billeting, the distribution of food and clothing, the manufacture of camouflage netting, salvage and national savings schemes, welfare services to the young, the old, the displaced, the sick, and other associated services.[235] The headmaster of Ivy Lane School, Chippenham, was requested by the Authorities to assist in the camouflaging of army nets in September 1941. By 13 October a consignment of nets had arrived from the military authorities and the teachers and boys' class had commenced camouflaging.[236] Making camouflage nets was a dirty, horrible job. The dust and fluff was choking and the dye stained both hands and clothes. The job left workers with bruised knees and aching backs. By November 1941 the Head Teacher had written to the Authorities to say that the children were too young to continue with camouflaging the army nets and he wanted them collected.[237] Pupils at Cricklade School also had to help make camouflage nets: '... the pupils were given brown and green strips of dyed sacking, which they had to weave in and out of coarse netting stretched out in advance.'[238] At the County School in Bromham the children were working on their camouflage nets for the Army in 'Handwork' lessons during mid October 1941. Two soldiers called at the school to collect the nets on 13 January 1942.[239] The Broughton Gifford WI tackled the task of camouflaging in 1942, managing to complete 40 nets for the army.[240]

The War Office had been asking the WVS to undertake the task of mending soldiers' socks in January 1942. The Wiltshire branch was gearing up to take on the work for the Salisbury Plain area. Their plans were to include the Sewing Circles and Housewives' Service in the work.[241] In Swindon the WVS were also active in the collection of aluminium and the formation of Street Savings Groups, and their emergency drivers 'had many demands made upon them.' The Trowbridge Branch of the WVS launched a campaign to aid the blitzed in Battersea.[242] The WVS' Rural Pie Scheme was established in 1942 and distributed over one million pies and snacks in 5,000 villages to farm workers.[243] The National Farmer's Union *Wiltshire Branch Record* of August 1942 was gladly reporting on behalf of the Wiltshire War Agricultural Executive Committee that '... pies under the above scheme sponsored by the Rural District Councils are now available in most parts of the rural areas.' Enquiries were to be made at the local bakers or village shop.[244]

WVS members felt that the skills they used at home had become invaluable additions to the war effort, as James Hinton reports, '... my careful economies are things to pass on, not hide as I used to', providing a 'local housekeeping service on a national scale'.[245] One sixteen year old from Trowbridge was working for the WVS at Holt in their cooking depot. 'We cooked meals there and we used to take them out to the schools. When Bath was bombed we had to take the meals down there.'[246] The WVS also helped with blood donation; in Swindon they were needing more volunteers by April 1940[247] and 'considerable help' was also given in the summer.[248]

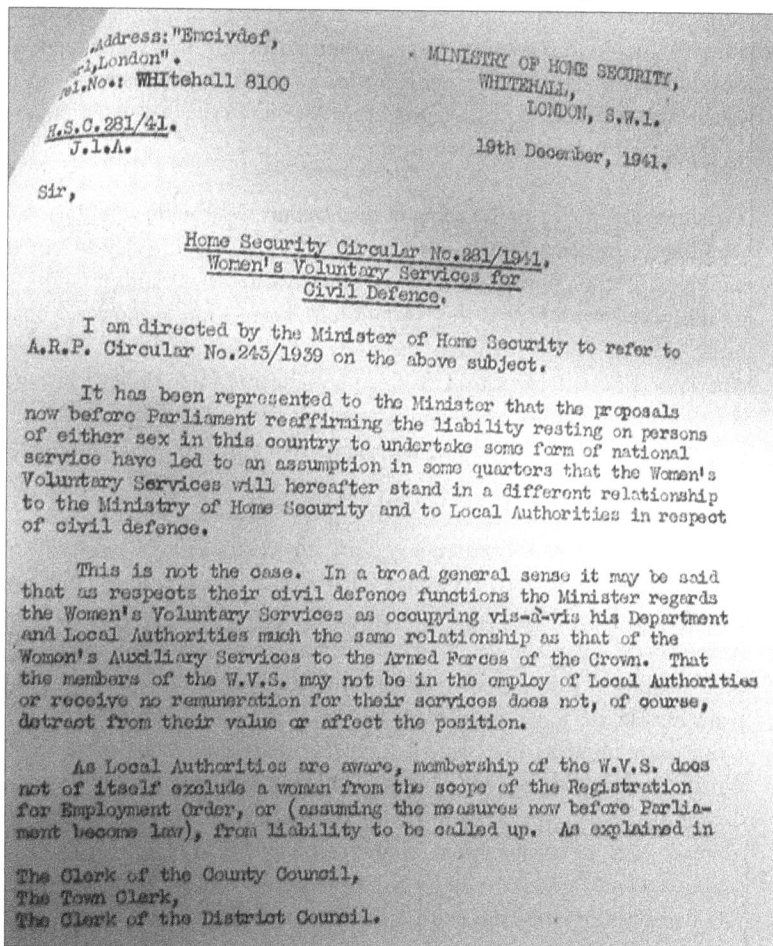

Circular from the Ministry of Home Security to all Clerks, 19 December 1941, re. the WVS' place and relationship within Home Security (WSA G24/225/28)

Between June 1943 and the end of the war there were almost one million WVS members across the UK.[249] Large numbers of working class women joined the ranks of the WVS, but like the Auxiliary Ambulance Service with its middle and upper class drivers, the WVS leadership remained fixed under the control of the upper and upper middle class.[250] Unlike the Women's Institute or Townswomen's Guild, the WVS did not encourage democratic participation; the organisation was run statutorily from a London HQ with Regional Administrators assisted by paid organisers overseeing the work of its local 'centre' organisers on the ground.[251] Most working class women would usually adopt a deferential attitude with the WVS leaders,[252] but this not was not to be the case for one Wiltshire woman. Eleanor Ritchie of Malmesbury, a company secretary before WWI, wrote to Lady Reading: 'you are giving all this work to one class of woman and not trying to enlist the professional woman who might be of so much use.' Hinton notes that the last straw was the appointment of a 70 year old; the county ladies running the Malmesbury branch had refused to look further than their own social circle.[253]

Friction could also occur when volunteers were in action, as was the case at the WVS' Swindon Welcome Club Canteen in March 1945 when what appears to be the Manager of the Club reported to the Town Clerk:

I feel I ought to report to you my first serious clash with voluntary helpers running the canteen. This occurred yesterday evening (Thursday March 1st). I had decided upon an interval in the Thursday cabaret as canteen takings were by no means as healthy as they should have been. I found, however, that my order had been countermanded; there was to be no interval because the canteen could not cope with the rush. I insisted upon the interval to the leader… though she threatened that her team would 'walk out'. The result was a meeting at ten o'clock between myself, and the helpers (twelve of them). Their argument was that they did not expect to work all that hard, that they could not cope with a rush (claiming that during last week's interval customers walked off with cake etc. without paying). My counter was that they could enjoy Club facilities any other night without work, but that the night of the rota was the night for work; that they had clamoured for a 'special' night, and must be prepared to meet its demand – but that the takings had not risen appreciatively since the cabaret attracted one of the week's biggest crowds. The leader said I must organise the team myself if I was not satisfied; I replied that I was willing to try. At this point the team as a whole was apparently coming round to a spirit of reason, but the leader (to whose tone I am afraid I take very strong exception) seemed determined not to let it rest at that. She charged me with not having shown a proper spirit of co-operation; whereupon I reminded them that this was the only team from which I had so far received two threats to 'down tools', the first having been when the evening was too quiet for them…. I have observed this particular team, and my own judgement is that too many of them do not want to work when they come to the Club. Other teams will literally slave in a rush-hour; these do not intend to do so. Moreover, I have no confidence at all that the leader will allow them really to pull together next week. I fear that the situation is dangerous – I should be happy if the Thursday team resigned en bloc, when I could fill their places with a smaller but less contentious team...[254]

WVS Offices in Blue Boar Row, Salisbury, courtesy of the British Council (WSHC P56039)

The Chippenham doctor Joan Hickson had seen the devastation of the Baedeker Bath raids in April 1942 at first hand. In her diary entry she told of an ex-nurse who left her first-aid point and that 'various WVS ladies had been driving about the town with labels on their cars getting extra petrol, just went off without a word, with the result that the conscientious ones left behind worked day and night on feeding, evacuation etc. These people did extremely well by all accounts.'[255] There was also trouble due to requisitioned property having a multi-purpose usage. The WVS was granted permission by the Swindon Borough Clerk to get their water from a cloakroom just inside the entrance of the Town Hall for use in the canteen. 'The caretaker has complained that some of our helpers spill water on the floor, and yesterday morning he locked the door against them.... I think this treatment rather drastic, considering the matter of spilling a drop of clean water on a tiled floor is not very terrible.'[256] The role of the WVS was one of the topics of an Open Discussion; a Ministry of Health course for Billeting Officers which included Swindon. 'It is useless to try to attract and hold the best types of voluntary worker unless you can offer a job which is constant challenge to their enthusiasm, initiative and individualism. But it really does not matter whether you are dealing with a paid staff or with voluntary workers: to get the best from them you must be prepared to preach the gospel of service, to make it a personal matter for each individual and to build up a tradition of pride in common achievement...' It was stated that the ladies of the WVS were 'doing admirable work in a variety of ways'.[257]

The main route into the WVS for working class women was via the Housewives' Service, accounting for 30% of national membership. It was easier for these women to find time to attend short training courses in first aid or home nursing, after which a card placed in their front window would proclaim their

Letter from the WVS for Civil Defence in Swindon detailing some of the work of the WVS and Housewives' Service, 17 January 1942 (WSA G24/225/28)

readiness, as Hinton reports, to 'offer to the community, all the gifts, experience, common-sense, which she has hitherto expended upon her home and family'.[258] They were to provide a point of contact for ARP wardens, take responsibility for the children of working mothers, make tea for emergency workers and help elderly neighbours to shelters. After the threat of aerial bombing lessened they were able to provide details of local services, visit the sick and elderly, invite neighbours to training sessions and talks, hold make do and mend sewing and knitting sessions etc.[259] In 1942 their name was changed to become the 'Housewives' Section of the Women's Voluntary Services for Civil Defence' as they had 'now become so vitally important a part of Civil Defence'.[260]

Although the Housewives' Service appears to have been generally well received by the ARP Wardens in Wiltshire, there were some problems in Calne in May 1942. Wiltshire County Council's Civil Defence Officer was reporting that 'there are one or two cases, like Calne, where the Head Warden looks at the movement with some suspicion.' To help put the Service on a 'firmer and more official foundation' it was suggested the Wardens could be informed that the Housewives' Service was being formed by the WVS in every town and village in Wiltshire; their presence would provide extra assistance nearby; they could supply water for stirrup pumps, shelter the wounded, or homeless, supply hot water for drinks; look after invalids, children or the elderly; direct people to Rest Centres and First Aid points; assist in gas cleansing. The housewives would be selected 'in consultation with the Head and Senior Wardens and [would] be given short talks on the local Civil Defence Organisations, Elementary First Aid, Anti Gas and Fire Fighting, Emergency cooking and the erection of outdoor stoves of brick and earth.' The Civil Defence Officer concluded by stating: 'This Service has been found of the greatest assistance in an emergency and Head and Senior Wardens are asked to give it every encouragement.'[261]

Three types of card were issued in January 1943 to be placed in the windows of WVS members. One indicated an unofficial First Aid Post by the WVS, another

to indicate the house of the Village, Group or Sector Representative, a third for the house of the Street Representative who would be the focal point of all WVS activities in that area.[262]

By May 1945 the Regional Administrator of the WVS in Bristol was writing to Swindon's Town Clerk to thank the town's Civil Defence workers for the help they had given. 'Although the war cannot be said to be over at the same time that particular phase of it (especially

WVS Street Representative card to be placed in the window of an appointed worker (WSA F5/530/17)

in connection with A.R.P. and Civil Defence) in which the W.V.S have been called into action, would appear to have come to an end... This help has been particularly appreciated during times of emergency and it is with a very thankful heart that we look forward to the days when these emergencies will be something belonging to a remote past.' At the beginning of July 1945 a film entitled *Willing Hands* was made by the Ministry of Home Security which documented the work of the Service.[263]

Robert MacKay notes that although the Local Authorities provided the framework for Civil Defence, it was the WVS who took charge of the post raid services. If not for their contribution, these services would have been non-existent.[264]

Letter from Herbert Morrison, Minister of Home Security, to Lady Reading re. the continuation of the WVS, 28 September 1944 (WSA G24/225/28)

The WVS managed to resist closure after the war by ensuring the organisation became indispensable to the Attlee Government,[265] organising the Home Help Scheme and the work of women's organisations during the fuel crisis of 1947, and settling the displaced persons of Europe.[266]

By 1951 the WVS in Trowbridge were describing their work as '[delivering] 'Meals on Wheels' for the sick, aged and infirm; a clothing exchange; the collection and dispatch of magazines for the troops abroad; and assistance in running the '60-Plus Club' and, once again, Civil Defence, call[s] for a steady response from members.'[267]

Women's Institute

IT HAD BEEN decided that the participation of the Women's Institute (WI) in the war would be severely restricted, as Anderson reports, 'out of respect of the beliefs of Quaker members' but this policy led to a drop in numbers from 332,000 in 1939 to 288,000 in 1942.[268] Interestingly, when the WI was formed in 1915 one of its principal aims was to become more involved in producing food due to the war.[269] The WI had begun plans for billeting and evacuation well before the Second World War began, but these were superseded by the WVS. Instead, they set up knitting and sewing circles and also lectures and day schools about make do and mend, cooking with rationed food, and domestic DIY instruction.[270] In Redlynch the WI were making plans at their meeting held on 6 September 1939, discussing what they could do to help. The following week they had decided to take home sewing or knitting to complete, forming a working party. By February 1940 this party had made over 70 garments which were sent to the Red Cross. By November the total had risen to an impressive 354 garments. They also helped the county's nurseries by answering the 1943 appeal to make 'knickers and overalls'.[271] The WI also established a comprehensive scheme to distribute fruit bushes and vegetable seeds, many of which were gifts from overseas. Collecting Centres were run for rose hips and herbs; from 1941 rosehip syrup was a familiar substitute for orange juice in Welfare Centres.[272] The Codford WI ran cookery classes at a cost of 2s. 6d. for eight sessions, designed to help women make the most of the produce available to them. They also discussed the distribution of meat pies at their meetings and a dried herb scheme, collecting and drying them for culinary and medical purposes, both for themselves and for wider distribution.[273]

The WI is best known for making jam, for which the Government provided much of the equipment and syrup. They implemented strict quality control regulations and by the end of the scheme 5,300 tons had been made. In February 1941 the Wiltshire Federation of the Women's Institute received a letter of appreciation by Lord Woolton, Minister of Food, thanking them for their work in fruit preservation. Work had been completed in 66 centres throughout the county. As a result of the efforts made by the WI, 19 tons of the fruit crop was saved and approximately 29 tons of jam made. The WI also made jelly, and bottled and canned fruits[274] with the help of tinning equipment sent from Canadian housewives and, perhaps appropriately, it was in fact the Canadians who had first devised the idea of the WI. Those not lucky enough to receive a Canadian gift had to raise the money to buy their own equipment.[275] In 1941 the Codford WI began a preserving scheme which ran for the rest of the war. They also formed a Fruit Preservation Committee for Codford and the surrounding villages.[276] The *Wiltshire Gazette* was reporting the work of the WI jam makers in Burbage on 22 October 1942, the group having made 1,403 lbs of jam. It also noted that the names of members who were willing to undertake milking in an emergency were provided.

The WI in Netheravon decided to set up a special committee after seeing soldiers evacuated from Dunkirk wandering around the village after their arrival at nearby RAF Netheravon, 'uniforms soaked in sea water, some without proper footwear... [having] nowhere to go...'. They found an old brewery and later recalled that '[n]ow it was all hands to the rescue. [The troops] helped us clean the old place up and whitewashed the walls. Then we approached the Ministry of Food and got permits for tea, margarine, cooking fat, and a little sugar... begged and borrowed cooking utensils, teapots, oil stoves and small tables, trestle tables and chairs. In an incredibly short time we were ready for business.' They opened every evening except Sunday from 6.30pm until 10pm with volunteers working on a rota. The soldiers were delighted; they had somewhere to sit and talk away from camp.[277]

The WI also appear to have been keen to get involved in the *Brains Trust* programme, the Tisbury branch asking for questions from its members on 'preserving the old' and 'building the new' in 1942 along with the topics of health, housing, schools, work etc. 'This means we want to know what you want saved and preserved of the old life, and what plans you want to make for the new.'[278] Representatives of the WI were also invited to participate in the Bradford and Melksham Rural District Council's plans for housing schemes in November 1944 regarding the design of houses. They had their own Housing Sub Committee and a 'stake in planning'.[279]

Townswomen's Guild

THE TOWNSWOMEN'S GUILD (TWG) was formed in 1929[280] for 'ordinary women living in the nation's towns and cities'.[281] At the advent of war the organisation felt they could be of little help and so decided to suspend their activities, leaving just one member of staff working at their headquarters. The Guilds themselves were unhappy about this; funds and encouragement poured in from all over the country. The Townswomen's Guild's activities recommenced in October 1939 when they began taking responsibility for projects such as digging up town parks for allotments. They also took part in the collection of herbs, especially nettles. Their Recruiting Centres for part-time workers were recognised by the Ministry of Labour as official Bureaux and they also provided Social Centres for evacuees and club rooms for visiting parents to spend their weekend visits.[282] In Trowbridge the Townswomen's Guild was not formed until 1947. Its aim was to '[e]ncourage [the] education of women and to enable them as citizens to contribute towards the common good...'[283]

Other clubs existed in Wiltshire towns. The Business and Professional Women's Club was formed in Trowbridge in 1944 and was:

> open to all employed women who are interested in public and international affairs and who enjoy worth-while speakers and discussions. It is not just a local affair, but part of a National Federation of over 220 clubs grouped in regions.
>
> There is also an international organisation, with groups in the U.S.A., and exchange gifts with one in Canada.
>
> Our recent programme has included Wiltshire history and records, an inquiry into the law regarding women, and enjoyable social activities.[284]

The club was still running in the early 1950s. By the early 1950s the Co-operative Women's Guild, established in Trowbridge in 1920, was being run for: 'The promotion and understanding among the nations' alongside keeping women informed on matters affecting women and the home, and felt that through the National Executive it had influenced those 'in authority' on child welfare. The Trowbridge Guild of Married Women had met since 1910 and knitted comforts for the troops such as socks during the Second World War, as they had done so in the First.[285]

Information Services

THE NATIONAL COUNCIL of Social Service was in discussion with national voluntary organisations by 1938 regarding how best to offer advice and clarification to the civil population. Local Centres were seen as the way forward and after the outbreak of war the Citizens Advice Bureaux (CAB) came into being, often in makeshift rooms borrowed for the task. The National Council of Social Service HQ provided a base from which reliable information could be collected, duplicated and channelled to the bureaux. Over 1,000 were set up and run by 100,000 staff, mostly volunteers. The CABs, as Anderson notes, needed to be 'adaptable and flexible, capable of adjusting to the rapid changes in social life brought about by the war'.[286] The Chippenham doctor Joan Hickson wrote in her diary in June 1943 of the Mayoress of Chippenham: '... she has a conscience about setting a good example to other people and has taken on too much. She started the Citizen's Advice Bureau and went there every morning, did all the visiting for soldiers' and sailors' families, besides endless billeting of evacuees, settling refugees and other mayoral duties.'[287] A newspaper report printed a record of the CAB in the South West during one month in 1942. 10,000 enquiries were answered, 1,500 rationing problems dealt with, 100 worries settled for relatives of POWs, 500 queries solved re. evacuees and billeting, expert and kindly advice given on 350 family and matrimonial problems. They also helped with enquiries regarding employment, allowances, insurance and pensions, income tax and price complaints,[288] which could cause a great deal of concern for those involved. In a letter to his mother from Alexandria in November 1942, Sergeant Bull of the 'A'

Squadron Royal Wiltshire Yeomanry (M.E.F.) was concerned over tax issues. 'The allotment still hasn't been officially stopped here yet and until it is I can't touch it, I had a shock a few weeks ago when I discovered I had £20 income tax. I've got to pay so much monthly, £2 I think it is, so at present I'm in debt a bit, but as soon as the allotment is stopped then I shall be alright, so you see I'll be no better off for stopping the allotment and I still had to pay income tax on it as you were not dependent on me, although this is the money from the R.A.F that all comes in, I don't know how much I've got in the bank now...'[289]

An Emergency Information Service was listed in the *After Raid Welfare* handbook for the Swindon ARP Area Scheme. Their job was to prepare Emergency Information Bulletins and distribute them through the Emergency Information Committee's contacts and services. There was also the Casualty Information Bureau run by Local Authority volunteers, set up to record the particulars of casualties. The 'Searcher Service' consisted of trained volunteers from offices, housewives and other organisations whose job it was to investigate all enquiries regarding casualties and missing persons not readily answerable by the Missing Persons Section 'and to trace with the help of the Household Register and 'Good Neighbour Arrangements' scheme, the whereabouts of all residents in a raid affected sector.'[290] Salisbury City Council was reporting on the use of Information Centres at well known central places, such as the Guildhall. It was felt to be essential that an Information Centre be opened as soon as possible after an air raid, opening for possibly two or three days. 'All persons requiring help or advice will be questioned at a table near the entrance to the Banqueting Room by members of the C.A.B./W.V.S., who [would] get to know the kind of information or help required. The Enquiry Form [would] be completed and handed to the applicant and the applicant directed to the appropriate officer in the centre... Persons who [had] to stay in the Centre for some length of time [would] be provided with a cup of tea and light refreshments (say biscuits or bread and butter or sandwiches)'; the words 'and butter' being crossed out.[290]

Services included:

Assistance Board – to help provide financial assistance to those temporarily in need.

Public Assistance Authority – to issue travel vouchers and arrange for the care of orphaned children.

Ministry of Labour – to issue unemployment books and deal with any questions relating to employment.

Ministry of Food – to deal with replacement ration books and issue an emergency card immediately.

NRO [National Registration Office?] City Council – to issue new identity cards, deal with requests for billeting allowances, to provide certificates for burial and deal with the removal of bodies.

WVS – for the provision of clothing for those 'rendered destitute', to take particulars of the missing not included on casualty lists and to answer casualty enquiries, enquiries from people outside the city and to help redirect letters.

Military Assistance Officer – to answer service enquiries from service personnel who were worried about family, to give assistance to servicemen on leave in the form of cash, extended leave, travel warrants, equipment etc.

Citizens Advice Bureau – to carry on their usual function of providing information and advice.

Ministry of Pensions – for advice on pensions for widows and dependant workers of ARP personnel who have died from injuries received in the course of their duties.[291]

The CAB had become so well regarded by the end of the war it was felt they would have a vital role to play when peace came[292] and continue to play an important role in local communities today.

The Soldiers and Sailors Families Association was founded in 1885 by Major Gildea of the Warwickshire Regiment who was unusual at the time in that he cared for the welfare of the families of those in his service. The Association was extended to all dependants of Army and Navy personnel and the RAF was included after its formation, changing its name to Soldiers, Sailors and Airmen Families Association (SSAFA). The Service proved invaluable after Dunkirk and an Overseas Service provided information for servicemen about their families at home, giving emergency help if required. The SSAFA also opened clothing depots and nurseries where needed.[293] In Swindon, an adviser was available to 'deal with all enquiries in respect of personnel of H.M. Forces; to give assistance to members of the Forces and/or dependants of Service personnel.'[294] By 1945 their numbers had grown to nearly 30,000 helpers, almost all voluntary. The majority were women and many were servicemen's wives.[295]

Home Defence

Home Guard

IN OCTOBER 1939 Churchill was concerned that middle-aged volunteers for war service were being overlooked and suggested that a 'Home Guard of half a million men over 40 should be formed'.[296] Eden broadcasted an appeal at 9pm[297] on 14 May 1940, with some volunteers arriving at Police Stations before the broadcast had ended.[298] The Chief Constable of Wiltshire had received a telegram from the Home Office at 12.25pm on 14 May, notifying him of the impending broadcast. A supply of forms were being forwarded and were to be sent to Police Stations across the county as soon as possible, 'in any case, in time for any applications which may be made first thing tomorrow morning'[299] but this did not give much time for Police Officers on the ground to get organised, and Wiltshire's residents were very keen. Police stations throughout the county were 'besieged by telephone calls and callers. The village inns did a roaring trade that night, and next morning the bewildered Police, some of whom had not heard the news, were hard put to it – sorting out applications and politely sifting out those who did not appear to conform to the very wide conditions of the service.'[300] In Chippenham amongst the first to enlist in the Local Defence Corps was the landlord of the Little George and a worker from the Westinghouse factory.[301] Major E. A. MacKay, Commander of the Home Guard's 4th Battalion, Trowbridge Company, and Secretary of the Wiltshire County Territorial Association compiled a report from each Home Guard District in 1945 covering its operations during WWII. It was noted that '... still the men came in. In three days, excluding Salisbury, the number mounted to 3,754.'[302] Peggy Pickford from Warminster was writing to her sister Elizabeth Martin in Australia on 23 May 1940 about her husband's new role. 'Austin joined the local defence volunteers ("parashots" in the papers!) directly it was announced. It seemed a chance to do **something** while carrying on the farm work, and it has more glamour than the A.R.P. (which isn't needed so much in the country anyway) because the volunteers are armed and have a uniform.'[303]

By June 1940, 15,879 men had joined up in Wiltshire and by December the number was 17,194. In May 1940 it was stated by the Chief Constable's Office in Wiltshire that Special Constables were not permitted to enrol in the Local Volunteer Corps. Members of the AFS and ARP were allowed, however, and needed to state their membership on application.[304] Many, such as Mr Porter from Newtown, Westbury, were a member of both the Home Guard and the ARP.[305] By July 1943 the Government had decided to allow 'aliens' to join the Home Guard without requiring to be vouched for by the Chief Constable of the district. Also newly eligible for enrolment alongside aliens were 'British subjects and nationals of Allied and neutral states who also possess the nationality of a state at war with Britain,' and 'Nationals of Allied and neutral states who are married to women who possessed at birth the nationality of a state at war with Britain.' In 1942 there had been confusion over the state of Czechoslovaks born before 28 October 1918 and classed as 'Austrian;' the Government wrote to Chief Constables to clear up the issue and stated that the exclusion of any Czechoslovaks was not intended. Citizens of Eire were another matter entirely, and the War Office had asked in May 1941 that any applicant's details be passed on to the Special Branch and Metropolitan Police to ensure that there is 'no adverse record against the individual.'[306] Numbers increased in Wiltshire after conscription to a high of 23,409 in September 1943.[307]

At first headquarters were located in rooms 'begged or borrowed', or in outhouses. Shepherd's huts were much in demand,[308] with platoons such as Codford's making the most of them.[309] One member of the Great Bedwyn platoon recalled their use of the hut. 'We had a shepherds hut... that we used during the summer months as an observation post. We spent two hours on duty and two hours off keeping a lookout for enemy paratroopers and crashed aircraft. We set up a telephone link between the hut and... home [of] our platoon's commanding officer...'[310] Others made their own with boards and rabbit netting as makeshift look out posts. 'Farm carts and wired knife-rests... were all that we had. But we did what we could in haste that was with us day and night, for, in a short month or so Holland had been invaded, France had fallen, and our Army, left in the lurch, came back to us from Dunkirk.' 'It was up to us to hold the fort while they reorganised.'[311]

The first danger appeared to be from Fifth Columnists,[312] and fear and uncertainty reigned. To the population at large it almost seemed as though a 'prospect of untold horrors' lay in store. Peter Hennessy notes the mood… '[F]ifth columnists dropping from the air, sabotage by British-born German sympathisers, invasion itself – seemed dramatically closer the day Churchill took power' and the Low Countries were invaded.[313] Even Churchill had declared in his speech on Dunkirk of 'this malignancy in our midst'.[314] Wiltshire County Council's County Civil Defence Organisation issued a statement entitled *Invasion*:

> The Prime Minister and the Government have told us repeatedly that Invasion is to be expected, and it is not for any individual to challenge or ignore their warning even if (in his ignorance or apathy) he wished to do so.
>
> When Invasion comes the battle-cry of the Civil population must be 'Stand Firm.'
>
> The enemy will do everything in his power to demoralise and stampede the people – by ruthless bombing, by the speed of his attack, by the use of gas, by fantastic rumour, by the threat of atrocities and by false instructions spread by Fifth Columnists.
>
> Each one of us must know how we are personally going to help beat the invader.[315]

This was to be achieved by keeping the roads clear by staying put. 'The urge to move must be restricted. Britain is a small island. When Invasion comes there is no better place to be than in the house where you now are.' A Commander of the Salisbury Plain District went on to describe the chaos in France due to the mass movement of the civilian population. Wiltshire's civilians were also asked to prepare now; to have a plan. What would they do for light and for cooking if the supply was cut off? What about water shortages due to a lack of supply? They were encouraged to think about burying some food to stop the invaders from taking it, and to offer their services to the Local Defence Committee to help with specific tasks such as fighting fires or looking after the elderly. 'It is better to do something to help, than just sit and imagine horrors.'[316]

But Fifth Columnists could already be within their midst. On 11 June 1940, the 10th Battalion of Wiltshire's Home Guard noted that: 'Two unshaven strangers speaking broken English, studying a map, in close possession of a large sum of money but boots worn out, were reported at closing time at the White Hart, Oare. Information received too late to apprehend them, so telephoned particulars to Marlborough.' The suspects were apprehended the following day and handed over to the Intelligence Authorities.[317] A story goes that two spies were arrested in Tisbury when a lady living on the outskirts of the village had two nuns call at her door asking for alms. The nuns proceeded to peer through her curtain at the Officer's Mess now stationed at her house and 'her suspicions were aroused still more as they departed by a sight of the heavy men's boots which were sticking out from under the nuns' robes'![318] In Minety a woman and her daughter were

LOCAL DEFENCE COMMITTEE.

A Defence Committee has been formed for this Parish to deal with the situation which might arise in the event of invasion. Unless invasion occurs this Committee will possess no executive powers but it will make preliminary plans to deal with the problems likely to arise in the event of the Parish becoming isolated ; these problems cover such matters as :

Co-operation with the Military.
Arrangements for wounded.
Arrangements for housing and sheltering homeless.
Food and cooking plans.
Collection of labour and transport to assist the military.

The Committee consists of :

REV. W. B. SMITH	P.C. BARKER
MR. OLIVER REED	MRS. LANE
MR. BREWER	MRS. LANDALE
MR. DABNEY	MRS. THOMAS
MR. HAZELTON	MRS. WILLIAMSON

and if you are in need of advice you should apply to the Committee.

The Committee instructs everyone in the event of invasion
NOT TO SPREAD RUMOURS,
NOT TO BLOCK ROADS BY BECOMING REFUGEES,

but it is the duty of everybody

TO CARRY ON THEIR ORDINARY WORK AS LONG AS POSSIBLE.
TO FOLLOW THE ORDERS OF THE POLICE, A.R.P., MILITARY AND HOME GUARD.
TO "STAY PUT" AND REMAIN IN GOOD HEART.

Printed by Bennett Brothers, Journal Office, Canal.

Poster advising of the formation of a Local Defence Committee in West Grimstead to deal with invasion (WSA 1988/24)

billeted with a local resident. The local Policeman had to warn the billetee several times to make sure she shut her curtains fully as they were often seen to let the light in. Then the daughter went missing and the tenant awoke in the middle of the night to find someone was trying to suffocate her with a pillow. She fought her off and the woman was arrested and taken away in a Black Maria. 'When her room was searched a two-way radio was found. No one knows what happened to this woman or her daughter. Their cases, clothes, and all their belongings were never collected.'[319] However, suspicion and rumour could misinform. A raid occurred in the village of Ham at the residence of Frances and Ralph Partridge, known pacifists living at Ham Spray House. On 23 June 1940, eight Police Officers arrived and 'went over the house from top to bottom... They would not say what were the grounds of suspicion, but they came to the conclusion it was village gossip, their having foreign friends, and... [one of them] wearing a beard.'[320] Many situations were also purely innocent. Frances Partridge noted in her diary that friends of hers had been stopped twice under the suspicion of being spies. 'At Bristol a woman saw them photographing a building and rushed to the police, describing them as 'an obvious Italian with a blond German-looking man." They were in fact on an errand on behalf of the National Trust; a seemingly mysterious organisation unknown at least to those who had stopped them![321] Frances also wrote of her meeting with some Brüderhof members on 13 May 1940. 'Everyone jokes about the likelihood of German parachutists landing in our Wiltshire fields dressed as nuns or clergymen – a good farcical subject on which to let off steam. This afternoon I was alone in the kitchen when the doorbell rang, and there on the step stood three tall bearded men who addressed me in strong German accents, and wore something between a clergyman's and military dress! Aha! I thought, the parachutists already. But when they asked for Mrs. Nichols I realised that it was some of the Brüderhof, a community of Christian Pacifists of all nations who live the simple life near Swindon. Curiosity was too much for me, so I asked them to have some tea... It was the maddest of mad hatter tea parties, consisting of me and these three Jesus Christs, all looking at me sweetly and speaking in gentle voices. I told them we were pacifists. 'Are you persecuted much?' they asked, rather taking the wind out of my sails.'[322] One Salisbury man felt at the time it was everyone's duty to look out for Fifth Columnists but that many innocent people were interviewed by the police on hearsay alone.[323]

The Local Authorities were trying their best to keep track of known aliens, the Passenger Transport Department in Swindon being asking in a memo if they were employing any aliens or conscientious objectors. Swindon's Medical Officer stated that he was aware of the presence of a lady with a German sounding surname in May 1940 in Swindon (she was actually Swiss), and it appears in Swindon that the Local Authority seemed to be confused over exactly who should be considered an alien, wondering if the citizens of Eire should be regarded as aliens too.[324] It was reported in the *Salisbury Journal* on 9 June 1944 that a German girl from Portsmouth, who was a member of the National Fire Service, had been summoned to court. It was alleged that she had failed to sign a statement as to her nationality, and also that she used a name other than that by which she was ordinarily known. She had travelled to Salisbury with her American GI. One 'friendly alien' was working in Salisbury for a War Office approved tailor. He was a naturalised German who had had to leave his wife and son behind. He had received only one letter from them in a year through the Red Cross. One of his co-workers was distressed to find the Police notifying him to go to his lodgings and collect his belongings to take for internment in the Isle of Man: 'this was at a time when there was real fear of invasion so 'friendly' aliens were being moved to a place of safety. When the danger passed he returned to us and stayed until the war ended.'[325] The internment of German citizens caused an outcry and the writer Heather Tanner from Kington Langley (who herself had given a home to a German Jew who was then interned), later stated that there was '[a]ngry protest' which the Government had to subdue by devising a number of categories for release: serious illness, an invitation to join the Pioneer Corps, work on the land: 'enemy alien transformed into loyal subject'.[326]

In May 1940 an ARP officer at Corsley had suggested using local farmers to help search for enemy parachutists. '... assuming that there is a definite possibility of an enemy landing in this country from aircraft and that patrolling the whole area by Army Units is impossible good use might be made of local farmers. These men know every inch of the ground, possess cars, shot guns and in most cases telephones, could be organised in districts to assemble quickly in bodies and would be interested in this active form of A.R.P.'[327] The Government had also been considering the benefits of using local knowledge on the ground; during the summer of 1940 a guerrilla role had already been assigned secretly to certain selected volunteers.[328] The civilian workers of the Auxiliary Units Special Duties Branch consisted of over 3,500 volunteers working as observers, runners and operators, working with around 150 Royal Signallers and members of the Auxiliary Territorial Service (ATS).[329] Over twenty Auxiliary Units were set up, consisting of army officers and 'cells' of the Home Guard who were trained in sabotage and the use of high explosives. They became responsible for dumps and hideouts stocked with guerrilla necessities.[330] The Aux Unit HQ had been established in Whitehall Palace, Westminster, until it was blitzed in 1940.[331] Lady Jane Pleydell-Bouverie, Personal Assistant to the London Controlling Section Committee, offered up Coleshill,[332] on the Berkshire/Wiltshire border. Coleshill was developed to train Auxiliers, Scout Sections and Group Commanders, often at weekends when they were not working. The training included hand grenade and shooting skills, camouflage, night stalking, the use of explosives, map reading and close quarters combat.[333] Those undertaking training disembarked at Swindon Station and were then transported to Highworth General Post Office. The postmistress telephoned Coleshill and a car would arrive to take them to their final destination.[334] Nearby Hannington Hall, sited in Wiltshire, was established as an 'ATTERY' for ATS personnel in 1942. They were part of the Auxunit Special Duties Section and Signals, but worked almost in isolation. They gained the nickname the 'Secret Sweeties'[335] which they hated.[336] The ATS personnel at Hannington worked as radio operators, passing on intelligence reports. They were also taught some spying techniques, including self defence and survival practice, and were expected to stay at their posts after the event of invasion even if the army had pulled back.[337] Also stationed at Hannington Hall was the niece of the Archbishop of Canterbury, Beatrice Temple, who had been given the role of Senior Commander. She would personally visit the subalterns in the field to check on their welfare and the standard of their accommodation etc.[338] In the field, observers were expected to leave their reports in 'dead letter drops' to be picked up and taken to secret wireless Out-Stations. The civilian operators stationed at these units would transmit the reports to military run In-Stations outside the occupied area. These In-Stations would be positioned approximately fifteen plus miles inland; the Out-Stations were no more than ten miles from the coast. In-Stations were usually located underground in dugouts, an example of one such is the underground wireless Auxunit Control Station at Hare Warren near Wilton which has recently been designated a Scheduled Monument. At three times larger than any other known unit, it is the only known Control Station of its type,[339] called a 'Super' Station and classed as an Inner Network Station of the Army Southern Command at Wilton House. It controlled an area of the coast from Portsmouth down to Lands End and up the Bristol Channel into Gloucestershire. This so called 'elephant shelter' was constructed by the Royal Engineers four feet below the surface, accessible via a vertical shaft.[340] Many of the original fittings are still in place, such as bed frames, operator positions etc. It was the last station to be built of the 'Special Duties' network, and was also the most 'advanced and complex',[341] having nine wireless aerials secreted in nearby trees.[342] The Auxiliary Units were disbanded in 1944[343] with Hare Warren closing in July,[344] and former Auxiliers went into the field to lead teams on operations into France like Captain John Merchant of the Wiltshire Regiment. With his team he parachuted into Brittany on 9 July 1944. John Warwicker reports that the mission was deemed an 'unqualified success'.[345]

It was the job of the Home Guard to remove or collect all signposts, and Fay Inchfawn at Freshford wrote of their removal just after Dunkirk in 1940. 'Even the milestone was tipped upside down over the hedge into the field.'[346] Sybil Eccles noted from Chute in May 1940: 'The signposts have all gone... Everything from signposts to aeroplane production is moving with unusual swiftness. This is satisfactory and at the same time madly irritating for it demonstrates so clearly that if we care to be efficient we can be so... a little while ago it would have taken three months to remove the signposts – now it has taken three days.'[347]

The removal was made under *The Removal of Direction Signs Order 1940*, dated 18 June 1940, under Regulations 4B of the Defence (General) Regulations 1939 which stated that:

> No person shall display or cause or permit to be displayed any sign which furnishes any indication of the name of, or the situation of, or the direction of, or the distance to, any place.
>
> For the purpose of this Article the expression 'sign' includes any direction post, place name and map.

Pile of Signposts after their removal from the area around Chippenham, c. 1940 (WSA F4/843/4 B/W)

2. It shall be the duty of the owner of any such sign and the occupier of any land or premises on or to which any such sign is placed or attached forthwith to remove the sign or to obliterate there from or conceal any such indication as is mentioned in Article 1 of this Order...[348]

The Westbury White Horse, along with the other iconic landmarks of the Wiltshire landscape, was camouflaged.[349] Hilperton resident Miss E. Berrett noted in her diary entry on 25 August 1940 that 'Westbury White Horse is also camouflaged with branches held in place with wire netting. It looks like a brown patch on the side of the hill.'[350] There was some concern over whether the sticks and bracken used for the purpose would stain the chalk, and would it prove effective?[351] A photograph taken of the Westbury White Horse during WWII proves that from a distance indeed it was! The Fovant badges that had been created by the Australian soldiers of WWI before they left for France were allowed to grow over and it was in fact the Home Guard who, in their spare time, endeavoured to restore the Fovant badges and add new ones for the Wiltshire Regiment after the war.[352]

At first weapons were few and far between, being the men's own weapons or ones they'd borrowed. In May 1940 6,000 rifles had been sent to local Police

Stations in the county for collection, divided between the districts of Chippenham, Corsham, Calne, Marlborough, Malmesbury, Warminster, Trowbridge, Bradford on Avon, Melksham, Devizes and Market Lavington. Interestingly at Marlborough the Police Station wasn't used; their allotted 1,000 rifles were kept safe at 'The Armoury, Marlborough College'. There were also 100 rifles kept safe with Lord Roundway at Roundway Park! Alongside the rifles were caps and overalls, but of these there were only 1,200 and 900 respectively; most clearly not enough to go around. By June 1940 the War Office was intending to broadcast an appeal for the loan of shotguns, to be handed in at the nearest police station.[353] Uniform consisted at that time of field service caps and arm bands which were also few in number and 'on many occasions it was necessary for men to wait their turn for some of these valuable articles before they were qualified to proceed on duty.'[354] The Salisbury platoon drew lots as to who got one.[355] The uniform itself was also slow in coming, and when it did it was often inadequate. The khaki denim uniforms started to trickle in from June 1940 to the 9th Battalion stationed in North Wiltshire, but it was some months before everyone was kitted out. The field service caps arrived only in small sizes. 'Can it be that in these early days Home Guards were so swollen-headed that the usual Army fittings were too small!'[356] The lack of adequate clothing took its toll on some men, such as one on duty at an Observation Post on top of Anstie's roof in Devizes who suffered frost bite and eventually lost a leg.[357] One of the first tasks of Commanding Officers was to reconnoitre their areas and note vulnerable points, and to take action to patrol them. Within a few days of being formed, it was not unusual for the 5th (Swindon) Battalion to do guard duty

Site of the camouflaged Westbury White Horse in WWII, reproduced by kind permission of Ivan Clark (WSHC P54010)

for three nights a week.[358] One task of the 8th (Salisbury) Battalion was Fire Guard duty at Salisbury Cathedral and the Infirmary.[359] The Home Guard were always on the look out for invading enemy parachutes, but not just for the threat of invasion. German bombers could crash and any surviving crew members needed to be captured. The Wiltshire farmer, writer and broadcaster A.G. Street joined the Home Guard and found himself chasing through the Wiltshire countryside around Wilton after a German airman who had bailed out. The German turned out to be 'a very ordinary, decent-looking lad...' Street realised on his way home that as a civilian who had just received his first real experience of war, he 'disliked it intensely'. He had been keen to hunt the airman down like a fox at the hunt, and would have shot him if necessary. 'But, somehow, when he was caught I had no further quarrel with him.'[360] It appears that Street was not alone; a letter to Wiltshire's Chief Constable from the Regional HQ in Bristol stated that there had been many instances of parachutists or those in crashed aircraft not being taken charge of quickly enough and 'opportunities have been allowed them, even in the presence of captors, to destroy maps and other documents, which, if seized, would have been of great value to our war effort. Instances have occurred in which such persons have been treated rather as benign guests than as enemies.'[361] At Fovant a German bomber crashed in 1941. The flight mechanic was found almost a week later despite search efforts.[362]

Some platoons initially thought it was their job to defend their villages, but their strength of numbers and lack of weaponry could not make this a viable option. Instead their job was to 'be mobile and to harass the enemy by any possible means, using their intimate knowledge of their own fields and areas near their villages.' Areas designated as 'anti-tank islands' were those whose through roads were to be denied the enemy.[363] Sybil Eccles of Chute lent one Local Defence Volunteer Platoon Leader her husband David's field glasses and bicycle. 'He didn't want guns or rifles. Apparently the chief task is one of accurate observation and prompt information.'[364] ARP wardens answered a call to help with manning the tank island of the 6th Battalion (located in East Wiltshire) and were training regularly with the Home Guard troops, alongside carrying out their ARP duties,[365] but the two services didn't always work in co-operation. On 6 September 1940 the 10th Battalion at Salisbury received a code word which was passed to the Wilcot platoon. They were ordered to sleep in the village hall in readiness: '... much to the annoyance of the A.R.P. warden, who complained to the Police and in turn the Police sergeant rang... up threatening to prosecute the Home Guard. On receipt of the letter that was signed by all the leading inhabitants of the village, the appointment of the warden as a special constable was cancelled and the Police sergeant was shortly afterwards moved to another station.'[366] The 4th Battalion in Central Wiltshire felt that their primary duty was to watch the countryside at night, if necessary giving the alarm. Identity cards were also examined at night 'and even the passengers in the omnibuses then running were checked, a proceeding not always appreciated by late travellers.'[367] The men manned road blocks and Observation Posts, often after working all day, and some had to be milking by 5am the next morning. No guard rooms were available for shelter or rest, and the blocks could be situated some miles from where they lived. In these cases, the summer night would often be divided into two four hours of duty. Private car owners, men and women, would help by transporting the first watch to the block at 9pm, bringing the relief at 1am and returning the first watch home, and returning to the block again at 5am to pick up the relief.[368] One Cricklade resident recalled that her father, one of the Cricklade Home Guard, manned a barrier which had been placed across one of the roads. He would often be on duty all night, still having to do a full day's work the next day.[369]

The majority of Wiltshire Home Guard Divisions were split up according to Police Divisions and each had its own group leader, later becoming a Battalion leader, commanded by a Group Organiser. In the Calne and Chippenham District a list was made up of retired officers and others who could be invited to take command of the parishes.[370] In the 9th Battalion at the north of the county, a man who had recently relinquished command at Aldershot was instructed by the War Office to organise the force.[371] The Grenadier Guards (currently based in the county) were entrusted with the task of organising the 4th Battalion, Trowbridge and Devizes District.[372] The Home Guard were initially known as the Local Defence Volunteers (LDV), dubbed by many as 'Look, Duck and Vanish'[373] but the LDV changed its name in July 1940 to the Home Guard.[374] At the end of 1940 the Wiltshire Battalions were given numbers;[375] military rank and commissions were introduced on 1 February 1941. In April 1942 compulsion was introduced[376] and some units such as the 4th Battalion in Central Wiltshire formed new companies due to the increase in their ranks.[377] The Conscription Act brought some disquiet to the 8th Battalion in Salisbury 'but few took advantage of the clause that allowed resignation from the force up to 16th February 1942',[378] although the 9th Battalion in North Wiltshire did lose some men due to resignations. In January 1942 Army Council instructions were issued to the effect that all Home Guard members over the age of 65 (except in very exceptional cases) had to resign or be discharged. In the 9th Battalion: 'This caused much heart-burning at the time, and necessitated the reorganisation of several commands.' Some left very much against their own wishes.[379]

As time went on Wiltshire's Home Guard were given help from troops stationed in the county for training and there became the 'ever present paperwork'.[380] Office work became essential and the service of Auxiliary Clerks was authorised by June 1941.[381] From July an Administrative Assistant was attached to every Battalion, paid for by a grant from the Territorial Army Association.[382] They worked closely and 'in harmony' with the Home Guard on the tasks of equipment, accounting and records.[383] In November 1940, permanent staff instructors were appointed and after January 1942 there were also Adjutants and Quartermasters.[384] One sergeant of the Cricklade Home Guard used his holiday leave to attend training courses, learning how to give lectures to his men. 'He kept a book with notes about these, plus diagrams such as the parts of a gas mask, gas drill, personal decontamination procedures, and so on. In April 1942 he attended a sten gun course at Highworth, and in July of that year spent a whole week at Woolacombe learning about Spigot mortar, an anti-tank weapon thought necessary after Dunkirk. His notes included instruction about ammunition, shells, bomb recognition, their handling and safety precautions.'[385] Most companies trained on Sundays and two evenings a week such as the 3rd and 9th Battalions.[386] [387]

The 1st Battalion of North Wiltshire found that the Colonel who had a regiment camped near Rudloe was always ready to send instructors anywhere, any time, to say nothing of arranging a battle. An expert on fighting in Spain gave a lecture at the Gaumont Cinema, Chippenham, early in 1941 to *c.* 1,200 of the 1st Battalion. On 4 May 1941 a competition was organised in the Chippenham Sports Ground for the Battalion, for the throwing of Molotov cocktails and number 36 grenades. Regular forces provided the judges.[388] One Salisbury platoon member later felt that 'making Molotov cocktails was all very amateur but at least we felt we were doing something.'[389] In 1941 the Government were informing Home Guard Battalions of their duty to immobilise petrol pumps in the event of an emergency, the order superseding an earlier directive given the previous year. Members of the Home Guard were to visit premises in the local area and liaise with them regarding their security measures, and to get themselves acquainted with the workings of the pumps. The 1st Battalion had made a list of the petrol pumps to be immobilised in their area.[390] The 2nd (Malmesbury area) Battalion's training exercises included rounding up parachutists at night and locating tanks in the woods around Malmesbury.[391] A large number of air crashes were occurring in the 4th Battalion's area of duty in Central Wiltshire. As a result lectures were provided in air rescue work with the emphasis on quick release of aircrew. Their training was put to good use many times. Their Battalion Intelligence Sections undertook training and the unit was 'transformed… from small bands of guides, whose duties were the supply of all local information to any Regular troops passing through the area, to established sections of well trained personnel.'[392] The 10th Battalion in Marlborough found that their training exercise 'The Battle of Marlborough' with some of the Canadian Bren Gun carriers (representing tanks) proved extremely informative. They discovered that Granham Hill was a weak point and thereafter it formed part of the town's defences.[393] On 2 October 1942 The *Salisbury Times & South Wiltshire Gazette* was announcing that the Home Guard in Salisbury were commended for their 'stout defence' at a training exercise. They took part in a simulated invasion with soldiers, Fire Guards and members of the WVS Housewives' Service. Surviving in Chippenham Borough Council's records at the Wiltshire & Swindon History Centre is a copy of the marching song *Britain's Home Guard*, composed by H. J. Falls and Cyril Howley, and written by Falls, including the lines:

> On village green and city square,
> They learn'd the way to fight,
> Rememb'ring how their fathers died,
> To break the German might;

Now veterans and youngsters too,
United here they stand.
To smash the invader,
Should he attack our land.[394]

The 13th Battalion, made up of Swindon's Great Western Railway employees, held their first training camp at Castle Eaton in August 1943,[395] closely followed by the 5th (Swindon) Battalion during August and September. It proved to be a great success.[396] The 6th (Marlborough area) Battalion's weekend camps were held at Winterbourne Bassett[397] and the 7th Battalion from Salisbury and its surrounding villages held their summer weekend camps at Fovant in 1944.[398]

Certificate of Proficiency issued to members of the Home Guard (WSA 1292/1)

During the summer of 1943 the 4th Battalion formed a Battalion Mobile Reserve consisting of the Bromham Platoon, as a response to the need for a 'swift moving, strong body of men that could be called upon at any time.' The Adjutant had been part of a cycling unit in 1915. He 'prepared a cyclist drill and this reserve very rapidly became a most valuable force, passing as they could through the countryside silently and rapidly to come into action at any point.'[399] By the end of 1944 the 5th (Swindon) Battalion had a Signal Section with wireless equipment, a Pigeon Service attached to the rifle section, an Intelligence Section, Transport and Ammunition Officers, a Press Officer, Medical Officer, Liaison Officer and even a military band.[400] The Home Guard was also charged with protecting factories and some military establishments, as at the EKCO Factory Works at Cowbridge, Malmesbury.[401] These units were not fully integrated into the Home Guard until 1942.[402] The 11th Battalion in Swindon was formed to protect industry; Messrs. Short Bros. at the GWR works, Messrs. Phillips and Powys Ltd. at South Marston and the head offices of Short Bros. in Stratton St. Margaret amongst others.[403] The 12th Battalion was comprised of employees of the Bristol Aircraft Company (BAC) and Birmingham Small Arms (BSA) factories at Hawthorn, Corsham.[404] Initially the 13th Battalion had been formed exclusively from GWR employees '... with, as its primary object, the defence of the G.W.R works against enemy attack and sabotage.' The GWR had realised the necessity of protecting lines of communication after Eden's speech and had issued an appeal for the defence of its railway bridges, signal boxes, junctions, lines, works and 'places of vital importance' to traffic. The response was immediate and almost overwhelming.[405] The 9th Battalion in North Wiltshire included companies at local airfields such as Wroughton, Lyneham and Clyffe Pypard.[406]

Swindon No.1 2lb Anti-Tank Gun Detachment, Mobile factory defence, 'C' Company, 11th Battalion, Wiltshire Home Guard, based at the GWR Works, Swindon, Wiltshire, c.1944. C Company's headquarters were at 24 Shop (WSHC P43759)

The Home Guard was to be mobilised using code words, the first being an 'Alarm Signal'. When this signal was received, 'half the immediate garrison [would] immediately be held available at 30 minutes notice by day and 15 minutes by night. The remainder [would] be available at 4 hours notice. 10% [could] be on leave at one time.' If the additional code word 'Stand To' was issued, all troops needed to be in a complete state of readiness at 3 hours' notice. No leave would be granted, but those on leave would not be recalled. If then the code word 'Action Stations' was issued, half the garrison would be available at 15 minutes notice, with the rest at one hour's notice. 'All the garrison [would] Stand To half an hour before blackout until half an hour after commencement. They [would] Stand To half an hour before blackout ends until half an hour after its finish.' Situation reports were to be sent to the area HQ half an hour after sunrise and at 1700 hours daily. The 1st Battalion were told that the defence of the Corsham area was to be 'active counter attack' and the Home Guard were not to impede any Officer through their Traffic Control Posts unless they were in doubt as to the person's credibility.[407]

Some members became disillusioned with the Home Guard. One such was the Chippenham doctor Eric Hickson. His wife Joan wrote in her diary in March 1944:

> Eric has resigned from the Home Guard. They have been badgering him to give a course of lectures on first aid for some time, which he has been trying to put off. He has done very little for them in the last year and the last straw was when they asked for a duplicate photograph in uniform and he hadn't got a uniform. As I had definitely turned down the GTC [Girls' Training Corps] myself I didn't feel I could press him. If we had both taken these jobs we should never be in for the evening together at all... with Eric doing so much night work already... it really is beyond a joke to take up anything else. I suppose the town think we are unsportsmanlike and unpatriotic. Perhaps we are in a way when you think of all the husbands and wives who are totally separated at the moment and who haven't even their homes.[408]

Farmers also had trouble combining long hours with their Home Guard duties. One farmer, a member of the Little Bedwyn Home Guard, recalled the summer of 1940. 'What a wonderful summer that was. In fact being on night duty was quite good as it was warm and clear, especially on moonlit nights. The great difficulty was trying to keep awake in the warmth after a hard day's work.'[409] Another, from Minety, was prosecuted for not attending Home Guard parades. His defence was that he had '12 cows, 9 in milk on 19 acres and [he] worked for other farmers using his lorry, working for 15 or 16 hours a day.' His appeal to the County War Agricultural Executive Committee was unsuccessful.[410]

Efforts were made by the 13th (GWR) Battalion to '... get the social side of the Battery going and dances were held'[411] and in Bradford on Avon a Civil Defence Quiz took place, won in February 1943 by three ARP girls.[412] In March 1943 an

ARP quiz was held in Malmesbury Town Hall. Fourteen teams from Malmesbury and the surrounding villages took part.[413] The Melksham Home Guard Social Section was discussing in March 1941 which events to hold. Suggestions included a sports evening and various competitions; darts, skittles, billiards and bagatelle. They would have to postpone the proposed dance as the hall was not free and the band they had approached was not available.[414] The *Wiltshire Times* was reporting in its 24 July 1943 edition that a Home Guard Sports event was to be held at The Courts, Holt, on August Bank Holiday 1943. There was to be a tug of war competition alongside other events and refreshments with proceeds going to the Holt Nursing Association. The B Company of the 5th (Swindon) Battalion performed the play *Zero Hour* on 26 January 1944. A local newspaper reported it as providing 'such lubricant in the liveliest manner for a large and enthusiastic audience… at the Commonweal School.'[415]

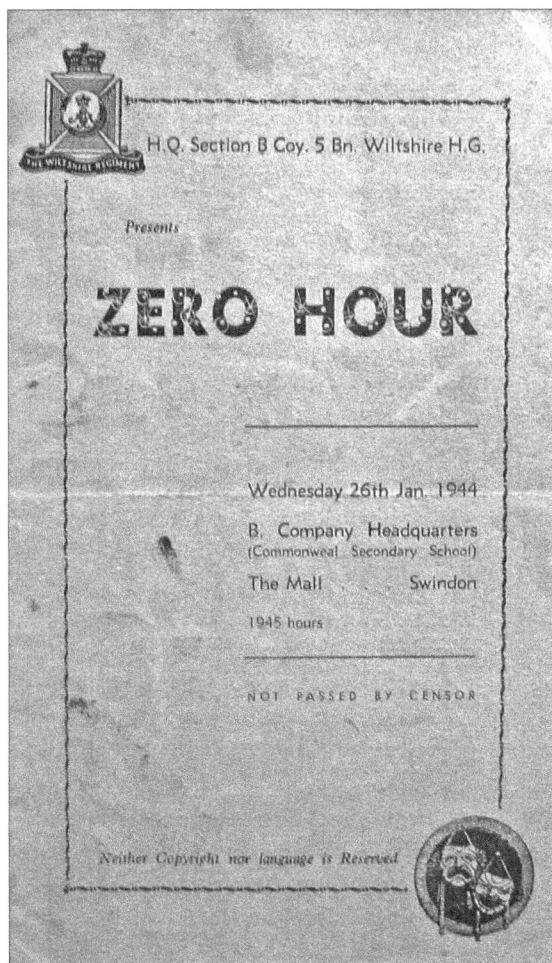

Home Guard units felt proud of their achievements. When tests were set, success leading to proficiency badges, the 4th Battalion (which covered the West and parts of Central Wiltshire) stated: 'The standard set down was a high one indeed, not fewer than six subjects had to be passed in which case a Commanding Officer's certificate was granted and a record made in Orders. It can safely be said that even in the Regular Army the standard was not so high as required of these part-time soldiers.'[416] Some of the 6th (Marlborough area) Battalion had not had a day's holiday, including Sundays, since the war began but felt it had been worth it when a regular Officer described a demonstration of Platoon battle drill as being up to the standard of men having

Programme for B Company of the 5th Battalion's (Swindon) production of Zero Hour, 26 January 1944 (WSA 2812/8)

spent six months training in the Army.[417] The 4th Battalion also felt proud that theirs was the 'strongest Battalion in the County' with a total of 3,055 members at its height.[418]

The 2nd Battalion from Malmesbury and the surrounding area paraded in front of Queen Mary at Malmesbury Abbey on 6 October 1940. A letter sent from the Queen's equerry at her request said that she was '... much impressed by their smartness on parade.' Further parades were undertaken for Weapons Week in 1941, Warship Week in 1942, Wings for Victory in 1943 and Salute the Soldier Week in 1944.[419] Many of Wiltshire's Battalions celebrated their third and fourth anniversaries by putting on parades and demonstrations. At Chippenham there was a big parade and march past followed by a display in Monkton Park which consisted of an attack on a farmhouse occupied by 'Germans'; the farmhouse was blown up and the prisoners captured. A collection at the gate raised £60 for the Wiltshire Regiment Prisoner of War Fund.[420] The first parade in Salisbury was reputed to have been 'a shambles', but with the help of WWI veterans there was a very quick improvement.[421]

It was arranged with the various American Units stationed at Charlton Park as to who would deal with parachutists[422] and the Home Guard was also to play an established part in emergency response, as set out in Chippenham Without's Parish War Book.[423] Some Home Guards had been confused between US helmets and German ones; the US personnel at Charlton Park were able to give them guidance on the matter.[424] The Home Guard's Trowbridge I Control Room was thought by some 'far too elaborate for practical purposes but this was proved false as on the occasion of the exercise 'Jupiter' in which a full force of American troops were employed, the battle was handled excellently in this control room, much to the surprise of the American senior officers present.'[425]

Initially women were not allowed to join the Home Guard and by November 1940 female Members of Parliament were asking questions. The loudest advocate was Edith Summerskill who tried to elicit definitive explanations as to why women were unable to join, but was, as Penny Summerfield and Corinna Peniston-Bird report, 'brushed off with statements suggesting it was due to 'matters of principle and organisation'. After asking for more specific answers, the argument centred on a lack of uniforms, equipment, supplies and instructors. Summerskill keenly felt that in wartime women should also be given the ability to learn to defend themselves as they too suffered from the threat of invasion.[426] Sybil Eccles noted in June 1940 at Chute: 'I can only speak for this one small village – but here the spirit is excellent and the courage and determination are high. Young Mrs King is a testimony of the Chute mood. Standing at her garden gate, arms akimbo, she says to me: "What I say is, give us all a gun. Why shouldn't the women shoot too – I'd like to learn to shoot, I would." Her eyes flash and one feels in advance quite a pang of sympathy for the hungry parachutist who is unlucky enough to knock at the Kings' front door.'[427] Edith Olivier from her house near Wilton noted in her diary: 'That is the happiness of living in this place, and indeed in any country place in England to-day. We are not cut off from the life-and-death struggle of our country, for has not this been called 'a war of little groups', in which the Home Guards and the housewives take their place behind the aircraft and the tanks?'[428]

By 1942 *The Times* reported that 'women were learning to shoot in 30 'Women's Home Defence Units' belonging to the Women's Home Defence organisation, and by December 1942 the number was thought to be 250. The War Office issued an order which was published in *The Times* on 12 November 1942. 'The War Office has sent an order to all Home Guard units that the training of women as unofficial Home Guard units has not been authorized. Weapons and ammunition in the charge of the Army or of Home Guard units must not be used for the instruction of women and the use of the name Home Guard is not permitted.' By late 1941 many Home Guard units needed recruits and Summerskill discovered that many male members were in favour of recruiting, some having already done so. Finally in 1943, women were allowed to become Home Guards, but only in an auxiliary capacity. They were to be between 18 and 65, but preferably over 45 and could only wear a plastic badge to define their role. Their job would be 'to perform non-combatant duties such as clerical work, cooking and driving'.[429] In September 1943 the Home Office was considering the suitability of certain classes of women employed in the Home Guard. There were two classes; Class 1 for 'Aliens, and British subjects who possess the nationality of a state at war with Britain, or whose husbands possess such a nationality, and women who have retained British nationality on marriage to aliens,' and Class 2 for 'British subjects not included under 1', subdivided into a) those to be employed on clerical or telephonist work and b) those employed in other work of a 'confidential' nature, 'and the Home Guard Commander is uncertain as to their suitability for it.' It was noted that: 'The criteria of suitability applied to women auxiliaries should be the same as those applied to recruits for the Home Guard itself, but as the Women will not be actually enrolled in the Home Guard, the procedure will be slightly different...'[430] The 5th (Swindon) Battalion employed three women at the time of the Stand Down[431] and in the 6th (Marlborough area) Battalion women assisted as clerks, telephonists and camp cooks.[432] The 7th (Salisbury area) Battalion enrolled 135 women as members of the Women's Home Guard Auxiliaries, performing various tasks such as helping in the orderly rooms and at feeding centres. 'Their work was greatly appreciated.'[433] The 8th (Marlborough area) Battalion had 34 nominated Women Auxiliaries by July 1943.[434] It was noted by MacKay in his published report of the wartime activities of the Wiltshire Home Guard that: 'In the tense summer of 1940, when it was known that first news of the attempted invasion might be an announcement on the wireless at any moment of the twenty-four hours, women took turns to sit up through the night by the silent but switched-on wireless, whilst their men-folk watched the countryside for parachutists.'[435] By 1944 there were 32,000 members of the Women's Home Guard Auxiliaries.[436] For those women who did join, many felt that they were indeed 'doing their bit', but women had been excluded from playing the part they wanted to in the war for three years. Research has shown that the role they played has long been ignored, and that public recognition has eluded them; their role being downplayed.[437] One female Home Guard member was noted at the Stand Down parade for the 2nd Battalion in Malmesbury. She was Chief Clerk at the Battalion HQ and was representing the Women HG Auxiliaries on the dais with others who had helped the Home Guard.[438] It appears that members of the Women's Home Guard Auxiliary did not march with their male counterparts.

Trowbridge Home Guard's Auxiliary Section (WSHC P43516)

By May 1942 every Wiltshire Home Guard man had either a personal weapon or some specialist role. 'Every man was expected to be efficient in his own weapon and also in one other.'[439] The 21 September 1941 issue of *Picture Post* was declaring that *The Home Guard Can Fight*, looking at the training given at Osterley Park near London. Events at the Park were 'something new and strange as to be almost revolutionary – the growth of an 'army of the people' in Britain – and, at the same time, something that is older than Britain, almost as old as England – a gathering of the 'men of the counties able to bear arms.'' The readers were told how the Home Guard would need to increase in numbers to enable them to undertake their new duties; to take over tasks currently done by the regular army; to become a combat force here at home... finally, they were being taken seriously.

There was also the 'Blue Line,' the defence along Wiltshire's Kennet and Avon Canal,[440] for which pillboxes had been erected along its route.[441] England's Tudor and Napoleonic coastal defences had been long neglected; WWI brought with it the construction of pillboxes along Britain's East Coast.[442] It was realised in WWII that an attack by invading troops would not only come from the sea.

The development of airborne parachute troops meant that if the enemy won the battle of the skies they could drop their troops on any part of British soil. On 10 May 1940 the Home Defence Executive was set up under Sir Edmund Ironside, Commander-in-Chief Home Forces, to deal with all matters of Home Defence. He noted that if the Luftwaffe won air superiority, they would be able to airlift 9,750 lightly armed men in one flight, travelling as far as East Anglia or Kent. He devised a Defence Plan which protected London and the Midlands by a GHQ (General Headquarters) line with, as Henry Willis notes, a series of Command, Corps and Divisional 'Stop-lines' between it and the coast. The Plan was completed by 12 June[443] and led to the construction of thousands of pillboxes and anti-tank blocks,[444] many of which still stand today. Alongside these defences were anti-tank ditches, giving the enemy an eleven foot drop into a ditch.[445] To construct the ditches a hole would be dug in the road, four feet deep and four feet wide, to be filled with concrete, and holes in the form of an upside down U were made. The 'construction' could be easily put into place as and when it was required; a piece of wood was placed over the holes to allow for normal use of the road at all other times.[446] Shallow ditches were also dug to prevent aircraft and gliders from landing[447] and sockets for tank traps appeared near pillboxes. Made from old railway lines they were about twelve feet in length and bent to a right angle.[448] Anti-tank obstacle trials were held at Westbury on 13 and 14 August 1941 where various obstacles were tested using live ammunition. The reinforced concrete cylinders worked best at withstanding the 2-pounder gunfire.[449]

DSCN3914 anti-tank cylinders at Woodborough Bridge on the Kennet & Avon, reproduced by kind permission of Tim Burge

The first line of defence was to be along probable invasion beaches, the second a line of road blocks, manned by the Home Guard. Stop-lines were created between the invasion zone and the GHQ Line, their aim to neutralise any enemy incursions inland. The GHQ line followed natural waterways such as canals and made the most of topographical features wherever possible to create an anti-tank obstacle. The only detailed list that exists of the GHQ line is for the Southern Command area. The list detailed three GHQ Stop-lines within the area; red which travelled from Great Somerford to Tilehurst; blue which went from Bradford on Avon to Tilehurst and green, going from Highbridge to Freshford and then on to Stroud, to a point near Gloucester. The Command and Corps stop-lines were also located: Taunton stop-line, from Bridgwater to Seaton; Salisbury stop-line, from Frome to Salisbury and then to Odiham; Ringwood stop-line, Christchurch to Salisbury; Oxford stop-line, Abingdon to Banbury. Corps stop-lines: Stalbridge –Blandford –Wimborne to Christchurch; Totton –Romsey –Michelmersh – Chichester –Midhurst to Petersfield and from Wadebridge –Bodmin to Fowey.[450] Major Green reports that the Stop-lines were constructed in 'frantic haste' due to the imminent threat of invasion at the beginning of the war, and work was halted in October 1940 after the Battle of Britain had been won. Their construction was probably meant as much a deterrence as a threat, being clearly visible to German air reconnaissance, but they may also have had the added bonus of raising the morale of the civilian population, to 'stiffen their will to resist'.[451]

One Bradford on Avon resident recalled: 'In addition to the pillbox by the Pack Horse Bridge, just to the north of this box, within a triangle formed by the river, Barton Orchard and the railway line, was a second pillbox, just off the river bank. Long since demolished, I don't think a trace remains. The interesting fact was that it had a red pantiled roof to disguise it as a cottage. Quite effective, apart from the tiles broken by myself and others climbing over it!'[452] The press were, perhaps understandably, not allowed to publish any details of wartime defences.[453] Wiltshire County Council's Planning Department had been considering the future of pillboxes and concrete obstruction pillars at Norton Bavant Farm in 1947 – should they be removed in the public interest? It appears not to be so, as it was reported that there was 'no hurry'.[454]

The remains of these defences can still be seen today, with examples including a pillbox in a field beside the River Avon in Chippenham. Others do not fare so well and many have been lost, but in 2010 a campaign by local historian John Girvan led to the listing of a pillbox on the Kennet and Avon Canal at Rotherstone, near Devizes. It was found to be in good condition and formed 'an integral part of a crucial defensive stop line'.[455] Stop-line Green is considered to remain remarkably intact and as such is a well preserved part of military archaeology.[456]

The Home Guard played a role in the lead up to D-Day, patrolling railway bridges looking out for saboteurs or enemy parachute troops. 'The men felt that they were doing a useful job of work, great keenness was shown and many were the night intruders brought in by these guards for failing to answer challenges,

Pillbox on the River Avon near Chippenham, taken by the author, 2014

etc.... directly contributing to the success of the overseas operations.'[457] They felt that at last they were involved in something that was worth doing.[458] After D-Day a month's holiday was given in August to rest many who had 'felt the long strain,' but musketry practice continued without pause. 'Training was resumed but we all felt that the Home Guard was passing, we were warned of the code word which would herald our dissolution and, at the end of October, we knew the 'Stand Down' was fixed for November 1st.' Final parades were arranged throughout the county for Sunday 3 December 1944.[459] The 1st Battalion's Stand Down Ceremonial Parade was to be held in John Coles Park, Chippenham, with General Sir Alexander Godley addressing and reviewing the troops at 11.45am. There would then be a march past by the Town Hall. As for transport arrangements to the site, Companies were asked to make arrangements for as much transport as they could, and 'the buses of Messrs. Thomas, Browning, Hopkins, Vaughan, Simmonds and Keen' had been reserved for the Battalion.[460]

Personal weapons, ammunition and all other equipment needed to be handed in by 31 December. Uniform was to be retained by members as personal property,[461] but initially this wasn't to be the case. '... it is regrettable that the authorities showed considerable reluctance in allowing Home Guards to keep their personal clothing. At first it was intended they should keep only their boots. Eventually, after representations from many quarters, Home Guards were allowed to retain their boots, battle dress, greatcoat, cap and gas capes.'[462]

A special Army Order was issued to the Home Guard with a message from the King on the day of the official Stand Down on 3 December. 'For more than four years you have born a heavy burden. Most of you have been engaged for long hours in work necessary to the prosecution of the war or to maintaining the healthful life of the nation... The Home Guard has reached the end of its long tour of duty under arms. But I know that your devotion to our land, your comradeship, your power to work your hardest at the end of the longest day will discover new outlets for patriotic service in time of peace. History will say that your share in the greatest of all our struggles for freedom was a vitally important

You will hand in all weapons, ammunition, clothing, equipment and Home
Guard Government stores in your possession at (place) ....
.... Neston Schools .... on (date) **Dec 10th** ....
at .. **10.00** .. hours, except the following items which you may retain :

Caps, F.S.	Boots, Ankle	Greatcoats
Battledress, blouse	Anklets, leather or web.	Capes, anti-gas No. 1, or
Battledress, trousers	Titles and Badges	Capes, Rubberised
	and Service Respirator until recalled	

You will bring with you
your copy of A.F. H.1158

(Signed) *E. Head*

for Comdg. **Neston** Pln./Coy.

Date **2 9 NOV 1944**

1st Bn. Wilts Home Guard

To be handed in with personal kit

I certify that I am not in possession of any articles of Clothing, Equipment,
Arms or any property except that for which retention has been authorised by
H.M. Government.

Date *6th December/44*   *R.G.W. Armitt.*

Signature

*Example of a postcard sent to each member of the Home Guard, detailing which items of
equipment to return (WSA 1292/7)*

one. You have given your service without the thought of reward. You have earned
in full measure your country's gratitude. George R.I. Colonel-in-Chief.'[463]

Membership of the Home Guard had not been without risk. Personnel
from the 6th Battalion in North Wiltshire received BEMs when their 'coolness
and disregard of personal danger, prevented casualties when mishaps occurred
on the bombing range.'[464] On 13 September 1942 a member of '… Alderbury
Company, lost his life whilst serving the throwing of No. 36 grenades by members
of an AA battery. He deliberately laid himself on a grenade which had rolled back
into the throwing position at the feet of the thrower. Lt. Foster's great gallantry
was officially recognised and on the 27 November it was announced by the BBC
that he had received the posthumous award of the George Cross.'[465] There were
numerous other near misses, such as at Purton where the platoon often accidentally
fired a stray bullet when cleaning or dismantling the guns. The platoon Sergeant
checked the guns each morning to ensure no bullets remained in the barrels.
'While carrying out this inspection early one morning, the person responsible…
accidentally pulled the trigger of a .22 rifle. The bullet which discharged remains
firmly imbedded in the wall of the butchers' shop at the top of Purton Hill to
this day.'[466] The Commonwealth War Graves Commission's list of civilian war
dead included members of the Rescue Service, Casualty Service, Home Guard,
Messengers and Firewatchers.[467]

Every Battalion had their own Stand Down parade and a few members
of most Battalions were sent to represent them at the ceremonial Stand Down
parade of the Home Guard in London[468] where a tribute concert was held in the
Albert Hall with stars such as Vera Lynn performing.[469] The final disbandment

itself came on 31 December at midnight. 'For the last time the officers and men of Britain's Home Guard met in town and village halls, remembering the last eventful years a little wistfully and determined that the comradeship formed should endure through the years to come.' What many had enjoyed most was the companionship that membership had brought; men such as those in Leigh who lived in isolated hamlets, rarely meeting anyone from outside their own village. 'Now, on Sunday mornings the whole Company marched, four abreast and carrying their rifles…'[470] [471] Many units continued as far as they could by establishing rifle clubs and taking part in shooting competitions,[472] such as the Hannington and Lushill Rifle Club, formed after Stand Down.[473] A Home Guard Certificate of Service would be issued to all those who could verify their membership of the Home Guard, but those who had been convicted of an offence under the *Defence (Home Guard) Regulations 1940* or for a disciplinary offence would not be eligible.[474] In 1946 applications were made for six Civil Defence workers from Malmesbury Borough to receive Defence Medals.[475]

After the war the 6th (Marlborough area) Battalion of the Wiltshire Home Guard compared the Home Guard's call to arms as to the time of the Napoleonic War.[476] Their feelings of life in the Home guard also summed up the experiences of many civil defence workers in rural England:

'Working it is true, from the blessed comfort of [our] unblitzed homes… men did the work of two men, preparing for the battle that was not to be.'[477]

Royal Observer Corps

THE ROYAL OBSERVER Corps (ROC) were originally known as The Observer Corps,[478] established in 1925 to enable the identification and monitoring of aircraft movements[479] with any findings communicated to a regional HQ.[480] The experience of aerial bombing in WWI had made the Government aware that an early warning system to spot and track enemy aircraft would be needed in a time of war. Experimental work was carried out with Special Constables and in 1934 the 'perceived threat' from Germany prompted a six-year programme of expansion.[481] The system began as an extension of the Police Force[482] with new recruits enrolled as Special Constables, such as in Malmesbury in 1938.[483] The Bradford on Avon Corps was set up in January 1938[484] and the post between Bodenham and Nunton, known as the 'Bodenham' post, was established in January too, the Earl of Radnor being one of those on duty during the war. The Head Observer was the landlord of the Radnor Arms.[485]

Two Observers would be on duty both day and night throughout the war,[486] watching for aircraft after they had passed the Chain Home radar system, and Calder notes that they were 'remarkably efficient' at it.[487] One Observer would watch and listen for aircraft whilst the other would identify and report in, although training in aircraft identification did not occur until the men themselves formed the Royal Observer Corps Club.[488] The Chain Home Radar System began development in 1935[489] by Robert Watson-Watt and his team of Meteorologists[490] with the Chain Home sites hugging the coast.[491] The first stage in the system involved the interception of aircraft in a Sector Operations Room, where a Controller was able to direct a Fighter Pilot to the general area of the target. At the same time a Controlled Ground Interception (CGI) Controller would, as Colin Dobinson notes, 'take over the fighter for close control', contacting the appropriate Chain Home Station to ensure that the target was hostile, then speaking to the pilot directly on a different VHF channel from the Sector Controller, 'directing him via the PPI' (Plan Position Indicator). This was the theory and it was not always successful, but it gave Pilots 'a new confidence in their work'.[492] A memorial stone has been erected in the honour of Watson-Watt and his colleague Arnold Wilkins, the dedication reading:

> Birth of Radar Memorial
> On 26th February 1935, in the field opposite
> Robert Watson Watt and Arnold Wilkins
> Showed for the first time in Britain that aircraft could be directed by bouncing radio waves off them, by 1939 there were 20 stations tracking aircraft at distances up to more than 200 miles later known as radar. It was this invention, more than any other, that saved the RAF from defeat in the 1940 Battle of Britain.[493]

Avebury was the location of a Controlled Ground Interception Station, but a new site was commissioned in September 1941 at Cricklade when Avebury became a training centre. Top priority was given to its erection.[494]

The Observation Posts of the ROC were positioned on high ground where there was also a wide field of vision, and they were linked by telephone to an operations room.[495] Due to their exposed position, some weather conditions could prove difficult, and the winter of 1939 was particularly harsh. A permanent screen was built to protect Malmesbury's Observers, consisting of blocks, as Charles Vernon notes, 'with half the platform open and the other half forming a covered shelter for two men'.[496] The Corps was granted the title 'Royal' in April 1941 in recognition of the valuable work they were contributing[497] and it was at this time that they parted from the Police and became administered by the RAF. New uniforms were issued, at first coveralls but in 1942 this changed to RAF style battle-dress.[498] It was also at this time that women became able join the Corps and by 1943 there were 2,700 female ROC workers.[499] As Margaret Dobson puts it, 'The Corps were the 'Eyes and Ears' of the Royal Air Force, essential for the effective working of the air raid warning system.'[500]

During the war there were 39 Observer Corps Groups around the country which controlled 30-50 posts each, with the number of personnel at around 34,000.[501] The *Aeroplane* reported on their importance after the end of the war. 'The general public knew nothing of the activities of the ROC… In fact the ROC was probably responsible for more damage to the enemy's war effort than most of our home-based military forces of a similar character, which must be unique in the annals of civilian national service.'[502]

MAIDEN

OBSERVER CORPS

Form of Agreement for Observer's Hut

AN AGREEMENT made this *first* day of *April* 1943 between **Walter L. Barton Agent to the 17th. Duke of Somerset** of **The Estate Office, Maiden Bradley, Warminster, Wiltshire** (hereinafter called " The Landlord ") of the one part, AND the Secretary of State for Air (hereinafter called " The Secretary of State ") acting by

WESTERN Area

Commandant Observer Corps of the other part.

WHEREBY the Landlord grants to the Secretary of State the right to erect maintain use and remove a portable wooden hut with right of access and egress thereto and from on the land described in the schedule hereto from the date of this agreement until the twenty-ninth day of September next following and thereafter from year to year but terminable by either party by three months' notice in writing to quit expiring on any Quarter Day at a yearly rent of **Forty** shillings the first payment to be payable in advance on completion of this agreement by the Secretary of State and subsequent payments on the twenty-ninth day of September in each year.

1. The Secretary of State agrees :—

    (1) To pay the said rent at times and in manner aforesaid.

    (2) To indemnify the Landlord against payment of any rates which may be assessed on the occupation by the Secretary of State of the said portable wooden hut.

    (3) To use the hut only for the purpose of sheltering members of the Observer Corps in the performance of their duties.

    (4) To pay fair compensation to the Landlord for all damage caused by the erection maintenance use and removal of the hut inclusive of damage to crops caused by the normal user of the hut. Claims for compensation shall be sent to the Area Commandant within fourteen days of the occurrence of the damage.

    (5) To remove the hut within one month of the termination of this agreement.

2. The Landlord agrees to allow the Secretary of State paying the said rent and performing and observing the conditions of the agreement granted quiet enjoyment of the rights conferred.

3. It is mutually agreed :—

    (1) That any dispute as to compensation for damage under this Agreement shall be referred to the Arbitration of a single arbitrator to be agreed upon by both parties, or failing agreement to be appointed by the President of the Charted Surveyors' Institution, subject to and in accordance with the provisions of the Arbitration Acts 1889 to 1934.

Form of Agreement for an Observer's Hut, No. 23 Group, E1 Post at Maiden Bradley, between the Duke of Somerset and the Secretary of State for Air, 1 April 1943, reproduced by kind permission of the Duke of Somerset (WSA 2056/4/12)

By the early 1950s it was realised that many posts were not positioned in the best of locations and many were not even classed as 'proper' Posts. In April 1951 411 Posts were due for re-siting and an additional 93 were to be built. This included the Bodenham Post which was moved to Pepperbox Hill and given the new name of 'Alderbury Post' (Bravo 2) but retaining its original purpose; to report aircraft.[503] It was linked to Wylye's Bravo 1, Broad Chalke's Bravo 3 and Tisbury's Bravo 4. By 1957 Monitoring Posts such as Alderbury's were moved underground due to the threat of nuclear war.[504]

Youth Organisations

DURING WWI THE Boy Scouts in Trowbridge had proved very willing to help the war effort.[505] In the autumn of 1939 the National Headquarters of the main youth organisations, under the approval of the Minister of Home Security and the National Youth Committee, arranged for the placement of Youth Liaison Officers to be attached to each office of the Regional Commissioners for Civil Defence. It had been realised that youth clubs were closing down; their meeting premises could often be requisitioned and their organisers were entering the services; there had also been a general lack of support for the clubs. It was reported that the 'youth movements must go on, old units must be re-vitalised wherever possible, and new units started where they are most needed.' The Local Education Authorities had a part to play, and 'every boy and girl needing mental, physical and spiritual recreation and guidance [should] know... just where to find it.' The youth organisations listed included the Boys' Brigade, the Boys' Clubs, the Boy Scouts, the Church Lads' Brigade, the Girls' Clubs, the Girls' Friendly Society and the Girls' Life Brigade, the YMCA and the YWCA.[506] In December 1941 young people aged 16 and 17 were required to register with Local Education Officers under 'Youth Registration' to encourage them to find the best way of doing their duty as citizens, but also as a way to channel their leisure activities into acceptable forms of pastime.[507] These young people took part in Civil Defence by joining the Army Cadet Force, Air Training Corps, Girls Training Corps or Youth Service Corps, assisting the Army and Civil Defence by digging gun emplacements, painting kerb stones white and collecting salvage, as they did in Devizes.[508] The Air Training Corps (ATC) was set up in 1941 when the Government took over the Air Defence Cadet Force which had been established by an RAF Officer in 1938. King George VI became their Air Commodore-in-Chief and approved the new badge, with the motto VENTURE ADVENTURE. Swindon was reported as being at the forefront of Wiltshire towns for the scheme just two days after its establishment. It was open to boys aged 16 to 18 and Cadets would be expected to join the RAF, Royal Navy or Fleet Air Arm when they became old enough, although it was expected that the RAF would get the highest proportion of recruits. The boys were issued a free uniform, but boys who joined under 16 would not receive it until they reached 16. The Army Cadet Force was established in February 1942, a full year after the ATC. The King also became their Colonel-in-Chief. A newspaper calling for recruits called them 'Local Lads

Eager to Join the 'Junior Home Guard." It reported recruiting in North Wiltshire in Swindon, Chippenham, Calne and Malmesbury. Recruits were to co-operate with the Home Guard in tactical operations and make use of their equipment, but retain a separate identity. In March 1943 Malmesbury's Town Clerk asked for the Cadets to be used as ARP messengers.[509] The Army Cadet Force in Codford used to meet with the Home Guard. Once, during an exercise, the Home Guard had to guard the railway line and the Cadets were told to filter through. '… All the boys knew the terrain, but so did the Home Guard, who were better than us.'[510] The Government finally realised in 1942 that an organisation should also be set up for girls, and the National Association of Training Corps for Girls came into being. Three Corps were established; the Girls' Training Corps (GTC), the Women's Junior Air Corps and Girls' Nautical Training Corps; again the recruits had to be aged between 16 and 18 years of age. With the help of prominent local ladies as leaders, these units proved very popular in Wiltshire. Swindon was again at the forefront with one of the first units. The Auxiliary Fire Service used members to act as telephonists and messengers.[511] 'Young Citizens' were formed into pools, usually working from a local school, called the 'Aftermath Messenger Service'. They were used in Control Centres and emergency mortuaries, and in June 1941 the Civil Defence Messenger Service was established, working from local posts and sent to where they were needed most. The Young Citizens were all aged 15-18; a lower age limit had been enforced due to the Government's concern over younger aged casualties.[512] In Trowbridge the Red Cross Girls' Cadet Unit was formed in 1942. The girls helped with domestic duties at the Trowbridge and District Hospital. The boys unit was formed in 1945.[513] The Girl Guides was already a long-standing organisation, having been established in 1910,[514] and in Trowbridge as early as September 1939 they were busy helping a group of blind evacuees with their sewing and mending.[515]

The social side of these youth organisations appears to rest with sport, and many boxing matches were arranged between various Air Training Corps and Army Cadet Units in Malmesbury. It also appears there were hockey matches between the Girls' Training Corps units in the area. Joint dances were held for members of all the youth organisations and they also took part in many parades. The GTC also performed a George Bernard Shaw play. The Naval Cadets do not appear as prevalent in Wiltshire, although one school in Malmesbury wanted to establish a corps as '[m]any boys in this neighbourhood are anxious to see a Naval Cadet Corps started here.' It appears no further action was taken, however. The ideals of these youth services are evident in the Girls' Training Corps song: 'We're here to help our country shoulder her heavy load, this is the way to victory, this is the surest road.'[516]

The Stand Down

WITH THE COMING of D-Day, the threat of invasion was over and the process of winding down Civil Defence Units began. A memorandum was sent by Wiltshire's Deputy County Medical Officer to Civil Defence workers on 15 September 1944 stating that 'no written instructions have been received confirming the relaxation of Civil Defence hours of duty from 48 to 12 per month, as announced by the B.B.C.' but guidance was given, stating that hours of duty could be reduced as announced and that those hours spent on duty should be used to carry out servicing, cleaning and maintaining any vehicles to ensure they were 'ready for the road', and also for staff training.[517] Demobilisation of Civil Defence services, apart from the Police and Fire services (and except London and the South East), began in November 1944. Those first to be released were men over 60 and women over 45, those working full-time and those who had additional 'household responsibilities'. The national Air Raid Warning System came to an end from 2 May 1945 but in Malmesbury, the Malmesbury Gas and Coke Company reported that they were unable to reinstate the street lighting due to staff shortages.[518] The Deputy County Medical Officer wrote to the staff of Wiltshire's First Aid Posts in May 1945 to express his appreciation of their efforts, for the '... enthusiastic help and co-operation they have given this Department since 1939. I am sure that, had any large air attack on this County been experienced, the First Aid Post Service would have given a good account of itself.'[519] In October 1945 the Ministry of Health at Whitehall was informing Salisbury's Town Clerk that the authority would be credited for any surplus Emergency Service goods or furniture that were sent to a Regional Store. Fire Guard office furniture down to wall clocks, hand towels and tea cloths were moved to the Council Offices at Bourne Hill, some for disposal. Clothing was also surplus to requirements, and the 5th Sarum Air Scouts were hoping to take advantage. They were writing to Salisbury City Council in July 1945. 'The official hat for our section of the Scout movement is the beret – and as we have great difficulty in obtaining supplies we are wondering whether you will have any disposal stock... to purchase.' They were in luck – there were 4 dozen 'part-worn' berets for disposal, and the Council were also selling 30 pairs of sheets at 17s. 6d. a pair and pillowcases at 1s. 3d. each. The Assistant Controller and ARP Officer were also hoping that the Government would re-purchase 72 'practically new' waterproof capes. Anti-gas equipment was also being retuned to the Home Office Civil Defence Regional Store in Reading under the terms of an ARP Bulletin.[520]

Details can be found on individual Civil Defence workers and members of the Home Guard in Wiltshire, such as their application forms, in the archive at the Wiltshire & Swindon History Centre. Major E. Mackay's book *The History of The Wiltshire Home Guard*, 1946, gives the names of all Platoon Commanders. Wiltshire's museums also hold various items and documentation relating to the County's Civil Defence units and their members.

Civil Defence was still felt to be an important part of the Government's Cold War defence in the immediate post-war era[521] and in November 1945 the Government was stating that Civil Defence services were only temporarily suspended.[522] A national campaign resulted in fifty thousand people being recruited during the period 1949-54[523] but the idea of Civil Defence in the minds of the British people had changed. Home life, the family and privacy meant that people would not undertake Civil Defence duties out of patriotism or a sense

Civil Defence and Food recruiting campaign Flying Squad demonstration in Market Street, Salisbury, 18 October 1957 (WSHC P5012)

of duty as during the Second World War.[524] The Government tried utilising this outdated 'call to arms' and failed in its 1949-51 campaigns.[525] The campaign of 1952-3 instead focused on fun and enjoyment, a place to find new interests and make new friends. There was also an emphasis on the contribution of Civil Defence towards promoting peace, and house-to-house canvassing was used to help drive recruitment.[526] Membership of the Civil Defence Corps and Auxiliary Fire Service in the 1950s was open to men and women aged 18 and over, although due to National Service, '[i]n the Civil Defence Corps men under 30 are at present accepted only (a) for the Rescue Station or (b) as Scientific Intelligence Officer or (c) if they have been found unfit for H.M. Forces but are fit enough for service with the Corps.'[527] The WVS in Warminster continued to run an Emergency Feeding Centre Feeding Exercise in the town in the early 1950s. The centre's organiser, Mrs Brely, was awarded the BEM in the Birthday Honours List of 1958 for her work with Hungarian refugees.[528] The Trowbridge Guide to the Festival of Britain in 1951 stated in a message from the Chairman of the Urban District Council that:

'I hope that this Festival of Britain year will be one of achievement that will leave the town better off at the close than it was at the beginning, with all its citizens roused to a greater sense of civic responsibility and a determination to make the fullest contribution possible to the general welfare of the town.'[529]

By 1957 the Government was asking *Civil Defence: Is it any use in the Nuclear Age?*[530]

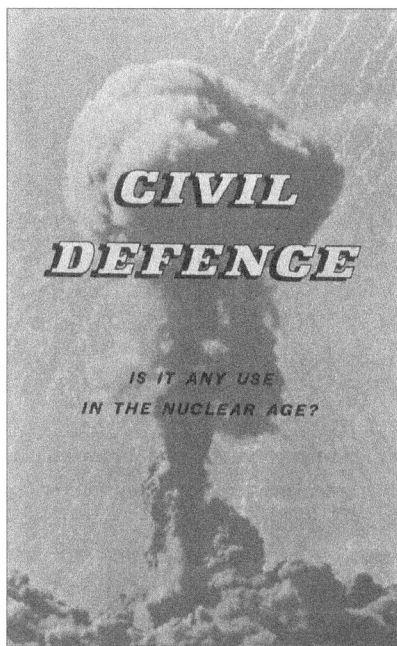

Leaflet for the Civil Defence Campaign of 1957 (WSA G23/231/1)

It appears that 1944 may not have marked the end for the Home Guard after all, as they were to be brought back into action during any further crisis. Civil Defence Circular 47/1950 dated 6 December 1950 was sent to all Clerks of Local Authorities, entitled *The Home Guard and Civil Defence Class Z (or equivalent) Reservists*. A statement had been made by the Minister of Defence in the House of Commons on 15 November 1950 as a consequence of the beginning of the Korean War.

2. It has frequently been represented that uncertainty about the reconstitution of the Home Guard has acted as a deterrent to Civil Defence recruiting…

3. The instructions to be issued to the Home Guard Advisers in Army Commands will provide, among other things, for the closest contact at Regional level with the Home Office in planning Home Guard units, their strength, sources of recruitment etc. Generally speaking, the object will be to secure that recruiting for Civil Defence is given priority in the big industrial areas and centre of population while in rural areas priority will be given to the potential needs of the Home Guard. The principles governing the transfer of men to the Home Guard will also be agreed between the War Office and the Home Office and implemented locally by the respective authorities in consultation.[531]

Home Office Circular 8/1951, dated 11 January 1951, was entitled *Recruitment of the Home Guard* and was sent to Wiltshire's Chief Constable. There was guidance on the proposed recruitment arrangements and thought was being given regarding repercussions for the Special Constabulary. It was hoped that '… suitable applicants wishing to join the Special Constabulary will not be rejected because they may indicate that if they are subsequently accepted for service in the Home Guard they would wish to transfer to that force.' The Home Guard were recruiting in Wiltshire in 1952. Wiltshire's Chief Constable was writing to the Home Office on 23 February: 'A number of Chief Constables have reported that they have been approached by local Home Guard Commanders and asked to 'screen' applicants for enrolment in the Home Guard.' There were concerns over the issue and it was noted that the 'Security Service' were at present screening potential members.[532] Civil Defence continued to play a role for some into the

1960s, but Matthew Grant notes that 'the level of new recruits in the hydrogen bomb era was typically only half that of the atomic age'.[533]

Although Wiltshire did not suffer heavy bombing during the war, its inhabitants aided those who were suffering and some carried with them the traumatic memories of those events. Of the Civil Defence workers themselves, one Wiltshire man summed up the feeling of Civil Defence during wartime. 'For myself, like so many others, it had to be accommodated in one's life. It was necessary and people adjusted to it.'[535]

Wiltshire County Council admitted that the cost of Civil Defence services was expected to total £54,070 between April 1939 and March 1940. All that was expected back from the Government was £38,320.[535] At a local level wartime Civil Defence left a financial legacy as well as a personal one.

Most memories of the voluntary work undertaken on the Home Front during the Second World War encompass those of the ARP and Home Guard; these groups were most visible in areas that were not heavily bombed. The WVS was also noted with thanks for the work they did, especially regarding their clothes banks, which provided practical help to householders regarding the evacuees they took in. From 1942 the Government had actively worked to send full-time Civil Defence personnel to the war industry for production work instead. The remaining staff in the various units of Civil Defence were then expected to work interchangeably to maintain strength of personnel. But those full-time members who remained did not have the chance to earn higher wages in industry or gain, as Calder puts it, the 'prestige and privileges of the armed forces'.[536]

The January 1945 edition of the *Great Western Railway Magazine* printed part of the Queen's Thank You speech when she addressed a representative assembly of women members of the Civil Defence Services on 6 December.

I believe strongly that, when future generations look back on this most terrible war, they will recognise as one of its chief features the degree to which women were actively concerned in it. The war could not be won without their help. This is a thought which gives me pride… British women have won laurels in many fields, but nowhere have they played a more distinguished and courageous part than in the many spheres of activity that go to make up Civil Defence here at home… To all of you I want to say, in the name of the country which you have served, and are serving, so gallantly, 'Thank you for a difficult job magnificently done.'[537]

7

The Menace from the Sky

Air Raid Precautions

IN 1934 WINSTON Churchill spoke of a possible future 'in which millions of people, bombed out of their homes in the next war, would aimlessly wander the countryside, creating a potentially explosive social and political situation and diverting scarce military resources.'[1]

Official Air Raid Precautions planning began in 1935 with the creation of an ARP Department at the Home Office, but work had been undertaken behind closed doors from the 1920s, when the Committee of Imperial Defence formed a sub-committee for ARP, chaired by John Anderson, the Permanent Under-Secretary of State for the Home Office.[2] The Committee had been established in 1904 but it was from 1924 that it began looking at the design of the country's air raid precautions. Included was the development of Auxiliary Fire Brigades, barrage balloons and trenches in city centres.[3] The Air Ministry gave 'bleak estimates' regarding the scale and extent of damage that could occur via aerial attack and on this basis much of the military and ARP planning was created.[4]

The Depression of the 1930s hampered progress with only a small amount spent on ARP, mostly for anti-gas research. The Office of Works had neither the funds nor the machinery to test shelter designs but in 1934 it was agreed by the Home Office Minister's Committee that it was the Exchequer who should pay for some ARP services, not Local Authorities. £92,000 of funding was allotted.[5] A circular was published by the Home Office in July 1935 which for the first time made secret preparations public, asking for suggestions from Local Authorities for their own wartime measures. It became a hot issue, debated in parliament and in the press, with the accusation that it had been made public deliberately to prepare the civilian population for war.[6]

Civilian respirators were being developed at Porton Down in Wiltshire as early as 1934,[7] an extension of the establishment's post WWI assessment of the condition of a million wartime respirators in the 1920s. In 1926 Porton's scientists also began looking at gas attack from the air. Staff at the site wrote the first five of the 1939 ARP handbooks published by the Home Office which not unsurprisingly dealt largely with anti-gas measures.[8] By 1936 the Government had announced that gas masks would be made available to the general public free of charge in the event of war, continuing its focus on anti-gas measures. For one scientific advisor to the Ministry of Home Security, J. F. Baker, focusing on gas 'was a shrewd political move'. Each member of the community would have his or her own protective device, costing only a little over two shillings per head. Joseph Meisel notes that Baker did not want to 'belittle in any way the remarkable achievement of those responsible for designing, producing, storing and distributing' civilian gas masks, and they may have deterred the enemy from using poison gas as a weapon, but Baker felt the result was a 'marked neglect of structural precautions'.[9]

The Ministry of Home Security took on responsibility for regional organisation which involved the co-ordination of Civil Defence activities such as the Police and Fire Brigades. It also oversaw the Air Raid Precautions organisations run by the Local Authorities and research, design, supply and finance functions. In 1940 a Parliamentary Secretary was appointed to deal with shelter policy; soon after one permanent Secretary was in control of all four main Divisions.[10] By September 1939 the Government had produced a set of ARP preparations which were designed to counter attack from the air.[11] Included in these preparations was a set of information leaflets for the public, published in July 1939. Leaflet No. 1 was entitled *Some Things you Should Know if War Should Come* to help people get prepared. Advice included what to do when an air raid warning was given, how to use a gas mask, the lighting restrictions which would prevail in the event of war, fire precautions, evacuation, identity labels and food. Leaflet No. 2 *Your Gas Mask* went into more detail, containing guidance on taking care of the equipment: 'Take care of your gas mask and your gas mask will take care of you'. Reassurance was given: '... it has been most carefully and fully tested, and will give you adequate protection against breathing any of the known war gases,' alongside advice on how to store it, put it on and take it off.[12]

With the Munich Crisis came the public appearance of gas masks and trenches. '[T]he Country went over to a war mentality, if not to a proper war footing' and there was an atmosphere of apprehension amongst the population. Mass Observation reports showed that many felt left in the dark by the authorities, and the rate of both wills and marriages soared.[13] Thirty-eight million gas masks were issued for men, women and children in 1938,[14] distributed by the ARP on 27 September between Chamberlain's second and third visit to Germany.[15] Post Office pillar boxes were coated in yellowish gas detector paint; Decontamination Squads were composed of street cleaners.[16]

The residents of Bemerton collected their masks from one of the outbuildings of Belvedere House, alphabetically in order of surname with varying sizes available.[17] The gas masks were 'grotesque combinations of pig-snout and death's-head' and smelt of disinfectant and rubber.[18] The 'Mickey Mouse' masks for children had 'red rubber face pieces and bright eye rims'.[19] A lady from Bemerton recalled that '[t]hey were horrible to have on, a strange sensation and

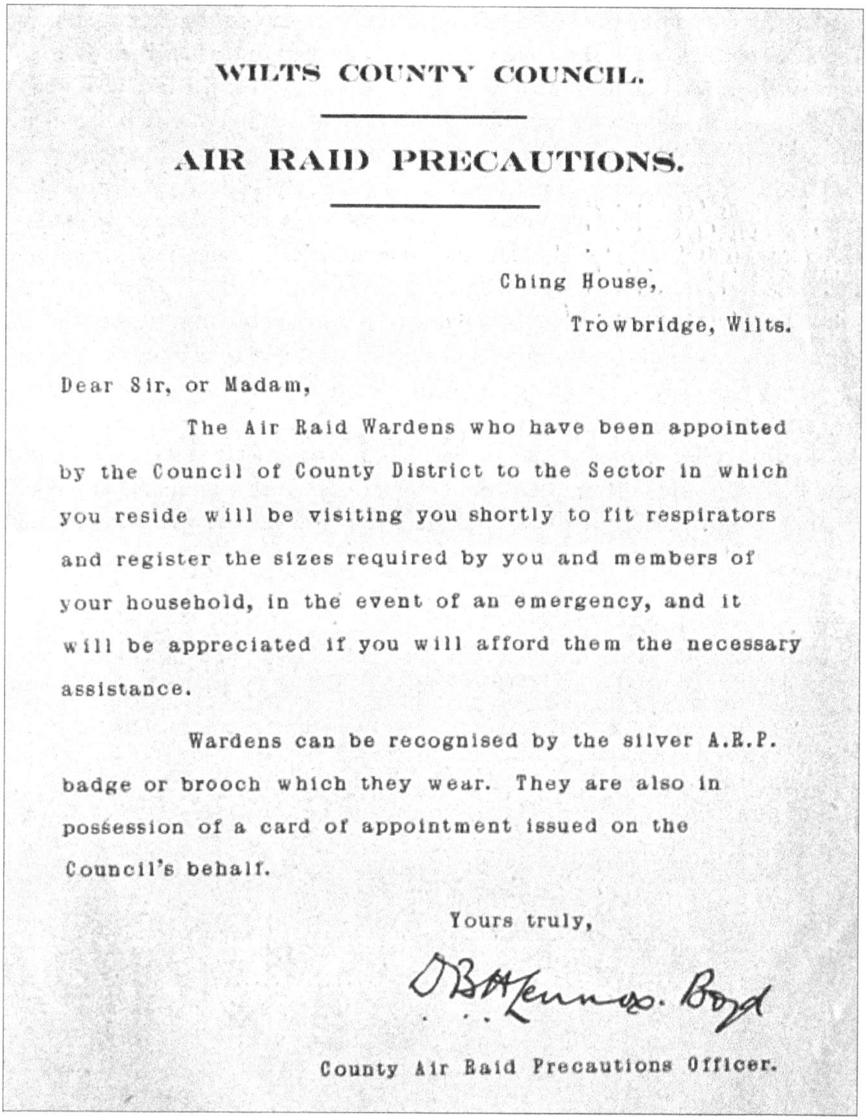

WILTS COUNTY COUNCIL.

AIR RAID PRECAUTIONS.

Ching House,

Trowbridge, Wilts.

Dear Sir, or Madam,

The Air Raid Wardens who have been appointed by the Council of County District to the Sector in which you reside will be visiting you shortly to fit respirators and register the sizes required by you and members of your household, in the event of an emergency, and it will be appreciated if you will afford them the necessary assistance.

Wardens can be recognised by the silver A.R.P. badge or brooch which they wear. They are also in possession of a card of appointment issued on the Council's behalf.

Yours truly,

B.H. Jennings Boyd

County Air Raid Precautions Officer.

A standard letter to householders by Wiltshire's County Air Raid Precautions Officer, advising of the imminent fitting of gas masks (WSA F5/530/28)

the goggles all misted up.'[20] One Wiltshire boy tried one on at home the night before he was due to have a gas mask drill at school. 'It seemed dreadfully tight and he said he 'didn't like it a bit and couldn't breathe in it.' From having longed to put it on he was almost in tears.'[21] There was an adequate supply of gas helmets for babies, whose mothers would have to pump in air via a bellows[22] but babies did not receive their gas 'tents' until March 1940.[23] Air Raid Wardens were expected to examine gas masks on a monthly basis, with individuals facing a charge if their mask needed repairing due to neglect, or had to be replaced through negligence.[24] People were asked to test their masks in gas vans or chambers where they were told to wear them for a quarter of an hour each week, but most felt that they would never be needed and with the 'Phoney War', many people didn't bother with them much.[25] A 'Wiltshire Resident' was writing in to the *Wiltshire Gazette* on 19 October 1939 about gas masks after a suggestion the previous week regarding carrying your gas mask at all times. 'I cannot agree with that. No one wants those things dangling across the shoulder. The poor children who are supposed to carry them everywhere, are to be pitied.' If an air raid was to occur '… there would be more danger if we had to stand in the streets, throwing everything down we had, get out the mask, put it on, instead of rushing to the nearest house or shelter.' However, June 1940 came along and with it Dunkirk; the carrying of gas masks had risen from 'virtually nil' to 30%.[26]

The children of Cricklade were taking part in gas mask drills in the schoolroom, putting the masks on under their desks. They soon found they could liven up these drills. 'If we blew out air in a certain way wearing these, we could

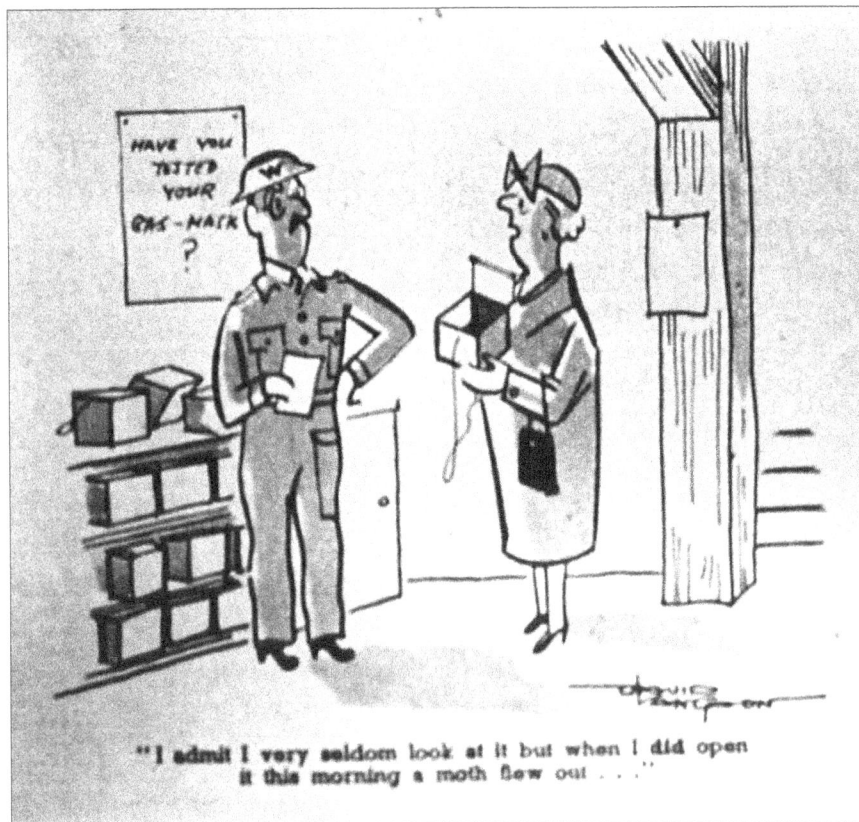

"I admit I very seldom look at it but when I did open it this morning a moth flew out . . ."

Newspaper cutting about gas mask testing by ARP Wardens, discovered in the Post Log Book of the Trowbridge ARP Western Sector (WSA G15/224/6)

make a noise like a 'whoopee' cushion which used to annoy our teachers.'[27] In fact, many of Wiltshire's school log books report regular gas mask inspections, such as St. Peter's School in Devizes.[28] By February 1941 Churchill was continuing to make the 'usual references to invasion and gas-attacks.'[29]

Choking Gases

    Phosgene and Chlorine are, alas
    Chloropicrin too, a deadly gas.
    Affects the lungs, affects the breath
    And very soon may lead to death.
    The only hope is perfect rest,
    Remember this and do your best.
    Pop on a mask, and quickly fetch her
    Without the least delay a stretcher.
    DON'T give her alcoholic drinks,
    Persuade her to have forty winks.
    And DON'T in spite of great temptation,
    Try artificial respiration.

Nose Gases

    DA., D.M.,-also D.D.
    You cannot smell, you cannot see:
    This makes it harder still to tell
    There's arsenic in them as well.
    It makes one snuff and sneeze and blow,
    It makes one very sad and low.
    Non persistent so won't endure,
    Pop on a mask and re-assure,
    Make several jokes and remove quick,
    Don't be surprised if they are sick.

Tear Gases

    Tear gases-first comes C.A.P.
    Then K.S.K. and B.B.C.,
    If you smell pear drops beware,
    For K.S.K. is in the air.
    These gases too, affect the mind,
    Explain why they are not really blind.
    Remove and re-assure, you 'oughter'
    Wash out the eyes with saline water.

Mustard Gases

    When you have heard the warning sound,
    That Mustard gas is on the ground,
    Pop on the mask that you possess;
    All helpers have protective dress.
    Remember, 'tis persistent gas,

Will last for weeks on road and grass.
The smallest splash upon your hand,
Will quickly to a sore expand.
If on a person there's a trace,
Rush him to the appointed place.
Take off his boots and clothes and suit,
And scrub him well from head to foot.
Then in another room he'll find,
Fresh clothes and boots…assistance kind. [30]

Verse to remind ARP Wardens of the dangers of gas. Discovered in the Post Log Book of the Trowbridge ARP Western Sector, 1940-44.

The first ARP circular to set out the framework for ARP planning and the relationship between Government, Local Authorities and even private industry before the Air Raid Precautions Act of 1937 contained an 'explicit refusal' to fund public shelters that could take a direct hit from a bomb. Householders were to protect themselves against the effects of near misses at a much cheaper cost. Prominent left wing scientists Julian Huxley and Charles Percy Snow denounced the plan as providing 'only a dangerous illusion of security'. The ARP Act compelled Local Authorities to draw up ARP schemes which were to be funded at a standard rate of up to 75%.[31]

The Munich Crisis of 1938 brought about not only the distribution of gas masks. It also highlighted the inadequacy of other ARP preparations, including shelters.[32] On 30 September 1938 the *Warminster Journal* was highlighting the lack of ARP provision when reporting the details of a Town Council meeting. 'What if Warminster were bombed: Demand that A.R.P. should be speeded up.' Local Authorities were told to make permanent those trenches that had been built in parks and public gardens by lining and covering them with concrete and steel, but they could not be kept waterproof and fell out of favour with officials. However, even with the fifty people inside 'sitting out an all night raid with stinking water lapping over shoes', they were preferred to the surface shelters. At least the trenches were underground.[33] In Salisbury the Greencroft shelters were dug by volunteers at this time. They were lined with pre-cast concrete slabs and fitted with seats and dim electric lighting. 'Most of the 'trench stewards' were older people prepared to do their bit, but they were no match for the courting couples who began to make use of the convenient facilities. The trenches were fitted with doors, opened only when the air raid warning had sounded.'[34] Trowbridge had opened seven public shelters in the town by 6 October 1939. The largest, in the basement of the bandstand in the Park, could hold 150 persons. The Blind House was also put to use, accommodating 20 people. All the shelters were protected with sand bags and their position indicated by illuminated signs.[35] The basements of public buildings were also utilised as shelters.[36] Children's books were published especially for use in air raid shelters. These 'Better Little Books' published by Raphael Tuck and Sons were illustrated 'chapbooks'. '…

children and their attendant parents, grandparents, or teachers conclusively seized on these twopenny diversions in the mad scramble to the nearest air-raid shelter'. Tuck himself explained in the introduction that: 'This series, now famous, was intended to supply a suitable diversion during air-raid alerts. Handy little books like these could be easily carried in the pocket, and handed on easily from one reader to another in shelters. At the same time, by their small size, the books made their most of the very limited quantities of paper then available.'[37]

Some of Wiltshire's inhabitants felt that others were worrying unnecessarily, and said so in the 19 October 1939 edition of the *Wiltshire Gazette*. 'An Air Raid won't descend on us like an April shower – I consider there is more fuss and signs of war in these country places than in London and other danger areas put together.'

The opposition parties felt that the Government had mismanaged shelter policy and should take responsibility for their construction. Critics of the Government's approach included John Burton Sanderson Haldane, who had studied the effects of modern bombs dropped in Spain during the Civil War. He strongly criticised the content of the Government's pamphlet *The Protection of Your Home Against Air Raids*, even to the fact that it did not include a pickaxe; invaluable in Spain for digging your way out of the rubble. Haldane disagreed with the idea that it was best to disperse people into small groups. He felt it was safer to shelter large groups underground in properly designed mass shelters but felt the Government were worried that large groups of people would induce high tension and emotion, even panic, in each other and that mass shelters would also prove a good target for the enemy. The Left Book Club became a vehicle for criticism of official ARP plans from as early as 1937, publishing research such as that of the Cambridge Scientists' Anti-War Group which revealed the shortcomings of commercial gas masks and also highlighted Haldane's work. John Anderson, the Minister of Home Security, convened an 'independent' conference, chaired by Lord Hailey in February 1939 to discuss the issue. What emerged from the Hailey Report was that the provision of 'heavy protection' could create a 'shelter mentality', thereby interrupting production or 'unduly diverting national effort from other [ie. active] measures of defence', the population being driven to shelters by the enemy to immobilise the country. The Government also felt that if a mass shelter received a direct hit it would be bad for the country's morale and that a shelter in the home soothed individual anxieties; most people would prefer to remain at home if they could. Criticism of Government shelter policy continued. Scientists and architects wanted to work with the Government, but instead had to criticise its under-activity in regard to shelters as 'a virtual scandal'. In 1939 Chermayeff felt that professionals like himself 'could have an important part to play in the urgent programme of the Government if they were given an opportunity'. Chamberlain had chosen John Anderson to coordinate ARP services in all departments on the outbreak of war[38] as Minister of Home Security[39] but Churchill deemed Herbert Morrison more able to cope with the Blitz[40] and Morrison took on the post on 3 October 1940.[41] The change was 'hailed as a victory' for all those who had protested against conditions in the shelters, and improvements did follow.[42]

The Ministry of Home Security published a booklet in 1940. *Your Home as an Air Raid Shelter* explained how blast splinters caused more casualties than direct hits and that a house could provide protection via a shelter. 'First, you can buy a ready-made shelter to bury or erect in the garden. Secondly, you can have a shelter of brick and concrete built or attached to the house. Thirdly, you can improve the natural protection given by your house by forming a 'refuge room.' The first two of these generally give better protection against bomb splinters than the third, but cost more; they may be the only way of getting proper protection if your house is very lightly built, say of timber. A properly-prepared refuge room can, however, give almost as good protection as a garden shelter, and is the method most householders are likely to adopt.'[43] The Institutions of Architects, Engineers and Surveyors represented on the Building Technical Advisory Committee had arranged a scheme whereby in some areas advice could be sought for some householders at an 'inexpensive' cost of half a guinea. A consultant would then visit to inspect the house and provide a written report on the type of shelter which would work best, 'describing ways within your means by which your protection can be improved.'[44] One Hilperton resident was taking things seriously, busy 'pack[ing] the glass & china we do not use in boxes as she is afraid it may get broken with the vibration' of aeroplanes which had been passing over them all day on 25 August 1940.[45]

Salisbury City Council issued its own booklet in 1941: *Notes & Advice on Air Raids: Before, During and After – Forewarned is Forearmed.* Plans had been made to 'minimise damage and to relieve promptly any distress which air attack on Salisbury may bring. But the success of these arrangements depends on every citizen knowing what to do, and doing it calmly, without panic.' Instructions included getting to know the Warden, keeping buckets and sandbags filled, purchasing anti-gas ointment and during a raid, turning off gas and electricity, being ready to shelter anyone in need and putting on a gas mask if outdoors. There was also guidance on where to go for help if, after a raid, ration books, identity cards etc. were lost.[46] One Warminster family remembered the precautions leaflets. 'Air raid shelters would be issued as soon as possible, but until then the safest place would be under the stairs... Molly had to manage herself and several times had to scrabble under the stairs with the children. The shelters eventually became available.'[47] Sandbags were stockpiled; provided by the Government as early as April 1939 'to enable Local Authorities to arrange for such additional protection as may be feasible for buildings, or parts of buildings, which it is essential to maintain and use in danger areas,' stored in local depots. Sandbag filling machines were also available for purchase, such as Faulkners Limited's 'Speed-up' model which was priced at £5 15s. 6d., for which Wiltshire's Chief Constable was placing an order in May 1939. The promotional leaflet assured it could help five men do the work of thirty. And many, many sandbags were needed. On 6 November 1939 the County's ARP Officer was asking the County Surveyor to release 1,600 sandbags to help protect Chippenham Hospital alone.[48]

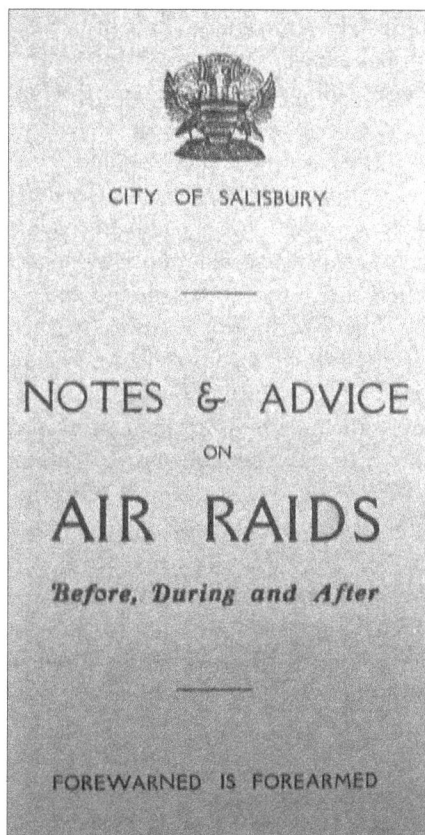

City of Salisbury Booklet 'Notes & Advice on Air Raids' (WSA G23/225/18)

One Wiltshireman who was working to reduce the threat of bombs was Charles Henry George Howard, the Earl of Suffolk, whose residence was at Charlton Park near Malmesbury. He had been working at the Nuffield Institute of Medical Research in Oxford in 1939 and in May 1940 had been requested by Herbert Morrison to 'bring to England a group of top atomic scientists, some valuable machine tools, industrial diamonds and a quantity of heavy water, the latter vital to atomic research'. After succeeding in his mission his next task, as Director of the Scientific Research Establishment,[49] was to 'look into ways of dismantling and disposing of bombs which had not gone off on impact with the ground, whether intentionally or otherwise'[50] as 'each new arrival from the skies was a separate and very dangerous puzzle'. Churchill later recorded:

'One squad I remember which may be taken as symbolic of many others; it consisted of three people, the Earl of Suffolk, his lady private secretary and his chauffeur. They called themselves 'The Holy Trinity'. Their prowess and continued existence got around among all who knew, and 34 unexploded bombs did they tackle with urbane and smiling efficiency, but the 35th claimed its forfeit. Up went the Earl of Suffolk in his Holy Trinity. But we may be sure that, as for Mr-Valiant-for-Truth, all the trumpets sounded for them on the other side.'[51]

Lord Suffolk was posthumously awarded the George Cross when the Holy Trinity were killed defusing a bomb on the Hackney Marshes on 12 May, 1941. A window was dedicated to him in the parish church at Charlton.[52]

By 26 August 1940 Frances Partridge was writing from Ham Spray that '[t]he news is now entirely concerned with air-raids. Inside every head in England the same questions are revolving: 'How many killed? How many injured? How is everyone 'standing up' to the raids?' Oh, the sordid horror of the news; now it is just one long description of destruction, smashing, mashing and killing... The Germans say we are being unduly optimistic about the mildness of their raids, and that we will change our minds 'in the next few days,' since they are revising their technique and bombing by night indiscriminately – the famous 'war of nerves.' Our newspapers tell us how wonderfully unshakeable our morale is.'[53]

At the same time as the trenches were being dug in the parks, barrage balloons were appearing over London[54] and elsewhere. Approximately 30 barrage balloons were put up in Salisbury; they were released each morning and taken down again every evening at about 6.30pm. People used to go and watch them being taken down. 'Their silver fabric reflecting in the evening sunlight made a very pretty sight.'[55] A barrage balloon was situated in the infant's playground at one of Salisbury's schools. '... and the soldiers slept in an army tent and cooked their own food. It was quite noisy when the balloon went up but especially when it was winched down. Everyone felt safer if the balloon was up while we were in the shelters, which could be three times a day.'[56] It is surprising to note that these balloons had another very different impact in Wiltshire; in the form of an escaped barrage balloon. The *Wiltshire Times* reported in its 2 December 1939 edition that it lost its mooring in the Midlands and drifted its way down to Wiltshire, its steel cables wreaking havoc. The balloon's cables were attracted by magnetism to the electricity cables and large areas of Melksham lost electricity along with Semington. The roofs of houses were damaged and a chimney was knocked down, not to mention the loss of clothes props! The balloon was finally captured near Bournemouth, Dorset. The 'Baedeker' raid on Bath in late April 1942 had repercussions for nearby Wiltshire communities, not just due to the number of evacuees they received. The Head Teacher at Ivy Lane School, Chippenham noted in his school log book that the gas supply had been turned off until further notice.[57] Fay Inchfawn living in Freshford described the raids:

> ... when over the peaceful valley, ominous and slowly, sounded the long banshee-like wail of the siren.
>
> Almost immediately the banging began. My first feeling was one of annoyance – then of dread. I sat up... Through the wide bay window saw great lights flaring in the sky and dropping slowly earthward, not in one place only but in many directions... The glass in the roof rattled and the whole house shook... Alas, a third time that night the Luftwaffe came – came in strength with the pitiless power and vengeance of which we had read, but which we had not experienced before.' Their neighbours came over to sit out the attack with them. The following day there was no gas and it was discovered that the whole village had been up all night. 'That Sunday night the raiders came again... This second attack was worse than the first. The glow in the sky opposite our front door was blood red, like the Northern Lights. Within myself I was thoroughly frightened. That fear-striking drone of heavy planes overhead – all those thunderous bangs and explosions – would they never cease?' ... The Village had, naturally, been up all night, and on Monday morning, in the absence of instruction but in the presence of such dire necessity, it was decided to open the Rest Centre, which had been carefully arranged and equipped ready for the catastrophe of invasion.[58]

Shelters

A FRIEND OF JOHN Anderson's, William Paterson, designed what was to become known as the 'Anderson Shelter', made of corrugated iron and designed to be erected in a back yard or garden to protect against the fallout of 'near misses'.[59] They had initially been planned for use inside the home, but this was prevented by technical issues. The Anderson consisted of 'two curved walls of corrugated steel met in a ridge at the top and bolted to stout rails.' They needed to be sunk three feet into the ground and covered with 18 inches of soil. The entrance incorporated a steel shield and an earthen blast wall, designed to shelter six people.[60] In Salisbury one family erected one in their back garden, fixing wooden seats on two sides. A deckchair was placed against the other wall for 'the wife'. The shelter was often used and the family dog would know when to go to the shelter and when to re-appear when the 'all clear' sounded.[61] Shelters were provided free of charge to 2.5 million families living in those areas classed as vulnerable, who were insured under the National Health Insurance Acts and had an annual income under a certain level (this increased if a family had more than two children of school age).[62] The first shelters came off the production line in February 1939 with production running at 50,000 per week.[63] From October 1939 the shelters could be purchased at £6 14s. to £10 18s. each for those earning over £250 per year, but under 1,000 were sold. Problems with the design included constant flooding and the lack of sound proofing. They were also rather small to sleep in. The steel shortage became a problem and finally stopped production.[64] One of the largest limitations of the shelter, however, was that it could not help those people living in blocks of flats or tenements.[65] Mass Observation pointed out that less than a quarter of the public had gardens.[66]

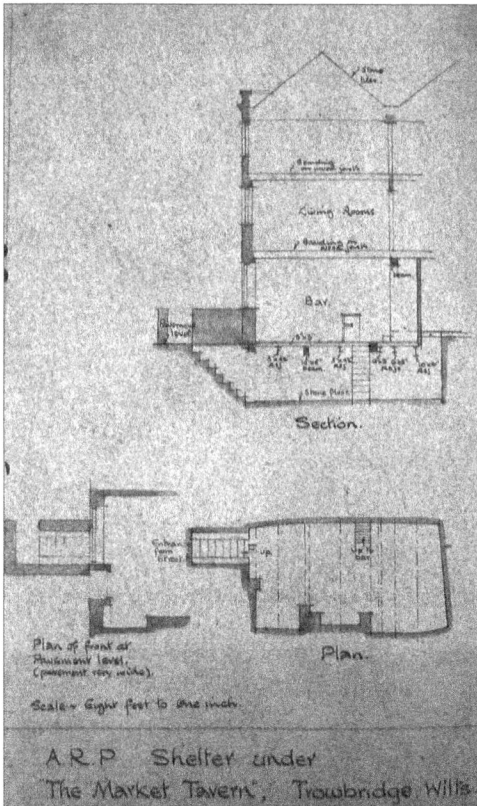

ARP Shelter under the Market Tavern, Trowbridge, by the Wiltshire County Architect, scale 8ft to 1"
(WSA G15/225/25)

In Bemerton:

When the first air-raid sirens sounded at night my mother, brothers and I got up, put our overcoats on over our pyjamas and went next door where the table was put on its side on the floor and Mrs Burton from next door, her daughter, my mother and us boys sat on the floor behind the table while Mr Burton and my father stood at the window looking for searchlight beams. Later on we could see the glow of fires at Southampton during the air-raids. After many nights of this my mother bought us dressing gowns, the front garden fence was cut and a gate made and fitted so that we could go more directly next door.

Sometimes they had to get up as often as four times in the night.[67] 'Siren suits', admired by Churchill, were introduced. They had puffed shoulders, baggy legs, elasticated bottoms and a hood, designed to keep the wearer as warm as possible when spending long periods of time in a shelter.[68]

Local Authorities were again empowered to take control of and prepare buildings for use as shelters and other ARP purposes under the Civil Defence Act

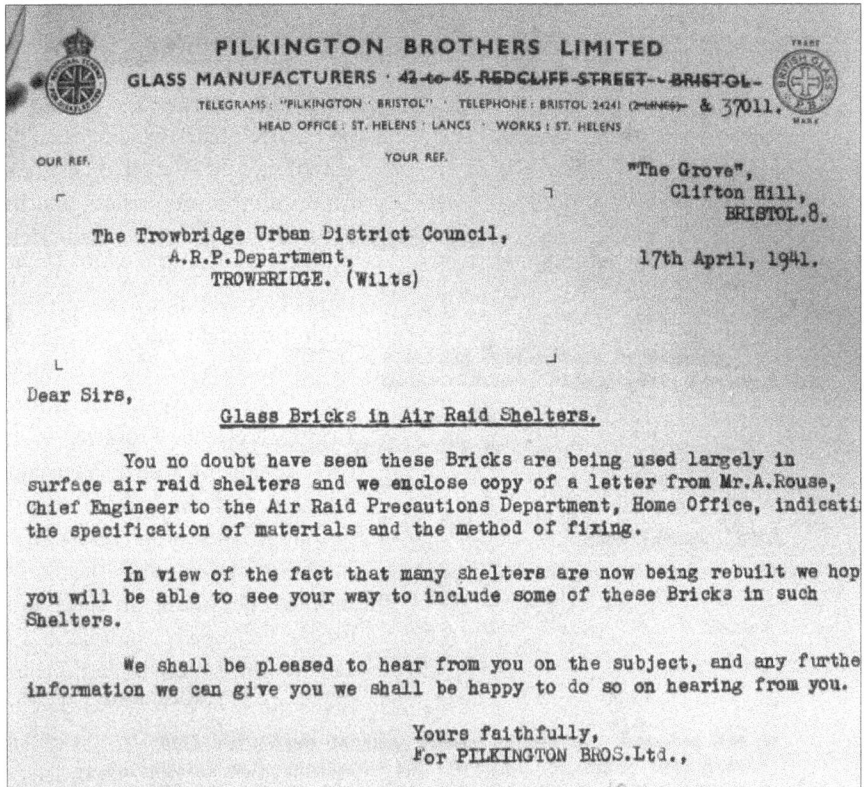

Letter from Pilkington Brothers Limited dated 17 April 1941, regarding their glass bricks for air raid shelters. They were hoping that the Trowbridge Urban District Council would consider them for their surface air raid shelters as many shelters were now being rebuilt (WSA G15/225/25)

of 1939. They could also provide material to reinforce some private basements and it became compulsory for employers to sort out their own ARP services and provide workplace shelters.[69] It was the Ministry of Health which was responsible for the sanitation, equipment, ventilation and order in the public shelters, appointed under the Ministry of Home Security.[70] In March 1940 the Government turned its attention to a new brick and concrete communal surface shelter to protect those living in blocks of flats or for the use of a single street[71] and it began urging Local Authorities to provide shelters for people caught out in the street during an air raid.[72] A small number of air raids had taken place since April and by June 1940 the controversy regarding shelters was back to haunt the Government again, this time from a shortage of cement.[73] On 31 December 1941 the Civil Defence Regional Technical Advisor of the No. 7 Region (based in Bristol) was enquiring whether the Trowbridge Town Council had any surface shelters in use which had been constructed with lime mortar. Circular 290/40 had requested that all such structures should be 'immediately examined for any defects or weakness' and that the Ministry was 'anxious to ascertain the distribution and magnitude of the problem...'[74]

Communal shelters were unpopular; they were cold, dark and damp with poor ventilation and could often collapse through poor construction.[75] In early December 1940 the Trowbridge UDC Clerk was having trouble finding both the labour and materials to build shelters. The Civil Defence Office of the Regional Commissioner in Bristol replied that its Technical Advisers felt that 'much can be accomplished by improvisation and the use of alternatives which will ensure a reasonable degree of protection, where homes are being adapted as shelters in accordance with H.S. Circular 163/40. Your attention is drawn in particular to the construction of *in situ* concrete walls or screens of sand-concrete in bags. Use might also be made of wattle for holding in earth filling, where supplies can be obtained.' In May 1941 the Civil Defence Regional Technical Advisor was looking at improved shelter design. The improvements were to be put into place as soon as possible as experience had shown that they greatly added to the protection already given by good shelters. The alterations were needed as the 'original designs were based on the fact that an H.E. Bomb within about 50ft of a shelter would in effect be a direct hit, but it ha[d] been found that many shelters ha[d] stood up to near misses at a distance of 15ft.'[76]

The shelters, a safe haven in times of need, were also a public nuisance to the Superintendent of Police at Trowbridge in 1942. He felt the need to write to the Council's Surveyor regarding 'nuisance' occurring at the shelter and suggesting it should be locked until needed. The Surveyor felt that it would be difficult to make adequate arrangements to get the shelter unlocked in an emergency and suggested that the problem may be exacerbated at the present time due to the dark conditions inside the shelter. He would make representations to the Wiltshire County Council departments that 'some form of internal lighting should be provided, even if only 'twilight' units as now used for street lighting.' In response to the charge that the shelters were often in a 'filthy condition', he stated that the shelters

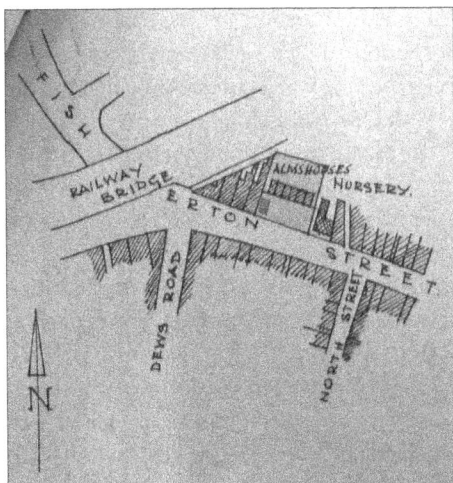

Site plan for scheme No. 4, Fisherton Street, Salisbury (WSA G23/225/16)

were inspected two to three times a week by the Council's 'road length-men', and cleaned if necessary. The location of the communal shelters in Trowbridge was being debated in September 1940 and there appears to have been overcrowding issues. The Town Clerk noted that '... an endeavour [was] being made, in order to relieve any congestion at the civilian public air raid shelters, to get the Military Authorities to issue instructions to the troops to shelter in the churches...' The Ministry of Home Security had also realised that overcrowding was a problem, issuing Circular No. 3 in January 1941 regarding ventilation conditions, having 'further considered the question of gas-proofing and ventilation in view of the circumstances that shelters are now liable to be occupied under crowded conditions for long periods during the night, and that heating has been approved for certain kinds of shelter. In these circumstances it is essential, in the interests of safety and health that the fullest possible ventilation shall be maintained at all times...'[77]

Anderson announced in Parliament on 12 June 1940 that the shelter programme, begun 19 months before, had been completed. Over half the country's civilian population of over 40 million were now able to find a space at a shelter simultaneously.[78] This does not appear to be the case in Wiltshire, however, as communal shelters were still being built, although they were being called 'Communal (Domestic) Shelters.'[79] Shelters were being planned for the inhabitants of parishes which were situated within 1,000 yards of an aerodrome, such as at Stanton St. Quinton near RAF Hullavington in October 1940. The landowner of Glebe Farm had given permission for a shelter to be built 'at the rear of the cottages on his farm.'[80] By 2 October 1940 the Home Office was directing Wiltshire County Council that on general principle, they were agreeable to allow the provision of 'public shelters in certain towns in Wiltshire, up to 5% of the existing population', resulting in towns such as Chippenham, Bradford-on Avon, Marlborough and Devizes requesting further shelters. There was concern in Melksham that the number of public shelters was wholly inadequate; seven shelters which could accommodate 160 persons, but '[t]he population of the Urban District [had] very considerably increased since 1939' from 5,500 to over 8,000. In a recent air raid alarm there were 'numbers of people in the main streets of the Town seeking shelter accommodation.' It was felt that capacity should be increased by at least 150%. Many were allowable with a grant, but others not so, such as a planned shelter increase to a total provision of 520 persons at the Corn Exchange, Devizes.[81] In August 1941 Salisbury City Council was writing to various businesses in the city, asking if they would be agreeable to having a communal shelter erected 'for the benefit of the occupants of certain houses in the neighbourhood.' The Council made it clear that it would remove the shelter 'within a reasonable time after the Government's declaration that the existing state of emergency is at an end,' and to restore the land as much as it could to its original condition. The scheme was large with each envisioned shelter given a scheme number, there being approximately 42 in all. Some landowners were given compensation for the disruption, such as the tenant of 105 Queen Alexandra Road, Salisbury who received £2 in Shelter Scheme No. 39.[82]

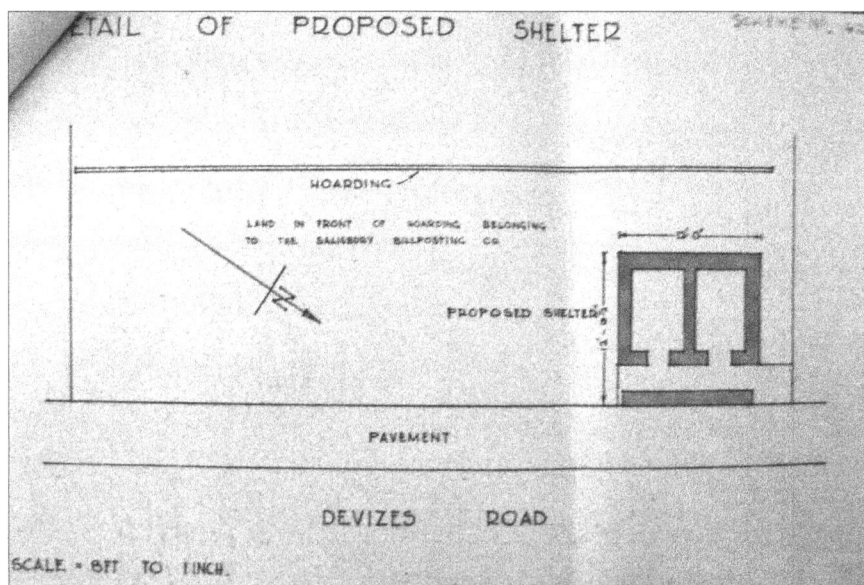

Detail of a proposed shelter for Scheme No. 42 at disused land in Devizes Road, Salisbury, scale 8ft to 1inch (WSA G23/225/16)

By the autumn of 1941 most of the dampness in the public shelters had been reduced and the Morrison shelter (named after Anderson's successor as Minister of Home Security) had been invented. It was, like the Anderson, provided free of charge for most and built as a family shelter, but this time it could be erected indoors. On top was a steel plate and the sides had wire mesh, 2ft. 9" in height. They could also be used as a table in the daytime.[83] Those residents of Bemerton who had one often used to drag in a mattress so that they could sleep inside.[84] One lady recalled that she only went in it once as a child: 'it was a bit frightening – like a cage.' Another Bemerton family 'painted the top to resemble Portland Harbour and then I could display my fleet of battleship, aircraft carrier, cruiser, destroyers and corvettes, entirely built from… old bits of wood, nails etc. and painted grey.'[85]

There had been over half a million Morrisons distributed by November 1941 and they proved of value to those who suffered in later attacks.[86] The *Salisbury Times and South Wilts Gazette* was reporting on the free distribution of Morrison shelters in Wilton in its 9 October 1942 edition, finding that '… the number of applications has been nothing like as many as the Ministry of Home Security expected … there might be some confusion about the issue of the shelters. The application forms which had been prepared by the Ministry were not very clear about the issue, which was definitely free, irrespective of the applicant's income.'

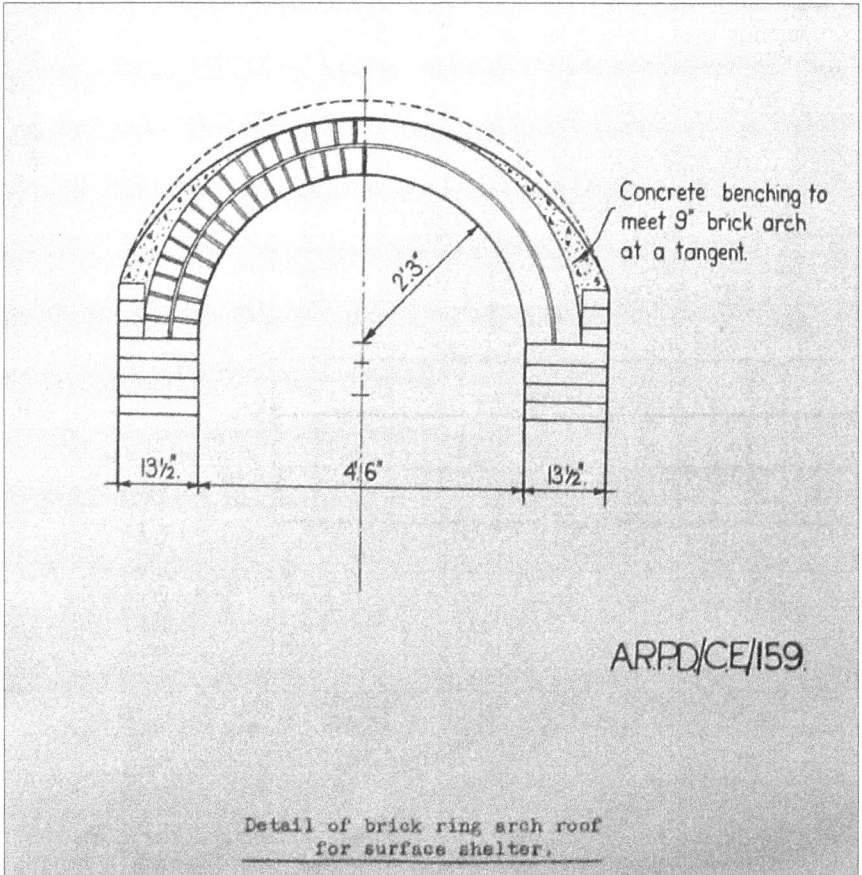

Concrete benching to meet 9" brick arch at a tangent.

2'3"

13½.   4'6"   13½"

ARP.D/CE/159.

Detail of brick ring arch roof
for surface shelter.

Technical specifications for the brick ring arched roof of a surface shelter (WSA G15/225/25)

Some of Wiltshire's school log books give insights into the ARP preparations undertaken during the war and the difficulties they created. In Chippenham, the Ivy Lane Head Teacher noted with frustration the number of trips that needed to be taken to the shelter during a school day, but on 2 September 1939 he did report that several bombs had been dropped on the town and on 27 February 1941 the children had to go to their shelters as machine gun fire had been heard in the locality of the school. On 15 September 1939 the school received a visit by a County ARP official as there had been complaints regarding a lack of places of shelter during an air raid. The sirens were not the only cause of shelter use; there were ARP practices and the children were assigned their places in the shelter on 12 November 1940. By 13 January 1941 a wall had been built immediately in front of the girls' porch and the school would disperse to seven stations in the time of an air raid; the two stations inside the school, the two shelters in the playground, to one under the railway arch next to the school, to a shop in the High Street and to one in Station Hill. The Station Hill location would presumably have been used by the evacuees who were being taught in the Wesleyan and Baptist Rooms on Station Hill due to overcrowding at Ivy Lane. By 22 January 1941 the Head was emphasising the need for 'constant attention' on the part of staff regarding gas masks. Definitive instructions were being given as to the procedure. Weekly inspections would take place. On 25 March 1941 the headmaster was noting that the children were using the shelters for approximately 12 minutes. The Police Sergeant then notified him that the children would not be allowed to use a public shelter during an emergency in school hours. Much more ARP practice was undertaken in early September 1941 due to the intake of over 100 new scholars.[87] Miss E. Berrett of Hilperton, a teacher and Firewatcher, noted in her diary on 5 September 1940 that needlework classes were being disrupted by air raids. 'We had an alert from 1.40pm-2.00pm this afternoon so most of the needlework period was spent on the floor.'[88] At

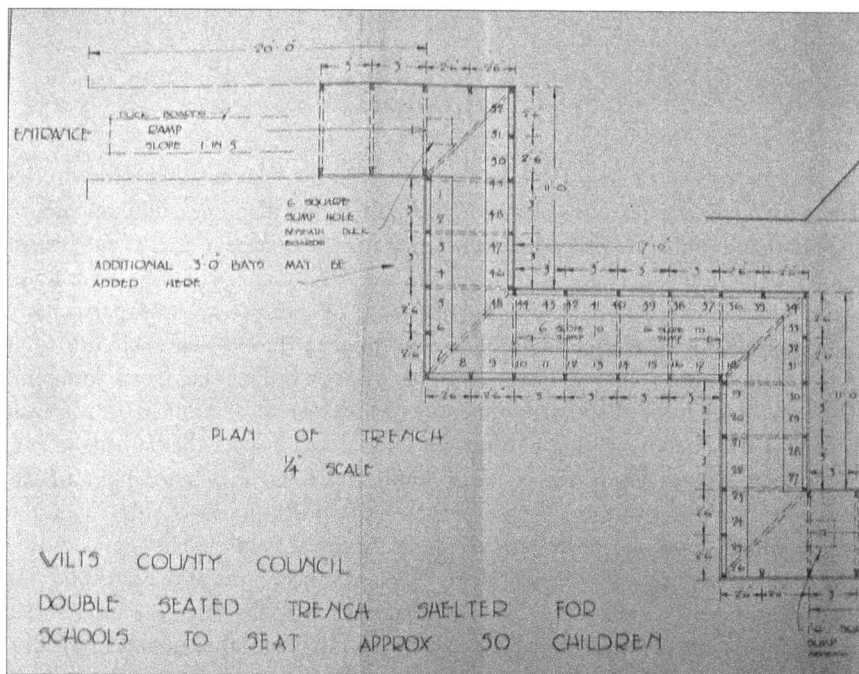

Wiltshire County Council Plan for a double seated trench shelter for schools to seat approximately 50 Children (WSA F8/600/292/1/26/2)

Highbury Avenue School in Salisbury: 'Shelters were dug out by hand by a gang of workmen, and when the siren sounded we would all assemble in classes on the playground and go into the shelters, which had a few dimly lit bulbs. The seats were rough to sit on: boys wearing short trousers developed sore legs behind their knees because the wood had not been planed, and there was also a very strong smell of creosote. At the corners were toilets behind a Hessian curtain, the toilets being a wooden seat and bucket, short cutting Izal paper and there were draughty vents. While all the children were in the shelters the teachers would be standing in the sloping entrances looking for German aircraft and occasionally a teacher would walk through the shelter to check we were behaving ourselves.'[89] The shelters at the South Wiltshire Grammar School in Salisbury were dugouts in the grounds. Children 'hated going into them because they were dark and claustrophobic.'[90]

Towns and villages suddenly looked very different. Houses had brick or concrete blast walls built in front of them as in Bemerton. 'Our house had white blast brick walls built to the tops of the ground floor windows and about one foot from the windows. There was also a wall at the front door and on each pane of glass was cross gummed tape so it was dark indoors.'[91] A blast wall was being built at Stratton St. Margaret School in June 1940 to protect the corridor which was being used as an air raid shelter.[92] A worker at the Avon Rubber Company in Melksham remembered the entire workforce coming out to watch a British fighter aircraft attacking a German plane overhead. The result... the apparent shooting down of the bomber near Bratton and the company quickly introducing rules to enforce the use of shelters![93]

Bombs

MANY OF WILTSHIRE'S inhabitants had become so familiar with aircraft flying overhead on its way to bomb Britain's cities that they could distinguish the German bombers' twin engined pulsating roar compared to that of the British planes. 'All we could make out in the sky were the planes coming, wave upon wave. I thought they were never going to stop.' 'On many occasions, particularly on a moonlit night, German bombers could be seen [in Cricklade] circling high above St. Sampson's Church, which must have been a brilliant landmark for them. They would seem to collect there, then proceed on towards the north.' In Marston Maisey it became an exciting pastime for children to inspect the damage left by the bombs. 'There were several sticks of bombs discarded after random air attacks within 1 or 2 miles of our village. At the first opportunity local lads, including me, would dash off on our bicycles to inspect the crater and perhaps collect some jagged shards of steel.' It was possible to collect dozens of fins of the phosphorous incendiary bombs in the fields around Cricklade.[94] In May 1944 the local Police Sergeant gave the children of Lydiard Millicent a talk about the dangers of picking up bombs found in fields.[95]

It wasn't just children who were interested in bomb craters, however. In Warminster: 'One morning we awoke to a great hubbub about, and apparently a couple of small bombs had been dropped in the woods by my school. It was the main subject of conversation and I bet the whole town walked to the woods to see the craters. It didn't look much to me, just a couple of depressions among the trees. Our teachers told us not to go near as it wasn't safe.'[96] It was important that the visual impact of these aerial attacks was kept to a minimum. The number of incidents must have been rising by 1940 in Wiltshire when the County Surveyor called on his Divisional Surveyors to try to minimise the amount of work entailed 'in camouflaging the increasing number of craters.' Elaborate camouflaging would not always be necessary and often positioning branches or turf to break up the shape seen from the air would suffice.[97]

The Government had been informing the public of the art of fire prevention in July 1939 with its Civil Defence Leaflet No. 1 entitled *Some Things you Should Know if War Should Come*. It suggested clearing the top floor of all flammable materials to prevent fire spreading, but the advice for incendiary bombs may have been slightly disconcerting: 'Water is the best means of putting out a fire by an incendiary bomb. Have some buckets handy. But water can only be applied to the bomb itself in the form of a fine spray, for which a handpump with a length of hose and a special nozzle are needed. **If you throw a bucket of water on a burning incendiary bomb it will explode and throw burning fragments in all directions.** You may be able to smother it with sand or dry earth.'[98] The Lord Privy Seal issued another booklet in August 1939, entitled *Fire Precautions in War Time*, explaining how civilians could help themselves if a fire bomb attack occurred:

> It is probable that in an air attack on this country an enemy would make use of fire bombs. The object would be not only to destroy property but also to create panic.
>
> A large number of these bombs might be dropped in a small space. A large proportion of them would fall in gardens, streets and open spaces where they would burn out without doing much damage. But in a built-up area some would fall on roofs of houses. One of those houses might be YOURS... In Civil Defence EVERYBODY has a part to play. This is especially true of fire-fighting. In every house there should be one or more people ready to tackle a fire bomb. So read what follows; read it again and again, make the preparations which are advised and see that everyone in your house knows exactly what to do.

It went on to detail how to deal with bombs.[99]

It may not be surprising, then, that in June 1940 the ARP Warden gave a talk to the children at the Minety School on air raids with particular reference to the dangers of incendiary bombs.[100] A meeting was to be held at the Town Hall in Melksham on Monday 3 February 1941 to discuss measures to be taken for detecting and dealing with incendiary bombs and the organisation of Fire Watchers and Fire Bomb Fighters.[101] In Freshford the Civil Defence Officer had already fitted gas masks, and 'now he had called to advise us concerning incendiary bombs. He asked us whether we possessed a stirrup pump... In the porch we had better keep a bucket of water and a sack of sand.'[102] The Home Office was reporting by August 1940 that the use of stirrup pumps for incendiary bombs was effective and they were increasing supply for use with ARP schemes. 'It is clear that the stirrup hand pump has proved to be a very effective appliance for dealing with the light incendiary bombs, which have been used in large numbers by the enemy; and it is important that as many of these appliances as possible should be quickly available at the scene of any attack…'[103]

On 23 November 1940 the Home Office was warning Wiltshire's Chief Constable of the dangers of approaching crashed enemy aircraft; a BBC broadcast was to be aired on the subject. A new type of bomb had been discovered on enemy aircraft: 'canisters of high explosive for the purpose of destroying aircraft after they have grounded' which could constitute a danger to the public.[104] In December 1942 the Principal Officer of the Regional Commissioner of Civil Defence issued a circular regarding home made phosphorous bombs which were being used for training and which had been the cause of accidents.[105] One such accident occurred when members of a Devizes Home Guard platoon were covered in glowing fragments when a bomb exploded on a course. The accident required a trip to hospital.[106] An ARP Circular had expressly stated that only those bombs approved by the Ministry should be used for training purposes. All such bombs needed to be handed in to the Police or Bomb Disposal Squad. The bombs would then be rendered innocuous by the Squad and issued from the Civil Defence Office of the Regional Commissioner in Bristol.[107] The *Air Raid Precautions Book* for residents of Devizes advised bombs to be carried (with great care, presumably!) to the Control Centre, to be taken onward to Roundway Down for detonation by the military.[108]

Some employees felt exposed to the risk of bombs, due to the fact that they were working in a job where they were required to remain at their post whatever happened, and/or that

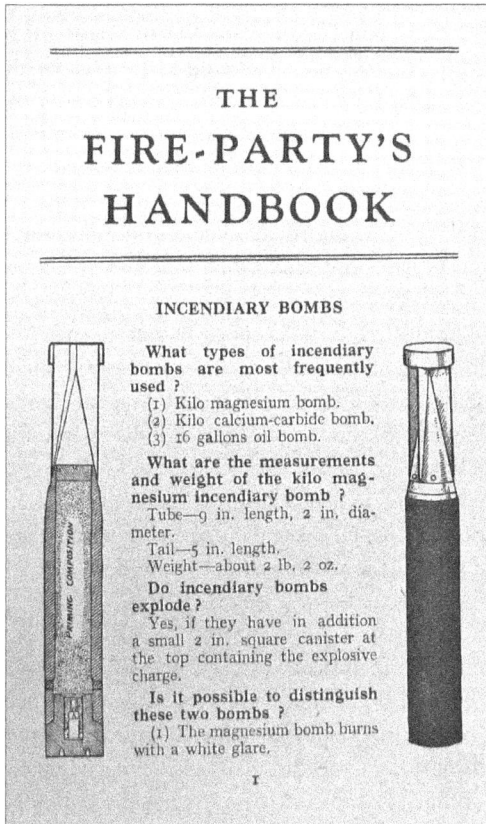

THE

FIRE-PARTY'S

HANDBOOK

INCENDIARY BOMBS

What types of incendiary bombs are most frequently used ?
(1) Kilo magnesium bomb.
(2) Kilo calcium-carbide bomb.
(3) 16 gallons oil bomb.

What are the measurements and weight of the kilo magnesium incendiary bomb ?
Tube—9 in. length, 2 in. diameter.
Tail—5 in. length.
Weight—about 2 lb. 2 oz.

Do incendiary bombs explode ?
Yes, if they have in addition a small 2 in. square canister at the top containing the explosive charge.

Is it possible to distinguish these two bombs ?
(1) The magnesium bomb burns with a white glare.

The Fire Party's Handbook: how to recognise and deal with incendiary bombs (WSA G14/225/6)

their place of work was situated next to possible bombing targets. In September 1940 the Matron at the Trowbridge and District Isolation Hospital was writing to the Clerk of Trowbridge Urban District Council regarding a routine which had been set up. The hospital was located adjacent to the Barracks and Camp and 'the latter can be seen from the Air and may be a target for the enemy.' She held the Home Office's Certificate as an Instructor L.G.A.C from her previous job in London and had been giving lectures to each member of staff in anti-gas measures, the use of the stirrup pump, giving first aid to casualties and familiarising them with the contents of incendiary bombs. 'At every siren patients take cover and a senior member of the staff other than the night staff has been on duty during the great number of the warnings we have had at night. We have no night porter here, so we do rely on our Warden nearby should something of a big character occur. I have been advised to appeal to you for some protection for the nurses heads who have to patrol these grounds at night. The wards are scattered over quite a big area. I have tried to buy tin hats.'[109] The Ministry of Health, Regional Offices, was looking into concerns raised by Swindon's Town Clerk over the standard of protection provided at First Aid Posts, Cleansing Sections and Ambulance Depots Sleeping Accommodation in May 1941. The Ministry of Home Security had agreed to 'take the matter in hand so far as it concerns the Ambulance Depots in your area, and immediate attention is promised.' As for the First Aid Posts, the Regional Architect had attended and work was recommended on the Pinehurst and Eastcott Hill First Aid Posts. In July 1941 work was recommended on four sites.[110]

In June 1942 the Women's Voluntary Service based in Swindon was writing to the Clerk of the Council asking for a table shelter to be provided in their office. They felt that as the office would be manned day and night in time of 'threatened invasion' it would be an advisable asset, having been warned that a heavy air attack might accompany any invasion attempt. 'We understand that in several towns in this Region, which have suffered under recent air attack, that certain W.V.S. personnel have found it necessary to remain on duty for several days without a break... I certainly feel that some protection at our post of duty is a reasonable request. We do not wish to leave to go to a public shelter.' They were surprised that their request had been turned down but would accept the reinforcement of the cupboard under the stairs as an alternative.[111] It wasn't just emergency workers who were concerned, as a petition by some Swindon residents shows. It was sent to the Swindon Council Offices and asked: 'In view of the imminence of air attack, we the undersigned citizens of Swindon demand the immediate provision of bombproof shelters.' The Council's comments on the matter were forthright:

It is assumed that the petitioners do not really mean 'bomb proof', as such shelters require at least 10' of concrete and even then, it is by no means certain that this thickness of concrete would resist a bomb.

The cost of the type of shelter which has been erected in the Park is approximately £3 per person, and thus the cost of providing shelters of this type for the population of Swindon, 60,000, would be very heavy.

The instructions of the Government to towns of the vulnerability of Swindon are that shelters should be provided for those persons likely to be caught in the streets at some distance from their homes.

This being the instruction of the Government, it is most unlikely that the Government would approve and pay grant on the provision of shelters for the entire population.

It would be exceedingly difficult to proceed now with the erection of shelters, owing to shortage of materials and labour.

Even if materials and labour were available, the time taken to construct the shelters is considerable, thus it took approximately five months to construct the shelters for 2,000 persons in the Park.

The clear instructions of the Government are that people, on an air raid occurring, should stay in their homes, which they have been instructed how to make reasonably safe.

Even if shelters were available, their existence would cause people to flock into the streets, thus constituting a danger.

The provision of some shelters for persons at home and not merely for persons in the streets would cause unfairness as between those rate-payers for whom shelters were provided and those for whom none were provided.

The acceptance of the idea that people would leave their homes to go to public shelters, when there are not enough public shelters for all, would cause overcrowding in the shelters, panic and probably injury and loss of life.[112]

A resident of Orchard Road in Trowbridge was asking the Council the same question in January 1941: 'if there is ever going to be any Air Raid Shelters on the Longfield Estate, as I think it is high time there was something done for this large community of working Class, it is because we are pushed in a corner out of the town or is it asking too much, there would be no place for any of these people to go should there be any bombing here, even if it is an reception area [*sic*], I think it is time this Estate was thought more of as there is no place immune from bombing these days...' The Council's reply relayed the 'dispersal' policy; for people to take shelter in their own home rather than concentrated in communal shelters.[113] The Vicar of Latton was handing out advice regarding what to do in the event of an air raid '...it would be a good idea, if a bomb was about to fall, to sit on a low stone wall and drop down on the opposite side when the bomb fell.'[114] The Colerne Parish Council was discussing the need for an air raid shelter at or near the school in 1941.[115]

Sybil Eccles from Chute noted in a letter of 17 November 1940 that 'Thursday was very noisy – guns all night long and a continuous drone of Huns overhead on their way, as we realised later, to brave and unfortunate Coventry.'[116] One boy living near Savernake Forest also recalled seeing the bombers on their way to Coventry. 'You could see the shells from the anti-aircraft guns exploding in amongst them. It was frightening because I thought if a plane was hit it would come down on our house.'[117]

Frances Partridge noted in her diary entry from Ham Spray in Ham on 15 November 1941 that: 'All last night the noise of bombers going over was incessant. They seemed to be streaming through the sky, yet there was never that menacing threat towards us in the sound of their engines. This sinister noise was so loud that sleep was difficult, and this morning we compared notes, and wondered if the Germans were up to some new horror. At lunchtime came the explanation. M.A.M. came in looking pale from listening to the news, and said there had been a tremendous raid on Coventry all night, and the middle of the town almost obliterated. She had to revise her basis for optimism.'[118]

Form W.D.P. 1 (Part 1), reporting damage to eight poultry huts, with four dwelling houses needing to be evacuated as a result of an air attack near the villages of Little Horton and Coate, Devizes, 16 March 1941 (WSA G5/225/6)

So, were the citizens of Swindon right to worry? In 1941 Wiltshire had been classified as a 'C' area for the Government's shelter programme, with the exception of the Borough of Swindon, which had been given an 'A' rating. The 'C' rated areas were due to face a 'drastic reduction' in size of the labour force allotted;[119] Swindon was most definitely considered to be a target for air attack. Swindon Borough Council held the Mortuary Superintendent's completed forms of death due to war operations, including civilians killed by enemy action but also Civil Defence personnel, giving names, addresses and location of death for both adults and children. The collection also includes an analysis of injuries sustained during air raids in 1942 and there are Medical Emergency Service forms with an individual's name, address, age and injuries sustained. The Forms *Authority to View* were to enable identification of the deceased. Contained within the records are some of the toe tags used on the casualties.[120] The Westbury register has also survived but it recorded only one casualty; that of a German airman.[121] Temporary mortuaries were set up by councils in the county, such as that at Gipsy Lane in Swindon[122] and some parish War Books incorporated mortuary accommodation in their emergency plans, such as those for Chippenham.[123]

Also to be considered are the individual stories of those involved. Two workers were making their way up Regent Street in Swindon in 1942 when an enemy raider started strafing the street at rooftop level. They huddled against a shop front, terrified, and continued on to work, very shaken. It was 'not a very good start to the day.' A GWR worker who lived near the works in Swindon had a Morrison shelter in their living room. The sirens sounded one night and his wife, the landlady, insisted their two lodgers join her under the table. The worker recalled: 'Suddenly there was a terrific noise and everything went dark. We were terrified but unhurt. After a while I ventured out from under the table and could see the kitchen was demolished, the apple tree from the garden through its roof. As I climbed the stairs in search of a candle I could see the night sky through the roof, but I didn't tell my landlady as she was very proud of her new home... A desolate scene met our eyes the next morning. Several people had been killed and there was a large gap in the row of houses, just a few doors away from our house, which itself was not habitable. A large crater behind the houses showed where the bomb meant for the railway works had fallen. This frightening experience and narrow escape brought home to me what it must have been like to have been bombed night after

Section of a map showing Swindon bomb sites (drawn as circles), 1951, drafted by Swindon Borough Council's Engineer and Surveyor, scale of 6 inches to 1 mile, showing Swindon Town's County Ground, centre right, and Rodbourne Cheney, top left (WSA G24/235/2)

night in the big cities.'[124]

It was 'sadly ironic' that two girls on holiday in Trowbridge from London should lose their lives due to a German bomb. It was dropped near the Town Bridge, narrowly missing it. Unfortunately it hit the British Legion Club instead (where the girls were staying) along with part of the Blind House and half of the Bear Inn. 'The attack occurred very early one morning before I had got out of bed. Hearing the blasts, I pulled my younger brother ... out of bed and tried to bundle us under it to afford some measure of protection if more bombs were dropped. As I did so the bomber flew over the Trowbridge Girls High School and past our bedroom window...' The licensee of the Bear was an ex-Naval man, and '[a]lmost as if the bombing were an everyday occurrence he invited me in, fished out an undamaged crate of beer bottles from under a table, [and] poured out glasses for both of us.' Four bombs had been dropped, one 50 yards from one family's shelter. It had been lucky for them that they had not been in it.[125] Another bomb 'landed yards from the main gasometer... all the buildings behind what was Sharp and Fisher were demolished and the windows were all blown out, virutally as far as Lloyds Bank and the other way virtually up to Bythesea Road. Those windows weren't replaced until the end of the war. In those days they sort of boarded the windows up and left like about two foot square, so that people could get a little bit of light in. All the windows up Wicker Hill, all through the war, were just with little glass peep holes.'[126] Most of Wiltshire's towns were bombed, and on one occasion the canal was breached between Staverton and Beanacre. The breach, though, had been minor and 'the only casualties were a few fish. The damage to Britain's war effort was nil.' A farm had also been half destroyed at Beanacre and a judge who was faced with deciding on the amount of rent reduction praised the courage of the farm girl who continued to live and work at the farm.[127] In May 1944 a 2,000 pound, six foot high Herman bomb landed in Bradley Lane, Holt. It failed to detonate and the Army Bomb Disposal Squad were called in to render it harmless.[128]

Bombing at Leigh Road, Westbury, October 1940, reproduced by kind permission of Ian Clark (WSHC P53989)

The roof of the Town Hall in Bradford on Avon had been the recipient of

Extended view of the same site in Westbury with a group of boys viewing the scene (WSHC P55201)

spent ammunition falling during an air fight. Those inside could hear the rattling noise it made.[129] A German aircraft tried to extinguish a local searchlight battery by bombing it. They missed and instead bombed the Marlborough to Broad Hinton Road. A Wootton Bassett man drove his Austin Riley car into the crater and had to be rescued and taken to Savernake Hospital.[130] At Ham Spray Frances Partridge noted in her dairy on 4 November 1940:

> We were sitting round the fire tonight when there was a noise like an old tank or a car passing very slowly overhead, rattling as it went. I thought: 'Yes, it's a bomb; but it's going over – it won't hit us.' Ran up to the nursery, and then came the CRASH…. and I was standing recovering when in came Joan, her hair loose and dishevelled. She looked flustered, and no wonder as she was bicycling up the avenue when she saw and heard the bomb go over. Soon after we had settled by the fire again there was another, and another – CRASH, plop, plop, plop. Good, I thought, I'm getting used to them. R. said 'Well twice may be a coincidence, but if they do it again it'll look as if they were aiming at something.' And they did. I see that one does, without trying to, learn something of the sounds of raiding planes and their significance. The nastiest moment is when, after a low flight, the engines shut off and there's total silence… Walked out to look at the craters. In the lane at the end of the avenue men were filling in quite a respectable one. They were very jolly. 'Only casualty a skylark,' said one. One of the last of the 'sticks' fell in the garden of one of the Ham bungalows, and a little boy, missed by a few feet, was sound

asleep under the debris.[131]

On a farm near Chippenham in August 1941: 'We had been harvesting that day and a long trailer of sacked up wheat had been left on the field at the end of the day. At about half past eleven we heard the approach of an enemy aircraft and suddenly realised we were being bombed. There were fires starting in the fields all round the farm and a number of large bombs had exploded. I suddenly found myself blown from my seat across to the door of the room…We all bravely went outside and found there seemed to be fires everywhere. We rather pathetically tried to put some out with buckets of water, but it was hopeless.' The following day there was a broadcast by the Germans to say that Hullavington aerodrome, about one mile away from the farm, had been almost completely destroyed.[132] In Salisbury 'I was on the top deck of a bus in town when the fighter planes came over with the guns firing – you could see them blazing. Then when I got back home to Bemerton there was lots of excitement because they had dropped a bomb which had bounced on the rail, gone through the wall and ended up in the allotments. Shrapnel had hit the water tank and there was water everywhere.' 'I was a small boy at school at Bemerton St. John when there was an air raid. In a lull we were sent home in the charge of a helper. I recall another lad and I were just crossing Skew Bridge when a German bomber came up the railway line spraying machine gun fire in all directions. But as he crossed the bridge where we two small boys were running the machine gun fire stopped… perhaps he was a father himself, perhaps he had just run out of ammunition… who knows? Anyway I am here to tell the tale.'[133] On 27 July 1942 villagers in Westwood and Wingfield were machine gunned.[134] Sybil Eccles noted that in September 1940: 'We've even had seven bombs in Chute, which thrilled the boys… 'We're in the front line, Mum, all the Morses' windows have been blown out'!! The young horrors imitate dive bombing, screaming bombs and siren warning all day. It's their chief pleasure and, bless them, they don't worry about it at all.'[135] At Ashton Keynes a bomb fell on a resident's house, killing him in the process.[136] On the first night of the Baedeker raid on Bath a stray bomb dropped in Silver Street, Potterne, killing an eighteen month baby and trapping five people inside the ruins. The water main in the street had received a direct hit.[137] The raids were in revenge for the RAF bombing of Lübeck and Rostock.[138]

For one newly arrived school girl in Swindon the air raid was a terrifying experience:

> When the first note of an air raid warning started up, we left our work and were quickly hustled from the classroom to line up by the pond. Our small wooden building had no suitable shelter, so we were led in an orderly 'crocodile' to Avenue Road, an adjoining road of houses with low walls enclosing tiny gardens.
>
> Before the warning, we had been told to knock on a front door and ask to be taken in while the air raid lasted. But now it was actually sounding, the

thought of opening a gate, walking up a strange garden path and knocking on an unknown door terrified me. I stood by a closed gate, lost and afraid; afraid to open it; afraid to move as the road emptied of children. The fear of meeting strange people was far greater than the threat of bombs and enemy planes.

Eventually, when my form teacher saw me standing there, she took me up a path, knocked on the door and handed me over to a kindly person; a sudden sense of warmth and protection flooded through me. I was safe once more.[139]

Devizes Control Centre Daily Log Book detailing a child fatality at Potterne, April 1942 (WSA G20/223/3)

Miss E Berrett, a Hilperton resident and Firewatcher, noted in her diary on 24 August 1940 that 'German planes were active last night & we had very little sleep. We heard gun fire and bombs dropping. Later we heard that one time bomb fell at [North] Bradley. Others fell on the old iron works at Westbury. Bradley bomb exploded at 1.15pm.'[140]

These stories, just some of the incidents which occurred across the county, give an idea of the impact that aerial attack had to lives and livelihoods in rural areas. Some evacuees found that their new rural surroundings could bring back memories of home. Children from Portsmouth had been evacuated to Clarendon House in Salisbury. They found in November 1940 that '... the bombing got worse. At night we heard the distant rumble of guns. The glow of Portsmouth burning lit the southern horizon. For me, it was frightening. For the other boys in my dormitory it was terrifying: their families lived close by the dockyard.' These boys were also subjected to a bomb falling 300 yards from their dormitory. 'A crash. An explosion. The building shook. Windows rattled. Bits of plaster fell about us. We tried to hide our terror...' The crater was six feet deep and 15 feet across.[141] Miss E. Berrett of Hilperton reported in her diary entry on 1 December 1940 that '[t]oday's wireless says that Southampton was heavily bombed last night. Our evacuee is very worried about her mother, sister & brother who live there.'[142] Peggy Pickford from Warminster was writing to her sister Elizabeth Martin in Australia regarding the searchlights on 1 September 1940.

> The searchlight effects are marvellous. One cannot help staying out to watch. We hear the Germans zooming about for hours on end... I was watching from the back door the other evening, after the warning had gone and I was admiring the complicated dance of the searchlights (I could count ten without moving my face and twenty eight on two sides of the house one evening) and shells bursting in the sky, just above the little fir plantation, and flashes like lightning right across the sky (guns, I supposed.) I wish I could draw. No, it's no good. I can't convey it. There were long sausage clouds and the lights either went through or behind them.... All the searchlights [became] concentrated to a point directly overhead, and there was a loud zooming from there too! So, I discreetly went in again, and to bed!'[143] One family moved to Purton in 1939. The children's mother asked if there was an air raid shelter for the children to go to whilst at school. The headmistress replied 'Oh, they wouldn't bomb our little school'... little did they know that Purton was 'a front-line centre of war factories and airfields, as the area was later described'.[144]

Salisbury Council's War Damage Register for 1941-1943 lists the damage done to properties in the city, with most of the damage appearing to relate to damaged window frames and glass, ceilings and plasterwork, and roof slates and tiles. Some houses needed demolishing but others, although seriously damaged were worth repairing. The Council's *Return as to Damage to Property Directly Consequent upon Bombardment for Air Attack from the Air* for 11 August 1942, listed

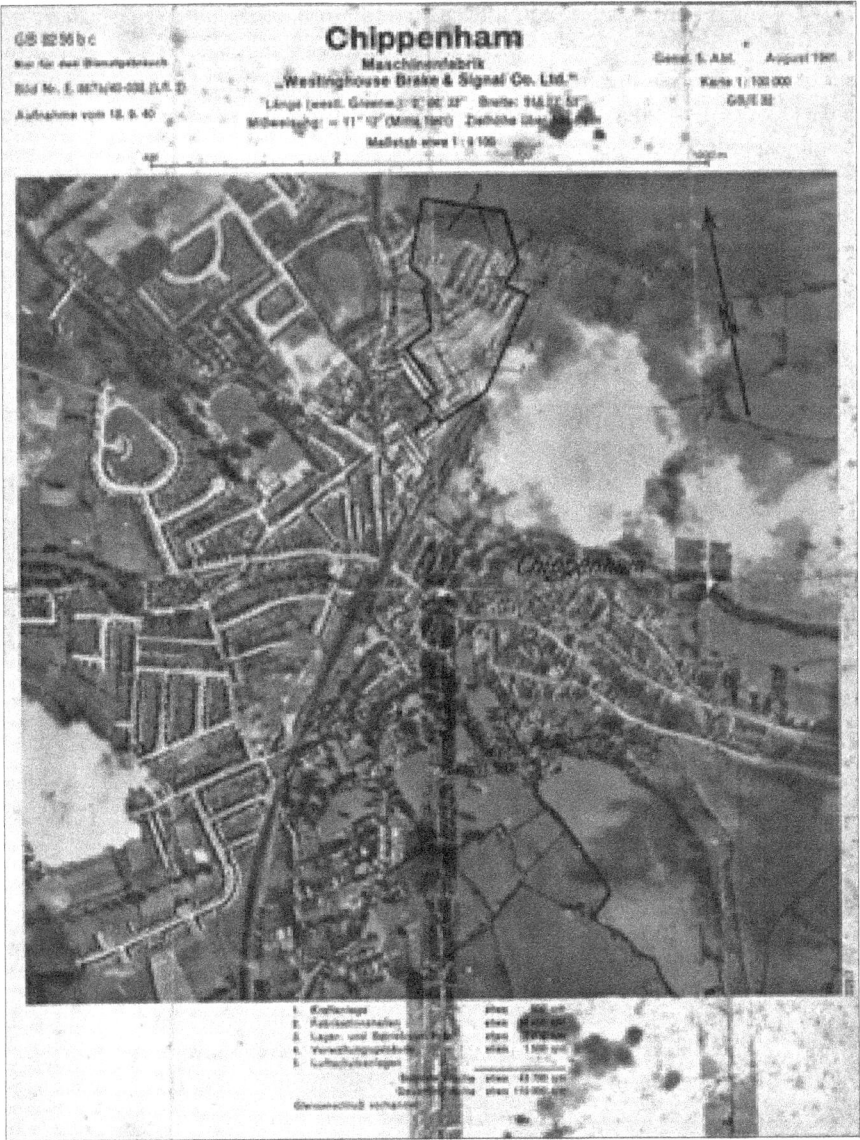

Aerial view of the Westinghouse site taken by the Luftwaffe (WSA 2514 - uncatalogued collection)

12 dwelling houses as needing to be evacuated, 303 houses as slightly damaged, and also included a small number of offices and industrial establishments.[145]

The Commonwealth War Graves Commission's list of civilian war dead includes 53 Wiltshire residents. Fatal incidents occurred in Ashton Keynes, Calne, Chippenham and Trowbridge, but by far the largest casualty rate was to be found in Swindon, where two raids at the end of 1940 and two in August 1942 took place in five streets.[146]

Interestingly, some falling objects from Wiltshire's skies from aircraft were more benign in nature. In January 1940 the Research Department at University College Exeter were warning the county's Chief Constable of a 'cardboard cylinder with a lid attached at one end. This contains a small black and white stocking flag... attached to a length of lead wire, which in turn is connected to a length of string to which is finally tied to a black parachute...' Perhaps understandably, the description did not further elaborate as to the intended use of the contraption, just

Photograph of the University College Exeter's cylinder, sent for identification purposes (WSA F5/505/29)

that it should be handed in to the nearest police station.[147]

The Wiltshire Council Emergency Committee was reporting in March 1943 that the average number of bombs dropped during school hours after an alert was 'less than one a year in every 400 miles.' It was concluded that as the risk was so small, no new school shelters would be needed. Warminster must also have been considered a relatively safe part of the county in 1943. The Council's Emergency Committee were reporting that supplies of Morrison and Anderson shelters were running low in Wiltshire by March 1943. It was decided not to provide Warminster with any new supplies.[148]

The press had been operating censorship on sensitive information throughout the war, and this included the damage caused by bombs. The readers of local newspapers were only told of 'enemy activity in the South of England' which included bombs. After the war when the censorship regulations were lifted, details were published in local newspapers.[149]

By December 1944 the Clerk of Trowbridge Urban District Council was being asked to cut back on the maintenance of the air raid shelters due to the improved military situation. A Government circular was received in May 1945 asking for the closure of shelters and also for demolition and relinquishment. As with the pillboxes, air raid shelters often remained standing long after the war ended. Many local councils wanted them demolished, but the request by Trowbridge in June 1945 was not successful. The County Architect reported to the Engineer and Surveyor at Trowbridge Urban District Council the same month stating that an application could not be submitted to demolish the shelters until the labour situation had improved.[150] By 1946 the shelter in the Pinehurst area of Swindon had partly collapsed and was being used as a toilet by young people. The Tenants' Association was making complaints.[151] Issues did not just include the anti-social use of the shelters however; a request was made to the Town Clerk by the Borough Surveyor in October 1945 that the public shelter at Swindon's County Football Ground had not been de-commissioned and the council was continuing to pay rent for it.[152] The steel used in shelter construction was an important commodity and a Civil Defence Circular sent to the Surveyor of Trowbridge Urban District Council in June 1946 urged the collection and storage of the material. A circular of April 1947 suggested it be used for housing.[153]

Mrs Matthews and daughter Joy surveying the bomb which had been defused after being dug up from their back garden at Hill Street, Hilperton, 1961 (WSHC P54037)

The story of bombs in Wiltshire did not end with peacetime. Newly discovered bombs were being unearthed even as recently as 1998 in Chippenham when local residents had to be evacuated due to discovery of two tallboys. The event was noted at the House of Commons by local MP James Gray.[154]

The Blackout

IT WOULD BECOME as difficult as possible for enemy aircraft to find their target; landmarks such as Wiltshire's famous white horses were camouflaged, and buildings such as Wiltshire County Council's headquarters at County Hall in Trowbridge[155] and Harris' factory in Calne were camouflaged too.[156] Miss E. Berrett of Hilperton described the new condition of the Westbury White Horse in August 1940. 'Westbury White Horse is also camouflaged with branches held in place with wire netting. It looks like a brown patch on the side of the hill.'[157] At Cherhill the landowner first laid an area of roof felt on the horse and then covered this with gorse from the hill. Next wire netting was placed over and it was pegged down.[158] Decoy sites were set up to confuse; to keep enemy attacks away from the true targets[159] and an enforced 'black-out' was to come into effect country-wide from 1 September 1939.[160] A decoy airfield was set up near Minety and the area was bombed, with one house getting a direct hit and one man being killed. It was never known if the decoy airfield was the cause, or if it was a bomber shedding his load. As one Minety resident later recalled: 'The farmers living near the airfield, had to agree, without any option, to this danger, in the hope of saving someone else's life. They carried on with their lives and work, knowing what could happen, but then, this sums up the spirit of the British Nation during those days...'[161] One lady returned to her village of Little Durnford after the war and noted: ' 'Nothing has changed,' you murmur happily – but that is a hasty judgement! The villagers, it is true, treat bombs in much the same spirit in which they endure the weather; something which happens and must be borne. They even point out with some pride the places where bombs fell; but, being less enduring then the weather, they are also considered less interesting! ... though one of the latter did achieve an unconventional spreading of artificial manure by bursting in a barn full of the stuff!'[162]

The threat of bombs in Wiltshire was not unfamiliar; by 1916 during WWI there had been a real fear that the larger Zeppelins would be able to reach western Britain. The German raids on Liverpool at the end of January 1916 left the Zeppelins moving across the midlands. Within 50 minutes of the attack Swindon residents had heard the news with the GWR hooter blasting out the alarm for 'lights out'. Householders drew their blinds and the police stopped motorists to ask them to turn off their headlights. By February 1916 the Borough of Marlborough was posting public notices requesting its inhabitants to keep lights to as low a level as possible and to keep blinds and curtains drawn during Zeppelin raids. 'Warning will be given at the approach of Zeppelins by sounding the Fire Alarm on the Town Hall 3 times in succession. When the alarm is sounded all Lights should be immediately extinguished, and everyone is strongly advised to remain indoors.'[163]

In July 1939 the Government was advising house owners on how to blackout effectively in its Civil Defence public information leaflet No. 2. 'Of course, the most convenient way of shutting in the light is to use close fitting blinds. These can be of any thick, dark coloured material such as dark blue or black or dark green glazed Holland, Lancaster or Italian cloth. If you cannot manage this, you could obscure your windows by fixing up sheets of black paper or thick dark brown paper mounted on battens... The simplest way of testing material, whether for blinds or curtains, is to hold up a piece against an electric bulb...' The last piece of helpful advice was to tell people not to delay when purchasing the required materials. 'If you wait you might find that you had difficulty in getting what you wanted... After all, it is only common sense to make our preparations in advance to meet a possible emergency.'[164] In early September 1939: 'The good citizen, already preoccupied with gas-proofing one of his rooms with cellulose and tape, or erecting an Anderson shelter in his garden, had to rush to the shops to buy blinds, curtains, blackout paint, cardboard, drawing pins, brown paper or whatever could be used to seal his windows at night. All these commodities rapidly became dear or unobtainable'.[165] Many households in Bradford on Avon had purchased blackout material by August 1939, with the price quickly increasing from 2s. 6d. to 3s. 11d. per yard. Jack Mock notes that 'the quality became noticeably inferior'.[166] After the declaration of war, small rolls of brown gummed tape could be purchased at the ARP offices in Swindon. One resident had purchased some the day before at a much higher price. A neighbour described it as '[p]rofiteering... that's what we said would happen. They've started already.'[167] Neighbours in the town were also busy talking to each other about how they were managing to fulfil the necessary tasks. Black curtains were pretty much unobtainable in the town and so residents had to make other arrangements. 'My father decided to construct wooden frameworks to fit downstairs windows, and cover with lino, which proved to be effective. Unfortunately this measure was not applied to the upstairs rooms, so at bedtime we had to undress in the dark.'[168]

The Headquarters Company of the Devizes Home Guard at Southbroom School with taped windows visible behind (WSHC P53735)

Householders had to get used to spending at least five minutes blacking out their home of an evening. If even a chink of light was visible from the street, an ARP Warden would be on the case. The disruption of evening life was commonplace. Bemerton's parish magazine records the blackout as a recurring theme with meetings cancelled, evening church services retimed to coincide with the full moon, and 'making use of the Parish lantern of old.'[169] 'Having struggled with drawing pins and thick paper, or with heavy black curtains, citizens might contemplate going out for supper – and then reject the idea, settle down for a long read and an early night.'[170] In Freshford on the Somerset/Wiltshire border: 'As a community we have been exceedingly strict with ourselves over the black-out. If through accident someone turns on the light in an unshuttered room, that someone rushes in a frenzy to draw curtains and drag down the blinds…'[171] One Corsham lady painted stars on the insides of her blackout blinds to make them look a bit more attractive.[172] There were also worries that visible light was not just due to an error on the part of a careless resident. People in Salisbury were becoming increasingly concerned that they had a spy in their midst as during the blackout a blinking light was continuously visible. The source was tracked down and turned out to be coming from a school, although the reason for this is not clear.[173] An article in the *Wiltshire Gazette* on 21 September 1939 suggests that in rural areas, the necessity for strict blackout rules was not clear to all, and there were suggestions that it was not being enforced strictly enough. A statement from the Ministry of Information was printed, pointing out the reasons why it was essential:

Although rural districts would not be the object of deliberate attack, there were 'important targets in county districts which might invite attack from the air if they could be located.'

Although not a target themselves, rural districts would 'if they retained their lights, be like buoys in an unlighted sea.'

If 'the cities and towns were blacked out but not the adjoining county districts, then the towns would be in a pool of darkness which from above would enable them readily to be located.'

'A relaxation allowed to country districts would begin to spread into suburban areas, and soon we should find that the black-out was no longer effective.'

It was often asked why normal street lighting could not be retained until an air raid warning was sounded. The answer; that a large town would probably be visible at a great distance due to the height and speed of modern aircraft. The Ministry's article concluded: 'The statement should satisfy those who, particularly in country districts, feel that the restrictions are unnecessarily severe and who, with this assurance of necessity, will continue to see that they in no way contribute to any danger to the country as a whole.'

In Devizes the street lights were painted blue to shield the lights. A template of the letter 'S' was used during the process so that it would be visible, indicating the direction of public shelters.[174] The total number of people killed in road accidents increased by nearly 100% in September 1939 after the blackout, this figure excluding those who had accidents such as falling into canals or into holes or down steps at night. From mid October members of the public were allowed to use dimmed hand torches, adapted by using a double thickness of white tissue paper, to be switched off during alerts. Masked headlights were also permitted.[175] A large Government campaign was run in the winter of 1940-41, urging people to carry or wear something white in the blackout. Only a minority did so.[176] A Salisbury resident noted that suddenly many devices came onto the market, all pertaining to help people find their way in the dark. '... so called luminous devices... guaranteed to shine in gloom. Many of them were useless but door-to-door salesmen had a field day for a few weeks.'[177] Curry's were advertising their blackout special offers in the *Wiltshire Gazette* on 27 August 1942.

It was decided in December 1939 that churches, markets and street stalls could be partially illuminated and a small amount of light could be used in shop windows. Illuminated signs could be used by restaurants and cinemas but all lights needed to be extinguished when the sirens sounded the alert. 'Glimmer' or 'star' lighting was also introduced; a pin prick of light pointing downwards in city centres and at road junctions. However, not all towns were prepared to 'bear the cost or take the risk'. By January 1940 the results of a Gallup Poll suggested that as many as one in five could attest to having sustained at least a minor injury as a result of the blackout.[178] Local newspapers were filled with reports of accidents, many fatal, taking place during blackout hours. One such report was in the *Wiltshire Times* on 4 November 1939; three fatal accidents in the Trowbridge district during blackout hours, all occurring within a few hours of each other. One was a 19 year old cycling through Holt, another an 80 year old pedestrian who was knocked down in Trowbridge and the third was a motor cyclist who collided with a cow at Wingfield. The Ministry of Information produced a leaflet telling of:

Danger in the Dark!
Lots of accidents happen in the blackout which don't get into newspapers.

They may be trifling bumps and bruises – or something more serious. But all are a hindrance to the war effort. So – look out in the black-out!

What do I do...?

I pause when I go out in the dark to let my eyes adjust themselves. I never cross roads until I know the way is clear.

I never flash my torch into the eyes

NOW IS THE TIME
TO BUY
SPECIAL BLACK-OUT
OFFERS

A.R.P. LAMPS (complete)   2/9
FRONT CYCLE LAMPS
            (complete) 3/6
LARGE TORCH & 3 SPARE
            BATTERIES 4/-
SIZE 8 TORCH & 1 SPARE
            BATTERY 2/3½
EXTRA LARGE TORCHES
            (complete) 3/6
We also have a few
FOOTBALL CASES (Size 5) 8/6
ROLLER SKATES from 6/6 pr.
ALL TYPES OF H.T.'s IN
            STOCK AT

CURRY'S
CHIPPENHAM

'Now is the time to buy...' Advertisement by Curry's in the Wiltshire Gazette, 27 August 1942 (WSHC Microform Collection)

of approaching drivers, and I remember I can see a vehicle approaching before the driver can see me.

If I drive, I take care my headlights are properly adjusted, and I drive at a speed appropriate to the limited range of vision.[179]

Local newspapers such as the *Wiltshire Times* on 15 July 1944 listed the following week's blackout times, pm and am, which in this case were at 10.53 pm to 5.33 am, altering by a couple of minutes each day.

In February 1940 summer time was introduced early, to be retained for the whole year. It was replaced in 1941 by 'double summer time' in the summer months, allowing the population to have extra daylight in the evening, but was no help in the morning. Buses and trains took on a new dimness and there were worries over the perceived increase in unlawfulness at night.[180] The Pinehurst Tenants Association in Swindon was concerned, writing to the Clerk (who sent a copy to the Police) about the need for extra policing in 1940. They felt that it was unsafe for their children to be outside after dark due to the 'reduced lighting service,' and wanted additional protection.[181] The blackout continued… and people got used to the inconvenience,[182] but it was particularly hard for those working outside at night, such as railwaymen. Factories found it difficult to achieve a full blackout, having to paint or cover all their windows with permanent material, reverting to the use of artificial light during the day. Angus Calder notes that ventilation was ignored quite often.[183] Many schools such as Heywood reported being fitted for blackouts[184] which disrupted school lessons. In April officials from the Council's County Hall in Trowbridge measured up one schoolroom and the hall for 'blacking'. The rooms were to be used for ARP exercises by the local fire organisation.[185] By spring 1940 Fay Inchfawn in Freshford reported that 'all [were] very tired of the black-out. The brown paper at the sides and tops of the windows was showing signs of wear. The gummed strips on the panes themselves held on most tenaciously, and it was pleasant to be able sometimes to open windows top and bottom, and really see the view all at once instead of seeing it in squares.'[186]

925,000 cases were brought to court countrywide regarding infringements of blackout restrictions over the duration of the war and there were a total of 1,000 cases involving lighting offences. 1940 was the peak, with 300,000 successful prosecutions.[187] The *Wiltshire Gazette* was reporting in its 19 October 1939 edition that seven men were brought in front of the magistrates at the Devizes County Petty Sessions for failing to have rear lights attached, breaching blackout regulations. Their defence was that they had been unable to purchase the necessary lamps.

But, finally, after a period of five years there was hope. The Chippenham doctor Joan Hickson reported in her diary entry of 7 September 1944: 'The papers today contain great news for the ordinary civilian. The blackout is to be considerably modified from Sept 7th, much more street lighting, and no absolute blackout required for windows, only ordinary curtains. This will lighten what has been one of the major burdens and annoyances of war for ordinary people.'[188]

'The long tyranny of the blackout' ended on 17 September 1944, replaced by a 'dim-out', but many people did not yet bother removing the blackouts from their homes.[189] By October 1945 the Consulting Surgeon in the GWR Medical Fund Society Hospital outpatients was complaining yet again that the blackout had not been removed in the room that he was using.[190] The blackout was one feature of WWII on the Home Front which uniformly affected the population as a whole. It has been described by one official historian as 'transfor[ming] conditions of life more thoroughly than any other single feature of the war'.[191]

The official historian of Britain's Civil Defence effort maintained that it had been a 'revolutionary' concept to provide civilians with the domestic air raid shelter, the gas-mask and the stirrup pump at national expense. The historian Meisel feels that if the plans were really 'revolutionary', compared to the alternative offered by those scientists and architects working outside the Government sphere, then the revolution was a conservative one.[192] In the week ending 11 September 1940, German bombs had claimed the lives of 1,211 civilians; an unparalleled number in Britain's history.[193]

Despite the work of the German bombers, London continued as an administrative capital; Portsmouth and Plymouth were still able to serve the Royal Navy, the Liverpool docks remained open and Coventry's war production work was maintained. Factory workers continued to turn up for work. Supply losses were not disastrous to the war industry or the population but Calder notes that '[t]he attacks on docks and railways, the side effects on public utilities and transport, nervous tension, casualties and sleepless nights, had results which could not be measured, though they were clearly significant.'[194] In Wiltshire the county was on the whole, relatively untouched, but bomb damage did occur. Residents had heard and seen the German bombers for themselves. They also knew of the small scale bombing which affected their local area, sometimes with fatal consequences. The people of Wiltshire also witnessed at first hand the real human cost; the evacuees, some who had moved from cities like Portsmouth, losing their homes, possessions, and sometimes family members or friends too, and Wiltshire people themselves were also injured or killed in the heavily bombed areas, such as student nurse Cynthia Walker from Bradford on Avon who was training at St. Thomas' Hospital in London in the summer of 1940. The hospital had prepared for air raids but the block Cynthia was in received a direct hit. She was one of six female medical hospital staff to lose their lives.[195]

Wiltshire people understood the cost and often wanted to do more to help. The 29 July 1944 issue of the *Wiltshire Times* was reporting how the county was helping the flying bomb victims. The request for volunteers from the Warden's Service to help in another part of the South of England 'met with a most gratifying response.' Malmesbury was one of those towns which were prepared to 'adopt' another which had been devastated by aerial attack. The WVS had been asked by the Ministry of Health to help re-equip homes in these areas and Malmesbury had adopted Battersea. In June 1944 until December 1945 the Warminster surveyor Geoffrey Butcher supervised the builders from the Warminster and surrounding district who had been sent to London to repair homes damaged by bombs. 'Houses which could be made habitable had to be provided with a living room, kitchen and one bedroom and a bathroom. It was [Geoffrey's] job to drive back to Warminster once a week, in the blackout, to collect the wages.'[196] At the end of 1944 the Malmesbury WVS' Head Housewife was appealing to her fellow townspeople. 'We are asked to give any useful household article we can spare to help the unfortunate people who have lost everything. Anything from a bed to a teaspoon will be accepted... The matter is urgent, so let us who – up to now – have been spared the horrors of a blitz do our utmost to make a Christmas present to those who have suffered so much.'[197]

The Commonwealth War Graves Commission was tasked by Royal Charter to produce a list of civilian war dead, to include the Civil Defence Services. The Roll of Honour contains over 60,000 names for the country as a whole.[198]

A different type of bomb became the focus of worry after VJ Day, and with it the emergence of the Cold War. The Ministry of Supply wanted to hold onto the underground factories at Corsham in the post war years, feeling in 1946 'that the policy is to hold on firmly to our best refuge from the atom bomb.'[199]

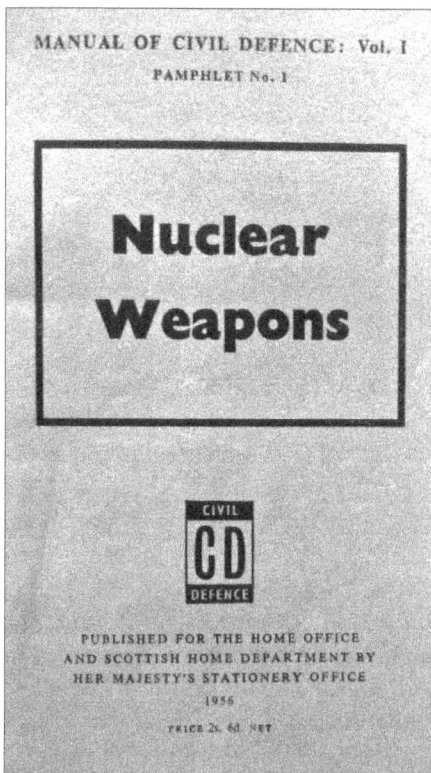

MANUAL OF CIVIL DEFENCE: Vol. I

PAMPHLET No. 1

Nuclear Weapons

CIVIL
CD
DEFENCE

PUBLISHED FOR THE HOME OFFICE
AND SCOTTISH HOME DEPARTMENT BY
HER MAJESTY'S STATIONERY OFFICE
1956
PRICE 2s. 6d. NET

Civil Defence Manual No. 1, 'Nuclear Weapons', 1956 (WSA G23/231/1)

8
Pulling Together

Rationing

R ATIONING HAD TAKEN place during WWI with controls over consumables such as sugar, butter, bacon and ham, necessary after growing food shortages led to rising food prices and queues. The Ministry of Food which had administered the scheme was abolished in 1921 when food control ended.[2] The Trowbridge publication *Trowbridge Roll of Honour* reports that food control was begun in the town in 1917 with Trowbridge having its own Food Committee to regulate and distribute foodstuffs. Before the scheme began, 'long queues of people, mostly women and children… waiting for hours outside the food shops… with the result, often, that numbers could get nothing, and only the favoured succeeded in what was sometimes a scramble.' After food control was introduced an individual was registered with a retailer and presented a food card for their allotted share.[2] Wiltshire's School Log Books mention rationing during WWI with an entry from 1 March 1918 at Salisbury St. Mark's Girls School stating: 'No attendance marked this afternoon, the school being required in connection with the 'Ration' Scheme & the teachers employed to assist with same.' On 11 June the school was closed so that the teachers could assist with the 'new food registration.'[3] The queues and unequal distribution were eliminated by the use of food control which set a 'just apportionment' for all. It was disliked but reluctantly accepted.[4] WWI rationing had proved successful, and the food queues diminished.[5] The experience of WWI had shown that industrial unrest would be triggered by the maldistribution of foodstuffs in wartime, leading to food queues. The British people would understand the necessity of a rationing system to enable the equal and fair provision of foodstuffs to every civilian.[6] In 1929 the Treasury was looking at possible wartime controls; the introduction of wage, price and import control to reduce consumerism and to encourage saving alongside higher taxation.[8]

Sir William Beveridge, permanent Secretary to the first Ministry of Food, was appointed Chairman to an influential sub-committee on rationing in 1936. It was decided that the successful system of food control used during WWI should be re-established in the event of another war, but the scheme would only be successful if every person was guaranteed their fair share.[8] The system of controls when shortages became apparent in WWI had been voluntary. E. M. H. Lloyd described the situation: 'delays in facing the problem brought the country near to disaster... A breakdown of food supplies in 1917, with all its unmanageable consequences, was only averted just in time.'[9] The findings of the sub-committee culminated in the creation of the Board of Trade Food (Defence Plans) Department in December 1936, its purpose to plan for the supply, control, distribution and movement of food. The aim of rationing was not just to curtail usage; it was also meant to guarantee supplies.[10] The Government also planned to keep inflation as low as possible. With an increased output during wartime, there were worries that inflation would rise. WWI had shown that high inflation could lead to social disruption and that maintaining price control was necessary to control the labour force. The 1941 budget announced that prices would be held at that year's level for the duration of the war, but only rationing could make the measure possible.[11]

Wartime rationing would follow along the lines of WWI with procedures put into place for the control of cereals, meat, sugar, fats and tea. A 'buffer' of bread, potatoes and canteen meals was to be made freely available to help provide for the different energy requirements of individuals. Government agents and shadow organisations would be set up with leading members of the food trade, responsible for the regular flow of food to retailers and consumers. The country would be divided into 19 divisions with Local Authorities helping to establish some 1,400 Local Food Control Committees. There would also be Divisional Food Officers responsible for food control. It was the job of the Local Committees to liaise with consumers, issue ration documents, supervise registration, allocate supplies and enforce regulations. The consumer-retailer 'tie-in' would be the *pièce de résistance* of the system, consumers registering with individual retailers to receive their goods.[12]

The pre-war planning of food policy gained momentum from 1936[13] with the establishment of the Food (Defence Plans) Department,[14] speeding up after the Munich Crisis of September 1938. Fifty million ration books had been printed before war had been declared[15] but the Government's planning under Sir Henry French was, according to Kevin Manton, a 'woefully limited version of what was necessary.' Targets had been set well below those Beveridge had recommended, and even these had not been reached. There were also no adequate plans in place,[16] and the policy was 'woefully inadequate.'[17] In September 1938 the Postmaster General was making enquiries of Calne's Town Clerk, asking if there were any vacant properties in the town which could be utilised as a Food Control Office.[18] The Town Clerk had been actively preparing for the act of hoarding in the event of war, with a letter to local tradesmen on 27 September 1938. 'In view of the intention of the Government to enforce a strict system of food control in the event of war breaking out, it is clearly desirable that any attempt to hoard food stuffs in advance of control should be resisted. Retail tradesmen would be fully justified in refusing abnormal supplies to their customers. Indeed, it seems to me to be their duty to do so.'[19]

By 1939 the Board of Trade Food was not ready to carry out even the limited functions placed under its control.[20] In July 1939 Civil Defence Public Information Leaflet No. 4 *Your Food in War-time* set out the Government's plans in the event of war. It looked at how householders could help, and covered details of the proposed rationing scheme. It stated that the Government had been purchasing 'considerable reserves of essential foodstuffs' as a precautionary measure and 'the necessary arrangements ha[d] been made to control the supply and distribution of food through the country immediately upon the outbreak of hostilities.' Traders were urged to maintain and/or increase their stock and it was suggested that the public store foods such as '[m]eat and fish in cans or glass jars; flour; suet; canned or dried milk; sugar; tea; cocoa; plain biscuits. When you have laid in your store, you should draw on it regularly for day to day use, replacing what you use by new purchases, so that the stock in your cupboard is constantly being changed… Any such reserves should be bought before an emergency arises. To try to buy extra quantities when an emergency is upon us, would be unfair to others.' Maximum food prices would be fixed by the Ministry for each controlled food, and would be clearly shown in shop windows. Certain foods, soon after the outbreak of a war, would be brought under a rationing scheme 'similar to that which was introduced during the latter part of the Great War.' Every householder would have to fill in an application form which asked them to give particulars of all those who were living in the house. 'These forms, when filled in, would be returned to the local food office… which would issue the Ration Books, one for each person. You would then register at a retail shop of your own choice for each rationed food.'[21] The Ministry of Food was established at the outbreak of war in September 1939.[22] It is interesting to note, however, that the Food (Defence Plans) Department at the Board of Trade had not initiated any detailed preparations in advance for the storage of food. The Ministry of Food was only able to make up the shortfall after war was announced by the delay caused by the Phoney War.[23]

In April 1939 a letter marked 'Secret' was sent from the Home Office to Wiltshire's Chief Constable, stating that the department was making preparations 'for the compilation of a complete National Register upon the outbreak of war' and wanted the help of the Police to enumerate homeless persons on the night of the National Registration Day. The procedure was to be similar for that of census recording. The day was set as 29 September 1939 under the National Registration Act of 1939.[24] The register can now be viewed online at Findmypast in association with The National Archives.

By the end of 1939 the ration books had been sent through the post and each citizen had registered with a grocer and butcher.[25] Dorothy Holman was writing from Norton Bavant to her daughter Elizabeth Martin in Australia on 20 October 1939 about rationing, the process which had just begun the previous month. 'Personally I think the Govt. is erring on the side of molly-coddling the public. I suppose they don't mean the profiteering etc. to go on like it did in the

SERIAL No.

V

NATIONAL REGISTRATION

INSTRUCTIONS

1. A return must be made upon this form by any *homeless* person who spends the night of National Registration Day in the street or open air, or in any arches or night shelter, and has not been included in any other return for the purposes of National Registration.

2. This form must be filled up and taken to a National Registration Office. If the person usually lives or works in any particular locality, the form should be taken to the National Registration Office for that locality. If help is desired in filling up the return, it will be given at the National Registration Office.

3. The form must be taken in person to the National Registration Office, and not sent by post. When it is handed in, the person making the return will be handed an Identity Card which he or she will need for various important purposes under conditions of national emergency, and must carry about.

Name..
(To be entered by the officer delivering the form.)

I, the above-mentioned person, declare that the particulars stated on the back are correct to the best of my knowledge and belief, and that I have not been included to my knowledge in any other National Registration return.

Signature ....

Date ....

Form for registering homeless people on National Registration Day (WSA F5/530/4)

last war and there are identity cards ready for rationing; petrol rations, free gas-masks, paid A.R.P people, free tin hats and oilskin suits (many will NEVER be used, I feel sure)...'[26] In June 1941 the Chief Constable of Wiltshire was keen to encourage members of the public to carry their identity cards with them at all times by introducing a procedure whereby Police Officers would routinely ask to see the identity card of anyone they needed to stop for whatever reason. Identity card numbers were also to be noted after the names of every person contained within an official report. An individual who was unable to show his identity card for inspection when asked was able to avoid prosecution if they brought it to a designated Police Station for inspection within a prescribed time period set by the Police Officer at the scene.[27] In Ham, residents were visiting the village hall to collect their new ration books on 14 May 1942. 'The new ration-books have just been issued by three brisk officious females... We troop like sheep, humbly, in to an atmosphere that seems to be telling us that we civilians and children are 'nothing but a nuisance' too, mere numbers of cards, and lucky to get any food allotted to us whatever!'[28]

A new identity card system was to be introduced in the summer of 1943, the Chief Constable of Wiltshire receiving a Government circular advising of the changes. Those persons over 16 who had held a buff coloured ration card were to be issued with a new, blue card. Those under 16 would retain their old cards. Civil Defence workers whose card did not contain a photograph would be issued a new form. By 1944 some Civil Defence workers, such as Wardens, First Aid Post, Ambulance, Control Centre personnel and members of the National Fire Service held a pale blue ration card but it did not give the holder any special status. They were merely to 'facilitate rapid identification.' The Police, including members of

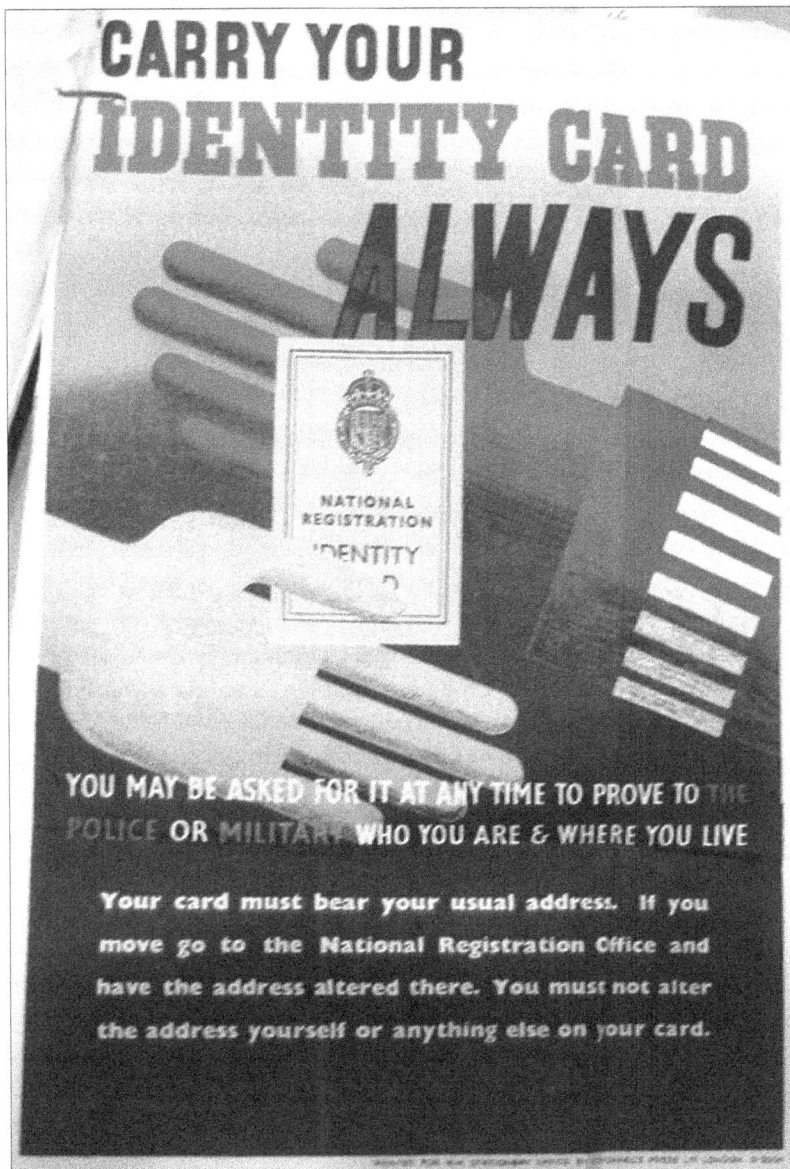

Poster for display in all Police Stations in 1941 'Carry Your Identity Card Always' (WSA F5/530/4)

the Women's Auxiliary Police Corps and Special Constables, held buff coloured cards which also contained their photograph.[29]

The RB1 form was to be filled in for children aged over six (later reduced to five) and younger children received the RB2. From 1943 an RB4 form was introduced for five to sixteen year olds. Additional allowances were given to pregnant and nursing mothers and there were also different books for those who could not register with a certain retailer, such as seamen.[30]

Beveridge's plans of 1936 had stated that food controls would be put into place within hours of the outbreak of hostilities but the Minister of Food William Morrison did not do so.[31] The first piece of legislation to be put into place was price control with the prices on some clothing and household goods being fixed in November 1939. The Ministry took the decision to subsidise food in December 1939[32] but rationing was not put into place until January 1940 due to the uncertainty of the Phoney War.[33] The uncertainty of food supplies appears to have been in the public mind by December 1939 when Sybil Eccles was noting in a letter that the Women's Institute at Chute was reporting a profit of 3*s.* 2½*d.* for teas in October: 'the whole of the rest of them is furiously concentrated on the problem of what they shall give their husband for his supper. A woman's life boils down to food and boots – boots and food, doesn't it?'[34] The *Wiltshire News* was announcing the start of rationing in its 5 January 1940 edition, due to begin on 8 January. Its 'housewives' guide at a glance,' showed what would and would not be rationed. The public were told to register with retailers by 8 January for meat and were assured that rations for this product would be 'well up to ordinary requirements' and appealed to consumers not to increase their demand for sugar before rationing started. There was also a separate article about the forthcoming meat rationing which was warning readers that: 'No one will quarrel with the fact that in distribution priority is given to the needs of the Services, and it is also necessary to maintain reserves against irregularities in future arrivals. There is therefore some reduction in the supplies of imported meat available for the public.' It also noted: 'As in 1918, meat will be rationed on the basis of value. The weight of the ration will therefore vary with the consumer's choice of quality.' Bacon, ham, butter and sugar were rationed first, followed by meat in March 1940.[35] One Warminster resident had her ration books registered at the Co-op, 'but the meat she had at two separate shops. That way, if there was anything going extra like sausages or offal which wasn't exactly rationed but in short supply she had two chances... Warminster was noted for their pork butchers. There were at least two good ones in the High Street where we got special pig products like faggots... and chitterlings.'[36] With July 1940 came the rationing of tea, margarine and cooking fats, followed by preserves and cheese in 1941,[37] but for those who did not have access to canteens such as agricultural workers, a supplementary cheese ration was provided.[38] The Wiltshire farmer and broadcaster A.G. Street was considering the rationing of cheese in 1943. 'One of the vexed questions in the countryside to-day is cheese, or rather the rationing of that useful food.' Farm workers were ensured an eight-ounce ration if they possessed an agricultural unemployment insurance card but he felt this was not enough for the older farm worker.

> He can get little or no extras to the ordinary ration of food, and by virtue of his work on the land he undoubtedly merits more than the full eight-ounce ration of cheese per week. For he has always been a cheese eater, in fact he is probably,

to use a modern way of putting it, more cheese-minded than either the younger man or the land girl. Moreover, he is doing a good job of work during this war, so good that the nation cannot do without him. Here is his argument, as he put it to me the other day.

'I could manage all right if I could get a bit more cheese. Thee do summat about it, maister. They gi'ed thic Hess chicken. I'd gi'e un chicken. All I got up yer while I be hoein' in these cold wind be some bread an' jam.'[39]

Hints on WAR-TIME SPENDING AND SAVING

Here are three ships

1

3

2

This one is loaded with foodstuffs and necessaries

This one is loaded with unnecessary goods

This one is loaded with munitions

By limiting your purchases of the goods contained in Ship No. 3, you leave more cargo space for the goods we need to win the war. Spend carefully then—buy what you must—but avoid spending on unnecessary things, particularly goods which come from abroad.

Result:

(1) You increase the shipping available for essentials.

(2) You have more money to invest in National Savings Certificates and the New Defence Bonds.

HOW TO LEND TO HELP WIN THE WAR

Lend to defend the right to be free

A Gallup poll conducted after the first wave of rationing in January showed that 36% were in favour of more rationing but 54% would prefer voluntary reductions in consumption.[40]

The Government had been considering rationing tobacco and bread but it was felt that no substantial savings would be made on bread and that rationing tobacco would be bad for morale.[41] However, it can be noted that tobacco was one of those goods like beer, spirits, wines, sweets and sugar which suffered price rises due to the increase in customs and excise duty.[42] The duty on a barrel of beer had been 24s. in 1939, reaching *c.* £7 in the second half of the war. It was also watered down considerably.[43] Cigarettes went up from 11d. in 1941 to 1s. 9d. in 1943.[44] Cigarette queues often formed in Bradford on Avon when there were rumours that the Co-op or Mr Summer's in the Shambles had received new supplies.[45] Most village pubs operated a counter system (a bar with room to house fixtures and equipment) to protect supplies for their regular local customers as the pubs often ran dry. Richard Meakin notes that:

Ministry of Food advert in the Wiltshire Gazette, 18 January 1940 'Hints of War-time Spending and Saving' (WSHC Microform Collection)

'It is said that when the New Red Lion... [at Minety] ran out of beer and the brewer's lorry had turned up, at opening time there would be a queue from its door to Taylor's Printing works (about 300 yards away but now demolished); the word had got round! The trouble was, once the queue had gone so had the beer. With convoys of troops moving through, some stopping for the night, or several days and nights, the demand was out of control.'[46] In Devizes there were 'long queues in the Little Brittox for fish and at the pork butchers in Maryport Street for sausages... the arrival of fresh supplies spread through the town like wildfire.'[47] There were also queues for cakes at the bakers in Sidmouth Street but '... they tasted like sawdust because of the inadequate ingredients.' Airmen often walked from Melksham to buy goods such as sweets and cigarettes, but when the Bath Road shop had run out, all they could provide the servicemen for their effort were jugs of water.[48]

Clothing had not been rationed during WWI[49] and this was a new venture for the Government.[50] The supply of clothing began at a stable level at the outset of WWII, but there was trepidation in the market and so prices rose steadily, in some cases to double their pre-war level[51] and eighteen months on the prices of some clothes had risen by a whopping 75%.[52] The Prices of Goods Act of November 1939 tried to address the issue of profiteering but it was only partially successful, leading to the Goods and Services (Price Control) Act of 1941. After the endorsement for a clothes rationing scheme in February 1941 an extension of rationing was called for in March.[53] Churchill felt it would be unpopular to ration clothes[54] and thought the British would become dressed in 'rags and tatters'[55] but it became necessary due to cotton shortages.[56] By the summer of 1941 a points rationing system had been introduced for clothes which consisted of consumers receiving a number of points (or coupons) for use at any retailer.[57] Each individual was entitled to an annual supply of 66 coupons,[58] later reduced to 60 as clothing shortages became more severe. Each item of clothing had a certain number of coupons required for it: 14 points for a woman's coat, 16 points of a man's, 7 for a skirt or dress etc.[59] with children's clothes requiring fewer coupons (they would need new clothes more often as they grew).[60] Margarine coupons had to be used for clothes at first until clothing ration books were introduced in 1942-3. From August 1941 second hand clothing was price fixed so that an exchange of coupons would be needed if the sale price was found to be above the fixed price. Hats were never rationed and so became very expensive and hard to obtain. By 1943 many women had no choice but to go out hatless.[62] The situation became so bad that the Archbishop of Canterbury decreed that the covering of women's heads in church would no longer need to be observed.[63] How an individual's wardrobe looked in 1941 had an impact on how they could cope with restricted clothing during the course of the war.[64] A mother from Wilton was woeing the need to have coupons for pocket handkerchiefs. 'They write up everywhere that 'Coughs and sneezes Spread diseases' and I don't know they do. Half the children at school haven't got a handkerchief, and they splash about everywhere. This poor little one comes back every week with a fresh cold...'[65] By 1942 a 'sombre mood' had gripped British fashion. The turn ups on male trousers had been banned and the ruling was proving deeply unpopular,[66] as was limiting the length of men's socks to nine inches.[67] The enthusiasm for clothes rationing was wearing thin and turning to anxiety.[68] The effect, however, was startling with the saving made through the elimination of turn ups, pleats and double cuffs etc. described as 'substantial'. Turn ups were reinstated in February 1944 and the length of socks returned to a normal length in November 1945 so that demobbed men would not have to return to austerity clothing after having served their country.[69]

During the Second World War many tried to improvise. Occasionally silk parachutes were on sale at Devizes market, much sought after for those intrepid make do and menders as '... the silk was of beautiful quality and was coupon free. The snag was that they were criss crossed with strong seams [*sic*], so that only small areas of silk could be salvaged, and making a garment was like doing a jigsaw puzzle. If one was very thrifty and even more patient, one could unpick the seams and not only have parachute silk but also a quantity of stout thread as well. The material was soft and hard wearing and much used for small garments.'[70] In fact the Government released a large amount of parachute material off coupon in 1945, and an advertisement claimed that it was possible to produce two nightdresses, two slips, two pairs of cami-knickers and four pairs of knickers from a third of a 24 panel parachute.[71]

Edith Olivier was reporting at Wilton that the talk of the town was mostly about coupons, one middle aged woman scoffing at the extravagance of purchasing 'Ready Mades,' pointing out the shoddy material. 'I would be ashamed to put it on my back. It has gone into rags before you can turn round in it...' She announced superciliously: 'I buy good stuff by the yard and make it up at home. I made this dress myself.'[72] One enterprising worker in the paint department at EKCO's near Malmesbury was very helpful regarding ladies and their shoes, often spray painting them as required. 'He did a rather limited palette, but would colour coordinate shoes wherever possible'![73] Office workers in Swindon sent for shoes which had been made for prisoners with a 'V' stitched onto them. The V's were unpicked and 'they made a very good pair!'[74] Others just made do. The Chippenham doctor Joan Hickson wrote of a dance she attended in the town, in aid of the hospital. 'On the whole it was a quite pleasant experience. Had to go in my embossed velvet dress, which was grubby and nine years old.'[75] Men had already begun to dress down and lose their dinner jackets in deference to those in uniform, making the case for women to choose shorter dresses for dinner. The little black dress became a necessity,[76] easy to accessorise as the situation demanded. Clothes became practical but chic with a military feel.[77] The Board of Trade announced in 1943 that England expected an economy in clothes and in coupons, but also an 'abundance of well dressed women'.[78] By 1942 patches on clothes were seen as patriotic rather than a sign of being disadvantaged with the society photographer and Berwick St. John resident Cecil Beaton remarking: 'Extravagant spending and waste, bad things at all times, are now downright heathenish. There is a biblical beauty about the way that the housewife gets the best result from slender means.'[79] Peggy Pickford from Warminster was remarking about her wardrobe to her sister Liz in Australia in a letter of 5 November 1941. 'I haven't had a new jumper for ages. I am now wearing the grey cable-stitch one I made on my honey-moon – five years ago! I have just had to darn the elbows! I also wear the one you made to the same pattern and dyed russet colour. They've seen me through several Winters.'[80] *Vogue* also did its bit, suggesting that patches could enhance a tired or worn item.[81] Women now regarded it as a matter of pride to rework 'unpromising' materials, transforming them into wearable garments. Blankets and blackout materials could be turned into coats.[82] A lady in Cricklade heard that the drapery stores in Swindon had some cot blankets which weren't on ration. 'I bought two, and took them apart and made dressing gowns for my girls.'[83] Vogue's *Knit Series No. 9* catered specifically for war workers. If they had time to make their own or knew someone to help, the 12 designs for 7*d.* had it covered, from smart sweater twin sets to waistcoats, tailored jackets and a 'practical' jacket and hood.[84]

For those women who had always been on a tight household budget, to 'make do and mend' had been done for years.[85] The Women's Institute helped the Government promote make do and mend with 'thrift classes' after the programme's launch in 1942, which was primarily aimed at women.[86] Peggy Pickford noted in a letter of 16 March 1942 to her sister Liz that: 'Things are getting so scarce that everybody is advertising for second-hand things, and turning out their lumber rooms to see if they can make an honest penny. Following the trend, I am advertising for a play-pen and push-chair and offering M's old portable Coronal which still goes perfectly. Typewriters are terribly scarce, so we might make a fiver of it!'[87] The Board of Trade introduced a puppet character called Mrs Sew-and-Sew, designed to be highly competent and able to offer advice. By 1943 she was featured in all the popular magazines[88] but by 1944 although it had become the norm, to make do and mend was becoming a 'tiresome necessity'.[89]

Canned foods came under points rationing in December 1941, proving an instant success[90] and becoming associated with praise and satisfaction.[91] The downfall of points rationing was that it had its uncertainties. There was no guarantee a consumer could purchase exactly what they wanted with them, but the advantage lay in their flexibility. They gave the consumer more choice by the ability to use them in any number of different retailers with the added bonus of creating competition within the marketplace.[92] Special provision was made for children and manual workers.[93] The scheme, according to Ina Zweiniger-Bargielowska, was a 'complete shock and surprise', but the initial feedback was positive.[94] Hancock and Gowing consider the points system to be 'one of the big home front successes of the war'.[95] Footwear was also rationed in 1941, along with a priority scheme for the provision of furniture and hollowware such as buckets and pans.[96]

Following not long behind was a scheme for chocolate and sugar confectionery in the summer of 1942.[97] Calne's Food Executive Officer must have enquired about the sugar confectionery situation on behalf of the town's shopkeepers in October 1942 as the reply from the Cocoa and Chocolate (War Time) Association made it clear that '[t]he reason why there is an apparent shortage of boiled sweets is that the demand for this type of confectionery is much heavier than normal... No doubt the demand will adjust itself to available supplies as soon as the position is realised'[98] – presumably when people stopped trying to purchase them, that is! The priority scheme often led to buyers competing against each other and Zweiniger-Bargielowska notes that 'the scramble of housewives... would probably produce as good a fit between real needs and actual purchases.' As the war continued, the Board of Trade was working to create a balance; economy versus the effect on morale by the severe shortage of essential items which led to the furniture utility policy in 1942. Utility cloth and clothes contained a distinctive mark, produced to certain specifications and of a high quality. The clothes were designed by top London fashion designers and were not standardised in colour or finish. Utility ware continued with: hosiery, footwear, knitting, bedding and household textiles.[99] The utility label needed to include the term CC41 (Civilian Clothing Order 1941, also known as Controlled Commodities). Reginald Shipp designed a logo in the form of two C's in the shape of round cheeses; it would prove to become the highly familiar 'double cheese' image of WWII. There was an emergence of patterns and checks for utility cloth. Stripes and patriotic motifs were also common.[100] Polychromatic scarves were popular and cost just two coupons.[101] Those who could have only afforded the poorest quality cloth before the war noticed that the quality of the cloth had improved,[102] and overall utility clothes were seen as smart and utilising simple designs, but there was a shortage of popular sizes.[103] Complaints were raised over the 'shoddiness' of some utility clothes, however, and utility stockings were considered a waste of coupons due to their poor design and quality.[104] Stocking repair shops sprang up in towns and cities, and magazines offered tips for repairing or re-dyeing odd stockings to create new pairs.[105] Utility furniture, however, proved popular and the opinion was that it was 'well designed for its functional purpose'.[106] Perishable food such as fish, fruit and vegetables were not rationed despite the public calling for a fairer system of distributing them.[107] One difficulty of the rationing system was the problem of maintaining an up-to-date record of registrations which retailers' buying permits relied on. There were also disruptions in supply due to the loss of shipping, bombed out retailers losing stock and individuals who mislaid their ration books or lost them in air raids.[108]

A scarcity of cloth meant scant supply for other uses, such as for needlework lessons at schools. At Ivy Lane School in Chippenham a needlework exhibition formed part of its Open Afternoon for parents in July 1941; by October the school's head teacher was reporting that on account of the war conditions, certain materials necessary for school use ie. art brushes and needlework apparatus could only be obtained with difficulty. 'We are carrying on as

The 1941 CC 'double cheese' label, reproduced by kind permission of Joy Bloomfield

best we can.' During April 1942 he was appealing to children for odd material and old garments for needlework.[109]

By 1942 consumer spending had reduced by approximately 15%. Expenditure on food had also fallen by 15% and for clothing it was at less than two-thirds of its pre-war level. Private motoring had 'virtually disappeared'.[110] Surveys of 1942-3 show that 54% approved of rationing, 27% had no criticism and only 14% were dissatisfied. Women were more satisfied with the scheme than men, as were those in rural areas. Manual workers were the group least satisfied.[111]

The wartime diet consisted of a large amount of brown bread (before the war the majority of people ate white), milk and potatoes.[112] The 'National Wholemeal Bread' was a compulsory brown loaf, produced to economise on wheat. It was unpopular throughout the war[113] but the Government was forced to introduce it due to a shipping crisis in 1942.[114] Even Ernest Bevin commented upon it at a meeting with the Deputy Prime Minister Clement Attlee. 'I say, Deputy Prime Minister, that loaf is indigestible. I can't digest this stuff in the middle. I throw it away: it's just waste.' The public appeared to agree, with the Ministry of Food receiving many complaints. Angus Calder notes that '[f]or a few weeks people indignantly ascribed every minor malaise from which they suffered to 'this nasty, dirty, dark, coarse, indigestible bread." Some experimented with it by sieving it through old silk stockings. 'I got all your vitamins out and gave them to the pigs'!'[115] Those on low incomes were used to a limited diet and it appeared that if the staples, bread and potatoes, remained off ration then people would cope.[116] Rationing touched everyone and it had to be adjusted for many individual needs, from expectant mothers and heavy workers to beekeepers. No food requirement could be ignored simply because the number of people affected was so small.[117] The official historian of the food campaign, R. J. Hammond later remarked: 'gastronomically speaking, nothing could be more pathetic' than the Ministry of Food's 'Victory Dishes' which utilised potatoes, dried egg and salted cod. Instead, most civilians tried to make do with spam, soya sausages, meat pies, tinned and powdered soup, fish paste, Bovril and cocoa.[118]

Egg consumption was reduced[119] and the quality of manufactured foods became poorer.[120] Lend-Lease supplies from the US helped and by 1943-4 the situation could have been far worse[121] although it was from the US that the most serious threat to British meat supplies came in 1942-3. The US made a decision not to honour their promise to replace the Australian meat supplies[122] which had been coming to Britain but which had been diverted to US troops in the Pacific.[123] They were also prioritising military shipments over civilian food cargoes. By May 1943 the US had introduced a meat ration for their civilian population and the US' Chief of Transport argued that the British were 'still living 'soft' and could easily stand further reductions.' However, the US ration stood at 28oz a week, double that of the British![124]

Zweiniger-Bargielowska reports that '[t]his virtual peasant diet was nutritionally adequate and healthy but also dull and monotonous'[125] with the lack of onions keenly missed. It was possible to grow onions domestically but they were

Housewives were encouraged to use potatoes in baking; 'potatoes in place of flour'. The Ministry of Food's 'Potato Plan Part 5' suggested potato pastry and also chocolate sponge pudding with potato. 'Flour costs ships… use home-grown potatoes instead', published in the Wiltshire Gazette, 18 February 1943 (WSHC Microform Collection)

prone to blight. They were placed under the newly formed Vegetable Marketing Company with the first commercial crop expected in 1941. Unfortunately the supply was mismanaged and the growing season was inclement for the crop, leading to the meagre amounts collected being left rotting in storage whist the company 'dithered.'[126] The Co-operative Society was advertising in the *Wiltshire Gazette*, 1 July 1942, that the quality of their tea was helping the ration. 'To-day – when two ounces of tea per week is your ration – only the best will do. That is why wise housewives are turning more and more to Co-operative Teas. These fine, rich blends, with their full body and flavour, do make the ration go further – do give you more cups of *better, tastier* Tea. All types – and prices to suit all pockets.' Housewives found the scarcity of fats particularly restricting as they were needed for pastry making, frying, and browning in cooking, as well as making sandwiches more appealing, but wartime rationing was not static and the amount an individual could obtain often altered depending on the national food supply, for example the sugar ration ranged from 8oz to 1lb per person over the course of the war.[127]

The public were not immune to shortfalls in foodstuffs. From October 1940 onwards there was evidence of widespread dissatisfaction with food shortages, rationed and unrationed food, particularly due to high prices and inequality of distribution. In January 1941, 42% had difficulty in obtaining unrationed foodstuffs as there were none in the shops, and another 16% because prices were too high. Discontent remained a feature throughout the spring and summer of 1941, but was alleviated by the expansion of food control. In August 1941 the Food Executive Officer of Calne Borough Council wanted to know the position regarding the purchase of unrationed goods at a certain retailer. 'Apparently, the assistants are refusing to serve unrationed goods to persons who are not registered with the shop for rationed goods, which I presume would be

Oxo's 'First Aid for the Larder', advertisement in the *Wiltshire Gazette, 11 January 1940 (WSHC Microform Collection)*

legal. At the same time, you have many regular customers who are not registered with you for Bacon who wish to continue buying unrationed goods.' The Officer was, however, enquiring because his wife was one of those being refused![129] The preceding month the Officer had come across another example, a grocer who also owned a café and refused to supply cakes from the café to those who were not registered at his grocers, and was asking the Ministry of Food's Enforcement Officer for his opinion. He had also sent on a letter from another two retailers who had stated that they felt it was acceptable to work a system that made it necessary to register for four commodities to be able to have a chance of obtaining unrationed items. The Divisional Food Officer had replied saying he had taken great exception to the case and that it was a 'totally improper' request. There was no mention of it being against the law, however, and by the evidence of a letter sent in August it appears that it was not so. The Food Executive Officer's feelings regarding the reply from the retailers in July suggests that they considered the public to be 'up to all sorts of dodges to try and get more rations and schemes of retail shopkeepers to try to check this in order to secure equitable distribution of commodities should, I think, be encouraged provided they are within the law.'[129] One Cricklade resident felt that 1941 was the worst year of the war for rationing, 'when cheese and preserves were rationed, then clothes, canned food, biscuits and cereals, soap and sweets. One local took advantage of the shortages and put up the prices of the water cress he collected himself, saying 'There's a war on!''.[130]

The situation had improved to the extent that in a Gallup poll of autumn 1941, 41% had no difficulty in obtaining unrationed foodstuffs, and those who did mentioned tinned foods, cereal and dried food. The Government responded with the points rationing scheme, launched in December 1941 and which ensured equitable distribution of those and other processed and packaged foods. It marked a turning point in popular attitudes towards food control.[131]

Home Front propaganda stressed that Britain's citizens should be both willing and proud to accept suffering and sacrifice to aid the war effort, but Home Intelligence reported in 1942 that although people were unhappy and unwilling to make voluntary sacrifices, they were willing to accept compulsory sacrifices without too much complaint. Zweiniger-Bargielowska reports that in surveys, food and general shortages were a big problem for both the Government and individuals during the 1940s with food being the largest concern before the supply situation stabilised during 1942. By May 1941 it had been fully realised that civilian morale had more to do with the difficulties of day to day living rather than events happening further afield.[132] Food became one of the chief topics of conversation for higher income groups whose standard of living was being reduced at the same time as a higher proportion of their income was being spent on food.[133] Fresh food was easier to come by in the countryside, especially for farmers. Peter Ginn notes that this fact remains as bitter memory for some town and city dwellers. However, the shop goods were easier to acquire in towns and cities, and harder to get hold of if you lived in the countryside.[134] One Great Cheverell resident recalled '... with home grown fruit and vegetables, in many cases home laid eggs and in some cases goats milk and home fed bacon it must be allowed that food was always sufficient if often dull and of inferior quality.'[135] Another country dweller spent an afternoon in the Wiltshire countryside in October 1940 'rough shooting,' collecting '50 rabbits, some pigeon, 3 partridges, a pheasant and 4 hares... We came home to eat a huge tea and marvel that when bombs are dropping one can still spend an afternoon like that.'[136] In Cricklade '[w]e had a large garden – nearly everyone did – to grow potatoes and green stuff. We'd salt down runner beans, store carrots and beetroot in sand, and potatoes in straw, picking out the rotten ones to give to the pigs.'[137] Grated potato could be used as a suet substitute, among other things.[138] Country dwellers also helped out their fellow townsfolk. In Cricklade, 'My mother would send her sister a whole rabbit in a parcel of brown paper tied up with string if she was desperate for meat. These had been shot on the farm. My uncle could skin them himself, and it was all quite legal because these were wild rabbits which meant there were not rationing restrictions. As farmers we did quite well; we always had plenty of fruit and vegetables.'[139]

Many people were envious of the clothing that Service personnel were given, feeling that 'at least the servicewomen get something decent to wear',[140] and the Government appeared to see that the issue could affect morale. Wiltshire Constabulary were advised in September 1941 by the Board of Trade who had 'collaborated with other departments,' that clothing coupons for full-time members of the Civil Defence services would cease for articles 'made in personal issue' even if they were not taken home. One exception would be the stockings of Policewomen when used on duty. By October the Board of Trade was sending out explanatory notes. '…the idea behind the scheme is simply fairness – fairness to people who do not have uniforms issued to work in. People who do not get them are therefore required to surrender a fixed number of coupons every year, a number which has nothing to do with the value of the uniform clothing received, but has been fixed to ensure that, at the end of the year, they will not be substantially better off than non-uniformed workers.'[141] When it came to service uniform, the WRNS' was viewed as the most chic and for many women entering the services, their full set of uniform totalled the greatest number of clothes they had ever owned.[142]

Between the autumn of 1942 and December 1944 many felt that the number of clothing coupons was inadequate and there were calls for extra coupons for household linen. Poorer working class people found it hardest to cope and were in real need of household linen like towels. It appears the Government was attempting to manage the crisis by the re-distribution of coupons. Housewives who had been dutiful at the outset of the war had found that by 1943 'if they had spent the money three years ago they would not now have to surrender coupons to replenish stocks, while people who had then bought heavily [were] 'sitting pretty'.'[143] In July 1943 the Industries and Manufacturer's Department of the Board of Trade were asking Local Authorities to obtain figures for the number of consumers who were buying goods coupon free. They would have to keep a record of all coupon equivalent documents issued and make quarterly returns. It was felt the new system would 'not increase the work of Local Authorities and the standard coupon equivalent declarations [would] greatly simplify the work of traders and the banks.'[144]

Shortages created a high degree of tension between the retailer and consumer with retailers feeling they were on the receiving end of a situation they had no control over. Customers felt that retailers would offer preferential treatment, especially towards the rich. There was widespread discontent over the practice of 'luxury feeding' by those who could afford it – the consumption of goods which were not rationed but could be obtained at extortionate prices. In 1942 a 5s. price limit was placed on restaurant meals due to concern over the effect on morale, but there was no evidence that it had any effect on luxury feeding. One criticism was that people with money could afford to buy quality clothing with the same number of coupons which would last twice as long.[145] A memorandum from the Ministry of Food summed up the situation. 'Rationing is essentially inequitable; it provides the same quantity of an article for each person without any consideration of their needs or habits or of their capacity to secure alternatives.'[146] In her diary entry of 11 June 1942 the Chippenham doctor Joan Hickson was debating the idea of necessity when thinking about new floor boards. 'Necessity is such a relative term... the prudent housewife in me says 'Keep up household replacements while you can, so that there will not be too much to do after the war when stocks will be scarce and expensive for a long time'. I would always go without anything in the house rather than pay a fancy price for it but having found some pre-war stock of Persian rugs at my price and colourings I am afraid I fell for them. With clothes the problem is easier. Having a definite rationing scheme one feels justified in having one's ration, though really there again is no 'necessity' to have anything new while one has a pair of shoes and a skirt that hang together at all. The same is true with food. People grumble and grumble and say they don't know what we are coming to, but scientifically there has been an adequacy of everything except vitamin C, and we must be by far the best fed nation in Europe.'[147]

Women found the cosmetics situation difficult. The output of cosmetics had been restricted, pushing up prices and making them a common commodity on the black market.[148] In some cases they had been disguised as medicines, others offered the unmixed ingredients for women to make up themselves.[149] In Malmesbury, the young factory workers at EKCO's were snapping up cosmetics as soon as they were put on the shelves.[150] Jack Mock notes that in Bradford on Avon some women '... melted down the end of lipsticks and tried beetroot juice as colouring. We even experimented with gravy browning over our legs to resemble stockings, and asked a friend to mark a 'seam' down the back of our legs with an eyebrow pencil. Off we went to the Town Hall dance, thinking we looked in the fashion. It wasn't quite so clever as it rained!'[151] A wartime social survey suggests that two thirds of women applied cosmetics: 'beauty as duty' was seen as necessary to maintain morale. Coping with austerity clothing, women used make-up and hair and coupon free accessories as a way to enhance a limited wardrobe,[152] as Calder notes, 'beneath the neck, fashion was almost impossible.'[153] The fashion editors of magazines focused on accessories such as scarves, and make up such as lipstick and nail varnish. Women would try hard to dress as an individual; customising and altering their attire as much as they could.[154] In 1944 the shortages of cosmetics had become so severe that *Vogue* began appealing to its readers to make the most of diet, exercise and relaxation to keep looking beautiful[155] – presumably it must have been a tall order for the majority to participate in the latter!

The writer Fay Inchfawn, living in Freshford on the Wiltshire/Somerset border noted in 1943: 'For a time we decided to wash and set our own hair just as we did in the days of perms and immaculate coiffures... A neat head really does give one a feeling of satisfaction...'[156] Lingerie had suffered in the war, becoming 'plain and serviceable' with a lack of whalebone for support. Factory workers were among those who suffered the most and the public demanded something should be done. The Corset Guild of Great Britain petitioned Downing Street and succeeded in getting measures introduced to help the industry help those most in need.[157] Gravy browning became a substitute for stockings and hair was tied up due to shortages of shampoo and hair dye.[158] One boy from Swindon remarked that his sister was 'coming to terms with more expensive silk stockings and cosmetics. I did have some sympathy for her as it was natural that she wanted to look her best, especially when there were so many servicemen around the town.'[159] The writer Barbara Cartland felt great sympathy for women in the services who were getting married, as the Government had refused to give them enough coupons to obtain a white dress. Getting married in an ill-fitting uniform would not see them at their best on one of the most special days of their lives. She organised and facilitated a 'wedding dress pool', purchasing over 70 dresses for servicewomen to use for the day and return.[160]

An additional problem, especially for parents, was the lack of toys for sale at Christmas. The importance of Christmas had become even more apparent in uncertain times and alongside presents the tree, decorations and a Christmas dinner were all especially needed, but in short supply. It was an anxious time for housewives who were worried that they would not be able to get enough food, and there was resentment over toy shortages.[161] But it was not just about toys; evacuation caused turmoil too. Sybil Eccles from Chute noted in a letter on Boxing Day 1940 that 'Christmas is nearly over. All about England tomorrow morning countless mothers will be waking with a sigh of relief – and many too, with tears that the stockings are emptied and they were not there to hear their children's cries.'[162] The price and quality of toys were also an issue, and in late November 1943 Zweiniger-Bargielowska notes that there was 'little hope of a turkey, and there [was] much resentment at the alleged 'black market' and unsatisfactory distribution' of Christmas goods.[163] In Swindon one boy remembered his mother talking about the short supply of turkeys. She was 'not unduly concerned for we were unable to afford one anyway.'[164]

By Christmas 1944 parents had no choice but to buy 'two bits of unplaned wood badly stuck together' for the extortionate price of 12s. 6d.[165] As ever, being inventive, DIYing and making the best of it was the course of the day. In Chippenham Joan Hickson reported in her diary entry of 19 December 1943 that 'Ruth and Biz [were] hard at Xmas presents, weaving with odd bits of wool and making shopping bags out of coloured sacking.'[166] With Christmas poultry in short supply many had to make do with a mock turkey or 'murkey' from a recipe given by the Ministry of Food. The murkey was made up of unrationed sausage meat in a stuffing mix shaped to look like a turkey.[167] One Swindon man remembered hearing as a boy in the run up to Christmas 1941 that '[s]ome poultry was hanging in two butcher's shops in Cromwell Street, where little crowds had gathered. 'But the prices they're asking!' [he] heard a lady say. Rabbits, unskinned, seemed plentiful. 'I likes to see 'em running about" said his friend, and he agreed.

A long queue from a temporary stall on the canal path stretched past the chipped and rather sorry looking Golden Lion effigy and down Bridge Street and beyond Keogh's shop. 'Oranges, they've got oranges!' somebody shouted, and we joined the queue. Each customer was allowed two, so we went home with a Christmas luxury for the four of us at home...'[168] Even the act of posting Christmas cards had become more expensive in 1940, with a Hilperton resident noting in her diary that the cost was due to rise from half a penny to one penny.[169] The Christmas of 1940, however, was seen as a 'relative success' and this pattern continued throughout the war, helped along by the work of Lord Woolton, Minister of Food, praised for having done a good job for the Christmas of 1941. The 'Austerity Christmas' appears to have improved by the late 1940s.[170] Lord Woolton had a 'talent for propaganda', enjoying talking to his audiences on his morning *Kitchen Front* broadcasts, promoting nutrition with humour[171] and was immensely popular during the war. One correspondent wrote that 'if ever a man deserved a halo it is Lord Woolton.'[172] He would always personally explain on the radio why each new policy was introduced.[173]

In February 1941 food queues were described by the Ministry of Information as 'a bigger menace to public morale than several serious German air raids.'[174] Queues were thought by Home Intelligence to weaken morale; a hotbed for complaints and talk of acquiescence towards the enemy, and with 'growing anger' amongst working women who did not have time to queue. The Ministry felt that queues were 'an unhealthy symptom, and inconsistent with the underlying principles of rationing.'[175] One WWII joke regarding queuing had a shopkeeper saying to a young lady: 'Excuse me, miss, are you pregnant?' She replies: 'Well, I wasn't when I joined the queue.'[176] Fay Inchfawn living in Freshford on the Somerset/ Wiltshire border noted in 1943 that shopping had become '... a daily task involving long waits and disappointments.'[177]

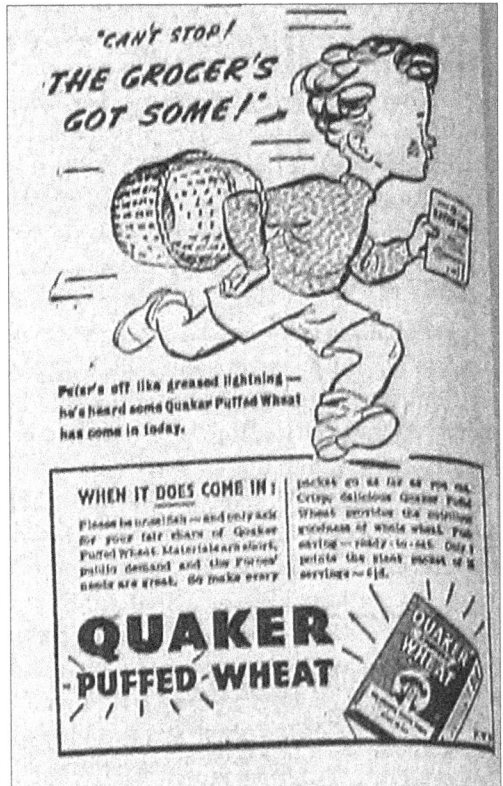

Advert in the Wiltshire Times, 3 June 1944, 'The Grocer's Got Some – when it does come in, buy Quaker Puffed Wheat!' (WSHC Microform Collection)

The Government was worried about the health risks to pregnant women of spending a long time waiting in queues and in September 1945 it established a priority scheme to enable them to go to the front of the queue. The queue itself was regarded as unfair when working women, the elderly and mothers with babies were less able to queue and so missed out on the best cuts of meat or the limited supply of unrationed foodstuffs.[178]

People working in towns such as Swindon would get to know a few of the shop girls and in this way could receive inside information such as when biscuits were going on sale. Coupons were required for biscuits alongside a good position in the queue. Often people would join a queue as soon as it formed, so as not to miss out, but it was common for them not to know exactly what they were queuing for until they reached the front! Shopkeepers who tried to be fair to all were appreciated. A Land Girl based near Cricklade could never get to the shops in time to buy anything at all and had no time to queue due to the long hours she worked. The shopkeeper would often keep her ration back for her at special times such as Christmas to ensure she got her fair share.[179] When shopping, the first food queue to line up in would be for unrationed goods as those were the ones most likely to run out of stock. Edith Olivier reported that all queues moved very slowly, more likely than not in absolute silence.[180] Many people spent the VJ Day public holiday queuing.[181] From Wilton, Edith published *Night Thoughts of a Country Landlady* in 1943, purportedly to be about an elderly neighbour. Whether real or not, the writings give an insight into life in this part of Wiltshire at that time. Edith reported that most queues were for food or for the bus, with the shopping bag being an absolute necessity due to the lack of paper for disposable shopping bags, popular before the war. Edith asserted that now every woman jealously guarded her shopping bag which had started out as a brightly coloured, jazzy affair but was soon reduced to a dusty, shabby looking item. She reported that at the beginning of the war, women would cordially meet and chat when out shopping; later there was none of this, just a rush to get to the shops to be first in an unfriendly queue, beginning with the bus queue. Those living in the villages further out would find it easy to get a seat, but nearer to town it became much, much more difficult. '… at every village on the road a little group is waiting by the post office… At last the bus appears round the corner. Futile umbrellas hail it, though these are obviously unnecessary, as the driver can plainly see the little crowd which now sways uncertainly into to the road. He quickens his pace, and the bus rattles heartlessly by… The tough ones resolve to make the best of it, and to walk. Others give up altogether and walk home; while the remaining few form themselves into a gaggle and gossip in the shelter until the next bus comes, an hour later.'[182] The Traffic Manager for Bristol Tramways Co. Ltd. was writing to the Marlborough Borough Council's Clerk regarding bus queues. 'I have been directed to write to your [*sic*] with reference to the congestion caused in the High Street here by persons waiting for the Swindon 'bus, and the scramble which takes place when the 'bus arrives…'[183]

Swindon's *Herald and Advertiser* was reporting on 1 October 1943 about the 'SOS' for more buses in the Malmesbury area. People living in rural villages nearby who had essential business in the town were being 'stranded.' The other side of the argument was noted; the need to conserve rubber supplies, and there was also the question of conserving fuel. The *Warminster Journal* was reporting on the reduction in train services as early as 29 September 1939 due to the war timetable. Trowbridge High School pupils were delayed for over an hour when their scheduled train for the school run did not run.

The black market inevitably appeared hand in hand with austerity when state control altered the economy and its price control mechanisms. One report appealed that '[h]onesty cannot be universally enforced by regulations. The black market not only in petrol but in any other commodity begins *and must end* with the man in the street…' The black market became a feature of 1940s Britain but less so than in some countries. Non-perishable items and home manufactured goods were notoriously difficult to control and were popular commodities, cosmetics among them.[184] Malpractice using clothing coupons was widespread, especially in the first year of rationing.[185]

Restaurants and hotels were able to exploit illegal opportunities to a high degree before the price limits on meals in 1942, but even this was not an adequate deterrent.[186] Wiltshire newspapers such as the *Salisbury Times*, 25 September 1942, contain many references to prosecutions, such as the Salisbury licensee fined for having butter obtained illegally in his cellar, the Salisbury coalman fined for overcharging and another found to have supplied unregistered customers. There was also the 'disturbing state of affairs' reported in the 20 August 1942 edition of the *Wiltshire Gazette* when local residents and pub landlords in the area around Christian Malford were in receipt of hams, evaporated milk, cheese, tea and sugar, all taken from a camp. The defendants pleaded that they did not know where the goods had come from, one stating that he had met a man in Christian Malford who 'told him he was a buyer and sold to stores at an aerodrome. He gave [the] witness the impression that he had a store of his own in London. The hams were not marked, and were taken from the back of the car. [The] Witness did not know until some time afterwards that [the man] was in the Air Force.' Ten people were charged; two were sentenced to a term of imprisonment and the others received what were described as 'heavy' fines. A Calne butcher was fined for having supplies in excess of his permits[187] and a Hilperton farmer for selling watered down milk.[188] One North Wiltshire farmer recalled that 'World War II started to disrupt everything. Milk, as well as petrol, went on ration, also feeding stuffs for cattle which could only be claimed according to your returns of milk production. I was therefore obliged, much against my will, to refuse my customers more than their ration, although they would have paid anything to get it. My ration of food for the cattle was based on the number of registered customers on my returns so that it would have been impossible to obtain extra cattle food to cover it. Had it not been for this I am sure I would have felt tempted to take the risk in many instances where in my opinion people were getting insufficient milk for their needs.'[189] Another farmer from Warminster did find a way. 'It wasn't too difficult to sell a gallon or two more than our permit allowed for by stating that we had fed milk to calves that we didn't have. I managed to get a 10 gallon churn of milk [from a neighbouring farmer]... I asked him how, being 10 gallons short, he would make it right on his books and he said he'd put down the tractor had accidentally backed into it and knocked it over.'[190] The *Salisbury Times* reported on 31 January 1941 that: 'The three weeks of milk rationing have revealed a difficult problem in Wiltshire... In many parts of the county practically the whole of the domestic milk supply is handled by producer-retailers. During these three weeks nearly all the producer-retailers were short of milk and had to buy from wholesalers in order to supply their non-priority customers with 90% of their requirements... It may be possible at times for producer-retailers who have surpluses to pass them on to neighbouring producer-retailers who require additional supplies to make up the permitted allocations to non-priority clients, but the transfer of supplies in this manner is not that easy. So far the surplus of Wiltshire produce-retailers during a period of milk rationing still constitutes an unsolved problem... During January there will be no milk for butter or cheese manufacture in Wiltshire.' It is interesting to note that on 7 February 1941 the *Salisbury Gazette* was reporting that cheddar cheese was to be produced in Wiltshire the coming summer. 'This industry has been virtually at a standstill for about three months because of the milk supply position, but owing to the high nutritive value of cheese, it has been decided to convert into Cheddar and other hard-pressed land-keeping cheeses during the summer months a large proportion of the milk surplus to liquid requirements... Farmhouse cheese-making in Wiltshire will be resumed, but the major portion of the production will be undertaken in creameries.'

Some people sold eggs unofficially, such as one resident of Cricklade, running the risk of being found out. 'One day his suspicions were aroused when he noticed a woman sitting in her car, and watching his cottage as a WAAF came to their door to buy eggs. He quickly told her to come back later and, sure enough, within a few minutes the stranger was trying to persuade him to sell her some, on the pretext that her mother was ill. Fortunately for him the wily Jack managed to fob her off!' Another resident kept poultry for the Christmas market, taking the shell eggs to Swindon Old Town. 'Unofficial' bartering was common; sugar in exchange for eggs etc. Cars could be stopped and searched, and the lady was asked what she was doing with her eggs. 'They're for my mother-in-law, for hatching.' The eggs did not have the required 'h' for hatching stamp, and she had to appraise her mother-in-law of the situation before the Authorities checked. Farmers who kept poultry were often better off. It was possible for hen keepers to consume quite a number of their own eggs as it was not easy to check how many each hen had laid.[191] Other Wiltshire residents had surprise windfalls. US soldiers were being housed in the estate yard buildings at a farm near Tottenham House when one day their cookhouse caught fire. The damaged food was meant to be destroyed, but one local managed to salvage some. 'We had whole round cheeses, dried fruit in sacks and lots of canned items. Most of the cans had their labels burnt off so it was always a surprise to find out what was inside. One tin may contain custard whilst another was full of baked beans – once a can was opened you had to eat its contents!'[192]

In 1945 the Police were called in to investigate a case of misappropriated items of rationed goods at a Land Army Hostel near Marlborough. Statements were taken from some of the girls to the effect that they had not been receiving their full ration since at least 1944. They finally complained to the Warden who ran the hostel and had since been given their ration of sugar, tea and jam, but not cheese and meat. After talking to another lady who worked at the hostel they had become suspicious and alerted the Police. Items including sugar, 'various brands of tea and a tin containing a quantity of soap flakes' along with pure honey, golden syrup, jam and a tin of corned beef had been found in the Warden's room and an office drawer. It also became clear after inspecting the contents of the Hostel's larder that the Warden had been falsifying her stock sheets; larger quantities of tea had been found than had been entered on the sheets. The testimony of a Land Girl also supported the findings. '… I have never seen a calf's head, ox heart or anything like the amount of tongue shewn on the Stock sheets.' The Police felt it 'quite likely' that the Warden had misappropriated items, but felt 'the information given by the girls is based largely on suspicion.' It was deemed that the matter would be best dealt with by the Wiltshire War Agricultural Executive Committee.[193]

Farmers were able to manipulate the system; most could get a limited petrol allowance for their car, to be used for farm purposes only. One Minety farmer used his car when visiting friends, making sure the trailer with the calf or pig came too, just in case he got pulled over by the police.[194] The *Wiltshire Times* was reporting on 8 July 1944 that a man from Trowbridge had been fined £10 for wrongful use of petrol. He had given a false statement to his employer for the purpose of obtaining petrol for travelling to work. Others took a different view. One Cricklade resident recalls: 'For private use we were only allowed sufficient petrol for one trip to Cirencester per week for shopping, and if the police stopped our car anywhere else we could be fined. With such limited use many felt that a car was not worth the tax and insurance, and decided to jack them up off their tyres for the duration of the war.'[195] Others were also having difficulty. The Chippenham doctor Joan Hickson wrote in her diary in May 1942 of the terrible trouble the local nurse was having obtaining petrol. 'They have been cutting her down and down and she has now run out, and the fool clerks at County Offices talk glibly about using a bicycle. Little do they realise what 24 hrs a day duty means year after year, when they arrive at 9.30am (or later) and take at least an hour's break for lunch, and shut up shop at 5pm. Nurse England does about three people's work on the district and is one of the few remaining fanatical people with a mission, no other aim or object in life than to do her work well. She never stops and is nearly at breaking point as it is. She is damned well going to get as much petrol as she wants if we have to write to *The Times* or our MP about it. There will be a public stink made by us about people getting it for church or shopping if difficulties are made about hers.'[196] Once petrol had been rationed the bicycle shops in Bradford on Avon saw an increase in trade for both sales and repairs.[197] Cycling as a sport appears to have gained in popularity during the 1940s too. An obsession with 'massed start cycle races' led to problems on the roads. A letter was sent to Wiltshire's Chief Constable's Office from the Home Office in August 1943, saying that the Secretary of State had 'under consideration, in consultation with the Minister of Transport, the subject of massed start cycle races on highways, which have taken place in a limited number of areas, but have recently, he understands, tended to become more numerous and widespread.' It further noted that the 'competitors ride in groups or pass and re-pass one another throughout the whole course of the race' which was 'likely not only to cause obstruction to traffic, but to be a source of danger both to the public and to the racers.' It was also considered a 'waste of police time'. It goes on, rather sneeringly: 'this type of racing has been discountenanced by leading cycling bodies, and for some years no pedal cycle races of any importance had, until recently, been run on the highways from a massed start' though it notes that the practice was increasing and asked Chief Officers of the Police to discourage the events and warn competitors they might be liable to prosecution for causing nuisance, obstruction and disorder. 'No facilities for this event can be given by the police.'[198]

On 27 November 1942 Calne Borough Council received a letter from the Ministry of Fuel and Power. 'I am directed by the Minister of Fuel and Power to state that, in view of the increasing operational needs of the armed forces of the United Nations [*sic*], the Government has decided upon a far-reaching and dramatic scheme of petrol economies, in which it is necessary for Local Authorities to play their part.'[199]

It was not hard to see why a large number of retailers worked the black market. The rationing system was based on the registration of consumers with a retailer but it was hard to keep track of registrations which were constantly changing. Retailers were often left with unclaimed rations, available to 'favoured customers'. Practices to gain favour included tipping. The lack of proper auditing meant that it was possible to play the black market with ease and explain discrepancies away. Retailers felt their situation was difficult, having to pay over the odds for produce from wholesalers. The wholesalers blamed the retailers and both accused the Ministry of Food who, they claimed, 'failed to attack the 'real racketeers''. There was also theft in transit; claims on the railway companies were fifteen to twenty times greater than before the war.[200]

Travellers, who had originally been able to hold a Traveller's Ration Book, had been able to move around the country without making contact with the National Registration or Food Rationing system and therefore the Ministry was unable to trace their movements. In 1941, to rectify the situation, the ration books were withdrawn and instead coupons were provided for four week's rations; a new application would have to be made each month.[201] By 1944 a list of the serial numbers of Identity Cards stolen since 1942 was held at the National Registration Enforcement Branch at Somerset House. The cards of deceased persons and those who had joined the Armed Forces should have been collected and forwarded to the Central National Registration Office to stop fraudulent use taking place. It was also noted in the confidential booklet issued to the Police *National Registration Identity Cards* that forms and official stamps had been stolen from National Registration Food Offices; the serial numbers of most had been registered at the Criminal Record Office. Further safeguards had been adopted against forgery:

(a) The title page is engraved, and not capable of being reproduced typographically.

The overprint on the title page makes photographic reproduction a difficult and expert task.

The overprint on the inner portion will show up mechanical erasures (by knife or eraser).

The colour is liable to run if a chemical eraser is used.

The material, which contains silk fibre, is not reproducible by forgery without expert manufacture of paper.

Each card contains a stock control number.[202]

Joan Hickson reported in her diary in January 1943 the story of a friend who had called her to say that she'd lost her bag (it was subsequently discovered to have been stolen). She was 'nearly frantic' as it held all her family's cards and coupons: identity, food, sweets, clothing, hen food. She would have to apply to many different authorities for replacement, each asking her to produce one of the others as proof of identity. She wasn't hopeful about getting any clothing coupons replaced.[203]

The tea rationing system, put into place in July 1940 to sustain morale, was being abused. Retailers were either selling it 'off ration' or overstating their sale figures to get inflated permits. By February 1942, between one and eight million excess tea rations were being released, reducing supplies significantly. The Government acted by introducing a coupon replacement scheme and the result was 'remarkable'. It was noted in September 1940 that the most common foodstuff to be the cause of rationing rule evasion was meat with customers being sold condemned meat, illegally slaughtered meat and other malpractices conducted by those in the meat industry. An auctioneer felt by 1947 that these now 'commonplace practices' were the result of the Government not policing or enforcing policy. Previously honest people felt there was no harm in what they were doing; they were 'being turned from decent honest citizens into dishonest people" with the result that it would make it harder for those who remained honest to make a living outside the black market. 'Butchers who did not buy black market rabbits or meat were losing customers.'[204]

The means of acquiring illicit food were 'many and varied' in the country, and bartering and exchange were often conducted between those home producers who had little access to money. To combat the black market in eggs the Government subsidised retail egg prices in June 1941 but some farmers retained their eggs; the black market remained a more effective way of making money.[205]

The Ministry of Food attempted to keep the black market under control with its enforcement organisation. Its main priority was towards the prevention of food crime by putting pressure on retailers and consumers with regular inspections, and to hunt out large-scale black marketeering. The nineteen Regions oversaw enforcement work in their area, working in close co-operation with the Police. The Food Control Committees worked with Local Authorities on minor offences committed by retailers and consumers, but this system proved inadequate at preventing large-scale crime. A Central Intelligence Bureau was established in 1942, its job to act as a 'clearing house' for information, its aim to cut off supply lines.[206] Warminster's Food Control Committee contained members who represented 'every food business in the town'. Bert Dawkins felt that they dealt with consumer complaints such as traders selling rationed goods unfairly.[207]

Ina Zweiniger-Bargielowska feels that the black market functioned as a 'safety valve' as there were limits to the amount of self-sacrifice an individual could undertake, and many people resorted to using it. However, those on low incomes were least able to reap the benefits, restricted by the inflated prices.[208]

The black market became even more extensive in the post-war period. Labour's policies were not sufficient to stop large-scale skirting of the control orders and any measure of wartime patriotism had long since disappeared.[209] The Minister of Food became concerned in May 1946 that food orders were 'generally being ignored and evaded more flagrantly now than at any time during the war' and that a significant number of the agricultural community continually ignored the Food Orders, feeling they were red tape to work around to their best advantage, but to the disadvantage of their community as a whole.[210] As a result enforcement staffing doubled, peaking in 1948. The number of prosecutions remained high throughout the wartime period and beyond, peaking in 1947-8. From 1950 prosecutions began a steep decline.[211]

There were also wartime difficulties in obtaining fuel for homes and schools. At the end of October 1940 the Director of Education in Swindon was urging all Head Teachers to 'avoid waste of heat by securing a maximum efficiency from the heating apparatus… The demand for fuel for industries engaged on war production has increased at a time when the output of coal has been reduced owing to the shortage of man-power at the pits, and supplies to non-industrial users, including schools, have been restricted, in order that the vital war industries may not go short. In other words, the Education Committee have precisely the same difficulties to face, but in an accentuated form, as the private householder.'[212] Coal was on Peggy Pickford's mind when she was writing from Warminster to her sister Elizabeth Martin in Australia on 28 November 1940. 'Coal is rather scarce and we are being allowed one cwt. a fortnight. Again we are lucky to live on a farm. We just go out and pick up as much wood as we want; we need never shiver for want of a fire. So far, we have been able to get paraffin alright, but it is not very good stuff. It makes the lamp glasses sticky and does not give so much heat. I wonder if the censor minds me saying all this. I am not grumbling, but just trying to tell you what it is like.'[213] The Chancellor had promised in the 1941 budget that essential services such as coal, gas and electricity would be stabilised, by subsidy if necessary. The Rent and Mortgage Interest Restrictions Act of 1939 had the effect of freezing rents at their 1939 level for all properties below a certain rateable value.[214] It was stated in a letter from the Mines Department to Calne's Town Clerk, 17 October 1941, that '[i]t is proposed to issue a new revised Schedule at an early date, together with a Coal Classification Schedule which will show the actual types of coal sold under each grade in the Schedule. It will then be necessary for the Enforcement Officers to carry out inspections in order to protect the consumer against the substitution of coals.' In December 1941 the Fuel Overseer reported to the Council Fuel Sub-Committee that the necessary restrictions on coal supplies for domestic consumers had taken place. 'In order to assist the flow of coal during the continuance of the present spell of weather; to expedite the clearance of wagons standing under load, and to permit the larger residential premises to acquire greater stocks of coal than has been possible under existing restrictions with a view to relieving the burden on transport later in the winter, it is proposed as a temporary measure further to relax the restrictions where conditions are favourable. This applies also to the small consumer, who may receive coal over and above the basic quantity.'[215]

Ministry of Fuel and Power advertisement in the Wiltshire Gazette, 18 February 1943 'Stop! The forces need that extra lump' (WSHC Microform Collection)

In July 1942 Calne Borough Council received a letter from the Electricity Commission stating that fuel rationing would not be happening as yet, but that a scheme would be put into place if it was felt necessary.[216] By September 1942 Chippenham's Joan Hickson was writing about the 'mad' publicity campaign for voluntary fuel rationing, 'which will mean that the conscientious will save till they are ill and the people with no social conscience won't take any notice. I am afraid we are rather the latter. Though quite prepared not to be wasteful and leave things on in unused rooms, we are not prepared to shiver unless everybody else definitely has to as well!'[217] By January 1943 Fuel Watchers were being appointed at a local level as the Ministry of Fuel and Power were contesting that: 'Experience has shown that the best results in fuel saving are achieved when the duties of checking consumption are placed on one person.'[218] Even food manufacturers were using fuel shortages to advertise their wares. An advert for Welgar Shredded Wheat in the *Wiltshire Times*, 15 July 1944, stated that '... it's easy to cut fuel and shopping bills – and time in the kitchen – whilst serving most nutritious breakfasts... The economical food that NEEDS NO COOKING.'

Some schools were running short of coal, such as Ashton Keynes School in February 1941 when its coal supply had been exhausted and there were no new supplies to be had. The school had to close – it got a new supply a week later. By March 1941 the school had been without coal yet again for one week. The School Manager kindly donated some.[219] At Ivy Lane School in Chippenham the staff were advised in September 1941 to use half their ordinary amount of fuel in the staff room as no further supplies would be available. Temperature charts were distributed amongst the staff the following month. By November there were no fires and the temperature had fallen to 52 degrees Fahrenheit. The School Medical Officer would have no option but to close the school if the temperature did not improve. The Vicar was doing everything he could to help but there was no coal to be found. The hall temperature reached 48 degrees Fahrenheit and the children were dismissed. In March 1942 the school was again having difficulty obtaining coke and firewood.[220] In Bemerton, one resident

Advert in the Salisbury Times, 21 February 1941 Coal Advert in the Salisbury Journal, 21 February 1941 'Coal Supplies: How You Can Help', issued by the Mines Department (WSHC Microform Collection)

recalled: 'Because coal was rationed a small fire would be lit generally about tea time, but in the very cold winters the small amount of coal stored would go very low, so my brothers and I would walk to the gas works taking a cycle and a sack with us, then we put the sack of coal on the cycle and pushed it home. Later we made a barrow using pram wheels and a large box and we would get the coke in that. The coke was mixed with a small quantity of coal. The only big fire we had was on Christmas Day.'[221]

Rationing also affected other utilities, albeit voluntarily. The Chairman of the Waterworks and Fire Brigade Committee at Swindon Borough Council was making a statement over water supplies in 1944.

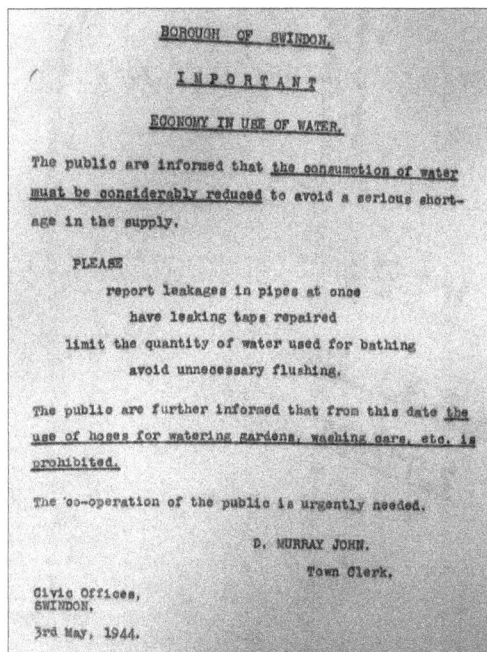

BOROUGH OF SWINDON.

I M P O R T A N T

ECONOMY IN USE OF WATER.

The public are informed that the consumption of water must be considerably reduced to avoid a serious shortage in the supply.

PLEASE
report leakages in pipes at once
have leaking taps repaired
limit the quantity of water used for bathing
avoid unnecessary flushing.

The public are further informed that from this date the use of hoses for watering gardens, washing cars, etc. is prohibited.

The co-operation of the public is urgently needed.

D. MURRAY JOHN.
Town Clerk.

Civic Offices,
SWINDON,
3rd May, 1944.

Notice to the people of Swindon from the Town Clerk, May 1944 'Economy in use of water' (WSA G24/225/12)

It is a matter of considerable regret to my Committee that they are forced to bring forward to the Council such a minute as this and to appeal to the public to make every effort to reduce the amount of water consumed in premises by our undertaking... circumstances which could never have been foreseen and are entirely outside the control of the Council have been responsible for the present situation... I desire first to emphasize that Swindon is not alone in facing a serious water situation. Not only towns in this part of the country, but almost every undertaking in the south of England is concerned with a similar position. So widespread is the threat and so serious that the Ministry of Health have addressed to all Local Authorities a circular letter stressing the need for an immediate curtailment of consumption and informing undertakings that emergency powers will be available to take extraordinary steps to meet the needs... Particularly in the class of bulk supplies has the increase, by reason of the present war, jumped to an extraordinary extent. In 1944 we are supplying forty times as much water in bulk supplies as we did in 1940... A great part of the answer to our present dilemma can, however, be found by the general public adopting a rigid system of self rationing at once.

Rainfall in 1943 had been six inches below average and in the first three months of 1944, only one third as much rain had fallen as for the same period in 1943, which itself was below average.[222]

Dig for Victory

ONE WAY THAT civilians could legally supplement their diet and help the war effort was by Digging for Victory!

> *Dig! Dig! Dig! And your muscles will grow big*
> *Keep on pushing the spade!*
> *Don't mind the worms*
> *Just ignore the squirms*
> *And when your back aches laugh with glee*
> *And keep on diggin'*
> *Till we five our toes a wiggin'*
> *Dig! Dig! Dig! To Victory*
> (Dig for Victory Song)[223]

The Defence of the Realm Acts in 1916 and 1920 paved the way for the Government to acquire land for use as allotments[224] and WWI had seen a rapid increase in gardening to increase the home production of food. The Board of Agriculture gave the go ahead to increase the number of allotments with Local Authorities gaining the power to take over land if required. Trowbridge residents were often new to gardening but they acquired gardening tools and 'worked hard'. A depot was also opened in Trowbridge in order to send fresh fruit and vegetables to the Navy at the Harwich Naval Base.[225] It was suggested by the early 1930s that allotments could be used to alleviate a 'hunger crisis' and stop social unrest by 'mitigating some of the worse [*sic*] consequences of unemployment'. The Allotments for the Unemployed Scheme had already been run by the Society of Friends since 1926. It was to become the best of a number of schemes set up to aid the unemployed and by 1932, 61,299 had been helped.[226]

During WWII the Government emphasised that food supplies would be increasingly important with Lord Woolton declaring it a 'food war'.[227] Civilians were inundated by a huge propaganda offensive; 10 million instructional leaflets being distributed in 1942 alone. The Dig for Victory Campaign resulted in a huge expansion of allotments, from 815,000 in 1939 to 1,400,000 in 1943[228] with the number of private gardens growing vegetables rising from three to five million.[229] A survey of manual workers showed that over half kept an allotment or garden in WWII.[230] W. T. Price, Wilshire's Chief Executive Officer, stated in 1939 that under the *Cultivation of Lands (Allotments) Order* 1939, County, Borough, Municipal and Urban authorities were empowered to take possession of unoccupied land (unused land which was not contributing to the rates) for food production. If no such land was available the authority could take possession of other land. In

Wiltshire, these powers were to be exercised by the War Agricultural Executive Committee, to be approached by Parish Councils in cases of difficulty, but the process does not appear to have been straightforward.[231]

Bradford on Avon Council had been requested by the Ministry of Agriculture and Fisheries in September 1939 to look at the question of allotments in their district 'with a view to ascertaining whether any further provision of allotments is necessary to augment Food Supplies in time of War.' By 30 September 1939 the Honourable Secretary of the Bradford on Avon District of the Gardeners' Mutual Improvement Society had been approached by Major Fuller who was hoping that local Gardening Societies would help the Area Committee to further the allotment scheme. The Society was prepared to assist in any way possible.[232] By October 1939 the National Allotments Society Ltd. were writing to the County's War Agricultural Executive Committee (CWAEC) and Local Authorities, keen to get in on the act and put forward their case:

> As is well known, the Government are anxious to increase the quantity of home-grown food, and so far as is possible to produce it under conditions that will relieve the transport of the country, thus involving the fullest possible use being made of allotments by the utilisation of much of the unoccupied land at present available.
>
> It will be remembered that, during the last war, and especially during the years 1917-18, this form of intensive cultivation added materially to the food supply of the nation – it is also common knowledge that, but for the help which Germany received by this means, she would have collapsed internally at least twelve months earlier than was the case.
>
> It seems to us that War Agricultural Committees will have their hands full in carrying out the Government's programme for ploughing out grass-land and large scale production, and that they and the various Local Authorities may be glad of the co-operation of organisations which have experience in dealing with allotment holders and other

Leaflet to apply for a 10-Rod allotment (WSA G13/132/61)

small producers.

> The National Allotments Society, Ltd. has in membership over 2,000 associations, with upwards of 200,000 members and is able to give material help in propaganda and organisation…[233]

In December 1940 they were writing to Calne's Town Clerk, stating that they 'would be pleased to co-operate with your Authority in any way possible. We shall be pleased to hear of any steps which your Authority may have taken to stimulate the demand for allotments; the methods employed and the measure of success achieved' regarding the Dig for Victory campaign of 1940/41.[234]

The Parish Council of All Cannings was having trouble finding allotment land. They had approached the vicar in November 1939 who had noted that 'in the past the demand for land had been very poor and consequently some of these allotments had become derelict… this Council had a certain amount of allotment land in the Parish which had originally been used for building purposes' but there had been no demand for the land and it had been let to just one person. Wiltshire's CWAEC reviewed the case and reported that a parish could make enquires regarding land and then 'consider the matter in light of local evidence, and decide whether or not it should require the land, under the powers that have been delegated to it, by the Ministry of Agriculture.' It was the Parish Councils who initiated enquiries and formed an opinion, related to local circumstances and according to need, indicated by the number of applicants.[235] In November 1939 the Wiltshire Federation of Women's Institutes was gearing up, arranging the co-operative buying of vegetable seeds for their members, but supplies were limited. By 1940 they were arranging potato growing competitions.[236]

In the village of Minety, like many, one family 'dug up about half an acre of land and turned it into a garden, this was extra to the large garden that we already had. This new garden was called 'Victory Garden'.' But it had been 'an overambitious venture, because it was never fully planted and the fruit trees that were planted only came into production after the war.'[237] The Chief Executive Officer of Calne Borough Council was reporting problems with allotments to the Divisional Food Officer in October 1940. The Town Council were 'doing their utmost to encourage the production of food-stuffs by allotment holders. They are experiencing, however, a good deal of trespass in the allotments and also pilfering.' They were hoping to obtain some barbed wire fence to erect around the allotments but had been unable to find any.[238] By June 1942 Swindon's Town Clerk was wondering if allotment claims for bomb damage were the same as those for bomb craters in agricultural fields. The answer from the Ministry of Agriculture and Fisheries was an affirmative.[239]

Robert MacKay calls the working of allotments during wartime a burden rather than a hobby 'on top of the long and arduous week already worked'.[240] The problems of wartime gardeners were many, especially finding time for weeding and controlling pests. Children were often put to task picking caterpillars off plants. If weeds got out of control enough to endanger the next door neighbour's

THE COLORADO BEETLE.

BEETLE

GRUB

EGGS

A DANGEROUS FOREIGN POTATO PEST.

If you find insects resembling those shown above, please send specimens at once to the Ministry of Agriculture, 10, Whitehall Place, London, S.W.I.

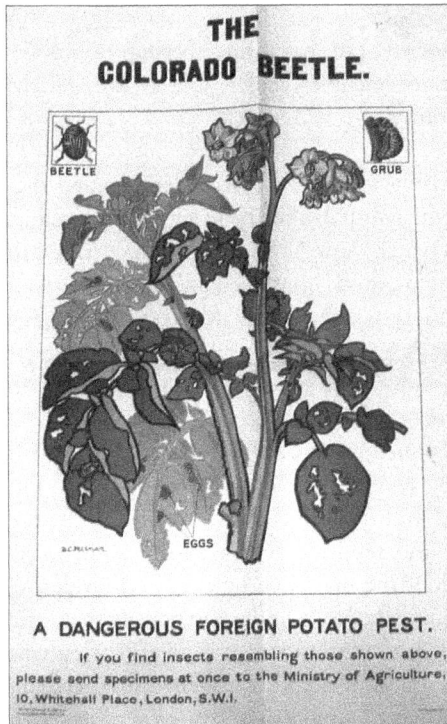

Posters announced that there were foreign invaders to look out for, such as the Colorado Beetle. Landford and Hampworth Women's Institute archive (WSA 1815/39)

crops a fine could be charged.[241] Some Wiltshire children were tasked with catching white butterflies as they could do quite a lot of damage. 'We were armed with old tennis racquets and allowed to go all over the gardens and grounds...' They were paid after their catch had been counted out. At the beginning of the season they were paid a halfpenny each, reducing to sixpence per hundred at the height of the season.[242] The June 1945 edition of Ministry of Agriculture's *Allotment and Garden Guide* was asking 'Are you watching out for the Pests?,' giving helpful advice about black fly.[243]

On 1 October 1941 the Ministry of Agriculture and Fisheries was writing to Local Authorities, informing them that the Dig for Victory campaign had been launched on 29 September. The objective was to attain the 'maximum possible addition to the number of allotments provided and cultivated', and to increase the production of 'essential vegetables in private gardens.' It was also stipulated that the Minister felt that a special appeal should be made to women and older children to 'assist or relieve the men in producing vegetables from allotments or gardens. It has been reported to Mr Hudson that one progressive authority has already set aside 300 five-rod plots for cultivation by women.' It was made clear that if possible, allotment land intended for women and children should be 'broken up' before it was handed over.[244] The Minister of Agriculture Robert Hudson gave a broadcast talk at the launch of the 1941/2 Dig for Victory Campaign on 29 September 1941:

This time last year I asked you to increase wartime allotments to the half-million. You got nearly 600,000. I urged that vegetables should replace flowers in gardens. That has largely been done. On the whole a splendid bit of work. The first thing, therefore, I want to say to-day is 'Thank You'.

But we can't afford to rest on our spades. Our farmers and land workers are going all out to provide things like milk, meat, bread, porridge, potatoes. That's not enough. We all need fresh vegetables, especially children. They must get them. I want you to look on yourself and your garden as a production unit on active service…

There are lots of fine <u>women</u> gardeners. Gardening is a job women can do well. It's not easy - but it's healthy. It's better anyhow than standing in queues.

I realise the call Civil Defence is making on men outside their ordinary working hours. So if your menfolk can no longer spare the time, will you lend us a hand? And your older children too…

Finally a word to employers. I know you're having a hard life these days, but I want your help urgently. Get your people digging for victory. If you've land round your works, help your workers grow vegetables on it – for their homes or your canteens. Put a keen man in charge. Let him arrange competitions and offer prizes. Set him a good production quota.

Make no mistake. Home-grown food supplies, and this is where every garden and every allotment counts, are <u>still</u> as vital as ever in our war effort. Our future depends as much on food as on tanks and planes and ships.[245]

The Minister of Agriculture's speech at the 1943 launching ceremony was again used as a call to women and older children. 'Women and the older children especially must roll up their jumper sleeves and play a full part. I know all the other things women have to do to-day… I ask British women to grow food because it means the well being of their children. Fresh food for the family will be vitally important next winter…'[246] It seems that the Ministry of Agriculture and Fisheries considered women every bit as capable as men to be in charge of an allotment, but those in the Ministry of Information envisioned a different story when it came to propaganda. WWII propaganda assumed that a man would be in charge of the garden. Women might 'dabble' and by doing so damage important plants.

Poster showing men taking a lead role in gardening, both during the wartime 'Dig for Victory' Campaign and in the post-war 'Dig for Plenty' campaign (WSA G13/132/61)

Women and children could help, but the expertise was meant to come from the men.[247]

By April 1940 the Ministry of Agriculture and Fisheries was sending a circular letter to Local Authorities praising the 'valuable work' which they had been undertaking. 'It is important, however, that Local Authorities should continue to make every effort to encourage their residents to redouble their efforts in this respect, and that these efforts should be made at once in the short time that still remains before the season is too far advanced... Where the lack of suitable unoccupied land has tended to limit action by your Council under the Cultivation of Land (Allotments) Order, 1939, in providing war time allotments for which there is an outstanding demand, I am to say that the Minister will be prepared to consider applications by your Council for his consent to take possession of occupied land...' By 1 July 1940 the National Allotments Society Ltd. was calling for a 'supreme effort,' but also noted that problems would arise if cultivators grew more produce than they could use themselves. A committee had been set up at the Ministry of Food to deal with the issue and the Society had been asked with the National Council of Social Service to work with the Women's Institute and Rural Community Councils to adopt a scheme in rural areas. The scheme involved setting up Produce Committees or Sub-Committees of existing committees to work with the above groups and representatives of the wholesale and retail fruit and vegetable trade to 'conduct propaganda' and deal with policy questions. It was also intended to market less perishable surplus products such as carrots, onions, turnips and parsnips via an official wholesale agent. It was advised that the more perishable green items should be offered as gifts to hospitals, school feeding centres, works canteens etc.[248] A further Ministry of Agriculture and Fisheries circular to Local Authorities on 8 July 1940 stated that even more needed to be done to 'substantially increase' the number of allotments, suggesting land on sports or recreation grounds if no other was available. Bradford on Avon appears to have been struggling to find space for allotments by January 1941 when a letter sent by the Ministry entitled *1940/41 Dig for Victory Campaign* relayed the message that during the first year of the war the Council had not stepped up to the mark by using its powers under the new Order... 'the returns made by your Council showing the number of applications... and the extent to which your Council found it necessary to exercise the powers conferred upon them... to provide land for such allotments, does not appear to reflect the actual potentialities of the situation in your Council's district, neither do the results secured compare favourably with those obtained in the same period in their local Government areas in the County.'[250]

Included in a Government circular of 8 April 1941 was a schedule of approved crops: Farm Crops – wheat, barley, oats, rye, mangolds, sugar beet, beans for fodder, peas for fodder, potatoes, turnips and swedes for cattle feeding, vetches; Market Garden Crops – carrots, haricot beans, gherkins, onions, red cabbage for pickling; Crops for Seed – any farm or vegetable crop for seed purposes for which a definite contract could be made.[251]

By the end of September 1943 the Wiltshire War Agricultural Executive

Committee was drawing the attention of the county's Local Authorities to the fact that food supplies would not increase and could even decrease in the future, including in the immediate aftermath of the war, and 'every effort is being made to assist those who are producing food for their own consumption.' The Committee was prepared to give assistance via lectures and talks, demonstration allotments and advice on gardening problems. The list of lectures was extensive; from glasshouse crops to fruit preservation in a multitude of forms; to manure, compost making, the management of a vegetable garden, the value of many types of crop; diseases and their control; the planning and planting of an orchard, pruning and cultivation of soft fruit. Wiltshire's CWAEC must have been on the ball. The 1944 Dig for Victory Campaign encouraged the 'intensification of publicity and educational measures' by Local Authorities with the aim of ensuring that efforts were not being relaxed; to provide advice and assurance to improve the fertility of soil with compost and to better cultivate and crop; to tackle pests. 'The Minister feels very strongly that a much better advisory service can be organised by some authorities for the benefit of their allotment holders and private gardeners.' There was also a statement at the Hot Springs Conference in the USA regarding the world shortage of food after the war. Home production would remain a necessity for some time to come. A further issue arose with the admission that the lack of water supply was 'tending to discourage some allotment holders and that authorities are being urged to remedy the lack. Materials are short, particularly galvanised piping, and labour scarce; in general therefore, water supply schemes should not be undertaken unless the lack will result in the land going out of cultivation.'[252]

The *Wiltshire Times* reported in its 14 April 1944 edition that gardeners were busy over the Easter weekend when '… thousands of potatoes and hundreds of packets of seeds were planted by those who had their ground already in trim, while others took the opportunity of making up for lost time by 'digging for victory' in real earnest, so that the appearance of many allotments and back-gardens was transformed.' Plots sprang up in front and back gardens, but any and every possible site was utilised including roadside verges, railway cuttings, public parks and school playing fields.[253] Devizes schoolboys were taught gardening to help on the allotments.[254] As early as 21 September 1939 the *Wiltshire Times* reported that London schoolboys were working to clear a Trowbridge slum site so that it could be used to grow food. In Chippenham, the County Horticultural Adviser visited Ivy Lane School in November 1940 to discuss the school's gardening groups for the coming years and by May 1941 permission was given to use the school premises as a cultivation school for the Service of Youth on Thursday evenings.[255] At Compton Bassett School they were receiving seed potatoes for the school garden in April 1942.[256] At one Salisbury school the children planted potatoes, cabbages and sprouts in plots between the air raid shelters[257] and at Stapleford they grew vegetables for school dinners.[258] The children had varying degrees of interest and success. Pupils at the school in Cricklade were given a plot of land to garden. 'The boys considered the whole activity a skive … and the girls were no better… We girls did our gardening right down at the bottom, and were given a patch each. I used to rake mine over and make it look nice and tidy, with all the cabbage plants above and the buttercups coming through beneath, so nothing I grew came to anything much!'[259] Schools in Swindon were visited as part of the Food Production in Schools Scheme. It was noted in 1940 that most of the 'ventures' were successful. The report for Sanford Street Boys noted, 'Very successful season. Dry summer affected some of the crops (beans, onions etc). Land requires liming this winter. Great credit to the boys in classes 1 & 2 & to teachers in planning and supervising. Hard work on difficult land'. The children at Westcott Mixed School were not quite so successful, with their King Edward potatoes not well suited for the soil. The report also noted: "Green-stuff' affected by summer pests. Spring cabbage partially destroyed by rabbits... Results very satisfactory considering very rough nature of ground at commencement of year – boys very enthusiastic.'[260] Children who had grown food as part of the wartime curriculum would often continue to do so much later in life; the Dig for Victory campaign influencing and encouraging them, a 'legacy that has stayed with them' throughout their lives.[261]

By April 1944 the Chippenham doctor Joan Hickson was remarking in her diary... 'An article in the paper today says there is a shortage of flower seeds and a large demand for plants, which are soaring to greatly inflated prices. Apparently after five years of war and little to buy in the shops, and few outings or amusements we feel we must have flowers and are prepared to pay for them.'[262]

The countryside itself was a resource. Ninety percent of plants used in medicinal drugs had been imported before the war and stocks had to be maintained. The National Herb Committees with help from the Women's Institute trained pickers in plant recognition and sent them out with children to gather herbs. Around 20 plant species were collected across the country with rose hips being used when the supply of orange juice ran short.[263] The Wiltshire Federation of Women's Institutes (WI) was providing gathering instructions. They should be 'red, firm, but not too soft.' They were not to be gathered in the rain as, if wet, the fruit would go off quickly, and only the fruit should be gathered; no stems or leaves. They had to be packed in dry sacks or cardboard containers that could withstand knocking in transit, and be despatched by train to a company in Basingstoke. The WI advised that '[r]ose hips are rich in the vitamins which keep us healthy and the Ministry of Health are asking for volunteers to harvest the rich crop in the hedge-rows. The campaign will open with a National Rose-hip week... and all are asked to help.' 'Do not delay in dispatching. The rose-hips will keep a day or so, but the fresher they get to the factory the more vitamin they will contain.'[264] The Broughton Gifford WI reported in October 1942 that they had sent 52 lbs of rose hips to the depot at Trowbridge. By 1943 the figure had risen to 70 lbs.[265] But herbs could also improve a bland austerity diet. The Ministry of Agriculture's *Allotment and Garden Guide* was looking at herbs in its December 1945 edition, suggesting that 'when planning your garden or allotment next year, bear herbs in mind. If you already have one or two kinds, try some of the less common, to give variety of flavour to your vegetables.' Included were some drawings of herbs with information on how to grow them.[266] Making wartime food more interesting could mean trying something altogether different... In May 1942 Joan Hickson '[m]ade some delectable cream of spinach soup, an egg cheese and rice thing for supper, a pie with the remains of mince and all the left-over vegetables for tomorrow's lunch, and a bean roast for Sunday night. Lucy actually enjoyed my supper, thought it was 'lovely'. Mrs Gillard is very conservative and refuses to taste anything new... I was tasting something and said 'Well it's all right, but not what I would call exciting,' and she looked at me very seriously and said 'Now I wonder what you mean exactly by exciting?' The idea that food could be interesting or exciting had simply never occurred to her.'[267] The Broughton Gifford WI had also been busy collecting parsley in 1943, sending 1lb of it and 'other herbs' to the Prisoners of War Depot.[268] The *Wiltshire Times* was reporting on 5 August 1944 that the Attendance Sub-Committee had been considering a communication from the Honourable Secretary of the Wiltshire Herbs Committee. He had suggested a

FOR OFFICE USE ONLY.		4488		1943
D/NO	Date		**CARRIERS RECEIPT**	

HORSE CHESTNUT COLLECTION
(Without Outer Green Husks)

Received from :—

Name ....

Address ....

....

Sacks of HORSE CHESTNUTS. Gross Weight .... cwts .... qrs .... lbs

Date .... Carriers Signature ....

IMPORTANT :—It is essential that this carriers receipt should be completed and posted to :—
MACLEANS Ltd., Great West Road, Brentford, Middx.

CONSIGNMENT NOTE

Date .... 194....

.... **Railway** .... **Station**

Please receive and forward the undermentioned goods at Company's risk
Carriage payable by consignee through London Ledger A/c.

SENDER	CONSIGNEE	No. of Sacks	DESCRIPTION	WEIGHT		
				Cwts.	Qrs.	Lbs
	MACLEANS LTD., Gt. West Road, Brentford, Middx.		Horse Chestnuts (Class 8)			

Carrier's receipt for horse chestnuts, 1943, Wiltshire County Council Education Department files (WSA F8/600/11/1/17/2)

two day school closure 'to enable the teachers to organise parties of school children to gather rose hips.' In reply it was stated that the teachers had 'so much work thrown on them, apart from the actual teaching, that they did not think they could ask them to organise these collections.' They recognised the value of the rose hips, and hoped that it could be organised in a voluntary capacity instead. Some communities had great expertise at herbing. Sutton Benger was one such example, with some villagers having begun herbing as a supplementary income during and after the First World War. Herbs were collected from the surrounding fields, woods and riverside, as well as gardens. They would then be brought to the village to be weighed after they had been cleaned, dried, checked for colour and dampness. Next they would be taken to Chippenham railway station and put on a train to Potters and Clarkes at London and Manchester to be made into medicines and ointments. In 1945 the prices paid to pickers ranged from 1d. for Parsley Piert, Scullcap and Toadflax to 10d for Burnet, Pilewort and Tormentil. The range of herbs was impressive; 66 items in total, from well known 'weeds' such as nettles and dandelions through to cowslip flowers, scarlet pimpernel, wood betony, fig wort and valerian roots.[269]

The Fruit Preservation Scheme 1941 put into action by the Women's Institute was set up principally to prevent the waste of surplus fruit. The WI was to set up Preservation Centres in rural areas and country towns. The centres would obtain a licence to manufacture jam and preserve fruit under Article 2 of Statutory Rules and Orders 1941 No. 591. Those schools, hospitals, British Restaurants and other premises which were authorised under the scheme would also require a licence.[270] The Landford Women's Institute was granted a licence in December 1939.[271] It was planned that those schools and hospitals which were preserving fruit grown in their own gardens would be able to keep the jam for their own use in addition to their rationed allowance but British Restaurants could not do so. Preservation Centres could not sell their produce directly to the public or to their members. Quality controls were set, there were standards for labelling and Ministry of Agriculture Inspectors would visit premises to inspect the produce. Local Authorities were tasked with providing instruction, and in Wiltshire this was being provided by a panel of Domestic Science Teachers and members of the WI who were already 'actively engaged in advising the general public.'[272] In Great Cheverell '[t]he Army avidly bought any garden surplus, which was collected weekly.'[273] At the County School in Bromham, 9 September, 1941, a group of children went to Spye Park to gather blackberries 'in accordance with a request by the Deputy Director to help with the Government Scheme for the preservation of wild fruits'. On 15 September they were gathering mulberries for the same purpose.[274] In October 1940 the eldest boys at Minety School were spending time picking up acorns to help the war effort, and blackberrying took place in September 1941[275] as had been done by Wiltshire children before them during the First World War.

With the high level of exposure given to the Dig for Victory Campaigns by the press, the Red Cross used the ongoing campaign to help to raise money for

FOOD FACTS

HARVEST HOME

Apple pudding on wintry days ? Runner beans for dinner in December ? This is the time to make sure you will have these dishes later on. Preserve every ounce of home-grown food you can spare for the winter. You are on a *fighting food standard* now. Nothing must be wasted. Gather in the garden harvest now, so you can enjoy your 'Harvest Home' in the winter.

ELDERBERRY AND APPLE JAM

Ingredients : 3 lb. elderberries, 3 lb. apples, 5 lb. sugar. *Method :* Remove berries from stalks and wash. Warm them to draw juice. Simmer for ½ hour to soften skins. Core apples and simmer until quite soft in another pan with very little water, pass through sieve or pulp well with wooden spoon, add apples to elderberries, reheat and add sugar. Stir until dissolved and boil rapidly until jam sets. Make first test for setting after 10 minutes.

Salting Beans

Salting is the best way of preserving runner or French beans. Use young fresh beans. Take a lb. of cooking salt to 3 lb. of beans.

Wash the beans, dry, string them and, if large, break into pieces. *Crush* the salt with a rolling pin. *Put a layer* of salt about 1 inch deep into the bottom of a crock or jar (any large jar will do). *Press* in a layer of beans, then another layer of salt ½ inch deep, and so on. The secret of success is to pack the salt well down on the beans. *Finish* with a layer of salt 1 inch deep. *Cover* with a cloth or paper and tie with string. *Leave* for a few days for beans to shrink.

Don't worry if contents become moist. *Just add* more beans and more salt until jar is full again. If beans are well covered with salt it doesn't matter how moist they are. *Re-cover.* Store in a dry cool place.

Before use, wash beans thoroughly in hot water, then soak for 2 hours in warm water. Cook in the usual way, but without salt.

RECIPE of the WEEK No.20

Marrow Surprise

Cooking time : 20 minutes. **Ingredients :** 1 medium sized marrow, 4 oz. grated cheese, ¼ pint household milk and vegetable stock, 2 tablespoonfuls flour, 1 oz. margarine, ½ lb. carrots, 1 cup sliced beans, salt, pepper. **Quantity :** Four helpings. **Method :** Peel marrow, unless garden fresh, remove seeds, slice beans and carrots, cut marrow into large pieces. Put carrots and beans in one saucepan with a little boiling salted water. Cover and cook till almost tender. Add marrow, cook for five minutes. **Cheese Sauce :** Melt margarine in a saucepan, blend in flour, cook for a few minutes, add milk and vegetable stock to make thick sauce, stir until smooth, add grated cheese. Pour sauce over marrow, carrots, beans. Brown under grill. Serve with potatoes.

Apple Rings

Here's a way of keeping apples that can be used for windfalls or blemished fruit. Wipe the apples, remove the cores and peel thinly. Cut out any blemishes. Slice into rings about ¼ inch thick. Steep the rings for 10 minutes in water containing 1½ oz. of salt to the gallon. Thread the rings on sticks or canes to fit across the oven or spread on trays. Dry very slowly until they feel like chamois leather. The temperature should not exceed 150° F. Turn once or twice during cooking.

Pears can be treated in the same way, but they must be cut in halves or quarters and spread on the trays.

DRYING HERBS

Parsley, mint, sage, thyme, marjoram and bay leaves can be dried and stored for the winter. Gather the leaves on a dry day. Wash small leaved herbs such as thyme, tie in muslin bags and hang by the fire to dry. Large leaved herbs such as bay leaves should be tied in muslin, dipped in boiling water. Then dried in a cool oven, this takes about 1 hour.

FREE — Ask at any of the Food Advice Centres or Bureaux for a free copy of the *Hedgerow Harvest* leaflet, or send a postcard to the Ministry of Food, London, W.1. The leaflet contains many useful recipes for preserving wild fruits and berries.

LISTEN TO THE KITCHEN FRONT EVERY MORNING AT 8.15.

How are you? FIGHTING *fit, thanks!*

THE MINISTRY OF FOOD, LONDON, W.1. FOOD FACTS No. 113

their cause with the use of Victory Garden Shows. The Horticultural Committee of the Red Cross Agriculture Fund produced leaflets on how to organise and run them but it appears that in Bradford on Avon at least, entering garden shows was not a popular pastime for local residents. In June 1943 the Clerk of Bradford on Avon Town Council was writing to the Red Cross about the attempt to organise a flower show. There had been some difficulty in obtaining organisers from the most likely relevant local organisations 'owing to so many of their members being engaged on essential work and having insufficient time to deal with the matter.' They were unable to assist. The Bradford on Avon Conservative Club had in fact also replied to the Clerk with more regrets; the fact that the Gardeners' Society had been disbanded for the period of the war, that it was too late in the season to carry out the suggestion, and that a show held in 1941 had proved a failure regarding entries.[276]

The Dig for Victory campaign assumed that the masses had little experience of gardening and would struggle without expert help. A panel of experts was asked to produce *Growmore Leaflet No. 1* to help people plan what to grow and make good decisions. The experts had many and differing views and the result was a compromise which Franklin Ginn

Ministry of Food advert for preserving fruit and vegetables and drying herbs in The Wiltshire Gazette, 3 September 1942 (WSHC Microform Collection)

notes was also 'riddled with misprints' and published in the winter when there was little gardening to do. Most gardeners relied on newspapers, other gardeners and gardening shows on the radio.[277] The first gardening advice was available through the Growmore Bulletin *Food from the Garden* in October 1939. Mr C. H. Middleton, 'The Wireless Gardener', was also on hand with his radio broadcasts and received huge audiences.[278] The Ministry of Agriculture and Fisheries hoped to control gardeners in the same way as farmers to avoid over production, but it was not a success.[279]

A survey conducted in the early 1940s shows that for 51% the motivation to grow food in a domestic setting was to get fresh food for the family. 15% wanted to help with the war effort and 14% because it was cheaper. 59% percent reported no difficulties growing more vegetables but 9% struggled with a lack of time and 9% said it was too much hard work, with 5% not wanting to spoil the flower beds. Those least likely to take part were from the manual classes; less likely to own a garden and also more likely to already be growing produce due to economic necessity. A Home Intelligence Report of 1943 discovered that the economies suggested by the Government in its food campaign were felt 'piffling' by the working classes and that 'such forms of thrift ha[d] long been imposed by necessity.'[280]

The Government wanted to control and organise everyday life with the Dig for Victory Campaign, hoping to achieve an all-year-round supply, but this was not achieved. The figures which were publicised to demonstrate the success of the Dig for Victory gardeners were based more on a best guess rather than fact but they were enough to encourage and boost morale.[281]

In November 1943 the National Allotments Society Ltd. was considering the planning of allotments post-war and the role that Local Authorities would play in this respect. The Society wrote to Wiltshire's Town Clerks and Clerks of the Council to represent their case… '[W]e are greatly encouraged by the interest which many Local Authorities have taken in allotments over a long period of years and the splendid efforts they have made and the results achieved in the 'Dig for Victory' Campaign.' They realised that there would be many competing interests for land and were asking that their interest be given equal consideration alongside others. 'Your attention is, however, specially directed to their social and recreational value. You will, we are quite sure, agree that it would be difficult to find a more healthy form of recreation or one which makes a greater contribution to food citizenship. Moreover, it is one of the very few spare-time occupations from which the whole family derives both pleasure and benefit. A community, well supplied with allotments, can show a much cleaner bill of health, judging from the reports of Medical Officers of Health in some of the larger centres of population… The provision of allotments for all citizens who need them should be regarded as a public duty and a social service just in the same way as the provision of parks, open spaces, recreational grounds, etc. is so regarded.' Contained within Wiltshire County Council's wartime files is a pamphlet by the National Allotments Society Ltd. entitled *Future of Planning: Allotments*, specifically aimed at Local Authorities and containing a 'model' layout with ideas for the future of allotments. The Society saw one possible barrier to the provision of permanent allotment sites. This was the cost of the land, which some Local Authorities regarded as being required for the 'highest use to which land can be put,' i.e. for building development.[282]

By 14 February 1946 a Ministry of Agriculture and Fisheries circular was stating that there was an urgent necessity to retain war-time allotments due to the world food situation. It was hoped that Local Authorities would continue to support the 'Dig for Victory over Want' campaign. 'The need for self-help is just as great as in the dark days of the war',[283] and in 1946 Warminster Urban District Council agreed to keep the spare ground at the Park in Warminster under cultivation.[284] By January 1947 the campaign was being called the 'Dig for Plenty' campaign of 1946/7.[285]

The June 1945 issue of the Ministry of Agriculture's *Allotment and Garden Guide* was reminding its readership of the growing world food shortage, 'but in these strictly utilitarian times we gardeners and allotment holders may feel that the sight of our vegetable plot coming along nicely with a variety of crops is not only a distinctly pleasant sight but a solid insurance premium against that threatened world food shortage which has now become a reality.' The December 1945 edition of the guide was noting the American influence on British gardening. 'No doubt owing to the American 'invasion' of this country many gardeners became much interested in sweet corn'… There were complaints about delayed ripening. On the Ministry's own plots 'which [were] by no means ideal, the variety 'John Innes Hybrid' which [was] early maturing, did well and aroused much interest.'[286]

In 1951 the National Council of Social Service published an advisory handbook on behalf of The National Association of Parish Councils. *Allotments* encouraged Parish Councils to fulfil their duty as laid out in the 1950 Act to provide allotments to people who needed them, thereby 'doing a most important job which, besides producing material results, is of real social value.' The old wartime *Dig for Victory* leaflets and *Growmore* bulletins were being made available if required.[287] By the time rationing had ended in 1954, allotments were being seen as 'anachronistic' and allotment use was in decline. This decade saw the last Allotment Acts and in 1957 Government funding and support for the allotment movement ended.[288]

Livestock

As with pig rearing, commercial poultry keeping suffered during the war. The cereals and beans the birds were fed on were considered luxury goods. The Government, however, was well aware of the health benefit of eggs and wanted to ensure supply. In December 1940 the Domestic Poultry Keepers' Council was set up, its aim to provide guidance and to encourage the practice of keeping poultry in a domestic setting. The use of registration meant that the Government could be more efficient with the limited rations of feed that were available. The Council recorded a membership of 791,000 in its first year[289] and by 1945 the number had risen to over one and a quarter million members rearing over 12 million hens. By 1944-5 domestic hen keepers accounted for approximately 25% of officially known egg supplies.[290] There was a reduction in rations for pigs and poultry during the 'desperately cold' winter of 1942/3 ensuring that egg production fell markedly. The situation had improved by the end of the war, but as Peter Ginn *et. al.* point out 'for many kitchens throughout the nation the horror of dried egg powder had become a distinct reality.'[291] Jack Mock notes that packets of dried egg were issued every two months in early 1941, arriving from the US. The ration was equal to approximately 12 eggs.[292] One of the bonuses of dried egg, however, was that it could be imported more easily, taking up less space on ships and it also weighed less. Shipping space was also reduced by devising new processing techniques for meat, helping to maintain Argentinean meat imports at their pre-war level.[293]

There was a dramatic reduction in the pig population over the course of the war, with numbers reducing by 2,500,000. They were not a cost effective animal to keep commercially as the amount of land that would be needed to grow pig fodder would be too great to make it a viable proposition.[294] The Ministry of Agriculture set up the Small Pig Keeper's Council in 1941, encouraging the formation of Pig Clubs.[295] Pig Clubs were a way of raising pigs without requiring feed as Club members used pigswill from their kitchens and gardens,[296] and by 1943 there was often a pigswill bin in urban areas for local residents to fill[297] (there were waste food bins on every street in Devizes).[298] As early as June 1941 in Calne it appears that the Borough Surveyor felt that there was 'very little swill available for collection' and that it was 'not a practicable proposition for the Council to undertake the boiling of it.' The Council did want to co-operate by making the swill available to farmers but did not want to be involved in any expenditure such as the provision of bins, collection and boiling. Farmers had shown great interest in the proposal of the town's swill to be collected and boiled by the council and sold at a 'reasonable price... owing to the tremendous shortage of feeding stuffs which now prevails.'[299] One consequence of the devastating foot and mouth outbreak was that pigswill then had to be more vigorously checked to ensure it had been adequately sterilised, and this had to take place on licensed premises.[300]

It was the job of the Small Pig Keeping Council to encourage people to set up Pig Clubs in town and in the country. Small amounts of pig meal could be purchased to aid the process but, as with the chickens, it proved too successful and the Ministry of Agriculture and Fisheries tightened up its regulations as too much feed was being used.[301] The number of Pig Clubs rose to 6,900 with thousands of members.[302] For the Eccles family in Chute, October 1940: 'The pigs arrived this morning – squealing and lively under a large net. Harris tucked them under his arm and bore them protesting to their new home. They've spent the rest of the day nosing round and grunting to each other uncertainly – I fancy they feel a trifle strange.'[303] Sybil Eccles was finding the Government controls troublesome by February 1941:

'I'm engaged in a colossal, wordy and apparently endless correspondence with various baby departments of the Ministry of Agriculture. All about our precious porkers. We are allowed to keep one whole pig for household consumption every three months. But we shall have to kill them both together owing to the food shortage... Short rations, poor fellow, and he wouldn't fatten... So we propose to have a wild fling with all the food we can muster, cram it down their willing throats until mid March and then slay them both – eat one and sell his brother to the Government meat supply...'[304] An article in the *Devizes Gazette* on 6 March 1941 was calling on pig owners to market their pigs at a lighter weight due to the shortage of feeding stuffs. Rations coupons for feeding stuffs were to be reduced to half their current figure.

In Minety one family built a pigsty out of concrete blocks for two pigs. Unusually, their village had its own slaughterhouse,[305] the number of which had dropped countrywide from 16,000 in 1939 to 600 by 1941.[306] The slaughtered pigs then came home and it was 'a very busy time for all the family and friends, whose help had been requested.' The majority of the pig was buried in salt in a lead lined box. It was common for the two hams to be salted too, occasionally pickled in large earthenware containers before being hung to dry from the ceiling. One half of the head was salted with the other and the 'Bath Chaps' (lower jaws or jowls) and trotters given fresh as presents. The intestines were not forgotten. Called chitterlings they were cleaned and cooked. Black pudding was made from the blood and faggots were made from the liver etc... 'Then in the evening we sat down to a beautiful meal of fresh pork and sweet meats, while boiling on the stove was the backbone and tail for stew the next day...'[307]

Company employees also took part in Pig Clubs, such as those at John Wallis Titt who kept theirs at their works, and Town Council staff who kept theirs at the old sewage works at Smallbrook Lane, both in Warminster.[308] Enfield Precision Engineering had two large pigsties on site; the smell from them was said to have been 'terrible'.[309] At the EKCO factory near Malmesbury pigs were kept and fed on kitchen scraps. After slaughter, half the food went to the Ministry of Food and half to the factory. It was noted that the two sets of pigs looked very different. One herd appeared very well fed whilst the other herd looked distinctly 'scraggy.' No prizes given as to which herd was destined for the Ministry![310]

It was not just the lack of foodstuffs for farm animals that was causing difficulty; domestic pet owners were also under pressure. The *Wiltshire Times* 29 September 1939 edition was reporting suggestions for feeding cats and dogs in wartime, suggested by the National ARP Animals Committee. '... so long as normal foods are available, they should be used. The Committee's suggestions are for emergency if ordinary food stuffs for animals should become unobtainable, and therefore the committee wishes again to stress that there is no need for animals to be destroyed on the grounds that there may not be enough food for them.' The Committee provided three specimen meals to be given on successive days to maintain variety. An advert in the *Salisbury Times* on 17 January 1941 offered help to pet owners, stating that when pets were destroyed en masse during the Spanish Civil war the country was overrun with vermin. Owners would have to register their pet with the local National ARP for Animals Committee which would provide them with a free numbered disc for the animal to wear. It also advised on what to do if dog and cat food supplies became scarce. 'Soak and boil rice in water for an hour or two (use 1 oz. of rice to a pint of water). Mix this with mashed beans – haricot or butter beans – or dried peas, boiled and mashed. To this mixture add the liquid made by stewing for twenty minutes in a little water any of the following: green vegetable leaves, dandelions, stinging nettles, carrot, spinach, swede or turnip tops. Use when cool with a little gravy or meat soup and a few pieces of dry rusk or toast if desired.' The Chippenham doctor Joan Hickson remarked in her diary in July 1943: 'Just happened to pass a fish and chip shop with a lot of fish and not much of a queue, and managed to get a lovely hake, about 3lb for 2 shillings and ten pence, with a head for cats.'[311]

During the war Local Authorities contributed 2,000,000 tons of kitchen waste for the war effort but by the end of 1945 in Swindon the amount had reduced and valuable feeding stuff was being lost.[312] The saving of kitchen waste became an urgent issue in May 1946. The Ministry of Agriculture and Fisheries made a broadcast, referring to the fact that the position had worsened as flour conservation measures had recently been introduced. As a result the feeding ration for pigs and poultry was to be drastically reduced in July 1946 from one-sixth of the pre-war supply to one-twelfth. A letter sent from the Directorate of Salvage and Recovery, Board of Trade to Swindon Borough Council stated: 'It is a matter of vital importance that the number of pigs and poultry in the country should be maintained during this difficult period at the highest possible level... every possible source of untrained [*sic*] feeding stuff must be explored if pig and poultry producers are to achieve this end. One of these sources is to be found in kitchen waste and it has been and continues to be the Government policy that wherever possible supplies of this valuable feeding stuff should be recovered through the medium of Local Authorities salvage schemes.'[313]

During the war rural inhabitants also kept rabbits for their meat and pelts. The animals were useful as, unlike poultry, they could be fed on vegetation.[314] The terms and conditions of the Domestic Poultry Keeper's Council were extended to cover domestic rabbits.[315] Some Wiltshire families had been commercially selling rabbits before the war, such as Charlie Wiltshire, Charlie Andrews and Herbert Bailey from Upavon who had sole rights to catch rabbits on Salisbury Plain for many years. They would transport the goods to London by train.[316] In Minety redundant poultry houses were used for rabbits that were fed on garden weeds and grass from the lawn and fields. They were sold to local hoteliers such as the Bell Inn at Malmesbury.[317] One Cricklade resident sold his rabbits for their meat as hotels were happy to buy them.[319] Some farmers from Wiltshire with thousands of rabbits on their land sold them to London hotels at inflated prices.[319] Rabbit meat had now become 'an integral part of the diet, whether wild or domesticated.'[320]

Bees were a good wartime investment, only needing minimal feeding and a colony could be acquired very cheaply. A common sight would often be two or three beehives in a domestic garden or an allotment with over one million active hives operating over the wartime period. The British Beekeepers' Association had lobbied hard for honey to be recognised as an important foodstuff and in 1943 keepers were allowed an additional sugar ration for their bees. Sugar was a real commodity and to stop illegal claims the police were required to check that actual beekeeping was taking place. The number of colonies was checked before the ration was granted. However, the Government still suspected that illegal practices were taking place and the bee sugar ration was coloured green in an attempt to prevent fraud. An unfortunate consequence was that the practice also turned the honey green, and so was discontinued! Domestic beekeeping dropped dramatically after the de-rationing of sugar in 1953.[321] One family in Minety had 35 bee hives. 'Some of the bees' sugar and honey were bartered for cream and butter.'[322]

Recycling and Salvage

RECYCLING WAS CLASSED as helpful to the war effort, and children were particularly useful for collecting goods for salvage, going door to door to collect material such as paper, with schools or Scout/Guide groups organising the effort. Feathers could be used as pillow stuffing for servicemen and scraps of knitting wool could be transformed into blanket squares. Clothes and shoes were sent to clothing depots and bones were collected for fertilizer.[323] Rubber could be 'turned into new' and any old rubber toys, golf or rubber cricket balls, old wellies, cycle and pram tyres, hot water bottles, garden hoses and rubber gloves were required if they could not be re-conditioned.[324] In August 1941 the WVS in Trowbridge was busy organising the collection of wooden cotton reels which the Army used as insulators.[325] By 15 July 1944 the *Wiltshire Times* was printing information from the Ministry of Information, urging people to remember to replace stoppers in used bottles when they were returned to the supplier. 'Every screw stopper from beer or similar bottles contains rubber... Every stopper replaced in an empty bottle and returned promptly to the supplier saves the need for a new one.' In Chute, July 1940, Sybil Eccles was reporting that they were 'doing [their] duty with scrap iron, wastepaper and bones. The Village Dump – in a corner of Mustey's field – [was] now an imposing sight.'[326] The writer Fay Inchfawn, living in Freshford on the Somerset/Wiltshire border wrote in 1943: 'We were now entreated by the Government to save bones and not to waste bread, but we were all of us so busy that only my mother found time to listen to the news.'[327]

Industry was also getting involved, with Alfred Bird & Sons detailing their Bird's Custard Tin School Saving Scheme to the Director of Education at Swindon in July 1942. Each school would act as a Collecting Centre with the more tins collected, the better the price paid. The company's aim was to re-use their tins instead of them being mixed with the general salvage as they were 'essential to [their] business.'[328] The Head Teacher of Ivy Lane School in Chippenham was reporting that a 'bones' dustbin had been received in March 1942 for the 'collection of bones for the national effort.'[329]

In July 1940 the first phase of the Battle of Britain was taking place over

WWI tank being broken up for scrap metal in Trowbridge Park (WSHC P14864)

the Channel which led to the 'Great Aluminium Scare'. Lord Beaverbrook used the newspapers for an appeal. 'We will turn your pots and pans into Spitfires and Hurricanes, Blenheims and Wellingtons.' Everyone was to hand in any article made fully or partly of aluminium to their local WVS' HQ… 'The need is instant. The call is urgent. Our expectations are high.' It was soon noted, however, that shops were still selling goods containing aluminium. Beaverbrook retorted that he could not 'pilfer' from shops, and in the end the high grade aluminium that was required would not come from the country's donations.[330] The drives for metal were more of a symbolic gesture rather than of any real practical value but the people felt they had 'done their bit' and the Government valued the rise in morale.[331] In May 1941 Warminster's Spitfire Fund raised £5,000 as a result of football matches, whist drives, dances, collections etc. and the Urban District Council raised £76 from the sale of waste paper, scrap iron, swill, rags and bones.[332] It was Salvage Week at Ivy Lane School in Chippenham in August 1941. The children were invited to bring along paper, bottles and other items. There were eight prizes of money offered by the Local Authority for the under 11s group.[333] The Spitfire Funds were not in need of money, but donations provided a very useful anti-inflationary effect for the Government. A Spitfire was 'priced' at £5,000 and the BBC announced a list of the latest donations after its news bulletins. The scheme had made £13 million by April 1941. By the end of the war nearly every large town in the country had named

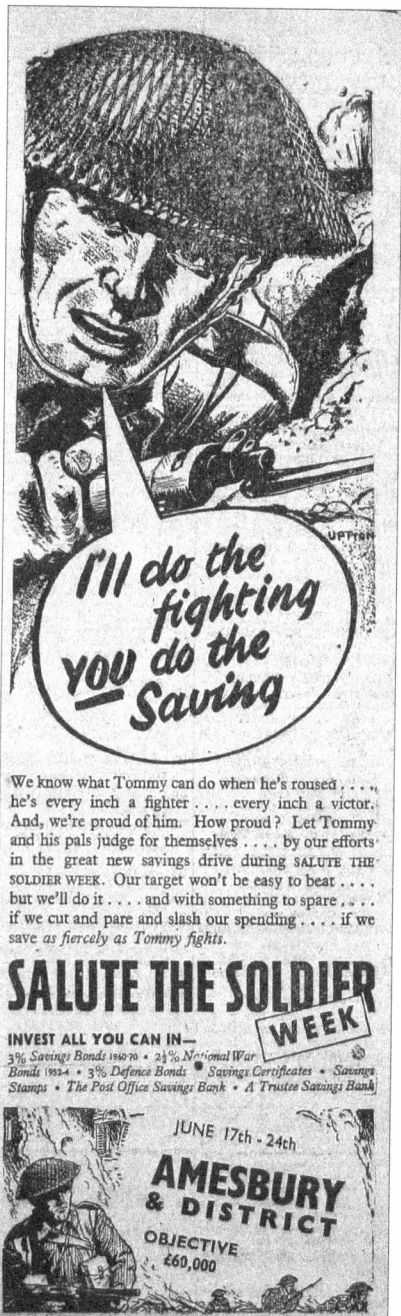

*Advert in the Salisbury Journal, 16
April1944, urging people in Amesbury and
District to beat their savings drive target
of £60,000 for Salute the Soldier Week
(WSHC Microform Collection)*

a Spitfire.[334] Ivy Lane School banked £1
2s. 1d. in January 1941 so that they could
wind up their Spitfire Fund.[335] Everyone,
as a Purton resident recalled, was 'saving
aluminium, old clothes, jam jars, bones,
paper and pig food'. Government posters
showed how the salvage would be used;
milk tops made aeroplanes, rubber made
paratroopers' boots, bones made cordite
for cartridges...[336] Dame Vera Lyn later
recalled that:

'The Government's 'model
housewife' was one who shopped with
'special care', wasted nothing, saved paper,
tin, bones etc. She would try to keep
herself and her house 'trim and cheerful',
taking special pains with the cooking to
keep 'the men's spirits up'. She sends the
children to bed early and will not stay up
listening for sirens, and reminds herself by
doing this she is helping to win the war.'[337]

The Malmesbury Branch of the
British Legion even received a letter
from Lord Beaverbrook, the Minister for
Aircraft Production, thanking them for
their donation of £5 towards the Spitfire
Fund.[338]

In the summer of 1940 Malmesbury
Town Council created a 'Tin and Metal'
day on alternate Mondays. By October
1940 Malmesbury's Rural District Council
(RDC) was reporting that only two of
its eighteen parishes were not salvaging
scrap iron and steel, and only Great
Somerford and Norton did not have a
dump. It appears their recycling scheme
was too successful, however, as it had to
be suspended the following month; they
were having problems selling the scrap.
By March 1942 Malmesbury RDC was
receiving complaints about the collection
of scrap metal from the dumps. The metal
was being taken and the tins were left lying
about. The Sanitary Inspector was asking

the Ministry of Works to get the contractors to do the job properly, but by April the metals were not being collected at all and 'butchers were clamouring for the collection of empty metal tins from their premises.' At the end of summer 1942 the Ministry of Supply was accusing Malmesbury RDC of neglecting salvage, calling it a 'defaulter'. Malmesbury claimed that with a population of fewer than 10,000 they should not have been included in the compulsory scheme.[339]

Swindon's Board of Education was keen to emphasise to schools their role in reducing waste. In their 1940 memorandum No. 17 entitled *Waste* they encouraged schools to remind pupils of the facts: shipping capacity was not unlimited and was urgently needed for war cargoes; imports needed to be paid for by exports and so the need to limit imports was great; hence the need to make the utmost use of everything that was bought. Schools were told to lead by example when collections of waste were organised, and in Wiltshire the Education Committee had arranged for the collection of waste paper from schools. In July 1942 the Board was

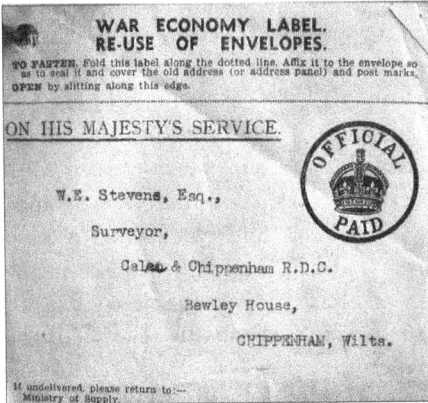

WAR ECONOMY LABEL.
RE-USE OF ENVELOPES.

The use of labels to enable the re-use of envelopes (WSA G3/761/63)

also looking for Head Teachers to 'influence the school children in Swindon to give help' out of school and to set up competitions such as writing salvage slogans or producing posters. The Ministry of Supply had asked all Local Authorities in Wiltshire to organise a salvage drive over the period 15-29 August 1942, and the Board would be appreciative if its schools could assist by receiving copies of the Ministry's *Lectures on Salvage* for distribution. By 1943 the situation appears to have deteriorated. It was being stated by the Cleansing and Salvage Superintendent to Swindon's Education Officer that: 'There is a serious shortage of waste paper in the country, and at the moment we are importing waste paper from abroad, while at home we destroy it by burning, or render of less value by placing it in the dustbin, where it is sometimes possible to extract it before it is tipped in the refuse collecting vehicle... 100,000 tons of waste paper and cardboard is needed by our Paper and Board Mills by June this year, this will save about 10,000,000 dollars. The need is urgent. Can you help?'[340] The paper shortage affected the publication of newspapers and magazines. Broadsheets such as *The Times* published at 8-11 pages throughout the war but London's 'dailies' fared worse, dropping from 24 pages to 6, then 4.[341] The shortage can be illustrated by the weekly publication *Picture Post*. By the autumn of 1939 the magazine had reduced from *c.* 75 pages to *c.* 60 pages. By the beginning of 1940 it was still managing around 60 pages but by July this had dropped to 40. Between September 1940 and the end of that year each issue contained around 38 pages and by the end of 1941 the number of pages had dropped again to around 28. 1942 saw between 24 and 28 pages published and this appears to have continued throughout the rest of the war.[342] Warminster's Peggy Pickford was explaining rationing to her sister Liz in Australia in her letter of 5 December 1943. 'Papers are all rationed. You cannot just go and buy one on the off-chance. They have to be ordered and even then you cannot always get them unless someone else drops out.'[343] The *Wiltshire Gazette* was reporting in its 22 August 1946 edition that as from 27 September the amount of newsprint which could be used by newspapers was due to increase. 'Under the revised rationing scheme, papers will be permitted for a period to print as many copies as the trade may require to meet the public demand... made possible by the purchase in Canada and Newfoundland of increased quantities for importation in 1947.' Through the revised scheme it was hoped that consumers would be able to buy their newspaper of choice.

It was Wiltshire's turn to have a 'Special Book Drive' in January 1944, with

An advertisement in the 1 July 1942 edition of the Wiltshire Gazette, using the fear of Fifth Columnists to alert people to the waste paper recovery competition in Chippenham (WSHC Microform Collection)

the people of Cricklade and Wootton Bassett being asked for 24,000 books. The drive had originated with Winston Churchill's tour of the Near East and what he could do to help the troops there. 'He was told that all kinds of reading matter was urgently required. As a result these 'Drives' were started. Millions of Books and Magazines have already been sent to the Navy, Army, R. A. F. and Merchant Navy, but millions more [were] needed...'[344] The Broughton Gifford Women's Institute (WI) contributed over 265 'Ship Halfpennies' and two and a half sacks of books in aid of Ships Libraries in 1942. The figure had risen to 400 halfpennies

WANTED
PRISM BINOCULARS
FOR THE
FIGHTING FORCES
The Public are invited to place
their Binoculars on
ACTIVE SERVICE
We are prepared to pay GOOD PRICES
for suitable Instruments, or Gifts will be
gladly accepted.

GLOUCESTERSHIRE :

F. STEEL, 9, Dollar Street, CIRENCESTER.
LEONARD JONES, Market Place, CIRENCESTER.
S. R. HYSLOP, 83, Regent Street, SWINDON.
Messrs. PARKER & Co., 25, Fleet St., SWINDON.
S. R. HYSLOP, 33, Wood Street, SWINDON.
S. W. FOWLES, Market Place, DURSLEY.
POOLE, George Street, STROUD.
W. G. MAROK, 9, High Street, STROUD.
Messrs. SEYMOUR, High St., CHIPPING CAMPDEN.
Messrs. MOODY, BELL & LAMB, 27, Clarence Street,
   CHELTENHAM.
G. JEFFS, Winchcombe Street, CHELTENHAM.
R. THOMAS, 369, High Street, CHELTENHAM.

Messrs. DOLLAND MITCHISON, The Promenade,
   CHELTENHAM.
Messrs. HARVEY Bros., 154, High St., CHELTENHAM.
Messrs. CHARNLEY & SONS, 42, Southgate Street,
   GLOUCESTER.
R. M. HILL Co-op. & Industrial Society, Brunswick Rd.,
   GLOUCESTER.
H. CANNON, 23, St. Aldgate Street, GLOUCESTER.
F. NORVILL, 7, Barton St., East Gate, GLOUCESTER.
A. R. WHEATLEY, Cheltenham Road, Longleaves,
   GLOUCESTER.
BANNISTER & THATCHER, 146/147, High Street,
   TEWKESBURY.
A. BARTON, 11, Market Street, CINDERFORD.

Binoculars wanted for the Ministry of Supply. 125,000 were required to be put on 'Active Service' (WSA G24/225/29)

in 1943.[345]

Heywood School helped the war effort by encouraging the children to collect money for various causes. Seven shillings and six pence were raised for the Finnish Relief Fund in March 1940. In December 1940 six pairs of wristlets were knitted by the children and sent to the Knitted Comforts Fund. By January

1942 the children were bringing in pennies to help buy wool to continue knitting for the forces. The following month children wrote notes to their parents about Warship Week which raised a total of £13 1s. 6d. (noted as a special effort), and in June seven scarves were knitted by parents and children, sent to the Merchant Navy.[346] The Broughton Gifford WI's working party had been 'very busy' during the year of 1942. '119 garments ha[d] been made or knitted and 35 parcels of comforts ha[d] been sent to soldiers from the village.' One hundred cigarettes had also been sent to HMS Goatfell.[347] In the Chippenham locality the target for the February 1942 Warship Week in March was £230,000; the cost of HMS Cyclops. The Ivy Lane School target was £200. The Head Teacher of the school noted in the school's log book on 6 March: 'We are subject to many 'disturbances' in these days – next week much attention will be devoted to 'Warship Week,' all consequent upon conditions arising out of the war'. Posters were displayed, and one of their boys was awarded first prize for 'best Warship Week poem.' The school managed to raise £190.[348] In May 1943, £39 was raised by the Heywood School Savings Group for the Wings for Victory week and a collection was made for the British Sailors' Society. By May 1944 the children were writing letters to their parents about Salute the Soldier week. Their target was to raise £50 but in fact they collected an amazing £293! The last collection during the war was for 'The Aid to China Fund' when 17s. were collected.[349] The Kington St. Michael schoolchildren were busy collecting paper salvage for the local paper mill at Slaughterford in September 1944[350] and in May 1944 the schoolchildren of Lydiard Millicent were involved in 'sports' in connection with the Salute the Soldier campaign.[351] A concert was given by the children of Stratton St. Margaret School in aid of the Stratton Soldiers' Fund in June 1940.[352]

By September 1941 the Clerk's Office in the Urban District of Melksham had received notification from the Ministry of Supply that it had decided to requisition 'all unnecessary iron and steel railings in the Country for scrap for use in iron and steel works and foundries,' and he directed the Melksham Urban District Council to carry out a survey and furnish the Minister with a schedule of iron or steel posts, chains, bollards, gates, stiles and similar materials in their area, of which all were to be called 'railings.' The Council's interpretation was that those railings not to be included fell into certain categories:
(i)   Railings which should be maintained for safety reasons.
(ii) Railings necessary to prevent cattle etc. from straying.
(iii) Railings of special artistic or of historic interest.'
Any objection raised by an owner would be subject to a 14 day appeal from 'the publication of this notice.'[353]

On 28 October 1941 the Architects Department of United Dairies Ltd. was anticipating the removal of railings, by writing to all Local Authorities 'in the areas concerned' that their iron railings, gates and burglar-proof rails were to be left intact by order of the Assistant Director of Emergency Works (Salvage). Melksham residents were beginning to get worried in January 1942 after reading about the Swindon 'Old Iron' collection in the press. '...my object is to enquire if railings will be taken in this present collection. If so, I shall be obliged if you would instruct the collectors that they will need to weigh those round my house. I shall need payment for them, and should have no hesitation to sue the Ministry, through your Council, for their worth. Their value, as you know, will be insignificant, but I object to the principle of compulsion in the scheme.'[354]

A copy of the Emergency Powers (Defence) Acts 1939 and 1940 *Requisition of Unnecessary Railings* had been received by Melksham Council by March 1942, along with correspondence in January regarding information by the Directorate of Emergency Works (Salvage) which was trying to clarify the situation for Local Authorities who were appealing to them for guidance. The Ministry of Works and Buildings had also noted from schedules received that Local Authorities were interpreting Government circulars differently. Guidance letters were produced and Local Authorities were asked to provide a supplementary schedule if necessary in light of this more detailed information. By November 1942 a representative of the Ministry of Works and Planning, the Emergency Works Officer for the Gloucestershire and Wiltshire Counties, had been to Melksham to review the Council's schedule. He felt that '[s]ince the Minister of Supply's instructions of last September the demand for scrap metal has become even greater and it is felt that additional railings and gates should be removed. I am, therefore, enclosing a Supplementary Schedule which I have prepared...' The need was felt to be so urgent that by 29 December the Ministry of Works and Planning was telling the Council that: 'It is essential that the maximum quantity of metal should be made available for war production purposes and I am to say that, in the absence of any observations from your Council within seven days of the date of this letter, the Ministry will authorise its local officer to requisition and remove the railings, gates etc., in question under the powers conferred by Defence Regulation 50B.' The Council's Clerk replied on 2 January 1943, stating that they would be unable to hold a special meeting of the Council within the time frame given; premises were already being used for other purposes such as training of Civil Defence volunteers. 'I feel, however, at this stage I must lodge a formal protest on the Council's behalf at being requested to deal with this important matter in the short space of 7 days in view of the fact that the original schedule was prepared in February of last year and that no further definite movement appears to have been made in the matter until this stage.' When the council were able to meet on 5 January they were unable to agree to the 'adoption of [the] Supplementary Schedule in its entirety' and invited the Ministry to send a representative to Melksham to discuss the matter further. Melksham Council's stand must have become common knowledge in the public sphere. A Chippenham resident wrote and congratulated them on their 'firm stand re the second schedule of ratepayers' railings. We the owners – occupiers, here are doing the same thing, my railings were not on the list of removals, now a hoard of men, and chits of girls have been around planning another loot... There are thousands and thousands of so-called scrap all over the country (not valuable) or they would not collect it. Here in our C. our fences have been ruthlessly torn down and walls damaged, then left as scrap on the flower beds staring the owners in the face... I hope to keep my rails a little longer, they are somewhat a protection after having a lorry also a car backing in the wall. In the corner bedroom, the plaster is down showing the red bricks this was done by the tanks ....' It appears that Local Authorities were having trouble reconciling some residents to the need to give up their railings. The Urban District of Melksham files also contain many letters asking for compensation.[355] Malmesbury's Town Council meeting of May 1942 was taken over by protestations over the recommendation for the 'wholesale clearance of iron railings in the town,' which the Council considered unnecessary. It was stated by one of the Aldermen that a Ministry of Supply official, 'a young married woman with no knowledge of local needs or conditions... visited the town and scheduled over 100 different lots of iron railings for removal. As far back as December 1941, the Council ha[d] scheduled 14 lots for removal.' During his life of three quarters of a century he had never heard of any such wholesale confiscation of private property, and the Ministry's schedule was 'contrary to its own original ruling that only 'unnecessary' railings should be removed.' It was noted by the Mayor that the members had never been so united on any subject, and they agreed the railings should stay. The Ministry wrote back asking for clarification. In December 1944 the Council heard that the removal of the railings was 'suspended indefinitely'.[356] There had also been several protests over the removal of railings in Bradford on Avon in 1942.[357]

In Devizes, railings were cut off with oxy-acetylene jets, producing nasty jagged edges on the remainder left behind.[358] In Swindon, 1943, one boy remembers the loss of the railings. 'Long lines of red-brick terraced houses, blue-slate roofs, and iron railings set on low brick walls, with iron gates, all neat, all nice, the little gardens separate and so defined. Then men came with acetylene torches and cut the railings from the walls, loading the iron onto lorries. 'They're taking our railings,' so the story went, 'to make tanks for Russia!' Suddenly the enclaved streets took on a new, more open look. We walked along the little walls, until people banged their windows.... Practical handymen unearthed sufficient bricks to raise the walls a little, or found wood to improvise some fencing.'[359] By May 1943 in Bradford on Avon it was being noted in a Council meeting that one Councillor was 'afraid that straying cattle in [Trowbridge Road] were causing havoc, people's gardens were getting in a terrible state.' The railings had been removed.[360]

On 31 July 1943 the *Wiltshire Times* published a letter written by the Local Panel Architect regarding the procedure they were following over the removal of railings. The tone of the letter suggests that the issue had been controversial to say the least, provoking a 'considerable expression of feeling.' He reported that he had 'reviewed carefully every example and ha[d] endeavoured to keep a just balance through the Districts... with the intention that not only should the best specimens be retained but that where nearly similar examples occurred in neighbouring areas, the best only should be kept if they were not in the 'front rank.'... It has been my policy to try and preserve for future generations specimens which could be of interest for their design and craftsmanship... It may be stated that in no case of reservation was acquaintance with the owner or occupier allowed to weigh with a decision.' He thanked all those who had co-operated in the removal of their 'aids to privacy.'

The residents of Cricklade were saddened by the loss of their two Crimean cannons which were located on either side of the town's war memorial and which were even complete with canon balls. The Parish Council decided to do its duty and dispose of them; the Home Guard tried to stop them by suggesting they would be useful as barricades but to no avail. The guns, along with some of the

Notice by the Bradford-on-Avon Rural District Council, 19 September 1941, advising of the removal of railings (WSHC Steeple Ashton WI Scrapbook Collection on Microfilm)

town's railings, disappeared, never to return. Cricklade's Parish Council were definitely keen on doing their bit, as they also notified the Ministry of Supply of two disused weighbridges in the town and of two large lead eagles situated on the entrance gates at Common Hill House, which they were happy to provide for 'war purchases'.[361] The removal of Malmesbury's 'German gun,' was a little more popular. It was to 'be manufactured into missiles for use against the enemy, it was hauled through the town.' Going with it was the Crimean gun which had been positioned at the entrance to the Abbey. 'A small gathering watched the departure of the relics with gratification, but their chief cause for joy was the departure of the German gun. 'Ought to have gone years ago' said a woman whose sons were in the Forces and who had a 'hostile spirit to anything German.' The Vicar wrote in the Council magazine: 'I am glad that the Crimean gun has gone... Guns are no emblem for the Christian Church to possess and exhibit.' The German gun raised £2 for the Council.[362]

Fundraising had also been undertaken during WWI when full use was made of the National War Savings Committee, raising money through War Weapons Week, War Loan Week and War Bonds Week. In Trowbridge, the town had been presented with a 'Fighting War Tank' by the National War Savings Committee for their contribution.[363] During WWII, drives such as 'Wings for Victory' cost a lot of money to run with massive targets to be met, but money was easy to raise as insurance companies and other financial institutions would easily exchange 'idle' cash for Government bonds. Parades and competitions using the theme of 'thrift' enlivened wartime life in rural areas. Events held in Melksham for the Wings for Victory week included an Opening Ceremony, RAF exhibition, RAF Concert Party, dance, children's procession, boxing match, whist drive, Home Guard shooting match, football match, Home Guard sports evening, ATC Open Evening, a free performance at the Melksham Picture House and a combined service at St. Michael's Church. The Melksham Committee were aiming high when they wrote to the Group Captain of the RAF at Rudloe Manor asking if a flyover by a 'flight of fighter planes' might be possible at their opening ceremony. Perhaps unsurprisingly, the answer was no![365] Selling Centres were set up at four places in the town; White's shop in High Street, Bridgman's shop in Lowbourne; the Gas Showrooms in Bath Road and the Women's Voluntary Service (WVS) Centre in King Street. The decoration of these premises was carried out 'in a most excellent manner,' the material and decorations 'including the miniature aircraft were all donated through private individuals.' Stock was collected via the local postmaster. There was a slight issue over losses of £2 10s. 0d. which could not be accounted for. Part of it was made up by the WVS Centre Manager and partly by the Secretary of the Selling Centres, but he felt overall that his team 'worked most enthusiastically for the good of the cause'.[365]

The leaflet sent out to Local Committees who organised their Wings for Victory Campaign from March to June 1943 stated that the drive would 'provide a great opportunity for the British people to give some expression to their admiration for the Royal Air Force. The appeal of these Weeks will be so strong that, with proper organisation, we can look forward to their results eclipsing those of earlier Campaigns.' To garner support, each Local Authority that took part in the campaign with a Local Savings Committee who reached its target would be presented with a trophy in the form of a plaque, specially designed for the campaign. The back of the leaflet contained a helpful list detailing the cost of different types of aircraft, from a troop-carrying glider at £2,500 to a Lancaster bomber at £40,000 or a four-engined flying boat at £50,000. To sum up, the leaflet proclaimed: 'The financial objective of the Campaign is to increase savings and investment in Government securities. But above all we must make it a tribute to the dauntless heroism of the Royal Air Force, to those who won the Battle of Britain and to those who are still winning it for us every day...' The Melksham Committee was commended by the Air-Vice Marshall in April 1943 as the sum they had raised, almost £114,000, had well beaten their target of £75,000 and 'must easily constitute a 'per capita' record for almost any town in England.' The presentation of the plaque took place on the Town Hall steps on 30 October 1943.[366] It wasn't just the Local Committees who received recognition. A Certificate of Honour was given to Durrington Church of England Junior School in 'recognition of special achievement during the Wings for Victory National Savings Campaign 1943'.[367] In May 1944 Wiltshire's Local Savings Committees were competing for the honour of holding a County flag, to be awarded to the Committee with the best amount of small savings per head of population during Salute the Soldier Week. The flag was to be inscribed with the name of the winning Committee and held by them permanently. Trowbridge were the winners.[368]

THIS

CERTIFICATE
OF HONOUR

IS AWARDED TO

The Junior School

SAVINGS GROUP

IN RECOGNITION OF SPECIAL ACHIEVEMENT

DURING THE

WINGS FOR VICTORY

NATIONAL SAVINGS CAMPAIGN 1943

I EXTEND MY THANKS TO ALL CONCERNED
IN THIS IMPORTANT NATIONAL SERVICE.

SECRETARY OF STATE FOR AIR

Certificate of Honour awarded to Durrington School for its achievement in the 1943 Wings for Victory Campaign (WSA F8/600/106/1/27/1)

It was May 1941 in Chute, and the villagers had 'been and are plunged into the midst of a ferocious war weapons week. So far we've taken £1,500 from the three villages (Chutes), isn't it good?... Last night we took a tank (with soldiers) and a band round Upper and Lower Chute and Cadley and collected stamps and certificates, more than £500 and only crept exhausted home to dinner at ten o'clock.'[369] It was announced in the *Wiltshire Gazette* in August 1943 that the Sherman tank which Malmesbury people had raised the money to adopt, and to which they had also given its name, 'had been successfully in action at El Alamein'.[370] The Red Cross also organised fundraising for the wounded and Prisoners of War with Churchill's wife Clemmie supporting its 'Aid for Russia' campaign.[371] Subscriptions from the Duke of Gloucester's Red Cross and St. John Fund were received at the County Office during 1944. It brought the total subscribed to £3,136 18s. 11d.[372] The Red Cross had also been a beneficiary during the Flag Days of WWI, when funds were raised at the annual 'Our Day' appeal in communities across the country, Trowbridge amongst them. At this time blankets had also been collected to be distributed to the troops on Salisbury Plain to protect them from the 'bitter cold'.[373]

When looking at correspondence relating to the various drives, it has been

An address taking place at the Town Hall, Trowbridge, during War Weapons Week, reproduced by kind permission of Mike Marshman (WSHC P55106)

noticeable how much planning went into them, and in Latton fund raising events changed the social scene of the village, as there had been none before the war. 'Twice a week we held little social evenings to raise money for the Red Cross in the village community hut. My mum organised them; we were very busy, very busy.'[374] Melksham's War Weapons Week typically consisted of many Sub-Committees: Schools, Street Savings, War Bonds, Works, Selling Centres, Publicity and Propaganda, Entertainment and Processions, all reporting to the Executive Committee[375] and all requiring staff. Many individuals who were asked to help said they were already very busy and therefore were not available, such as the Joint Managing Director of Avon India Rubber when asked to serve on Melksham's

Salute the Soldier Week Committee in 1944. The availability of distinguished members of the armed forces to give speeches was also an issue. The Melksham Salute the Soldier Committee had wanted a serving officer of high rank for its 1944 campaign, but if not a retired officer of high rank would do.[376] The Melksham Wings for Victory team wanted the Wiltshire Regiment Band to play at their Wings for Victory parade, but they were away from their Barracks in Devizes at the required time.[377] Malmesbury was busy 'smashing' their Wings for Victory target in May 1943, raising £32,380 over their target of £75,000.[378] By 9 March 1945 the Flag Day Department of the Joint Committee for Soviet Aid were thanking their helpers in Pewsey for their efforts in raising £134 0s. 1d. for Red Army Flag Day. 'We realise that these flag day collections make a good deal of extra work for you, and we are sincerely grateful. Thanking you very much indeed for returning the boxes and for bearing the cost of the carriage.' Flag Day had been run since 1943, set to coincide with Red Army Day in February. The money would be used to '... pay tribute to the Red Army for the tremendous part it has played in our common struggle, we hope to provide medical aid for its ten million wounded.' It appears that Pewsey Rural District Council had taken part the previous year, with the Clerk noting on 8 December 1943 that '... every effort should be made to make this a great success in order that medical and other comforts may be provided for the gallant armies and peoples of Soviet Russia. Through their victories and great sacrifices, the people of this country have undoubtedly been saved a great many of the horrors of war, and it is felt that the residents in this district will want to show their appreciation and admiration in a practical manner.'[379] All over the country people had celebrated Red Army Day in 1943 with parades and speeches, with enthusiasm for Russia running high in an 'Anglo-Soviet mania' of the common people.[380]

The Local Committees wrote many letters to both local and national companies who had business associations with their town, having most success with local banks. Many local businesses would only support their home

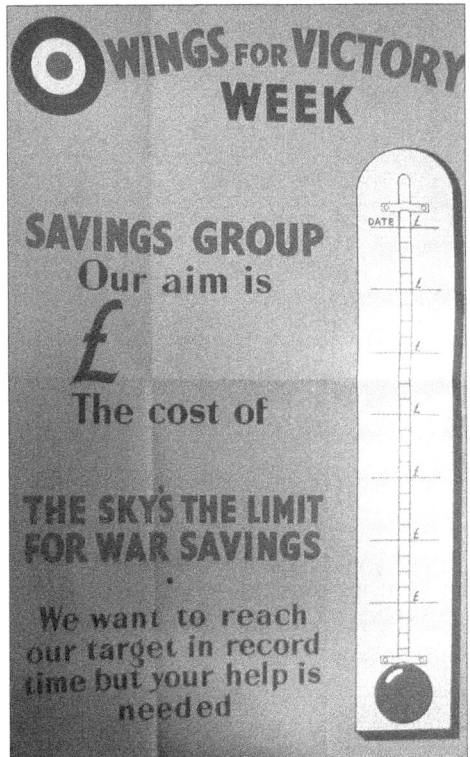

Wings for Victory poster, specially produced for the region including Wiltshire with only a limited quantity available (WSA G14/225/1)

town, and national businesses felt they could not help at a local level, such as WH Smith who replied to Melksham in 1944. 'Owing to the fact that we have a large number of branches all over the Country where local campaigns are organised, we have been obliged not to make any investments centrally and not to participate in local campaigns.'[381] Public liability insurance was also required, taken out by Melksham for its War Weapons Week in 1941.[382]

Melksham's War Weapons Week in April 1941 hoped to raise £30,000. The National Savings Committee relayed that the object of the week was 'the focusing of local attention, by a week's special activities, on the vital need for economy, the need for a reduction of consumption, thereby freeing labour and materials for the production of armaments and war purposes generally, and for the subsequent saving and investment in State securities.' Local Committees were given a free rein but the National Savings Committee spelt out the activities which were usually adopted: 'Parade; luncheon with speaker; exhibits of weapons and trophies in public places, shop windows, Municipal Buildings etc; exhibition of photographs; competitions; selling centres; agencies in shops; intensive press, poster and leaflet campaign; cinema slides and film; presence in town of service units; bands; prominent sales indicator; speeches at works, cinemas etc.; meetings; circularisation of likely bigger investors by a special War Bonds Committee, usually consisting of Bank Managers and leaders of professional bodies; use of all possible local influence to secure the objects set out above.' In Melksham the various investment opportunities available for the War Weapons week were War Bonds, Savings Bonds and Defence Bonds (for the big investor), and National Savings Certificates, deposits in Post Office Savings Banks and Trustees Savings Banks for smaller investors.[383]

Posters were to be put up around the town, including in the air raid shelter opposite the Town Hall. There appears to have been contention over the service which was to be held at St. Michael's Church. The Vicar felt that the 'Drum-Head Service' should be left out of the 1941 War Weapons Week. 'The aim of the Christian Church is to keep before our people the Spiritual aims of the conflict – This we did on the day of National Prayer, and it would only confuse their minds if this Service took place.'[384]

By April 1941 Melksham's campaign was progressing, and included two senior girls of Lowbourne School who sent the Committee's Honourable Secretary £2 'to be forwarded to the Minister of Air Craft Production as their gift to the Nation during War Weapons Week, to buy screws for an aeroplane.' Another pound was given to the Clerk of Melksham Council 'by an old lady who was insistent that it should be treated anonymously. She desire[d] to give the same as a Gift to the Nation.' He duly posted it on to the Financial Secretary of the Treasury in London.[385] It was announced at the beginning of May that the £30,000 target had been surpassed and the total raised was £62,979 0s. 6d. In May 1941 thirty children from Yatton Keynell school were taken to Chippenham to see an exhibition of 'War Weapons'.[385] At Ivy Lane School in Chippenham subscriptions were being collected every morning during War Weapons week at the end of May

1941. The week concluded with a school concert.[386]

Making your money count could also help the war effort. The Government's budgetary analysis of 1941 concluded that to combat an inflationary gap of £500 million, half this amount would have to be recovered via personal savings. The smaller saver could make full use of the readily available National Savings Certificates and Defence bonds.[387] Luckily, the shortage of all kinds of goods meant that some had money to save and by 1943 Calder notes that saving was 'an even more obvious national obsession than salvage.' The National Savings campaign spent more on advertising than the Ministry of Food and the BBC broadcast a *Weekly Savings News* every Sunday. During the war individual savers were able to save as much as a quarter of their disposable income after tax, compared with less than five per cent before.[388] The Malmesbury Savings Committee was re-formed in 1941, wanting to set up a savings indicator in a prominent part of the town to 'show the progress of the savings campaign locally.' Interest in saving was high; there were over 50 savings groups in the Malmesbury area. A greater effort would be required for the next year, but the Committee felt sure that the people of Malmesbury would have both the 'keenness and spirit' to succeed.[389]

Practical skills also came into good use. As in WWI, knitting comforts for the troops was a task many set to with gusto, but the wool was often hard to find. It was reported in the *Wiltshire Times* on 21 October 1939 that the wife of the Commanding Officer, 2nd Battalion, Wiltshire Regiment, was asking for help from the 'good ladies of Trowbridge' to provide knitted comforts for the men who were now at the Front. It was suggested that the newly arrived blind evacuees would be good at the task if wool could be provided. It was noted, however, that 'there is now such a demand for wool (especially in khaki colour) that unless this appeal is quickly answered there may be a difficulty in obtaining this wool.' The Wiltshire Comforts Fund reported to the Women's Institute (WI) in August 1940 that arrangements had been made for the working parties to buy their wool directly from the Personal Service League in London. The supplied wool would consist of Khaki, Navy, RAF and Grey 4 ply fingerings along with 'special sock mixtures as preferred by the Service Authorities.' There was also 'wool-in-oil' for sea-boot stockings and coarse white scoured wool for long stockings to be worn over rubber boots. The Wiltshire Comforts Fund was prepared to subsidise the cost of the wool. The Personal Service League could provide a book of official patterns for all three services.[390] Miss E. Berrett from Hilperton was having trouble purchasing wool by the end of October 1940, however, as there was 'very little to be had.' It would appear that to be lucky depended on when a visit to the shop took place as allocations were received at the beginning of each month. By the end of the month the shelves were looking 'very bare with most... empty.'[391] The situation had become so difficult that the WI even suggested collecting dogs' hair with wire brushes and using it for spinning.[392] By July 1941 the Fund was running short of money but 'the necessity for continuing the good work is urgent.' They were appealing to Lady Radnor, President of the Wiltshire Women's Institutes to support the fund by using her influence to get the various Wiltshire WI branches to raise funds and organise whist drives, dances and other entertainments.[393] The *Wiltshire Times* reported criticism of the fund in its 1 April 1944 edition with soldiers saying that they had received no comforts, but the Committee explained that it was their job to give the family and friends of the soldiers the goods for them to post. 'We cannot possibly know where all the men are serving.' The Committee had raised over £1,000 to provide comforts which included woollen goods, hand knitted by 'zealous' ladies, and cigarettes. Money had also been raised by sales, such as the Red Cross gift sale for Prisoners of War held in April 1944 at Trowbridge, for comforts in the form of Red Cross parcels. By 19 August 1944 the *Wiltshire Times* was reporting that knitting wool was being distributed at the Bromham Women's Institute meeting 'for the members to knit garments for the children of liberated Europe.'

The mood of the Home Guard was to continue to do more, as noted by the 10th Battalion's Stand Down speech in December 1944. 'Let us congratulate ourselves, that we have done our bit towards the war but remember that even when standing down we can do a bit more. An extra row of potatoes, an extra acre of corn, economy in fuel, salvage, readiness to lend a hand, where wanted, letters to relatives in the Forces. They all help and we must go on doing what we can.'[394]

WHAT DO I DO . . . to go "all out" for victory?

I SAVE everything I can for my local salvage campaign —paper, metal, bones, food scraps.
I SAVE gas, electricity, coal, paraffin and water.
I SAVE money wherever possible and put it into War Savings.
I SPEND every ounce of energy and every minute I can spare in War-winning work. I help local voluntary organisations and, if I can, I dig for victory.
I KNOW that everyone, including *myself*, can do *something*.

This space is made available by Wadworth & Co., Ltd.

Advertisement in the Wiltshire Gazette, 7 January 1943 'What do I do... to go "all out" for victory?' (WSHC Microform Collection)

Salvage Drives were still in operation in 1948 with Swindon's Education Officer asking school Head Teachers on behalf of the Salvage Superintendent to 'make a special clearance of old school records, correspondence and other waste paper, especially during May while the special salvage drive is being carried out [and] to appeal to children to impress upon their parents the urgent need for saving paper for salvage collection.' However the schools were not required to ask children to collect from their homes. A memorandum from Swindon's Town Clerk to the Education Officer in October 1952 gave details of a 'Speed the Scrap' campaign for more scrap iron. 'It is felt that there must be many tons of scrap iron, steel and non-ferrous metals, both in depots and offices which are of no further value in their present form, and an appeal is made to all Chief Officers to arrange to salvage every bit of available scrap.'[395]

Rationing in the post-war period became more restricted than it had been during the war. The end of Lend-Lease, the world wide food shortage and Britain's balance of payments difficulties led to a reduced consumption of all foods, the exceptions being fish, sugar, potatoes and fruit during 1946 and 1948.[396] Rationing and controls were kept in place post-war to achieve an anti-inflationary and dollar economy policy, part of Labour's wider commitment to economic planning and fair shares. The 'Convertibility Crisis' of 1946 led to immediate food, petrol and even film cuts.[397] By 1946 British people were so sick of austerity food that they would rather eat too little than eat the food they could get hold of.[398] Zweiniger-Bargielowska feels that the policy objectives of import reductions and an 'export drive', coupled with Labour's socialist agenda meant that rationing was continued until the change of Government in 1951,[399] although it remained in a reduced form until 1954.

During wartime civilians had acquired less than four years the normal clothing supply and it was less than three years for household goods.[400] Perceived food deprivation became rife during the difficult year of 1947 and the topic was constantly debated.[401] Bread was rationed for two years from July 1946 with potatoes being controlled in the winter of 1947/8.[402] Despite rationing there were post-war domestic improvements in the kitchen. In 1951 a Mass Observation study found that the average housewife spent a quarter of her 75 hour week in the kitchen discovering the usefulness of new inventions, from teabags to the vacuum cleaner. The refrigerator was still too expensive for most families to own, but some did own a television.[403] In 1950s Bradford on Avon housewives would pop into their Southern Electricity Board showroom to 'pay their bills and watch encouraging cookery demonstrations on the new appliances,' and some households had a 'meat safe,' a cupboard with a metal grill on the front to allow air to circulate. Of these modern gadgets, the vacuum cleaner would have been an expensive buy. Only 33 % of homes had a washing machine.[404]

Peter Hennessy reports that the post-war period should not be seen as one of complete drabness and misery. 'True there wasn't much in the shops and there was even less money around to spend then. But to be young, alive and unwounded was a joyous experience…'[405]

Success at reducing consumption has been considered one of the most important consequences for the Home Front during WWII together with air raids, evacuation and the disruption of family life.[406] Even from 1942 rationing was thought to be the Second World War's finest achievement, pivotal in maintaining morale[407] and it was the 'most successful Government public relations exercise' that Hennessy has ever encountered.[408] It has been shown that inflation during WWII was lower than that in WWI; the Government's aim of stabilising inflation appears to have been met. This in turn aided Britain's post-war inflation position which Forrest Capie and Geoffrey Wood think could have been far worse. It appears that rationing was the key and without it both subsidies and price controls would not have worked.[409] It is also worth noting that Britain's longstanding connections to countries spanning the globe helped it feed the nation. Although it reduced its imports by weight, 56% of the calories consumed on British soil were imported.[410] The fashion industry found that the war and austerity years inspired British design in a positive way[411] and the utility scheme resulted in the introduction of regulated standards for materials and manufacture with consumers beginning to feel a right to demand value for money.[412] Make do and mend was not always miserable – some women felt proud of their achievements when their creativity was put to the test.[413] Food control had been essential to the British war effort and post-war reconstruction.[414]

When it came to austerity, housewives took on more than their share of the burden. The task of shopping and managing the family's meals and budget became extremely difficult due to rationing, shortages and queues. The pains they took to maintain the health of their families and to keep up morale were vital for the war effort and as in WWI their standing in society rose as a result.[415] Inequalities regarding the food consumed and the nutrients contained within them disappeared during WWII. After rationing ended the nutrient content and the quantity of food consumed remained similar between different classes and it was the family size which became a determining factor regarding the expenditure on food per head.[416] There is a myth that common purpose and 'universal sacrifice' occurred on the Home Front in regard to the consumption of goods, but in reality that sacrifice remained uneven at times. Many did not consider rationing to be fair, especially for those who had little money to spare[417] and abuse of the system did occur. However, the Government's food controls meant that consumption of goods and with it society at large became more equal than in the inter-war period. The Government's policy of food control had been essential to sustain morale on the Home Front.[418]

9
Home Front Health

AT THE OUTSET of WWII, one of the aims of the Government's food control policy was to supply the minimum necessary in order to maintain the health of its population.[1] A healthy civilian population would be able to work harder and give more for the war effort. The Executive Committees drew up the food policy after consultation with the Ministries of Food and Shipping. They also gained scientific advice about balanced diets.[2] In 1919 the Ministry of Health had been created and the National Health Insurance Scheme worked in conjunction with child welfare clinics and the school health service. The issue of nutrition had been looked at in the inter-war period and had been largely ignored, the Government trying to blame ill heath amongst the poor on ignorance rather than an inadequate diet, as Lizzie Collingham notes, 'bad cooking, bad marketing [and] bad household economy'. Now the war had forced the issue and these experts found themselves giving advice to the Ministry of Food, finally able to exert pressure in the decision making process.[3]

Health and Nutrition

THE BOARD OF Education had set about assessing the malnutrition of children in the 1930s alongside its provision of school meals and milk, but John Welshman reports that the issues remained unresolved by 1939. To monitor the effectiveness of the Government's aim to keep the civilian population healthy it called upon the physiologist and nutritionist Dr Hugh Sinclair to undertake a survey of the nutritional status of those most at risk of malnutrition in the UK population through the Oxford Nutritional Survey. In fact two surveys were conducted and the nutrition of pregnant women was looked at between 1942 and 1944. The findings showed that almost 25% of the women followed in 1942 were deficient in protein, and over 60% deficient in iron and vitamin A. This led to the Ministries of Health and Food bringing in a food supplementation policy. By the end of 1942 pregnant women were given additional access to fruit, dairy produce and cod liver oil tablets.[5] In 1940 Tisbury WI were reporting in their Committee

Minute Book that they had been recruited by the Public Health Department to advise mothers and infants of the extra foods they might be entitled to, to 'make known to all it may concern and point out that it is very important for the good of the health of mothers and children.'[6] The *Our Towns* Report of 1943 recommended that access to school meals needed to be widened; that restaurants, pubs, milk and potato bars (establishments set up for the consumption of milk and potato based food and drink) needed to be set up in working class areas, and that a permanent policy on nutrition based around the wartime rationing system should be put into place. Welshman feels that evacuation proved a catalyst for change to policy in this area in the early 1940s.[7] The biochemists Elsie Widdowson and R. A. McCance were also busy looking at how far the diet of 1939/40 could meet the needs of the civilian population to maintain health and fitness, experimenting on themselves and concluding that the current levels were adequate in all but calcium. Britain's leading nutritionists Professor E. P. Cathcart, Professor Sir Edward Mellanby and Sir John Boyd Orr were included on the 1940 formed Scientific Sub-Committee on Food Policy, mainly concerned with food production, but Jack Drummond, Nutrition Biochemist at University College London was appointed Chief Scientific Advisor. A long-term plan was created to ensure the nutritional quality of the wartime diet. By 1941 the system was beginning to work well, recognising the importance of animal protein in the diet and giving these products priority when it came to food imports. Work to fortify food with vitamins and minerals was also taking place.[8]

Hand in hand with austerity came the extension of nutrition in food, and during the early 1940s a planned policy of nutrition emerged which added vitamins to margarine and flour, and extended communal feeding. A scheme using milk and eggs was launched in 1941 to raise the intake of protein, calcium and vitamins for expectant and nursing mothers, children, adolescents and invalids. The Vitamin Welfare Scheme of December 1941 entitled expectant and nursing mothers and children under five to free fruit juices and cod liver oil or vitamin tablets,[9] but the milk, fruit and juice schemes had their origins in the inter-war period.[10] There was free orange juice for under 5s from 1942 and those aged under 11 received free orange juice and cod liver oil from 1946 onwards.[11] Lily Cooper from Warminster recalled that '[e]very morning our teacher doled out the compulsory medicines. These were things like Cod Liver Oil and Malt, Parishes Food, or Scotts Emulsion.'[12] At school in Bemerton: 'The nurse would sit in the cloakroom and we would queue to be given a teaspoon of cod liver oil.'[13] By 1943 only one in five of those eligible were actually claiming their allowance. Following an aggressive advertising campaign this figure had risen to a half.[14] In Warminster schools Lily Cooper notes that 'the milk came in a churn with a one third of a pint measure to use to fill earthenware cups. I was really pleased to be given this to do when it was my turn to be 'milk monitor'.'[15] One Cricklade resident remembers the free milk provided at school; each child had to bring in a mug to use. The children took turns being milk monitors, '... carrying a small churn into the various classrooms, and ladling the milk into the children's mugs with a tiny third-of-a-pint measure. If there was any left over, they'd annoy the teachers by giving out second helpings. With no hot water, the mugs were then swilled out under the tap and put back, so that by the weekend they needed a good scrub at home.'[16] The 1944 survey found that with supplementation the proportion of women who were suffering from vitamin deficiency had fallen but that protein and iron concentration had actually declined. This possibly indicated a lack of meat which corresponded with Government figures suggesting a fall in the average consumption of meat between 1942 and 1945. The results influenced the Government's policy on food both in wartime and after.[17] In Mere during the immediate post-war period one resident remembered that at school: 'Every day we had to line up for a spoonful of Cod Liver Oil. We also had a small bottle of milk given to us by the pupil milk monitor for the day.' Her mother had to fetch cod liver oil and concentrated orange juice for her pre-school sister. She collected it from the local Ration Office.[18] The Ministry of Food's concern over standards led to improvements in safety and in the quality of milk,[19] and on 10 July 1940 the County Analyst was visiting the County School in Bromham to take away a milk sample.[20]

The County School in Bromham was receiving its quota of orange juice for under 5s in accordance with a Board of Education Memorandum, 16 December 1943 (WSA F8/500/42/1/2)

Food manufacturers were making the most of the nutrition campaign, combining it with the difficulties that came with living in wartime Britain. Rowntree's Cocoa was advertising its product in the *Wiltshire Times*, 24 June 1944, by printing a housewife's tips on how to manage 'good meals'. The article went on to state: 'To drink we always have Rowntree's Cocoa – we take it in a flask when we go on a picnic. It's a wise decision, Rowntree's Cocoa. So many things we drink at meal-time contain no nourishment at all! But Rowntree's Cocoa contains protein (bodybuilding food); fat; carbohydrate, which gives energy (in the way *sugar* does); and iron for the blood…' Printed in the *Salisbury Gazette* on 31 January 1941 was an article entitled *Health in your Shelter this Winter by a Doctor of Science*. It warned of the health hazards and discomfort of shelter life in winter, the exposure to draught and damp, together with 'nerve tension and anxiety, call for some extra protection of our well-being. This protection is afforded by appropriate foods. It is here that the food beverage 'Ovaltine' can be most helpful. It is made from natural foods. It is simple to prepare. It is delightful to take. But the main reason is that it combines the nutritive food properties of two almost perfect foods – milk and eggs – and the highly digestible… barley malt together with the rich health protective enzymes, and minerals of these foods, in perfect organic unity…'

Milk had been regarded as one of the most important dietary provisions for children. The National Milk scheme which was launched just after Dunkirk was providing free milk to the poorest families and by September 1944 the majority of those entitled were taking up their provision.[21] Children under five could have seven pints of subsidised or free milk and children aged 5-17 were entitled to 3.5 pints per week alongside their school allocation from the milk-in-schools scheme which had been established in the 1930s. It has been estimated that just over 50% of children took school milk before the war; the figure had risen to 76% by 1944 and continued to rise in the immediate post-war period.[22] Milk supplies were sometimes low and some of Wiltshire's school log books reported problems with supply due to a period of drought, such as at Compton Bassett in September 1940 when they received no milk for a week.[23] At Ivy Lane School in Chippenham the Head Teacher noted that in September 1941 the milk began to be delivered in pint bottles, taking more time to prepare. 'In these days much more time is absorbed by the School Medical Officer, by National Savings' drives and by other national schemes eg. Salvage collection – on account of the time in which we live.' The Head Teacher found that the amount of clerical work involved with health and the evacuees was 'almost overbearing.' 'The School Medical Officer makes many demands – one re. diphtheria immunisation cards could not be carried out. I informed the Deputy Director of Education of the amount of clerical work required on the occasion of the CO [County Office].' Head Teachers were being put under severe pressure due to a lack of supply teachers. By January 1942 both of the teachers at Ivy Lane were again absent and supply teachers were 'at a premium.' 'Apart from that County Office expects schools to 'carry on' during the temporary absences of teachers.'[24]

Medical services were overstretched during the war and hospital care, school medical services, maternity and child welfare clinics found it difficult to maintain services with staff shortages. A Government enquiry in 1943 found that the standard of medical service for the civilian population had become 'dangerously low,' but the ability of the people to eat more nutritiously and be more aware of hygiene made a difference.[25] In 1939 there was a new awareness that school medical inspections could not give an accurate assessment of nutrition, but Civil Servants were determined to use it as a method of measurement during the war until 1944 when the issue again became apparent.[26] The Chippenham doctor Joan Hickson was constantly called upon to undertake school medical inspections. She revealed her feelings in a diary entry of 7 May 1942. 'What can possibly be the good of counting up the number of tonsils or adenoids only as opposed to both together and with or without glands in the neck? Going through the damned cards 8 or 9 times, never getting the wretched statistics right – and feeling I am too old now to do it any more for the money… Anyway I loathe the work so intently and feel it is so useless and a waste of a doctor's time. An intelligent nurse or mother could sort out any problems and send the child to their own GP with much better results.'[27] She noted in a diary entry of January 1945 how the war had been taking

DRIED EGGS

The Ministry of Food package contains 12 eggs for 1/9d. or 1⅛d. each.

This dried egg is pure fresh egg with no additions, and nothing but the moisture taken away. It is pure egg, spray dried.

Eggs are a very highly concentrated form of food. They contain first-class body-building material. They also help us to resist colds and other infection because of their high pro-tective properties.

Eggs are easily digested, and for this reason are especially good for children and invalids.

Dried eggs are just as good as fresh eggs, and should be used in the same way. They are very useful for main dishes. Here are some recipes for a variety of appetising dishes in place of meat, fish or cheese and which are particularly suitable for dried egg.

HOW TO RECONSTITUTE DRIED EGG

1 level tablespoonful egg powder
2 „ „ water
} equals 1 egg.

Mix the egg and water and allow to stand for about five minutes until the powder has absorbed the moisture. Then work out any lumps with a wooden spoon, finally beating with a fork or whisk.

TREAT LIKE FRESH EGGS

After reconstituting the egg use at once. Do not reconstitute more egg than necessary for immediate use.

METHOD OF COOKING

Use in recipes exactly as fresh eggs, beating as usual before adding to other ingredients.

STORAGE

Keep the egg powder in a tin with a tight fitting lid, and store in a cool place. Do not keep dried egg in a refrigerator.

Information from the Ministry of Food regarding the use of dried eggs (WSA G15/225/2)

its toll. 'Domestically things are still pretty hard. All through January I worked a 14 hour day with only the briefest intervals for food and never dared sit down, but got through it with the aid of sleeping pills at night and benzedrine in the day... The prevailing recollection of all this time is fatigue.'[28]

School children had been measured and weighed regularly during school medical inspections since the end of the 19th century[29] when the knowledge gained by the Victorians (and later the Edwardians) through mass schooling led to interest in a new 'child study movement', looking towards collectivist ways of solving social problems. Government legislated on school feeding during the early part of the 20th century. During the inter-war years the Government attempted to influence the behaviour of adults by gaining access to them through their children.[30] Reformers had tried to tackle public health issues before the war, but according to Peter Ginn their efforts had been 'stifled'.[31] Dairy farmers had been actively resisting the introduction of regulations seen as essential for health reasons such as milk pasteurisation, which was not fully introduced until 1949 on commercial grounds due to successful lobbying through the Ministry of Agriculture. Pasteurisation was intended to reduce the spread of milk-transmitted tuberculosis, and was called by Dr Summerskill the Milk (Save the Children) Bill.[32] In 1936 William Beveridge had seen rationing as a way of 'tackling the serious hunger-induced health issues of the day'; the wartime diet was seen as not just about survival but for a healthier life.[33] Lord Woolton, the Minister of Food, had lived in the Liverpool slums himself and had been greatly affected by the death of his next door neighbour due to starvation. Angus Calder notes that '[h]is interest in nutrition was deep and sincere'; his arrival at the Ministry of Food in 1942 led to the top officials in the Ministry being trained to see the need to view even small decisions in a nutritional context.[34] He found himself in the position to use his power, as Collingham notes, to 'stamp out all the diseases that arose from malnutrition, especially among children'.[35] Dietary experts had discussed how best to feed the nation in the event of war. Suggested methods included increasing the production of products such as milk, meat and eggs or curtailing the production of these products to enable the expansion of crops such as cereals and potatoes, but the Government was far more focused on the 'ploughing up' campaign than in specifics of nutrition.[36] The Government targeted large families and gave additional support to vulnerable groups. Ina Zweiniger-Bargielowska notes that the 'fitness of babies and school children was particularly striking'.[37]

The BBC broadcast *The Radio Doctor* from 1941, which continued to air for 10 years and educated listeners on what was healthy to eat and what was not, but it seems that this propaganda message was not getting through to over 8,000 workers surveyed in 1942. When asked which food was most important for their health, many asked that the question be repeated and/or to explain what was meant. Two thirds of the men said 'meat' and more attributed a greater importance to tea than beans or lentils. The results indicated that people were not overly concerned with what was good for them; the foods they considered essential to their well-being were, as Calder puts it, the 'items of their traditional diet which they missed most'.[38] But for one housewife in Swindon, the message did appear to be getting through. 'Too much use of the frying pan was frowned on by the health advisers and mother was once again listening to the Radio Doctor...'[39]

Good health, however, was not just about the consumption of food. Mothers found it particularly hard to clothe their children with the worst item being footwear, and this was a constant grievance throughout the war. Children were given additional coupons but they were often not enough.[40] Ina Zweiniger-Bargielowska reports that 'Harass[ed] mothers... worried about serious foot deformities resulting from the shoe shortage'. Footwear issues remained critical throughout 1942 and it was felt that the Government showed, as Zweiniger-Bargielowska notes, 'no sign whatsoever of understanding the difficulties of the growing child'. 'Make do and Mend' leaflets helped by giving tips on how to repair children's clothes and make new ones out of unwanted adult clothing.[41] A Trowbridge mother was writing to the *Wiltshire Times* in disgust on 7 August 1943 regarding the shoe situation. 'Surely it's time someone in authority did something about the rubbish we are sold for boots. The average life of a pair of child's boots or shoes is three weeks, whatever price you pay. I have three children, and to keep them shod is a proper headache; all their coupons are needed for footwear alone. My coupons have all been spent on kiddies' shoes, except for three required for my uniform coat. Repairs are now taking a month to six weeks, as there are no men home to do them for us. Provide us with decent footwear for our kiddies... Every mother knows that bad or ill-fitting shoes can ruin a child's feet for life.' The Education Department in Swindon was also well aware of the footwear shortage. In December 1941 they wrote to all their Head Teachers, stating that, 'owing to the Clothes Rationing Order,' it may be necessary to provide an additional supply of shoes 'so that Physical Training shall not suffer through the lack of suitable shoes... it may be possible to supply a sufficient number so that any one class may be equipped at a time.'[42] After the Japanese had cut off the British supply of rubber, the height of heels on shoes was restricted to two inches. Wooden soles were also introduced to help ease the situation but they were awkward to walk in. Clogs made a comeback; they were hard wearing and coupon free.[43] The clothing exchanges run by the Women's Voluntary Service from 1943 attempted to ease the footwear situation but the problem remained and continued into the post-war period. When the *Sunday Pictorial* ran *100 Families to speak for Britain* in 1946, the inability to purchase shoes was raised, with one lady trying twenty different shops without success.[44]

Inadequately shod children could also struggle to get to school and there were the health implications of spending too much time in cold, wet apparel, although this problem had been a long standing issue in rural areas. By December 1943 ten pairs of wellington boots were applied for by the Head Teacher of a school in Heywood from a number 'sent to this Country as a gift from America and Canada.' The school received eight in January 1944 with a further two pairs to follow. Another five pairs were received at the beginning of 1945 'for children who have a long distance to come to school.'[45] In Brinkworth, November 1944, the

Head Teacher of the school applied to the Women's Voluntary Services Clothing Depot at Calne on behalf of the children who needed wellington boots.[46] By 1950 well fitting shoes were available to all who needed them.[47]

Form C. 5 for the supply of boots and clothing for evacuees, 1943 (WSA F8/600/11/1/17/2)

Supplements and Communal Feeding

THE WILTSHIRE FEDERATION of Women's Institutes was giving out instructions for the gathering of rose hips in September 1941 to run alongside a national campaign, 'Rose-hip Week' on 28 September. WI members, Scouts, Girl Guides and schoolchildren were all asked to help. The manufacturers would pay 2s. a stone and any ripe hips would do, even from the garden.[48] Devizes schoolchildren collected rose hips in the autumn 'to provide vitamin C for babies and small children'.[49] The children of Heywood School also helped by picking rose hips, collecting twenty four and a half pounds in November 1944. Almost

FOOD FACTS

Thank the farmer—

bless the weather—for

plenty of green vegetables *NOW!*

A mild season has advanced the crops — that's why health-giving green vegetables are top-of-the-bill this week. Make the most of them while they last! We all need all the Vitamin C we can get, *and* more variety in our diet. Make cabbage a "special" tonight. Make greenstuffs a daily "extra" while they stay plentiful and cheap. It's nothing but common sense to go for the good things while they are at their cheapest and most abundant. So fill your shopping-basket at the greengrocer's!

4 RULES FOR COOKING GREEN VEGETABLES

1 Don't soak green vegetables before cooking. Wash them thoroughly in cold salted water.

2 Cook them as quickly as possible.

3 Use only enough water to keep pan from burning. A teacupful is usually enough.

4 Bring water to the boil, put in shredded greens, put the lid on the pan and cook steadily for 10 to 15 minutes. Give the pan a shake once or twice during that time. Serve at once.

National Milk Scheme. Important. Apply to the Food Office this week for authorised to free year old milk for expectant mothers, and free milk for children holding R.B.1 green books. Take us send the ration book when you apply. Expectant mothers must also produce medical certificates. R.B.1 before are eligible for free supplies of liquid milk and not vary.

LISTEN TO THE KITCHEN FRONT EVERY MORNING AT 8.15

THE MINISTRY OF FOOD, LONDON, W.1 FOOD FACTS No. 14

Ministry of Food Advertisement in the Wiltshire Gazette, 4 February 1943 'Food Facts Thank the farmer – bless the weather – for plenty of green vegetables now!' (WSHC Microform Collection)

a year later the school received 4s. 1½d. for them.[50] The 'Dig for Victory' campaign had a medical aspect too. The Dig for Victory Leaflet No. 32 *How to Grow Small Fruits* emphasised the fact that these fruits, especially blackcurrants, were 'valuable sources of the important vitamin C, which prevents scurvy.'[51] An early Government poster proclaimed 'Women! Farmers can't grow all your vegetables. You must grow your own. Farmers are growing more of the essential crops – potatoes, corn for your bread, and food for the cows. It's up to you to provide the vegetables that are vital to your children's health.'[52]

Herwald Ramsbotham, the Board of Education's Private Secretary, noted in June 1940 that making school meals popular would be '… an important educational advance'. Schools meals were seen to be an integral part of the Communal Meals Division at the Ministry of Food, necessary as part of an integrated policy of nutrition which included British Restaurants and factory canteens. By July 1941 school meals were being viewed as a permanent feature of the educational system; Local Authorities had a duty to provide both school meals and milk, and to employ a School Meals Organiser under the 1944 Education Act.[53] The number of children taking school meals rose from *c.* 160,000 before the war to 1.6 million in 1945. These subsidised meals provided children with up to 1,000 calories a day[54] and meant that from only 4% of children receiving a school meal, by the end of the war 40% were now doing so, helped by a rise in quality. School meals had finally lost their association with poverty and had, according to Zweiniger-Bargielowska, 'became an integral part of school routine'.[55] Welshman notes that during the war a 'transformation of attitudes' occurred regarding the provision of school meals and milk which would continue into the 1960s[56] but it appears that in 1944 Wiltshire County Council were reporting on the 'devastating' cost of school meals in the 25 February edition of *The Salisbury and Winchester Journal*. There was an estimated increase of £42,000 for the provision of the meals which it was hoped would be somewhat recoverable by £26,300 in sales. By 1945 over one in three children were fed at school.[57] In April 1943 *The Lady* Magazine reported that: 'Many wives and mothers are able to give their families better and more regular meals under war conditions than ever before.'[58] The ration levels brought every person up to the consumption level of a skilled worker.[59]

Communal feeding was a way to provide nutrition for adults and pre-school children too, whereby needy groups could be fed with a nutritional meal and the Government could 'influence the dietary'. Churchill was not impressed with the term 'communal feeding', and wrote to Lord Woolton, Minister of Food. 'I hope the term 'Communal Feeding Centres' is not going to be adopted. It is an odious expression, suggestive of communism and the workhouse. I suggest you call them 'British Restaurants'. Everybody associates the word 'restaurant' with a good meal, and they may as well have the name if they cannot get anything else.'[60]

Poster advertising a British Restaurant (WSA G22/225/4)

The energy requirements of ordinary consumers were supplemented by the development of British Restaurants. These non-profit organisations were set up by Local Authorities and were run voluntarily by the WVS[61] until March 1941 when all Feeding Centres were transferred to the Ministry of Food, run by the WVS and/or paid staff.[62] At their peak[63] in 1943 they were serving over 600,000 subsidised meals a day in over 2,000 restaurants. The nutritional standard was meant to be high and it was aimed at stopping fathers taking their child's meat ration at home. Communal feeding was also used to help evacuated families.[64] By 1943 men working in heavy industry were complaining that they did not get enough meat to eat and British Restaurants alongside factory canteens were used to address the problem.[65] The Women's Voluntary Service's Rural Pie Scheme also addressed the issue for agricultural workers in the fields. The Scheme peaked at an average distribution of one and a quarter million meals a week to *c.* 5,000 villages. The provision of the British Restaurant as a non-profit making concern meant that the Local Authorities who were left to provide them could be slow and apathetic in doing so,[66] as appears to have been the case in Malmesbury, where the Town Council were accused of 'steadfastly refus[ing] to make a move'.[67] The atmosphere in those that were created was described as friendly, and that, combined with their good food, made them popular.[68] Bradford on Avon's British Restaurant was the first to open in the West Wilts. area. Bob Randall recalls: 'The meal was remarkable, not only for its low price and high quality but also for the generous size of the helpings...'[69]

There was also an increase in industrial canteens, with *c.* 1,500 before the war becoming *c.* 18,500 by 1944, but the quality of the food was variable and many workers stuck to their old ways of taking a packed lunch to work.[70] On 24 May 1941 the British Growers' Publicity Council was advising Local Authorities that it was working on a national food campaign of wartime vegetable recipes for Community Feeding Centres and Canteens. Their leaflets, specially prepared by the Council's expert and approved by the Ministry of Food, were then sent directly to Local Authorities.[71]

PATRIOTIC SOUP

8 pints stock or water.	1 lb. minced beef.
¼ lb. fine chopped onion or leek.	6 ozs. oatmeal (medium or coarse).
2 lbs. grated carrots.	Seasoning.
2 tablespoonfuls meat or vegetable extract (optional).	

Method. Place the minced beef in the pan. Heat slowly, stirring until some fat is extracted. Add onion and cook for a few minutes. Add the oatmeal and continue cooking for 3 or 4 minutes, without browning. Add the grated carrot, stock and salt. Simmer gently 1½–2 hours. Add the meat or vegetable extract and more seasoning if necessary.

Issued by the British Growers' Publicity Council, 68 Victoria Street, Westminster. S.W.1. April 1941

The British Growers' Publicity Council recipe for 'Patriotic Soup', 1941 (WSA F2/850/10)

Marlborough was getting ready for a new British Restaurant at The Green in February 1942. The Ministry of Food had approved the proposals and estimates for equipping the restaurant, totalling £1,235 6s. 8d., which included a potato peeling machine and a large mincer. The Ministry was prepared to make a payment to the Council for the cost 'as soon as substantial progress has been made with the equipment in the kitchen.' A condition of accepting capital expenditure reimbursement from the Government was that a 'monthly income and expenditure

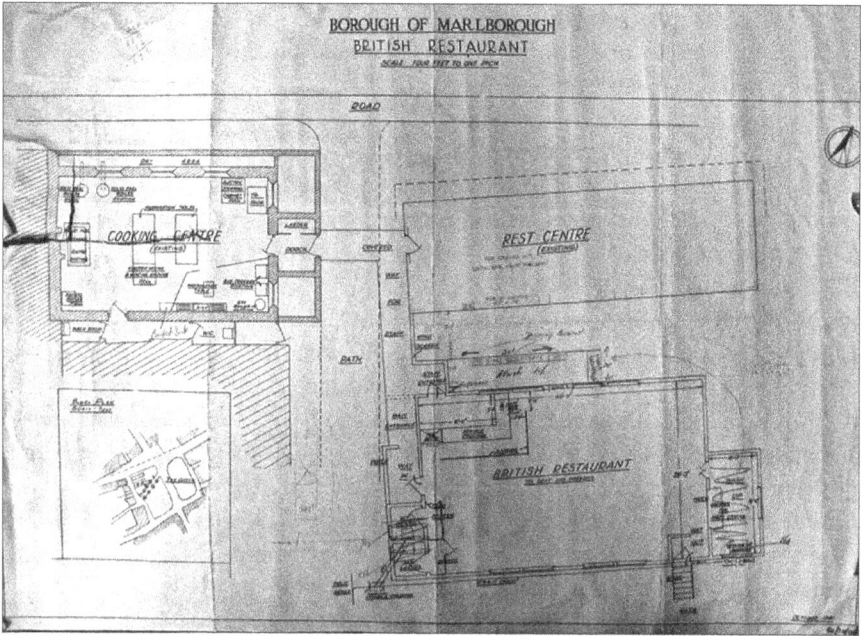

Plan, Scale 4ft to 1', October 1941, for a Cooking Centre, adjacent to the Rest Centre and British Restaurant, to seat 100 persons (situated below the Rest Centre). Also a location plan for the British Restaurant, 1:1,250 situated in a road off The Green, Marlborough (WSA G22/701/12PC)

account and balance sheet, certified by a competent official, [should] be forwarded to the Ministry.'[72]

Cooking Depots such as the one at Holt were used to produce food to supply schools and other establishments that required it. A Depot supplying 500 meals a day would be staffed by 5-7 persons. By February 1943 the Wiltshire County Council Emergency Committee was reporting that both the Holt and Wilton Depots were producing approximately 1,000 meals per day. Wiltshire County Council was under the impression that although they were responsible for the running of the county's Depots, it was the Ministry of Food who would drum up demand for the meals, except in the case of schools. It was noted that a Depot would not be able to run at a profit unless it was supplying a minimum of 2,000 meals per day. The Minutes of Wiltshire County Council's Emergency Committee on 7 January 1943 stated: 'That the Ministry be informed that the County Council only undertook to operate Cooking Depots on the distinct understanding that the whole of the loss would be borne by the Ministry; and that the Committee ask, in the light of recent circulars issued by the Ministry, to have a re-assurance on this point, that if a satisfactory guarantee cannot be given that the number of meals will be augmented and that the loss in running will continue to be paid by the Ministry, they will have no alternative to considering the question of closing the [Holt] Depot.'[73] Cooking Depots appear to have been a good way to supply local schools with meals. In March 1943 the parents of 26 Public Elementary Schools in the Pewsey area were anxious for their children to receive a mid-day meal at school. The General Education Committee was urging the Emergency Committee to open a Cooking Depot at Pewsey.[74] Vans were provided to transport the meals to the schools but, as in the case of July 1943, they were often second-hand vehicles and there were often not enough vans to cover all the routes. Councils needed a permit to purchase the vans and these could take a long time to be granted.[75] Schools were provided with emergency rations in case the school meals transport broke down.[76] In January 1945 the school at Heywood received two six pound tins of meat and one five pound tin of biscuits from the Catering Office to be used to feed the children in an emergency. That very same month bad weather made the roads impassable and no hot meals were brought to the school. The emergency food was used instead. Five days later no hot meals arrived and the children had to be sent home.[77] Schools such as Leigh[78] reported problems receiving the school meals on time; it often played havoc with the school timetable. In Brinkworth, hot meals at school began in November 1942[79] and in May 1942 the County Canteen Organiser visited Stratton St. Margaret School to organise school dinners for pupils. They were taken at the Methodist Hall.[80] In Brinkworth, the School Meals Organiser had arranged for meals to be delivered to the school. This was causing problems by July 1944 when the dinners from the Wootton Bassett 'cooking area' arrived late again, causing the dinner hour to overrun. His Majesty's Inspector called in September to discuss help with dinners; the school needed paid help or Women's Voluntary Service (WVS) assistance.[81] The Ministry of Food's Ford Emergency Food Vans Scheme was terminated in July 1945 but the Wartime Meals Division noted that the demand for vehicles for 'essential services' still exceeded supply. 'It has therefore been agreed with the [Ford Emergency Vans] Trust that the vans will be offered to Local Authorities now using them at the price of £155 each.'[82]

It appears in 1943 that the Ministry of Food was worried about the level of care and maintenance given to equipment used in Cooking Depots and British Restaurants, suggesting that both over scrubbing and inadequate cleaning were causing problems. The Marlborough Borough Council Clerk received a standard letter from the Ministry in September stating: 'From reports received it would seem that insufficient care is being taken of insulated containers, field boilers... Insulated containers are particularly important since their good condition depends not only on their lasting properties but also the transporting and good condition of food to school, British Restaurants etc. ... If the tinning has worn away, it will be necessary to send the containers to the manufacturers for re-tinning. Where, through neglect, signs of rusting are visible, the use of a non-abrasive cleaning powder will usually suffice to restore the container to good condition.'[83]

Members of Trowbridge Urban District Council were visiting a British Restaurant in Bath on 9 September 1942 with a view to opening their own. They had come back very impressed with the smooth running of the Restaurant, and had been advised to ensure that they opened with sufficient staff to prevent customers having to queue and become dissatisfied. Also advised was the use of paid staff rather than soldier's wives: '... as they want time off every time their husbands are on leave, causing disorganisation & dissatisfaction among the other staff.' Equipment that was an absolute necessity was a cold storage room and refrigerator. 'Without one or the other it would be impossible to prevent a serious waste of food.' The planned site was to be at the lower end of the Park where a public footway passed through. Two Nissen huts would be used, one to be the main dining hall seating 250 (63 tables seating four in a yellow colour; the chairs would be green). The second hut would be the kitchen block, the buildings being inter-connected by covered lobbies. As for toilets, these were considered a 'luxury and unnecessary,' especially as there were public toilets nearby. Staff toilets would be provided. The Restaurant would provide a 'cash and carry home' and a 'cash and carry Restaurant Service' via a separate counter in the kitchen block. There would also be another counter in the kitchen, accessible via the restaurant. The diner would first need to obtain a ticket for the meal they desired before exchanging it at the food counter.[84] Due to paper shortages[85] the Ministry of Food decided to change to plastic colour coded tokens in 1942.[86] Examples of the tokens used at Marlborough British Restaurant survive.[87]

The Ministry of Food was to supply the tables and chairs, service trays, washing-up cloths, wagons for dirty crockery, service counter containers, solid fuel boilers, gas hot cupboards, gas heated 'safe sets' (for tea and coffee), etc. It was the Council's job to provide a 'dish washing machine, washing-up [equipment] and buckets, sinks..., heating apparatus..., wireless set, kitchen equipment, crockery, cutlery, general stores etc.' It was also noted that emergency tinned food would be required for use in case of invasion. One of the dishwashers that the Council was looking at '[took] full size racks with full size dishwashing and rinsing capacity.' There was also a specification for an Euk Dishwashing machine and it was noted that a 'Hovis' clock was going to be one of the fittings along with a radio installation[88] which the Ministry of Food would authorise.[89] The Restaurant was re-opened by the County Council in Trowbridge on 9 August 1943 after it was closed by the Urban District Council. Cash takings amounted to £74 8s. 1½d.; more than expected. A sandwich man had been employed to display placards in the town on the opening day and direction signs were due to be erected as soon as a sign-writer could be found. The Ministry of Food had also been asked to sanction a ladies toilet at the Restaurant. Customer numbers for week one totalled 1,500; week two 2,974 and week three 1,213.[90]

The Ministry of Food's Wartime Meals Division even went as far as to give suggestions regarding the decoration of British Restaurants, stating that this could be a problem area, especially for those premises which had been requisitioned and adapted for the purpose. 'There remain some British Restaurants which are by no means as cheerful or, it may be added, as successful as they might be were a little more attention given to their general appearance, and a number of Local Authorities, fully alive to this, have indicated to the Ministry of Food that they would welcome some guidance on the subject of decoration.' The guidance notes

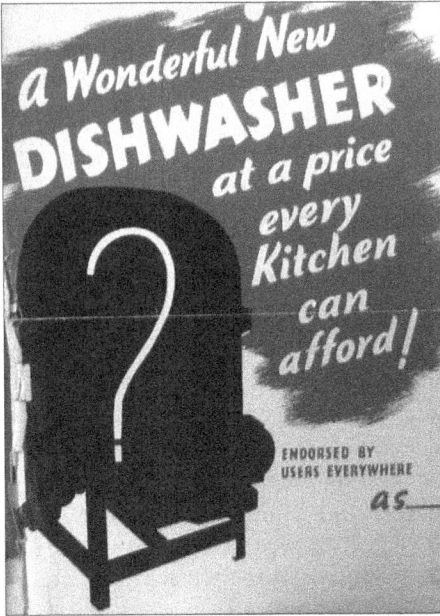

Advertisement for a dishwasher (Hobart model), discovered in the Surveyor's Wartime Correspondence files of Trowbridge Urban District Council, 1942 (WSA G15/225/22)

stated that 'the importance of light cannot be over stressed' and that 'even a notice board, for instance, if painted a bright, gay, colour, gives off more light than one finished in dark brown or black' and that light should be diffused. '[F]ew things are more depressing in a room than scattered 'pockets' of semi-darkness.' The colour tone of walls was discussed, using one striking colour to dominate and 'bring other colours into relation with it.' It was also suggested that wall decoration such as murals, painted panels or lithographs would brighten up 'difficult interiors.' Murals were highlighted in the work already done across the country by Art College students and local artists who were working with schoolchildren on the projects, also advising on the main colour scheme. 'It is generally agreed that the most pleasing designs are those which are on the lighter and more cheerful side, being neither too ponderous in conception nor too frivolous in treatment... Among the most successful themes are those based on incidents in history and traditions of the neighbourhood.' If it was not possible to do this, the Council for the Encouragement of Music and the Arts (CEMA) would be preparing a number of lithographs 'designed by distinguished living artists' in the form of events taking place over months of the year, such as tree felling in October or a picnic in May. Also being produced were collotype reproductions of 'paintings by masters of the past'. Some Local Authorities had decorated their British Restaurants with paintings loaned by local art galleries. 'The value of good lettering, both inside and outside their British Restaurants, has been well appreciated by many Local Authorities. Good lettering, appropriately coloured, can indeed play a not inconsiderable part in the general decorative scheme of the interior.'[91]

By July 1943 Corsham's Parish Council was asking for a British Restaurant in the town such as the one in Chippenham. The *Wiltshire Times* reported in its 24 July edition that the Parish Council thought it would be useful for the town's female war workers. '... [M]any married women in Corsham are now part-time workers, and consequently they have difficulty in preparing the mid-day meal.' Members of the Calne and Chippenham Rural District Council did not agree, however. They felt that it would be extremely difficult to find volunteers to run the

Restaurant, as 'they could not even get sufficient volunteers to serve cups of tea in the canteen for Service visitors to Corsham.' They also noted that the last British Restaurant had been run at a loss before being forced to close. One member went so far as to state that: 'Judging by the number of women walking about Corsham now he should think they had time to cook their husbands' meals themselves.' Workers had their own canteen where they could get meals at reasonable cost, and the Council Member did not see why they should be called upon to provide a Restaurant for women who were 'too lazy to cook their own dinners'. The Wartime Meals Officer at the Regional Offices of the Ministry of Food in Bristol was asking Calne's Town Clerk on 10 July 1945 what would be happening regarding the schoolchildren who regularly used the town's British Restaurant which was due to close. 'As a Local Authority, I am sure you would be as loath as we should be as a Ministry to cause hardship to children who have been relying on the restaurant for their midday meal'. The Town Clerk replied two days later stating that they had managed to keep the Restaurant open with voluntary help but that the Methodist Church who had given their schoolroom over for its use during the war badly needed it back.[92]

To April 1947 850 British Restaurants had survived but the Government had withdrawn its financial responsibility for communal feeding, leading to the gradual decline of the scheme, although a British Restaurant Service opened to the public at the Community Centre in Chippenham in 1951.[93] Approximately 10% of rationed food was consumed in catering establishments during the war.[94]

Medical Services

ANGUS CALDER NOTES that the provision of medical stores in general terms had been called the 'most remarkable achievement' of British war production with large increases in output using specialised technology. New drugs were created or imported and stocks replenished.[95] The US set up a hospital at Chiseldon which included an improved pharmacy. The staff reported on 13 January 1945 that they had encountered new British drugs which they began using with the help of the British Pharmaceutical Journal and telephone calls to the pharmacy at the local RAF hospital,[96] presumably RAF Wroughton. Seven million children received vaccination against diphtheria under the Emergency Hospital Scheme which, over the course of the war, made more people eligible for free treatment.[97] The County School at Bromham saw the doctor visiting to give the first of the diphtheria innoculations on 7 January 1940.[98]

During WWII the 'Goodtime Girls' caused a health scare and VD rates soared in autumn 1942 to 58 cases per 1,000 troops per annum,[99] although in September to November 1943, 910 arriving US soldiers had been hospitalised as soon as they got off the boat for VD at the infectious stage. The high rate of VD infection before reaching British soil was the cause, according to David Reynolds, of the biggest official grievance against the US Army on the part of the British.[100]

The Ministry of Health sent out discreet notices and a radio broadcast.[101] Many in the British military were worried that the US perception of Britain would be a 'nation of prostitutes' and British Welcome Clubs were introduced as a fix to introduce US troops to 'nicer' girls.[102] *The Salisbury and Winchester Journal* was reporting in its 25 February 1944 edition on the cost of treatment for VD cases which had increased by £1,100 in the annual budget. It was also reported that due to 'lax morality' the Council were now having to care for 'a large number of unwanted children' with a budget rise of £9,100 in child welfare to make this possible. The Wiltshire Women's Institute were discussing the value of 'sex instruction' at their County Conference in April 1944[103] and the Ministry of Labour and National Service in Swindon were so concerned for the welfare of women and young girls that they hoped an expert on sex education would undertake some talks in local factories.[104]

The Ministry of Health had been looking to make health care more widely available from the inter-war period. It was hoped to create a regional structure, placing the hospital at the 'apex of the system'[105] and had looked at the possibility of providing specialist medical services for all in 1936.[106] The Emergency Hospital Service was planned in 1938 but only began being utilised when the bombs started falling, revealing the differing standards in health care between regions.[107] The 'surgery boy' of one medical practice in Warminster described it as it was just before the war: 'Entering the surgery door, there was a tiled passage. The first room to the left was Dr Blackley's consulting room, and up the steps on the left, in the house, was Dr Hogan's consulting room. This was opposite the posh persons' waiting room. They would come in through the front door... To the right of the surgery door was the dispensary and my office.'[108] The Emergency Medical Service put into place during the war was a unification of the public and private hospital systems.[109] It was state funded and supervised by the Ministry of Health,[110] leading in the post-war period to a sytem which was administered regionally but which had a marked dependence on state funding.[111]

The Government's Memorandum No.2 issued by the Emergency Medical Services in 1939 and entitled *Emergency Hospital Organisation* stated that the hospital arrangements for an emergency were to be organised by the Minister of Health following liaison with the Local Authorities and representatives from the voluntary hospitals. Medical Officers of the Ministry, known as Hospital Officers, were appointed in June 1939 to prepare an Emergency Hospital Scheme suitable for their individual areas. Hospital accommodation was to be co-ordinated on a regional basis: 'the conception of casualty clearing stations and base hospitals... understood in previous wars, is not altogether applicable to modern warfare' and as such every hospital in the country needed to be prepared to play its part. Those in the immediate vicinity were to give first aid and those outside the danger zone would be the ones to receive casualties and any other long-term patients who needed to be transferred.[112] Not all hospitals were to be included in the Scheme, and those that were would be told which classification they came under. Different classifications had different purposes: Class 1A included all larger hospitals and

Class 1B small hospitals; Class 2 hospitals were those not suitable for the initial reception of casualties but were to be used for convalescence or chronic cases; Class 3 hospitals were for some infectious diseases hospitals in outer areas.[113] It was planned that during an emergency, ambulances would 'in conjunction with the first aid parties, collect casualties. Lightly injured casualties would be dealt with on the spot or directed or conveyed to the first aid posts, one of which it [was] hoped [would] be situated at or near to every casualty receiving hospital; and serious cases

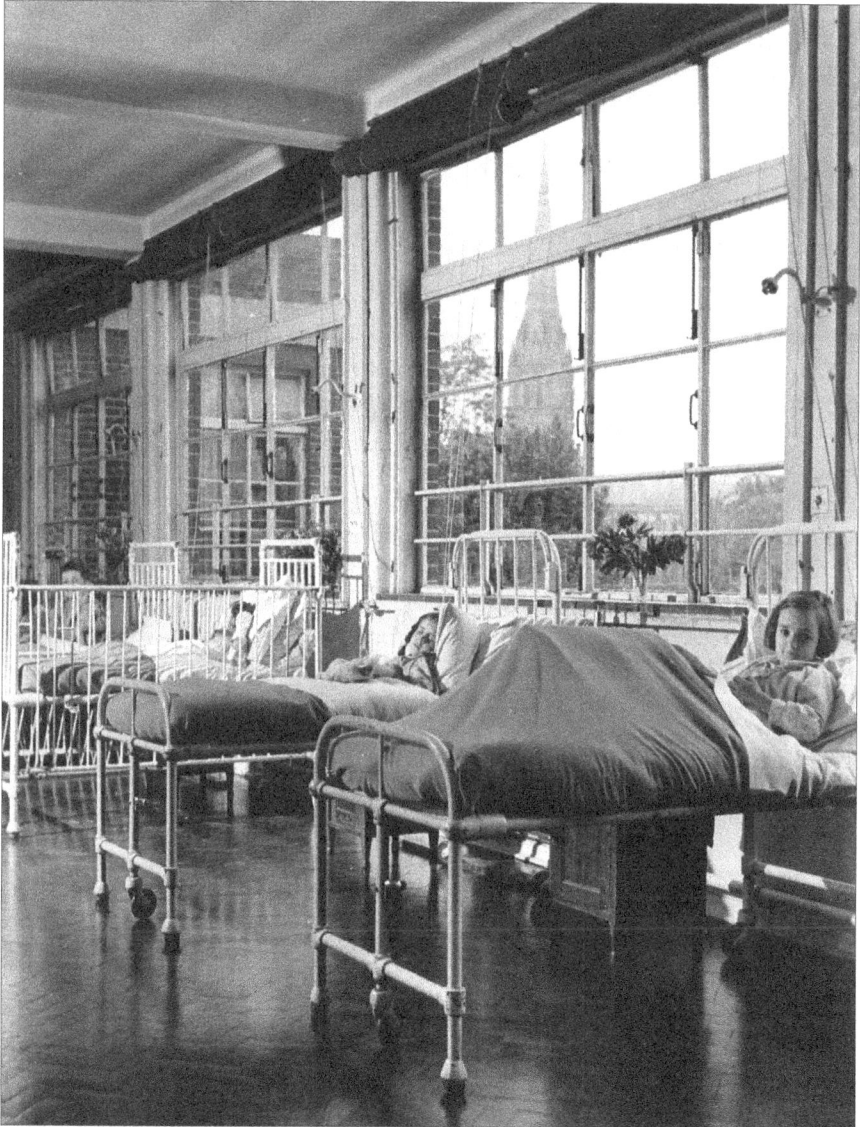

The children's ward at Melksham Hospital, 1942, courtesy of the British Council (WSHC P55951)

would be brought in the ambulances to the nearest class 1A hospital. If serious cases arrived at the aid posts, they would be received but subsequently transferred to a casualty hospital...'[114] By 1941 the Minister of Health, Ernest Brown, was announcing in Parliament the Government's aim to create a comprehensive hospital service as soon as possible after the war, with appropriate treatment available to all who needed it, and the Beveridge Report of 1942 included a free National Health Service, a 'crucial weapon' with which to tackle the Five Giants: Want, Disease, Ignorance, Squalor and Idleness.[115] The Scheme was initially meant to treat air raid casualties but took on greater roles such as immunisaton and free treatment which was extended. The Scheme maximised the benefit of scarce resources[116] and had brought together the public and voluntary hospital systems by 1943[117] but it was also a useful tool to raise morale. Mass Observation had suggested that civilians viewed healthcare as important and a concern.[118] In 1944 the Government published its White Paper, *A National Health Service*.[119]

The Great Western Railway's Hospital in Swindon opened in 1872 and its Medical Fund was registered as a statutory Friendly Society.[120] During 1943 it admitted 778 patients and performed 459 major operations, working closely with the town's St. Margaret's Hospital. Before any Government healthcare schemes medical contributions were paid by a married man which covered his wife and dependant children, but could also cover employees who had retired due to old age or infirmity, for example as a result of an accident at work, and also their wives and dependants. It was noted of the scheme that it 'began in 1847 with the kindness of the men in work who tried to help their less fortunate brethren over the doctor's bill.'[121] Ruth Marshall notes that before the war in Trowbridge: 'There were two ambulances... The ordinary ambulance that took you to Trowbridge hospital and the fever ambulance. Now the fever ambulance was a little brown old van that used to strike horror into people, because it took you up to the fever hospital...' A local grocer was the ambulance man. Before the NHS people, like this Trowbridge resident, 'paid into a scheme, there was the Pioneer and the West Wilts Conservatives ... you paid so much a week... when it came to you had help with paying for the doctor and that. I think a bottle of medicine was 3/6, which was a lot of money, when you didn't have much money. If you went in hospital it was ever such poor food and your family were expected to bring you in eggs and nourishing food.'[122] A branch surgery operated in Colerne for local residents, the main surgery being situated in nearby Marshfield, just over the border in Gloucestershire. During the inter-war period the doctor ran a club costing a couple of pence weekly for those who were not covered by the National Health Insurance Scheme[123] which had been set up in 1911 for wage earners.[124] As there was no local chemist, the doctor had to dispense medicines also, essential in rural areas when emergencies arose.[125]

One Warminster resident described his stay in the cottage hospital before the war. 'There were two main wards, a male and a female ward, with about 16 beds in each... there was a very nice atmosphere of competence and support.'[126] The Chippenham doctor Joan Hickson wrote of her feelings on 30 September

1942 after seeing a newspaper article about 'improved' medical services after the war which insinuated that at the present time the rich received the best treatment. 'Such articles make me see red, or any that insinuate that doctors do good work only for fees… It is absolutely untrue and libellous to suggest that medical staff scamp their work in voluntary hospitals in order to run off and see private patients. Quite the reverse is the case. Nearly all the consultants I know are much more interested in their hospital work than their private patients because the work is more interesting with less society small talk… The voluntary hospitals and still more the county institutions could be vastly improved in the way of general comfort and amenities and less red tape and institutional regulations, but I think it would be difficult to better the actual medical treatment of serious cases. Much could be done in the way of home helps for minor cases at home, more possibilities of convalescence at the sea after illness, and housing, food and hygienic conditions of all sorts need to be improved. Not that I am in favour of the voluntary hospitals continuing unaltered, far from it. I have always thought it very wrong that the medical staff should not be paid, but this is quite a different matter to having them all under bureaucratic red tape.'[127] By 23 March 1944 Wiltshire County Council's Emergency Committee was reporting that the Senior Regional Officer at the Minstry of Health felt it would not be necessary to retain the Emergency Hospital at Calne.[128]

The physical health of the nation had been improving, but mental health was another matter. Joan Hickson noted in October 1942 that '… mild neuroses are increasing again. At the beginning of the war it was not so noticeable as so many people had jobs which diverted their interest from themselves for the time being. Now they are all getting sick of it and tired and unable to cope with the difficulties of ration books etc, and are collapsing again.'[129] A diary entry in June 1944 told of '[a]nother case of Doodlebugitis for me in pm. A woman who had come down from Croydon worn out and must rush to have her glasses changed after two days. She had no proper sleep for nearly a fortnight and said no one could have a bath or go to the loo in peace. It was far worse than 1940… Finally I persuaded her to go off with a prescription for sleeping tablets…'[130] Mental stress could be caused from the loss of sleep from bomb alerts as well as the attacks themselves, and this included Civil Defence workers who also had day jobs[131] but Robert Mackay reports that neurotic illness, perhaps unexpectedly, did not rise during wartime[132] and Angus Calder notes that suicide rates fell from 12.9% in 1938 to 8.9% in 1944.[133]

The mental health of returning service personnel and those who had been affected by war in other ways, such as evacuees and Civil Defence personnel, would have ramifications for both their families and society at large when peace came. Fathers returning from battle might have been psychologically affected by the horrors of war and subsequently seem distant and strange to their children.[134] One Wiltshire soldier recalled in his memoirs the battle of El Alamein and the burial party that set out after the battle in October 1942. 'They came back with some very grisly stories… In the hardened state that everyone was in, these stories would not have worried us a bit had they concerned the enemy but since it was friends and mates who a few hours had been joking and laughing with us, they certainly subdued us, and had a depressing effect which lasted several days.'[135] When meeting a man in Chippenham who had fought with the Wiltshire Regiment in Normandy, an acquaintance noted the horror that was still apparent on his face. 'When he spoke to me of those terrible days in Normandy, his eyes were full of tears...'[136]

Unfortunately newcomers coming into the county such as evacuees brought with them infectious diseases. The Malmesbury Rural District Council reported its first outbreak of paratyphoid in over 20 years in October 1941. Cases of pulmonary tuberculosis came via carriers from Bristol. The cases were brought under control by the Medical Officer with assistance from the American Red Cross.[137] The school log books of Wiltshire include many regular entries regarding inoculations. The Head Teacher of Ivy Lane School in Chippenham reported in November 1940 that the school had been having problems with diphtheria since 1939.[138] Compton Bassett School was closed each Monday and Friday throughout July as part of the summer vaccination scheme of 1940 and in May 1942 they were immunising children for diphtheria at the school. Immunisation had taken place, but unfortunately one boy had died of the disease.[139] On 7 August 1943 a notice was published in the *Wiltshire Times* regarding the protection of children from diphtheria by immunisation. 'I think it is only right that you should know that diphtheria is a poisonous disease... In Great Britain diphtheria killed 3,155 persons in 1940. It killed 3,158 persons in 1941 and 2,116 persons in 1942. Of those deaths in 1942, 1,888 were children under 15.' In the 22 July 1944 edition of the *Wiltshire Times* the Trowbridge and District Isolation Hospital Committee was reporting the death of a child who had not been immunised. They viewed one case in particular as '... a life needlessly thrown away. In my opinion those people who, in their ignorance are attempting to dissuade parents from accepting the benefits of this service are taking upon themselves a very terrible responsibility, for there is no questioning the fact that by so doing they are jeopardising the lives of children. Seven million children received vaccination against diphtheria under the Emergency Hospital Scheme which, over the course of the war, made more people eligible for free treatment.'[140] The *Wiltshire Gazette* was reporting on the need for more blood donors in Wiltshire on 24 August 1946. The Army Blood Transfusion Service had been responsible for the supply of blood to the armed forces and civilians through local hospitals. The Ministry of Health took over the service in the post-war period, estimating that it required 4,500 donors a year to meet the needs of the county. It is presumed that medical advances or the new health system led to an increase in demand; a hospital which used 80 bottles a year before the war now required 80 a week. One lady from Mere became critically ill in 1944 following the birth of her second child. Blood donation saved her life via a transfusion from the US army's supplies.[141] The arrival of the US troops on British soil aided the health of local communitites in other ways too. The US army hospital at Odstock became a civilian hospital after the war. The

Bemerton Local History Society reports that: 'We were very lucky in Salisbury to have the Americans because they built the hospital at Odstock. If it hadn't been for them I don't think we'd have the great hospital we have there today...'[142] The US huts were later replaced by permanent buildings on the same site.[143] Not initially intended as such, their wartime use had transcended into their permanent use, and the locals were grateful for it.

An article was published in the *Warminster Journal* in 1944 to reassure readers that voluntary hospitals would continue under post-war planning 'without loss of their identity or autonomy.'[144] Most hospitals under the new state post-war system would be run by Regional Hospital Boards. Executive Councils would be responsible for GPs, Dentists and Opticians, and Local Authorities would be in charge of vaccinations, ambulances, community nursing and home help.[145] The medical profession was worried that they would become public servants under Local Authority control.[146]

A Healthy Environment

THE LIMITING OF petrol for the public at large meant a return to the bicycle or travelling on foot which helped keep people fitter.[147] The day to day life of war workers could take its toll; the hard physical labour of the Land Girls and the repetitive nature of factory jobs. At the EKCO factory near Malmesbury, the management realised how the mental state of its workers could affect production, and noted complaints regarding a lack of sunlight in the new assembly shop, which could not be avoided due to restrictions such as anti-shatter material covering the Government specified small windows. In the old building it had been possible to '... have all the windows open and look out on the lawn... and the fresh air came in in the summer. It's all clammy down here and you never see the sun any more...'[148] The company brought in a Mass Observation worker to look at the situation and suggest improvements.[149] Enfield Precision Engineering at Westwood was using sun lamps to aid the health of their workers who were employed underground.[150] The letters of Peggy Pickford of Warminster to her sister Liz in Australia are a heartfelt reminder of how the rigours of wartime life affected those living through it.

> 18th December 1941.
> Dear Liz and Nick,
> You will both have had my cables by now, and I do hope you were not too worried or shocked. I tried to put it as gently as possible in the few words of a sentence. I'll try and tell you how it happened, and will start right from the beginning.
> When mummy found that Red Cross job at Warminster didn't materialise, she determined to do something. So she went to the Labour Exchange here, and they put her in touch with a munitions factory in Trowbridge...
> She said she was willing to do any work but what she felt she could be

of most use at was welfare or first aid. The woman she saw said there were two of them doing that, but they badly needed someone else to help (dealing with cuts and hysterics etc) and that if she would come and work 'at the benches' for a little while they would probably be able to wangle her in. They assured her that the work in the factory was within her capabilities...

Ma was quite happy about it, but feeling 'journey-proud' as she put it, wondering what on earth it would be like at the factory...

I put in all this because I think the apprehension about her new job and the packing up, and the nervous tension generally, may have had something to do with bringing on the stroke...[151]

Sadly Peggy and Liz's mum passed away not long after the stroke she suffered in December 1941.

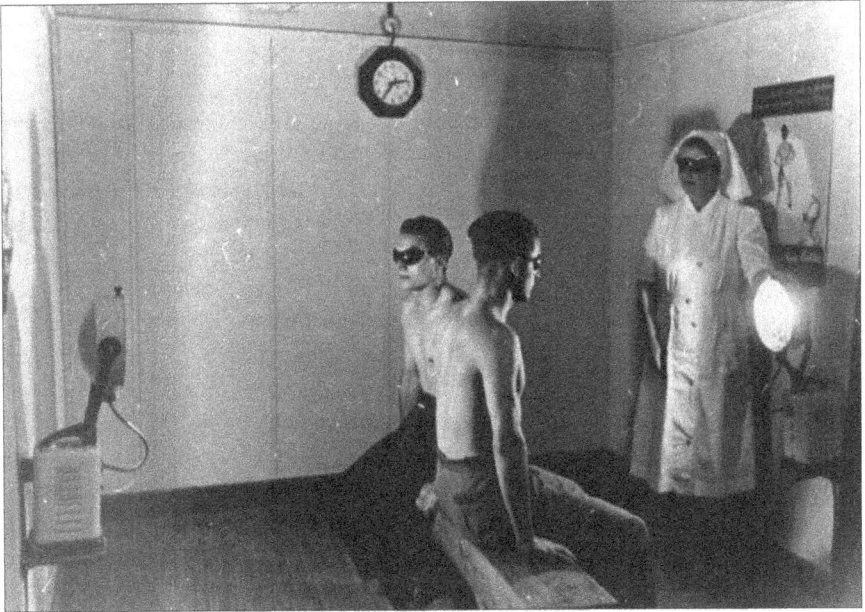

Compulsory sunray treatment for Enfleild Precision Engineering Workers, 1941-1945, from Eddie Baker archive with kind permission (WSHC P41845)

There was a shortage of housing for wartime workers and evacuees moving into Wiltshire, which could sometimes affect their health. In April 1943 the Warminster and Westbury Rural District Council received a letter from a lady who was living at a farm in Edington and who wanted help to move herself and her family to Westbury. She reported: 'I am living in a condemne[d] house that is not fit for pigs to live in when it rains we get wet through...' The lady, bombed out of London, also reported that 'we have been very ill as we have no water only a brook and the cows and horse they drink and stand and do things in it...' The Council discovered that the family had been given the cottage by a local family when they 'arrived from London one wet night and had nowhere to go, and out of pity were let into the condemned cottage as a temporary measure.' The Council had not requisitioned the property and advised the owner that they should not have let them in. By doing so they were all breaking the law.[152] In *c.* 1944 a tenant in Bishopstrow was writing to the Council regarding the School House at Norton Bavant. 'My wife is eagerly looking forward to the day when it will become vacant. Well Sir I have heard that a few more people are going after the School House now, one or two expectant mothers, but I was first to go after it, and owing to the fact that it was personally promised by Mr Finch & you I am not worrying how many try for it. I think I am quite a deservant case as any. I have a boy aged (7) seven who is subject to epileptic fits and since I left the service the wife & child have been pushed around from pillar to post...'[153] It was reported in August 1944 at a Wiltshire Building Sub-Committee meeting that a newly built prefabricated hut at Malmesbury Secondary School was found to be unsatisfactory 'with the quality and workmanship of the hut, and felt that as this matter was a matter of national policy, the Chairman was requested to draw the attention of the Advisory Committee of the County Councils' Association to this matter.'[154] One man who was working for the Bristol Aeroplane Company underground at Corsham during WWII moved his family to a prefab in the town. When they saw the building for the first time his wife remarked that the garages were nice. 'They are not garages' he said, 'they are the prefabricated bungalows that we are going to live in.' Their daughter suffered from bronchiectasis and had to take much time off school, as well as spending fourteen months in Frenchay Hospital at Bristol.[155]

The inadequate provision of piped water was an ongoing problem which was prevalent throughout the war, as can be seen in a letter from the residents of Atworth who had become so desperate by August 1945 they were writing to the Minister of Health, Aneurin Bevan. 'Sir, It is with great regret I write to you. Knowing what great things you have to do. But representing the hard working housewives of this village I enclose a protest signed by a few of us, who wish to appeal to you to get something done for us. For ten years we have asked our Parish Council and Rural District Council to give us a water supply. 'We are desperate'. They put us off with the answer 'water is coming'. There is enough water in this village to supply everyone. But it was turned down. Our M.P. Mr. Grimston has been appealed to. He has all the details of our troubles. But still every little while we are without water. No one seems to be able to put things in order. Hoping you will spare us time to go into this matter.' There is a note with an additional fact. 'The people here pay one shilling per week for a bath often to be told sorry there is no water.' An Engineer and Surveyor had reported to the Bradford and Melksham Rural District Council in March 1944 stating that the proposed scheme could not go ahead as the Water Board was unable to guarantee the required volume of water 'owing to the exceptional heavy demands, (of what is thought to be wartime duration only,) now being made upon their present system' and due to the 'very strict embargo being laid on all constructional activities not directly concerned with the war effort'.[156] The Ministry of Health's *National Water Policy*, published in

1944, stated that in rural areas the 'prime object of organisation and planning' for domestic supplies was to ensure that as many houses as possible could be readily connected to the public mains. 'In our great cities and in urban areas generally piped water supplies are practically universal. This is not so in the countryside. Despite the improvement in the past decade, nearly 30 per cent. of those living in rural districts are still not reached by the mains. Thus, water supplies in the countryside are still much below the level of adequacy which modern standards demand, and large extensions of piped supplies in rural localities, and also of sewerage, must form an important part of water policy as an accompaniment of a progressive housing and agricultural policy.'[157]

On 2 May 1941 the Air Ministry was writing to Devizes Rural District Council regarding the water supply for Melksham's RAF Hospital and RAF Keevil, asking if it was possible for the Council to make available 50,000 gallons per day from their present resources. Regarding Keevil: 'It is understood that this Site is outside your district, but that the Authority in whose area it is situated has no water supply available...' By 1 September 1941 the Intelligence Officer of the 2/ Lt. Royal Engineers was writing from the Headquarters of the Salisbury Plain Area to all Boroughs, Urban and Rural District Councils in Wiltshire regarding the county's water supply. 'For obvious reasons it is desired that a complete knowledge of all sources of water supply within the County of Wiltshire shall be in the hands of the Military Authorities. The magnitude of the task of collecting this data will be as obvious to you as the need for the data and therefore it has been decided to appeal to you, who have so much of this knowledge about your finger tips, to give us all the information you can about your own Council area.' The military required information regarding the location of wells, reservoirs and pumps, public and private; the capacity and the normal supply of each alongside figures regarding the population supplied.[158] In Corsham in 1941 the taps could not be used on a local farm from 7-9pm because of drought restrictions. This caused huge problems when a plane crashed in the farmer's field. Water problems became worse due to the increase in population.[159] Many had trouble with water pressure. One family living in a farm near Cricklade found that the pressure was so low from the Ashton Keynes pumping station that they had to install a small hand pump. 'That was my punishment every day – a half hour on the pump!' Even in Wiltshire towns such as Cricklade, some residents had to rely on just one water pipe connection to the house, and one cold tap.[160] By 26 March 1942 the Ministry of Health was writing to Wiltshire's Town, Urban and Rural District Councils alongside the Joint Water Boards Committee regarding economy of use in water. Rainfall over the past year had been lower than average and the Ministry realised the difficulties. 'In addition to any difficulties arising out of the low rainfall of recent months, they have to face unexpected demand for water for military purposes, increased domestic demands owing to the influx of munition workers, evacuees or other new population, increased industrial demands for water for factories engaged in essential war work and for other war purposes. It is consequently more than ever necessary that [those undertaking works] should be cautious about depletion of supplies either by pumping more than is necessary or by unduly drawing down impounded reserves. They should take all necessary steps to restrict undue consumption of water before the position becomes acute and should not hesitate to put restrictions on supply into operation…'[161] On 7 May 1943 George North, Assistant Secretary at Ministry of Health was writing to the Clerks of England's Rural District Councils regarding water supplies and sewerage, wanting to obtain up to date information about the availability of piped water supplies for domestic use in rural parishes. 'The Minister is mindful of the staffing and other difficulties of Local Authorities and the appended questionnaire is limited to simple questions. A question as to sewerage is also included.'[162] The lack of availability of water for domestic use had health implications for the residents of Wiltshire during WWII and beyond. Families in rural areas were also still managing without electricity during war years.[163]

Austerity continued into post-war Britain and in the population at large there was a widespread feeling of deprivation even though the British diet had been the healthiest ever.[164] There was a reduction in the consumption of all foods except fish, sugar, potatoes and fruit in the working class diet of 1946-8.[165] The Medical Research Council's National Survey of Health and Development taken in 1950 from a cohort of 4,419 children born in 1946 discovered that there were in fact both social and regional differences which were resistant to post-war food restrictions. Inequalities of food distribution and consumption which were 'considerable' before the war had only partially been eradicated and social factors such as access to kitchen facilities appeared to make a difference. A child's social class also appeared to have affected their intake of milk,[166] orange juice, fruit and vegetables, even though rationing delivered a more even distribution of meat and fats. There were also found to be 'significant differences' between the diets of children from different regions, possibly due to cultural factors, food distribution and the seasonality of supply.[167] Infant mortality rates fell in England and Wales from 59 per 1,000 in 1939 to 46 per 1,000 in 1944.[168] The nutrient content of the post-war diet remained well within the British Medical Association's (BMA) recommendations for most items.[169] However, by March 1947 a Scientific Officer in the Ministry of Food was claiming that 'nutritional standards had fallen so badly as to have halted the physical improvements made by children during the war'.[170] A British Medical Report of the late 1940s looking at the availability of food during the years 1941-8 concluded that there had been a significant deterioration; with spring 1946 came a shortage of fats and less palatable foods which increasingly led many to a less appetising diet.[171] The BMA had noted some 'small regressions' in a few areas in the early and late 1940s with growth rates,[172] but reported in 1950 that 'it would appear to be a fair conclusion that the health of the population as a whole, despite the trials and tribulations of recent years, has been well maintained'.[173] It appears that the medical community was divided on the issue.

WWII was a major turning-point in the history of the British diet. The increase in consumption of brown bread, milk, and vegetables alongside added nutrients resulted in a healthier diet with no one falling short of basic nutritional requirements. The wartime food policy led to an equality of consumption. Post-war full employment and other food schemes ensured that the public remained healthy.[174] Rickets had virtually been eradicated over the wartime period. The Ministry of Food had effectively shown that a Government had the ability to tackle public health issues, and public expectations altered because of it.[175] Lizzie Collingham reports that by the end of the war a social consensus had been reached whereby many in the Government understood that the state should take responsibility for the diet, health and welfare of its citizens.[176]

10
Morale of the Masses

The Ministry of Information

WILLIAM MAXWELL AITKIN, Lord Beaverbook, became the first ever Minister of Information in February 1918, using the press as a propaganda tool to promote the allied cause towards the end of WWI.[1] The Ministry of Information (MOI) was formed again at the outbreak of WWII to ensure that the public received a positive presentation of events and to stop the circulation of defeatist or demoralising rumour. Robert Mackay states that they were given the task to 'stimulate the war effort and to maintain a steady flow of facts and opinions calculated to further the policy of the Government in the prosecution of the war'. The Ministry was able to use various sources to achieve this aim: reports from its Regional Information Officers, surveys carried out for it by the independently run Mass Observation organisation[2] (a venture begun in the 1930s),[3] Police 'duty-room' reports via the Home Office, postal censorship of mail going abroad and the BBC's Listener Research Department reports.[4] The Home Intelligence Division (within the Ministry of Information) had two arms. The Home Intelligence Unit prepared reports on the morale of the civilian population, essential to plan the Ministry's home publicity and to aid the work of other Government departments. The other department was responsible for social survey and was set up to assess the effect of the Ministry's poster campaigns and as Cantwell notes, to make 'direct inquiries about morale.' These attempts were ridiculed in the press, leading to a change in emphasis; later surveys concentrated on market research. The Postal and Telegraph Censorship Department became independent in April 1943; censoring communications provided helpful intelligence and prevented information from falling into enemy hands.[5] The staff at the Ministry were not career Civil Servants, but writers, academics and journalists.[6]

In June 1940 the British Board of Film Censors set up their own Film Censorship Division which also allowed for positive 'falsification'. Factory workers could find their machines taken over for a short spell by what Angus Calder terms 'glamorous young women in ministry-approved war worker outfits who performed for the benefit of the cameras'.[7] In the first few years of the war the Government heavily restricted the information that was passed to the media. Newspapers were dependent on the information that the MOI chose to provide or that of commercial news agencies which were themselves already censored. It was better to run any other material past the Censorship Division of the MOI as it was an offence to gather, record, communicate or publish information which could be of possible use to the enemy. The media felt resentment at the Government's distrust of their practices, but over time the Ministry learnt to use subtler and more successful techniques to gain control through censorship, persuading the media to self-censor. The Government still imposed control over the sources of information available, but it also became more communicative and less nervous of the media. The Government used a similar approach for the film industry, but awarded contracts to those companies whose views were similar to their own.[8] News about new weapons and the movements of Winston Churchill remained understandably highly censored;[9] also censored was information about bomb disposal[10] and the weather.[11] Robert Mackay notes: 'In all its dealings with the media the Government never seriously departed from the principle of freedom of expression: censorship applied to facts not opinion.'[12] The BBC's Chief Censor stated that the Americans broadcasting from London found the process to be 'kindly and sensible' in comparison to that of Germany and Russia. However, Peter Hennessy notes that 'never before and never since has a British Government taken so great and so intrusive a range of powers over the lives of its citizens… [including] what they read in the newspapers, what they could hear on the wireless sets'.[13] In September 1939 the Director of the Censorship Division of the Ministry of Information, based at Senate House, London, was writing to Swindon Borough Council regarding arrangements for the application in war of 'security' censorship of films. 'A Ministry of Information has been formed comprising amongst others a Censorship Division which will be responsible for the Censorship of the Press, Broadcasting and Films.' Included was notification that '[t]he Regulations make it an offence in any manner likely to prejudice the efficient prosecution of the war to obtain, possess or publish information on military matters, the term "military" being used in its widest sense. False information is covered by the prohibition equally with true information.' Specific details were mentioned such as the movement of troops, information about defence measures, POWs, munitions etc. 'The Regulations also prohibit any attempts to influence public opinion (defined as including the opinion of any section of the public) in a manner likely to be prejudicial to the efficient prosecution of the war.' The Division would be able to authorise an Order to prevent or restrict publication in such cases. 'The makers and exhibitors of films have the responsibility respectively as to what they make and exhibit and will incur liability by the production or exhibition of any films containing information which might be directly or indirectly useful to the enemy.' The renters and distributors of films could ensure compliance by dealing only in censored films. The Board's Examiner would be carrying out the security censorship which included imported and exported films alongside those made for the home market, although films for export would incur a 5s. fee per reel. A certificate would be issued for every film which passed the security censorship process.[14] The Chippenham Doctor Joan Hickson realised that censorship was taking place in the newspapers over the V2 rockets. Noting in her diary entry of 17 November 1945 she writes: 'The powers that be are at last releasing a bit of news about the V2 rocket bombs, which have been hitting London since September. Nothing whatever in the papers but people coming out of London have been telling of other different 'explosions' which come without warning. Now the news has been released that these are V2 rocket bombs, which travel to a great height (60-70 miles) and that there is no sound of them coming.'[15]

But it wasn't just the press who had to be censored; citizens needed to be circumspect too. From 1939 the Ministry of Information began 'Keep Quiet' campaigns, supported by the local press. The *Wiltshire Gazette* was announcing in its 21 September 1939 edition that:

"Walls Have Ears!'

There is too much talking! Information which might be of great value to the enemy is being passed on every day in hotels, public houses and general meeting places.

Sailors, soldiers and airmen are forbidden to talk shop – why should you? It is every citizen's duty to refrain from discussing with his friends such information as movements and numbers of troops and the names and nature of units and stations.

The enemy has a spy system. Chance remarks are often dangerous. Failure to comply with this request may result in severe penalties. Stop talking!'

The Ministry of Information also saw its role as that of convincing people that Britain would win through. It began to experiment, producing pamphlets which were a longer-lasting information source. It began work as soon as it came into being, with the addition of leaflets into some published titles, such as the short polemic *Fifty Facts about Hitler* in which leaflets were inserted and copies distributed by the Foyles' Book Club. Dr. Henry Irving notes that this early experimentation resulted in an 'increasingly professional approach to publishing' with success via titles such as *The War at Sea* in March 1940, 470,000 copies of which were sold by July, followed by *The Battle of Britain* by author Hilary Saunders which sold 300,000 copies within its first week of release in March 1941. The revised edition was even more popular with its illustrated cover and 'eye-catching' diagrams and photographs. Dr. Irving notes the MOI's Controller of Production G. S. Royds as stating in 1944 that the series 'began as something new on the bookstalls, a new kind of book in British publishing; today they are part of the country's reading'.[16] By early 1941 the results of a Gallup poll showed that 80% still believed that Britain would be victorious, but as there were 'no grounds for optimism,' the Ministry wanted to use the idea of post-war reform as a Government 'pledge' motivator. Churchill was against the idea and would not allow the Ministry to do so. The arrival of a new Minister of Information in June 1941 heralded a change in emphasis which turned away from morale propaganda, deeming it unsuccessful. Instead the emphasis would be on 'explanation and education'; that the public would be happy to suffer sacrifices if they were clearly explained and felt to be fair to all. There was a feeling that the initial strategy had been one of mistrust and fear of the public reaction, as Robert MacKay reports: 'question[ing] its courage and confus[ing] its grumbling with defeatism... the people did not need to be chivvied into calmness and courage'. Also, the 'Big Blitz' had ended and the need to alleviate panic and defeatism turned into a need to tackle apathy and war weariness.[17]

From mid 1941 the MOI actively encouraged the idea of a new Britain after the war, believing it to help morale. The Ministry also felt that the quality of life of the people should be included in war aims. However, Robert MacKay notes that any talk of reconstruction did not match Churchill's idea that the Government should not 'deceive the people by false hopes and airy visions of Utopia and Eldorado.' This view hampered the MOI in its efforts to work with the public when excitement was created by the publishing of the Beveridge Report, and it also affected the BBC's work. J. B. Priestley was soon to become 'too vocal' about his ideas for a post-war society in his *Postscripts* of 1941. The radio series brought with it angry memoranda from the Prime Minister to the MOI and Priestley's contract was not renewed.[18]

But by 1943 everyone, including the press, was talking about post-war Britain. MacKay reports that: 'The entire country, it seemed – was discussing reconstruction in one form or another.'[19] Churchill was also against the most successful of graphically designed printed wartime ephemera, Abram Games' *Your Britain: Fight for It Now* of 1942, which was to become what Jim Aulich describes as an 'iconic symbol of the Welfare State'.[20] Even Churchill himself broadcast his *Four Year Plan* on 21 March 1943.[21] The use of pamphlets, posters and illustrated books made available through bookshops, kiosks, on the street, in factories, at rallies, meetings and lectures enabled a social environment where all classes could exchange ideas and talk about progressive politics.[22] The MOI also focused on how the Government was actively helping people cope with the pressure of war; creating fair shares for all with food control, increasing wages and creating full employment.[23] The Department was also helping to shape Government policy by passing on relevant information from social surveys to empower the Government to act to sustain morale,[24] for example by bringing in the five shilling rule whereby a price limit was placed on restaurant meals, seen as a way to stop black marketeering in restaurants[25] after learning of it as an issue through social surveys.

By 1941, J. B. Nicholas, Chairman of the Advertising Services Guild, was encouraging the Government to use propaganda more vigorously. He condemned the Government's domestic poster campaigns as being neo-romantic, individualistic and formalistic. He commissioned a Mass Observation Report entitled *Home Propaganda*, and the findings (which he agreed with) were that Home Front propaganda was 'diffident and occasionally patronising.' He wanted 'pictures for the people and of the people in their everyday lives.' The ensuing debate in 1942 was dubbed 'Respectability vs. Vulgarity', and Aulich reports that

Nicholas was criticised for 'competitive commercialism' and 'the degrading values of brutal aggression'. Nicholas continued with his campaign to influence the Government to be direct in their communication with the public; for 'hard-sell realism' and more engagement from artists. Aulich feels that what emerged was a more commercial, legible, illustrative and realist style of mass culture.[26]

The Government soon realised the value of a strategy that would consider entertainment as a way of raising morale and countering war weariness. Mass Observation results concurred; people needed some form of light relief to help them cope with the emotional strain and physical austerity of wartime life. Cinema became part of this strategy.[27] Also included was radio and the idea of bringing music and the arts to the masses through organisations such as the Entertainments National Service Association (ENSA). At Ham Spray House in Ham, Frances Partridge noted in her diary that: 'Music is my great solace…'[28] William Rossiter operated a jazz radio station from the basement of his electrical shop in Bradford on Avon during the war, alongside his Chief Fire Officer duties. His broadcasts continued into the 1950s.[29]

Radio

JIM SMITH RECALLS that the 1930s marked the start of the home radios boom. Each set needed an accumulator made up of glass and metal plates which needed to be charged weekly, alongside a high tension battery. It had been Jim's job to do the 'battery rounds' on a Saturday for Parsons and Gould in Castle Street, Salisbury, whereby he would cycle round and sort out the accumulators at a cost of sixpence each.[30] During WWII the difficulties that came with going out in the blackout meant that people became, as Arthur Maidment from Salisbury recalls, 'radio addicts'.[31] The BBC's content changed, moving towards easy listening, popular music, variety and sport, with some news and advice programmes. Presenters, women amongst them, used a new, informal tone. The popularity of comedy shows such as *ITMA* (It's That Man Again) and *Hi Gang!* whose audience exceeded more than 16 million listeners a week encouraged the BBC to produce a second service, the *Forces Programme*. By 1941 six out of every ten listeners were tuning in to the *Forces Programme* rather than the *Home Service*, especially those aged 16-20.[32] One Cricklade resident remembers how *ITMA* with Tommy Handley captured the public's imagination. The programme '… affected the language, as every one spoke in the catch-phrases stolen from the regular characters'.[33] Peter Hennessy notes that in 1940 Churchill 'commandeered the English language for war'.[34] Printed on the back of a postcard published by Valentine & Sons Ltd. during the war is a quote by 'The Prime Minister.' 'We shall continue steadfast in faith and duty till our task is done.'[35] The statement was part of a speech given by Winston Churchill to the Allied Delegates at St. James' Place, London, on 12 June 1941.[36] It is generally acknowledged that Winston Churchill's speeches helped to raise morale, but Marion Parsons noted that 'I believe Tommy Handley was even more effective; he diverted us from reality every week.'[37] Joan

Hickson noted in her diary entry on 10 May 1942, however, that: 'Really very glad to get home and get a bit of a sit as it is fire-watching night. At 9pm we listened to Churchill's two years in office speech. I have never heard him so optimistic. He was almost rollicking and made us rock with laughter. A great relief as any highfalutin' stuff would not have gone down well in our state of fatigue.'[38] *Music While You Work* and *Workers' Playtime* were popular with factory workers.[39] The BBC chose J. B. Priestley to bring morale to the masses. His down-to-earth manner and Yorkshire accent could, as Mackay states, 'effortlessly reach the minds of the people by speaking of their courage, humour and quiet determination... striking a sympathetic chord with the public and helping to create for the British people an image of itself which, idealized though it doubtless was, served as a model to be aimed at for the testing times which lay ahead.'[40] The *Radio Gardener*, Mr Middleton, was popular. One Bradford on Avon resident remembers one of his rousing Sunday afternoon broadcasts, stating that 'onions and potatoes were munitions of war as surely as bullets and shells.'[41] Radio news broadcasters became national celebrities. Their names were announced so that listeners would begin to recognise and trust their reports. The *Radio Times* gave details of their backgrounds and pastimes alongside photographs so that listeners could identify with them more easily. As Peter Lewis puts it: 'Trust was all-important'.[42] William Joyce's Nazi English language broadcast featuring Lord Haw Haw became popular, with one sixth of the listening public tuning in during autumn 1939. The broadcasts were meant, as Angus Calder notes, to 'undermine British confidence in the news' and to undermine Churchill, but were often 'ludicrously inept'.[43]

With the advent of radio, WWII became the first war in which it was possible for the enemy to project information directly into the homes of the enemy population.[44] It was also possible for the British Government to do the same, both at home and abroad. Overseas publicity was undertaken by the Ministry, divided into geographical areas: Empire, America, Latin America, Soviet Relations, Far East, Middle East and Europe.[45] The Political Warfare Executive was established in August 1941 as a covert operation under the Foreign Office, amalgamating parts of the BBC and Foreign Publicity Department at the MOI alongside Special Operations 1, part of the Special Operation Executive (SOE); its task to undermine enemy morale using propaganda methods.[46] The Executive broadcast 160,000 words of news in 23 languages to continental Europe[47] every 24 hours. Every effort was made to make the broadcasts appear genuine, with falsehoods and black propaganda sent out across the airwaves.[48] Work on enemy and enemy occupied countries was initially the task of the Political Warfare Executive, later coming under the remit of the Ministry of Information. The Ministry worked closely with the News Department of the Foreign Office. The Home Planning Division took care of the Home Front and after the arrival of large numbers of American troops an American Forces Liaison Division was set up.[49] A 'joke embargo' was imposed on the radio for references to the Home Guard, black market, Police, US soldiers, the ATS, WAAFs and WRNS amongst others.[50]

The *Brains Trust* came on air in 1941 (originally called *Any Questions?*)[51]

and consisted of a set of fielded questions sent in by listeners to be discussed by panellists with a 'Question Master'. During 1943 the programme gained a regular weekly audience of 10-12 million[52] with 3,000 postcards arriving per week from both civilians and service personnel.[53] One Swindon resident recalled that: 'Father was not particularly interested in classical music but enjoyed a programme called 'The Brains Trust'.'[54] It wasn't just on-air that discussions were becoming popular. The format moved to local venues countrywide and to the forces abroad. As Peter Lewis argues, its 'questioning, slightly sceptical look'[55] to discussions was engaging and refreshing, filling a need within society at large. The *North Wilts Herald* was reporting in its 26 September 1941 edition on the Swindon Discussion Group's 'Brains Trust' meeting. Panellists gave their opinions on a wide ranging set of questions from attendees. Examples included 'Can science be reconciled with religion?' and 'Why is the Southern Cross only visible in the Southern Hemisphere?' The Tisbury Women's Institute was planning a Brains Trust event at their Committee meeting of 3 September 1942, asking that members please send in questions 'written on a Post Card [to be sent] to the office'. Subjects for discussion included housing, health, schools and their work.[56] The Army Bureau of Current Affairs was encouraging troops to take part in debates, seen by the servicemen as a way to get respite from military duties.[57] In August 1942 two teams from Wootton Bassett and Broad Hinton were pitted against each other on a question programme aired by the BBC's *Home Service*. The Interrogator was Wiltshire's A. G. Street, the well-known broadcaster on farming and agricultural adviser to the University of Bristol.[58] It was reported in the *Wiltshire*

Advertisement in the Wiltshire Times, 2 December, 1939, for Wiltshire manufactured 'Ekco' radios. Many shops were advertising radios for Christmas in this issue. Franks of Trowbridge were noting 'In times like these nobody wants a set to go "dead" in the middle of a news bulletin, and it's no joke being without radio entertainment these evenings' (WSHC Microform Collection)

Times on 19 August 1944 that Lady Ludlow-Hewitt had presided over a 'Brains Trust' event at Bromham's Women's Institute meeting. 'Some excellent questions were sent in by the members, dealing with religious education, and some were humorous. All were dealt with in a business-like manner and satisfactorily answered.'

One Purton resident remembered as a child: 'Our solid brown Bakelite wireless set gave regular reports, and I saw my parents in the dining room listening to the damning news: German armies continuing their surge forward, fighting their way into northern France, retreating allied troops pouring into Dunkirk...'[59] She was conscious of the programmes coming from the wireless, *ITMA*, *Monday Night at Eight*, *Henry Hall's Guest Night*, and more '...I didn't really listen to them. But the laughter made life seem normal... So, like everyone else, we coped with daily life...'[60] In Minety, 'my father tuned in the radio as often as he could, during which time silence had to prevail. The radio was kept in good working order by much servicing, with one of the two accumulators... always on charge.' The family found that the *Picture Post* and *Pathé News* through the cinema were other sources of information. Films were shown at the village hall and the *Pathé News* was always included.[61] They followed the events of the war on the radio and in newspapers. 'Father also had a large map, mounted on a soft backing that would easily accept pins... Little flags, Union Jacks, Stars and Stripes, Swastikas etc. would be moved daily.'[62] The reach of propaganda was widespread, the BBC utilising Wilfred Pickles' travelling talks as *Billy Welcome* for propaganda purposes. He was asked to go to war factories and use his programme to incite patriotism and a national fervour, which Pickles himself found rather disturbing, especially when, after hearing 'personal endeavour stories', he had to pat the person on the back. 'How I loathed it, and how embarrassed I felt.'[63]

Children from Swindon made the most of Tommy Handley's *ITMA* catchphrases. 'Most of us could imitate the hoarse Cockney charlady, Mrs. Mopp, and her regular salutation 'Can I do you **now**, Sir?' The children often looked through telephone books at local kiosks, pestering the teachers once they had managed to save enough for the calls with what they hoped were mysterious '... guttural mutterings of the cryptic message "Funf has spoken"'. It was the alcoholic 'Colonel Chinstrap' who provided them with the greatest form of amusement. Form 2.1 'claimed a great triumph when, during a French lesson, the stern Miss Boby rebuked a girl who had not completed her home work with the words "and I saw you on Saturday afternoon, playing hop-scotch in the street!" "Scotch?" the entire Form claimed to have chorused, "Scotch? Don't mind if I do!"'[64]

Everyone knew how important the news was, and those who did not have a radio could have been at a disadvantage, although one local remembers '...on the day that we knew that details of the Atlantic Charter would be broadcast, I joined a knot of people in a street in Warminster to hear the announcement from a radio in a room where the owner purposely opened the window. That was mid-1941.'[65] One man from Swindon remembered how the radio was used when the submarine *Thetis* failed to resurface in 1939. 'Those with radio sets in their homes relayed the latest news to us in the early afternoon...'[66] He also remembers the day that war was declared. 'Everybody in our house was astir early the following morning. 'A lovely September day,' announced my mother, 'such a shame ...' Mr Richardson called soon after we had finished breakfast, to tell Dad that there was going to be a special announcement on the wireless at ten o'clock, and Dad could go in there to listen to it if he liked.' His father talked to him about the war: 'I don't want you worrying about this war. I don't want you getting worked up, and worrying like you did about the *Thetis*... I'm going to see about a wireless set tomorrow,' he said, 'then we'll have all the latest news.'[67] By January 1945 Joan Hickson was noting in her diary entry: 'In the middle of January the Russians struck through Poland faster than the Germans had gone the opposite way in 1939. We hung on the wireless again and stuck pins on maps until they were at the Oder, less than 50 miles from Berlin.'[68]

Cinema

MONEY SPENT ON entertainment had risen by approximately 120% from 1938 to 1944, with the most popular pastime being a trip to the cinema.[69] Cinemas and theatres were closed at the outbreak of war, but were allowed to reopen shortly after.[70] A wartime survey discovered that 70% of adults took a trip to the cinema,[71] and every week ticket sales reached 25-30 million.[72] As well as the news, cinema goers could be informed by short documentaries, made to focus on a certain service such as *Fires Were Started* in 1941 looking at the Auxiliary Fire Service.[73] Film was also used as a means of escapism from day to day life in wartime Britain.[74] In Salisbury queues became a regular occurrence at all three cinemas after the arrival of service personnel[75] and queues were also commonplace in Malmesbury[76] and in Chippenham.[77] Bob Randall recalled that '[q]ueues formed down Red Hat Lane [in Trowbridge] if a George Formby film was being screened.'[78] At Tidworth House the tennis courts were used to show films and theatrical performances to the troops.[79] The Gainsborough melodramas were the films that drew the largest audiences; they did not include political or even social content.[80] The Crown Film Unit (formerly the GPO Film Unit) attached to the MOI made films for the domestic market and to export abroad. *Next of Kin* was meant to discourage careless talk; *Millions Like Us* focused on female munitions workers and *Spring Offensive* targeted the rural market, considering the life of a farmer who took on evacuees and became involved with the War Agricultural Executive Committee.[81]

In April 1943 the Ministry of Agriculture had been exporting its wartime gardening know-how, announcing in its *Dig for Victory News* that Dig for Victory and farming films shown in the UK over the last year or two were now being shown at the New York Museum of Modern Art. When announcing the film showings, the Museum authorities were to state: 'Since the outbreak of war in 1939 the United States has given large quantities of vegetable seeds to England, which now reciprocates by sending to this country ten short films which show in the most practical fashion how to get the maximum value from seeds and gardens, how to store vegetables for winter, in fact, how to wage a victorious war with the weapon of food production.'[82] As well as the cinemas in towns and villages, civilians also had access to films through touring cinemas visiting village halls[83] and also at the new factory sites, such as the Bristol Aeroplane Company site at Neston where local people could pay sixpence to visit the onsite cinema.[84]

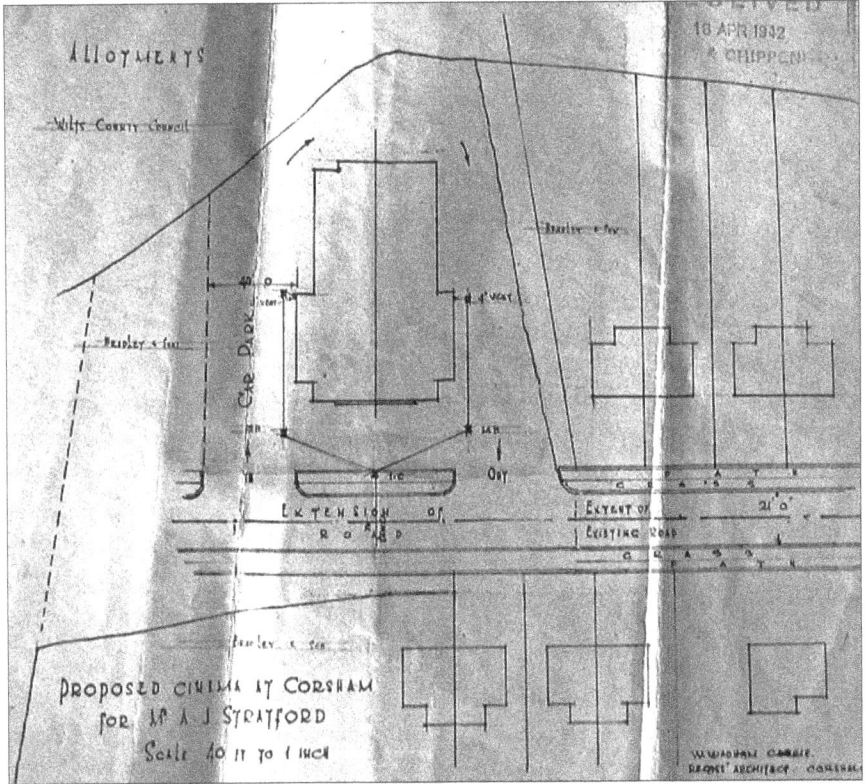

Site for a proposed cinema in Corsham, 1942. Scale 40ft to 1 inch, drawn by W. Wadham, registered architect, Corsham (WSA G3/760/1164)

Some children in Trowbridge were so desperate to get into the cinema that they asked the US soldiers for money. The best place to do this was 'Up the Red Cross'. The writer Maureen Duffy reports that 'It was a few minutes before any more game appeared, two soldiers together, warm and sleek in their light khaki… 'Gotta penny, mister?' Said Arthur. One of them looked down. 'You kids oughta be home out of this cold.' 'Go on, mister, gi's a penny.' 'What d'you want a penny for, son?' 'Aw, come on, Sel, let's git.' 'Me and my sister wanna go to the pictures.' 'If I give you sixpence now you run along home?' 'Yeah.' The American dug in his pocket and fished out a sixpence…. Now we felt we were getting somewhere. 'You try the next one,' said Arthur. 'Go on, it's easy." The children were always on the lookout for the Police, but managed to watch Charlie Chan and a 'Bowery Boys classic'.[85] A cinema was being planned for Corsham in 1942 but the plans for the site near Pickwick Road were still being looked at in April 1946.[86]

Public Houses

B EFORE THE WAR, visiting the public house was a custom; part of the life of perhaps three quarters of the nation's men and fewer of its women, at the end of the working week. Due to the supply of beer becoming erratic, drinking during the war became spread throughout the week, peaking when new supplies were rumoured to have arrived. Working class drinkers began to move themselves to the saloon bar rather than residing in the cheaper public bar. They now had more money to spend and supplies were to be found more often in the expensive bars which were also more likely to have a fire. This trend was not to be reversed in the post-war period, with many new pubs being built without a 'public' area.[87] Before the war few young women looked on the pub as a place to spend their leisure time. It was a venue that was particularly frowned upon by the middle classes in terms of female usage. Women did recall, however, memories of visits to country pubs in terms of what could be described as 'acceptable' drinking locations.[88] Interwar figures place female pub usage at between 12.5% and 41.5% of total pub usage, influenced by the location and type of pub with the average female drinker being a working class woman aged over 40.[89] During wartime the difference in gender roles narrowed and this was also true of their leisure experiences. Mass Observation noted in 1943:

'War-jobs are not by any means the only places in which women have become entrenched during the war. They have not only taken over men's activities in working hours, but to a very considerable extent in leisure hours too. Perhaps one of the most significant changes is the extent to which they have entered during the war in to the life of public houses.'[90]

The figures show that the increase was found to occur in urban and industrial

The Pheasant Inn, Salisbury, September c.1944, courtesy of the British Council (WSHC P55950)

areas. Many young women were mobilised, moving away from home to work in factories or in the services. Claire Langhamer notes that they were often 'set adrift from established social networks and the institutions which had served their leisure interests in the pre-war years'[91] and had access to wages which were often higher than in their previous occupations. One woman commented to Mass Observation in 1943: 'I visit pubs much more regularly than before the war because there is less to do... I often spend an evening 'pub crawling' instead of our old occupations'. Opposition to young women drinking did remain, with one 30 year old woman noting to Mass Observation that: 'All this old fashioned prudery – it's disgusting. Women are doing just as much in this war as the men...'[92] By the late 1950s drinks advertisers were actively targeting young women.[93]

Sport

FOOTBALL MATCHES WERE a popular pastime with league football resuming after being shut down at the beginning of the war, although on a reduced level with only small crowds allowed[94] and also on a regional basis to restrict travelling time. Standards of play were lower due to a loss of players to the Forces. Other spectator sports became popular with horseracing getting a bad name as it was said to foster gambling and waste petrol with people visiting racing venues. It was banned for three months after the fall of France. Racing, however, continued to attract large crowds and the BBC began broadcasting commentaries again on most of the major events. Greyhound racing, the most popular working class spectator sport after football, remained popular, albeit with restricted fixtures, and crowds still arrived to attend cricket matches at Lords.[95]

Dance

AS WITH CINEMAS, by December 1939 the dance halls became packed again.[96] In Salisbury dances were held almost nightly at the Assembly Rooms, Cadena Café Ballroom and Wilton Road Ballroom. An enterprising garage owner at Amesbury hastily converted the designs for his new car showroom so that it became a first class sell-out ballroom. Arthur Maidment notes that he 'soon possessed his own band, the Melville Christie Dance Orchestra, which could be heard regularly on the popular radio feature *Workers' Playtime*.'[97] On 13 May 1945 Harry Smith was writing to Swindon's Town Clerk from his home in Rosebery Street, notifying him that the BBC were calling at the Welcome Club to audition his orchestra. The BBC representative was 'very favourably impressed, and assured me that he would recommend the Orchestra to... London Studios, who [are] directly responsible for the feature "Saturday Night at the Palais"... he seemed very optimistic that we should be given an opportunity, also he was very impressed with the orderly crowd present at the dance.'[98] Access to entertainment was easier than ever for some, like those working in Wiltshire's underground factories who had access to a cinema, theatre come ballroom and bar on site.[99] Those working in the underground factories such as the Enfield Precision workers at Westwood Quarry, '... were miles away from anywhere, right out in the country, and it was essential to have some social activities like a billiard room and facilities for tea and coffee as well as a bar. We had a large assembly room with a dance floor, Saturday hops with a military dance orchestra in uniform and we were eligible for Entaco shows with top entertainers... Sometimes we had musical evenings – I played the violin.'[100]

In Cricklade so many dances were held that the bigger dance bands were not always able to attend. Local dance bands came to the rescue, such as the Rhythmic Dance Band formed by individuals who had been giving musical concerts for charity, but on seeing the enormous demand for dance bands, decided to form their own in 1940. They played in Poulton, Meysey Hampton and Kempsford (Gloucestershire), Marston Meysey as well as Cricklade which became their regular haunt, as they realised that the Blakehill Farm troops needed 'somewhere to relax on a Saturday night.' At least one member of the troupe must have found it to be a punishing, if somewhat enjoyable schedule, as she was also a Land Girl and had to be '... back for milking as early as 5am the same day!' They also played at Down Ampney (Gloucestershire) where the airmen would often put their drinks on the piano. 'On one occasion a little black airman came up and asked Sydney's father if we would play something that he could sing to... this lad seemed so nice he agreed. Well, he sang beautifully – one of the tunes we'd been playing – and behaved impeccably too.' One of those who attended dances in Cricklade recalled: 'They had dozens and dozens of troops at the Town Hall for dances, and because of their hobnailed boots they put blocks under the floor to save the spring.' Another resident felt that the dances were fun. 'Those were the days of the war that you could really say you enjoyed.' The town was 'thronging' with troops, 'very different from how it had been before!' and the dances meant that the troops got to know the local girls, inviting them to the Down Ampney base for dances in a large Nissen hut. 'Diana Dors [from Swindon] came to these, but she wasn't famous then – just one of the girls.'[101] Dances were held in Malmesbury at the Town Hall every Saturday

Letter from the BBC regarding their visit to the Welcome Club in Swindon (WSA G24/225/4)

with music by Charlie Comley's 'all-star' Swindon band. The cost of admission was 1s. 3d. Whist Drives were also popular in the town, especially during winter evenings.[102]

The majority of songs from the WWII period were cheerful (*Roll out the Barrel, Bless 'em all*) or sentimental (*We'll Meet Again, Moonlight Becomes You*), but Peter Lewis feels that there were few songs of quality compared to that of the First World War. WWI songs such as *Pack Up Your Troubles* and *Keep the Home Fires Burning* made a come-back, to be joined by the highly popular and notable pre-WWII German song *Lili Marlene*. Some songs became better known because of the events of war, such as the cabaret song *A Nightingale Sang in Berkeley Square*, which became associated with the London bombings; the glass had been shattered in Berkeley Square and it became a popular song to sing in shelters. There were some witty songs produced, the most notable according to Lewis was Noel Coward's *Don't Lets be Beastly to the Germans*, the irony of which was so subtle it passed over the heads of the Ministry of Information![103]

ENSA/CEMA

B EFORE THE WAR, state involvement in performance and the arts was virtually non-existent, with public money only used for purchasing works of art and to maintain museums. Funding for music and drama came from private sources. The Entertainments National Services Association (ENSA) had existed during WWI and was brought back to life to serve the troops once more, but nothing had been done for civilians; in WWII work had to start from scratch. In September 1939 the Treasury and Board of Education began talking about the need to preserve, as Leventhal noted, 'the national framework of culture, with special reference to music, drama and the arts' to sustain the morale of the civilian population. At the beginning of the war many theatres and concert halls were closed and travel restricted due to the blackout, threatening the livelihoods of professional performers.[104]

The Board of Education saw the need for a speedy resolve, but the Treasury felt uneasy about committing itself to the support of cultural activities, eventually agreeing that in principle they would be prepared to supplement any funds raised from the private sector, but in an unofficial capacity.[105] The exemption of books from purchase tax in 1940 and the fact that the amount of entertainment tax put on theatre seats was less than for cinema stalls was one way of helping to sustain the arts.[106] The Treasury agreed to work with the Pilgrim Trust, whose aim was to aid amateurs and as F. M. Leventhal reports, carry the 'best of the arts to the provinces.'[107] ENSA provided light entertainment for factory and service workers,[108] gaining in the process the title 'Every Night Something Awful'.[109] Although ENSA had acquired some big celebrities such as Gracie Fields and George Formby, most of its performers were 'near-amateur' talents who liked the security of an ENSA contract, if a poorly paid one. There were complaints over the low quality of the humour, and it was found that the Council for the Encouragement of Music and

The Guildhall Concert Party of Salisbury rehearsing on stage, c.1944, courtesy of the British Council (WSHC P56744)

the Arts (CEMA's) classical concerts were more popular. ENSA had a disc-lending service which increased the growth of gramophone clubs and its classical arm also undertook factory canteen concerts from 1943.[110]

CEMA became an offshoot of the Pilgrim Trust, operating under the Board of Education[111] and was set up in 1940[112] as the Committee for the Encouragement of Music and Arts. The Committee's aim was 'to rescue those cultural activities and interests which are threatened with extinction by war-time conditions and to secure that the opportunities afforded by those very conditions are not wasted'.[113] The *Warminster Journal* announced on 22 March 1940 that: 'The formation of a concert party to tour the military camps and depots in and around Warminster is the object of a well known stage artiste and dance instructress, Miss Renee Terry, who is lately come to reside in Warminster. Miss Terry is looking for amateur and semi-professional artistes who are prepared to entertain troops on payments of expenses only.'[114] The Athelstan Players debuted in April 1940 in Malmesbury, performing to a crowded audience and raising money for charity. In May 1941 Mrs Besly produced three short plays by the Athelstan Players which packed out the Town Hall for two nights running. The acting was said to have been almost faultless. By 1944 their performances were so keenly anticipated that tickets were sold out days in advance.[115]

At first the premise was to use professionals in an auxiliary role to encourage amateur activity, but there were those, such as John Maynard Keynes, who wanted

CEMA to raise the standards of artistic performance by using professionals.[116] In its first year of existence during WWII, CEMA juggled its task of encouraging amateur activity whilst at the same time promoting professional performances to meet the increasing demand for its services with limited resources. Concert parties began their factory tours and small bands of volunteer musicians visited air raid shelters and rest centres. It was noted by one observer: 'I saw C.E.M.A. artists come into rest centres full of men and women stunned into apathy by their experiences… and, by the sheer grace and sympathy of their art, warm them first to clapping, then to singing, and – within an hour and a half – to joyous cheers and radiant laughter. If ever a body of men and women helped to revive and sustain the morale of the English people, during a time when this was most needed, those C.E.M.A. artists did.'[117] As for aiding the amateurs: after its first year of operating, CEMA did not pursue this aim. Instead by 1941 the Carnegie Trust was supporting the National Council of Social Service, amongst others, to help with this strategy at a more local level.[118] Keynes took on the role of managing CEMA and during this time the organisation became, as Leventhal reports, 'less populist, concentrating on quality and professional standards…' He launched a supplement known as 'Art for the People' which consisted of travelling exhibits of art work.[119]

The two organisations ENSA and CEMA brought to the British people a 'wealth of cultural diversion,' including the Sadler's Wells Ballet, London Philharmonic Orchestra, Royal Opera, exhibits of sculpture by Henry Moore and paintings by Graham Sutherland.[120] The Ballet Rambert (under the auspices of CEMA) performed at the Garrison Theatre, Salisbury.[121] The Salisbury Playhouse was sold in 1939 to the military but in 1943 ENSA took it over and it became the Garrison Theatre Southern Command. Arthur Millie and Jane Ware describe this as the first of the theatre's 'golden periods' with stars such as Peter Ustinov and Laurence Olivier appearing and the performance of a play by Noel Coward. The Arts Council took over the theatre in 1945 and it was named the Arts Theatre. There were financial difficulties during the post-war austerity period and a 'punishing' schedule tour to local towns did not help. Under the direction of Peter Potter and Denis Carey the theatre gained national prestige but due to the expensive touring programme Millie and Ware report that the Arts Council 'withdrew from the management of the theatre' in 1951. Luckily local enthusiasts continued where the Arts Council had left off.[122]

One Chiseldon resident remembered being taken by the US troops to Chiseldon Camp as a child to watch a show featuring Bob Hope. 'We children were sat on the grass between the officers and the stage.'[123] A US Club was set up in the wool stores at Codford and ENSA visited to perform, including Gracie Fields. They gave their performance in the large repair depot in the paddock of the Manor House.[124] News got around that Gracie Fields was coming to visit the troops in Codford. Two inventive boys 'liberated' two US Army uniforms from the dump and sneaked in to watch the performance. Amazingly they got away with it![125] Cricklade residents could often be found watching ENSA shows at the Down Ampney airfield. Jimmy Edwards, in the RAF and later to become an actor, was often to be seen on stage. His act, according to locals, was 'fairly wild, and very popular.' Just after the war a lady from Cricklade went to see him on stage in London, but complained that she'd seen his act before at Down Ampney for free![126] One Swindon boy felt that: 'Our appreciation of music and culture suddenly blossomed as classical music concerts flourished... At school we welcomed the visit of an orchestra as we were urged to attend the school's matinee concert. Needless to say, the whole class suddenly became music lovers and quickly gave their names to attend. We then promptly looked to see what lessons we would be missing. On reflection, it became clear that our music mistress had played classical music for us to spark an interest in the music of the masters.'[127]

The Fovant Youth Club was established in the late 1940s and had a major emphasis on drama with shows and pantomimes being performed both in Fovant and in Dinton and Wilton. Members of the club would entertain at the piano in

Members of Little Cheverell Youth Club, 1940s (WSHC P1130)

pubs at which they stopped on their day trips to the coast.[128]

Art was also used to enliven an austere environment, such as subterranean factories, or to brighten up drab British Restaurant interiors; art was becoming more visible to the public at large. In 1943 the artist Olga Lehmann was invited to paint murals onto the walls of the Bristol Aircraft Corporation's underground factory in Corsham. She painted many and varied scenes, including prehistoric animals, horse racing, 19th century sailors and mermaids, and the circus.[129]

Some artists became official war artists; others were conscripted[130] or joined the Forces. The artist Rex Whistler was in the Welsh Guards, and stationed for a time at Codford. He painted murals and pictures on the walls in the Officer's Mess at the Camp[131] before leaving for Normandy only to die on his first day of action in July 1944.[132] The War Artists' scheme had proved very successful in WWI and so a War Artists' Advisory Committee was set up and the exhibitions of war artists, held in London and the provinces, were, according to Angus Calder, 'remarkably popular.' They also had the effect of enabling a wider public to view the work of good modern painters than would have been possible in peacetime.[133] The Ministry of Information also worked with other Government departments in terms of information provision and public relations. Its Home Publicity Division worked on campaigns requested by other Government Departments and regional campaigns, alongside those it developed itself. Artists were utilised for producing campaign material and worked out of the General Production Division. In 1942 £4 million was spent on publicity, £120,000 of which went on posters, art and exhibitions with the Home Intelligence Division gauging the public reaction to the material.[134]

CEMA and ENSA soon came became rivals through their work in factories. CEMA's performances, described by Ernest Bevin as 'high brow', were of a classical theme, in the form of repertoires. ENSA's shows were of the variety type, including humour and popular songs. ENSA became synonymous with low class offerings and CEMA with artistic integrity. By the beginning of June 1940 the Ministry of Labour intervened to ensure that effort was not duplicated and that the largest number of civilians could gain access to entertainment at work, but CEMA was asked to do this through ENSA. Difficulties also ensued due to the fact that CEMA members were paid higher fees than those in ENSA. By the beginning of 1941 Ministry officials realised that this system had been counter-productive and were encouraging CEMA to increase its factory performances after giving it back its independence.[135]

The London Philharmonic Orchestra became very popular and research conducted by the BBC found that listeners were increasingly turning to classical music. They increased its airtime. Robert MacKay feels that '[t]he changes to people's working lives, the reality and sense of shared experience, new and improvised arrangements for the presentation of the arts – brought more people into contact with serious music (and the other arts) or encouraged them to sample things outside their usual diet.'[146] CEMA had proved with its wartime work the receptivity of the British public towards the arts. It maintained art as part of British culture and raised morale with the help of its dedicated members who toured the length and breadth of the country.[147] Factory concerts came to an end in 1946.[148] Sir Malcolm Sargent, star of *The Brains Trust*, pointed out the greater attraction for classical music during the war had been 'because it ha[d] been made available to them in the places they ha[d] been in the habit of visiting in search of entertainment – theatres, music halls, and cinemas.'[149]

The art and artefacts in vulnerable areas were considered by the Government before the war. Plans were made by the Museums and Galleries Air Raids Precautions Committee to move items to safe locations. A 'National Register' had been put together as early as 1935. Houses were assigned items, the move in fact taking place only hours after war was declared. The scheme became unworkable, however, when those receiving the items discovered that the Treasury expected them to foot the bill for any repairs and additional security that would be required.

Museum staff also wanted to work with the items and house owners often received an unexpected 'guest' to be accommodated free of charge. The idea of housing 'treasures' underground was politically sensitive; the Government was worried that civilians would feel it was putting objects before lives, but eventually sites in Wales and at Westwood Quarry were acquired by the Museums and Galleries Air Raids Precautions Committee. By the middle of 1942 all the treasures of the British Museum, the Victoria and Albert Museum, the National Portrait Gallery, the Science Museum, the Imperial War Museum, the British and Bodleian Libraries and 40 of London's other museum, galleries and archives had been relocated.[150]

J. B. Priestley contributed his plan for Britain in 1941's *Picture Post*, entitled *When Work is Over*, detailing his idea of leisure in post-war Britain. Along with more holidays, he felt there should be more facilities in which to study the arts, with the establishment of civic centres for music, drama, film and talk.[151] During Keynes' tenure of CEMA, he looked forward to the reorganisation of CEMA as a peacetime organisation, with establishment by Royal Charter.[152] The Charter to the Arts Council was granted by King George VI in August 1946, guaranteeing CEMA a permanent existence with the British Government doing more to support the arts than it had done during the previous 150 years.[153] The newly arrived *Wiltshire Life* magazine was noting the opening of Swindon's new Arts Centre in its Christmas 1946 issue. It was the first in the country to be owned by a Local Authority.[154]

The Printed Word

ARTHUR MARSHALL RECALLED that '[r]eading of any kind was a solace'.[155] Sales of *Penguin Specials* peaked in 1942 and by 1945 sales had nose-dived to the point where they were suspended.[156] The New Left Book Club revealed an interest in written information, but the increase of photography and newsreel marked a shift from the written word to the image.[157] Detective fiction writers were aware that their readership could be subject to traumatic situations and, as Elizabeth Willis puts it, 'subject to official propaganda on a daily basis'. Readers did not want too much flag waving in their 'rare and valued lighter moments' of reading.[158] The classics became highly popular once more: Jane Austen, Anthony Trollope, Charles Dickens. Tolstoy's *War and Peace* was a huge wartime hit. To be mentioned on the BBC's *Brains Trust* meant a surge in demand, and Maureen Waller notes that the *6d. Penguin Specials* paperbacks were very successful.[159]

New broadcasting techniques meant that the visual became increasingly important to the Ministry of Information.[160] Adprint were a book company who were looking at new technology as a way of publishing high quality, illustrated books which would also be cheap to buy.[161] Hilda Matheson, the BBC's director of talks, was pivotal in establishing the Adprint-designed *Britain in Pictures* series in 1943 as 'cultural propaganda', and Jim Aulich notes, 'political manipulation of a popular cultural form'.[162] The *Picture Post* worked with the Ministry of Information, producing issues on topics that the Ministry wished to be seen by its

5 million readership.[163] Local stories containing good propaganda value made it into the national press, such as the story of a 'titled lady' who was helping to build the runway at Keevil airfield.[164]

Publications which looked at 'nostalgia' Britain had become a trend, with publications such as *Britain in Pictures*, which worked to highlight the beauty of British topography (including architecture) in an attempt to maintain morale.[165] The civilian population was also reliant on newspapers as well as the radio for information. Farmers routinely tuned in to Wiltshire's A.G. Street or read publications like *Farmers Weekly* or *Farmer and Stockbreeder*.[166] Local newspapers such as the *Wiltshire Gazette* gave advice on food preservation and many other matters. A letter from Warminster's Peggy Pickford to her sister Elizabeth Martin in Australia on 1 November 1939 notes that 'Ma's been buying *Punch*, and if you really want a true picture of England during the war, *Punch* is as good as anything

Photograph of Lacock during WWII, published by the Central Office of Information (WSHC P1397)

at giving it to you.'[167]

Poetry gained in popular appeal during the war. It was light to carry and useful to peruse during a tea break or between housework. People expected the emergence of wartime poets such as WWI's Rupert Brooke or Wilfred Owen but none materialised. Instead, a writer of another genre would have to do and Richard Hillary filled the void with *The Last Enemy* (1942), his story as an RAF pilot in the Battle of Britain and of the surgery he endured for burns. Like Owen, he returned to the war where he died aged 23.[168] War poets were finally discovered, among them the newly emerging Roy Fuller in the Royal Navy who noted: 'The trouble is I seem to have escaped the war again.' RAF Squadron Leader John Pudney, whose books of poetry were popular, became attached to the RAF's Public Relations. Other well known young poets included Sidney Keynes and Alun Lewis. The most highly acclaimed, but less well known at the time, was Keith Douglas. He died in Normandy in 1944. As Calder points out, there was a trend towards the 'retreat from politics in poetry' and the 'reversion to romanticism' from painters such as Graham Sutherland, composers such as Michael Tippett (who later moved to Wiltshire) and poets such as Dylan Thomas.[169] The journal *Horizon* was published in January 1940 to maintain cultural standards in wartime as Calder notes, a 'stand against cultural austerity'. Its publisher, Connolly, denounced state control of the arts. He felt that although the appreciation of art was growing, those producing the work: the Brains Trust, war artists, journalists, the BBC, Penguin books, the MOI, were not producing 'true' art as the artists themselves were denied 'independence, leisure and privacy'.[170]

By 1943 the number of newspapers bought per head of population was higher than it had ever been with four out of five men and two out of three women seeing a paper on any one day. Other media had their uses, but it was the printed word that could be, as Calder notes, 'studied so as to form the basis of a considered opinion.' Newspapers, though, had to be reduced in size as the war continued due to paper shortages. Before the war newsprint and periodicals had been using up to 23,000 tons of newsprint weekly. This fell at first by one third and then from summer 1940 in much greater numbers, to reach rock bottom in February 1943.[171] *Picture Post* became thinner and thinner as the war progressed, reducing from 75 page editions in August 1939 to *c.* 60 pages in October 1939; to 38 pages in December 1940 and *c.* 28 pages through 1943-1945.[172] Circulation restrictions were also put into place and the only way for the newspapers to increase sales was by limiting the number of pages produced. The Royal Commission on the Press (first assembled between 1947 and 1949) noted that over the course of the war newspapers had reduced by as much as 80% in size. The Commission realised that a lot of news needed to be suppressed, and that distortion and inaccuracy were unavoidable. An enraged *Daily Express* cynically noted that Britain would need to drop leaflets on itself to let its populace know how that war was progressing.[173]

Paper shortages were also affecting books. Publishers were limited to 60% and then 40% of the paper they had access to before the war. Official publications were taking up a lot of paper and at the height of the war effort less than 22,000 tons were available for books. This, at a time when the popularity of novels was on the increase, and newly published copies of the classics such as Jane Austen and Trollope were hard to find. New books became shorter and the Ministry of Information's pamphlets lauding the people and the war became bestsellers. It is noted by Calder that the demand for books was so large that even minor titles sold out as quickly as greater titles, but a lack of paper supply meant that it could not be capitalised on.[174] Agatha Christie's autobiography shows that she identified with some of those in society who were 'being side-lined as too old to participate' in her work,[175] and her books 'set the tone' in early post-war Britain.[176] The *Daily Mirror* leapt to success by 1943, its circulation reaching two million and increasing to three million by 1946. Inspired by American journalism, David Kynaston reports that it '[c]ater[ed] for short tea-breaks and even shorter attention spans'.[177] The *Wiltshire Gazette* was reporting the easing of paper rationing in its 22 August 1946 edition. 'From 22 September the amount of newsprint which may be used by newspapers will be increased... But as the newsprint available is still extremely scarce it is essential to avoid the printing of unused copies... This release of additional newsprint has been made possible by the purchase in Canada and Newfoundland of increased quantities for importation in 1947.' New newspapers were a different matter, however; still covered by the Control of Paper (No. 70) (Economy) Order, and still limited to 8 cwts. in a four month period. The increase in pages printed would not cover sports papers or sports editions, but the restriction on their circulation would be lifted on 22 September, although the new publication *Wiltshire Life* was lamenting the paper shortages in its very first edition, Christmas 1946. '... To maintain the high standard of illustrations in the magazine we need good art paper. We are allowed only 8 cwts for 4 issues.' They had also had problems with distribution. The paper was being produced in Scotland and had to be left in sidings during blizzard conditions. When it arrived, the paper was a 'mass of useless sodden pulp. We are sure that our readers will appreciate the difficulties under

The National Savings Committee's 'Squanderbug' campaign to encourage the purchase of Savings Certificates. Advertisement in the Wiltshire Gazette, 7 January 1943 (WSHC Microform Collection)

which we labour and forgive the use of inferior paper'.[178]

Newspapers relied on advertising, and although commercial revenue was down, the Ministry of Information became a steady financial provider, fully utilising newspapers for its advertisements. The 'Dig for Victory' campaign became so well known that its name still resonates with the British public today.[179] 1943 saw the emergence of the 'Squander Bug', a cartoon character portrayed through the newspapers as Calder describes, 'inciting housewives to waste money and wearing a swastika to show which side he was on'.[180]

The well-known slogan 'Keep Calm and Carry On' was introduced to the public at large between 27 June and 6 July 1939 by the Ministry of Information. It was part of a set of posters to be issued in the event of war which also included 'Your Courage, Your Cheerfulness, Your Resolution; Will Bring Us Victory' and 'Freedom is in Peril; Defend it with all Your Might'. 2.45 million copies of the posters were printed late August/early September 1939 but none were ever distributed.[181] The phrase has made a comeback in the 21st century.

The Ministry of Information found that the best way to boost morale was to focus on the provision of, as Ina Zweiniger-Bargielowska puts it, 'full and honest news'.[182] The Meeting Minutes of Wiltshire's Civil Defence and Welfare Committee in October 1941 noted that there were representatives of the Ministry of Information on Local Defence Committees, acting as liaison between Defence Committees in Rural Districts and their Information Committees. The Defence Committee noted that the possibility of invasion could still not be discounted at this time and that the graveness of the situation would rise further come the spring. It was noted that '[t]he question of how far the propaganda to the public should be pursued is a difficult one to determine since circumstances have modified in the past few weeks.'[183] Joan Hickson was noting in her diary in June 1944 that she felt so exhausted with suppressed emotion at the news coming through after D-Day. She wrote: 'The point being that I cannot write about the Invasion, though I feel it is just the sort of thing that might be of interest to the children and their children in future years, to know what we were doing and feeling in these momentous days. The trained journalists are just the opposite, rejoicing at having so much 'copy' at last and being able to pour it all forth in a spate of words and impressions. I shall have to put in newspaper cuttings as I have dried up so much. I can feel nothing except slightly sick, and do nothing except what I have to do.'[184]

The written word in a different form could also aid morale. It was often hard for mothers, wives or other family members to juggle home life with the rigours of life in wartime without the support of those who were now serving their country in the Forces. Letters were essential 'lifelines' for those at home and away, easing anxiety and helping people to cope in difficult times. The creation of the Airgraph in January 1941, microfilmed by the Eastman Kodak Company to reduce the size of letters (a printed facsimile was made for the recipient),[185] helped to make transportation over long distances both viable and swifter.[186] Morale could take many forms. Joan Hickson also worked in Bath and reported in her diary after the Baedeker Raid of the 'blitzed sweet shop man who escaped with his life received a consignment of chocolate and biscuits the next day so he made them up into equal parcels and sold from a table in the street. Ice cream people appeared who were very welcome.'[187]

The Church could often see itself, as G. Machin puts it, as a 'guardian' of the moral and spiritual welfare of the people.[188] It was difficult for the Church to have a voice during wartime due to the dilemma of pacifism versus the justification for patriotism,[189] and the need to support those parishioners whose loved ones were on the front line. In Melksham there was to be a 'Drum-Head' service to raise funds for War Weapons Week, to be held at St. Michael's Church. The feelings of the Vicar, sent to the Clerk of Melksham Urban District Council, illustrate the difficulties involved:

'We called a meeting of the Ministers of the Town this morning to discuss more fully your request... We want the Committee to be under no misapprehension that we are not equally with them convinced of the justice and righteousness of the cause to which the Nation is committed, but we all feel it is inappropriate for the Christian Church to start the propaganda of the War Weapons Week with a religious service.

The Business of the Christian Church is to strengthen the moral and spiritual aims of the war and to keep before the people the high ideals for which the nation entered the war... A Service of the suggested kind would be to us formal and unreal, but to read into our action any obstruction to the aims of the week would be entirely unjust...

We might add we are very jealous of any further encroachment on Sundays, which are more and more being taken up for various purposes some of them very necessary, but could not a parade of this kind take place on Saturday afternoon?'[190]

For some members of the British population during wartime religion could provide a certain amount of comfort and support; for others it raised doubts. The Church played a role in morale building during WWII by giving some the means to keep going despite all they were enduring, both physically and mentally.

The Royal family did much to boost morale during the war and Queen Mary visited Wiltshire many times. She was living in Badminton, Gloucestershire, for the duration of the war and wanted to be photographed 'among my people.' One such visit was to Haden's in Trowbridge and was attended by a reporter from the *Wiltshire Times*. 'So, on a grey afternoon with the light fading rapidly, Queen Mary, surrounded by workers, stood in a space between buildings with a lot of metalwork around – and I, on a ledge above, wondered if the picture I was taking would be sharp enough to print. It was sharp enough, but it was never printed in any newspaper. The censor decreed that publication of it would disclose information of value to the enemy.'[191]

The 'Austerity Britain' of peacetime 1945 left most looking for escapism. The West End theatres were sell-outs, dance halls were as popular as ever and the country's cinemas attracted an all-time peak of 1,635 admissions in 1946. The radio shows were still going strong with *ITMA*. Tommy Handley had since relocated to *Tomtopia* and was continuing to amass huge listening figures.

Workers gathered around Queen Mary on her visit to Hadens in Trowbridge, 1940, reproduced by kind permission of Mike Marshman (WSHC P55103)

David Kynaston notes that: 'The high cultural mood, accurately reflecting the prevailing sense of fatigue amid the pleasure seeking, was one of isolation and retrenchment.'[192] *Women's Hour* debuted on 7 October 1946, at first called 'uninteresting, waste of time, full of old ideas' by the *Daily Mirror*.[193] *The Light Programme* was planned to replace the *Forces Programme* in July 1945.[194] *Country Questions* of 1947 featured the celebrated Wiltshire farmer and journalist A. G. Street commenting on listeners' questions about the countryside.[195] *The Archers* was first broadcast in 1951 and *The Goon Show* started out in the same year, called *Crazy People*.[196] Radio had become crucial to the quality of life of the nation and during the war and it had produced, as Peter Hennessy puts it, 'the single greatest cultural change in the country since the development of railways a century before had opened up the nation to the national newspaper'.[197] The Penguin *New Writing* magazine, with a readership of 100,000 in 1946, saw a swift fall in circulation, the editor and publisher lamenting the hope that 'given the formula an enormous public was now ready to devour what would have been almost entirely highbrow fare before the war.'[198] Reading was not popular with the working class especially, many not finding books that would interest them.[199] The publisher Geoffrey Faber wrote in the *Spectator* in 1948 '... I found myself wondering out loud where 'literature' had got to. Almost every book seemed to deal with some more or less specialised subject.'[200] Newspapers remained popular in the post-war period, the most successful being the *Daily Mirror*, the *News Chronicle*, the *Daily Herald* and the *Daily Express*. Television returned to the screen on 7 June 1946.[201]

The Pay Act of 1938 and the austerity years had left many people with money to spend and time to spend it in. Butlins made the most of this market, ensuring that the camps were 'within reach of millions'. The late 1940s were the time of spectator sports, with millions going to football matches, motorcycle speedway and the dog tracks. Cycling club members got on their bikes to make the most of the clear roads free of cars due to the continuance of petrol rationing.[202] Cycle speedway became popular after the war when Control Boards and Local Leagues were established and tracks set up, often initially in bombed out areas.[203] Wiltshire had both a League and Championship by the 1950s which was attracting teams from its towns and villages as well as from neighbouring counties. Protesters against the proposed motorcycle speedway track in Blunsdon, 1948, were arguing that it would take up good agricultural land which was needed for food production and would spoil the peace and quiet of the area. They also noted that whilst they had been unable to get a playground built for their children, the track which was for commercial use and for 'outsiders' was going to take place against their wishes. The site was due to be called Blunsdon St. Andrew Abbey Stadium. The plans also

A Cleverton Hornet in a race with three Eastward Eagles from Swindon, taking part in a League event at Marlborough, 1958/9 season, reproduced by kind permission of Trevor House (WSHC P53341)

had their supporters too.[204]

Labour Party memos show that the Government were discussing the need for a leisure policy, concerned about the popularity of the cinema and gambling as 'passive' pursuits and drawing the conclusion that many types of escapist entertainment or recreation were encouraged by, as David Kynaston notes, the 'drabness, insecurity and hopelessness of everyday life.' The Arts Council's offerings were not as popular as their wartime counterparts, with 80% of their former wartime audience discontinuing their patronage. By 1947 the Council was reporting that its activities were not reaching the working class and its regional outreach was curtailed. In 1946 the BBC's new 'high culture' radio channel, the *Third Programme* was not listened to by the working class and by 1947 was, as Kynaston notes, 'too remote' and 'too heavy' to engage with ordinary working people.[205] The *Wiltshire Times* was reporting the launch of an 'interesting social experiment' on 19 August 1944. A new Committee had been established, the Calne Community Council. 'Its growth is being carefully watched from outside, and it may well be the forerunner of very similar movements in other towns. The London Organiser of the National League of Social Service has already asked to be informed of its progress, and the Ministry of Information has also evinced interest in it... the Community Council particularly lends itself to expansion in the post-war period. Its constitution, as drawn, has among its objects to promote the general good of the community in the Borough of Calne and surrounding districts, with the aim of advancing education, developing physical improvement, further health, promoting healthy leisure, and pursuing any charitable objects.'

During the Convertibility Crisis of 1947 the Board of Trade put a 75% import duty on foreign films to save currency and encourage home-grown talent. The Americans replied by boycotting Britain, necessitating a turn around, but they did agree to restrict their British earnings to £4.25 million a year. Harold Wilson established a National Film Production Council late in 1948 with funding on the proviso that 45% of films were British made; those produced included *Brief Encounter*.[206]

The post-war era provided the people with, as John Lehmann put it, '... A Socialist Government, besides doing practically nothing to help artists and writers, has also quite failed to stir up either intellect or imagination; the English renaissance, whose false dawn we have so enthusiastically greeted, is further away than ever...'[207] Paul Addison notes that the 'bridge' connecting art to the people during the war 'was in fact crumbling'.[208] The British population at large felt little need to, as Kynaston reports, 'abandon [its] cultural hierarchies' in the immediate post-war era.[209]

Leisure time in the 1950s was spent reading, listening to the radio, knitting, needlework and gardening. The development of the transistor radio revolutionized post-war Britain, making portable music available, and cheaply too.[210]

Did the Ministry of Information (MOI) do its job well? It appears that it was of value. Robert Mackay notes that the overall picture gained from the MOI charting of public morale was clear: 'morale held up through the years of tedium and deprivation as it had through the traumatic period of military defeat, threatened invasion and mass bombing... the overwhelming impression is of a willingness to see the business through, to endure the strain and the boredom, and comply with the orders and regulations which those in charge said were necessary.' The leadership of the Government was an important factor, as was the policy of raising the standard of living for the poorer sections in society. The Ministry of Information acted as a connection between the Government and the people, enabling the war to become a 'truly people's war'.[211] However, MacKay feels that the Government's obsession with morale was unnecessary and the effect the Ministry of Information produced was 'probably marginal'.[212] Of course, this ending was not solely down to the MOI; individual temperaments also played their part, and as we have seen, some played a greater and fairer part than others. The official historian of the Second World War, Asa Briggs, felt that the Ministry of Information was viewed as an unpopular wartime invention, making a conscious appeal to the country's historic past at the beginning of the war.[213]

By February 1945 the journalist and author James Lansdale Hodson felt that the minds of the people had moved to the left, looking towards a new future rather than turning back to the pre-war past. 'The love of good books and music has grown. Our A.B.C.A [Army Bureau of Current Affairs] and other discussion groups in the Forces have encouraged a number, at all events, to enjoy arguments and the methods of democracy, and our production committees have worked similarly in factories.'[214]

11
Victory is Here!

VE Day

O N 30 APRIL 1945 the Home Office was writing to Wiltshire County Council's Clerk with Circular 97/1945 regarding plans to mark the 'Celebration of the Termination of Organised Hostilities in Europe.' The Government wanted Local Authorities to begin making local arrangements, understanding that although the war was not yet won, the general public would wish to celebrate 'the victorious end of the European campaigns before turning with renewed energy to the completion of the tasks before it.' It had already been planned that news of the cessation of hostilities in Europe would be announced by the Prime Minister on the radio. At 9 o'clock in the evening of the same day the King would 'speak to his peoples throughout the world.' It was hoped that churches in the country would arrange for bells to be rung. The King wished the following Sunday to be 'observed as a day of thanksgiving and prayer' with victory parades organised to include 'as many aspects as possible of the national effort'. It was also noted that due to the shortage of fuel and labour it would not be possible to restore full street lighting, and instead Local Authorities were given permission to utilise any forms of temporary lighting such as flood lights where they could. It was hoped that the military would assist in this regard. There would also be no objection to the use of bonfires. The Government was considering licences, stating that dance venues should be allowed to open later than usual, and that Local Authorities should also be sympathetic to the applications from sellers of 'intoxicating liquor'. The remainder of the day of announcement 'which will generally be known as VE-Day' would be classed as a public holiday.[1] The Downton Parish Council Minutes of April 1945 relayed the possibility of having a combined Church Service with the bells rung for 'V-Day'.[2]

There appears to have been some initial confusion as on 5 May 1945 Wiltshire's Chief Constable received a message from the Inspector of Bath Police (on behalf of the Regional Police Staff Officer) advising that on receipt of the message 'MILLENNIUM' certain information should be passed to all Local Authority Clerks in Wiltshire. Two days later another message was received from

Poster announcing a public meeting to be held in Westbury regarding Victory Celebrations, 6 May 1945 (WSA G17/225/2)

Bath stating that there would in fact be no coded message. 'V.E. Day as given out by the B.B.C. will be announced by the Prime Minister at 1500hrs. Tuesday 8th May, 1945. The whole of Tuesday & Wednesday will be public holidays.'[3]

Sudden delays and confusion amongst the Allies meant that the VE Day announcement came later than expected. King George VI had returned to London on Sunday 6 May 1945 in readiness for the 'great day' on the Monday. The Prime Minister Winston Churchill found Monday 7 May to be a frustrating time. He wanted to make it VE Day, and had his speech ready and waiting, but he was hampered by the Americans and Russians. It was, as Peter Hennessy notes, an 'anti-climax'. On what became the official day, Tuesday 8 May, crowds packed into Trafalgar Square and Whitehall to hear Churchill's announcement at 3pm, with Churchill telling the crowd that it was 'their victory'.[4]

Frances Partridge wrote in her dairy at Ham Spray House in Ham on 1 May 1945 that she had just switched on the late news at 11pm to hear that Hitler was dead. On 5 May she was '[w]aiting, waiting for the end' after two days of disturbed sleep, waking with her heart beating wildly, hoping to hear the church bells pealing for victory. On 7 May she reported that they had been kept 'on the hop' all day, radio announcements telling them that the Germans had signed the unconditional surrender, but no announcement was made. 'If the war is over, then it is over, and I am bewildered to explain this fever of anticipation. The voices of the B.B.C. announcers betray increasing irritation, and everyone is on tenterhooks waiting for the inevitable...' Finally it came; the report that Churchill would announce the end of the war in Europe at 3pm. 'It's all very flat,' she went on. 'We've just been drinking a little weak gin.' Frances did, however, feel a sense of peace at the news.[5]

The Chippenham doctor Joan Hickson was writing in her diary on 7 May. 'Everyone on tenterhooks all day, waiting for the announcement of cessation of hostilities in Europe. The wireless keeps saying it will not be very long, so we dare not turn it off but kept popping back between patients to be greeted by the most futile of radio plays or music. Finally at six it was said that 'No further announcement was to be made tonight', so we turned it off. The result was that at 8pm it was announced that Churchill would speak at 3pm tomorrow... As usual I am completely drained of emotion and can feel nothing.' She noted that there had been a little 'drunken singing' in the town that evening. On Wednesday 9 May: 'Went up the town last night to see what people were doing. Crowds everywhere, dancing and singing in the market place. There was very little drunkenness and no hooliganism... not even a broken window. On the whole people showing their good taste and sense. Family parties out for the evening to enjoy themselves and to show their children the lights on the trees on the islands by the bridge, all reflected in the water and very lovely. Few children have ever seen any lights at night.'[6]

About one third of the population tuned in from 3.20pm to 4pm on 8 May to hear the 'Bells and Victory Celebrations'. The majority of listeners appear to have enjoyed it. David Kynaston notes that it was 'vivid, noisy and inspiring', bringing everyone, including invalids and those who lived in the remotest parts of the country, into the spirit of festivity in London and the other cities visited. Some, however, did find the commentary rather tiresome.[7]

Victory Scarves were produced by Arnold Lever with patriotic designs to mark the end of war in Europe[8] and the Board of Trade announced that it would be allowing the people to purchase red, white and blue bunting without coupons

VE Day celebrations in the Guild Hall Square, Salisbury, courtesy of the British Council
(WSHC P53874)

until the end of the month.[9] VE Day celebrations in Mere included celebrations in the local pub and in The Square, and linking hands around the triangle of Mere town clock and singing Auld Lang Syne. The US troops fired off light flares into the sky. One boy remembered being 'hoisted onto his uncle's shoulders and jigged around the Town Clock high above the crowd.'[10] In Bishopstone the locals had a few drinks and held a party on the playing field.[11] The VE Day celebrations at Longbridge Deverill included fireworks at the crossroads.[12]

Jack Mock reports on Bradford on Avon's VE Day celebrations on 8 May when the streets were '... thronged with thousands of folk, old and young, with hearts full of joy and thanksgiving for the great victory... Practically every building was lavishly adorned with the flags of all the Allied nations, patriotic messages, and electric and other forms of illumination. In the centre of the town, long festoons of flags and decorations stretched across the streets, in which children waved flags, adults adorned their dresses and hats with rosettes... Stretched across the river were hundreds of gaily coloured lanterns, which in the dark produced a fairyland scene as the flickering lights reflected on the water.'[13] In Devizes flags and bunting were put up, along with pictures of the King and Queen, displayed in shop windows, but the Town Council was criticised for not organising any official celebrations. However, many impromptu celebrations took place and hotel and restaurants put on Victory suppers. Pubs were allowed to stay open late, but soon ran dry. The Prime Minister's speech was relayed by loud speaker from St. John's Church and there was a bonfire on Roundway Down with floodlights in the town and flares at The Crammer. The children of Sheep Street were given free ice creams by local residents,[14] as also occurred in Meadow Road, Salisbury. The celebrations in the locality of Meadow Road, Sidney Street and York Road were reported to have been perhaps the liveliest in the city.[15]

The Head Teacher of Kington St. Michael School noted in the school's log book that (perhaps unsurprisingly) after the two-day VE celebration the children had returned to school 'too tired to do work.'[16]

The war in Europe had ended, but with relief came anxieties about the future. Joan Hickson wrote in her diary:

'Today one can't find any general relief or trust in the future. Quiet thankfulness that the immediate killing is over – yes, though perhaps not for those of us with sons who will have to help beat Japan. No sense of security that civilisation is fundamentally decent. Starvation and chaos and physical ruin indescribable all over Europe with typhus and TB rampant. Already people voicing suspicions that 'It will be Russia next time' and that next time may mean the complete obliteration of a country by a V bomb and rockets before even war is declared.

I can feel nothing **but** gloom and apprehension about the future. Is this merely my age, having a son in the Navy destined for Japan, or more insight than some? I hope not the latter.'

The *Wiltshire Times* reported on VE Day in their 12 May 1945 edition, stating that the day was celebrated in towns and villages across the county with crowded thanksgiving services and great rejoicing. It was also noted:

'Wiltshire has been spared many of the hardships which have been the lot of London and other large cities, and of the coastal districts of the South and East, and has suffered comparatively little from air attack: but it has borne a full share of the "toil and sweat and tears" which the Prime Minister said was all that he could promise the country when he took office in the dark days of 1940. Her sons have served in every theatre of war, from the Far East to North Africa, and Europe, and have gained distinction in some of the bitterest fighting, from El Alamein to the Rhine and beyond. Her people at home have paid a noble part on farm and in factory, and in the various voluntary services, to further the nation's war effort.'

VJ Day

ON 10 AUGUST 1945 the Home Office was again writing to Local Authority Clerks, stating that although it was impossible to say when the termination of hostilities with Japan would take place, Local Authorities were to refer to Circular No. 97/1945 of 30 April 1945 when making arrangements. 'The Secretary of State recommends that local authorities should endeavour to make such arrangements as are possible, in the time available, to promote in each locality all such methods of public rejoicing and festivity as may be practicable, and for this purpose it is hoped that it may be possible for local authorities to arrange to provide bands, to light bonfires and to take other appropriate means of celebrating this historic occasion. It is hoped that Churches will be able to arrange for Church bells to be rung throughout the Country.' At the end of hostilities, the two working days immediately following were to be classed as days of paid holiday in Government factories and for those working in Government service.[18]

David Kynaston notes that days of negotiations took place after the Japanese surrender on 10 August, and by 14 August there was an expectation that the war would end in a matter of hours. At midnight the Prime Minister Clement Attlee announced Peace. Due to the late hour of the announcement, many people began their trip to work the next day without realising that it was the start of a two day public holiday. The King's speech was broadcast on 15 August[19] which was declared VJ Day.

Corsham Parish Council's Committee had been set up to prepare for the VE Day preparations but found they had little time to prepare for VJ Day. Community singing and a second bonfire in the park were hastily arranged, and again there was dancing outside the Town Hall. The Community Centre organised a children's sports day the following day and a United Service was again conducted in the town.[20] The opposite was true of Devizes Town Council who were more prepared the second time around and laid on a 'comprehensive programme' with entertainments for the children in the Market Place and a tea party which included a 3cwt. iced Victory Cake decorated with Allied flags. Coloured lights adorned the fountain and Market Cross. With the evening came dancing in the Corn Exchange and Drill Hall, and a bonfire and fireworks on the Green.[21]

Jack Mock notes that the VJ Celebrations at Bradford on Avon were similar to those of VE Day and would '... long be remembered. Buildings were decorated in fine style. The river lights were a joy and the island illuminated with a huge "V.J." Again the Scouts organised a huge bonfire at Jones Hill, and a torchlight procession was held which attracted a large crowd. The fire was lit and a small firework display was held... there was dancing in the car park near the baths.'[22]

Vera Lynn recounted the reflections of a Somerset housewife on VJ Day. '... in spite of the joy one can't help reflecting that our larders are bare, there are no houses for our returning soldiers... Everyone's house needs painting and replastering, our clothes are shabby, and one can't buy a sheet or blanket unless one is bombed out or newly wed... we are all exhausted.. The best minute of the day has been just to sit down and realize that the war is over.'[23]

The Home Secretary later wrote a message to the Police of England and Wales, thanking them for their work on the two VJ Days:

'I know that you ask no thanks for a job which, you will say, was "all in the day's work"; but I think it right that the police should know how great is the appreciation of the good-tempered efficiency with which they discharged their heavy, and sometimes difficult, duties on this occasion.

At the time of national holiday, you had to remain on duty. At a time when the country as a whole was taking a rest from its labours, your burdens were increased. You did your duty splendidly...'[24]

The 'Victory Celebration'

The Home Office was reporting the plans for Victory Celebrations in a letter to Local Authorities on 18 February 1946, the day that the Prime Minister announced in the House of Commons that the official Victory Celebrations in London would take place on 8 June 1946. This date would be a public holiday across the country and it was presumed that Local Authorities would wish to undertake arrangements for their own local celebrations. A national parade would be taking place in London to 'represent as many phases as possible of the national war effort and [would] include representatives from the various parts of Great Britain.' Open air entertainments would be provided in the Royal Parks in London and the Ministry of Works were looking to illuminate certain public buildings in the capital between 10pm and midnight from 8 to 15 June 1946. No objections would be made if Local Authorities were to match these national plans. It would also be possible for bonfires to be lit using items of no salvage value, and Local Authorities were also advised to look at ways to include those less able to take part, such as the elderly, infirm or those in hospital. On 29 April 1946 Devizes was planning for a parade, to form in the Market Place at noon and march through the town. There would also be sports competitions to include a marathon and mile races.[25]

Many nations took part in the National Parade in London on 8 June 1946, but for political reasons the servicemen and women from the Polish Forces were sadly not invited to attend, and the Poles, for a time, felt betrayed.[26]

12
The Post War World

After the War
1946

Now let us lick our wounds
The hurts we took and bore
For we that have been made
Are whole and sane once more.
We've done our best and worst
We've fought and killed and died
As though we were accursed
Or lost to ought beside.
Set blame upon no man
For blame belongs to all
Active or passively
In great degree or small
Let's strike a joyous note
A jubilant encore
For we that have been mad
Are whole and sane once more.

Poem by JR Hooper of Mere written in 1946, published in *There's a Wind Upon the Downs?*[1]

S IR WILLIAM BEVERIDGE felt in 1943 that national unity had been the greatest moral achievement of the Second World War. Kenneth O. Morgan notes that J.B. Priestley and Harold Nicolson 'agreed that the war years were creating a vast cultural transformation in the British people'.[2] Sonya Rose reports that the wartime working class felt a mixture of emotions when thinking of the post-war world. There was the hope in a fairer society and wartime slogans and Government reports talked of a redistribution of wealth, but there was also the feeling that nothing would change; that vested interests 'would see to that'.[3] Orwell wrote in 1944: 'Everyone expects not only that there will be a ghastly muddle over demobilization, but that mass unemployment will promptly return... Everyone wants, above all things, a rest.'[4] Fay Inchfawn of Freshford on the Somerset/Wiltshire border noted in her 1943 publication *Salute to the Village* that England was in the process of remaking itself, getting ready for a new England which as yet, was still to be fashioned. 'We hate to think that the England which our forefathers made for us is passing away; but nothing in it which is worth preserving need ever pass away – that is, if, as a nation we will keep it alive.'[5]

J. B. Priestley announced that WWII had been a 'People's War'[6] and now it was to become a 'People's Peace', but what exactly would this emerging post-war world bring for the people?

Election

THE WARTIME COALITION Government remained in place after VE Day. Churchill then dissolved it on 15 June and called a General Election.[7] Voting began on 5 July 1945 but the count did not begin until 26 July due to Service votes requiring further checking for duplication.[8] The total number of civilian and Service voters in Britain was 32,353,319.[9] The Tisbury Women's Institute was asking how they could obtain information about just what the political parties stood for in their Committee meeting of 7 June 1945. The answer: 'my Committee advise adherence to our previous policy of keeping party politics outside the Institute movement.'[9a] Peggy Pickford was writing from Trowbridge to her sister Elizabeth Martin in Australia on 26 July 1945:

'They are just announcing the election results and so far Labour seems to be sweeping the board (it's midday only). This rather shocks me. It was the Labour people who clamoured for a second front to help Russia, when we were obviously not prepared – can they know enough to finish off the Japanese war successfully? And do they really care? I think they are terribly self-centred and may get us in an awful mess if they do get in.

I don't think now is the right time for them to begin their experiments of a Utopia, although I agree with some of their plans. But the way the dockers and miners strike even against their leaders' advice does not portend well for unity in their ranks. They seem to strike needlessly because they are getting good money, and they know it is hindering the Japanese war effort. However, what I think doesn't signify.'[10]

On 27 July 1945 *The Times* confirmed 'The Nation's Verdict;' Labour had won by a landslide of 394 seats to the Conservatives' 210.[11] The newspaper reported: 'It had been expected that the National Government would be hard pressed, but because of Mr. Churchill's great prestige as a leader of the war-winning Coalition even the Labour Party had not expected to achieve a victory on this scale.'[12] Due to the war, Peter Lewis feels that men who would never have joined the forces had seen up close the attitude and (sometimes inept) performance of their middle class officers. They felt the upper classes did not deserve the deferential attitude or respect that had once been taken for granted.[13] Morgan's research finds that 60% of British servicemen actually voted.[14] J. B. Priestley's novel *Three Men in New Suits* (1946) included one of the demobbed servicemen stating that the people at home were not so different after the war, but that they themselves were. They wanted different men in charge, planning and co-operation.[15]

Peter Hennessy feels that the shift to Labour in the General Election was down to the nation's experience of total war in times of stress and shortage.[16] The social historian Jose Harris states that historians remain divided on the cause of the Labour landslide, suggesting a turning point between citizens and the state, a break from the past, the ability of the Labour party to maintain support more successfully during the war than the Conservatives, a delayed reaction against the deprivation of the 1930s, a reflection of the sociological changes the war brought with it, or a new moral and philosophical state of mind between society and the state…[17] It could have been one or many of these things.

Labour concentrated its election manifesto on housing, social insurance and full employment, also emphasising the need for modernisation and central planning.[18] David Kynaston reports that its 'energetic message of can-do fairness' was another factor in its success.[19] The *Wiltshire Life* magazine chose to use a knight in shining armour for its first ever issue, Christmas 1946. The accompanying text wondered: 'Romance and chivalry. Will they ever return again to save us from the chaos which besets us?… In this age of grim reality we sorely need men of enterprise and knightly endeavour'.[20] Claire Waring feels the statement was a 'lament for the bankrupt state of the country's emotions', but possibly also a note to the loss of Churchill and the introduction of Attlee's new ministerial style.[21]

The Demob

THE VICTORY PARADE in London on Saturday 8 June 1946 provoked criticism, but there were approximately 6 million spectators.[22] Across Wiltshire; indeed, across the country, towns and villages had been preparing to welcome home demobbed servicemen and women. Many wanted to show their appreciation and set up a 'Welcome Home Fund' with the help of the Government's War Charities Act 1940. Parishes were required to apply to their County Council to register their Welcome Home Fund, with any objections to be sent in writing to the Council within 14 days of notification in the local newspaper. In Lea and Cleverton a meeting was held on 9 May 1945 between the Lea and Cleverton and Garsdon Parish Councils, the object of which was to raise funds to provide members of His Majesty's Forces with 'a suitable welcome home on their return.' The Administrative Centre for the scheme was proposed as the village hall in Lea and by June 1945 they were in the process of opening a bank account for the Fund. It was agreed that competitions would be organised to raise money; a skittle and bowling competition, a darts match and raffle with the Youth Movement (a club for young people) holding a fête, baby show and slide show.[23] In Calne the Mayor

THE PARISH OF BROMHAM
"Welcome Home"
Fund

At a Parish Meeting held in the Village Hall on December 13th last it was decided to open a fund for the welcome home of our men and women in the fighting services. It was decided to make our target £1,000, so that each service man and woman on returning would be given at least £5. The same would be given to the next-of-kin of any making the supreme sacrifice

Bromham is pulling its full-weight in the War Effort, but those of us who have not had to leave our homes, our businesses and our families owe a special debt of gratitude to the men and women in the services

We appeal to the business man, farmer and small-holder, who has been able to carry on his job, though under difficulties. How much has it been worth to you to be home while they have been fighting for victory ?

We appeal to the householder, who, thanks to our fighting men, still enjoys the pleasures and comforts of family life and has been spared the horrors of air-raids

Your collector (....)
will be calling during MARCH for your first contribution, and will call again in SEPTEMBER for any further sum you may like to give

Help us to prepare a really memorable home-coming by giving as generously as possible

R. H. ANGELL, Chairman
A. M. BARTLETT, Secretary

Bromham's Welcome Home Fund (WSA 3061/31)

inaugurated a fund. 'All serving members of the forces, including ex-prisoners of war, would receive a gift and a certificate to mark their long absence in the call of duty... Collecting boxes were mustered, labels for them were printed, and appeals went forth for folk to have fund raising events... The gift of an initialled wallet and a signed certificate was handed out to all returning ex-servicemen and women. A dinner was given in the Lansdowne Hotel on 6 June 1945 to ex-prisoners of war.'[24]

It appears that each parish could choose its own way to personally thank those who had served. In Alderbury it was decided to frame 133 certificates in the form of an 'illustrated address' but there was some contention over whether this was the most appropriate way to show the appreciation of the people of the parish. A number of people signed a petition stating that: 'We, the undersigned, residents of Alderbury and Whaddon, wish to register our disapproval of the suggested scheme of presenting the returned members of H.M. Forces an illuminated address. We are quite sure that the returning members would prefer some article of utility, which by every day use would bring them into closer co-operation with us. We suggest therefore that the Welcome Home Committee convene a public meeting at which this whole matter can be debated.' It is not clear whether a meeting took place, but the presentation of the addresses went ahead, with a couple of recipients writing to show their appreciation:

I thank you for the gift of money & the framed Illuminated address from Alderbury and her sister parishes.

It was indeed a welcome surprise because although I have and still love Alderbury and it holds tragic memories for me I never realized I was classed as 'One of You'.

People that reside in the village not of their birth are often alienated from the rest of the inhabitants but after fourteen years I think I can safely refer to Alderbury as my home village (after all I was born a Wiltshireman, in point of fact, a Cityman of Sarum).

The address is hung where I can always see it & will be always treasured in memory of a village that did not forget.

Thank you.[25]

The framing company, Photoframes: Sullman of London, congratulated the parish on the quality of their certificates, remarking that they were 'the finest I have handled so far.'[26]

In September 1946 forms were being sent out in Bradford on Avon for inclusion in a list of persons entitled to participate in the Welcome Home Fund. Questions asked included: date of joining the Forces, date of discharge, address at joining and current address, and details of the Unit or Service served in.[27] By 22 August 1946 the *Wiltshire Gazette* was reporting that Melksham had raised £2,100 for distribution and had also used a questionnaire to discover how the ex-service people wanted the amount distributed, resulting in a cash payment. Corsham presented their serving townspeople with a booklet entitled *War Records of Corsham 1939-1945*. The Chairman of Corsham Parish Council was asked to write the Foreword. In it he noted: 'The memory of our sons who fell in battle has been fittingly observed. Thanks to a gift by Miss. A Tennant and Miss L. Rigden, a 'Garden of Remembrance' has been designed in Station Road... Tribute must be paid to the Welcome Home Committee which raised £2,360 during the war.' This was equally divided among the town's servicemen and women on their return, working out at £3 5s. 0d. per person to include those who were not able to return (the money was given to their families). The Chairman concluded by stating that the book was the 'town's recognition of their contribution towards a victory which preserved our land and our homes.'[28] It was not just individuals who were honoured; the City of Salisbury organised an event to honour the Wiltshire Regiment which took place on 3 December 1947 when the Title Deed of the City was presented, conferring the right to march through the streets of Salisbury on all ceremonial occasions.[29]

Returning service personnel would need both a home and work. As Minister of Labour during WWII Ernest Bevin supported a number of schemes to ensure that demobbed servicemen got the job they wanted. He created two classes for demobilisation. Class B were builders and those who were urgently required for construction work; the rest joined an orderly queue dependent on certain criteria.[30] Universities also had an influx of students with the Government offering demobbed soldiers grants.[32] Demobbed servicemen and women could also have their degree entry qualifications waived;[33] the numbers of demobbed service personnel attending university began to stretch resources.[34]

The symbol of demobilisation became the unmistakable 'demob suit', comprising a Trilby hat and a classic suit.[35] A man from Broughton Gifford who had served with the Royal Navy remembered it very well. 'These suits, made out of a striped material similar to that used for making deckchairs, were hung in racks. A selection of capes or waterproof hats completed what was on offer from a grateful

Government – in both large and small sizes. The option of a cash alternative was not available! I refused to have any of these garments, but the person in charge simply had to get a signature from me, and from the back of the stock produced a sports jacket and flannels which I reluctantly walked out wearing.'[36]

Between mid 1945 and mid 1947 over four million servicemen were demobbed; a very slow process some thought. Servicemen could find that their pre-war jobs had not been kept open, and they were often not viewed as heroes by a war weary civilian population. Support and advice could be hard to come by[37] and the letters and diaries of newly demobbed soldiers show how bewildered they felt. The Britain they had left behind was not the same as the one in which they were now trying to make a fresh start.[38]

Women found it difficult to adapt to domestic life after the war ended, their lives often becoming more restricted after the return of their husbands, with their newfound freedom at work now commonly coming to an end. James Hinton records one Women's Voluntary Service Organiser from Nottingham writing in her resignation letter; "This is the most miserable letter I have ever had to write… It is a real heart break to me – but I have to choose between WVS and keeping my home going…' She had a husband who wished her to concentrate solely on her domestic duties.[39] Other wives were just getting to know their husbands after a brief romance followed by a quick wartime marriage and long separation, and many husbands could be greatly altered by their experiences. The men in turn could often miss the comradeship of their wartime lives and some found it hard to settle back into a world of peace with around 30,000 demobilised men contacting the Resettlement Advice Service per week by the end of 1945 needing help with their return to civilian life.[40] One demobbed serviceman who had come home to Devizes from North Africa and Italy in the Royal Wiltshire Yeomanry recalled: 'Although I had a good responsible civilian occupation to jump into on my release from the army, I found it extremely difficult to settle back into civilian life, and was very tempted to rejoin my Regiment despite all the trials and tribulations of the war. Had I been a single man I would have had no hesitation in doing so.'[41] Another, having worked as an Infantry Despatch Rider who had travelled from his home town of Trowbridge all over the world, felt that he was leaving his family when the time came to leave, and had a tear in his eye as he waved goodbye to his comrades. He kept his greatcoat as he could not bear to part with his 'good friend', keeping it as a 'lucky omen'.[42] For those Service personnel returning home, the memory of wartime experiences could be very difficult to live with in civilian life, affecting their work and those close to them too. One Broughton Gifford man found it difficult to settle back into his old life. 'When I returned to work at the Avon Rubber Company in Melksham, after demob, I could not bear the thought of office work and so went into the factory on production.'[43] Servicewomen could also miss life in the Forces which had brought with it new responsibilities and camaraderie. The uniforms had also given them a newfound status.[44]

To help ease the difficulties of returning servicemen into civilian life, there were a series of programmes on the *Home Service* radio. *Can I Help You?* covered the problems most likely to be encountered by demobilised service personnel. 'We've got to remember that civilians have been shifted about a bit as well... You and I are not the same individuals as 2, 3, 4 years ago – and we mustn't expect men who've been fighting over half the world to be the same either... we've got to scrap the idea that any of us is 'coming back' to something we left, or that there's any real difference between the serviceman and the civilian.' There was advice for those who had been waiting at home too. The Reverend Elliot wrote in the *Sunday Graphic*: 'All these years they have been dreaming of home, living for letters, solacing their lonely hearts... And don't worry if for a little time he seems disillusioned, even with his home, even with you.' In October the *Daily Mirror* published *Advice on nervous Returning Servicemen from the Wife of one of Them*, listing:

'Be glad to be back
Be prepared for civil restrictions
Be appreciative
Take over some of the family responsibility
Be prepared for changes in her
Be affectionate.'[45]

Wartime indiscretions by women could affect peacetime relationships and by 1945 the divorce rate was two and a half times that of 1938 with the cause of 70% being stated as adultery, over half of cases being brought by husbands.[46] The passing of the Legal Aid Act in 1945 made divorce a viable option and by 1947 the figure reached a peak of 60,000.[47]

The Military Recruitment Department at the Ministry of Labour and National Service was responsible for dealing with cases of refusal by employers to reinstate those who had completed military service.[48] Returning servicemen could often find themselves homeless, and by March 1946 the situation had not improved.[49] In 1946 ex-servicemen wanted to set up businesses on new housing estates in Swindon but were refused as priority was being given to housing.[50] The Purton Branch of the British Legion was drawing the attention of the Cricklade and Wootton Bassett Rural District Council to the plight of ex-servicemen c. 1946. 'The National Executive Council of the British Legion are particularly concerned regarding the urgency of the question of Housing, and local Legion branches are requested to impress upon Local Authorities, the increasingly serious position which is arising with regard to men and women returning from the Services on the re-establishment of family life and homes... It is therefore urged that 'ex-service' applicants should receive special consideration and that if the 'Points System' is being adhered to in the selection of tenants for completed houses, then the reward for devotion to duty and service to the mother country should warrant at least six points and thereby replace the present low allocation of merely three points.'[51] W. R. Davidge and Partners of London, Planning Consultants, were urging Devizes Rural District Council to consider the re-use of old wartime temporary buildings. 'No doubt the Council could use them for some temporary purpose for example housing ex-service men etc.'[52] Some ex-servicemen wanted to make use of 'self-build' schemes to build their own housing. In 1955 ex-servicemen wanted to build

12 houses in Swindon. All those taking part would be craftsmen in the building trade. Circular 44/52 from the Ministry of Housing and Local Government, April 1952, talked of Housing Associations and Self-Help Groups, considering their contribution to local housing needs. 'The Minister said in the House of Commons on 19th February, 1952, that he would like to show some practical appreciation of the initiative and determination of the members of 'Self-Help' Groups to help themselves.' Swindon had its own Swindon and District Self-Build Housing Association and in April 1955 they were handing over the keys to their very first house.[53] The Hilperton Self-Build Association was established in 1953 as a co-operative to build 40 homes at Marshmead, funded principally by a loan from the Bradford and Melksham Rural District Council.[54]

Self-Build Opening Ceremony in Hilperton, 1953 (WSHC P55200)

The Winter of Discontent

THE NEXT GREAT post-war trial was to be the 'Winter of Discontent.' The winter of 1946 had been rather unusual; decidedly wet and then surprisingly warm, but in December it turned extremely cold with temperatures dropping to 8°F (-13°C). The New Year came and went, and on '23rd January it began to snow... on the 26th Jan it was described as 'something else', and it stayed for over seven weeks.'[55] The snow storms and drifts caused severe disruption to the supply of goods and services, especially to rural communities. With rationing in place, few had any reserves left to see them through, and coal was already in short supply...[56] The following winter also appears to have been difficult with the Slade family battling the snow at Blakehill Camp near Cricklade in February, the month their daughter was born. 'Dad had to cycle off in the snow in the middle of the night into Cricklade to get the district nurse.'[57]

The Government had been warned in June 1946 that coal stocks were reducing fast and could reach the level of 3,000,000 – 4,000,000 tons by the spring of 1947.[58] As early as 2 December 1946 Sutton Benger Parish Council had been asked to make a reduction in their street lighting of 50%. 'After a lengthy discussion the clerk was instructed to write and ask for suggestions as to how this could be done.'[59] 'Fuel crisis' became the term used to describe a whole range of problems that culminated in the early weeks of 1947, but at Whitehall the term specifically detailed events from the second week of February when statutory fuel and power restrictions were put into place, until the beginning of March when power was fully restored to industry, although some industries were still well under their 1946 levels of activity in April.[60] Industry was hit hard, the consequence being a rise in unemployment from 400,000 in mid January to 1.75 million the following month.[61] The bleak winter of 1946/7 saw limited agricultural production and the need to increase production became paramount after the devaluation of the pound in 1949, raising the cost of food imports.[62] It was noted at a Ministry of Works Regional Building Committee Conference in Swindon on 27 February 1947 that: 'There can be little doubt that the effect of the fuel crisis will be felt for a long time in the building materials industry... It is, in fact, conceivable that, modest as the 1947 programme may appear to many Local Authorities by comparison with their own proposals, shortage of essential materials may dictate curtailment as the year proceeds.'[63]

By the time of the Government's nationalisation of coal on 1 January 1947, there had been difficulties finding manpower and a high absenteeism rate. 29 January, the coldest day for over 50 years, marked the beginning. Lights went out across the country and coal was strictly rationed.[64] Electricity supplies were regulated on Friday 7 February for London, the Midlands and the north-west, with restrictions placed on householders in these areas. Supplies would not be available from 9am-12 noon and from 2pm-4pm daily.[65] People began working in offices by candlelight. Fires went out, and cooking was limited with no one able to use their electric stoves during the times of restriction.[66] These restrictions were extended throughout February and the wartime blackout was reimposed over 80% of the country during the crisis.[67] Soon the whole of the country's households would have no electricity for five hours a day. Magazine production was curtailed, newspapers again shrank in size, fewer radio programmes were broadcast and some sporting activities were hampered due to electricity being prohibited.[68] The winter of 1946/7 had indeed been bleak; the Observatory at Kew had recorded no sunshine at all between 11 and 23 February, and Mass Observation was reporting the mood of the people: cold, miserable, depressed.... And to top it all, after the freeze came the thaw, and with it the floods which also broke records.[69]

The miners worked hard to raise production levels with those from the South Wales collieries being particularly praised for voluntarily working a double shift on 'Coal Sunday', 16 February 1947.[70] The weather stayed bitter until March, but industry got back on its feet and most of the temporarily unemployed were able to return to work. For householders, restrictions remained until the end of April, backed up by legal sanctions, and the general public felt helpless and frustrated. The mid-week sporting event restrictions were proving very unpopular.[71] The Conservative press pronounced 'Shiver with Shinwell and Starve with Strachey' during the crisis. Peter Hennessy notes that it was the first 'heavy blow' to the Labour Government and had showed Emanuel Shinwell, the Minister of Fuel and Power, as capable of a 'spectacular' level of complacency.[72] The economic losses to the country due to a downturn in exports were a major setback for the country, but for the Government, its loss of esteem due to the crisis was short lived.[73]

Rationing and the 'New Look'

THE AUTUMN OF 1945 brought with it the scarcity of yet more goods and also disaffection; a cynicism that the hard-won peace was proving difficult to live with.[74] Food shortages became uppermost in the public mind during the years 1946-8, along with clothing problems, queuing[75] and fuel.[76] Alongside the end of lend-lease and Britain's balance of payments came the reduced consumption of all foods except fish, sugar, potatoes and fruit for working class people.[77] Britain needed to increase its exports to narrow the 'dollar gap', but for those people who had wartime savings to spend, it was hard to accept the necessity to divert many consumer goods for export.[78] The 1946 *Britain Can Make It* Exhibition of industrial design at the Victoria and Albert Museum gained the alternative name 'Britain Can't Have It!'[79] By the winter of 1946 there was very little comfort to be had as austerity was moved up a

Ministry of Food Advert reminding everyone of the 'Bread Code', Wiltshire Times, 18 May 1946 (WSHC Microform Collection)

notch, and those who had been willing to accept discipline for a period in post-war Britain were now finding it hard to manage.[80]

There were ration cuts in bacon, poultry and eggs, resulting in a 'housewives revolt' by the British Housewives' League. The next big issue was bread. The results of a Gallup poll showed that half of the population were not in favour of rationing, and the subject of bread had become a 'national obsession'. But the wheat shortage was acute and therefore a two pound loaf would be reduced to one and three quarters – with the price remaining the same![81] The Ministry of Food was telling the housewife all she needed to know in its advert in the *Wiltshire Times*, 13 July 1946. 'Bread rationing isn't as difficult as it may seem. Bread and flour and cakes and scones and buns are going on a new points scheme called Bread Units – BU's for short.' There was advice on how many BUs each individual would receive per week ranging from a child under 1 year with 2 units to a male manual worker with 15 units and supplementary coupons to be obtained from their employer. 'Remember, bread is being rationed to make sure of our share.' The bread rations were generous and little wheat was saved above pre-rationed levels, but the policy was understandable given the post-war international food shortage.[82] Dried eggs were available again and on points by 20 June 1946, a Ministry of Food advertisement in the *Wiltshire Times* stating they were now at 8 points a packet. There was good news too; the sweet ration had been increased from 12 to 13oz and there would also be additional sugar available for jam making, although the soap ration was being cut for all except children of a certain age (including those

Inscribed stone plaques giving the price of bread per gallon from 1800-1971 on the wall of St. Giles Church, Great Wishford. Note the subsidised price of 1946-48 is the lowest of any (WSHC P10548)

under the age of one). An additional meat ration was given to underground coal miners, a contentious policy but perhaps justifiable when the Government faced a severe labour shortage and an impending fuel shortage.[83] By 1951 the general meat ration was 'exceptionally low'.[84] Peter Hennessy reports that: 'The shadow of food – or, rather, its absence – dimmed even the brightness of that summer [1947] and the pen portraits which have captured it for future generations.'[85] By 1948 everyone was getting thoroughly sick of rationing[86] as austerity reached its height. Ina Zweiniger-Bargielowska notes that George Orwell's *Nineteen Eighty Four* captured the bleak image of the time (the title was a date reversal of 1948 and was published in 1949)[87] as well as what Thomas Pynchon reports as 'Orwell's despair over the post-war state of socialism'.[88]

The South African fish Snoek became synonymous with the unpalatable food of post-war Britain,[89] introduced as a replacement for sardines. The Ministry of Food promoted it to the public with posters and published recipes in May 1948, but there appears to have been a lack of enthusiasm for it, and with so many tins to shift, the Government made a tin of Snoek five points less than household salmon.[90] Cigarettes were still not rationed but the cost of them rose greatly.[91] A Compton Bassett man recalled that in the April 1949 budget the cigarette tax was to be raised so that cigarettes would cost far more than they had previously 'so I put what cigarettes I had in the fire and have not bought any since.'[92]

By January 1947 the scarcity of cotton yarn due to a fall in production meant that the issue of Police uniform would be adversely affected with a 50% reduction. The wait for 'worsted' materials was also lengthening, estimated at 12 months. By April 1947 the Home Office was again reporting that problems of supply would continue because of 'the severe restrictions recently imposed upon electricity supplies, the production of cotton yarn has been seriously affected.' In response to the difficulties the textile industry was facing, the Board of Trade issued *The 1947 Clothing Quiz* booklet which detailed how the public could use their clothing coupons and listed the principal coupon free articles, from academic robes and butter muslin to jock straps and wooden soled footwear. Also included was a notice that as from 1 March 1947 coupons were to be given up for sheets or cotton blankets, although people in priority classes would be able to apply for 'coupon equivalent certificates'. There was also a question and answer section at the end. The Foreword was used to reassure that clothes rationing would end as soon as production had risen. The position of cotton yarn had not improved by July 1947.[93]

Sweets were de-rationed in April 1949 but the shortages were so high that they were placed under restriction again in August.[94] The late 1940s saw the relaxation of policy over prams and toys.[95] The de-control of bread, potatoes and preserves occurred in 1948 with milk and soap following in 1950.[96] From 1949 food worries appear to have reduced, replaced by anxiety over rising prices which figured highly in the political agenda until the mid 1950s.[97] When the Conservatives came to power in 1951 they had no choice but to continue with rationing due to balance of payments constraints, and even cut imports of unrationed foods. The remaining rations schemes were ended during the period of 1952-4 alongside the end of controls over distribution, imports and the manufacture of food. By 1954 only one fifth of food expenditure was price controlled.[98] The National Registration Identity Card had been discontinued in 1952.[99]

Vogue was sporting the new Paris fashion of autumn 1947 which incorporated long flowing skirts. This 'New Look' was to sweep over Britain the following year and Mass Observation noted that despite rationing, 10 million women in Britain either had or wanted to have the new style.[100] Utility clothing actually became more popular after the war, with 50% of those surveyed in 1948 and 1950 keen to have an increase in utility clothes as they helped those who could not afford high prices.[101] The National Housewives' League was 'very cross' about the post-war New Look... 'because here was Christian Dior, lowering the hemlines almost to the ankle with enormously full skirts and little slim tops... and nothing that we had in the cupboard was any longer in fashion and an awful lot of us said, 'Oh, we can't afford it, and we can't buy it', but of course we did.'[102] The New Look required 30 to 40 metres of material and a new corset, currently still classed as a luxury garment.[103] Utility schemes came to an end in 1952.[104]

Expectations were high that a normal life could be resumed at the end of the war, and this included the end of queuing, but it did not materialise, and Joe Moran notes that the 'hardships that had been reluctantly endured became openly politicized'. The Mother's League was established in July 1945 to campaign against queuing; the British Housewives' League was a little more militant, organising a revolt in August of the same year. Their complaints still lay with the shopkeeper whose power remained pretty much absolute. In 1945 the *Sunday Graphic* described him as 'the recalcitrant, domineering, bureaucratic shopkeeper... the man to whom a queue outside his shop is the breath of life, because it bolsters up his self-conceit.' Churchill used the queue for political gain, relating it to 'the essence of Socialism' in 1949 and he used the term 'Queuetopia' during his unsuccessful 1950 electoral campaign. The British Housewives' League lost impetus after 1947. The end of rationing in 1954 and the advent of self-service finally put a stop to queuing for consumer goods, although people were initially worried that self-service would mean more queuing. This was not the end of the queue, however, as the newly emerging welfare state of the post-war period led to queues for the family allowance benefit and the old age pension, amongst others, at the Post Office... 'carping about the Post Office became "a national pastime".'[105]

When it came to rationing, morale was waning in the post-war period[106] and the Government produced extensive propaganda under the campaign 'We work or want' which Ina Zweiniger-Bargielowska feels ultimately failed.[107] This was due to the many changes put into place by the Government which destabilised and disrupted civilian life in the post-war period, at odds with wartime stability.[108] By 1948 the black market 'spiv' was becoming more acceptable and people began to wonder if a high moral stand was as necessary as it had been in time of war.[109] Ealing Studios made *Passport to Pimlico* in 1949 which looked at rationing, the storyline following the residents of Pimlico as they discovered a treasure trove and set themselves up as a restriction-free state. The film fuelled resentment over rationing and Peter Hennessy thinks it would be interesting to know how much it contributed to the 'dramatic shrinkage' of Labour votes in the 1950 election.[110]

But for all this, there was also hope in the post-war world. Despite the shortages, people felt lucky to be alive and in one piece, to be young and able to look forward.[111]

The Five Evils

THE WARTIME EMERGENCY Medical Scheme, planned in 1938, had paved the way with its shift towards the regional and local control of healthcare.[112] William Beveridge had become Chairman of the Reconstruction Committee of the Social Services in 1941. His White Paper Report, published in December 1942,[113] categorised itself as a plan to 'abolish want' and Peter Lewis reports it was 'hailed as a prophet of Utopian Britain',[114] seen by many as a new social Magna Carta.[115] It tackled the five main 'evils' of social life: Want, Disease, Ignorance, Squalor and Idleness[116] with a focus on social security.[117] For Beveridge it meant an end to means tested welfare, a hated relic of the pre-war years. Instead it would be contribution based.[118] The Beveridge Report got everyone talking, and the views were mostly positive. One in four adults listened to the radio series regarding full employment, broadcast in 1944.[119] The Stationery Office was overwhelmed and a White Paper record of 635,000 copies were sold. Beveridge introduced his report to the public via the BBC radio broadcast *Postscripts* and he continued by broadcasting further summaries for the public in twenty-two languages.[120] Army commanders began to ask for additional supplies for their troops.[121] In 1942 Home Intelligence Reports showed an 'almost universal approval' by the British public, 86% of whom felt that it should be put into effect. Even those who had least to gain such as employers and the upper-income groups were in strong support. Mass Observation discovered that the public had been won over by Beveridge's inspirational attitude, but the Conservatives had not, with only William Morrison, Minister for Town & County Planning, being a committed supporter.[122] With the wartime appointment of Ernest Bevin, former General Secretary of the Transport and General Workers' Union and his working class roots, and later the post-war socialist Labour Government, a link was established between the Government and working people, almost completely missing during WWI.[123] Beveridge had the ability to capture and reflect the spirit of the time. Harry Hopkins later noted that the coalition Government, thinking they had requested an 'innocuous technical survey of social insurance, thus found itself saddled with what in effect was a declaration of Human Rights…'[124] In a 1944 Gallup poll, 55% of the public approved of the proposal for a National Health Service with 32% in favour of no change.[125] The public mood was for change, and the writings of Frederick Hayeck the economist, social theorist and political philosopher who protested over the expansion of state control as illiberal, were found to be laughable by the public. It is interesting to note that Hayeck's views on economic freedom and consumer choice had become popular by the mid 1950s.[126]

The *Financial Times* was reporting in 1946 that these new 'social services' would become a burden for the country in years to come,[127] and post-war pensions were set too low to eradicate impoverishment.[128] However, at the time viewing the Government as a provider was thought a way to ensure fairness of supply for all.[129] Lizzie Collingham feels that after 1945 the Government never fully recovered from the expectations it gained in wartime; that its responsibility was to continually 'do something' in all aspects of social care, and that it was 'right and proper' for the state to take responsibility for its citizens.[130]

The Chippenhm doctor Joan Hickson was awaiting the printing of the Beveridge Report. Her diary entry of 30 November 1942 records: 'The Beveridge report on Social Security published at last. It had been eagerly awaited for many months and was expected to be violently opposed by those whose 'vested interests' were attacked. The summary so far available sounds most mild and sensible.' The following day she noted: 'Reception of Beveridge report good on almost all sides, this showing how moderate it is. If it is mild enough for even the Conservatives not to dispute it can't go very far.'[131] By 19 February 1944 she had read the White Paper, considering it to be:

'[v]ery vague and will perpetuate the difficulties of the dual system. The public think it all sounds very nice as it is for everybody, but they may not like it when they get it. If we are to have our incomes halved and work as civil servants, then we must insist on conditions comparable with other civil servants. The work as work will doubtless be quite well done as far as the actual treatment of disease goes, but medicine is so much more than that. To be a good doctor at present, one's practice has to be one's hobby and one's religion, intimately bound up with one's whole life. If it is to be merely a 'job' with a salary, no one is going to stand the intrusion of the telephone... Perhaps taken over the whole country the standard of actual physical treatment of disease will be better, but if medicine is only to do this, there will need to be a vastly increased army of 'guides, philosophers and friends' recruited from somewhere else.'[132]

In April 1944 Joan had noticed a change in attitude. 'Another meeting at the RUH [Royal United Hospital, Bath] to discuss the White Paper. Resistance seems to be stiffening against it, we were glad to see. The discussion was on principles only, no finance involved yet. It went on till nearly midnight....'[133]

The printing of the Beveridge Report sparked one Wiltshire resident (also a doctor) to write to the *Wiltshire Times*, published on 22 July 1944. He took exception to the constant remarks in the 'abridged version' of the paper stating that the social security scheme would be free. It would be paid for by a compulsory levy and also from rates and taxes. 'From the swollen sums thus mulcted from the public a large rake-off will be taken by the augmented bureaucracy required to operate the service. It is to be emphasised that the levy will be made on **every individual** whether he chooses to take advantage of the service or not. The new levy will be many times larger than the relatively modest contribution exacted by the Insurance Acts and the victimisation of the public will be correspondingly greater' and by 1944 there was growing resistance to the proposed changes from the British Medical Association.[134]

Anuerin Bevan, Minister of Health and tasked with implementing the proposals, had to go head to head with the GPs and they remained at loggerheads throughout 1947. Remaining unconvinced, many GPs voted against the NHS at British Medial Association polls. It was the Consultants who tipped the balance, working with Bevan, and after some amendments the British Medical Association had no choice but to give in,[135] although David Kynaston states the feeling that it was Bevan who capitulated, not wanting to fight a battle on two fronts.[136]

The Family Allowance Act was set up in 1945[137] and the National Assistance Act of 1948 effectively abolished poor law.[138] On 5 July 1948 the Health Service and National Insurance Scheme became fully implemented.[139] The first Family Allowance Day was set for August Bank Holiday 1946 and on that day 2.5 million families claimed their entitlement.[140] The British population had been overwhelmed by Government propaganda leading up to the day. Bevan had also sweet-talked the women's magazines into publicising the issue positively. The Government's hard work must have paid off; as early as March 1948 a Gallup poll was reporting that 61% saw the NHS as a good idea, and only 13% as a bad one.[141] By 1959 most people had accepted the NHS, as Hennessy puts it, as a 'natural feature of the British landscape'.[142]

The NHS was the first health system in the Western world to offer free health care to all[143] and the Beveridge Report is seen by some as the key to post-war social policy.[144] Hennessy reports that Bevan's time at the Ministry of Health has been lauded as his 'finest hour'; his ability to fashion it into a 'shining instrument' was a true transformation.[145] Sean Glynn and Alan Booth feel that public opinion became more radical and idealistic during the war, leaving space for professionals to push for reforms.[146] A doctor who started at a Warminster practice in 1946 stated that: 'Visiting was an essential part of the job. Fifteen to twenty-five home visits every day was the rule (sometimes more) and I had a list of chronic patients I visited once a month. By going to the patients in their homes, it was possible to see the circumstances in which they lived and meet other members of the family and even have a cup of tea, a practice which my predecessor… had encouraged.'[147] As for Warminster's dentists, one remarked that '[w]hen I was first in practice, after the Second World War, people looked on their teeth as an expensive nuisance. They would get rid of their teeth as soon as possible and have snappers fitted. Before the Health Service came in, they paid into a fund to help meet the cost of treatment. After 1948 everything was literally free.' He also noted that the 1950s was a time of expansion for dentists and he was able to appoint assistants. He could also offer them accommodation – a huge bonus. The NHS had brought with it advances in dentistry, as at the beginning of the war 'we didn't even have electric drills; one used a foot pump.'[148] One Warminster doctor noted that after the introduction of the Health Service in 1948 the doctors at the hospital had greater access to the consultants from Bath, who began to visit regularly and support the local doctors.[149] After 1948 all of Warminster's hospitals were controlled by the West

Wiltshire Hospital Management Committee. Their Secretary 'provided unfailing help and support to the hospitals, and would turn his hand to anything, working all hours and doing everything from helping with admissions to sorting out the central heating. Although the beds in all three hospitals were usually full, he nearly always managed to bring cases back from Bath to be nursed locally, near their families.'[150] One optician was having difficulties moving back to Swindon, writing to the Town Clerk on 7 December 1946. His firm had purchased a property to enable him to set up his practice again after he had been demobbed, but it had been requisitioned by Swindon Council for evacuees.[151] Before the creation of the NHS patients paid into a fund to meet the cost of treatment such as dentistry. After the war, everything was 'literally' free - then small payments began to be necessary.[152] Bevan resigned in 1951 when the Government first started charging for false teeth and glasses, feeling that it spelt out the destruction of the social services which had marked Britain out, according to Asa Briggs, as the 'moral leadership in the world'.[153]

Change in education had begun before the war. Local Authorities were responsible for running the education system and some had been innovative and progressive, forcing the Government's hand.[154] The Hadow Report of 1926 concluded that technical studies should be included in education. This report established a precedent for the 1940s when the Butler Act was being formulated and led to a continuation of existing patterns of provision[155] but it had been the 1936 Education Act that set a date in 1939 for raising the school leaving age to 15, not met due to the outbreak of WWII.[156] The educational sociologist Jean Floud noted that the chances of a child getting a free place at a higher education establishment were still overly dependent on their place in the social hierarchy.[157] The Education Bill, introduced in 1943 and passed in 1944 again aimed to provide secondary schooling for all up until the age of 15.[158] The Norwood Report looked into the curriculum at secondary schools to advise what should be taught, with the Butler (Education) Act 1944 working to expand secondary education for all children. However, the Fleming Report of 1944 relating to public schools resulted in limiting any chance of curtailing the independent sector.[159] The 1944 Education Act was designed with input from lobbyists who helped to maintain the current status quo rather than bring in changes,[160] with no provision to increase the number of grammar schools, nor any guarantee regarding the quality of the education received[161] even though the Percy Report of 1944 stated that a doubling in the output of engineering graduates would be needed in the post-war period, followed by the Barlow Committee Report in 1946 which recommended a doubling of the supply of scientists and technologists.[162]

What was put into place was a triparte system; effectively grammar schools for the 'elite', a secondary modern for the unskilled majority and a small number of technical schools for the rest. An IQ test, the 11 Plus, was used to direct a child to the correct school. This test was based on the later discredited psychologist Cyril Burt's work.[163] The children of semi and unskilled workers were under-represented at grammar school[164] but as a result of the system the middle classes did fare better in the post-war era with one in seven getting a place at University compared to one in sixteen before the war, although the rate of those attending from poorer backgrounds remained the same.[165] The public schools and Oxford and Cambridge Universities still retained closed scholarship (places available only to students who fulfilled certain credentials such as having attended a certain school) and there was a heavy bias towards humanities subjects.[166] The Education Act brought the need for more schools and more teachers but the war had taken its toll, with a shortage of books and equipment.[167]

In 1945 there remained a need for more teachers - an estimated 70,000 were required.[268] *Picture Post* was reporting the need for teachers in its 7 October 1944 issue, quoting the figure of 70,000 teachers with priority being given to teaching candidates in demobilisation. Recruits would have to be 'vigorous, enthusiastic, optimistic, devoted. None but the best [would] be good enough, for no job matter[ed] more than theirs.' They were to come from the Forces and war factories. Training centres were established and training schemes of various kinds rose with demobilisation.[169] By July 1947 the ex-US army hospital site at Burderop Park near Wroughton had been turned into a Ministry of Education Emergency Teachers' Training College with more land at the site being requested for use as a temporary secondary modern school. Squatters and the Ministry of Labour's Mobile Labour Services were occupying the remainder of the site.[170]

In Salisbury, a School Development Plan was being devised in September 1946 in conjunction with the 1944 Education Act. The Free Churches of the City of Salisbury were asking that a school be built on the east side of the city to conform with Section 76 of the Education Act; to make it as easy as possible for parents to send their children to the school of their choice. They were unhappy with the proposed siting of the new St. Thomas' and St. Edmund's schools. The Development Plan was submitted to the Minister of Education on 1 August 1946. By 16 August 1946 E. G. Powell, Honourable Ministerial Secretary of the Salisbury and District Free Church Federal Council and member of the Wiltshire Education Committee was printing a *Statement of the Position of the Development Plan*, explaining the difficulties of keeping Salisbury City Council informed. 'The local Diocesan Council of Education was fully consulted about the plan for their own schools, but the City Council were not permitted to be consulted, or even allowed to receive any information about the development plan for the city schools. I felt this procedure to be unfortunate, for in order to make a success of the Act it is necessary to get the goodwill and co-operation of all concerned. Consequently, I pleaded in the County Education Committee meeting that, since the Act did not permit consultation with the City Council, a copy of the proposals for Salisbury might be sent to the Town Clerk for information. I asked not for an act of law, but an act of grace. This was firmly refused... Any action which the City Council may now contemplate about the plan must be taken within two months of August 1st, 1946, and then by petitioning the Minister of Education.'[171]

Ellen Wilkinson, Butler's successor as Minister of Education, set up HORSA (Hutting Operation for the Raising of the School-leaving Age), the Emergency

Training Scheme for teachers and SFORSA (School Furniture Operation for the Raising of the School-leaving Age), meaning that a large number of new schools could be built[172] but the influx of wartime workers and their families had already been putting huge pressure on local schools and utilities in Wiltshire. By spring 1942 pressure was mounting for the construction of new primary schools at Box, Chippenham and Corsham. Plans for the schools at Chippenham and Box were submitted in 1943.[173]

The Director of Education at Wiltshire County Council was writing to the Clerk at Bradford and Melksham Rural District Council (RDC) in September 1946 regarding the problem of additional school accommodation for new housing estates. 'It may be that existing school accommodation will be sufficient to meet these needs, but on the other hand housing developments in a particular district where there is already pressure on the school accommodation may mean that extra school provision will have to be found.'[174] There were no improvements in Cricklade. At a meeting of the School Managers on 31 October 1952 the current situation was relayed. '... accommodation of the Cricklade (M.V.C.) School will shortly be quite inadequate. With the present roll of 155 it is necessary to use the school Hall as a Classroom... During the next few years the situation will become progressively worse... even with an unaltered housing situation the increase of school population will, in the next four years bring the total to near 200... Further, it has been announced that as soon as building land becomes available the balance of the Cricklade quota of houses will be commenced... immediate steps should be taken to provide not only the necessary accommodation, but also the extra furniture and fittings which will be needed. The problem of staffing will also arise and is a point to be borne in mind.'[175] The difficulty in obtaining iron and steel throughout the 1940s severely restricted construction of hospitals and schools.[176] Unfortunately in Cricklade, those children who failed the 11-Plus could not move on to a Secondary Modern school as no spaces were available. The problem was not solved until 1962 when Bradon Forest Secondary School was opened at Purton.[177] A temporary school had been set up after the war to serve the newly arrived civilian population at Blakehill Camp. By October 1955 it was due to be closed but as there was still so much overcrowding at Cricklade Infants School it had been suggested that the 'comparatively good premises' at Blakehill be used. The idea proved wholly unpopular with the Cricklade parents, and an alternative was suggested; to hire the Cricklade Congregational Church Schoolroom which was located very near to Cricklade Infants.[178]

What is apparent in Wiltshire in the immediate post-war years is that the wartime and post-war influx of families led to pressures on education provision and services.[179] Documents appear to highlight that the changes made after the Education Act of 1944 created an even greater need for educational facilities and teachers.[180] Wiltshire County Council's Director of Education was writing to the Planning Consultants W. R. Davidge in London on 10 February 1947 regarding the county's School Sites Planning Scheme. He would do his best to provide the required information regarding school sites but wanted him to appreciate 'that this is a rather big problem involving as it does not only sites for new schools, but sites for extensions to existing schools.'[182] The lack of accommodation post-war also had an impact on education. Wiltshire County Council's Education Committee was concerned about the Blakehill site near Cricklade in September 1947, and writing to the Cricklade and Wootton Bassett Rural District Council. 'I am sorry to bother you again about the above temporary housing estate. I require to know the degree of urgency in the matter of provision of temporary school accommodation...' In Chippenham, 25 January 1946, the Education Committee were asking that the military Camp at Hardenhuish Park be de-requisitioned to enable them to use the site so that they could put into effect the re-organisation due to the raising of the school leaving age. A similar case was being put forward in Swindon for The Lawn site which also had military accommodation, for use as an annexe to the College until the building of a new Secondary Grammar School which would release accommodation.[183] On 22 February 1946 the sites of some temporary huts for use as schools had been agreed: one hut on allotment land behind Amesbury Church of England School; two huts to be erected on the site of Hardenhuish Camp, Chippenham; one hut to be erected in the corner of a playing field at Purton Church of England School; one hut to be erected on a narrow strip of school garden at Salisbury St. Edmund's School; one hut to be erected on a garden belonging to the convent at Salisbury St. Osmund's Roman Catholic School; one hut to be erected in the playground at Wootton Bassett Church of England School; one hut to be erected on the playground at Wroughton Church of England School. By 24 May 1946 the Marlborough Common Camp hutments were also being considered by the Wiltshire Education Committee as the site for a temporary Secondary Modern School to meet the raising of the school leaving age.[184]

On 23 April 1948 Wiltshire's Director of Education was advising the Ministry of Education in London that a large number of Polish families would be arriving at Keevil Aerodrome, thought to include approximately 100 children who would remain at the site indefinitely. 'This number of children cannot be accommodated at the local schools. It is likely that we shall be able to use a building on the aerodrome for school accommodation and... the only way to deal with the problem will be to establish a temporary County School as at West Wells'[185] which had been a wartime site of industry.[186] The Council was hoping to recruit some teachers from among the adults in the group, but was concerned that they might not find enough. By the end of the month the Education Officer of Southern Command, British Army, was noting that a case had been put to the Ministry of Education. The School would only be catering for Polish children; the Local Education Authority had been asked to set up what was in effect a 'Special School' and that 'it was rather inequitable since the cost of this would have to be borne by local ratepayers.' It was found to be the case that provision could be made under the Polish Resettlement Act 1947.[187] The Camp was used to house 500 Polish refugees. Betty Smith reports that "[t]hey were pitifully poor and wasted after years of walking across Europe as refugees from the Russians and Germans, hiding from enemy forces and being bombed... Families were broken up and many lost... When they first came to the camp they lived communally until they could speak sufficient English to enable them to fend for themselves'. After a time many were able to find work in the factories and local farms in Trowbridge, but local residents found that the buses had become increasingly overcrowded. By 1956 the Polish had left the camp and it was again used to house refugees, this time as a consequence of the Hungarian uprising.[188]

Swindon Borough's Education Officer was trying to fulfil his obligation to accommodate teaching staff in October 1947, but at least one teacher was having trouble. 'I have been teaching in Swindon for almost a year during which time I have been unable to find accommodation in the town for my wife and children. They are now living in rooms in Swansea, thus entailing considerable expense and hardship.' The Borough Education Officer outlined the problem in a letter to Swindon's Town Clerk in April 1948. 'In normal circumstances, while the loss of two young qualified and able teachers would be regrettable, it would not be without remedy. Under the present circumstance, however, the loss becomes a very serious matter. The Ministry of Education have labelled Wiltshire, including Swindon, as an area in which no further appointments of women teachers can be made even to fill vacancies until the establishment has dropped by 96. At the same time good calibre men teachers are very scarce. The Committee cannot, therefore, afford to lose the services of these two teachers from their already slender staffing resources, particularly with the imminent prospect of increased numbers of children in the schools...'[189] There was a similar situation in Purton as by 1952 two teachers had already been lost 'through their inability to find suitable accommodation in Purton and when appointing new teachers the post ha[d] often been refused by the best applicants through there being no house to offer.'[190] In February 1948 the Director of Education was looking to employ teachers at a school opening for the children of European Volunteer Workers who were being accommodated at the West Wells Hostel at Hawthorn, Corsham. 'From our experience in similar circumstances it will be extremely difficult to obtain the services of teaching staff unless we can offer some likelihood of obtaining living accommodation.'[191] A letter of March 1949 from a Wootton Bassett School Headmaster to the Cricklade and Wootton Bassett Rural District Council gives an idea of the real impact in Wiltshire regarding education and the frustrations of those who had to cope with them. 'Those here are refused housing so left and went to districts that were more sympathetic.' They were very good teachers... 'The policy of ignoring the claims of the teaching staff when allocating houses is working to the detriment of the town and in particular that very important part of it - the children.'[192] It was not just housing allocation that was considered unjust; in Corsham there were complaints regarding the starting age for children in the town. Children of long-standing residents were able to start at age four but the children of newcomers could not start until five. Additional temporary school rooms were being promised to solve the issue.[193]

Some of the prefabricated huts in Lydiard Park that had been used by US troops were converted by the Wiltshire Education Committee and in September

1952 became a temporary school, opening with a class of 24 children between the ages of five and seven years. In May 1954 the school was reorganised for both juniors and infants and consisted of three temporary buildings separated by what were described in 1957 as 'uneven ill-kept patches of grass' but this was rectified in 1958. In two of the buildings were three classrooms, cloakrooms and a small office while the other provided toilets and washing facilities. There was a hard surfaced playground and a colourful garden created by the teachers and pupils with a caretaker to keep it clean and well looked after. According to a HMI report of 5 November 1957 it provided 'the one civilizing influence on this very ramshackle estate where there do not appear to be any other amenities.' A high moral tone was laid out in the report. 'Not only are the children taught the basic skills and appreciation of pleasant surroundings, but they are also trained in good social habits.' The area, being four miles from Swindon, was very isolated, with little public transport and no telephone; some of the families were itinerant, some children aged up to nine arriving at the school having attended no other.[194]

The Secondary Modern Schools were meant to equip children with the ability to use their leisure time constructively and look after their homes well. The Grammar Schools soon became the holders of far greater prestige, had more money to spend, and more middle class pupils.[195] The Ministry of Education's pamphlet *The Nation's Schools*, published on VE Day, upheld the distinction between the traditional Grammar School and the rest, and went so far as to argue the case against the Multilateral (Comprehensive) School system.[196] In 1947 the issue of Multilateral Schooling raised its head again at the Labour Party Conference. Some Local Authorities wanted Comprehensive Schools to be established and the National Association of Labour Teachers issued a report called *The Comprehensive School* in 1948.[197] Robert Mackay states that the Education Act helped to deny the country the most efficient use of its intellectual assets and denied schools a fair and equal share of allocated resources.[198]

Industry and Economics

IT HAS BEEN estimated that one quarter of Britain's wealth was destroyed during wartime[199] and there were now acquired debts of £3,000 million. Domestic capital had reduced by the same amount and any overseas investment had been used up; exports had also dropped to one third of their pre-war level.[200] Wealth and capital had been lost but the increase of wartime administrative infrastructure and resources enabled post-war growth and productivity to rise at the rate of twice its interwar level, restoring losses more quickly than expected, but Britain would never regain its pre-war wealth.[201] *The Spectator* reported to its readers: 'We have exhausted a great part of our gold reserves, we are overdrawn on foreign accounts, we have to re-equip and get going on export industries, and meet the huge expense of bringing back and demobilising our overseas forces.'[202]

The economist John Maynard Keynes issued a gloomy memo in August 1945, the contents of which stated that Britain now faced an 'economic Dunkirk'.

He warned that without US aid the nation would become very nearly bankrupt with the public's hopes dashed.[203] Lend-Lease was withdrawn by the US Government suddenly on 19 August 1945. From then on all goods imported from the US had to be paid for on delivery.[204] After the US dropped Lend-Lease it was hoped that they would instead help via a loan with easy terms, but the US had many claimants for its generosity, and Britain was way down the list.[205] A bail-out loan was approved with repayment to the US starting in five years time and which was to continue for the next 50 years.[206]

From July 1947 sterling had become fully convertible into dollars, and there began a quick drain on dollars and a run on the pound.[207] The Government managed to persuade the US to suspend convertibility, which finally took place eleven years later, but the damage had been done.[208] The crisis brought with it a deepening period of austerity[209] and had also undermined reconstruction,[210] slowing the Government's housing programme still further.[211] The US General George Marshall's speech on 5 June 1947 at Harvard was pounced on by Bevin, and, becoming one of his greatest moments in politics, led to Marshall Aid.[212] This aid was pivotal in allowing western European nations, including Britain, to avoid, as Peter Hennessy puts it, 'choking off their nascent booms' in the decisive year of 1947 so that they could continue with reconstruction.[213] By March 1948 production was booming, a trend that was to last for the next four years.[214] By 1948 the Government was maintaining only those controls which were essential to secure a proper distribution of materials which remained in short supply, but the Korean War of 1950-1953 saw a partial reintroduction of price control, finally dismantled in 1952 and 1953. Pre-war consumer spending was reached in 1950 and it was during this decade that a consumer boom began, but people could not spend their money as they would have liked due to shortages and many found that quality in goods was lacking.[215] Household appliances started to become available in Britain at this time.[216]

The Attlee Government's post-war economic policies have long been seen as austere, spelt out by the Chancellor of the Exchequer Stafford Cripps in 1948: 'You will see, then, that as long as we are in this impoverished state, the result of our efforts in two world wars, our own consumption requirements have to be last in the list of priorities. First are exports... second is capital investment in industry; and last are the needs, comforts and amenities of the family.'[217] Jim Tomlinson has shown that the same is true of the welfare state, with West Germany, Austria and Belgium spending more of their national income on social welfare in 1950 than Britain.[218] Labour committed itself to a 'huge' rearmament at the time of the Korean crisis and budgetary disputes followed.[219] In the wake of the Korean War there was a 'commodity price explosion' which compounded the problem that had begun in 1949 with the devaluation of the pound.[220] Keynes felt that the officials at Whitehall did not have the skill to effect the necessary economic methods that were required in the post-war era.[221]

There was general confusion by planners regarding the meaning of economic planning in peacetime. Herbert Morrison was purportedly in charge

Clement Attlee speaking in Trowbridge Park, 1951 (WSHC P12252)

of planning, but the Ministry of Labour and the Trade Unions were unhappy about working together, and coupled with the Government's unwillingness, the issue remained unresolved. It did not help that labour, machinery, building and material allocations remained tightly controlled.[222]

A series of private Nuffield conferences on reconstruction were held throughout the war, organised by the Oxford don and socialist George Douglas Howard Cole. Attendees included a great variety of individuals from the world of industry, the trade unions, academia, economics and the political arena with all three main parties involved.[223] A number of employers refused to attend, thinking it was, as Daniel Ritschel notes, a 'left wing conspiracy to hijack business opinion on behalf of reconstruction', a way to discover who amongst them held the same interests as the intellectuals so as to support their case. Many employers realised, however, that the public mood was for change and if they did not take part in the gathering debate their role would be seriously reduced in a post-war society. The first published statement of the Nuffield Conferences was published as *Industry and Education* in early 1943, followed by a published report called *Employment Policy and Organization of Industry after the War*. William Beveridge used the Conferences as a sounding board for his *Full Employment in a Free Society*, published in 1944 for which he credited the assembled experts as having served as the critical inspiration for much of its contents.[224] What came out of the Nuffield conferences was the realisation that a planned strategy for industry to include modernisation would be necessary for resurrection after the war. The means to ensure how this came about was the cause of much debate, the business community favouring the self-governing approach. This proposal became the subject of great controversy during the period of national debate on reconstruction and produced a hostile response with worries that industry would have little incentive to modernise, instead safeguarding their least efficient members from open competition.[225]

Cole managed to aid the progress of social reform by persuading policy makers to 'accommodate imperfections'[226] and the agreement was the end product of sustained negotiation involving distinct and often conflicting interests. Ritschel, however, feels that although the attendees managed to agree on a 'broad vision of progressive social and economic reconstruction', by doing so they whittled away at some of the more important elements, giving 'debilitating concessions' to those who were especially needed to implement the vision.[227] The Engineering Unions can be seen as radical advocates of planning. From 1945 to 1949 the National Engineering Joint Trades Movement and the Confederation of Shipbuilding and Engineering Unions wanted a system of targets for the sectors of the engineering industry to be turned into targets for individual factories. They received little support.[228] Prominent individuals such as Cole were determined to make the most of the opportunity for change, and a consensus was reached, albeit with a lot of bargaining. It was, however, not as complete as many had hoped.[229]

The Conference Statement published in 1943 stated that extensive changes were required in industry to restore Britain's waning economic position abroad and to provide the resources for full employment at home. There were three categories according to business type. The first covered small-scale and newer industries, left to grow and develop in an almost free market environment. The second covered key national utilities such as rail, coal, water and gas. These were to come under public ownership, administered by independent public corporations and headed by administrators already working in management roles. The third consisted of large-scale private industry, felt to be the sector that was best able to govern itself, but the Government also acknowledged the need for society to be on guard for abuse of 'monopoly powers'.[230] Labour had tried to put into place the Nuffield vision through industrial modernisation in the private sector but it was unsuccessful. Its strategy of tripartite co-operation between Development Councils and the business alternative of industrial self-government led to a policy stalemate.[231] A good example of this was the computer industry. Britain produced the first computer in 1948 and also the first commercially delivered computer in 1951, but British firms lacked the resources and domestic market necessary for commercial viability. In the US, IBM received military contracts totalling £350 million from their Government, compared to the British Government's £12 million sponsorship.[232] The Board of Trade's *The 1947 Clothing Quiz* booklet emphasised in the Foreword that: 'The textile industries are short of workers, modern machinery and fuel. The output of these industries must therefore be increased by the return of former textile workers, by the recruitment of new workers, by the re-equipment of the mills with modern machinery, and by the combined efforts of all engaged in the industries.'[233]

Among the Government's ambitious nationalisation programmes was road and tranport, bringing together rail, road, haulage and waterways under one banner, the British Transport Commission, unheard of before in any country and a new experiment.[234] The railways were nationalised under the Transport Act of 1947. After the damage and under-investment that had been inflicted on the rail system during the war, a massive investment was required, but this was delayed by shortages. The 1955 modernisation plan was not a success; the costs were higher than expected.[235] Work on developing the country's motorway system, which transformed British travel and with it rural areas, was begun in the mid-1950s with the first stretch becoming operational in 1958.[236]

The Conservatives retained Labour's nationalised industries when they came to power in 1951 and the broad measures of Keynsian economics also survived[237] but by the 1950s Britain's outdated economic structure was apparent.[238] The Labour Government had been unprepared for the tumultuous times ahead. No plans had been made to deal with nationalisation and there was little understanding about how to deal with inflation. There had also been no realisation of how important the lack of imports would become.[239]

The British people had a mixed view of their relationship with the world in this post-war period. For military and strategic matters, it was the US which was all important, but when it came to matters of, as Hennessy puts it, 'tradition, emotion and affection', then the Commonwealth was top of the list. When thinking of security and peace, it was Europe which mattered most. Britain felt itself to be a superpower, but the reality was very different and not shared by the rest of the world. Times remained uncertain. The roots of the Cold War began in the late 1940s[240] and the Korean War from 1950-1953 increased Britain's worries.[241] Sybil Eccles, wife of David Eccles the Government's Principal Economic Adviser during WWII, and resident of Chute, summed up her thoughts of a post-war Britain in her wartime letters to her husband in July 1941. How insightful they were.

> Here, the thoughtful, the practical, the energetic and the knowing, are beginning to talk in terms of an American-made peace, of an American-controlled future-they may throw in a word for England now and then, by way of comfort to themselves and consolation to their audience – 'England will supply the wisdom, the experience,' etc. – but it doesn't ring true – half of them don't believe England will supply anything. We shall struggle painfully with domestic reconstruction while America blows a trumpet call to the world. I oppose this view with angry obstinacy fortified by the conviction that at any rate I must have Mr Winston Churchill on my side. But I expect it's a losing fight and you and the rest of them have seen the unhappy truth.[242]

The New Jerusalem

THE SO CALLED 'New Jerusalem',[243] a Britain that would be better than, as Peter Malpass puts it, the 'disillusioned decades of unfilled promises between the wars'[244] which would rise from the ashes in the post-war era was being considered as early as 1941, with editorials such as the Picture Post's *A Plan for Britain*. J. B. Priestley had been reminding his listeners in 1940 of the broken promises after WWI regarding jobs for 'heroes' – a great betrayal.[245] José Harris feels that WWII was a unique chance for intellectual and reformist groups keen on social and Government reconstruction to act.[246] This was the time of the Planner, and it was the economists, social engineers and technocrats who 'came to the fore' when post-war reconstruction was being discussed during the war.[247] Angus Calder notes that town planners and architects became 'honoured and valued figures' after the publication of the *Barlow Report* in 1940 on the geographical distribution of industry and the *Scott Report* (1942) on town and rural development which attracted a great deal of attention.[248] The establishment of the Ministry of Town and Country Planning took place in 1943.[249] The *Scott Report* caused controversy with its attempt to combine modern agriculture with conservation and aesthetics.[250] The *Uthwatt Report on Land-use* was published in 1942. It recommended a system of land nationalisation which could have altered the balance of land ownership, but which Hennessy notes led to 'nowhere and nothing'. The Government instead put its faith in Silkin's 1947 *Town & Country Planning Act*, but this was poorly funded.[251] For the Attlee Government, planning became essentially the way of dealing with scarcity. Peter Hennessy feels there was no effort to use planning for economic regeneration.[252] He notes that war brought with it the Ministries capable of creating the 'most ambitious - and successful

Harvesting wheat at Manor Farm, Wedhampton near Urchfont, 1951 (WSHC P17789)

- regional policy ever' in terms of planning. Britain was classified from scarlet regions (overcrowded locations where no new production was permitted) through red, amber to green (depressed localities which required new industrial production to be established along with a mobile labour force).[253]

In March 1943 the Minister of Health issued Circular No. 2778 asking Local Authorities to formulate plans for housing construction 'so as to be in a position to make a quick start with housing construction immediately conditions permitted, whether during or after the war.' The Minister wished to be informed regarding how many houses each Authority planned to construct in their first year's programme and of any sites they would need to acquire. By August 1943 Swindon Borough Council was recommending that the Borough Surveyor be authorised to prepare plans for new housing on specified sites.[254]

Wiltshire had been looking at planning since the introduction of the Town and Country Planning Act in 1932, and by 1933 the 24 District Councils had begun planning schemes for their areas. It was soon realised that a 'combined operation' to co-ordinate all the districts would be necessary and the Joint Planning Committee was established.[255] In March 1940 the counties of Wiltshire, Gloucestershire and Somerset had been liaising with the Bristol University Research Group, undertaking a conference and Nuffield Reconstruction Survey. A further conference on post-war planning stated that Wiltshire wanted to control development; the war needs of Government were causing considerable concern. The Wiltshire Joint Planning Scheme had been considering the issue before the war and by 1946 it was clear that only Swindon was intended to be industrial; all other areas in Wiltshire were meant to remain agricultural. It was supposed to be clear cut, but military establishments had sprung up all over the county. 'Wartime towns springing up at Corsham and Westwood…no new town sites are desired'.[256] As early as 1942 the Wiltshire Joint Committee had felt that:

'In view of the extensive war-time development which has taken place in the neighbourhood of Corsham and at Westwood, Bradford on Avon, they feel that some definite national statement of policy is desirable in order that the Regional Committee may be appraised of the Government's intentions with regard to permanency or otherwise of these developments.

A very large area of the County has, as you know, been acquired or requisitioned by various Government departments for war purposes, and until a definitive national policy is evolved, the Committee feel it would be inappropriate for them to take definite steps in the matter.

They would, therefore, desire to stress the necessity for an early declaration of Government policy with regard to a national plan for post-war planning.'[257]

The *Wiltshire Times* was reporting in its 24 July 1943 edition a plan to create a Town Development Committee to look at schemes for post-war planning in Trowbridge. One resident noted: 'After the war is over Trowbridge, as the centre of county administration will, I predict, develop into one of Wiltshire's most important towns…' In view of this he felt certain that there would be a housing problem and that a committee would be well placed to consider appropriate sites, and ensure that sufficient houses would be built to accommodate the 'large influx of workers which would result.' It wasn't just housing; he also felt that a modern bus centre was 'essential'.

Nick McCamley feels that this vast wartime increase in housing capacity turned Corsham 'from a rural village to a town almost overnight'. Wiltshire County Council was extremely concerned about this development foisted on the county; effectively uncontrolled development leading to the urbanisation of a rural area. A committee headed by Lord Justice Scott met to investigate the issue during the wartime period. The Clerk of Wiltshire Council replied to a query from Lord Justice Scott's Committee in February 1942. 'I am not surprised at the anxiety shown by Lord Justice Scott's inquiry of what is happening to many of the beauty spots of this county. The position is an extremely difficult one because the town planning committee, whilst deprecating to the full the shocking development which has taken place not only in Corsham but also in many other parts of the County, they feel that nothing must be done to hinder the successful prosecution of the war.'[258]

Industries which had moved into the county during wartime often remained. Some, such as Vickers-Armstrong at South Marston had no choice, the Government refusing to let them return to their bombed out Southampton site.[259] On 19 July 1946 the firm was providing Swindon Borough Council with their estimate of requirements for housing and labour. 'As South Marston will become the headquarters of the Supermarine organisation, with its own Designing, Experimental and Production Departments, the transfer of our permanent staff and key employees is essential.' The transfer would happen gradually over the following two years, largely controlled by the housing and billeting facilities in and around the Swindon area. On 31 January 1947 Swindon's Town Clerk was writing to the Financial Secretary to the Treasury, hoping to speed up the housing programme in Swindon on behalf of Vickers. 'When it was announced some eighteen months ago that Vickers-Armstrong Ltd. were taking over permanently the factory and aerodrome at South Marston just outside the Borough, the Corporation were gratified since this was felt to be a step in the right direction, namely, the diversification of the industry of Swindon and district... if Vickers' Armstrong needed a speedier provision of houses for their employees then they must persuade the Ministry of Supply to bring pressure upon the appropriate Government departments to permit the Corporation to move more rapidly and to reinforce the local resources...' The Council had heard nothing further and felt that 'since the Corporation has made the generous gesture of allocating a proportion of their houses to Vickers-Armstrong's' employees, it is only reasonable that every effort should be made by the Government Departments to expend and speed up our housing programme.' The reply from the Treasury on 21 March 1947 was dismissive. The Department had 'no specific responsibilities in the matter' and had been advised that in fact the building labour supply situation did not compare unfavourably with the country as a whole and that in fact, 'the rate of meeting demands is slightly above the average.'[260] By 1950 the firm was trying to expand the site further as they were putting into production their new jet fighter. On 14 November 1950 the Clerk of Highworth Rural District Council was writing to the Under-Secretary of State at the War Office. 'This Council are fully aware of the urgent need for housing accommodation for Industrial Workers, and this matter has been pressed with the Ministry of Health, but the Council appreciate that the difficulties generally in this Region prevent more being done than the Ministry of Health have allowed at the present time'. By July 1951 it was being estimated that Vickers would need a minimum of '1,000 dwelling units with an immediate demand for 400 dwelling units to enable the Factory to expand to meet its commitments under the re-armament programme.'[261]

Others, such as Marine Mounting Limited at Wroughton were keen to expand by 1950, but could not do so due to the housing situation. On 30 June they were writing to the Clerk of Highworth Rural District Council. 'We are writing to you with regard to the housing situation in the Wroughton area, which makes it extremely difficult for us to obtain key workers. As soon as we obtain men they only remain for two or three weeks, after finding that it is well-nigh impossible to get a house in this area. This is having a serious effect upon our production.' Plessey in Swindon were also experiencing similar problems[262] and, like Vickers, had notified Swindon Borough Council regarding their plans. Their first enquiry was a letter to the Town Clerk on 31 October 1945. 'We are steadily transferring certain work from our Ilford factory to Swindon, in consequence of which our personnel who are specialists in these particular channels will also have to take up residence in Swindon. The most intricate problem is housing, and I am wondering whether you could advise me or let me have your views in this connection.' On 5 March 1947 the Manager of Plessey's had made 'urgent representations' regarding their housing requirements. 'The firm now employs 950 persons, and they need 500 additional employees.' The Town Clerk had explained that the Ministry of Supply had been giving 'urgent representations' over housing for Vickers-Armstrong, and that Plessey's would need to buy houses privately for their employees; the council would 'consider sympathetically those which were cases of housing need, particularly married men with families living in lodgings or separated from their families.'[263]

As early as 1 April 1944 the *Wiltshire Times* reported that the Ministry of Health was causing delays to post-war housing plans in Trowbridge. The Council's chosen sites had not yet been approved for the first two year programme. It was noted that the Prime Minister in his recent broadcast had assured the public that 'housing sites had been acquired.' '... The whole thing seemed to be quite simple from the Prime Minister's broadcast – almost 'child's play,' – that we can have the land for building sites, and that sites not already purchased can be purchased at the 1939 value... The Town Properties Committee does seem to be overburdened, and that some Sub-Committee should be appointed to go into the question of housing to get something done so that the Council will be prepared to go right ahead without any delay.' On 16 November 1946 the *Wiltshire Times* was reporting that the Wiltshire Federation of Women's Institutes was addressing housing problems

WH/BB

14th July, 1949

Dear Sir,

You may possibly remember that at the recent
Housing Conference at Plymouth, I mentioned that I would
appreciate an opportunity of again re-opening with the
Ministry the question of providing houses to meet Industrial
needs in this area, and I shall be grateful if you will let
me know when it would be convenient to see you.

The position is becoming very acute affecting
Vickers Armstrongs Limited, as the Government have refused
to allow them to re-establish their Works at Southampton
Water which were, I understand, completely blitzed and these
Works have to be transferred to South Marston in this
District to comply with Government policy. If you can
possibly spare me a few minutes, I feel I could justify the
urgency of this matter.

Would it be possible to come down on Monday next
the 18th instant ?

Yours faithfully,

C.H.H.Smith Esq.,
Principal Regional Officer,
Ministry of Health,
Regional Offices,
19, Woodland Road,
BRISTOL, 8.

Letter dated 14 July 1949 in the Clerks Correspondence files of Highworth Rural District
Council stating that Vickers-Armstrong Ltd. was unable to re-establish their works at
Southampton (WSA G6/132/12)

at a full day's conference in Devizes Town hall. The discussions were reported as
being 'well informed.'

By 1946 Wiltshire was zoned into urban, intermediate and rural zones, a
blue line indicating which land was intended to be made available for immediate
development. It was noted that the highest graded land for fertility would not
be included in any area marked for development. A study of the varying types of
agricultural land had been undertaken during the war, from which it had been
discovered that about nine-tenths of the county was agricultural land rather than
industrial.[264] In terms of house building, the Government's National Building

Programme split the country into Local Authority Zones with Regional Building Committees. Swindon fell into Zone 4. The Programme itself had been set out in a White Paper and was governed by the supply of materials and components, and the supply and output of labour. The aims of the Regional Building Committee in 1946 were to expand the building labour force by provision of sufficient new house building work 'within travelling distance of their homes;' to develop the Local Authority as the 'main agency' for housing provision, and to emphasise allocation to those families in greatest need; to stimulate and develop the production of building materials and components; to gain the experience of carrying out planning and preparatory work. Ministry of Labour trainees for the building industry were qualifying by February 1947. They were to return to their home town on completion of their training at the Government's Training Centres. The building force had been expanded and the 'Local Authority machine' had accelerated after a slow start to such an extent that the building and materials industry could not keep pace. 'But, the achievement of these aims has not been secured without cost. So far as our Programme is concerned, the cost may be measured in the over-commitment of the building industry with the consequent under-manning of contract, the slowness of completion of our new houses, and the uneven spread of house contracts, as between different Local Authorities, in the light of size and relative need. In fact, a premium has been placed upon ability to make an early start and to take first dip into the labour bag, at the expense of those Local Authorities who, notwithstanding urgent need, were faced with exceptional initial difficulties.'[265]

The *Wiltshire Times* was reporting on 9 November 1946 that labour shortages, especially of bricklayers, were hindering progress for house building in Trowbridge. The Ministry of Health's aim of 1947 would be to seek 'to relate building plans to building capacity, to obviate the over-commitment of the building and materials industries, to ensure greater equality in aims and achievement, with due regard to relative need, and to reduce delays in completion of contracts, with consequential saving in costs' which would

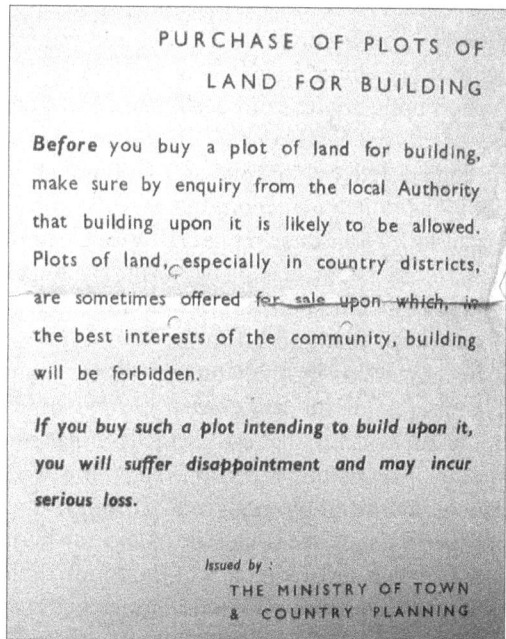

PURCHASE OF PLOTS OF LAND FOR BUILDING

Before you buy a plot of land for building, make sure by enquiry from the local Authority that building upon it is likely to be allowed.

Plots of land, especially in country districts, are sometimes offered for sale upon which, in the best interests of the community, building will be forbidden.

If you buy such a plot intending to build upon it, you will suffer disappointment and may incur serious loss.

Issued by :
THE MINISTRY OF TOWN & COUNTRY PLANNING

Poster c. 1946 warning potential buyers of land that it may be subject to restrictions for building (WSA G5/132/12)

result in 240,000 permanent houses completed nationally. It was noted that the number of houses it had been possible to allocate for 1947 was disappointing but inevitable.[266]

Local Government records show that post-war planning policy in Wiltshire favoured development for those villages with a population of over 600.[267] The population of Calne, Chippenham and Wootton Bassett approximately doubled between the years 1931 and 1961. From a population of about 62,000 in 1939, by 1961 Swindon had reached 91,775. Malmesbury appears to be the exception, with only a small population increase between the years 1931 and 1961,[268] surprising as wartime industry did move to the outskirts of the town. Corsham was a case in point, with a population of 3,754 in 1931 rising to a massive 9,309 by 1951.[269] A preliminary survey by the Technical Planning Committee of industry in Wiltshire, dated January 1944, suggested that Swindon was the only place which could locate new industrial estates. The summary suggests a total of workers in the county as 12,146 in 1938 and 23,428 in 1943.[270] Swindon Borough Council welcomed new industry, the Town Clerk feeling in 1946 that Swindon was a one industry and one class town and 'urgently need a more balanced community'. It was felt that this could be done by a greater diversification of industry.[271] A memo regarding the *Barlow Committee Report* and expansion of small towns can be found in the Wiltshire County Council files of 1946. Included is a questionnaire sent to Wiltshire towns about the subject. In reply, Westbury Urban District Council wanted substantial development of 10-12,000 population growth. They wanted the Town and Country Planning Association to bring their views before the appropriate Government Department. Devizes also wanted substantial development in their reply of November 1946. Calne, in February 1947, also wanted expansion of their 10,000 population as did Melksham, to 15,000, also requesting that their views be sent to the Government. They noted that any assistance would 'undoubtedly be appreciated' by the council. Marlborough in March 1947 wanted only minor additions to its population, but they did consider their area capable of industrial expansion. From these replies the Vice Chair of the Town and Country Planning Committee began making a shortlist in August 1947; of the twelve towns who were sent the questionnaire, six replied and it was suggested that either Westbury, Trowbridge, Bradford on Avon, Warminster or Melksham should be chosen. In a memorandum by the Country Towns Committee of the Town and Country Planning Association in Covent Garden it was noted that: 'The Committee has abundant evidence that the Councils of many small towns in purely rural areas feel that they are bound either to expand or die… the Committee strongly urge that serious consideration be given to the future of the country towns of Great Britain. It believes that in the large scale re-location both of industry and population which is part of the declared policy of the Minister and of the President of the Board of Trade, the country towns and not merely the small towns within the orbits of the large cities, should receive a substantial share.'[272]

Parish Councils were asked for their views on where they would like new housing to be situated.[273] Cricklade Parish Council came to the fore in the post-war period regarding the delays in post-war housing[274] and Sutton Benger Parish Council were deciding at a meeting in June 1946 that there was an urgent need for more houses in the parish.[275]

The Town and Country Planning Act 1947 gave Local Authorities the ability to reconstruct and redevelop.[276] It was decided to build 14 New Towns in Britain to help ease the housing shortage and to create what had begun with the Garden City movement, the idea, as David Kynaston puts it, of 'economically self contained and socially balanced communities' and these were designated between 1946 and 1950.[277] The Town and Country Planning Act of 1947 did not facilitate public engagement with planning; it only gave the right to object to the development plan after its publication.[278]

It was the Blitz that provided the impetus for conservation in planning. Lists of historic buildings were first written up to help the salvage workers in bombed areas prioritise the most important buildings, including those of historic value. It was, however, the establishment of the National Buildings Record in February 1941 which was to become a long lasting legacy for built heritage. Its aim was to conduct a photographic survey of all historic buildings to produce a permanent record – a huge task (and one that is still ongoing to this day) for architecture of importance, fulfilled by English Heritage (now Historic England) for buildings old through to modern. The Town and Country Planning Act 1947 had introduced the idea of lists of historic buildings of 'special architectural or historic interest' to be produced as guidance for Local Authorities. It also gave the lists statutory powers; they had to be compiled and property owners could not have right of appeal if their property was listed.[279] Conservation was also to play a role in planning, as the case of Salisbury's 1950 rebuilding shows.[280] Pevsner's *Buildings of England* pocket volumes, published between 1951 and 1974, did much to educate the general public about the idea of heritage[281] and introduced in the Civic Amenities Act 1967 was the concept of designated Conservation Areas to restrain development. Local Authorities could further protect the buildings within them to help preserve the character and appearance of an area without consulting Ministers.[282]

Nature conservation was also a consideration. W.R. Davidge and Partners, Planning Consultants from London, were asking the Devizes Rural District Council in February 1946 on behalf of the Wiltshire Planning Scheme's Joint Committee if any Nature Reserves or land of 'natural scientific importance' had been damaged by bombing. They acknowledged: 'It is very difficult to estimate what the Ministry have in mind as no definition of the word 'Nature Reserve' is given.' To assist, the firm had drawn up a list of headings to help the Council assess the situation in their area.[283] In 1946 the Wiltshire Joint Planning Committee was noting the area of the Avon Valley which ran from Castle Combe to Box in the south and Limpley Stoke in the west; Savernake Forest; Longleat and Stourton, and the 'spacious uplands of the Downs' as 'unsurpassed for their scenic beauty'. The Wiltshire Joint Planning Committee was looking at the preservation of trees in July 1947 when the Council for the Preservation of Rural England was highlighting the felling of the woods at East Knoyle. A resolution was passed on 15 July 1947 '[t]hat the Planning adviser be requested to press for the regulations by the Minister providing for the proper re-afforestation of land on which timber is felled and for the provision for complete liaison between the Forestry Commission and the Planning authority.' By October 1947 the Wiltshire Joint Planning Committee was reporting on the designation of twelve National Parks. It was noting that the Marlborough Downs would be designated as a Conservation Area.[284]

Jo Little studied social class and planning policy in the 1980s by looking at two Wiltshire villages, concluding that countryside planning had a part to play in rural deprivation,[285] and noting that the views of middle class 'newcomer populations' were well represented in both the planning process, also dominating local institutions.[286] Post-war planning had not helped the rural poor with its emphasis on agriculture and conservation. The interests of the dominant classes prevented rural development to the detriment of local people, with those benefiting the most being those who already had, as Mark Shucksmith notes, 'privilege and wealth'. Shucksmith feels that the countryside can be seen as a construction of the middle classes who 'benefit disproportionately from this imagery.'[287] [288] The upper class dominance in rural life had been declining in the pre-war years with the break up of large estates through tax reform. The changes to the middle classes resulted in the standing of the upper class in the community diminishing after the war.[290] Peter Ambrose is one of a number of voices who state that the political power of the elite was lost. He feels that the country passed through a revolutionary phase of social change during the 1930s to 1970s.[291]

In 1944 C. S. Orwin noted in the study *Country Planning: A Study of Rural Problems* that villages had remained unaltered whilst small towns in rural areas had prospered; the tendency of English villages to shrink meant that they were unable to keep up with the changing standards in society at large. Car ownership rose in the mid to late 1950s from 18% to 32%,[289] and rural depopulation ceased in the 1960s. What came with it was the absorption of urban life into rural areas[292] which took place through widespread car ownership.[293]

The Swindon Borough Clerk had been particularly worried about the new wartime housing proposals. By 9 June 1941 he was writing to the Regional Estate Surveyor in Bristol to communicate that although he wanted to 'further the national effort' he also wanted to protect town planning and housing standards, including density.[294] The Regional Officer, Ministry of Aircraft Production, had been making a close study of Swindon in 1946 and was attempting to act on lessons learnt during WWII. 'Can we take it that due consideration is being paid to the increased supplies where they be necessary in drainage and sewage systems, water supplies, provision of an adequate number of Communal Restaurants, whether any increase has been thought of towards the establishment of additional Community Social Centres and if consideration has been given towards the catering for the additional educational facilities that will be required. In this direction it is anticipated that a large number of incoming workers will be married with young families.'[295] Swindon was designated as an overspill town from London under the 1951 Town Development Act. Over the following years the population doubled in size, the centre of the town moved away from the GWR works and the character of the town altered.[296]

A chalk quarrying area at Westbury had been in the ownership of the War Department and tentative talks took place regarding its possible use as a cement works in autumn 1945, but the military were opposed due to its proximity to their firing ranges on Salisbury Plain. Government pressure was forthcoming and the Ministry of Town and Country Planning finally waded in in the summer of 1946. The Minister chose to hold a public enquiry regarding The Associated Portland Cement Manufacturer's Ltd.'s planning application.[297] On 5 December 1946 the Clerk of Westbury Urban District Council was asking if the Minister required their views 'or whether these should await expression at the Local Inquiry which my Council presumes, and hopes, will be held before a decision is made.'[298] Local people had questions to be put forward for the enquiry. One Westbury resident was asking in November 1946:

1. What area is likely to be affected by dust from the works?
2. Is the dust likely to cause serious damage to pasture land and crops, and cause abortion and sterility in cattle?
3. What amount of water would actually be required per day? (There appear to be varying amounts stated, ranging from 140,000 to 350,000 gallons).
4. If the Local Authorities cannot see their way clear to provide the necessary water, has the Company any plans to obtain water on their own account?
5. How do they propose to house their employees?
6. How long (approximately) do the Company think they would be working the chalk in the district?[299]

The company's solicitor wrote to the Clerk of Westbury Urban District Council on 12 December 1946 to state: 'I have noted from the Press today the terms of the recent decision of your Council that no objection would be taken to siting of a Cement Works at Westbury subject to various conditions... the Minister, in finally adjudicating upon the Application, will deal with any necessary conditions although I have no doubt he will be fully influenced by the views of your Council in the matter.' There was strong public opposition to the project and even though it was one of the earliest acquisitions under the new provisions of the 1947 Planning Act, many delays caused by the War Department meant that it would not be until 13 years later that the works went into operation.[300]

The Housing Crisis

GOING HAND IN hand with planning came housing, but house building during wartime had 'virtually ceased' and by the end of 1945 there had been 60 million changes of address among the civilian population necessitated by the war.[301] As early as 1940 Lord Woolton felt that there would be trouble with housing. 'I think there's going to be grave trouble, and the danger is that if the machine of Government which can spend money so recklessly in engaging in war, fails to be equally reckless in rebuilding, here will be both the tendency and the excuse for revolution.'[302] Beveridge highlighted housing in his 1942 Report as a problem of 'the first magnitude' and by 1944 Ministers had become even more anxious regarding its urgency. Lord Woolton stated in a memorandum on 5 September 1944: 'Of all the problems facing the Home Front, housing is the most important from the point of view of future stability and public contentment.' Churchill agreed.[303]

Civil servants within Central Government Departments had been working on the housing issue since 1941 with three sub-committees of the Central Housing Advisory Committee looking at temporary dwellings, design standards for post-war reconstruction and the role that private enterprise had to play. With experience of the post-WWI era came the realisation that state intervention would have to come to the fore when considering post WWII housing.[304] The vow of 'homes for heroes' which was unmet after WWI had not been forgotten.[305] Local Authorities were tasked with implementing the post-war housing policy as they had done after WWI, but this time around the Government would put into place a framework to control both labour and materials specifically for house building. They would rely on private building firms to deliver production.[306] Anuerin Bevan, Minister of Health and Local Government and responsible for the housing programme, noted in the House of Commons in October 1945: '... This means that we shall ask the Local Authorities to be the main instruments for the housing programme... It is... a principle of the first importance that the Local Authorities must be looked to as the organisations and source for the building of the main bulk of the housing programme.' He felt that '[t]he Local Authorities are admirably suited for this purpose.'[307]

The post-war policy on housing was being formed by 1942 with what Peter Malpass describes as 'very ambitious' targets. The Ministry of Health's paper on long-term policy announced: 'It is certain the country will expect an even more vigorous policy after this war... Every family who so desires should be able to live in a separate dwelling possessing all the amenities necessary to family life in the fullest sense, and special provision must be made for old people and single women.'[308] The commitment was later enshrined in the Housing White Paper of March 1945. It was announced in 1943 that a total of 3-4 million houses would be required in England and Wales during the first 10 years following the end of the war, providing a target of 300,000-400,000 houses to be built each year. This must be considered in the context that even in the rapid housebuilding period of the mid 1930s only 350,000 house builds were reached annually and at that time the Government had also relied on the private sector.[309] After the economic crisis of 1947 the housing programme was cut back and Jim Tomlinson notes that it 'thereafter bore a disproportionate share of the squeeze on resources going into 'social' investment'. West Germany was investing more in housing than Britain by the late 1940s.[310] The reality was that annual completions in the post-war period continued below the rate of 300,000 per year until 1953.[311]

The Ministry of Health conducted a Housing Census on 31 December 1945, using form P.1, its purpose to 'obtain complete and up-to-date information of the Housing position throughout England and Wales... The information obtained for this Return will be kept up-to-date by monthly Progress Reports which Local Authorities will be requested to complete at the end of each calendar month (Form P.2) beginning at the end of January 1946.'[312] During the war, families had been living in houses which would otherwise have been condemned and many others were living in properties which had received minimal repairs. Overcrowding was also a problem,[313] and these issues continued during the immediate post-war period. A Government circular of 31 March 1947 found in the records of Devizes Rural District Council stated in article nine that '... as the problem is so acute and urgent, cottages which have been condemned could be made habitable for the time being, by re-conditioning...'[314] One lady living in Malmesbury felt she had no option but to squat as her current lodgings were overcrowded; 10 people sharing a living room, kitchen, two bedrooms and an attic.[315]

A Gallup Poll taken in summer 1945 showed that 41% of electors felt that housing was the most pressing issue, above that of full employment or social security.[316] Labour's success in the polls had much to do with its stance on housing, but it was to be their biggest failure.[317] Macmillan and his Conservative Party's pledge to build 300,000 houses per year was a key part of the 1951 successful election programme.[318] In the immediate post-war years, house hunting, flat hunting or even room hunting could take a long time and many young couples were desperate for a house. The Government had announced that house building would be the new 'military operation', but the building industry was not a coherent unit which could work systematically and it was difficult to organise.[319]

The British people did not ask for much; just to have a little privacy in their homes, and hopefully a garden too.[320] Swindon was one town which still had to provide boarding out rooms during the post-war period, causing a great deal of friction.[321] One tenant explained she needed new accommodation as her landlady was 71 and 'couldn't be bothered with a baby'.[322] The requisition of properties continued during the post-war period with Aneurin Bevan appealing to householders to once more share their homes.[323] Mass Observation reported one young lady saying at a Post-war Homes Exhibition held in London that '... I'm so desperate for a house I'd like anything... four walls and a roof is the height of my ambition.'[324] One young couple were writing to the Cricklade and Wootton Bassett Rural District Council in November 1947 asking for a converted army hut. '... like most young couples we are anxious to get a home of our own and with another baby arriving we shall be more than overcrowded.'[325] The old Nissen huts used by the US forces in Dinton were the target of a campaign to get them converted into houses. 'There were no houses for young people at that time, and many were squatting where they could, so my husband and I went early one morning and moved into one of the huts. When other young couples saw what we had done they followed suit... We were the first ones in and the last ones out.

We were there eight years.' The huts shared just one tap and one toilet between them.[326] At Blakehill the camp had been requisitioned for Ministry of Aircraft Production workers, who had already been 'thrown together as a result of the war.' They had endured sharing with strangers or substandard accommodation, and the converted huts 'seemed like heaven to many of the tenants. Just to have their own front door key, electricity, hot and cold water laid on and an inside toilet was a luxury.' The majority of them were young couples with families.[327]

Only around 12% of newly married couples were able to live in a home of their own in 1945/6[328] and desperate people turned to desperate measures. The Government was caught on the hop by the squatter movement, highlighted by the Communist squatting of luxury flats in Kensington, and soon it was commonplace to see the occupation of old Service or Government camps in the summer of 1946. By September Harry Hopkins reports that the squatters had become 'like spam, an accepted part of the life of the times'[329] as by early October around 50,000 people were occupying over 1,000 military properties.[330] Ministry of Health Circular 174/46 stated the Government's position on 16 September 1946; that 'both civil and criminal law ha[d] been violated' and '[i]t [was] the duty of the police to take every step within the limits of their resources to prevent breaches of the law, and they ha[d] been instructed to take appropriate action to prevent further forcible entries.' 'The Minister expressly requests that Local Authorities would withhold all facilities from any 'squatters' entering into occupation of property under their control.'[331] It appears that lessons were learnt. Leafield Camp, part of HMS Royal Arthur near Corsham, was due to be relinquished by the Admiralty in 1949. The Clerk of the Council was writing to the Commanding Officer in December asking that steps be taken to stop squatters moving in. 'I am informed by an officer of the regional offices of the Ministry of Health, Bristol, that his head office in London have asked the Admiralty to maintain a guard if these buildings are vacated in order that their occupation by unauthorised persons may be prevented. The Council understand there is a real danger of squatters taking possession as soon as the premises are left without protection.'[332]

Longhedge Farm Camp, Amesbury Road, Salisbury, was a case in point. It appears that the War Department were in the process of disposing of the site early in 1946 but there were delays with the transfer. The camp became occupied by squatters on 16 August 1946 and the War Department was unable to disconnect the gas, electric and water supplies, which was now a matter for Amesbury Rural District Council. It appears, however, that essential supplies were not fully operational as a survey of the camp on 27 August showed that although families had electricity wired into the huts they were having to use candles and lamps. Water supplies to the huts were also not turned on and there was as yet no provision for refuse disposal. One camp resident was writing to the council in April 1947 regarding the site, which the residents had done their best to make their homes 'fit to live in'. 'Since we have been in these Huts we have paid our Rates which no time was lost in sending, also now we have the rent upon us and no-think [*sic*] has been done to help us out in the camp in any-way [*sic*]. We ask

To all Housing Authorities
County Councils for information
(England).

17 SEP 1946
CALNE&CHIPPENHAM
R.D.C.

Circular 174/46

MINISTRY OF HEALTH,
WHITEHALL,
LONDON, S.W.1.
16th September, 1946.

Sir,

"SQUATTERS"

I am directed by the Minister of Health to refer to the recent seizure and occupation of premises, particularly in London, by unauthorised persons; and to inform local authorities of the decisions taken by His Majesty's Government and of the action which local authorities should take wherever necessary in conformity with those decisions.

As announced in the statement issued from No. 10, Downing Street:

"His Majesty's Government take a very serious view of the forcible seizure and occupation by unauthorised persons of private premises in London, especially those required for housing or other public purposes. This action has been instigated and organised by the Communist Party and must result in hindering rather than in helping the arrangements made for the orderly rehousing of those in need of accommodation.

His Majesty's Government are advised that both the civil and the criminal law have been violated. Unless steps are taken to check lawless measures of this sort, the rights of the ordinary law-abiding citizens are endangered and anarchy may result.

It is the duty of the police to take every step within the limits of their resources to prevent breaches of the law, and they have been instructed to take appropriate action to prevent further forcible entries.

Writs have been issued in the High Court on behalf of the Minister of Works and the Minister of Health against trespassers in the premises known as the Duchess of Bedford House and Fountain Court respectively, claiming damages and an injunction to restrain the continuance of the trespass, and immediate steps will be taken to enforce any orders that may be made by the High Court.

In addition, a report of all the facts has been submitted to the Director of Public Prosecutions, who is considering in the ordinary course of his duties the question of instituting proceedings for criminal conspiracy against the organisers of or participators in this unlawful movement."

The Minister expressly requests that local authorities should withhold all facilities from any "squatters" entering into occupation of property under their control. In particular, the Minister asks that in such cases local authorities should not provide gas or electricity, and should cut off these services where they are already available at the time of occupation.

Premises should be securely locked, and the police summoned if any suspicion of attempted seizure arises. Where accommodation in the possession of local authorities is illegally occupied, immediate action should be taken to secure eviction, if necessary by legal proceedings.

The Government are confident that local authorities will take firm and prompt action on these lines in defence of ordered government and the principles of social justice on which the system of allocation of available housing accommodation is based; and that in taking it they will have the full backing of public opinion in the localities.

The great majority of the 192,000 homes so far provided under the re-housing programme - by new building, conversion and adaptation, requisitioning and repair of uninhabitable houses - have been made available for letting to the families in greatest need. These allocations are made by the local authority, as the elected representatives

/of

The Clerk to the Authority.

Ministry of Health Circular 174/46 regarding squatters, sent to all County Council Housing Authorities in England (WSA G3/132/3)

you gentlemen is it right, we need homes and decent ones for our wifes who have to at the moment make do for cooking on what we may have [*sic*], when you were out at the Huts you asked what was needed at each Hut cant some of these things be done in one way or another as it is very urgent, for us to live in them as one would like to [*sic*].'³³³

The unfortunate situation of residents of the Police and Army Quarters at Hudswell, Corsham, went all the way to Whitehall in 1947. The site had been taken over by civilians for housing but the premises had remained Crown property. The residents were facing eviction as of 31 August 1947; they had signed a petition and got the local MP David Eccles involved. They describe their plight on their petition dated 12 August 1947:

> Sir or Madam
> We the undermentioned, wish to make an appeal to the Committee to press the case for alternative accommodation on behalf of us people who are unfortunate to be living in the Police and Army Quarters of Hudswell and are threatened by eviction… The laws governing premises of this nature are very stringent, and should the County Court Judge rule against us, it would cause very great hardship as there are amongst us some necessitous cases such as expectant mothers and ailing wives…
>
> The point in question is that we were issued with tenancy agreements after we were made redundant, and the whole thing in my opinion seems a farce, pressing for our eviction while there is so much Crown property in the area lying idle, also the spending of public money to renovate Pookeredge House for an officers canteen whilst there are so many people wanting homes, who in lots of cases bore very great hardships by bombing and losing their homes. This necessitated evacuation to a district where work was available, and now for thanks we are to be turned out. The bulk of us are ex-servicemen with children who have done good work in this war.' The petition was sent to the Ministry of Health at Whitehall so that they could 'make representations to the War Department' on the matter.³³⁴

The Clerk of Castle Combe Parish Council agreed, writing to the Clerk at Calne and Chippenham Rural District Council about the Upper Combe hutment in April 1945 which was rumoured to be closing down soon.³³⁵ In July 1945 the Warminster and Westbury RDC were looking to military camps to help solve their housing problems. 'The Council have been doing their best to get accommodation and they are very keen on getting the War Office to hand over the Bury Camp at Codford which is a small camp and would, with slight conversion, provide housing accommodation for all the cases which I have in mind at the moment, but having approached… the War Office and the Ministry of Health were informed that this camp is not at present surplus to Government needs *despite the fact that it has been lying empty for about twelve months*… Incidentally we have asked them to release portions of the Knook Camp at Heytesbury and the Longleat Hospital but the reply to all is the same.'³³⁶ By 31 March 1947 Devizes Rural District Council were noting that '[a] source of considerable accommodation lies in Service hutted camps, which have been vacated by troops. These are to be found all over the country, and are usually fully equipped with the necessary services,

Letter From the Clerk of the Castle Combe Parish Council regarding the use of part of the Castle Combe Camp, known as Upper Combe, 27 April 1945 (WSA G3/132/40)

(water, electricity etc.) and should be utilised wherever possible as an immediate form of housing.[337]

Peter Hennessy reports that most Local Authorities turned a blind eye, 'glad to have some kind of safety valve which eased the everyday pressure on their housing departments',[338] but as Wiltshire's Local Authority records show, the situation was by no means that simple...

The Deputy Clerk of the Calne and Chippenham Rural District Council was considering the squatters at the Hardenhuish and Langley Burrell Without Camps in April 1948. 'The Council do not consider these camps are suitable for taking over for housing accommodation but feel, I think, that they are of some small assistance in providing houses for very distressing cases.

The Council has an arrangement with the Ministry of Health that upon any of these hutments becoming vacant the same are demolished.' A letter dated February 1950 shows the intent of the Council; to rehouse those from Langley Burrell into the Hardenhuish Camp. 'The Council have decided that the occupiers of huts at Langley Burrell Camp shall be rehoused into Hardenhuish Camp as accommodation becomes available...'[339]

RAF Blakehill was one ex-military site which the council had been earmarking for conversion, although in December 1947 it was noted that '53 of the converted Nissen Huts on this Camp are now occupied, and various repairs are essential from time, to time... This camp is causing considerable additional work on the Council's already over-burdened staff...'[340] There had been around 150 huts which were suitable for conversion, costing approximately £241 per hut. The site was still being used as a satellite airfield in 1948; planes would fly out of the site if the airfield at South Cerney was too wet.[341] The Chief Financial Officer of the Calne and Chippenham Rural District Council was unhappy with the situation of squatters at E. Site Camp at Thickwood, Colerne, in April 1948. 'You will know that the Council have taken over this camp, although they do not accept the huts as providing a standard of accommodation which they think is satisfactory or sufficient to justify expenditure to convert them into temporary housing accommodation. The Council will, however, provide essential services to satisfy general health requirements…'[342]

Squatters moved into Anzac Camp, London Road, Devizes in September 1946 but the War Department had not surrendered it to the Council. They did in fact 'urgently require' it for military purposes and suggested that Devizes Rural District Council re-house the squatters at the St. Edith's Marsh Camp at Bromham. It appears that the Council tried to fulfil the request, but at least two of the squatters were not happy with the accommodation offered at St Edith's Marsh. They thought it damp and not 'in any way suitable for human habitation,' and opted to stay where they were.[343]

The land that hutted sites were on had been requisitioned by the military, and in some cases the former land owners were not happy about their new use. This was true of the owners of Ashley House in Box. They were writing to the Calne and Chippenham Rural District Council in October 1946 to state their case:

> I understand that there is a possibility that the R.D.C. may take over the military huts in the field near this house for temporary housing purposes.
>
> This field belongs to my wife and myself, and is right in front of the house, which looks down on it. Furthermore there is a pool bordering it on which I keep wild duck, and this pool is to us one of the great amenities of our home.
>
> It was a bad blow when the military established themselves there, but we were promised full re-instatement at the end of the war. You will understand that this new development, if it takes place, will be a bad blow again.
>
> On view, however, of the housing shortage, I feel that we must respect the situation…
>
> Will you please inform me what financial arrangements are contemplated, as the capital value of the house will be greatly reduced.[344]

Merton College, Oxford, owned land which had been requisitioned for military use. Perhaps understandably, the owner did not expect any recompense. The site, Stratton St. Margaret Camp, had since been occupied by squatters and in a letter to the Highworth RDC the Estates Bursar pointed out that they 'presumably pay a rent to the Council. I understand that a rent of 12s. 6d. a week is being paid for each hut. The Council is probably making a profit out of the rent received and if this is the case I do not see why the land owner should not receive some portion of the money.'[345]

'Fontainville' in Westbury had been requisitioned for US troops during the war. The house became disused soon after, although the temporary accommodation in the grounds was taken over by squatters. The house became dilapidated and was later knocked down.[346]

It wasn't just the old military camps that were causing problems. The Pinehurst Estate (Swindon) Tenant's Association was bringing the subject of 'aluminium type prefabs' to the notice of the council. Tenants were finding the conditions at home very difficult in February 1947.[347]

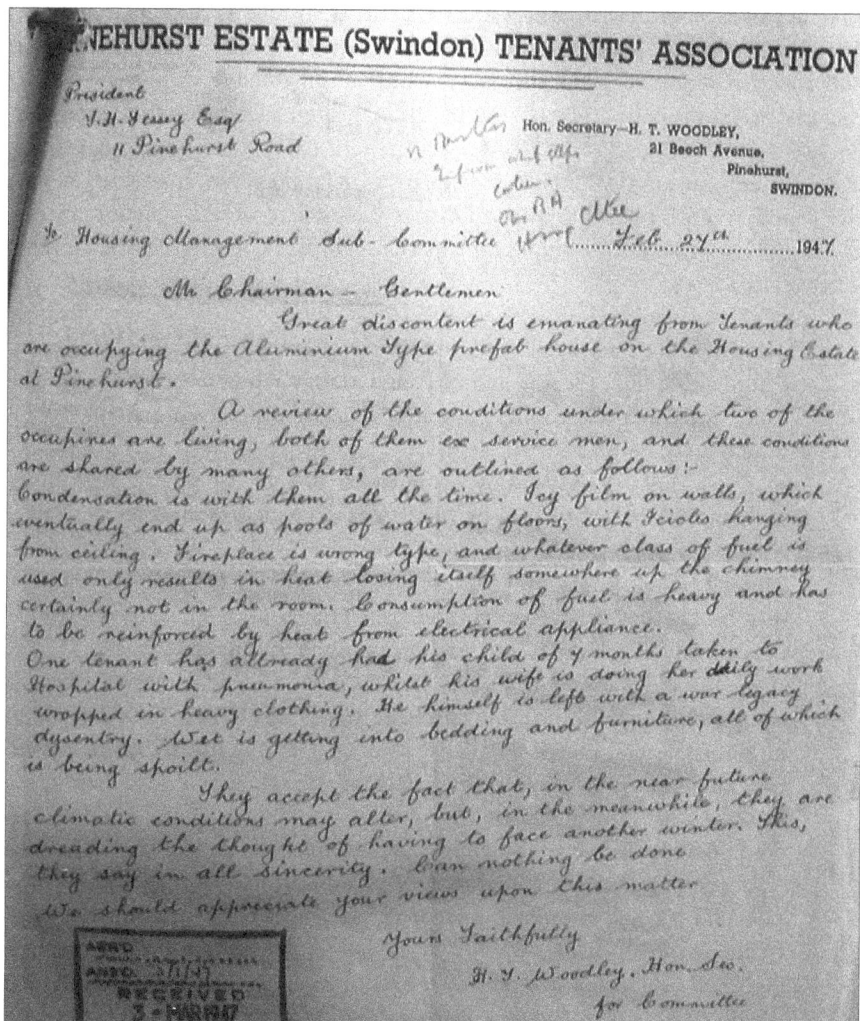

Letter from the Pinehurst Tenants' Association to Swindon Borough Council, 27 February 1947, regarding condensation and poor heating in prefabs at Pinehurst, Swindon (WSA G24/132/332)

The Swindon Borough Clerk felt it would be unfair to prioritise squatters: 'There are very many cases of families on the list who have equal if not greater need as persons who have taken matters into their own hands and become squatters. It is unfair to give them priority and might encourage the practice.'[348]

There were certainly many people wanting ex-service huts; the Local Authority records for Wiltshire held at the Wiltshire and Swindon History Centre are full of handwritten applications in the form of written correspondence in the late 1940s. The Ministry of Local Government and Planning's Regional Offices in Bristol were advising the Clerk of Highworth Rural District Council in March 1951 to ensure that when squatters had been rehoused their huts would not be taken over. '... as each family is rehoused, the Council will take prompt and effective action to make the vacated huts uninhabitable to prevent further unauthorised occupation (e.g. by partial dismantling, such as removal of doors, windows and roofs...'[349]

There was another side to the squatters' tale, however. Contained within the Calne and Chippenham Rural District Council records is a report by the Housing Department regarding their experience with squatters at Castle Combe, written circa 1948:

The problem of 'squatters' is one which Local Authorities in Rural areas have had to tackle since the war, and as a matter of interest here, briefly, is how the Calne and Chippenhm Rural District Council have met the situation in recent months.

In July 1948, persons commenced illegally to take possession of hutments formerly occupied by the R.A.F. at Castle Combe, and as is usual when a military camp becomes redundant, the whole camp is offered to the Council by the Ministry of Health. After hearing reports from its Officials, members of the Housing Committee visited the camp and recommended that the council take over four dispersed sites and the Communal site.

At the end of July, 1948, representatives of the Council, along with the Officials, met on the camp all the 'squatters' and talked over the position as it then stood. The result of that meeting was that the 'squatters' elected from among themselves a Committee of Management, and submitted to the Council a list of materials they would like in order to convert the huts into temporary dwellings.

Approval was obtained from the Ministry of Health to the proposed expenditure, and eventually materials were supplied including portable cooking ranges, etc. The whole of the work was carried out by the occupiers themselves, and it is interesting to note what a grand spirit exists between each family; resources and manpower were pooled, each family helping a family who perhaps by reason of old age or illness were not able to carry on.

Upper Combe and District Community Association (the official title of this new community) will stand as a memorial to the good relations between a Local Authority and its Officials, and the occupiers of the hutments themselves who by their own efforts have made a contribution to the community...[350]

The Council's Housing Manager disliked intensely the word 'squatter'... 'These people', he says, 'are only different from other members of society in that they were desperate for housing accommodation. In all other respects they are decent members of the community, and it has been a pleasure to help them.'[351]

Local Authority files contain lists of these squatters, such as those at

Hardenhuish Camp in Chippenham, giving the names of the family, where they were employed, the date they first entered the camp and their address previous to squatting. At Hardenhuish Camp the majority were working in Chippenham, many at Westinghouse and some at the Wilts Bacon Company. Many had been previously living in villages surrounding the town, but some had been living relatively nearby, suggesting they were moving out of overcrowded properties. It is interesting to note that, with one exception, none had been on the housing list of the Calne and Chippenham Rural District Council. Perhaps unsurprisingly, one of the first to arrive at the camp was a family already living nearby (the husband worked at the local veterinary surgery), having moved out of their old premises in July 1946. Forms were given to householders to complete for annual surveys of houses and premises, showing that Polish workers were amongst those resident at Hardenhuish Camp in May 1952.[352] The *Wiltshire Gazette* reported on the takeover on 29 August 1946. The squatters had defied a 'Trespassers will be prosecuted' notice. The first person to move in was a man who had served in the No. 1 Spanish Company with the British Army and who had been given no choice but to vacate a farm cottage which he and the three other men in his Company who had joined him had been living. He had approached the Council who could not find him a house, and had chosen to move into the camp instead of living on the streets. Of those families who then joined him on the site, most had been living in the area for some time, either in rooms or in overcrowded houses.

Travel continued to be a difficulty for some in the post-war period. Marion Parsons reports in her research of Blakehill Camp that a coach did operate at the site for employees of local firms Vickers Armstrong, Plessey and Garrards, and also to local schools. There was also a bus service operating from Swindon to Cirencester. However, she noted that those working in other local employment would need to cycle to work.[353] A resident at Blakehill Camp was finding she could not get a job due to the lack of nursery provision and bus services. She also mentioned that her husband was an 'ex-serviceman with a 33% disability pension and owing to his disability is off work a great deal. In these circumstances it is essential that I try and earn something but the expense of running this hut which leaks and is damp is beyond me.' All the families living at Blakehill were finally re-housed in July 1956.[354] By 14 November 1945 in Sutton Benger the Parish Council were drafting a letter to ask for an improved bus service[355] and in 1953 Swindon residents were petitioning for the reintroduction of one of its bus services which had been cut during the war.[356]

Peter Malpass reports that housing in post-war Britain has been viewed as the 'wobbly pillar' of the welfare system, undertaken alongside but completely separated from the construction of a 'coherent' welfare state. He feels that detailed planning went into the area of house construction during the war, but it was not connected in any way to social policy, even though both were run by the Department of Health in the 1940s and the State had embraced housing alongside health, education, social security and social services. The housing policy became overrun by 'quantitative imperatives' rather than 'systematic reform objectives'.[357]

Hut 22, Site 5,
Blakehill ,
Cricklade,
Wilts.

January 15th 1948.

Dear Sir,

In August last year I had some correspondence with you
with regard to housing accommodation. The Wootton Bassett Council
in conjunction with yourselves put me in one of these huts as
there was not a house available, although the Wootton Bassett
Council let a house at Broad Town to a single man and as far as I
know he still occupies this with 2 bedrooms being used for storing
tomatoes.

I want to inform you as at present is that the hut we
occupy leaks when the rain is heavy and is extremely damp.

I am finding it too expensive to run as together with the rent
of 13/10 plus electricity 7/- weekly plus 2 cwt coke and 1 coal
£1. The grates just roar the firing away and it does not heat the
rooms all over. There is no fireplace or anything in the bedrooms
to keep the beds aired. My husband has had to take a job in Swindon
and live at Stratton Hostel which means he is keeping 2 homes
going as there is no work round here and no transport at the right
times.

I have tried myself to get a job as my work is Shorthand
and typing but cannot find a nursery to take my child of 2 years.
I have two other children going to school and 1 boy of 16 who has
just joined the Navy.

Even if the Swindon Nursery would take my baby, (and they
say they have a waiting list) the first bus passing here is 9.30
a.m. which is too late.

I am at my wits end what to do as I am getting into debt.
This week I cannot meet my grocery bill.

I might mention that we have had our name down on the

/Amersham

*Letter by a resident of Blakehill Camp near Cricklade, written in January 1948 and
highlighting the difficulties and pressures living in rural Wiltshire in the post-war era. The lady
notes that she is 'not the only one complaining of leaks' (WSA G4/132/4)*

It has been said that keeping housing under the Ministry of Health until 1951 can
be been as Attlee's 'greatest administrative error'. Although the construction of
one million permanent new houses between 1945 and 1951 can be seen as a great
achievement after the devastation of WWII, when housing is viewed alongside the
other key social policy areas, it can be seen as having been quickly used to address
need, but not as part of a long-term strategy to reform the housing system. Malpass
views the lack of reform of housing policy in the post-war period as 'striking'; the

Attlee Government recognised the social and political importance of housing, but did not modify the sector in any way,[358] although Ian Cole and Barry Goodchild note that Bevan was concerned about social housing, wanting to develop a 'universal basis' for public housing provision, to run in parallel with initiatives in state education, health and social insurance. He had hoped that Local Authority housing would predominate for all social classes,[359] urging young couples in the post-war period to wait for a council house and avoid the burden of a mortgage[360] but in the 1950s private developers again began building for owner-occupation and local councils became the main provider for those in need. Housing did not gain the same foothold as health and education provision in the post-war era.[361]

Advertisement in the Wiltshire Times, 'loans for home buyers', 18 May 1946 (WSHC Microform Collection)

The idea of a 'property-owning democracy', Skelton's pre-war phrase which had been taken up by Eden in 1946, began to gain momentum in the early 1950s when revisionists were looking at the inequality between the owners of property and wage earning capacity. Sophie Jackson notes that the unequal distribution of property was seen to contribute an 'unequal distribution of security, freedom, and status' and the turn way from housing being viewed as a social need had begun.[362]

There had been major problems with water supplies during wartime and the supply of water to rural communities was a problem which hadn't yet been solved. The water requirements at Burderop Park had been causing Swindon

Borough Council difficulties in July 1942. 'It is regrettable that, even in these days, no notice is taken of responsible Authorities operating such matters as the supply of water, and I regret to add that there appears to be no co-operation between the various Military Authorities dealing with the matter of camps in this district.'[363] Local Authorities were fully aware of the need for utilities during wartime but the problems they faced in the post-war era were also many and great. A letter from the Ministry of Health in December 1943 stated that the purchase of land for water supply and sewerage in the Highworth area was so urgent that they '[would] entertain applications as schemes are so urgently required,' to be progressed at the earliest possible date after the 'cessation of hostilities in Europe and necessary labour and materials can be made available.'[364] As early as 16 August 1944 Devizes Rural District Council had been writing to the Ministry of Works in London, begging to inform them that the water supply to Great Cheverell was causing 'some anxiety owing to the fact that the yield has fallen considerably below the normal, and for some time the Council have had to pump almost continuously day and night in order to keep their consumers supplied.' They were asking whether the Ministry would permit them to take some water from the hospital at Erlestoke.[365] Wiltshire County Council was writing to the Rural District Councils in frustration on 5 June 1945, requesting that they advise the County Council of their schemes regarding water supplies and sewerage under the Rural Water Supplies and Sewerage Act 1944. Only four had done so, and of these, some covered only a small portion of their area; others had not taken into account the sewerage problem. 'The qualifying period for grants out of the £15,000,000 Fund has not started, so it is important to get applications sent in without delay. The County Council realise the urgency of the matter in many districts and are most anxious to help in any way they can…' A dairy farmer in Bishops Cannings was writing to Devizes Rural District Council in October 1945. 'My main supply is dangerously low. At any time I may find it exhausted. If I were an ordinary person with no dairy farm the matter would seem serious enough to warrant the immediate laying on of water. But I am dependent for my living on dairy farming and I must have water and plenty of it if I am to carry on…' The Parish Council had also been requesting that a supply be provided to the village as many of the village wells had dried up.[366] In April 1947 the Wiltshire Federation of Women's Institutes was writing to the Clerk of Devizes Rural District Council to draw attention to the issue. A resolution was passed at their Annual Meeting which '… urge[d] the Authorities concerned to supply their cottages with a piped water supply as efficiently as they supply their farm buildings and fields.'[367] Local people used their MP to access information regarding their own plight, and David Eccles, MP for the Calne and Chippenham Division, raised the issue of rural water supplies in Parliament.[368]

Sewage systems existed on the new military camps and it was hoped that wartime military supplies could be utilised for post-war housing. This did not always prove to be the case as the sites were often found to be in isolated areas; housing sites were meant to be selected for their proximity to existing communities and their amenities. 'It might have been thought that war-time provision of public utility supplies could have been utilized for post-war housing purposes. In point of fact this has not proved possible or desirable, except in a few cases, as the greatest possible care has necessarily been taken to select sites for post-war houses in locations where there are a proper complement of communal facilities e.g. in existing villages.'[369] In November 1945 Devizes Rural District Council were hoping to take a supply of water from the Cherhill source for Bromham residents, but the Cherhill source could not be obtained until the Air Ministry released it.[370]

The Town Clerk of Calne Borough Council was writing to the Ministry of Health in July 1944, voicing concerns over their proposed housing scheme. 'I have recently been in correspondence with the Calne Water Works Company Ltd. with regard to the layout of 11 acres of land for housing purposes, and at the same time I have been pressing the Company for a reply to the oft repeated question as to whether they will be able to give us a sufficient supply of water for the 140 homes to be erected on this site... We are being pressed to proceed with our housing scheme and we do not even know whether the Company will be able to supply water to the houses or not...'[371]

The Financial Officer of Malmesbury RDC noted the 'cost of supply is out of proportion to the population served'. It was stated that the Ministry of Health urged a contribution from the 'General Rate'.[372] By 1947 it was noted of the village of Yatton Keynell that 'the present method of sewerage disposal constitutes a danger to health.'[373] A notice was published in Chippenham and District Committee's 1951 *Festival of Britain* Brochure regarding the town's water supply. 'Chippenham and District obtains its water supply from boreholes of a depth of approximately 150-200 ft. and every drop of water for public supplies has to be raised by pumping to a total height of about 300 ft. which means the use of manpower, fuel and power, which ought to be expended as economically as possible.' It urged the townspeople to co-operate to help them provide water as efficiently as possible.[374] By February 1948 a report on the water supplies in Wiltshire had been submitted to the Minister of Health. It considered the abolition of small undertakings to be of paramount importance. What was required was to concentrate on the development of larger sources; to improve the efficiency of distribution and eliminate waste; to introduce regular sampling; to rely on natural water boundaries rather than Local Authority boundaries; and to ensure the adequacy of well qualified and experienced waterworks staff. It was expected that approximately £1,750,000 would be needed to provide 'in so far as practicable, all persons living in the County with a piped water supply and to enable the vital farming industry to be conducted on a safe, sound and hygienic basis. It [was] essential that [the] expenditure and the results of such expenditure should be under expert and unified control.' It was noted in an accompanying letter that the Ministry felt 'there is a great deal of leeway to be made up throughout the rural areas of the County before the water supplies can be regarded as being of a reasonable standard...'[375]

The 1947 Electricity Act which nationalised the Electricity Generating Boards had the effect in southern England of introducing a social obligation towards electricity and encouraged those institutions (such as Local Authorities) who worked with the boards to also meet these obligations. By the early 1950s much of the work done by the Southern Electricity Consultative Council was towards rural electrification. The Council had been set up to protect customers from the 'monopoly powers' which had effectively been granted when nationalisation took place. Clive Collier notes that the work was mainly undertaken because those in need found it hard to gain the required capital contribution and revenue guarantees; the effect of the Government's 'stop-go' behaviour during the post-war period. As most capital was given to areas where high numbers of people would benefit, small rural communities were overlooked. The Council worked to their statutory role of providing 'fairness and social justice', ensuring that the Standard Commercial Block Tariff was modified in 1953 for churches and village halls. They also tried to bring in a fairer system for old people's homes and other institutions.[376] The Wiltshire Joint Planning Committee was noting in 1946 that the war had brought with it an expansion of electricity supplies in the county[377] but in rural areas the Electricity Boards often had to balance their statutory duty of supply with the changes to the landscape they brought with it. Avebury (now a World Heritage Site) had its electricity supplied via the local garage proprietor, supplying 230 volts DC to the village population of 79. Overhead lines were used which ran via any possible means of support such as telegraph poles or trees. The Ministry of Works Ancient Monuments Division had not allowed the Wessex Company to supply the village in 1946, stating that it would need to be brought in underground at the company's expense. This was still the case in 1949, although now the Rural District Council had agreed to overhead lines but the County Planning Authority still wanted the work done underground. Many interested parties, such as the National Trust and the Ministry of Fuel and Power had a say in the negotiations. After five years of ruminating, the cables were positioned overhead along the line of the road.[378] The Wiltshire Joint Planning Committee were wanting electricity cables to be placed underground as much as possible within the confines of villages, but 'in view of the technical and financial difficulties which it is known will confront the electricity undertakers in adopting this policy, no action be taken except to continue to press for cables to be placed underground in places of special importance.'[379]

The Labour Shortage

T HE 40,000 DISPLACED persons in the country now came under the heading 'European Volunteer Workers', many of whom were Poles, drafted in from the Polish Resettlement Corps.[380] On 5 September 1946 the Wiltshire Constabulary were being advised that the Polish Air Force would be taking over the air base at Castle Combe, totalling approximately 1,300 men. They were to come under the auspices of the Polish Resettlement Scheme. The Constabulary was to be advised whenever Polish troops were moving, including one of the Infantry Battalions and Field Ambulance Units at Tilshead, again in September 1946. Approximately

5,600 Polish troops were due to arrive in the county during the second half of the year. Brigadier Watkins of Southern Command was reporting in a letter of 15 May 1948 that the Polish Resettlement Scheme was winding down. Its job had been to 'afford officers and men a period of not more than two years in which to get resettled into civil life, either in this country or abroad.' Almost 13,000 Polish Resettlement Corps Officers had already been demobilized into civilian life with a further 7,000 to follow by the end of 1948. It was estimated that 10,000 dependants would also be making their permanent home in the country, some arriving in Wiltshire in the autumn of 1946 in 'distressing circumstances.'[381] Robin and Heather Tanner of Kington Langley had taken in a Jewish German refugee in April 1939. After the war he trained as a teacher and his bilingual skills came into use at the newly established School for the Children of Volunteer Workers from Eastern Europe and the Baltic states at Hawthorn near Corsham.[382]

Harry Hopkins reports that many Eastern Europeans arrived in Britain to do domestic service, 'bridging the gap' that had appeared during the war. By 1956 the Hungarian community in Britain was six times as large as it had been before the war[383] but the housing situation was causing conflict. The National Federation of Building Trades Operatives (Swindon) were writing to Swindon Borough Council on 24 March 1955 regarding the Poles, stating that 'whilst we welcome close integration of these people into civic life, we are disturbed that local press reports may be taken to infer that some special priority is to be given them in the matter of housing.' They were also worried about local and London overspill applicants also adding to housing pressure,[384] Swindon being classed by the Government as an overspill town in the 1950s.[385] The Local Authority felt for Polish families, but equally for non-resident workers in Swindon as they could not find accommodation. They felt that the Polish were a national problem and that Government assistance should be provided. By March 1955 the newspapers were insinuating that 'some special priority is to be given to the provision of housing accommodation for Polish families.' The Clerk of Swindon Borough Council was quick to point out: 'Whatever may have given rise to such inference is certainly not founded on fact and you may accept my assurance that there is no intention to give any priority to the detriment of the housing of the other classes of housing applicants for which my authority is responsible.'[386] Jamaicans began arriving in Britain in the early 1950s and by 1956 annual immigration from the Caribbean had reached 26,000. Their arrival coincided with a time of acute house shortages.[387] The Government brought in the British Nationality Act of 1948 to re-affirm its place as head of a Commonwealth structure that was changing. An unexpected result was the arrival of the Windrush from Jamaica in June with 495 immigrants on board. The Government began to look at the issue by buck passing.[388] David Kynaston feels the Government were not overly concerned, especially as over 51,000 white European Voluntary Workers were already placed in the agricultural sector,[389] although Peter Hennessy notes that the Colonial Office had been calling it a 'disaster'.[390] A petition was sent to Attlee by 11 MPs asking for controls on immigration to be set if it became necessary,[391] but the post-war migration from the

Caribbean to the British Isles that began with the Windrush continued, remaining constant at around 1,200 per annum until 1951 when it rose to 2,200.[392]

One émigré came to live in the UK from Jamaica in 1956, settling in Trowbridge. He remembers that he and the other Jamaican workers were paid at a lower rate than white men doing the same work. The Trade Union supported the immigrants in getting equal pay for their labour. He recalls that although the employers wanted black workers, they felt that 'Caribbean workers always should be lower than the English'.[393] Another came to the UK in 1956 to find work in response to advertisements for people to leave Jamaica and fill jobs in the UK. His first problem on arrival was finding somewhere to stay and he was keen to move to better accommodation as he was sharing one room with five other men. However his search for rooms in Trowbridge was not successful. He came to an address in Poultney [Poulton] Lane in Bradford on Avon where his friend used to be lodging, but had moved on. He knocked at the door and an 'English' lady opened it. '... she said I won't have no more of you lot in here.' Some other friends were also living at the address and threatened to move out unless she acquiesced. 'So it was a bit, really difficult and [in] that room where we used to live there was 6 of us living in there, so it was really, really bad.'[394]

Born in Jamaica, Hugh grew up with his father and siblings helping on his father's farm and then working at a sugar factory until he came to Trowbridge in 1961. He moved to the UK for work in response to appeals in Jamaica for workers from Commonwealth countries to help rebuild the country after the Second World War. 'Jamaica been ruled by the British for three hundred and six years, we were part of the old commonwealth system, you know the old colonial rule. And we were told that British, that England is the mother country, so that's why we were all invited here after the world, the second war, to come and help, back, to build Britain back....So that's why so many of us came here because we were all invited. In Jamaica, every travel service you go, we didn't have television like we do here you know, no it was radio, it was advertising on the radio, how many jobs in England, . . . fifteen thousand people needed for trains, buses whatever have you [sic]. So they need us to come here to fill all those gaps you see and that's why so many, so many, of us came here.'[395]

Many local people in Wiltshire appear to have viewed the system for housing allocation as unjust. The prefabs built for EKCO workers near Malmesbury were given to the Local Authority after the war. Although they were for the use of townspeople too, EKCO could continue to place their workers in any prefabs which became available and from the townspeople's point of view, this was queue jumping. They called the site 'tin town'.[396] Cricklade Parish Council was among those who were very keen for new houses to be built in their area. In April 1946 they were writing to the Clerk of the Cricklade and Wootton Bassett Rural District Council to inform him of a motion that had been passed at their recent meeting, 'That an appeal be made to the Rural District Council to requisition land for a housing scheme at Cricklade, which is in need of houses, and that we may have a reply to discuss at our next meeting.' By October 1947 they were voicing strong opposition to delays, registering their disgust to the Rural District Council Clerk at the way in which tenants were allocated houses and the slow progress of completion, 'whether for Blakehill persons or the many other applicants,' and that there were more deserving cases than houses.[397] The Cricklade and Wootton Bassett Rural District Council were explaining themselves to the Chippenham MP David Eccles in July 1950 over their housing policy for the Blakehill site.

'When the huts at Blakehill were ready for occupation they were allocated in the usual way and at that time it was decided that the families thus housed should be considered to have been housed. It was never the position that they should be put into Blakehill until such time as the Council houses were built, and they could then move into Council houses.

Many of the families applying for huts at Blakehill were unsuccessful, and the Council are working through their list and housing the applicants as premises become available.

All applications are dealt with scrupulously and allocations made with a full knowledge of all the circumstances at the time of allocations.

There is no favouritism, as is alleged, and a very large percentage of the people in need of houses accept this.'[398]

Various types of industry such as engineering firms, public transport, utility companies as well as the Police and Fire Services were all wanting priority for housing. The style of their correspondence to the Local Authority is very telling; pointing to how public services would be brought to a halt if housing was not provided, including a letter from the Ministry of Fuel and Power to the Swindon Borough Clerk in June 1949. 'It is not necessary for me to emphasize the extreme importance of the grid system and general progress to industry in general...'[399] The British Electricity Authority was also adamant in February 1949, writing to the Clerk of Swindon. 'In making this request I have in mind the absolute necessity of the provision and maintenance of the supply of electricity without which all other industries, and indeed many public services, are brought to a standstill.' The Chief Constable was writing to the Clerk of Swindon Borough Council in January 1946. '... it is not only impossible to house these police officers but also to post Police Officers to localities where their services are particularly needed, owing to lack of houses in that locality. I would point out that these Officers for whom I am asking for houses are all returned or returning ex-service men and are therefore in exactly the same category as other returned service men from whom you have received application... proper and adequate policing is essential for the welfare of the community.' By May it appears that further explanation was necessary. 'The secretary of State for Home Affairs has represented to the Minister the importance from the point of view of securing an efficient police service of adequate housing accommodation being available for members of the Police Force...' 'In view of the present increase in crime and the impossibility of posting Police Officers to the localities (which include Swindon) in which the major part of the crime is being committed...'[400] Firemen complained bitterly that the Police were given priority, refuted by the Clerk. The firemen gained the support of the Fire Brigade's Union and Swindon Trade Council and by May 1947 the Fire Force Commander of the National Fire Service Area HQ at Highworth was stating in a letter to the Clerk of Swindon Borough Council that many of his officers were 'separated from their wives and families and [were] unable to enjoy the usual amenities of the civilian… in the majority of cases these are men returning to the Fire Service from H.M. Armed Forces.' Twelve were in 'dire need of housing.' The Council's reply in June 1947 was that their waiting list numbered over 3,000 with some already waiting several years.[401]

A meeting was held on 29 November 1946 regarding houses for Vickers Armstrong workers. It was reported that Swindon Borough Council expected to be in the position of having 50 'Howard' type houses, 142 B.I.S.F. (British Iron and Steel Federation) type houses, both now termed as 'non-standard construction' properties, and 100 permanent houses. A further 200 temporary houses would be in place by February 1948. It was noted that no further B.I.S.F houses would be allocated and 'the prospects [of obtaining] were very small for all other types of houses for Urban Authorities, with exception of the Airey type house (of prefabricated reinforced concrete, hence the term 'prefab', for temporary use only), the supply of which would be unlimited during the next year, and may possibly be offered to Urban Authorities because of this fact.' There followed a discussion on temporary aluminum bungalows, which the Housing Officer was against due to:

1. Costly production.
2. The flow and interference with other types of houses.
Its construction.
Aluminum was in short supply, as was the steel which would replace the aluminum.
Floor accommodation was sub standard.

Reasons for the B.I.S.F type of bungalow were as follows:

1. There is room for expansion in production of this type of house.
Little skilled labour is needed for either production or erection.
It makes full use of factory labour, during the change over from war to peace.[401a]

It was noted that the situation in the Highworth Rural District area was just as bad as Swindon's, 'with great concern over clearance etc. and [it was] wondered if it was better… to view Blakehill Army Camp which consists of 175 huts which were on the water, sewer, and electric light and may be possible for conversion into housing accommodation for Vickers Armstrong Co., it was agreed by various officials concerned that arising from the discussion on the matter this was the only bright spot of the evening, that the Vickers Armstrong Co., could look immediately into the position at Blakehill and possibly arrange for immediate use by conversion of 150 Army Huts.'[401b] As has been seen, Blakehill near Cricklade

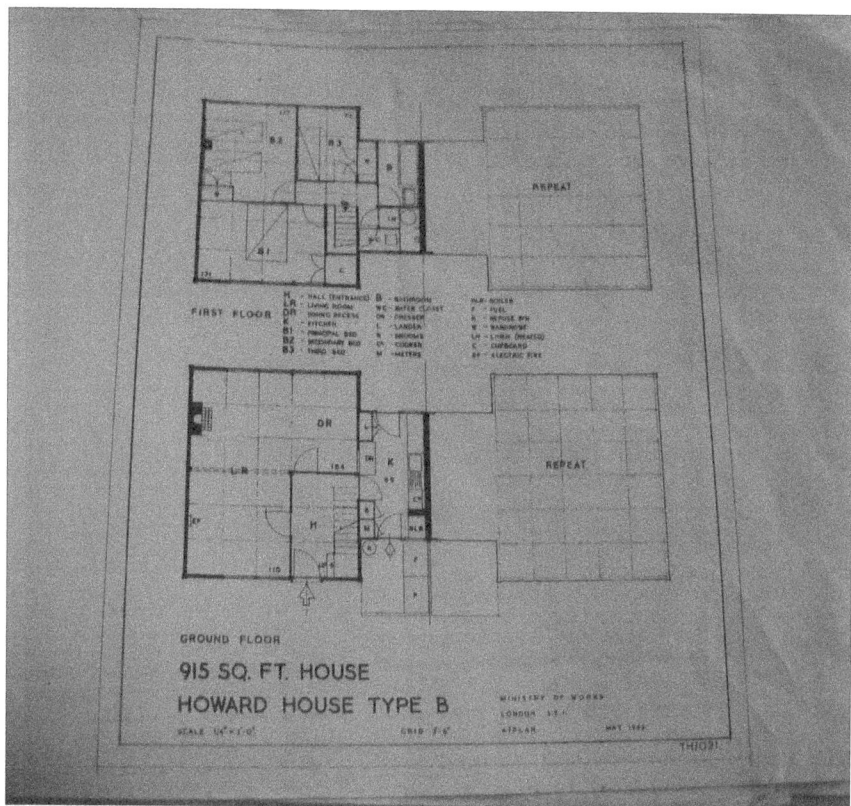

Plan of a Howard House Type B by the Ministry of Works, May 1945 (WSA G24/132/333)

was utilitsed as temporary housing and in fact the site was still in use by the RAF at this time.

The B.I.S.F type house has stood the test of time, with many still in use today. Unlike the prefabricated designs such as the Airey, which is classed as defective under the Housing Defects Act of 1984,[401c] the B.I.S.F. houses are not defective and are viewed by some as 'one of the most successful and sound buildings of post war construction'.[402] The Howard House is also not classed as defective under the Housing Defects Act.

By June 1951 the Central Ammunition Depot (CAD) were still looking at housing for their civilian workforce at Corsham who were in need. 'We have been notified by the War Office that the Ministry of Local Government & Planning is prepared to make an allocation to your Council of 50 non-traditional houses and that it remains for your council to allocate these 50 houses between essential W.D. civilians and occupants of hutted camps. Further, it is within the discretion of your Council to issue, out of the 50 houses allocated, 10 for erection under licence by private individuals, and essential W.D. employees will be permitted to make application.' The CAD had some individuals in mind.[403]

On the whole, it does appear that the Local Authorities were trying to adhere to the system and 'play fair', but the number of cases was overwhelming. There were voices, such as those in Swindon Borough Council, who wanted to obtain a certain type of tenant for hutted accommodation. They 'should be occupied by a type of tenant who can be relied upon to take special care of the property otherwise serious maintenance costs will rapidly be incurred.'[404]

No. 5 Site 4,
Blakehill, Cricklade,
Nr. Swindon,
Wilts.

17th May, 1950.

Dear Sir,

I wish to bring to your notice the unfairness, by which the Cricklade and Wootton Bassett Rural District Council has allocated the 14 new houses at the Village of Leigh.

The most glaring case is that of allocating one to a councillors daughter who is not yet married. Surely, Sir, there are more deserving cases in the district. The unofficial excuse being given by councillors is "That the couple would have been married a year ago had their mother in laws let them live with them" If all young couples wishing to get married are given a house on such a poor excuse, it will be years before couples with families get houses. There are people living in these Nissen Huts at Blakehill, with 2, 3 and 4 children in overcrowded conditions, surely one of these families should have been rehoused and let the young married couple have a hut. Another case is a young couple with one child, already living in a bungalow, and not under notice to quit, has been allocated one, again this is causing a lot of unrest in the district.

When we took these Nissen Huts at Blakehill, 3 years ago we were told we should be rehoused as and when new houses were built, so far only one family has be rehoused by the Council, and that on medical grounds. Surely the Council could start rehousing now. Whilst some of the families that have been allocated houses at the Leigh are genuine cases, most of them refused to live in these Huts at Blakehill. The view held by Blakehill residents is that we should be rehoused, and other families moved to the Huts, and rehoused in rotation. I may add that I wrote to the Cricklade and Wootton Bassett Council about this matter on the 20th April, but have not had a reply. I should be glad if you will take this matter up with the Council to ensure that future allocation of houses are more fair than has been up to the present.

Yours truly,

Letter from a resident at Blakehill Camp in May 1950 commenting on the perceived unfairness of housing allocation. Cricklade & Wootton Bassett RDC stood by their system (WSA G4/132/20)

In 1944 Churchill had promised the British population that half a million new prefabs would be built[405] and in Wiltshire by April 1944 the Local Authority had been busy designating sites in accordance with Circular 7 issued by the Ministry of Town and Country Planning. The new sites would be required to 'fit into a neighbourhood unit' and would not jeopardise any future planning policy. Approximately 67 towns and villages were earmarked for new housing.[406] The number of prefabs built countrywide between 1945 and 1949 was 156,623. Some people felt they looked very ugly, like pigsties or hen houses, but others appreciated the modern conveniences; fixed bath, hot water on tap, a refrigerator and a garden.[407]

One resident at Blakehill initially had no choice but to share a house in Swindon, the only place where rooms were available. She and her family had to share with two other families; kitchen and toilet. There was no bathroom. When they were finally allocated their hut at Blakehill it was '... like a palace to us'.[408] Another family at Blakehill also had a very different experience. Margaret Monk, still resident in Wiltshire today, was born at the Blakehill Camp in 1948. 'When there was such a shortage of accommodation after WWII, several large employers in the area (eg Vickers Armstrong, GWR, Plessey) were allocated some of the housing units for their workers'. The Nissen huts had became available when RAF Blakehill was closed as a full-time airfield at the end of the war and the huts were converted by the Swindon Borough Council:

'Mum and Dad moved to Site 6 Blakehill during 1947, and were thrilled to have their own place and privacy. Like many other young couples, having their own front door key was very precious. Some couples had been living in very cramped shared accommodation which was quite grim.

The Nissen hut was cosy, and had red flag stone floors which Mum polished proudly. When her mother came to visit from Birmingham, wondering what to expect in the middle of a field, she was quite impressed! Mum always spoke fondly of Blakehill days, which sounded like the happiest time of her life.'[409]

Aneurin Bevan, responsible for both health and housing, disliked prefabs and wanted to build permanent homes of a high standard.[410] He did, however, agree to the permanent non-standard construction type buildings that were of the British Steel design and also traditional permanent houses.[411] A Government circular of 31 March 1947 found in the records of Devizes Rural District Council stated that: 'The widest possible publicity should be given to the 'Airey' house, which is designed, and is especially suitable for, erection in rural areas. Stocks of the component parts are immediately available, and the average cost is less than most prefabricated houses, despite the fact that it is a permanent structure. It has the advantage of speedy construction, with the minimum of semi-skilled labour.'[412] Airey houses were being pushed at a Ministry of Health Conference in April 1947, reported by the Wiltshire Branch of the Rural District Councils' Association. It was noted at the conference that 93% of Rural District Councils had begun building new houses and were 'ahead of all other types of Local Authorities.' It was noted that one in every three houses built in rural areas in the next 18 months would need to be an Airey house, and RDCs were urged to apply for them, with 6,000 at present still unallocated. By 1950 Cricklade and Wootton Bassett RDC were being told by the Costain Concrete Co. Ltd. that under the new Ministry of Health Scheme they had a panel of builders in the Southern Area of England who would erect Airey houses at a cost of £1,250.[413]

By the end of 1945 the production of prefabs was gaining momentum and by 1948 nearly 125,000 had been erected,[414] all equipped with the latest mod. cons. The British Electrical Development Association was certainly on the case with their *Electric Kitchen Plans for Low Cost Post War Hom*es. On the inside cover was a view of their modern dining-kitchen with a quote from Lord Woolton, Minister of Reconstruction, February 1944. 'In our plans for the post-war world we expect to make great strides to ensure that electricity will be generally available.... Let scientific application be used to reduce domestic labour, waste and bad living conditions. The house, which for the poorer people has so often been a matter of domestic drudgery, can by the use of science be made into a place where a woman has leisure and pleasure. I believe a nation of our great manufacturing capacity can produce labour-saving devices in bulk and at standards and prices within the reach of the mass of people.'[415] The *Salisbury and Winchester Journal* was reporting in its 16 April 1944 edition that women should take a greater role in the planning of houses. Speaking at a lecture arranged by the Salisbury Diocesan Training College, Mr A. C. Townsend F.R.I.B.A., Head of the School of Architecture at the Southern

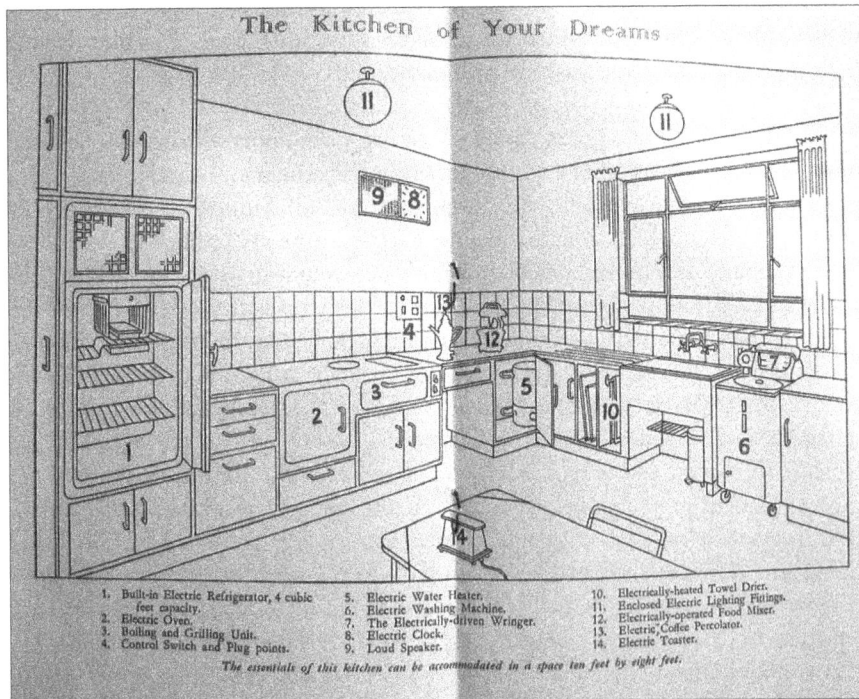

The Kitchen of Your Dreams

1. Built-in Electric Refrigerator, 4 cubic feet capacity.
2. Electric Oven.
3. Boiling and Grilling Unit.
4. Control Switch and Plug points.
5. Electric Water Heater.
6. Electric Washing Machine.
7. The Electrically-driven Wringer.
8. Electric Clock.
9. Loud Speaker.
10. Electrically-heated Towel Drier.
11. Enclosed Electric Lighting Fittings.
12. Electrically-operated Food Mixer.
13. Electric Coffee Percolator.
14. Electric Toaster.

The essentials of this kitchen can be accommodated in a space ten feet by eight feet.

The Post War 'Kitchen of Your Dreams' by BEAMA, c. 1944 (WSA G4/132/20)

College of Art, Winchester, spoke of the realisation that it would be '... much easier... to wash and cook in a kitchen which has modern equipment than in one that ha[d] no conveniences. We shall see great developments after the war, and no doubt many will be due to the increased interest which women are taking in the planning of their own homes...' The leaflet *A peep into the Future... everything for the electric home*, published by the British Electrical and Allied Manufacturers' Association *c.* 1944 asked the question 'What will our post-war homes be like?' The answer revealed the latest electric domestic appliances: the new electric cooker, refrigerator, oven, washing machine, vacuum cleaner, food mixer, toaster, coffee percolator and much more...[416] The *Wiltshire Times* was reporting on the Trowbridge Exhibition of Household Goods and Equipment arranged by Knees at the Red Hat Lane Showroom in its 16 November 1946 edition. Included was a picture of a 'modern kitchen,' fully equipped. The mid to late 1950s saw the proportion of people owning fridges rising from 6 to 16% and washing machines from 25% to 44%.[417]

The Minister of Agriculture was present at the Ministry of Health conference in April 1947, stating that there were not enough houses available for agricultural workers. He could not agree that '... houses to be provided for agricultural workers should be inferior to those provided for the urban population'.[418] There was still a need for more housing for agricultural workers in the post-war period. The National Farmers Union Wiltshire County Branch was stating in April 1947 that '... the acute shortage of housing accommodation for agricultural workers has been giving the Agricultural industry considerable anxiety for some years. It has been established beyond doubt that one of the principal factors in alleviating the present very acute food position is a more adequate supply of permanent British Agricultural labour. In this connection, the most serious limiting factor is the grossly inadequate housing situation.'[419]

But housing, whatever its style or purpose, was often delayed. Labour shortages also created problems. There was a post-war shortage of both skilled and unskilled labour.[420] The pre-war labour force of one million in the building industry had been reduced to 340,000, most of whom were working on the bomb damaged housing of the South East. Many more were still being retained in the forces or factories.[421] On 27 March 1947 Swindon's Borough Surveyor was reporting the use of POWs for the development of the town's housing sites since the 'inceptions of the Post War Housing Scheme.' He felt it unlikely that the POWs would be available for much longer.[422] By the end of 1947 *c.* 25,000 German POWs had been repatriated[423] and although in 1948 some POWs remained in Britain, this former large workforce would need to be replaced.[424] Aneurin Bevan attempted to speed up the demobilisation process for key building workers[425] but to help combat labour shortages and to try to get building projects started where they were most needed the Government rationed the right to use building labour and materials with the introduction of Building Licences and Industrial Development Certificates.[426] The use of these controls was tightened in 1947 to curb excess demand from the previous two years.[427] The need for Labour Permits was the cause of a meeting in 1945 between the Ministry of Health and a Swindon delegation.[428] Plans for housing development in 1945 had also met with delays due to the necessity of a Housing Census and Building Applications. A letter from the Ministry of Health on 17 January 1948 to the Clerk at the Cricklade and Wootton Bassett Rural District Council regarding the housing programme stated that '... the amount of timber imported in 1948 will govern the number of houses which can be completed in 1949... in considering whether approval can be given to the commencement of houses in any particular area, regard must be had to the amount of work in hand in relation to available local resources. After careful consideration of the position in the Swindon zone it is not possible to agree to the commencement of erection of any traditional houses...' (temporary Airey houses were already allocated for the area).[429] Cricklade and Wootton Bassett RDC was bound by legislation such as the housing quota – in 1949 the Council had exhausted its quota of private enterprise licences for new homes and could not approve a site at Lydiard Millicent.[430] In some cases landowners slowed down the progress of post-war house building. Cricklade Parish Council were asking – why should 'two local landowners be allowed to hold up building houses here'?[431] However in October 1947 the Principal Officer at the Ministry of Health's Regional Offices in Bristol was writing to the Cricklade and Wootton Bassett Rural District Council as 'Very Urgent,' asking why delays were occurring with their house construction programme.[432]

In Swindon the continued acute shortage of housing meant that the council had powers to requisition any unoccupied property for emergency

POWs at Lypiatt, Corsham, post-war (WSA 3572/3)

housing purposes. The records of Swindon Borough Council held at the Wiltshire and Swindon History Centre contain letters notifying the council of unoccupied properties; the Council then investigated the case.⁴³³ The Council noted in a letter regarding one such property in April 1947 that '... the housing situation continues to be most difficult, and the Corporation are obliged to ensure that the best possible use is made of all existing accommodation.' But overcrowding continued to be an issue as unauthorised sub-letting was also taking place, driven by need, and as some felt, also by greed. A letter from a tenant to Swindon Borough Council in January 1948 gave an idea of the 'racket' that was unauthorised sub-letting. '[W]hy is this kind of thing allowed to continue...' and the difficulties of lodging: '... we would willingly go from here if there was any place available as it is far from pleasant living with this person...'⁴³⁴ Swindon Borough Council was doing its best to get houses built. By October 1945 they had arranged for 50 permanent Howard houses to be built with the Howard company all set to begin. On 20 October 1945 the Borough Surveyor was having no choice but to delay the work. He had applied for a sanction from the Government to obtain POW labour for the laying of the groundworks and foundations, necessary for a development of this size. 'The deputation was very surprised to be informed that at present, the Ministry could not give any sanction to the erection of the houses and were given to understand that there were some technical difficulties which the Ministry required overcoming before such sanction was given. Further, there appeared to be the question of the allocation of houses not being made until the requirements of all Local Authorities in England had been ascertained.' The Council then had to explain themselves to the Minister of Health. 'In view of the extreme urgency of alleviating the demand for housing accommodation in the borough, it was felt that if it were possible to arrange for the delivery and erection of a number of these houses before the end of the year, steps ought to be taken in that direction.' By 19 October 1945 representatives of Swindon Borough Council had gone to London for an interview at the Ministry of Health in which they 'emphasised the urgent need for labour permits regarding German Prisoner of War labour.' The official show house opening was finally possible by 30 April 1946 with the first keys being handed over in April.⁴³⁵

Cricklade and Wootton Bassett Rural District Council were also requesting that householders take in lodgers and in 1950 had produced a number of lists of council house tenants who were either living alone or with up to a couple of lodgers. One lady had made herself 'ill with worry' after she had received a letter from the Council telling her she must sub-let a room. She was almost 90 years old and did not feel able to have anyone stay in her house. A Purton resident also felt unable to take in lodgers due to her nerves. 'I have considered the matter many times and appreciate the fact that there are still 547 applicants for council houses.' Another lady from Wootton Bassett already had several married couples lodging with her, difficult as they needed to go through her living room to reach their sitting room. She was away from home from 8.30am to 4pm at work and could only really consider 'one business lady' who would work similar hours to herself. It was the Council's policy not to consider any applications for housing unless they had been on the housing 'file' for at least a year. It appears that applicants would have to wait a lot longer than that, as one lady at Cricklade was asking for help after having her name down for just over a year. 'Im living in a 2 berth Caravan, with no drainage, no fire, and no running water, I also have no room for to put the baby's cot, and I don't think it's right for me, and my husband to have him sleeping with us. I have 1 churn of water in two day's... I have to walk over a mile away, to get baby's washing done... the Welfare have been out and looked over the Caravan, & they said it was no place for a baby. My baby has been in hospital for a fortnight... and I brought him home, and he's not well again... It's even breaking up my marriage where I worry so much, & then take it out on my husband.'[436]

Government Ministers were expressing concern over the slow rate of house completion,[437][438] suggesting by 1952 that Local Authorities did not apply a continuous and uniform flow of work.[439] In January 1952 the Minister of Housing and Local Government was writing to Local Authorities imploring them to get houses completed more quickly. 'This is the greatest and the most pressing of our social needs today... House production must be increased as rapidly as the resources of material and labour will allow... It is my hope that your Council will do all you can to expedite the completion of houses now under construction or under tender. In addition, will you make the necessary plans for an expanding programme over the next three years?' What is striking is that two years earlier the very same Cricklade & Wootton Bassett RDC was in dispute over the housing allocation for 1951 with the local MP David Eccles getting involved. The Council desperately wanted to build more houses but could not do so as they had been given a 'nil' allocation. Eccles wrote from the House of Commons on 20 October 1950 that he was '... horrified at the Minister's attitude and [would] certainly do everything possible to get [the Council] an allocation.'[440] In 1955 Local Authorities were able to decide themselves how many houses they wanted to build (G4/132/14). The slowness of post-war housing projects did not only cause concern at a national level. Local Political Parties and Parish Councils also voiced their opinions.[441][442][443]

After a year in Government, Atlee's departments were

Letter regarding the slow progress of housing construction at the Rudloe Estate near Corsham, 1 August 1946 (WSA G3/132/3)

getting rather muddled over housing. *Picture Post* reported the issue.[444] The Chancellor of the Exchequer was responsible for providing the capital for the housing subsidies; the Minister of Works directed the building industry: builders, materials, the provision of temporary and permanent non-standard construction and traditional built homes; the Minister of Labour provided the workforce; the Minister of Town & Country Planning had the say over the siting of housing; the Minister of Agriculture became involved in rural housing; the Ministry of Supply was in charge of materials (there was a severe shortage); the President of the Board of Trade was asking questions and requiring forms to be filled in for those builders employing over 50 men and the Lord Privy Seal also played an unknown and rather obscure role... On top of this, the Local Authorities were the Government's eyes and ears on the ground, some having very limited experience of housing projects on such a scale as was needed. They were overwhelmed by the scale of correspondence coming out of Whitehall.[445] On 6 March 1947 the Regional Officer at the Ministry of Health in Bristol was writing to Swindon's Town Clerk about the possibility of obtaining Technical Assistants to help the Council in the preparation of their new housing schemes. 'It is regretted that the Ministry of Health is unable to loan technical assistants to the Council at the present time, and in fact it has been found impossible to recruit sufficient technical officers to satisfy this Department's own requirements, which have greatly increased because of the pressure of housing work.' The Ministry of Supply would be contacting the Council about their position.[446]

Peter Hennessy feels it is unlikely that any of the Government measures such as the Industrial Development Certificate or Building Licence preference would have been possible if not for the acceptance of control during the climate of total war and the effects felt in its aftermath.[448]

Interestingly, new housing estates in towns also appear to have had problems regarding a lack of local amenities in the immediate post-war period. No shops were allowed to be built, the emphasis being on building houses only.[448] Some newcomers to villages complained they had to walk five

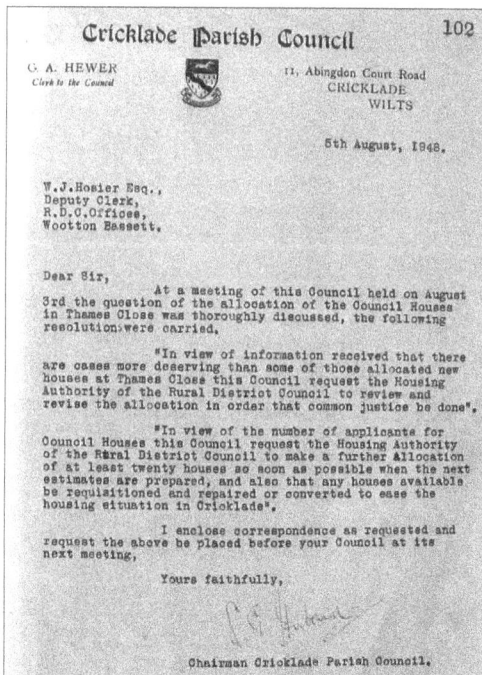

Letter from Cricklade Parish Council to the Deputy Clerk of the Cricklade and Wootton Bassett RDC in August 1948 asking for more houses (WSA G4/132/21)

miles to the shops[449] and a Presbytery in Swindon had parishioners scattered over the district. They wanted to build a church hall.[450]

What is apparent is that the conflict over housing during wartime continued and even strengthened during the immediate post-war years, especially regarding sub-letting and housing allocation.[451] Wartime military use caused post-war conflict, such as in Lyneham, where the Parish Council felt that they should have been getting more houses as the Air Ministry had pulled some down.[452] There was also a great deal of unrest with the quality and condition of housing, mainly from those living in the old military camps and even between camps.[453]

It was known that the hutments which were built or turned into living accommodation were only ever meant to be temporary with a short lifespan, but as the years went by it became evident that health issues would arise from their use. In February 1959 the Medical Officer of Health for the North Wiltshire area was writing to the Clerk of the Calne and Chippenhm Rural District Council about the Corsham Married Quarters Site 1A:

'Further to my certificate dated 15 Jan 1959 concerning the above, I have enclosed details of medical certificates I have received in recent years from Local Medical Practitioners in respect of the occupants of these properties.

The summary, I think, makes it clear that there has been a considerable amount of illness associated with these bungalows.' It was stated that 33% of the total of 106 dwellings had been associated with illness such as bronchitis.[454]

A husband was writing to the Calne and Chippenham RDC in December 1949 about the ill health of his wife at Hardenhuish Camp. 'I wonder if it is plausible for your council to fix another water point near the top end of the camp where we live, my wife suffers much ill health, & her Dr says she had not to exert herself, twice this year she has been in Royal United Bath for operation for her health, my wife finds it to much carrying water all that distance especially when I am at work [sic]…'[455]

	Nature of Illness	Date of Med.Certificate.
WARD ROAD		
1.	Paralysis of legs & bladder trouble.	10. 5. 56.
8.	Chr.Bronchitis.	1.11. 52.
WELLER ROAD		
1.	Naso-Pharyngitis & Tonsillitis	12.12. 53
4.	Chr. Bronchitis	21. 9. 57
13.	Haemosiderosis (not T.B.)	2. 5. 58
1	Pulmonary Tuberculosis	27. 7. 51
17.	Lumbago & Fibrositis	1953
21.	Chr. Bronchitis & Catarrh	9. 6. 58
14.	Respiratory Infection	12. 6. 57
27.	Pulmonary Tuberculosis	22. 1. 57
43.	Bronchitis	?
49.	Rheumatism & Bronchitis	17. 3. 58
53.	Pulmonary Tuberculosis	23. 9. 54
TUPMAN ROAD.		
2	Chr. Bronchitis & Asthma	22.11. 51
OTHER AVENUE		
2.	Fibrositis	15.12. 53
3.	Epilepsy	4. 2. 56
5.	Pulmonary Tuberculosis	12.10. 55
8.	Asthma	?
9.	Raynaud's Disease, Bronchitis & Fibrositis.	20. 3. 54
11.	Chr. Bronchitis	5. 9. 50
20.	Chr. Bronchitis	?
22.	Rheumatic Fever & Fibrositis	20. 3. 51
24.	Pneumonia & Bronchitis.	21. 3. 54

Health Certificates relating to the Corsham Married Quarters site (WSA G3/132/64)

A mother with her two children moved into a disused war-time day nursery in Malmesbury St. Paul Without in August 1946 due to the overcrowding in the property they were living in beforehand. There were ten people sharing a two bedroom house which consisted of a living room, kitchen, two bedrooms and an attic.[456] It appears the premises had been adapted by the council, although a letter from the Ministry of Health to the Clerk of the Malmesbury RDC (the Principal Housing Officer of the Ministry of Health in Bristol had submitted proposals for the site in February) suggests that they felt it was not wholly adequate. 'The layout of the huts makes it difficult to create a reasonable number of self-contained dwellings at low cost or with the economic use of labour and materials. Moreover, it is unlikely that the converted premises would remain acceptable to tenants for any long period, and the cost of maintenance would be high.' It was not only the Ministry of Health that was concerned. The owner of The Priory had written to Malmesbury RDC in September 1945 raising concern over the site which had been his but which had been requisitioned 'very much against my will, in full view of The Priory.' He wanted the council to buy his house, garden and garage as 'I cannot expect to sell the house (which I am trying to do) with such a hideous erection which completely dominates the view...'[457]

One resident of an ex-US Nissen hut at Dinton described the conditions. 'There was no heating, no lighting and no water available. The Council agreed at a later date (for a small rental charge) to modernise the huts, and consequently five inner walls were constructed to make them habitable, with two bedrooms, a kitchen with a sink and cold tap, a bathroom with zinc bath and cold tap, and an old-fashioned grate and oven, set in the centre of the hut. To complete the happy abode, there was an outside toilet.' She recalls the flimsiness of the walls, especially during one gale. 'That night, with only two layers of galvanised tin overhead, we really thought we were going to be carried away!' She did have some happy times there, but the medical condition of her family was a constant worry. 'My one big fear had always been keeping healthy, but we managed... My daughters had the usual children's' ailments, including my elder daughter developing a 'touch of pneumonia' (as the doctor termed it)... He told me to try and keep the temperature between 60° and 65° - yes in a Nissen hut with two layers of tin, and in the winter, icicles hanging from the roof! We had to keep the fire grate burning night and day – but we survived.'[458] One resident of Blakehill also remembered the cold. 'To keep warm we'd get the turf from outside, and, once we'd got the fire going, burn that on top day and night to keep it in. Even though our hut was cold, it was our own place and we did the best we could with it.'[459] One Blakehill boy recalls his surprise at the conditions at the Blakehill site. 'During 1947, our 'home fit for heroes' became available at Site 6, but was not as grand as I'd expected. The rain used to make a terrific noise on the Nissen hut roof, and I remember having to run from the bath to the range before I froze to death, trying not to slip on the bakelite-type floor!'[460] Interestingly, Salisbury and Wilton Rural District Council had been discussing the standard of prefabricated housing in 1944, which was reported in the 9 June edition of the *Salisbury and Winchester*

Journal. One member had visited an experimental 'make-shift' model emergency house on exhibition in London and although the appearance was commendable, steel sprayed with a grey asbestos substance to make it appear like stone, he had come back seriously unimpressed. '... the paint already beginning to show signs of wear... The ventilation was poor and the fittings in the kitchen needed adjustment...' He thought the project had been an 'extravagant experiment; they estimated it would last ten years... He would not, himself, he said, like to live in it during its second and third years' and thought it not worth the money.

Hutted accommodation at Westbury, reproduced by kind permission of Ivan Clark (WSHC P54000)

The need for a review of hutted accommodation was understood by Local Authorities but the housing shortage meant that its life had to be extended. One tenant commented on Swindon Borough Council's plans to extend the life of her bungalow in 1950, saying they '...practically condemn them and on the other hand prolong their life. The first essential of living accommodation is damp proof. How could the Council do it if they have the health of people at heart?' However, it is interesting to note that she was one of only 34 tenants to reply to a survey sent out to 540 at the Moredon Estate in 1950, all of which were complaints.[461] The Principal Regional Officer of the Ministry of Local Government and Planning in Bristol was writing to the Clerks of the District Councils regarding hutted accommodation on 19 September 1951. 'Many Local Authorities are faced with the problem of camp hutments which are prone to progressive deterioration... it is in some cases essential to give a measure of priority to the re-housing of families whose camp accommodation is likely soon to become uninhabitable.'[462] By 21 October 1949 the Clerk of Cricklade and Wootton Bassett Rural District Council was writing to the Ministry of Health Regional Offices in Bristol about the huts at Paul's Croft Camp, Cricklade and Cove House Camp, Ashton Keynes. The Council was of the opinion that 'in both these cases it would be better in the long run to erect houses to rehouse these tenants, than to spend further money on repairs...'[463] A local MP was writing to the Salisbury and Wilton Rural District Council in April 1948 regarding the accommodation at the Shute End Squatters' Camp, Alderbury. The roofs had been tarred but 'much of the tar was coming through some of the cracks, and was dripping on the floor, and in some instances on the beds and bedding... Apparently, now that it has rained, the huts are leaking badly, and I do think they need further investigation, as they are not really fit for habitation unless something is done...' He had already written to the Clerk on 10 February 1948 regarding repairs that needed doing. The agent of the Earl of Radnor, owner of the site, had visited to see if there was anything they could do, but it was noted that the land had been requisitioned. The issue of alternative accommodation was mentioned for what he termed the 'inmates.' He was 'well aware of the fact that the District Council knows only too well the sad state of housing in Wiltshire, and also that their hands are entirely tied by the elimination of building as imposed by the Minister of Health at the present time.'[464]

But it wasn't just the prefabs... In April 1947 a demobbed serviceman was living in a condemned house in Ashton Keynes as he could find no other accommodation:

> ...part of the roof has fallen in, and the only thing the Landlord have done is to put a piece of tin over it but the rain still comes in. And the floor in the kitchen is like a springe the water comes up from the floor when it is raining, now the rain is coming in on our bed [sic]. We have got a young baby 19 months old and my wife is expecting a baby in July... I got called up in Sept. 39 I had a house but when I was away a few months it was given up and I have had to live in a condemned house. I have been wondering since I have been home what we were fighting for, it is plain to see that the ones that stopped [are] better off...[465]

Another lady was writing about the cottage she was renting with her husband, an agricultural worker, in Castle Combe in August 1951:

> I am sorry to trouble you as I know you are very busy, but our cottage is got in such a terrible state & we can get nothing done about it from the owner... We are nine in family (10 most weekends). The oven in my range split from top to bottom 6 weeks ago, I have neither been able to roast or bake since. The boiler has a hole in the bottom & I can't manage without that.
>
> I have no decent window in the house, as all the leads are rotted, I can't even get a new lavatory bucket which ran out several weeks ago, & I reported it to the Sanitary Inspector; and the floors & walls are really awful. I want to get it distempered & painted but the walls in the front room are so bad it is not worth spending the money on...

I would be grateful if you could get something done for us, or we shall have to move from here, as the house is in such a state, no one else would live here and my husband does not want to leave his job if he can help it.[466]

State here your National Registration No. (as shown on your Identity Card)

You are on the .... CRICKLADE & WOOTTON BASSETT RURAL DISTRICT .... Council's list of applicants for housing accommodation. The list is being reviewed at the request of the Ministry of Health.

DO YOU WISH TO REMAIN ON THE LIST?

Answer Yes or No ....

Signature ....

Date ....

This form should be refolded and returned to the Council. Postage need not be prepaid.

You may receive more than one copy of this form. If you do, please fill in and return each of them.

If this form is not returned WITHIN 14 DAYS, it will be assumed that you no longer wish to remain on the list.

Local Authority's Housing Reference No. (If any)

FOR OFFICIAL USE

Form to remain on the Cricklade and Wootton Bassett Rural District Council housing list, c. 1949 (WSA G4/132/1)

Many of Wiltshire's Parish Councils desperately wanted houses in the immediate post war period, but by the 1960s the situation had changed. The Parish Council of Blunsdon St. Andrew was protesting fiercely over the proposed use of the former squatter camp as a caravan park. They wrote to the Council for Europe Consultative Assembly, Strasbourg, over the issue.[467] Kington Langley Parish Council was protesting over planned housing development by the early 1960s.[468]

Instability… and Celebration

B Y THE LATE 1940s an International Gallup Poll showed that 58% of under 30s would emigrate if they were 'free to do so'.[469] The percentage for the population as a whole who would choose to emigrate was 42%, compared to 19% of all people at the immediate end of the war.[470] Mass Observation had been undertaking a study during wartime regarding the kind of reconstruction people wanted after the war compared with what they expected to get. They wished the post-war world would be the age for 'equality of opportunity, better housing and education, socialism, security, abolition of unemployment' and the idea of planned redevelopment.[471] One Trowbridge man was looking optimistically towards the development of his town after the war. He wrote to the *Wiltshire Times*, published on 24 July 1943, hoping that there would be a 'People's Theatre for the development of the arts and music: a Youth Centre, wider recreational facilities, including a well-planned shopping centre… to make Trowbridge a better and brighter place for the workers, their wives, and families.' The Beveridge Report brought hope, but with hope came fears; that the experiences of the period immediately following the Great War would come again. Five people were feeling pessimistic for every optimist member of society.[472] As in the summer of 1939, there was a marriage boom once the war was over.[473]

By the summer of 1946 there was a general feeling that the cooperative working which had taken place during wartime was unravelling. There was little sense of stability or meaning in the post-war world. It was reported that a crime wave had engulfed the country at the end of 1945 which continued into 1946, especially for burglary.[474] In 1951 crime reached its peak with 524,000 indictable cases reported,[475] and the topic was proving an emotive one,[476] although the threat of crime was not as real as the newspaper headlines led its readership to believe.[477]

The bleak winter of early 1947 made evident the ongoing weariness of the British population. The song *Open the Door, Richard* of March 1947 became synonymous with the restrictions of daily life in the immediate post-war period.[478] One consolation was the pre-war Holidays with Pay Act which over half the population made use of to take a week's break away from home.[479] The onset of the Cold War in 1947/8 affected the mood of the people, but also the Government's relationship with them. In May 1947 the Prime Minister Clement Attlee chaired a Special Cabinet Committee on 'subversive activities', culminating in the systematic investigation of Civil Servants, with Communists dismissed from public office and academic posts.[480]

Not everything was as bleak as it seemed. The post-war period brought with it the revival of team sports to local communities and local teams such as Cricklade Football Club which had been suspended during the wartime period.[481] The 6 July 1946 edition of the *Wiltshire Times* was reporting the efforts of Wiltshire's County Football Association to reinstate matches during their first meeting since 1940. They were struggling with a shortage of referees and there was also a shortage of playing equipment. It was thought the coupons for the purchase of kit could be obtained via the English Football Association and advised all Wiltshire clubs to look into the matter. The *Wiltshire Times'* 7 September 1946 edition noted the beginning of the football season with a 'fine start' by Trowbridge. Enthusiastic football fans turned out in their thousands, including 1,000 alone for the Chippenham v Bristol Rovers' Reserves. Cricklade Town Hall was also well used after the war for concerts, dances and film shows, continuing to boost morale as they had done during the war. Times had changed, however, and the old pre-war ball dances were once again resurrected, but not just for those who had the money to afford them; they were open to all.[482]

The Festival of Britain was held in 1951, a means of celebrating a Britain which had survived to become a successful, settled society. It was based on the Great Exhibition of 1851 and, like 100 years before, it aimed to showcase the designs, architecture and technologies of the future. Morrison was the organiser, wanting to use the event to ... 'do something jolly... we need something to give Britain a lift' but the idea was also criticised as 'Morrison's Folly' which was costing £11 million of public money; it was also entirely the affair of the middle classes in its design and execution. Although based at the South Bank in London,[483] Corsham Parish Council were holding public meetings in 1950 hoping that, if funds allowed, they would be able to provide local festivities to mark the occasion. There doesn't appear to have been much local enthusiasm for the project. The appeal for donations cost the council over £20 and they received donations of just £5 in return! The plan was abandoned.[484] Lord Bath at Longleat House was hoping to get his hands on the Festival's 'Skylon' in December 1951 to place at Heaven's Gate as a tourist attraction. The plans had been reported in *The Times* and there were concerns, with a letter from the Council for the Protection of Rural England to the Council asking their position on the matter.[485]

David Kynaston reports that social and cultural divisions remained, and had perhaps been strengthened by the war. Harold Wilson noted after VE Day that 'class feeling and resentment are very strong'[486] and in 1946 Orwell noted: '... Allowing for the general impoverishment, the upper classes are still living their accustomed life.'[487] The Second World War had strengthened the popularity of the Royal Family and the 'wisdom of the establishment'.[488] By January 1947 many were against the proposed marriage of Princess Elizabeth to Philip Mountbatten, but by October those criticising the marriage had reduced in number. Viewing the wedding dress and presents became popular.[489] Lieutenant Philip Mountbatten was stationed at HMS Royal Arthur in Corsham when his engagement to Princess Elizabeth was announced. He was sent a congratulatory telegram on behalf of the parish.[490] The residents of Corsham had a special place in their affections for the Prince, who performed his first public engagement in the town whilst serving at HMS Royal Arthur. He too appears to have enjoyed his time there, later returning to the base and requesting to meet up with his old skittles team after his royal duties had been performed. On 2 June 1953 Corsham people were amongst those celebrating the Coronation of Queen Elizabeth II. There was a fancy dress competition, whist drive and sports including a marathon race and football tournament. The Scouts gave a display and the Fire Service and St. John's Ambulance Brigade gave demonstrations with a bonfire and fireworks concluding the celebrations.[491]

The Fovant branch of the Mother's Union marked the Coronation by making a linen tablecloth and embroidering it with the signatures of all its members in varied colours.[492] The residents of Corsham donated £23 to the King George VI Memorial Fund and £127 to the Coronation Appeal. A procession and service was held the day before the Coronation, and also a children's sports event, a marathon race, a bonfire and firework display with every child in the parish getting a souvenir.[493] In Warminster, families were making a beeline for those who had televisions. 'The pageant in the Park in the evening was a washout as it poured with rain. We all got a Coronation mug, and went to see *The Queen is Crowned* at the cinema.'[494] Chippenham residents could purchase a Souvenir Programme at a price of 1s. 6d. It described the history and workings of the Coronation Service with photographs of the Coronation Mug and Crown Piece, minted for the occasion and presented to the parents of all babies born in the town on the day or to those who were celebrating their Diamond or Golden Wedding. Chippenham's celebrations included a service in the parish church, a cricket match, the planting of two trees at St. Andrew's hospital, a march-through by the Royal Wiltshire Yeomanry, football matches and displays, dancing demonstrations, a public broadcast of the Prime Minister's Speech, a torchlight procession, fireworks, bonfire and dancing. The following days also included an 'Old Folks Tea', theatre production, talent spotting competition, exhibition and Coronation Dinner.[495] Members of the Salisbury Over 60s Club received the surprise gift of a souvenir Coronation Beaker. Celebrations in the city included a fire-lit image of Queen Elizabeth and Prince Philip as part of a fireworks display in Victoria Park.[496] Wiltshire's villagers also celebrated with a fancy dress parade at Atworth, Semington and Horningsham; flags and bunting were on display in Steeple Ashton; sports and a tea for the children of Biddestone; a tea for the children in Grittleton. The children at Hilperton were given a tea and a Souvenir Beaker – in Kington St. Michael it was tea and a Souvenir Mug; the over 60s at Horningsham were able to see events on a television; in Chitterne there was a tea for the children and a lunch for the adults. The children at Slaughterford were given a Silver Crown Souvenir and the over 60s at Southwick received a Coronation Canister of tea. The Commandant of the nearby Married Families' Camp at Lypiatt invited the residents of Neston to see the televised Coronation Service in the morning, followed by a tug of war and 'comic' football match with a tea in the village (together with the Lypiatt Camp families). In Trowbridge the parade included detachments of the RAF, WRAF, Royal Wiltshire Yeomanry, Home Guard, Women's Royal Army Corps, Army Cadet Force and Junior Flying Corps. Television sets were erected in the Town Hall and there was a fly past by the RAF followed by dancing and fireworks in the Park that evening.[497] The *Wiltshire News* reported the event in Trowbridge in its early June edition, noting that the townspeople saw 'a great demonstration of loyalty to the Crown.' Church towers put flags aloft and children 'swarmed into the streets waving flags.' The Royal British Legion Bugle Band took part and at 8.30am a peal was rung in the parish church. The Royal Wiltshire Yeomanry Band was at the front of a parade by the RAF from Bythesea Road to the Town Hall, where at 9.30am a message was read out for the Queen:

'We, the chairman and members of the Urban District Council of Trowbridge, on our own behalf and on behalf of the residents of Trowbridge, desire to express to your Majesty our loyal and dutiful attachment and our most sincere congratulations on the Coronation of Your Majesty…'

Again Bradford was lit up by lines of multi-coloured lights in the form of illuminated jam jars over the River Avon, in Middle Rank and Tory with buildings being floodlit.[498] [499] Warminster had a carnival and the residents of Melksham were dancing in the rain in front of the Town Hall in Market Square at the culmination of festivities which had taken place throughout the previous week. The residents of Westbury were dancing in front of their Town Hall too; the Morris Men with their folk dances, followed by a torchlight procession to the White Horse on Bratton Hill for a bonfire seen for miles around.[500]

Kenneth Morgan feels that the immediate post-war period was one of a 'suspicion of change and the paralysis of self-doubt'.[501] He states that most modern interpretations of the post-war period have viewed it as a time of decline rather than affluence.[502] The basic class structure remained the same; assets such as property held most value post-war, especially due to housing shortages.[503] Peter Hennessy reports Sir Ralf Dahrendorf's view that the post-war labour Government was the right Government at the wrong time; to continue with the redistribution policies begun in the interwar period was correct in social terms but wrong in economic terms.[504] However, Asa Briggs feels that this post-war world was not just one of austerity, it was one of improvement too. The broken promises after the Great War did not reappear. A land fit for heroes *was* begun this time around with employment opportunities, a rise in the standard of living and control over inflation, not forgetting, of course, the welfare state.[505]

Living in post-war Britain can easily be seen as a period of hardship, but it could also prove to be a time of 'revelation'; with the reappearance of the banana and pineapple, the first washing machine or TV… 100,000 bananas arrived from Jamaica for distribution in Bradford on Avon in December 1945. Queues quickly formed in many shops as they were the first bananas to be been seen in the town since 1941.[506]

Hennessy records that '[t]he world opening before us was not a pale imitation of one we had lost, but a lucky dip of extraordinary things we had never seen before.'[507]

13
Postscript

THE EFFECT OF Total War during the period of 1939-1945 caused great upheaval for the whole of Britain, both urban and rural areas. With the mass movement of people and wartime restrictions, Government control was absolute and freedoms were curtailed with a view to fairness to all during this tumultuous time in British history. Richard Titmuss wrote in 1950 of the 'Dunkirk Spirit' of the time with the war bringing with it solidarity and a mood for social change.[1]

WWI had caused a great deal of introspection in the inter-war period and many of the Government policies of WWII had their origins in the experiences gained during the Great War, although plans could also be based on unknown quantities, such as the Air Ministry's estimates of possible aerial bombardment which WWI had shown was possible. Even so, the Government was not prepared for the declaration of war in 1939 and Local Authorities took the brunt of this inadequacy, working hard but often with conflicting or uncertain advice or under tight timescales, the Government sometimes asking for more than they were able to give. Their duties far outweighed their experience, but in Wiltshire they appear to have held their own, fighting their corner as much as they could when necessary during wartime in respect of evacuation and industry, and in the post-war era, especially on housing. The Urban, Borough and District Clerks worked with many Local, Regional and National Government departments, private companies, military authorities and local residents, attempting to keep a sense of order and stability for the local communities in which they served. In its turn the Government worked hard to keep up morale, and connected with the people in a far greater way than it had ever done before, enabling WWII to truly become a 'People's War.' Even so, the idea of fairness was not held by all; human nature would see to that and the view that everyone worked together during WWII is not a realistic one. What can be said is that the Government (both National and Local) tried its best to make it so, and ensured that the British population was aware of the fact. Those who chose to suit themselves were probably in the minority, although it appears to have become harder to stay on the strait and narrow in the Austerity Years of 1945 to 1951.

The mass movement of people: evacuees, war workers and the military, caused social upheaval for both the individuals concerned and the local communities which hosted them. It appears that in Wiltshire, local people did their best but times were difficult. There has been a feeling that life in rural areas during WWII was easy; no bombs, plentiful fresh food... but although this is true, pressures were placed on rural dwellers. Additional duties included Civil Defence; there was also queuing for goods, Digging for Victory, the blackout, and taking strangers into their homes. It was hard for some to adjust, exhausting for others, and the period of 'duty' was often much longer than expected. Friction was common with the daily difficulties of living in a wartime society and the obligation of 'keeping mum' meaning that local people often had no idea what their lodgers were doing to help the war effort, with the misunderstandings that could ensue. Zwinieger-Bargielowska reports that '[a]ir raids, food shortages, shopping difficulties, queues, factory conditions, evacuees and hosts, these are the things about which the British public thinks and feels most.'[2]

Rural life could often be isolating for its permanent residents but the new second 'occupation' of Civil Defence duties brought people together as never before, alongside fundraising and other community events. Newcomers to Wiltshire brought with them their experiences and views of the world, the permanent residents of the county having their horizons widened if the reality of war itself at home and abroad was not already doing so. A rural county suddenly became a crowded county with busy roads, new industry and development; louder, bustling, sometimes lively... both town and village could look and feel very different. But also suddenly rural life held a new value – the importance of agriculture had grown in the eyes of the nation.

WWII brought with it many groundbreaking achievements on the Home Front. The evacuation of up to 10% of the civilian population had been the largest single movement of a population ever to take place. The conscription of women had been considered one of the most groundbreaking aspects of the war.[3] Government controls on the agricultural industry transformed British farming. The mobilisation of the population for Civil Defence and the acceptance of restrictions and conscription; the ability of the majority of British people to allow themselves to be controlled and utilised as the Government saw fit all are a testament to their resilience and resolve. That quintessentially English sense of fairness was typified by the queue, and the British have been well known for it ever since. Creativity, problem solving and innovation were also at the heart of wartime endeavour, in the domestic environment as well as for war production. The 'Make do and Mend' mentality which came to the fore during WWII was to become part of the British psyche for many years to come.

Wartime did bring permanent changes for Wiltshire. The military brought with it new jobs in the Civil Service. Industry, which had relocated for wartime purposes, often remained in the county. This could mean new job opportunities for local people, but also relocation or a permanent home in the county for others. The military also brought with it new infrastructure and amenities which could be utilised for civilians after the war, although not always in locations that were most beneficial to local people. Regional planning had begun pre-war but continued apace during wartime and beyond. The Second World War meant that unplanned development had occurred and this had to be managed. It can be seen that pressure on housing caused conflict during the war and especially in the immediate post-war period. Both the physical changes to the environment and the newcomers moving into it permanently altered the make-up of local communities. Wartime brought with it changes that became permanent, and also the diversity that came with those changes.

Socialist policies which had begun in the pre-war period by both the Government and individuals would not have moved on so quickly if not for WWII. There has been great debate as to whether Total War brought with it social changes which had a long-lasting effect. Views have altered from Harry Hopkins in the early 1960s claiming that 'social revolution' was a fair term to use,[4] to Angus Calder's reassessment in the late 1960s suggesting that war did not 'sweep society on a new course but instead hastened its progress along the old grooves.'[5] Newly accessible material became available in the 1980s and social historians began to review and revise further, with Arthur Marwick amongst others feeling that the Dunkirk Spirit argument could not explain the changes that had taken place during WWII, and that the forces for change had begun in the pre-war era. Many agreed, however, that wartime changes and experiences had helped to define how British society wanted to move forward, with Correlli Barnett coining the phrase 'New Jerusalem', encapsulating the idea of social reform, and it became an ideal time for the intellectuals, reformers[6] and planners to come to the fore. Although the British class structure blurred a little, to be called the 'endless middle',[7] there was little change in the upper class structure, clearly visible with the lack of change in the public school system and class ratio of university attendance. In rural areas the dominance of the upper classes had been declining in the pre-war years, resulting in the influence of the upper classes diminishing after the war, to be replaced by the arrival of those new class sets that had a voice in planning and parish matters, often to the detriment of the poorer members of rural communities. Skelton's pre-war idea of a property-owning democracy[8] which began to work alongside capitalism in the marketplace led to housing being viewed as a commodity for investment or leisure rather than as a basic necessity. Rural depopulation ceased in the 1960s due to the absorption of urban life into rural areas,[9] widespread car ownership and the motorway network speeding up the changes. It must be noted, however, that villages have constantly been evolving over time with change dictating their survival, C. S. Orwin noting the need for villages to grow to keep up with modern standards of living.[10]

Social historians have been grappling with the complex issues of how and where social change took place during WWII, but the majority feel that the effects were not fundamental enough to become permanent. Sociologists and social geographers note that social change did occur in rural communities, but that often these changes had begun pre-war. The majority agree, however, that wartime Government planning policies affected the rural population, especially in terms of rural deprivation, continuing with post-war rural planning focusing on agriculture and conservation[11] and the slow progress of utility provision in rural areas. There are many factors which cause change in society. The concentration of issues relating to housing, planning and industry found in the archives of the Wiltshire and Swindon History Centre for the period 1939-1955 can be seen as one piece of a larger picture, but an important one.

Post-war came and with it greater hardship and austerity, but also a period of renewal and change, although not as great or as quickly as had been hoped, and at a price, both in terms of Britain's standing in the world and the debts that war had brought. The post-war austerity years were hard to bear, and the post-war period which began with the hope of change ended with a decline in morale over rationing in which the family took precedence over the social commitments of Civil Defence in the anxious time of the Cold War era. Changes had occurred with nationalisation, the welfare state and a rise in the standard of living, but in other ways little had changed and housing was an issue that proved difficult to resolve. Britain had lost its position in the world but all was not lost. The euphoria of victory and peace had also led to a time of revelation and new technology which was to revolutionise the lives of Britain's inhabitants. Hardships had been endured but there were opportunities to come.

Notes

Preface

1 Briggs, A. (2000). *Go to It: Working for Victory on the Home Front 1939-1945*. London: Octopus Publishing Group Ltd.

1 Introduction

1 Calder, A. (1992). *The People's War: Britain 1939-45*. London: Pimlico (Original work published 1969), pp. 22-24. [WSHC 941.084].
2 Ibid., pp. 25-26.
3 Ibid., pp. 32.
4 Nicholl, P. (1973). *Britain's Blunder: How England Lost the Second World War: An Objective Study of the Second World War – Its Cause, Conduct and Consequence*. East Orange (USA): Communications Archives, Inc. (Original work published 1946).
5 Weber, M (1983). President Roosevelt's Campaign To Incite War in Europe: The Secret Polish Documents. *The Journal of Historical Review*, 4(2), pp. 135-172.
6 Hoggan, D. (1983). President Roosevelt and the Origins of the 1939 War. *The Journal of Historical Review*, 4(2), pp. 205-255.
7 Pleshakow, C. (2005). *Stalin's Folly: The Tragic First Ten Days of World War II on the Eastern Home Front*. Boston: Houghton Mifflin Harcourt.
8 Charmley, J. (1999). *Chamberlain and the Lost Peace*. Chicago: Ivan R. Dee.
9 Irving, D. (1987). *Churchill's War Volume One: The Struggle for Power*. London: Veritas Publishing Ltd.
10 Inchfawn, F. (2010). *Salute to the Village*. Monkton Farleigh: Folly Books (Original work published 1943), pp. 91. [WSHC XIN.921].

2 The Unexpected Guests

1 Hammel A. and Lewkow, B. (Eds.) (2012). *The Kindertransport to Britain 1938/9: New Perspectives*. Amsterdam: Rodopi, pp. 126.
2 Gartner, N. (2012). *Operation Pied Piper: The Wartime Evacuation of Schoolchildren from London and Berlin 1938-1946*. Charlotte (USA): ISA (Information Age Publishing), pp. 8.
3 Ibid., pp. xvii.
4 Hammel A. and Lewkow, B. (Eds.) (2012). *The Kindertransport to Britain 1938/9: New Perspectives*. Amsterdam: Rodopi, pp. 126.
5 Gartner, N. (2012). *Operation Pied Piper: The Wartime Evacuation of Schoolchildren from London and Berlin 1938-1946*. Charlotte (USA): ISA (Information Age Publishing), pp. 9.
6 Ibid., pp. 26.
7 Ibid., pp. 27.
8 Ibid., pp. 29.
9 Ibid., pp. 29.
10 Ibid., pp. 32.
11 WSA F2/850/1. [in file A]
12 Ibid., [copy of the minutes of the meeting is available at WSHC in file A].
13 Ibid.,[in file A].

14 Ibid.,[in file A].
15 Ibid.,[in file A].
16 WSA F2/850/1. [in file B].
17 Ibid., [in file A].
18 Calder, A. (1992). *The People's War: Britain 1939-45.* London: Pimlico (Original work published 1969), pp. 25. [WSHC 941.084].
19 Gartner, N. (2012). *Operation Pied Piper: The Wartime Evacuation of Schoolchildren from London and Berlin 1938-1946.* Charlotte (USA): ISA (Information Age Publishing), pp. 30.
20 Gartner, N. (2012). *Operation Pied Piper: The Wartime Evacuation of Schoolchildren from London and Berlin 1938-1946.* Charlotte (USA): ISA (Information Age Publishing), pp. 32-33.
21 Wheatcroft, S. (2008). Children's Experiences of War: Handicapped Children in England During the Second World War. *Twentieth Century British History,* 19(4), pp. 488. [doi: 10.1093/tcbj/hwn017].
22 Gartner, N. (2012). *Operation Pied Piper: The Wartime Evacuation of Schoolchildren from London and Berlin 1938-1946.* Charlotte (USA): ISA (Information Age Publishing), pp. 32-33.
23 Wheatcroft, S. (2008). Children's Experiences of War: Handicapped Children in England During the Second World War. *Twentieth Century British History,* 19(4), pp. 488. [doi: 10.1093/tcbj/hwn017].
24 WSA F2/850/1. [in file B].
25 Ibid., [in file A].
26 WSA F2/850/1.
27 Sylvia Hewlett, oral communication, 23/07/2014; WSA F2/850/1. [in file B].
28 Slocombe, I. (n.d.). *Belgian Refugees in Wiltshire in the First World War.* Unpublished. [WSHC AAA.949].
29 WSA F8/500/263/18/3.
30 Tanner, H. and Hanff, D. (1995). *Out of Nazi Germany.* London: Impact Books, pp. 19. [WSHC XTA.921]
31 Ibid., pp. 25.

32 Ibid., pp. 19.
33 Ibid., pp. 40.
34 Ibid., pp. 44.
35 Ibid., pp. 26.
36 Ibid., pp. 36.
37 WSA F2/850/1. [in file B].
38 Samways, R. (ed.) (n.d.). *We Think you Ought to Go.* London: Corporation of London, pp. 8-9. [WSHC 940.53161].
39 Gartner, N. (2012). *Operation Pied Piper: The Wartime Evacuation of Schoolchildren from London and Berlin 1938-1946.* Charlotte (USA): ISA (Information Age Publishing), pp. 34.
40 Gartner, N. (2012). *Operation Pied Piper: The Wartime Evacuation of Schoolchildren from London and Berlin 1938-1946.* Charlotte (USA): ISA (Information Age Publishing), pp. 50.
41 Gartner, N. (2012). *Operation Pied Piper: The Wartime Evacuation of Schoolchildren from London and Berlin 1938-1946.* Charlotte (USA): ISA (Information Age Publishing), pp. 36.
42 Gartner, N. (2012). *Operation Pied Piper: The Wartime Evacuation of Schoolchildren from London and Berlin 1938-1946.* Charlotte (USA): ISA (Information Age Publishing), pp. 36.
43 WSA F2/850/5.
44 Ibid.
45 *Wiltshire Times,* 30.9.1939. [WSHC Microform Collection].
46 Duffy, M. (1983). *That's How it Was.* London: Virago (Original work published 1962), pp. 64. [WSHC AAA.823].
47 WSA G5/225/6.
48 *Wiltshire Times,* 30.9.1939. [WSHC Microform Collection].
49 *Wiltshire Times,* 2.12.1939. [WSHC Microform Collection].
50 Vernon, C. (2011). *Malmesbury versus Hitler: The Town's role in the Second World War.* Malmesbury Civic Trust: Malmesbury, pp. 130. [WSHC MAL.949].
51 WSA G15/225/2. [Lord Privy Seal's Office, unpagingated].
52 WSA G24/225/1.
53 *Wiltshire News,* 8.9.1939. [WSHC

Microform Collection].

54 WSA G24/225/1.

55 WSA G18/225/9.

56 Ibid.

57 Gartner, N. (2012). *Operation Pied Piper: The Wartime Evacuation of Schoolchildren from London and Berlin 1938-1946.* Charlotte (USA): ISA (Information Age Publishing), pp. xxviii.

58 Burnett, D. (1978). *Longleat: The Story of an English Country House.* London: Collins, pp. 175). [LON.940].

59 WSA G15/225/14.

60 WSA F2/850/10.

61 Janis Packham, personal communication, 17.11.2014.

62 WSA F1/850/1. [File B].

63 WSA G24/225/1.

64 WSA F2/850/10.

65 Wiltshire Federation of Women's Institutes (1993). *Wiltshire Within Living Memory.* Newbury: Countryside Books, pp. 218. [WSHC AAA.949].

66 Wheatcroft, S. (2008). Children's Experiences of War: Handicapped Children in England During the Second World War. *Twentieth Century British History*, 19(4), pp. 489. [doi: 10.1093/tcbj/hwn017].

67 WSA F2/850/5.

68 Bemerton Local History Society. (2006). *Memories of Bemerton in Wartime.* Bemerton Local History Society with support of the Big Lottery Fund, pp. 15-16. [BEM.949].

69 Calder, A. (1992). *The People's War: Britain 1939-45.* London: Pimlico (Original work published 1969), pp. 57. [WSHC 941.084].

70 WSA F2/850/5.

71 WSA G24/225/1.

72 Street, A. G. (1950). *In His Own Country.* London: Eyre & Spottiswoode, pp. 211. [WSHC XST.824].

73 Inchfawn, F. (2010). *Salute to the Village.* Monkton Farleigh: Folly Books (Original work published 1943), pp. 9. [WSHC XIN.921].

74 Inchfawn, F. (2010). *Salute to the*

Village. Monkton Farleigh: Folly Books (Original work published 1943), pp. 13-14. [WSHC XIN.921].

75 Inchfawn, F. (2010). *Salute to the Village.* Monkton Farleigh: Folly Books (Original work published 1943), pp. 19-20. [WSHC XIN.921].

76 Inchfawn, F. (2010). *Salute to the Village.* Monkton Farleigh: Folly Books (Original work published 1943), pp. 25-26. [WSHC XIN.921].

77 WSA F2/850/5.

78 WSA F2/850/5.

79 Inchfawn, F. (2010). *Salute to the Village.* Monkton Farleigh: Folly Books (Original work published 1943), pp. 26-27. [WSHC XIN.921].

80 Partridge, F. (1978). *A Pacifist's War.* The Hogarth Press: London, pp. 60. [WSHC HAM.927].

81 Wroughton History Group (2009). *Stories from Wroughton.* Wroughton History Group, pp. 104-5. [WSHC WRO.940].

82 Smith, B. (1989). *Our Wiltshire Village: Steeple Ashton.* Gloucester: Alan Sutton, pp. 136-7. [WSHC STE.940].

83 Coleshill, W. (2008). *Memoirs of World War II in Castle Combe.* Unpublished, pp. 4. [WSHC CAC.949].

84 Parsons, M. (2005). *Cricklade Revealed: Part 5 - Social Life during the Second World War.* Marion Parsons, pp. 31. [WSHC CRI.949].

85 Forbat, J. (2012). *Evacuee Boys: Letters of a Family Separated by War.* Stroud: The History Press, pp. 10. [WSHC AAA.949].

86 Pickford, P. and Pickford, R. (Ed.). (1995). *Letters to Liz.* Newnham, Tasmania: Attic Press, pp. 8. [WSHC WAR.949].

87 WSA G24/225/1.

88 Welshman, J. (2010). *Churchill's Children: The Evacuee Experience in Wartime Britain.* Oxford: Oxford University Press, pp. 102.

89 Barnett, C. (1996). *The Audit of War: The Illusion and Reality of Britain as a Great Nation.* London: Pan Books, pp. 200.

90 WSA F2/850/5.
91 WSA F8/500/65/4/1.
92 Cooper, L. (2009). *A Little London Evacuee*. Diss, Norfolk: Data Tech D.T.P., pp. 53-55. [WSHC WAR.921].
93 WSA G15/225/16.
94 Calder, A. (1992). *The People's War: Britain 1939-45*. London: Pimlico (Original work published 1969), pp. 46-47. [WSHC 941.084].
95 WSA G12/225/1.
96 Ibid.
97 WSA F2/850/5.
98 WSA F8/500/141/1/1.
99 WSA G24/225/1.
100 WSA G15/225/16.
101 WSA F8/500/258/2/2.
102 WSA G24/225/1.
103 WSA G15/225/16. [Letter from Ministry of Health to Local Authority Clerks, 27.9.1939].
104 Gartner, N. (2012). *Operation Pied Piper: The Wartime Evacuation of Schoolchildren from London and Berlin 1938-1946*. Charlotte (USA): ISA (Information Age Publishing), pp. 36.
105 Gartner, N. (2012). *Operation Pied Piper: The Wartime Evacuation of Schoolchildren from London and Berlin 1938-1946*. Charlotte (USA): ISA (Information Age Publishing), pp. 110.
106 WSA F8/500/30/7/1.
107 Inchfawn, F. (2010). *Salute to the Village*. Monkton Farleigh: Folly Books (Original work published 1943), pp. 32. [WSHC XIN.921].
108 Calder, A. (1992). *The People's War: Britain 1939-45*. London: Pimlico (Original work published 1969), pp. 45. [WSHC 941.084].
109 Gartner, N. (2012). *Operation Pied Piper: The Wartime Evacuation of Schoolchildren from London and Berlin 1938-1946*. Charlotte (USA): ISA (Information Age Publishing), pp. 111.
110 Calder, A. (1992). *The People's War: Britain 1939-45*. London: Pimlico (Original work published 1969), pp. 46-7. [WSHC 941.084].
111 Gartner, N. (2012). *Operation Pied Piper: The Wartime Evacuation of*

Schoolchildren from London and Berlin 1938-1946. Charlotte (USA): ISA (Information Age Publishing), pp. 112.
112 WSA G24/225/1.
113 WSA F2/850/5.
114 Lewis, P. (1984). *A People's War*. London: Methuen London Ltd., pp. 14.
115 WSA 1815/40.
116 Ibid.
117 WSA F2/850/6.
118 Ibid.
119 WSA G15/225/16.
120 WSA F2/850/5. [11.1939].
121 WSA F2/850/10.
122 WSA F2/850/6.
123 Ibid.
124 WSA F2/850/5.
125 WSA G24/225/1.
126 Ibid.
127 WSA F2/850/5.
128 MacKay, R. (1999). *The Test of War: Inside Britain 1939-45*. London: UCL Press, pp. 125.
129 WSA F2/850/7.
130 Brown, M. (2005). *Evacuees: Evacuation in Wartime Britain 1939-45*. Stroud: Sutton Publishing, pp. 8.
131 Samways, R. (ed). (n.d). *We Think you Ought to Go*. London: Corporation of London, pp. 11-12. [WSHC 940.53161].
132 WSA F2/850/6.
133 Samways, R. (ed). (n.d). *We Think you Ought to Go*. London: Corporation of London, pp. 11-12. [WSHC 940.53161].
134 Ibid.
135 Samways, R. (ed). (n.d). *We Think you Ought to Go*. London: Corporation of London, pp. 17. [WSHC 940.53161].
136 Ibid., pp. 29.
137 Brown, M. (2005). *Evacuees: Evacuation in Wartime Britain 1939-45*. Stroud: Sutton Publishing, pp. 59.
138 Brown, M. (2005). *Evacuees: Evacuation in Wartime Britain 1939-45*. Stroud: Sutton Publishing, pp. 64.
139 Calder, A. (1992). *The People's War: Britain 1939-45*. London: Pimlico (Original work published 1969), pp.

409. [WSHC 941.084].

140 WSA F2/850/10.

141 WSA G15/225/14.

142 Inchfawn, F. (2010). *Salute to the Village.* Monkton Farleigh: Folly Books (Original work published 1943), pp. 27. [WSHC XIN.921].

143 WSA F2/850/5.

144 WSA F2/850/10.

145 WSA G15/225/11.

146 Ibid.

147 WSA G15/225/11.

148 WSA F2/850/8.

149 Vernon, C. (2011). *Malmesbury versus Hitler: The Town's role in the Second World War.* Malmesbury Civic Trust: Malmesbury, pp. 127. [WSHC MAL.949].

150 WSA F2/850/6.

151 Ibid.

152 WSA F2/850/8.

153 WSA F2/850/6.

154 WSA G24/225/6.

155 WSA G15/225/11.

156 WSA F1/100/34/3.

157 WSA G12/225/1.

158 WSA G24/225/6.

159 WSA G24/225/29.

160 Lane, C. and White, P. (1999). *Warminster in the Twentieth Century.* The Warminster History Society: Warminster, pp. 26. [WSHC WAR.949].

161 WSA G15/225/16.

162 Mass Observation (1987). *War Factory.* London: The Cresset Library (Original work published 1943), pp. 16. [WSHC SAI.684].

163 Calder, A. (1992). *The People's War: Britain 1939-45.* London: Pimlico (Original work published 1969), pp. 36. [WSHC 941.084].

164 WSA G15/225/11.

165 Ibid.,

166 WSA F2/850/1. [File B].

167 Nicholson, H. (2000). *Prisoners of War: True Stories of Evacuees: Their Lost Childhood.* London: Gordon Publishing, pp. 1-2. [WSHC AAA.949 (BL)],

168 Wiltshire Federation of Women's

Institutes (1993). *Wiltshire Within Living Memory.* Newbury: Countryside Books, pp. 220. [WSHC AAA.949].

169 Wiltshire Federation of Women's Institutes (1993). *Wiltshire Within Living Memory.* Newbury: Countryside Books, pp. 221. [WSHC AAA.949].

170 Wiltshire Federation of Women's Institutes (1993). *Wiltshire Within Living Memory.* Newbury: Countryside Books, pp. 220. [WSHC AAA.949].

171 Cockbill, T. (1989). *Our Swindon in 1939.* The Quill Press: Swindon, pp. 35. [WSHC SWI.949].

172 Came, M. (1986). Experiences as an Evacuee. Unpublished, unpaginated. [WSHC AAA.949 (Ephemera folder)].

173 Hinton, J. (1998). Voluntarism and the Welfare/Warfare State. Women's Voluntary Services in the 1940s. *Twentieth Century British History,* 9(2), pp. 286-287.

174 WSA F8/500/65/4/1.

175 Bemerton Local History Society (2006). *Memories of Bemerton in Wartime.* Bemerton Local History Society with support of the Big Lottery Fund, pp. 14. [BEM.949].

176 Duffy, M. (1983). *That's How it Was.* London: Virago (Original work published 1962), pp. 71-72. [WSHC AAA.823].

177 Hickson, J. and Skrine, R. (Ed.) (2013). *Carry on Coping: Diary of a Doctor 1942-1945.* Bradford on Avon: Ex Libris Press, pp. 23. [WSHC CHP.611. Original diaries are also available at WSA 4236/1-5].

178 Welshman, J. (2010). Churchill's Children: The Evacuee Experience in Wartime Britain. Oxford: Oxford University Press, pp. 91.

179 Hickson, J. and Skrine, R. (Ed.) (2013). *Carry on Coping: Diary of a Doctor 1942-1945.* Bradford on Avon: Ex Libris Press, pp. 60. [WSHC CHP.611 Original diaries are also available at WSA 4236/1-5].

180 WSA G5/132/52.

181 WSA G24/225/1.

182 Duffy, M. (1983). *That's How it*

Was. London: Virago (Original work published 1962), pp. 64. [WSHC AAA.823].

183 F2/850/5.

184 Brown, M. (2005). *Evacuees: Evacuation in Wartime Britain 1939-45*. Stroud: Sutton Publishing, pp. 2.

185 WSA F8/500/38/1/2.

186 WSA F8/500/263/31/1.

187 McKay, R. (1999). *The Test of War: Inside Britain 1939-45*. London: UCL Press, pp. 216-217.

188 Annetts, S. and Annetts, R. (2013). *Evacuated to Bratton*. Unpublished, pp. 14. [WSHC BRT.922 (BL)].

189 Vernon, C. (2011). *Malmesbury versus Hitler: The Town's role in the Second World War*. Malmesbury Civic Trust: Malmesbury, pp. 129-130. [WSHC MAL.949].

190 *Wiltshire Times*, 5.8.1944. [WSHC Microform Collection].

191 Vernon, C. (2011). *Malmesbury versus Hitler: The Town's role in the Second World War*. Malmesbury Civic Trust: Malmesbury, pp. 128. [WSHC MAL.949].

192 Ibid., pp. 128.

193 *Wiltshire Times*, 28.10.1939. [WSHC Microform Collection].

194 *Wiltshire Times*, 18.11.1939. [WSHC Microform Collection].

195 WSA F8/500/65/4/1.

196 Calder, A. (1992). *The People's War: Britain 1939-45*. London: Pimlico (Original work published 1969), pp. 48. [WSHC 941.084].

197 WSA F8/500/65/4/1.

198 WSA F8/500/42/1/2.

199 WSA F8/600/11/1/17/2.

200 Meakin, R. (2002). *Minety at War*. Richard Meakin, pp. 31. [WSHC MIN.949].

201 WSA F2/850/6.

202 Ibid.,

203 Ibid., [Meeting with Wiltshire Local Authorities and other representatives including the Ministry of Health, London County Council and Portsmouth County Council, held on 5.3.1940 at the request of the

Government].

204 MacKay, R. (1999). *The Test of War: Inside Britain 1939-45*. London: UCL Press, pp. 217.

205 Calder, A. (1992). *The People's War: Britain 1939-45*. London: Pimlico (Original work published 1969), pp. 542. [WSHC 941.084].

206 Came, M. (1986). Experiences as an Evacuee. Unpublished, unpaginated. [WSHC AAA.949 (Ephemera folder)].

207 Ibid.

208 Wiltshire Federation of Women's Institutes (1993). *Wiltshire Within Living Memory*. Newbury: Countryside Books, pp. 221. [WSHC AAA.949].

209 Meakin, R. (2002). *Minety at War*. Richard Meakin, pp. 26. [WSHC MIN.949].

210 WSA G18/225/24.

211 Calder, A. (1992). *The People's War: Britain 1939-45*. London: Pimlico (Original work published 1969), pp. 49. [WSHC 941.084].

212 Meakin, R. (2002). *Minety at War*. Richard Meakin, pp. 30-32. [WSHC MIN.949].

213 Wroughton History Group (2009). *Stories from Wroughton*. Wroughton History Group, pp. 104-105. [WRO.940].

214 Martin, M. (2008). *Evacuee School*. Unpublished, Unpaginated. [WSHC STV.949 (BL)].

215 Vernon. C. (2011). *Malmesbury versus Hitler: The Town's role in the Second World War*. Malmesbury Civic Trust: Malmesbury, pp. 125. [WSHC MAL.949].

216 WSA G24/225/4.

217 WSA F2/850/6.

218 Ibid.

219 Welshman, J. (2010). *Churchill's Children: The Evacuee Experience in Wartime Britain*. Oxford: Oxford University Press, pp. 90.

220 Ibid., pp. 91.

221 Lewis, P. (1984). *A People's War*. London: Methuen London Ltd., pp. 14.

222 Welshman, J. (1999). Evacuation,

Hygiene, and Social Policy: The Our Towns Report of 1943. *The Historical Journal*, 42(3), pp. 787.

223 Ibid., pp. 781.

224 WSA F2/850/5.

225 WSA F8/500/8/1/2.

226 *Wiltshire Times*, 30.9.1939. [WSHC Microform Collection].

227 *Wiltshire Times*, 7.10.1939 and 28.10.1939. [WSHC Microform Collection].

228 WSA F2/850/5.

229 WSA G24/225/1.

230 Urchfont Parish Millenium Group (2001). *Urchfont by any Other Name: A History of the Parish*. Urchfont Parish Millenium Group, pp. 156. [WSHC URC.940].

231 Parsons, M. (2004). *Cricklade Revealed: Part 4 - Social Life during the Second World War*. Marion Parsons, pp. 26. [WSHC CRI.949].

232 Steele, P. (2000). *Down Pans Lane: The History of Roundway Hospital 1851-1995*. P. Steele, pp. 74-76. [WSHC DEV.612].

233 WSA F13/232/6.

234 WSA G12/225/1.

235 Mock, J. (1997). *Bradford on Avon & District: The War Years (1939-1945)*. J. H. Mock, p. 53. [WSHC BRD.949].

236 White, A. (1940). *Christmas - In Spite of it All*. *Picture Post*, 9(12), pp. 11-12. [WSHC Reminiscence Collection].

237 Samways, R. (ed). (n.d).*We Think you Ought to Go*. London: Corporation of London, pp. 12. [WSHC 940.53161].

238 White, A. (1940). *Christmas - In Spite of it All*. *Picture Post*, 9(12), pp. 14. [WSHC Reminiscence Collection].

239 Samways, R. (ed). (n.d).*We Think you Ought to Go*. London: Corporation of London, pp. 12. [WSHC 940.53161].

240 Devenish, D. (1948). *A Wiltshire Country Home: A Study of Little Durnford*. London: BT Batsford Ltd., pp. 102-103. [WSHC DUN.727].

241 Calder, A. (1992). *The People's War: Britain 1939-45*. London: Pimlico (Original work published 1969), pp. 427. [WSHC 941.084].

242 Inchfawn, F. (2010). *Salute to the Village*. Monkton Farleigh: Folly Books (Original work published 1943), pp. 148-149. [WSHC XIN.921].

243 Browning, B. (2005). (2010). *EKCO's of Cowbridge*. Malmesbury: Cowbridge Publishing, pp. 107. [WSHC MAL.620].

244 WSA G24/225/5.

245 Ibid.

246 WSA G12/225/1.

247 WSA G15/225/14.

248 WSA F2/850/5.

249 WSA G14/225/11.

250 WSA F2/850/5.

251 WSA G15/225/11.

252 WSA G12/225/1.

253 Ibid.

254 Ibid.

255 Ibid.

256 WSA G15/22/516.

257 WSA G12/225/1.

258 Ibid.

259 WSA F2/850/12.

260 WSA G12/225/1.

261 Gartner, N. (2012). *Operation Pied Piper: The Wartime Evacuation of Schoolchildren from London and Berlin 1938-1946*. Charlotte (USA): ISA (Information Age Publishing), pp. 135.

262 Vernon, C. (2011). *Malmesbury versus Hitler: The Town's role in the Second World War*. Malmesbury Civic Trust: Malmesbury, pp. 131. [WSHC MAL.949].

263 MacKay, R. (1999). *The Test of War: Inside Britain 1939-45*. London: UCL Press, pp. 216.

264 WSA G15/225/16.

265 WSA F1/100/34/3. [WCC Emergency Committee Minutes].

266 WSA G5/132/42.

267 Vernon, C. (2011). *Malmesbury versus Hitler: The Town's role in the Second World War*. Malmesbury Civic Trust: Malmesbury, pp. 131. [WSHC MAL.949].

268 Ibid.

269 Lane, C. and White, P. (1999). *Warminster in the Twentieth Century*. The Warminster: Warminster History

Society, pp. 24. [WSHC WAR.949].

270 Welshman, J. (1999). Evacuation, Hygiene, and Social Policy: The Our Towns Report of 1943. *The Historical Journal*, 42(3), pp. 783.

271 Gartner, N. (2012). *Operation Pied Piper: The Wartime Evacuation of Schoolchildren from London and Berlin 1938-1946*. Charlotte (USA): ISA (Information Age Publishing), pp. 144-145.

272 Welshman, J. (1998). Evacuation and Social Policy during the Second World War: Myth and Reality. *Twentieth Century British History*, 9(1), pp. 53.

273 Ibid., pp. 50.

274 Gartner, N. (2012). *Operation Pied Piper: The Wartime Evacuation of Schoolchildren from London and Berlin 1938-1946*. Charlotte (USA): ISA (Information Age Publishing), pp. 139.

275 Ibid., pp. 141.

276 Ibid., pp. 138-139.

277 Lewis, P. (1984). *A People's War*. London: Methuen London Ltd., pp. 11.

278 Wheatcroft, S. (2008). Children's Experiences of War: Handicapped Children in England During the Second World War. *Twentieth Century British History*, 19(4), pp. 480. [doi: 10.1093/tcbj/hwn017].

279 Lewis, P. (1984). *A People's War*. London: Methuen London Ltd., pp. 11.

280 Cooper, L. 2009). *A Little London Evacuee*. Diss, Norfolk: Data Tech D.T.P., pp. 66). [WSHC WAR.921].

281 Inchfawn, F. (2010). *Salute to the Village*. Monkton Farleigh: Folly Books (Original work published 1943), pp. 32-33. [WSHC XIN.921

3 The Friendly Invasion

1 Calder, A. (1992). *The People's War: Britain 1939-45*. London: Pimlico (Original work published 1969), pp. 51. [WSHC 941.084].

2 Devizes Local History Group and Haycock, L. (Ed.). (1995). *How*

Devizes Won the War! Devizes Local History Group, pp. 6. [WSHC DEV.949].

3 Calder, A. (1992). *The People's War: Britain 1939-45*. London: Pimlico (Original work published 1969), pp. 51. [WSHC 941.084].

4 *Conscription Introduced*. (2014). Retrieved July 5, 2014 from the BBC History website http://www.bbc. co.uk/history/british/britain_wwtw_/ ff1_conscription.shtml

5 Calder, A. (1992). *The People's War: Britain 1939-45*. London: Pimlico (Original work published 1969), pp. 54. [WSHC 941.084].

6 *The Women's Royal Naval Service*. (2002). Retrieved March 13, 2015 from the Royal Naval Museum website http:// www.royalnavalmuseum.org/info_ sheets_WRNS.htm

7 *Women's Royal Air Force (WRAF) 1918-1920*. (2013). Retrieved March 13, 2015 from the RAF Museum website http://www.rafmuseum.org.uk/ research/online-exhibitions/women-on-the-air-force/womens-royal-air-force-wraf-1918-1920.aspx

8 Summers, J. (2015). *Fashion on the Ration*. London: Profile Books in Partnership with the Imperial War Museum, pp. 43.

9 *Women's Auxiliary Air Force (WAAF) 1939-1949*. (2013). Retrieved March 13, 2015 from the RAF Museum website http://www.rafmuseum.org.uk/ research/online-exhibitions/women-of-the-air-force/womens-auxiliary-air-force-waaf-1939-1949.aspx

10 Summers, J. (2015). *Fashion on the Ration*. London: Profile Books in Partnership with the Imperial War Museum, pp. 43.

11 Calder, A. (1992). *The People's War: Britain 1939-45*. London: Pimlico (Original work published 1969), pp. 267. [WSHC 941.084].

12 Ibid., pp. 268.

13 Ibid., pp. 52.

14 Nicholson, H. (2007). A Disputed Identity: Women Conscientious

Objectors in Second World War Britain. *Twentieth Century British History*, 18 (4), pp. 424. [doi: 10.1093/tcbh/hwm013].

15 Partridge, F. (1978). *A Pacifist's War*. London: The Hogarth Press, pp. 13-14. [WSHC HAM.927].

16 Buchanan-Dunlop, R. (2011). *Ham: the story of a Wiltshire village*. Ham: Buchanan-Dunlop, pp. 149. [WSHC HAM.940].

17 Calder, A. (1992). *The People's War: Britain 1939-45*. London: Pimlico (Original work published 1969), pp. 52. [WSHC 941.084].

18 Wyeth, R. (1995). *Sterner Days: Codford during the Second World War*. Warminster: Bedeguar Books, pp. 47. [WSHC COD.949].

19 Ibid., pp. 12-13.

20 Ibid., pp. 47.

21 WSA G24/719/4.

22 Vernon, C. (2011). *Malmesbury versus Hitler: The Town's role in the Second World War*. Malmesbury: Malmesbury Civic Trust, pp. 156. [WSHC MAL.949].

23 Ibid., pp. 133.

24 Cockbill, T. (1989). *Our Swindon in 1939*. Swindon: The Quill Press, pp. 13. [WSHC SWI.949].

25 Buckton, H. (2008). *Salisbury Plain: Home of Britain's Military Training*. Chichester: Phillimore & Co., pp. 1. [WSHC ABP.353].

26 James, N. (1987). *Plain Soldiering*. Salisbury: Hobnob Press, pp. 156-158. [WSHC ABP.353].

27 Buckton, H. (2008). *Salisbury Plain: Home of Britain's Military Training*. Chichester: Phillimore & Co., pp. 81. [WSHC ABP.353].

28 Ibid., pp. 85.

29 Ibid., pp. 96.

30 Ibid., pp. 87.

31 Devizes Local History Group and Haycock, L. (Ed.). (1995). *How Devizes Won the War!* Devizes Local History Group, pp. 74. [WSHC DEV.949].

32 Bailey, D. (2005). *The Story of Chiseldon Camp: Part Two*. Chiseldon: Chiseldon Local History Group, pp. 25. [WSHC CHS.949].

33 Warwicker, J. (Ed.). (2002). *With Britain in Mortal Danger: Britain's Most Secret Army of WWII*. Bristol: Cerberus Publishing Ltd, pp. 217, 220. [WSHC AAA.949 (BL)].

34 Adie, K. (2003). *Corsets to Camouflage: Women at War*. London: Hodder & Stoughton, pp. 139-140. [WSHC 355.22082].

35 Priddle, R. (2003). *Wings over Wiltshire*. ALD Design and Print, pp. 326. [WSHC AAA.354].

36 Adie, K. (2003). *Corsets to Camouflage: Women at War*. London: Hodder & Stoughton, pp. 139-140. [WSHC 355.22082].

37 Priddle, R. (2003). *Wings over Wiltshire*. ALD Design and Print, pp. 326. [WSHC AAA.354].

38 Adie, K. (2003). *Corsets to Camouflage: Women at War*. London: Hodder & Stoughton, pp. 139-141. [WSHC 355.22082].

39 Buckton, H. (2008). *Salisbury Plain: Home of Britain's Military Training*. Chichester: Phillimore & Co., pp. 102. [WSHC ABP.353].

40 Curtis, L. (2004). *Her Autobiography*. Walton on Thames: Red Kite, pp. 52-53. [WSHC. SAL.921].

41 Adie, K. (2003). *Corsets to Camouflage: Women at War*. London: Hodder & Stoughton, pp. 142. [WSHC 355.22082].

42 RAF Museum (2013), *Women of the Air Force* (retrieved 13 March 2015 from RAF Museum website); Adie, K. (2003). *Corsets to Camouflage: Women at War*. London: Hodder & Stoughton, , pp. 149.

43 *Dakota FZ692 'Kwicherbichen'*. (2015). Retrieved March 13, 2015 from the RAF Museum website

44 Wiltshire Federation of Women's Institutes (1993). *Wiltshire Within Living Memory*. Newbury: Countryside

Books, pp. 199, 201-202. [WSHC AAA.949].

45 Ibid., pp. 204.

46 Ibid, pp. 202-203.

47 Ibid.

48 WSA F1/100/40/1.

49 WSA G18/991/1.

50 McCamley, N. (2010). *Subterranean Britain: 2WW Secret Bunkers.* Monkton Farleigh: Folly Books, pp. 163. [WSA AAA.354].

51 Day, R. (2007). *Savernake at War: A Wartime History of Savernake Forest 1940-1949.* Hungerford: Roger Day, pp. 7-9. [WSHC SAV.949].

52 Tyrer, N. (1996). *They Fought in the Fields.* London: Sinclair-Stevenson, pp. 158. [WSHC 331.4830941].

53 Day, R. (2007). *Savernake at War: A Wartime History of Savernake Forest 1940-1949.* Hungerford: Roger Day, pp. 10, 13. [WSHC SAV.949].

54 Ibid., pp. 18.

55 McCamley, N. (2010). *Subterranean Britain: 2WW Secret Bunkers.* Monkton Farleigh: Folly Books, pp. 128. [WSA AAA.354].

56 Summers, J. (2015). *Fashion on the Ration.* London: Profile Books in Partnership with the Imperial War Museum, pp. 66-67.

57 McCamley, N. (2010). *Subterranean Britain: 2WW Secret Bunkers.* Monkton Farleigh: Folly Books, pp. 161. [WSA AAA.354].

58 Dobson, M. (2011). *Bradford Voices: Life in Bradford on Avon 1900-2010.* Bradford on Avon: Ex Libris Press, pp. 149. [WSHC BRD.949].

59 McCamley, N. (2010). *Subterranean Britain: 2WW Secret Bunkers.* Monkton Farleigh: Folly Books, pp. 162. [WSA AAA.354].

60 McCamley, N. (2007). *Secret Underground Cities.* Barnsley: Pen & Sword, pp. 154. [WSHC COR.949].

61 McCamley, N. (2010). *Subterranean Britain: 2WW Secret Bunkers.* Monkton Farleigh: Folly Books, pp. 163. [WSA AAA.354].

62 Whalley, P. (1995). *History of Royal Naval Store Depot Copenacre.* Unpublished, pp. 29-39. [WSHC COR.354].

63 DCSA (2006). *Corsham Tunnels: A Brief History.* Corsham: Corporate Communications (Crown Copyright), unpaginated. [WSHC COR.949].

64 Ibid., [Corsham Tunnels, Burlington Bunker].

65 Catford, N. (2012). *Burlington.* Bradford on Avon: Folly Books Ltd., pp. 1. [WSHC COR.949].

66 Dobson, M. (2011). *Bradford Voices: Life in Bradford on Avon 1900-2010.* Bradford on Avon: Ex Libris Press, pp. 150. [WSHC BRD.949].

67 McCamley, N. (2010). *Subterranean Britain: 2WW Secret Bunkers.* Monkton Farleigh: Folly Books, pp. 171. [WSA AAA.354].

68 Berryman, D. (2002). *Wiltshire Airfields in the Second World War.* Newbury: Countryside Books, pp. 9. [WSHC AAA.352].

69 Ibid., pp. 19.

70 Ibid., pp. 54.

71 Ibid., pp. 122.

72 Ibid., pp. 63.

73 Ibid., pp. 171.

74 Ibid., pp. 208.

75 Ibid., pp. 19.

76 Rattray, J. (2012). Blakehill – direct link to a bygone era. *Wiltshire Wildlife Trust Magazine,* Summer 2012, pp. 10. [WSHC WWT Magazine].

77 Ramsden-Binks, T. (2004). *A Short History of RAF Blakehill Farm.* Cricklade Historical Society, pp. 9. [WSHC CRI.352].

78 Berryman, D. (2002). *Wiltshire Airfields in the Second World War.* Newbury: Countryside Books, pp. 244-261. [WSHC AAA.352].

79 Ibid., pp. 15.

80 Pope, R. (2004). *Pewsey History in Pictures.* Pewsey: System Smart, pp. 4. [WSHC PES.771].

81 Meakin, R. (2002). *Minety at War.* Richard Meakin, pp. 74-76. [WSHC MIN.949].

82 Berryman, D. (2002). *Wiltshire Airfields*

in the Second World War. Newbury: Countryside Books, pp. 55. [WSHC AAA.352].
83 Priddle, R. (2003). *Wings over Wiltshire.* ALD Design and Print, pp. 131-132. [WSHC AAA.354].
84 Ibid., pp. 80.
85 Ramsden-Binks, T. (2004). *A Short History of RAF Blakehill Farm.* Cricklade Historical Society, pp. 9. [WSHC CRI.352].
86 Hide, J. (2002). *What's-Her-Name?* Salisbury: Wessex Books, pp. 29. [WSHC AAA.921].
87 Buckton, H. (2008). *Salisbury Plain: Home of Britain's Military Training.* Chichester: Phillimore & Co., pp. 110. [WSHC ABP.353].
88 Thamesdown Borough Council (n.d.) *Lydiard Park the War Years: an account of the military requisition of Lydiard Park during World War II and its aftermath.* Thamesdown Borough Council, pp. 5. [WSHC LYT.949].
89 Crowman, D. (1991). *A History of Tidworth and Tedworth House.* Chichester: Phillimore & Co Ltd., pp. 53. [WSHC NOT.940].
90 Berryman, D. (2002). *Wiltshire Airfields in the Second World War.* Newbury: Countryside Books, pp. 17. [WSHC AAA.352].
91 Day, R. (2007). *Savernake at War: A Wartime History of Savernake Forest 1940-1949.* Hungerford: Roger Day, pp. 5. [WSHC SAV.949].
92 Wiltshire Federation of Women's Institutes (1993). *Wiltshire Within Living Memory.* Newbury: Countryside Books, pp. 195. [WSHC AAA.949].
93 George, A. (c. 1993). *130th Station Hospital History.* In Harman (ed.). 130th Station Hospital Reunion Dayton, Ohio, October 15-18, 1993. Unpublished, pp. 1-2. [WSHC AAA.949 (BL)].
94 Bailey, D. (2005). *The Story of Chiseldon Camp: Part Two.* Chiseldon: Chiseldon Local History Group, pp. 69. [WSHC CHS.949].
95 George, A. (c. 1993). *130th Station*

Hospital History. In Harman (ed.). 130th Station Hospital Reunion Dayton, Ohio, October 15-18, 1993. Unpublished, pp. 1-3. [WSHC AAA.949 (BL)].
96 WSA G24/225/11.
97 George, A. (c. 1993). *130th Station Hospital History.* In Harman (ed.). 130th Station Hospital Reunion Dayton, Ohio, October 15-18, 1993. Unpublished, pp. 1. [WSHC AAA.949 (BL)].
98 Bailey, D. (2005). *The Story of Chiseldon Camp: Part Two.* Chiseldon: Chiseldon Local History Group, pp. 71. [WSHC CHS.949].
99 Berryman, D. (2002). *Wiltshire Airfields in the Second World War.* Newbury: Countryside Books, pp. 18. [WSHC AAA.352].
100 Wiltshire Federation of Women's Institutes (1993). *Wiltshire Within Living Memory.* Newbury: Countryside Books, pp. 187. [WSHC AAA.949].
101 Thamesdown Borough Council (n.d.) *Lydiard Park the War Years: an account of the military requisition of Lydiard Park during World War II and its aftermath.* Thamesdown Borough Council, pp. 4-5. [WSHC LYT.949].
102 George, A. (c. 1993). *130th Station Hospital History.* In Harman (ed.). 130th Station Hospital Reunion Dayton, Ohio, October 15-18, 1993. Unpublished, pp. 2. [WSHC AAA.949 (BL)].
103 Ibid., pp. 9.
104 Buckton, H. (2008). *Salisbury Plain: Home of Britain's Military Training.* Chichester: Phillimore & Co., pp. 101. [WSHC ABP.353].
105 Ibid., pp. 96.
106 Berryman, D. (2002). *Wiltshire Airfields in the Second World War.* Newbury: Countryside Books, pp. 175. [WSHC AAA.352].
107 Ambrose, S. (2001). *Band of Brothers.* London: Simon & Schuster, pp. 46-47.
108 Buckton, H. (2008). *Salisbury Plain: Home of Britain's Military Training.* Chichester: Phillimore & Co., pp. 107.

[WSHC ABP.353].

109 Devizes Local History Group and Haycock, L. (Ed.). (1995). *How Devizes Won the War!* Devizes Local History Group, pp. 87. [WSHC DEV.949].

110 WSA G11/132/21.

111 Bailey, D. (2005). *The Story of Chiseldon Camp: Part Two.* Chiseldon: Chiseldon Local History Group, pp. 79. [WSHC CHS.949].

112 Meakin, R. (2002). *Minety at War.* Richard Meakin, pp. 59-62. [WSHC MIN.949].

113 Randall, B. (2003). *A Patchwork of Memories.* Bob Randall, pp. 11. [WSHC TRO.949].

114 Priddle, R. (2003). *Wings over Wiltshire.* ALD Design and Print, pp. 145-146. [WSHC AAA.354].

115 Ambrose, S. (2001). *Band of Brothers.* London: Simon & Schuster, pp. 46.

116 Ibid., pp. 31.

117 Ibid., pp. 46.

118 Day, R. (2007). *Savernake at War: A Wartime History of Savernake Forest 1940-1949.* Hungerford: Roger Day, pp. 49. [WSHC SAV.949].

119 Ibid., pp. 18.

120 Hide, J. (2002). *What's-Her-Name?* Salisbury: Wessex Books, pp. 10. [WSHC AAA.921].

121 WSA 2860/3.

122 WSA L7/310/2.

123 Buckton, H. (2008). *Salisbury Plain: Home of Britain's Military Training.* Chichester: Phillimore & Co., pp. 101. [WSHC ABP.353].

124 James, N. (1987). *Plain Soldiering.* Salisbury: Hobnob Press, pp. 151. [WSHC ABP.353].

125 Annetts, S. and Annetts, R. (2013). *Evacuated to Bratton.* Unpublished, pp. 12. [WSHC BRT.922 (BL)].

126 Parsons, M. (2006). *Cricklade Revealed: Part 6 - Social Life during the Second World - Social Life during the Second World War.* Marion Parsons, pp. 1-2. [WSHC CRI.949].

127 WSA F9/120/23.

128 Parsons, M. (2006). *Cricklade Revealed: Part 6 - Social Life during the Second World War.* Marion Parsons, pp. 1-2. [WSHC CRI.949].

129 Wyeth, R. (1995). *Sterner Days: Codford during the Second World War.* Warminster: Bedeguar Books, pp. 91. [WSHC COD.949].

130 Reynolds, D. (1996). *Rich Relations.* London: Harper Collins, pp. 112. [WSHC AAA.949].

131 WSA F4/500/16.

132 Berryman, D. (2002). *Wiltshire Airfields in the Second World War.* Newbury: Countryside Books, pp. 14. [WSHC AAA.352].

133 White, K. (1992). Women During World War Two. *Wiltshire Folklife,* 25, pp. 40-41. [WSHC Wiltshire Folklife Journal].

134 Randall, B. (2003). *A Patchwork of Memories.* Bob Randall, pp. 11-12. [WSHC TRO.949].

135 Priddle, R. (2003). *Wings over Wiltshire.* ALD Design and Print, pp. 270. [WSHC AAA.354].

136 WSA F4/500/27.

137 Dinton Historical Society (2003). *Days of Cowslips and Skylarks: Dinton Looks Back.* A & D Media, pp. 55. [WSHC DIN.940].

138 WSA F4/500/28.

139 Day, R. (2007). *Savernake at War: A Wartime History of Savernake Forest 1940-1949.* Hungerford: Roger Day, pp. 18. [WSHC SAV.949].

140 WSA F4/500/28.

141 Ibid.

142 Wakefield, K. (1994). Operation Bolero: the Americans in Bristol and the West Country, 1942-1945. Manchester: Crecy Publishing, pp. 35. [WSHC AAA.949 (BL)].

143 WSA F5/530/6.

144 Meakin, R. (2002). *Minety at War.* Richard Meakin, pp. 14. [WSHC MIN.949].

145 Pellett, M. (2014). *Last Stop Before Destiny: the 101st Airborne Division in England 1943-44.* Matthew Pellett: CreateSpace Independent Publishing Platform, pp. 93. [WSHC AAA.949

(BL)].

146 Berryman, D. (2002). *Wiltshire Airfields in the Second World War.* Newbury: Countryside Books, pp. 175. [WSHC AAA.352].

147 Dawkins, B. (1989). *When Warm Milk Was Fresh Milk.* Bert Dawkins: Warminster, pp. 101. [WSHC WAR.949].

148 Inchfawn, F. (2010). *Salute to the Village.* Monkton Farleigh: Folly Books (Original work published 1943), pp. 41. [WSHC XIN.921].

149 WSA 1815/40.

150 WSA F5/530/6.

151 Parsons, M. (2005). *Cricklade Revealed: Part 5- Social Life during the Second World War.* Marion Parsons, pp. 12. [WSHC CRI.949].

152 Parsons, M. (2006). *Cricklade Revealed: Part 6 - Social Life during the Second World War.* Marion Parsons, pp. 17-18. [WSHC CRI.949].

153 Heath, N. (1999). *Life and Herbing in Sutton Benger: Memories of a Wiltshire Village.* Nesta Heath, pp. 20. [WSHC SUB.949].

154 Wyeth, R. (1995). *Sterner Days: Codford during the Second World War.* Warminster: Bedeguar Books, pp. 27. [WSHC COD.949].

155 Ibid., pp. 74.

156 Dewhurst, R. (2005). *Crosstracks to Hindon.* Salisbury: Hobnob Press, pp. 95-98. [WSHC HIN.940].

157 Hall, A. (1993). *Land Girl.* Bradford on Avon: Ex Libris Press, pp. 98. [WSHC AAA.949].

158 Meakin, R. (2002). *Minety at War.* Richard Meakin, pp. 13. [WSHC MIN.949].

159 White, J. and Russell, D. (2008). *Longbridge Deverill Parish Memoirs.* Longbridge Deverilll Local History Group, pp. 92. [WSHC LOD.949].

160 Reynolds, D. (1996). *Rich Relations.* London: Harper Collins, pp. 112. [WSHC AAA.949].

161 WSA F4/500/28.

162 Crowman, D. (1991). *A History of Tidworth and Tedworth House.*

Chichester: Phillimore & Co Ltd., pp. 54. [WSHC NOT.940].

163 Wyeth, R. (1995). *Sterner Days: Codford during the Second World War.* Warminster: Bedeguar Books, pp. 52. [WSHC COD.949].

164 WSA F4/100/23.

165 Price, J. and Price, J. (1999). *Dearest Sweetheart: Letters from a GI to his wife during World War II.* Paducah, KY: Turner Publishing Company, pp. 55. [WSHC NOT.921].

166 Olivier, E. (1943). *Night Thoughts of a Country Landlady.* London: B.T. Batsford Ltd., pp. 28. [WSHC XOL.824].

167 WSA F2/250/95.

168 Meakin, R. (2002). *Minety at War.* Richard Meakin, pp. 79. [WSHC MIN.949].

169 WSA F2/250/95.

170 WSA F4/550/35.

171 Day, R. (2007). *Savernake at War: A Wartime History of Savernake Forest 1940-1949.* Hungerford: Roger Day, pp. 36. [WSHC SAV.949].

172 WSA L7/244/2.

173 Parsons, M. (2005). *Cricklade Revealed: Part 5 - Social Life during the Second World War.* Marion Parsons, pp. 8. [WSHC CRI.949].

174 Devizes Local History Group and Haycock, L. (Ed.). (1995). *How Devizes Won the War!* Devizes Local History Group, pp. 78. [WSHC DEV.949].

175 Devenish, D. (1948). *A Wiltshire Country Home: A Study of Little Durnford.* London: BT Batsford Ltd., pp. 106. [WSHC DUN.727].

176 Bailey, D. (2005). *The Story of Chiseldon Camp: Part Two.* Chiseldon: Chiseldon Local History Group, pp. 36. [WSHC CHS.949].

177 Wyeth, R. (1995). *Sterner Days: Codford during the Second World War.* Warminster: Bedeguar Books, pp. 30. [WSHC COD.949].

178 Collins, J. and Miller, M. (n.d.). *Chiseldon Memories: Part One.* JMC and MMH, pp. 45. [WSHC

CHS.949].

179 Bemerton Local History Society (2006). *Memories of Bemerton in Wartime*. Bemerton Local History Society with support of the Big Lottery Fund, pp. 22. [WSHC BEM.949].

180 Buckton, H. (2008). *Salisbury Plain: Home of Britain's Military Training*. Chichester: Phillimore & Co., pp. 86. [WSHC ABP.353].

181 Wyeth, R. (1995). *Sterner Days: Codford during the Second World War*. Warminster: Bedeguar Books, pp. 41. [WSHC COD.949].

182 Dewhurst, R. (2005). *Crosstracks to Hindon*. Salisbury: Hobnob Press, pp. 95. [WSHC HIN.940].

183 Buckton, H. (2008). *Salisbury Plain: Home of Britain's Military Training*. Chichester: Phillimore & Co., pp. 87. [WSHC ABP.353].

184 Bailey, D. (2005). *The Story of Chiseldon Camp: Part Two*. Chiseldon: Chiseldon Local History Group, pp. 25. [WSHC CHS.949].

185 Reynolds, D. (1996). *Rich Relations*. London: Harper Collins, pp. 432-433. [WSHC AAA.949].

186 Wakefield, K. (1994). Operation Bolero: the Americans in Bristol and the West Country, 1942-1945. Manchester: Crecy Publishing, pp. 25. [WSHC AAA.949 (BL)].

187 Grinton, P. (2004). *US Army/Army Air Force: Units from UK Station List 1944*. Retrieved November 7, 2014 from D-Day Museum, Portsmouth website http://www.ddaymuseum. co.uk/d-day/d-day-and-the-battle-of-normandy-your-questions-answered [WSHC AAA.949 (BL) – Wiltshire Extract].

188 Berryman, D. (2002). *Wiltshire Airfields in the Second World War*. Newbury: Countryside Books, pp. 174-175. [WSHC AAA.352].

189 Ibid., pp. 235.

190 Bailey, D. (2005). *The Story of Chiseldon Camp: Part Two*. Chiseldon: Chiseldon Local History Group, pp. 80. [WSHC CHS.949].

191 Buckton, H. (2008). *Salisbury Plain: Home of Britain's Military Training*. Chichester: Phillimore & Co., pp. 103. [WSHC ABP.353].

192 Bailey, D. (2005). *The Story of Chiseldon Camp: Part Two*. Chiseldon: Chiseldon Local History Group, pp. 46. [WSHC CHS.949].

193 James, N. (1987). *Plain Soldiering*. Salisbury: Hobnob Press, pp. 149. [WSHC ABP.353].

194 Wakefield, K. (1994). Operation Bolero: the Americans in Bristol and the West Country, 1942-1945. Manchester: Crecy Publishing, pp. 125-126. [WSHC AAA.949 (BL)].

195 Ivan Clark, personal communication, 5/4/2014.

196 Wiltshire Federation of Women's Institutes (1993). *Wiltshire Within Living Memory*. Newbury: Countryside Books, pp. 217. [WSHC AAA.949].

197 355th Engineer Regiment (c. 1945). *Headquarters 355th Engineer General Service Regiment APO 350, U. H. Army: Unit History for period 1 November 1943 to 8 May 1945*. Reproduced from the Unclassified/Declassified Holdings of the National Archives Ref: V-531 Env 2, pp. 1. [WSHC AAN.949 (Ephemera folder)].

198 Bemerton Local History Society (2006). *Memories of Bemerton in Wartime*. Bemerton Local History Society with support of the Big Lottery Fund, pp. 73-74. [WSHC BEM.949].

199 Ambrose, S. (2001). *Band of Brothers*. London: Simon & Schuster, pp. 44.

200 Pellett, M. (2014). *Last Stop Before Destiny: the 101st Airborne Division in England 1943-44*. Matthew Pellett: CreateSpace Independent Publishing Platform, pp. 28. [WSHC AAA.949 (BL)].

201 Ibid., pp. 20.

202 Ibid., pp. 23.

203 Ibid., pp. 165.

204 Thamesdown Borough Council (n.d.) *Lydiard Park the War Years: an account of the military requisition of Lydiard Park during World War II and*

its aftermath. Thamesdown Borough Council, pp. 1. [WSHC LYT.949].
205 Day, R. (2007). *Savernake at War: A Wartime History of Savernake Forest 1940-1949.* Hungerford: Roger Day, pp. 34. [WSHC SAV.949].
206 Wiltshire Federation of Women's Institutes (1993). *Wiltshire Within Living Memory.* Newbury: Countryside Books, pp. 187. [WSHC AAA.949].
207 Reynolds, D. (1996). *Rich Relations.* London: Harper Collins, pp. xxix. [WSHC AAA.949].
208 Martin, M. (2008). *Evacuee School.* Unpublished, Unpaginated. [WSHC STV.949 (BL)].
209 Bemerton Local History Society (2006). *Memories of Bemerton in Wartime.* Bemerton Local History Society with support of the Big Lottery Fund, pp. 45. [WSHC BEM.949].
210 Reynolds, D. (1996). *Rich Relations.* London: Harper Collins, pp. 152. [WSHC AAA.949].
211 Langhamer, C. (2003). A public house is for all classes, men and women alike: women, leisure and drink in second world war England. *Women's History Review,* 12 (3), pp. 424. [doi: http://dx.doi.org/10.1080/09612020300200367]
212 Pickford, P. and Pickford, R. (Ed.). (1995). *Letters to Liz.* Newnham, Tasmania: Attic Press, pp. 106. [WSHC WAR.949].
213 Reynolds, D. (1996). *Rich Relations.* London: Harper Collins, pp. 151. [WSHC AAA.949].
214 Mass Observation (1987). *War Factory.* London: The Cresset Library (Original work published 1943), pp. 91. [WSHC SAI.684].
215 Reynolds, D. (1996). *Rich Relations.* London: Harper Collins, pp. 176. [WSHC AAA.949].
216 Ambrose, S. (2001). *Band of Brothers.* London: Simon & Schuster, pp. 44.
217 Day, R. (2007). *Savernake at War: A Wartime History of Savernake Forest 1940-1949.* Hungerford: Roger Day, pp. 34. [WSHC SAV.949].

218 Reynolds, D. (1996). *Rich Relations.* London: Harper Collins, pp. 37-38. [WSHC AAA.949].
219 Ibid., pp. 151.
220 Lewis, P. (1984). *A People's War.* London: Methuen London Ltd., pp. 205-206.
221 Reynolds, D. (1996). *Rich Relations.* London: Harper Collins, pp. 173. [WSHC AAA.949].
222 WSA F5/530/6.
223 Ibid.
224 Reynolds, D. (1996). *Rich Relations.* London: Harper Collins, pp. 159. [WSHC AAA.949].
225 Ibid., pp. 190.
226 Price, J. and Price, J. (1999). *Dearest Sweetheart: Letters from a GI to his wife during World War II.* Paducah, KY: Turner Publishing Company, pp. 55. [WSHC NOT.921].
227 Crowman, D. (1991). *A History of Tidworth and Tedworth House.* Chichester: Phillimore & Co Ltd., pp. 54. [WSHC NOT.940].
228 Ibid., pp. 53-54.
229 Buckton, H. (2008). *Salisbury Plain: Home of Britain's Military Training.* Chichester: Phillimore & Co., pp. 106. [WSHC ABP.353].
230 Parsons, M. (2005). *Cricklade Revealed: Part 5 - Social Life during the Second World War.* Marion Parsons, pp. 13-14. [WSHC CRI.949].
231 Ramsden-Binks, T. (2004). *A Short History of RAF Blakehill Farm.* Cricklade Historical Society, pp. 5. [WSHC CRI.352].
232 Adie, K. (2003). *Corsets to Camouflage: Women at War.* London: Hodder & Stoughton, pp. 156-157. [WSHC 355.22082].
233 WSA G24/225/4.
234 Ibid.
235 Mass Observation (1987). *War Factory.* London: The Cresset Library (Original work published 1943), pp. 81. [WSHC SAI.684].
236 WSA G24/225/4.
237 Ibid.
238 *Wiltshire Times,* 29.4.1944. [WSHC

Microform Collection].

239 WSA G24/225/4.

240 Devizes Local History Group and Haycock, L. (Ed.). (1995). *How Devizes Won the War!* Devizes Local History Group, pp. 8. [WSHC DEV.949].

241 *Salisbury Journal*, 22.10.1942. [WSHC Microform Collection].

242 Ibid., 9.10.1942.

243 Reynolds, D. (1996). *Rich Relations.* London: Harper Collins, pp. 214. [WSHC AAA.949].

244 Wyeth, R. (1995). *Sterner Days: Codford during the Second World War.* Warminster: Bedeguar Books, pp. 46-47. [WSHC COD.949].

245 Waley, M. (c. 1965). *Great Cheverell: A retrospect.* Unpublished, pp. 194. [WSHC GRC.940].

246 Reynolds, D. (1996). *Rich Relations.* London: Harper Collins, pp. 265-267. [WSHC AAA.949].

247 WSA F5/530/6.

248 Reynolds, D. (1996). *Rich Relations.* London: Harper Collins, pp. 426. [WSHC AAA.949].

249 Ibid., pp. 263.

250 WSA G24/225/4.

251 Rose, S. (2003). *Which People's War? National Identity and Citizenship in Wartime Britain 1939-45.* Oxford: Oxford University Press, pp. 73.

252 Eccles, D. (1983). *By Safe Hand: Letters of Sybil and David Eccles, 1939-1942.* London: Bodley Head, pp. 118. [WSHC CHU.928].

253 Sokoloff, S. (1999). "How are they at home?" community, state and servicemen's wives in England, 1939-45. *Women's History Review*, 8(1), 38-39. [doi http://dx.doi. org/10.1080/09612029900200196].

254 Reynolds, D. (1996). *Rich Relations.* London: Harper Collins, pp. 191-192. [WSHC AAA.949].

255 Sokoloff, S. (1999). "How are they at home?" community, state and servicemen's wives in England, 1939-45. *Women's History Review*, 8(1), 38. [doi http://dx.doi.

org/10.1080/09612029900200196].

256 Price, J. and Price, J. (1999). *Dearest Sweetheart: Letters from a GI to his wife during World War II.* Paducah, KY: Turner Publishing Company, pp. 59. [WSHC NOT.921].

257 Wyeth, R. (1995). *Sterner Days: Codford during the Second World War.* Warminster: Bedeguar Books, pp. 35. [WSHC COD.949].

258 Buckton, H. (2008). *Salisbury Plain: Home of Britain's Military Training.* Chichester: Phillimore & Co., pp. 110. [WSHC ABP.353].

259 Inchfawn, F. (2010). *Salute to the Village.* Monkton Farleigh: Folly Books (Original work published 1943), pp. 42. [WSHC XIN.921].

260 Reynolds, D. (1996). *Rich Relations.* London: Harper Collins, pp. 216-218. [WSHC AAA.949].

261 Ibid., pp. 224.

262 WSA F5/530/6.

263 Day, R. (2007). *Savernake at War: A Wartime History of Savernake Forest 1940-1949.* Hungerford: Roger Day, pp. 28. [WSHC SAV.949].

264 Dobson, M. (2011). *Bradford Voices: Life in Bradford on Avon 1900-2010.* Bradford on Avon: Ex Libris Press, pp. 148. [WSHC BRD.949].

265 Day, R. (2007). *Savernake at War: A Wartime History of Savernake Forest 1940-1949.* Hungerford: Roger Day, pp. 28. [WSHC SAV.949].

266 Thamesdown Borough Council (n.d.) *Lydiard Park the War Years: an account of the military requisition of Lydiard Park during World War II and its aftermath.* Thamesdown Borough Council, pp. 5. [WSHC LYT.949].

267 WSA F5/530/6.

268 WSA G24/225/4.

269 Lewis, P. (1984). *A People's War.* London: Methuen London Ltd., pp. 210.

270 Duffy, M. (1983). *That's How it Was.* London: Virago (Original work published 1962), pp. 122-124. [WSHC AAA.823].

271 Ibid., pp. 132-133.

272 Parsons, M. (2005). *Cricklade Revealed: Part 5 - Social Life during the Second World War.* Marion Parsons, pp. 11. [WSHC CRI.949].

273 Chase, E., Munro, D. and Munro, J. (1999). *Whiteparish: 100 Years of an English Village.* Whiteparish Historical & Environmental Association, pp. 118. [WSHC WHI.949].

274 WSA F8/500/8/1/2.

275 Wiltshire Federation of Women's Institutes (1993). *Wiltshire Within Living Memory.* Newbury: Countryside Books, pp. 217. [WSHC AAA.949].

276 Wyeth, R. (2007). *Sword and Ploughshares: Codford during the Twentieth Century.* Codford: Gemini, pp. 166. [WSHC COD.949].

277 Wyeth, R. (1995). *Sterner Days: Codford during the Second World War.* Warminster: Bedeguar Books, pp. 37. [WSHC COD.949].

278 Reynolds, D. (1996). *Rich Relations.* London: Harper Collins, pp. 258-259. [WSHC AAA.949].

279 Ibid., pp. 283.

280 Ibid., pp. 197.

281 J. Bloomfield, personal communication, 26.4.2013.

282 Annetts, S. and Annetts, R. (2013). *Evacuated to Bratton.* Unpublished, pp. 12-13. [WSHC BRT.922 (BL)].

283 Wiltshire Federation of Women's Institutes (1993). *Wiltshire Within Living Memory.* Newbury: Countryside Books, pp. 189. [WSHC AAA.949].

284 Lane, C. and White, P. (1999). *Warminster in the Twentieth Century.* The Warminster History Society: Warminster, pp. 26. [WSHC WAR.949].

285 Day, R. (2007). *Savernake at War: A Wartime History of Savernake Forest 1940-1949.* Hungerford: Roger Day, pp. 18. [WSHC SAV.949].

286 Wiltshire Federation of Women's Institutes (1993). *Wiltshire Within Living Memory.* Newbury: Countryside Books, pp. 217. [WSHC AAA.949].

287 Wyeth, R. (1995). *Sterner Days: Codford during the Second World War.*

Warminster: Bedeguar Books, pp. 12. [WSHC COD.949].

288 Eccles, D. (1983). *By Safe Hand: Letters of Sybil and David Eccles, 1939-1942.* London: Bodley Head, pp. 268. [WSHC CHU.928].

289 Reynolds, D. (1996). *Rich Relations.* London: Harper Collins, pp. 184. [WSHC AAA.949].

290 George, A. (c. 1993). *130th Station Hospital History.* In Harman (ed.). 130th Station Hospital Reunion Dayton, Ohio, October 14, 1993. Unpublished, pp. 1-2. [WSHC AAA.949 (BL)].

291 White, J. and Russell, D. (2008). *Longbridge Deverill Parish Memoirs.* Longbridge Deverilll Local History Group, pp. 92. [WSHC LOD.949].

292 Day, R. (2007). *Savernake at War: A Wartime History of Savernake Forest 1940-1949.* Hungerford: Roger Day, pp. 46. [WSHC SAV.949].

293 Reynolds, D. (1996). *Rich Relations.* London: Harper Collins, pp. 184. [WSHC AAA.949].

294 WSA F5/530/6.

295 Buckton, H. (2008). *Salisbury Plain: Home of Britain's Military Training.* Chichester: Phillimore & Co., pp. 110. [WSHC ABP.353].

296 Crowman, D. (1991). *A History of Tidworth and Tedworth House.* Chichester: Phillimore & Co Ltd., pp. 54. [WSHC NOT.940].

297 Bemerton Local History Society (2006). *Memories of Bemerton in Wartime.* Bemerton Local History Society with support of the Big Lottery Fund, pp. 10. [WSHC BEM.949].

298 English Heritage (2014). *Advice Report: Hare Warren Control Station.* English Heritage: Unpublished, pp. 3-4. [WSHC Archaeology Department].

299 Berryman, D. (2002). *Wiltshire Airfields in the Second World War.* Newbury: Countryside Books, pp. 191. [WSHC AAA.352].

300 Ambrose, S. (2003). *Pegasus Bridge.* London: Simon & Schuster, pp. 66.

301 Parsons, M. (2006). *Cricklade Revealed: Part 6 - Social Life during the Second World - Social Life during the Second World War*. Marion Parsons, pp. 5. [WSHC CRI.949].

302 Coward et. al. (2007). *The Donheads Past and Present*. East Knoyle: Hobnob Press, pp. 75. [WSHC DOM.940].

303 Day, R. (2007). *Savernake at War: A Wartime History of Savernake Forest 1940-1949*. Hungerford: Roger Day, pp. 36. [WSHC SAV.949].

304 Lynn, V. (1994). *We'll Meet Again: A Personal and Social History of WWII*. London: MacMillan, pp. 173.

305 Day, R. (2014). *Membury Airfield*. Retrieved 16 November, 2014 from Ramsbury at War website http://www.ramsburyatwar.com/ramburyairfield.htm

306 Day, R. (2007). *Savernake at War: A Wartime History of Savernake Forest 1940-1949*. Hungerford: Roger Day, pp. 34. [WSHC SAV.949].

307 Priddle, R. (2003). *Wings over Wiltshire*. ALD Design and Print, pp. 258. [WSHC AAA.354].

308 Crittall, E. (Ed.). (1959). *Victoria History of England: Wiltshire, Volume 4*. London: Oxford University Press, pp. 266. [WSHC AAA.940].

309 Day, R. (2007). *Savernake at War: A Wartime History of Savernake Forest 1940-1949*. Hungerford: Roger Day, pp. 36. [WSHC SAV.949].

310 Parsons, M. (2005). *Cricklade Revealed: Part 5 - Social Life during the Second World War*. Marion Parsons, pp. 5. [WSHC CRI.949].

311 Burchell, R. (2013). *Saucepans on our Heads: Growing up in Swindon during World War 2*. Bradford on Avon: Ex Libris Press, pp. 102-103. [WSHC SWI.949].

312 Ambrose, S. (2001). *Band of Brothers*. London: Simon & Schuster, pp. 61.

313 Bemerton Local History Society (2006). *Memories of Bemerton in Wartime*. Bemerton Local History Society with support of the Big Lottery Fund, pp. title page. [WSHC BEM.949].

314 CBC/Radio-Canada (2014). *Second World War*. Retrieved June 12, 2015 from CBC Digital Archives website http://www.cbc.ca/archives/categories/war-conflict/second-world-war/d-day-canadians-target-juno-beach/king-george-vi-addresses-his-subjects-on-d-day.html [King George address].

315 Partridge, F. (1978). *A Pacifist's War*. The Hogarth Press: London, pp. 186. [WSHC HAM.927].

316 Reynolds, D. (1996). *Rich Relations*. London: Harper Collins, pp. 392. [WSHC AAA.949].

317 Crowman, D. (1991). *A History of Tidworth and Tedworth House*. Chichester: Phillimore & Co Ltd., pp. 54. [WSHC NOT.940].

318 Thamesdown Borough Council (n.d.) *Lydiard Park the War Years: an account of the military requisition of Lydiard Park during World War II and its aftermath*. Thamesdown Borough Council, pp. 1-2. [WSHC LYT.949].

319 WSA G24/132/78.

320 Ivan Clark, personal communication, 2014.

321 Reynolds, D. (1996). *Rich Relations*. London: Harper Collins, pp. 408. [WSHC AAA.949].

322 WSA F5/530/6.

323 Reynolds, D. (1996). *Rich Relations*. London: Harper Collins, pp. 407. [WSHC AAA.949].

324 White, J. and Russell, D. (2008). *Longbridge Deverill Parish Memoirs*. Longbridge Deverilll Local History Group, pp. 92. [WSHC LOD.949].

325 Whalley, P. (n.d.). *Corsham Memories 2: The Prefab Years 1930/40*. Patricia Whalley, pp. 82. [WSHC COR.949].

326 Bailey, D. (2005). *The Story of Chiseldon Camp: Part Two*. Chiseldon: Chiseldon Local History Group, pp. 91-92. [WHSC CHS.949].

327 James, N. (1987). *Plain Soldiering*. Salisbury: Hobnob Press, pp. 160. [WSHC ABP.353].

328 Buckton, H. (2008). *Salisbury Plain: Home of Britain's Military Training*.

Chichester: Phillimore & Co., pp. 111. [WSHC ABP.353].

329 WSA G12/132/12.

330 Henderson, P. (1995). *100 Years in Corsham Parish*. Corsham Parish Council, pp. 85. [WSHC COR.940].

331 King, M. (1999). *Stand by your Beds*. Swanage: Finial Publishing, pp. 1. [WSHC DEV.359].

332 Ibid., pp. 5.

333 Ibid., pp. 17.

334 Wakefield, K. (1994). *Operation Bolero: The Americans in Bristol and the West Country, 1942-45*. Manchester: Crecy Books, pp. 26. [WSHC AAA.949 (BL)].

335 Reynolds, D. (1996). *Rich Relations*. London: Harper Collins, pp. 431. [WSHC AAA.949].

336 Ibid., pp. 433-435.

337 Price, J. and Price, J. (1999). *Dearest Sweetheart: Letters from a GI to his wife during World War II*. Paducah, KY: Turner Publishing Company, pp. 55. [WSHC NOT.921].

338 Hennessy, P. (1992). *Never Again: Britain 1945-51*. London: Penguin Books Ltd., pp. 353. [WSHC 941.0854

339 Carter, G. (1992). *Porton Down: 75yrs of Chemical & Biological Research*. London: HMSO, pp. 39. [WSHC IDM.354].

340 Ibid., pp. 169.

341 Willis, E. (2005). English Detective Fiction and the "People's War". *Forum for Modern Language Studies*, 42(1), pp. 15. [doi: 10.1093/fmls/cqio33].

342 Berryman, D. (2002). *Wiltshire Airfields in the Second World War*. Newbury: Countryside Books, pp. 50. [WSHC AAA.352].

343 Ibid., pp. 73.

344 Ibid., pp. 191.

345 Ibid., pp. 126.

346 Ibid., pp. 145.

4 Wartime Workers

1 Calder, A. (1992). *The People's War: Britain 1939-45*. London: Pimlico

(Original work published 1969), pp. 51. [WSHC 941.084].

2 WSA G24/225/29.

3 Calder, A. (1992). *The People's War: Britain 1939-45*. London: Pimlico (Original work published 1969), pp. 269. [WSHC 941.084].

4 Calder, A. (1992). *The People's War: Britain 1939-45*. London: Pimlico (Original work published 1969), pp. 235. [WSHC 941.084].

5 Glynn, S. and Booth, A. (1996). *Modern Britain: An Economic and Social History*. London: Routledge, pp. 144.

6 Calder, A. (1992). *The People's War: Britain 1939-45*. London: Pimlico (Original work published 1969), pp. 236. [WSHC 941.084].

7 Ibid., pp. 267-269.

8 Randall, B. (2003). *A Patchwork of Memories*. Bob Randall, pp. 44. [WSHC TRO.949].

9 Calder, A. (1992). *The People's War: Britain 1939-45*. London: Pimlico (Original work published 1969), pp. 452-454. [WSHC 941.084].

10 Lewis, P. (1984). *A People's War*. London: Methuen London Ltd., pp. 131.

11 Calder, A. (1992). *The People's War: Britain 1939-45*. London: Pimlico (Original work published 1969), pp. 283. [WSHC 941.084].

12 Lewis, P. (1984). *A People's War*. London: Methuen London Ltd., pp. 131.

13 Calder, A. (1992). *The People's War: Britain 1939-45*. London: Pimlico (Original work published 1969), pp. 316. [WSHC 941.084].

14 WSA G4/132/103.

15 WSA F2/250/95.

16 Postan, M. (1952). *British War Production*. London: HMSO, pp. 97.

17 Summerfield, P. (1983). Women, Work and Welfare: A Study of Child Care and Shopping in Britain in the Second World War. *Journal of Social History*, 17(2), pp. 249. [doi: 10.1353/jsh/17.2.249].

18 Paxman, J. (2013). *Great Britain's Great*

War. London: Viking, pp. 143-144.

19 Calder, A. (1992). *The People's War: Britain 1939-45*. London: Pimlico (Original work published 1969), pp. 235. [WSHC 941.084].

20 Lewis, P. (1984). *A People's War*. London: Methuen London Ltd., pp. 113.

21 Calder, A. (1992). *The People's War: Britain 1939-45*. London: Pimlico (Original work published 1969), pp. 268. [WSHC 941.084].

22 Lewis, P. (1984). *A People's War*. London: Methuen London Ltd., pp. 115.

23 Ibid., pp. 110.

24 Ibid., pp. 113-115.

25 Avon Rubber (1985). *Avon 1885-1985: In Pursuit of Excellence*. Unpublished, unpaginated. [WSHC MEL.678 (BL)].

26 Lewis, P. (1984). *A People's War*. London: Methuen London Ltd., pp. 116.

27 Gazeley, I. (2006). The Levelling of Pay in Britain during the Second World War. *European Review of Economic History, 10, pp. 75-76*.

28 Lewis, P. (1984). *A People's War*. London: Methuen London Ltd., pp. 115.

29 Sokoloff, S. (1999). "How are they at home?" community, state and servicemen's wives in England, 1939-45. *Women's History Review*, 8(1), 30. [doi http://dx.doi. org/10.1080/09612029900200116].

30 Lewis, P. (1984). *A People's War*. London: Methuen London Ltd., pp. 113, 115.

31 Wiltshire Federation of Women's Institutes (1993). *Wiltshire Within Living Memory*. Newbury: Countryside Books, pp. 210-211. [WSHC AAA.949].

32 Cattell, J. and Falconer, K. (1995). *Swindon: Legacy of a Railway Town*. London: HMSO, pp. 134. [WSHC SWI.385].

33 Anderson, B. (1994). *We Just Got On With It: British Women in World War II*.

Chippenham: Picton Publishing, pp. 63. [WSHC AAA.949].

34 Calder, A. (1992). *The People's War: Britain 1939-45*. London: Pimlico (Original work published 1969), pp. 335. [WSHC 941.084].

35 Baker, E. (n.d.). *Enfield Precision Enginering*. Unpublished, unpaginated. [WSHC WEW.629].

36 Browning, B. (2005). *EKCO's of Cowbridge*. Malmesbury: Cowbridge Publishing, pp. 57-58. [WSHC MAL.620].

37 Calder, A. (1992). *The People's War: Britain 1939-45*. London: Pimlico (Original work published 1969), pp. 335. [WSHC 941.084].

38 Anderson, B. (1994). *We Just Got On With It: British Women in World War II*. Chippenham: Picton Publishing, pp. 66. [WSHC AAA.949].

39 Hopkins, H. (1964). *New Look: A Social History of the Forties and Fifties*. London: Secker & Warburg Readers Union, pp. 45.

40 Rose, S. (2003). *Which People's War? National Identity and Citizenship in Wartime Britain 1939-45*. Oxford: Oxford University Press, pp. 114.

41 Ibid., pp. 121.

42 Wiltshire Federation of Women's Institutes (1993). *Wiltshire Within Living Memory*. Newbury: Countryside Books, pp. 207. [WSHC AAA.949].

43 Smith, H. (1984). The Womanpower Problem in Britain during the Second World War. *The Historical Journal*, 27(4), pp. 935-936.

44 Ibid., pp. 941-942.

45 Ibid., pp. 944.

46 Nicholson, H. (2007). A Disputed Identity: Women Conscientious Objectors in Second World War Britain. *Twentieth Century British History*, 18 (4), pp. 411. [doi: 10.1093/tcbh/hwm013].

47 Ibid., pp. 415.

48 Ibid., pp. 409-410.

49 Ibid., pp. 423.

50 Ibid., pp. 426.

51 Harris, C. (2000). *Women at War 1939-*

1945: *The Home Front.* Stroud: Sutton Publishing, pp. 74.

52 Calder, A. (1992). *The People's War: Britain 1939-45.* London: Pimlico (Original work published 1969), pp. 315. [WSHC 941.084].

53 Harris, C. (2000). *Women at War 1939-1945: The Home Front.* Stroud: Sutton Publishing, pp. 74.

54 Ibid., pp. 80.

55 Avon Rubber (1985). *Avon 1885-1985: In Pursuit of Excellence.* Unpublished, unpaginated. [WSHC MEL.678 (BL)].

56 Inchfawn, F. (2010). *Salute to the Village.* Monkton Farleigh: Folly Books (Original work published 1943), pp. 124. [WSHC XIN.921].

57 MacKay, R. (1999). *The Test of War: Inside Britain 1939-45.* London: UCL Press, pp. 175.

58 Sheridan, D. (1987). Introduction. In Mass Observation. *War Factory.* London: The Cresset Library (Original work published 1943), (unpaginated). [WSHC SAI.684].

59 Davis, J. (2013). *To Locate and Evaluate Local Government Archive Material for North Wiltshire held at the Wiltshire and Swindon History Centre, to Discover its use as a Source for Studying Social Change from 1939-55.* (Unpublished master's dissertation). University of Aberystwyth, Aberystwyth, pp. 20.

60 Mass Observation (1987). *War Factory.* London: The Cresset Library (Original work published 1943), Preface. [WSHC SAI.684].

61 Ibid., pp. 5.

62 Ibid., pp. 85.

63 Ibid.

64 Ibid., pp. 86-87.

65 Ibid., pp. 80-81.

66 Vernon, C. (2011). *Malmesbury versus Hitler: The Town's role in the Second World War.* Malmesbury: Malmesbury Civic Trust, pp. 175. [WSHC MAL.949].

67 Ibid., pp. 177.

68 Browning, B. (2005). *EKCO's of Cowbridge.* Malmesbury: Cowbridge

Publishing, pp. 71. [WSHC MAL.620].

69 Williams, D. (2004). *Gwendolin. Lifestory,* pp. 17. [WSHC COR.922].

70 Ibid., pp. 41.

71 Ibid., pp. 45.

72 Ibid, pp. 15.

73 Wilson, T. (1998). *The Hawthorne Aero-Engine Underground Factory 1940-1945.* Unpublished, pp. 24. [WSHC COR.949 (BL)].

74 Williams, D. (2004). *Gwendolin. Lifestory,* pp. 21-22. [WSHC COR.922].

75 Ibid., pp. 91.

76 Ibid., pp. 21.

77 Ibid., pp. 19.

78 Ibid.

79 McCamley, N. (2007). *Secret Underground Cities.* Barnsley: Pen & Sword, pp. 194. [WSHC COR.949].

80 WSA 3572/3.

81 McCamley, N. (2007). *Secret Underground Cities.* Barnsley: Pen & Sword, pp. 199. [WSHC COR.949].

82 Henderson, P. (1995). *100 Years in Corsham Parish.* Corsham Parish Council, pp. 90. [WSHC COR.940].

83 WSA F2/1230/21.

84 Hall, A. (1993). *Land Girl.* Bradford on Avon: Ex Libris Press, pp. 124. [WSHC AAA.949].

85 Lynn, V. (1994). *We'll Meet Again: A Personal and Social History of WWII.* London: MacMillan, pp. 154.

86 Summers, J. (2015). *Fashion on the Ration.* London: Profile Books in Partnership with the Imperial War Museum, pp. 24-25.

87 Ibid., 68-69.

88 Condé Naste Publications Ltd. (c. 1940). Vogue Knit Series No. 9: Warm Jumpers and Woolies for War Workers [Special issue]. *Vogue.* London: Condé Naste Publications Ltd. [WSHC Local Studies Reminiscence Collection].

89 Lewis, P. (1984). *A People's War.* London: Methuen London Ltd., pp. 116.

90 Summerfield, P. (1983). Women, Work and Welfare: A Study of Child

Care and Shopping in Britain in the Second World War. *Journal of Social History*, 17(2), pp. 253. [doi: 10.1353/jsh/17.2.249].

91 Summerfield, P. (1989). *Women Workers in the Second World War: Production and Patriarchy in Conflict*. London: Routledge, pp. 67.

92 Summerfield, P. (1983). Women, Work and Welfare: A Study of Child Care and Shopping in Britain in the Second World War. *Journal of Social History*, 17(2), pp. 253. [doi: 10.1353/jsh/17.2.249].

93 Summerfield, P. (1989). *Women Workers in the Second World War: Production and Patriarchy in Conflict*. London: Routledge, pp. 75.

94 Ibid., pp. 77.

95 Summerfield, P. (1983). Women, Work and Welfare: A Study of Child Care and Shopping in Britain in the Second World War. *Journal of Social History*, 17(2), pp. 253. [doi: 10.1353/jsh/17.2.249].

96 WSA G24/225/51.

97 WSA F8/500/157/1/2.

98 Summerfield, P. (1983). Women, Work and Welfare: A Study of Child Care and Shopping in Britain in the Second World War. *Journal of Social History*, 17(2), pp. 254. [doi: 10.1353/jsh/17.2.249].

99 WSA G24/225/51.

100 Ibid.

101 Ibid.

102 Ibid.

103 Ibid.

104 Ibid.

105 Eccles, D. (1983). *By Safe Hand: Letters of Sybil and David Eccles, 1939-1942*. London: Bodley Head, pp. 347. [WSHC CHU.928].

106 Ibid., pp. 373.

107 Summerfield, P. (1983). Women, Work and Welfare: A Study of Child Care and Shopping in Britain in the Second World War. *Journal of Social History*, 17(2), pp. 256-257. [doi: 10.1353/jsh/17.2.249].

108 Inchfawn, F. (2010). *Salute to the Village*. Monkton Farleigh: Folly Books (Original work published 1943), pp. 2. [WSHC XIN.921].

109 WSA G24/225/51.

110 Summerfield, P. (1983). Women, Work and Welfare: A Study of Child Care and Shopping in Britain in the Second World War. *Journal of Social History*, 17(2), pp. 256-257. [doi: 10.1353/jsh/17.2.249].

111 WSA F2/852/17.

112 Hickson, J. and Skrine, R. (Ed.) (2013). *Carry on Coping: Diary of a Doctor 1942-1945*. Bradford on Avon: Ex Libris Press, pp. 90. [WSHC CHP.611 Original diaries are also available at WSA 4236/1-5].

113 WSA G24/225/51.

114 WSA G8/132/31.

115 Vernon, C. (2011). *Malmesbury versus Hitler: The Town's role in the Second World War*. Malmesbury: Malmesbury Civic Trust, pp. 139. [WSHC MAL.949].

116 Summerfield, P. (1989). *Women Workers in the Second World War: Production and Patriarchy in Conflict*. London: Routledge, pp. 77.

117 WSA G24/225/51.

118 Smith, H. (1984). The Womanpower Problem in Britain during the Second World War. *The Historical Journal*, 27(4), pp. 941.

119 Kynaston, D. (2007). *A World to Build: Austerity Britain*. London: Bloomsbury, pp. 98.

120 Summerfield, P. (1989). *Women Workers in the Second World War: Production and Patriarchy in Conflict*. London: Routledge, pp. 69.

121 WSA G24/225/51.

122 WSA F2/852/17.

123 Ibid.

124 Smith, H. (1984). The Womanpower Problem in Britain during the Second World War. *The Historical Journal*, 27(4), pp. 941.

125 WSA G24/225/51.

126 Kynaston, D. (2007). *A World to Build: Austerity Britain*. London: Bloomsbury, pp. 99.

127 Ibid., pp. 209.

128 Summerfield, P. (1989). *Women Workers in the Second World War: Production and Patriarchy in Conflict.* London: Routledge, pp. 99.

129 Calder, A. (1992). *The People's War: Britain 1939-45.* London: Pimlico (Original work published 1969), pp. 389. [WSHC 941.084].

130 Summerfield, P. (1989). *Women Workers in the Second World War: Production and Patriarchy in Conflict.* London: Routledge, pp. 99.

131 Summerfield, P. (1989). *Women Workers in the Second World War: Production and Patriarchy in Conflict.* London: Routledge, pp. 103.

132 Summerfield, P. (1983). Women, Work and Welfare: A Study of Child Care and Shopping in Britain in the Second World War. *Journal of Social History*, 17(2), pp. 259. [doi: 10.1353/jsh/17.2.249].

133 Ibid., pp. 260-261.

134 Mass Observation (1987). *War Factory.* London: The Cresset Library (Original work published 1943), pp. 95. [WSHC SAI.684].

135 Hickson, J. and Skrine, R. (Ed.) (2013). *Carry on Coping: Diary of a Doctor 1942-1945.* Bradford on Avon: Ex Libris Press, pp. 143. [WSHC CHP.611 Original diaries are also available at WSA 4236/1-5].

136 Summerfield, P. (1983). Women, Work and Welfare: A Study of Child Care and Shopping in Britain in the Second World War. *Journal of Social History*, 17(2), pp. 261. [doi: 10.1353/jsh/17.2.249].

137 WSA F8/500/65/4/1.

138 Summerfield, P. (1983). Women, Work and Welfare: A Study of Child Care and Shopping in Britain in the Second World War. *Journal of Social History*, 17(2), pp. 262. [doi: 10.1353/jsh/17.2.249].

139 *Kelly's Directory*, 1939, pp. 100, 268, 298.

140 Cattell, J. and Falconer, K. (1995). *Swindon: Legacy of a Railway Town.* London: HMSO, pp. 1. [WSHC SWI.385].

141 Chandler, J. (1983). *Endless Street: A History of Salisbury and its People.* Salisbury: Hobnob Press, pp. 150. [WSHC SAL.940].

142 Bracey, H. (1952). Social Provision in Rural Wiltshire. London: Methuen and Co., pp. 28. [WSHC AAA.361].

143 *Kelly's Directory*, 1939, pp., 44, 58, 71, 162.

144 Whiles, J. (1995). *Calne at War 1939-1945.* John Whiles, pp. 35. [WSHC CAL.949].

145 Bemerton Local History Society (2006). *Memories of Bemerton in Wartime.* Bemerton Local History Society with support of the Big Lottery Fund, pp. 46. [WSHC BEM.949].

146 Lane, C. and White, P. (1999). *Warminster in the Twentieth Century.* The Warminster History Society: Warminster, pp. 168. [WSHC WAR.949].

147 Cooper, L. (2009). *A Little London Evacuee.* Diss (Norfolk): Data Tech D.T.P., pp. 42). [WSHC WAR.921].

148 Devizes Local History Group and Haycock, L. (Ed.). (1995). *How Devizes Won the War!* Devizes Local History Group, pp. 77. [WSHC DEV.949].

149 McCamley, N. (2007). *Secret Underground Cities.* Barnsley: Pen & Sword, pp. 154. [WSHC COR.949].

150 Calder, A. (1992). *The People's War: Britain 1939-45.* London: Pimlico (Original work published 1969), pp. 324. [WSHC 941.084].

151 Schaardenburgh, van, C. (2013). Shadow factories of W2 British motor industry. *Engineering and Technology Magazine*, 8(10). Retrieved September 10, 2015 from E&T website

152 Calder, A. (1992). *The People's War: Britain 1939-45.* London: Pimlico (Original work published 1969), pp. 324. [WSHC 941.084].

153 WSA F2/250/68, F4/500/33.

154 Randall, B. (2003). *A Patchwork of Memories.* Bob Randall, pp. 11. [WSHC TRO.949].

155 Phipp, M. (2011). *Wessex Aviation Industry.* Stoud: Amberley Publishing, pp. 282. [WSHC AAA.388].

156 Marshall, R. (1999). *Trowbridge Voices.* Stroud: Tempus Publishing Limited, pp. 90. [WSHC TRO.949].

157 Phipp, M. (2011). *Wessex Aviation Industry.* Stoud: Amberley Publishing, pp. 250. [WSHC AAA.388].

158 Maidment, A. (1993). *Under Salisbury Spire.* Salisbury: *Salisbury Journal,* pp. 177. [WSHC SAL.949].

159 Calder, A. (1992). *The People's War: Britain 1939-45.* London: Pimlico (Original work published 1969), pp. 446-448. [WSHC 941.084].

160 Postan, M. (1952). *British War Production.* London: HMSO, pp. 166.

161 Calder, A. (1992). *The People's War: Britain 1939-45.* London: Pimlico (Original work published 1969), pp. 450. [WSHC 941.084].

162 Phipp, M. (2011). *Wessex Aviation Industry.* Stoud: Amberley Publishing, pp. 260. [WSHC AAA.388].

163 WSA G24/225/6.

164 Phipp, M. (2011). *Wessex Aviation Industry.* Stoud: Amberley Publishing, pp. 261. [WSHC AAA.388].

165 McCamley, N. (2010). *Subterranean Britain: 2WW Secret Bunkers.* Monkton Farleigh: Folly Books, pp. 137. [WSA AAA.354].

166 Baker, E. (n.d.). *Enfield Precision Engineering.* Unpublished, unpaginated. [WSHC WEW.629].

167 Ibid.

168 Exton, C. (2007). *The Secret War Factory: Cowbridge Confidential.* Milton Keynes: Author House, pp. 19. [WSHC MAL.949].

169 Ibid., pp. 26-28.

170 WSA G24/225/6.

171 Wilson, T. (1998). *The Hawthorne Aero-Engine Underground Factory 1940-1945.* Unpublished, pp. 20-21. [WSHC COR.949 (BL)].

172 Dobson, M. (2011). *Bradford Voices:* *Life in Bradford on Avon 1900-2010.* Bradford on Avon: Ex Libris Press, pp. 153. [WSHC BRD.949].

173 Wiltshire Federation of Women's Institutes (1993). *Wiltshire Within Living Memory.* Newbury: Countryside Books, pp. 210. [WSHC AAA.949].

174 Sheridan, D. (1987). Introduction. In Mass Observation. *War Factory.* London: The Cresset Library (Original work published 1943), (unpaginated). [WSHC SAI.684].

175 Vernon, C. (2011). *Malmesbury versus Hitler: The Town's role in the Second World War.* Malmesbury: Malmesbury Civic Trust, pp. 138. [WSHC MAL.949].

176 Avon Rubber (1985). *Avon 1885-1985: In Pursuit of Excellence.* Unpublished, unpaginated. [WSHC MEL.678 (BL)].

177 Westinghouse Brake and Signal Company Ltd. (c. 1945). *The War Production Record of Westinghouse Brake & Signal Company Limited.* Westinghouse, V (back page). [WSHC CHP.620 (BL)].

178 Nock, O. (2006). *A Hundred Years of Speed with Safety. A Hundred Years of Speed with Safety,* pp. 127-128. [WSHC CHP.620].

179 Avon Rubber (1985). *Avon 1885-1985: In Pursuit of Excellence.* Unpublished, unpaginated. [WSHC MEL.678 (BL)].

180 Dobson, M. (2011). *Bradford Voices: Life in Bradford on Avon 1900-2010.* Bradford on Avon: Ex Libris Press, pp. 130-132. [WSHC BRD.949].

181 Briggs, A. (1994). *A Social History of England: New Edition.* London: Weidenfield & Nicholson (Originally published in 1983), pp. 16.

182 Lane, C. and White, P. (1999). *Warminster in the Twentieth Century.* The Warminster History Society: Warminster, pp. 185. [WSHC WAR.949].

183 WSA F14/001/1.

184 WSA G4/132/83.

185 WSA G24/225/12.

186 Browning, B. (2005). *EKCO's of Cowbridge*. Malmesbury: Cowbridge Publishing, pp. 52. [WSHC MAL.620].
187 WSA G24/225/11.
188 Ibid.
189 Calder, A. (1992). *The People's War: Britain 1939-45*. London: Pimlico (Original work published 1969), pp. 316. [WSHC 941.084].
190 Glynn, S. and Booth, A. (1996). *Modern Britain: An Economic and Social History*. London: Routledge, pp. 147.
191 McCamley, N. (2007). *Secret Underground Cities*. Barnsley: Pen & Sword, pp. 194, 196. [WSHC COR.949].
192 Ibid., pp. 127-130.
193 Parsons, M. (2006). *Cricklade Revealed: Part 6 - Social Life during the Second World War*. Marion Parsons, pp. 14. [WSHC CRI.949].
194 McCamley, N. (2007). *Secret Underground Cities*. Barnsley: Pen & Sword, pp. 196. [WSHC COR.949].
195 Wilson, T. (1998). *The Hawthorne Aero-Engine Underground Factory 1940-1945*. Unpublished, pp. 23. [WSHC COR.949 (BL)].
196 WSA F4/100/23.
197 WSA F4/760/747.
198 Brown, M. (2005). *Evacuees: Evacuation in Wartime Britain 1939-45*. Stroud: Sutton Publishing, pp. 29-30.
199 Dobson, M. (2011). *Bradford Voices: Life in Bradford on Avon 1900-2010*. Bradford on Avon: Ex Libris Press, pp. 143. [WSHC BRD.949].
200 Inchfawn, F. (2010). *Salute to the Village*. Monkton Farleigh: Folly Books (Original work published 1943), pp. 33. [WSHC XIN.921].
201 Mass Observation (1987). *War Factory*. London: The Cresset Library (Original work published 1943), pp. 13. [WSHC SAI.684].
202 Ibid, pp. 16.
203 Vernon, C. (2011). *Malmesbury versus Hitler: The Town's role in the Second*
World War. Malmesbury: Malmesbury Civic Trust, pp. 137. [WSHC MAL.949].
204 Mass Observation (1987). *War Factory*. London: The Cresset Library (Original work published 1943), pp. 15. [WSHC SAI.684].
205 Ibid., pp. 81.
206 Browning, B. (2005). *EKCO's of Cowbridge*. Malmesbury: Cowbridge Publishing, pp. 64-65. [WSHC MAL.620].
207 Exton, C. (2007). *The Secret War Factory: Cowbridge Confidential*. Milton Keynes: Author House, pp. 24. [WSHC MAL.949].
208 Mass Observation (1987). *War Factory*. London: The Cresset Library (Original work published 1943), pp. 100-102. [WSHC SAI.684].
209 Longmate, N. (2002). *How we Lived then: History of Everyday Life during the Second World War*. London: Pimlico, pp. 62.
210 WSA F2/850/10.
211 Mass Observation (1987). *War Factory*. London: The Cresset Library (Original work published 1943), pp. 101. [WSHC SAI.684].
212 Ibid., pp. 98-99.
213 Ibid., pp. 101.
214 WSA G24/225/5.
215 Mass Observation (1987). *War Factory*. London: The Cresset Library (Original work published 1943), pp. 105. [WSHC SAI.684].
216 Vernon, C. (2011). *Malmesbury versus Hitler: The Town's role in the Second World War*. Malmesbury: Malmesbury Civic Trust, pp. 147-149. [WSHC MAL.949].
217 Mass Observation (1987). *War Factory*. London: The Cresset Library (Original work published 1943), pp. 106. [WSHC SAI.684].
218 WSA G24/225/5.
219 WSA G24/225/6.
220 WSA F1/100/34/3.
221 WSA G24/225/6.
222 Ibid.
223 WSA G24/225/34.

224 WSA G24/225/35.
225 Ibid.
226 WSA F4/550/12.
227 Randall, B. (2003). *A Patchwork of Memories*. Bob Randall, pp. 11-12. [WSHC TRO.949].
228 WSA G24/225/9.
229 McCamley, N. (2007). *Secret Underground Cities*. Barnsley: Pen & Sword, pp. 194. [WSHC COR.949].
230 WSA G24/225/5.
231 WSA F2/250/68.
232 Phipp, M. (2011). *Wessex Aviation Industry*. Stoud: Amberley Publishing, pp. 288. [WSHC AAA.388].
233 Bracey, H. (1952). Social Provision in Rural Wiltshire. London: Methuen and Co., pp. 31. [WSHC AAA.361].
234 WSA G6/132/12.
235 Phipp, M. (2011). *Wessex Aviation Industry*. Stoud: Amberley Publishing, pp. 263. [WSHC AAA.388].
236 Trowbridge Urban District Council (1951). *Festival of Britain: Souvenir Programme - and Handbook*. Trowbridge: *Wiltshire Times*, pp. 26. [WSHC.394].
237 Phipp, M. (2011). *Wessex Aviation Industry*. Stoud: Amberley Publishing, pp. 250. [WSHC AAA.388].
238 Ibid., pp. 282.
239 Baker, E. (n.d.). *Enfield Precision Enginering*. Unpublished, unpaginated. [WSHC WEW.629].
240 Avon Rubber (1985). *Avon 1885-1985: In Pursuit of Excellence*. Unpublished, unpaginated. [WSHC MEL.678 (BL)].
241 Bracey, H. (1952). Social Provision in Rural Wiltshire. London: Methuen and Co., pp. 31. [WSHC AAA.361].
242 Rose, S. (2003). *Which People's War? National Identity and Citizenship in Wartime Britain 1939-45*. Oxford: Oxford University Press, pp. 140.
243 Lane, C. and White, P. (1999). *Warminster in the Twentieth Century*. The Warminster History Society: Warminster, pp. 185. [WSHC WAR.949].
244 Bracey, H. (1952). Social Provision

in Rural Wiltshire. London: Methuen and Co., pp. 42. [WSHC AAA.361].
245 WSA G24/132/57.
246 Lewis, P. (1984). *A People's War*. London: Methuen London Ltd., pp. 148.
247 Glynn, S. and Booth, A. (1996). *Modern Britain: An Economic and Social History*. London: Routledge, pp. 156.
248 Gazeley, I. (2006). The Levelling of Pay in Britain during the Second World War. *European Review of Economic History*, 10, pp. 178.
249 Briggs, A. (1994). *A Social History of England: New Edition*. London: Weidenfield & Nicholson (Originally published in 1983), pp. 57.
250 Glynn, S. and Booth, A. (1996). *Modern Britain: An Economic and Social History*. London: Routledge, pp. 156.
251 Ibid., pp. 181.
252 Wilson, Smith, D. (2006). A New Look at the Affluent Working Mother in Post-War Britain. *Twentieth Century British History*, 17(2), pp. 217.
253 MacKay, R. (1999). *The Test of War: Inside Britain 1939-45*. London: UCL Press, pp. 225.
254 Wilson, Smith, D. (2006). A New Look at the Affluent Working Mother in Post-War Britain. *Twentieth Century British History*, 17(2), pp. 216.
255 Ibid., pp. 210.
256 Ibid., pp. 217.
257 Glynn, S. and Booth, A. (1996). *Modern Britain: An Economic and Social History*. London: Routledge, pp. 279.
258 MacKay, R. (1999). *The Test of War: Inside Britain 1939-45*. London: UCL Press, pp. 220-221.
259 Smith, H. (1984). The Womanpower Problem in Britain during the Second World War. *The Historical Journal*, 27(4), pp. 937-940.

260 MacKay, R. (1999). *The Test of War: Inside Britain 1939-45*. London: UCL Press, pp. 223.

261 Marshall, R. (1999). *Trowbridge Voices*. Stroud: Tempus Publishing Limited, pp. 48. [WSHC TRO.949].

262 Westinghouse Brake and Signal Company Limited (1946). *Westinghouse: Engineering as a Career*. Westinghouse, pp. 1. [WSHC CHP.620 (BL)].

263 Wilson, Smith, D. (2006). A New Look at the Affluent Working Mother in Post-War Britain. *Twentieth Century British History*, 17(2), pp. 212.

264 Ibid., pp. 210-211.

265 Ibid., pp. 208.

266 Summerfield, P. (1983). Women, Work and Welfare: A Study of Child Care and Shopping in Britain in the Second World War. *Journal of Social History*, 17(2), pp. 263. [doi: 10.1353/jsh/17.2.249].

267 MacKay, R. (1999). *The Test of War: Inside Britain 1939-45*. London: UCL Press, pp. 224.

268 Glynn, S. and Booth, A. (1996). *Modern Britain: An Economic and Social History*. London: Routledge, pp. 1.

269 Glynn, S. and Booth, A. (1996). *Modern Britain: An Economic and Social History*. London: Routledge.

270 Morgan, K. (1990). *The People's Peace*. Oxford: Oxford University Press, pp. 9-10.

271 Calder, A. (1992). *The People's War: Britain 1939-45*. London: Pimlico (Original work published 1969), pp. 564. [WSHC 941.084].

272 Ibid., pp. 392.

273 MacKay, R. (1999). *The Test of War: Inside Britain 1939-45*. London: UCL Press, pp. 83.

274 Glynn, S. and Booth, A. (1996). *Modern Britain: An Economic and Social History*. London: Routledge, pp. 164.

275 Briggs, A. (1994). *A Social History of England: New Edition*. London: Weidenfield & Nicholson (Originally published in 1983), pp. 19.

5 Toil in the Fields

1 Street, A. G. (1950). *In His Own Country*. London: Eyre & Spottiswoode, pp. xvi. [WSHC XST.824].

2 Ginn, P., Goodman, R. and Langlands, A. (2012). *Wartime Farm*. London: Mitchell Beazley, pp. 14.

3 Collingham, L. (2011). *The Taste of War: World War Two and the Battle for Food*. London: Penguin Books Ltd., pp. 67.

4 Ginn, P., Goodman, R. and Langlands, A. (2012). *Wartime Farm*. London: Mitchell Beazley, pp. 14.

5 Tyrer, N. (1996). *They Fought in the Fields*. London: Sinclair-Stevenson, pp. 3. [WSHC 331.4830941].

6 Street, A. G. (1950). *In His Own Country*. London: Eyre & Spottiswoode, pp. xvi. [WSHC XST.824].

7 Calder, A. (1992). *The People's War: Britain 1939-45*. London: Pimlico (Original work published 1969), pp. 419. [WSHC 941.084].

8 Street, A. G. (1950). *In His Own Country*. London: Eyre & Spottiswoode, pp. 6. [WSHC XST.824].

9 Ginn, P., Goodman, R. and Langlands, A. (2012). *Wartime Farm*. London: Mitchell Beazley, pp. 17.

10 Martin, J. (2000). *The Development of Modern Agriculture: British Farming Since 1931*. Basingstoke: Macmillan Press Ltd, pp. 6.

11 Street, A. G. (1950). *In His Own Country*. London: Eyre & Spottiswoode, pp. 29-30. [WSHC XST.824].

12 Martin, J. (2000). *The Development of Modern Agriculture: British Farming Since 1931*. Basingstoke: Macmillan Press Ltd, pp. 12.

13 Calder, A. (1992). *The People's War: Britain 1939-45*. London: Pimlico (Original work published 1969), pp. 420. [WSHC 941.084].

14 Martin, J. (2000). *The Development of*

Modern Agriculture: British Farming Since 1931. Basingstoke: Macmillan Press Ltd, pp. 24.

15 Ginn, P., Goodman, R. and Langlands, A. (2012). *Wartime Farm.* London: Mitchell Beazley, pp. 17.

16 Martin, J. (2000). *The Development of Modern Agriculture: British Farming Since 1931.* Basingstoke: Macmillan Press Ltd, pp. 24.

17 Manners, L. (1973). *A Countryman Looks Back.* Minety: Taylor & Sons, pp. 122. [WSHC. MIN.921].

18 Ginn, P., Goodman, R. and Langlands, A. (2012). *Wartime Farm.* London: Mitchell Beazley, pp. 17.

19 Manners, L. (1973). *A Countryman Looks Back.* Minety: Taylor & Sons, pp. 121. [WSHC. MIN.921].

20 Calder, A. (1992). *The People's War: Britain 1939-45.* London: Pimlico (Original work published 1969), pp. 420. [WSHC 941.084].

21 Street, A. G. (1942). A Year of my Life. London: Eyre & Spottiswoode, pp. 34-36. [WSHC XST.921].

22 Martin, J. (2000). *The Development of Modern Agriculture: British Farming Since 1931.* Basingstoke: Macmillan Press Ltd, pp. 13.

23 Ibid., pp. 17.

24 Calder, A. (1992). *The People's War: Britain 1939-45.* London: Pimlico (Original work published 1969), pp. 418. [WSHC 941.084].

25 Cantwell, J. (1993). *The Second World War: A Guide to Documents in the Public Record Office.* London: HMSO (Original work published 1972), pp. 29. [WSHC 16.94053].

26 Manton, K. (2009). Sir William Beveridge, the British Government and Plans for Food Control in Time of War, c. 1916-1941. *Contemporary British History,* 23(3), pp. 379.

27 Martin, J. (2000). *The Development of Modern Agriculture: British Farming Since 1931.* Basingstoke: Macmillan Press Ltd, pp. 23.

28 Ibid., pp. 30.

29 Ibid., pp. 196.

30 Ibid., pp. 30.

31 Ibid., pp. 26-28.

32 Ibid., pp. 28-30.

33 Ibid., pp. 36.

34 Martin, J. (2007). George Odlum, the Ministry of Agriculture and 'Farmer Hudson'. *Agricultural History Review,* 55(II), pp. 233. [WSHC MAN.630 (BL)].

35 Ibid., pp. 240.

36 Street, A. G. (1950). *In His Own Country.* London: Eyre & Spottiswoode, pp. 213. [WSHC XST.824].

37 Ibid., pp. 213-214.

38 Tyrer, N. (1996). *They Fought in the Fields.* London: Sinclair-Stevenson, pp. 117. [WSHC 331.4830941].

39 Cantwell, J. (1993). *The Second World War: A Guide to Documents in the Public Record Office.* London: HMSO (Original work published 1972), pp. 29. [WSHC 16.94053].

40 Calder, A. (1992). *The People's War: Britain 1939-45.* London: Pimlico (Original work published 1969), pp. 420. [WSHC 941.084].

41 Tyrer, N. (1996). *They Fought in the Fields.* London: Sinclair-Stevenson, pp. 4. [WSHC 331.4830941].

42 Street, A. G. (1943) *Hitler's Whistle.* London: Eyre & Spottiswoode, pp. 16-17. [WSHC XST.630].

43 Calder, A. (1992). *The People's War: Britain 1939-45.* London: Pimlico (Original work published 1969), pp. 420-421. [WSHC 941.084].

44 Whatley, C. (1940). The Farmer's War. *Country Life,* April 20, 1940, pp. 404. [WSHC AAA.630 (Ephemera)].

45 Calder, A. (1992). *The People's War: Britain 1939-45.* London: Pimlico (Original work published 1969), pp. 421. [WSHC 941.084].

46 Olivier, E. (1943). *Night Thoughts of a Country Landlady.* London: B.T. Batsford Ltd., pp. 84. [WSHC XOL.824].

47 Wiltshire National Farmer's Union (1942). *Wiltshire NFU Record,* 10(8). [WSA 2309/120/9].

48 Collingham, L. (2011). *The Taste of War: World War Two and the Battle for Food*. London: Penguin Books Ltd., pp. 92.

49 Wiltshire National Farmer's Union (1942). *Wiltshire NFU Record*, 10(11), August. [WSA 2309/120/9].

50 Whatley, C. (1955). *Farm, Fox and Fireside*. Swindon: The Swindon Press Limited, distributed by the National Farmers Union Offices, Devizes, pp. 17. [WSHC AAA.630].

51 Calder, A. (1992). *The People's War: Britain 1939-45*. London: Pimlico (Original work published 1969), pp. 422. [WSHC 941.084].

52 Price, W. (1944). War-time Farming. *Ministry of Agriculture Journal*, pp. 3. [WSHC AAA.630 (BL)].

53 Calder, A. (1992). *The People's War: Britain 1939-45*. London: Pimlico (Original work published 1969), pp. 422. [WSHC 941.084].

54 Ibid., pp. 421.

55 Sketch, W. (1938). Manitoba in Wiltshire: A Fully Mechanised Farm. *Country Life*, September 17, 1938, pp. 269-270.

56 Calder, A. (1992). *The People's War: Britain 1939-45*. London: Pimlico (Original work published 1969), pp. 421. [WSHC 941.084].

57 Price, W. (1944). War-time Farming. *Ministry of Agriculture Journal*, pp. 8. [WSHC AAA.630 (BL)].

58 Calder, A. (1992). *The People's War: Britain 1939-45*. London: Pimlico (Original work published 1969), pp. 422. [WSHC 941.084].

59 Whatley, C. (1940). The Farmer's War. *Country Life*, April 20, 1940, pp. 406. [WSHC AAA.630 (Ephemera)].

60 Ginn, P., Goodman, R. and Langlands, A. (2012). *Wartime Farm*. London: Mitchell Beazley, pp. 48.

61 Price, W. (1944). War-time Farming. *Ministry of Agriculture Journal*, pp. 2. [WSHC AAA.630 (BL)].

62 Barber, W. (1944). Flax-Growing in England. *Country Life*, November 3, 1944, pp. 766. [WSHC AAA.362

(Ephemera folder)].

63 Price, W. (1944). War-time Farming. *Ministry of Agriculture Journal*, pp. 2. [WSHC AAA.630 (BL)].

64 Marshall, R. (1999). *Trowbridge Voices*. Stroud: Tempus Publishing Limited, pp. 93. [WSHC TRO.949].

65 Wiltshire Federation of Women's Institutes (1993). *Wiltshire Within Living Memory*. Newbury: Countryside Books, pp. 213. [WSHC AAA.949].

66 Price, W. (1944). War-time Farming. *Ministry of Agriculture Journal*, pp. 4. [WSHC AAA.630 (BL)].

67 Hall, A. (1993). *Land Girl*. Bradford on Avon: Ex Libris Press, pp. 74. [WSHC AAA.949].

68 Wiltshire Federation of Women's Institutes (1993). *Wiltshire Within Living Memory*. Newbury: Countryside Books, pp. 209. [WSHC AAA.949].

69 Wiltshire National Farmer's Union (1942). *Wiltshire NFU Record*, 10(5). [WSA 2309/120/9].

70 Barber, W. (1944). Flax-Growing in England. *Country Life*, November 3, 1944, pp. 766-768. [WSHC AAA.362 (Ephemera folder)].

71 Devizes Local History Group and Haycock, L. (Ed.). (1995). *How Devizes Won the War!* Devizes Local History Group, pp. 75-77. [WSHC DEV.949].

72 Barber, W. (1944). Flax-Growing in England. *Country Life*, November 3, 1944, pp. 766. [WSHC AAA.362 (Ephemera folder)].

73 WSA F2/1226/3.

74 Ginn, P., Goodman, R. and Langlands, A. (2012). *Wartime Farm*. London: Mitchell Beazley, pp. 44-46.

75 Price, W. (1944). War-time Farming. *Ministry of Agriculture Journal*, pp. 2. [WSHC AAA.630 (BL)].

76 Wiltshire National Farmer's Union (1942). *Wiltshire NFU Record*, 10(4), August. [WSA 2309/120/9].

77 Price, W. (1944). War-time Farming. *Ministry of Agriculture Journal*, pp. 4-5. [WSHC AAA.630 (BL)].

78 Garland, K. (2010). A Short History

of Greyhound Racing in Salisbury. *South Wiltshire Industrial Archaeological Society Historical Monograph*, 20, pp. 3. [WSHC SAL.799].

79 Price, W. (1944). War-time Farming. *Ministry of Agriculture Journal*, pp. 5. [WSHC AAA.630 (BL)].

80 Calder, A. (1992). *The People's War: Britain 1939-45*. London: Pimlico (Original work published 1969), pp. 422. [WSHC 941.084].

81 Collingham, L. (2011). *The Taste of War: World War Two and the Battle for Food*. London: Penguin Books Ltd., pp. 91.

82 Buchanan-Dunlop, R. (2011). *Ham: the story of a Wiltshire village*. R. Buchanan-Dunlop, pp. 149. [WSHC HAM.940].

83 Whatley, C. (1940). The Farmer's War. *Country Life*, April 20, 1940, pp. 405. [WSHC AAA.630 (Ephemera)].

84 WSA 2865/1.

85 Whatley, C. (1955). *Farm, Fox and Fireside*. Swindon: The Swindon Press Limited, distributed by the National Farmers Union Offices, Devizes, pp. 18. [WSHC AAA.630].

86 WSA 2865/1.

87 Martin, J. (2000). *The Development of Modern Agriculture: British Farming Since 1931*. Basingstoke: Macmillan Press Ltd, pp. 34-35.

88 Whatley, C. (1940). The Farmer's War. *Country Life*, April 20, 1940, pp. 405. [WSHC AAA.630 (Ephemera)].

89 Price, W. (1944). War-time Farming. *Ministry of Agriculture Journal*, pp. 1. [WSHC AAA.630 (BL)].

90 Rogers, R. (1957). *Some Aspects of West Country Farming: Wiltshire*. Royal Agricultural Society of England, pp. 20. [WSHC AAA.630 (BL)].

91 Street, A. G. (1950). *In His Own Country*. London: Eyre & Spottiswoode, pp. xvi. [WSHC XST.824].

92 Calder, A. (1992). *The People's War: Britain 1939-45*. London: Pimlico (Original work published 1969), pp. 423. [WSHC 941.084].

93 Ibid.

94 Collingham, L. (2011). *The Taste of War: World War Two and the Battle for Food*. London: Penguin Books Ltd., pp. 91-92.

95 Price, W. (1944). War-time Farming. *Ministry of Agriculture Journal*, pp. 5-6. [WSHC AAA.630 (BL)].

96 Ibid., pp. 2-3.

97 Ibid., pp. 2.

98 Collingham, L. (2011). *The Taste of War: World War Two and the Battle for Food*. London: Penguin Books Ltd., pp. 98.

99 Whatley, C. (1955). *Farm, Fox and Fireside*. Swindon: The Swindon Press Limited, distributed by the National Farmers Union Offices, Devizes, pp. 18-19. [WSHC AAA.630].

100 Street, A. G. (1943) *Hitler's Whistle*. London: Eyre & Spottiswoode, pp. 39-40. [WSHC XST.630].

101 Calder, A. (1992). *The People's War: Britain 1939-45*. London: Pimlico (Original work published 1969), pp. 424-425. [WSHC 941.084].

102 Ibid, pp. 425.

103 Cantwell, J. (1993). *The Second World War: A Guide to Documents in the Public Record Office*. London: HMSO (Original work published 1972), pp. 30. [WSHC 16.94053].

104 WSA 2028/76.

105 Tyrer, N. (1996). *They Fought in the Fields*. London: Sinclair-Stevenson, pp. 60. [WSHC 331.4830941].

106 Martin, J. (2000). *The Development of Modern Agriculture: British Farming Since 1931*. Basingstoke: Macmillan Press Ltd, pp. 41-42.

107 Tyrer, N. (1996). *They Fought in the Fields*. London: Sinclair-Stevenson, pp. 60-64. [WSHC 331.4830941].

108 Street, A. G. (1950). *In His Own Country*. London: Eyre & Spottiswoode, pp. 324. [WSHC XST.824].

109 Calder, A. (1992). *The People's War: Britain 1939-45*. London: Pimlico (Original work published 1969), pp. 425. [WSHC 941.084].

110 Tyrer, N. (1996). *They Fought in the Fields*. London: Sinclair-Stevenson, pp. 4. [WSHC 331.4830941].

111 Calder, A. (1992). *The People's War: Britain 1939-45*. London: Pimlico (Original work published 1969), pp. 425-6. [WSHC 941.084].

112 WSA 3061/8.

113 Hennessy, P. (1992). *Never Again: Britain 1945-51*. London: Penguin Books Ltd., pp. 44. [WSHC 941.0854].

114 Ginn, P., Goodman, R. and Langlands, A. (2012). *Wartime Farm*. London: Mitchell Beazley, pp. 18.

115 Martin, J. (2000). *The Development of Modern Agriculture: British Farming Since 1931*. Basingstoke: Macmillan Press Ltd, pp. 45-46.

116 Martin, J. (2007). George Odlum, the Ministry of Agriculture and 'Farmer Hudson'. *Agricultural History Review*, 55(II), pp. 235. [WSHC MAN.630 (BL)].

117 Martin, J. (2000). *The Development of Modern Agriculture: British Farming Since 1931*. Basingstoke: Macmillan Press Ltd, pp. 45-46.

118 Martin, J. (2007). George Odlum, the Ministry of Agriculture and 'Farmer Hudson'. *Agricultural History Review*, 55(II), pp. 234. [WSHC MAN.630 (BL)].

119 Whatley, C. (1940). The Farmer's War. *Country Life*, April 20, 1940, pp. 405. [WSHC AAA.630 (Ephemera)].

120 Calder, A. (1992). *The People's War: Britain 1939-45*. London: Pimlico (Original work published 1969), pp. 425-426. [WSHC 941.084].

121 Ginn, P., Goodman, R. and Langlands, A. (2012). *Wartime Farm*. London: Mitchell Beazley, pp. 18.

122 *World War One: The Few that Fed the Many*. (2015). Retrieved February 12, 2015 from the National Farmers' Union website http://www.nfuonline.com/the-few-that-fed-the-many-wwi-report/ [p. 7].

123 Ginn, P., Goodman, R. and Langlands, A. (2012). *Wartime Farm*.

London: Mitchell Beazley, pp. 18.

124 Price, W. (1944). War-time Farming. *Ministry of Agriculture Journal*, pp. 8. [WSHC AAA.630 (BL)].

125 Ginn, P., Goodman, R. and Langlands, A. (2012). *Wartime Farm*. London: Mitchell Beazley, pp. 22.

126 Calder, A. (1992). *The People's War: Britain 1939-45*. London: Pimlico (Original work published 1969), pp. 426. [WSHC 941.084].

127 Ginn, P., Goodman, R. and Langlands, A. (2012). *Wartime Farm*. London: Mitchell Beazley, pp. 22.

128 Foot, W. (1994). *Public Record Office Readers' Guide No. 9: Maps for Family History*. London: PRO Publications, pp. 54. [WSHC 929.1].

129 Calder, A. (1992). *The People's War: Britain 1939-45*. London: Pimlico (Original work published 1969), pp. 426. [WSHC 941.084].

130 Ginn, P., Goodman, R. and Langlands, A. (2012). *Wartime Farm*. London: Mitchell Beazley, pp. 23.

131 Calder, A. (1992). *The People's War: Britain 1939-45*. London: Pimlico (Original work published 1969), pp. 426-427. [WSHC 941.084].

132 Martin, J. (2000). *The Development of Modern Agriculture: British Farming Since 1931*. Basingstoke: Macmillan Press Ltd, pp. 64.

133 Calder, A. (1992). *The People's War: Britain 1939-45*. London: Pimlico (Original work published 1969), pp. 427. [WSHC 941.084].

134 Martin, J. (2000). *The Development of Modern Agriculture: British Farming Since 1931*. Basingstoke: Macmillan Press Ltd, pp. 64.

135 Martin, J. (2007). George Odlum, the Ministry of Agriculture and 'Farmer Hudson'. *Agricultural History Review*, 55(II), pp. 230. [WSHC MAN.630 (BL)].

136 WSA F9/150/4.

137 Foot, W. (1994). *Public Record Office Readers' Guide No. 9: Maps for Family History*. London: PRO Publications, pp. 57. [WSHC 929.1].

138 Martin, J. (2000). *The Development of Modern Agriculture: British Farming Since 1931*. Basingstoke: Macmillan Press Ltd, pp. 46-47.

139 Vernon, C. (2011). *Malmesbury versus Hitler: The Town's role in the Second World War*. Malmesbury: Malmesbury Civic Trust, pp. 154. [WSHC MAL.949].

140 Collingham, L. (2011). *The Taste of War: World War Two and the Battle for Food*. London: Penguin Books Ltd., pp. 96.

141 Martin, J. (2007). George Odlum, the Ministry of Agriculture and 'Farmer Hudson'. *Agricultural History Review*, 55(II), pp. 250. [WSHC MAN.630 (BL)].

142 Ibid., pp. 229.

143 Ibid., pp. 237-241.

144 Collingham, L. (2011). *The Taste of War: World War Two and the Battle for Food*. London: Penguin Books Ltd., pp. 90.

145 Martin, J. (2007). George Odlum, the Ministry of Agriculture and 'Farmer Hudson'. *Agricultural History Review*, 55(II), pp. 241. [WSHC MAN.630 (BL)].

146 Ibid., pp. 229.

147 Ibid., pp. 236.

148 Ibid., pp. 250.

149 Ibid., pp. 241-242.

150 Ibid., pp. 246.

151 Ibid., pp. 243.

152 Ibid., pp. 248.

153 Ginn, P., Goodman, R. and Langlands, A. (2012). *Wartime Farm*. London: Mitchell Beazley, pp. 24.

154 Foot, W. (1994). *Public Record Office Readers' Guide No. 9: Maps for Family History*. London: PRO Publications, pp. 53. [WSHC 929.1].

155 Calder, A. (1992). *The People's War: Britain 1939-45*. London: Pimlico (Original work published 1969), pp. 425. [WSHC 941.084].

156 Ibid., pp. 427.

157 Ibid., pp. 420.

158 Ibid., pp. 427.

159 WSA G2/132/37.

160 Price, W. (1944). War-time Farming. *Ministry of Agriculture Journal*, pp. 8. [WSHC AAA.630 (BL)].

161 WSA G2/132/37.

162 Ibid.

163 WSA G7/132/14.

164 WSA G5/132/73.

165 WSA G2/132/19.

166 Vernon, C. (2011). *Malmesbury versus Hitler: The Town's role in the Second World War*. Malmesbury: Malmesbury Civic Trust, pp. 154. [WSHC MAL.949].

167 Martin, M. (2013). *Hilperton Marsh in the Early 1940s*. Unpublished, pp. 1. [WSHC STV.949 (BL)].

168 Inchfawn, F. (2010). *Salute to the Village*. Monkton Farleigh: Folly Books (Original work published 1943), pp. 161. [WSHC XIN.921].

169 Ibid., pp. 164.

170 Hickson, J. and Skrine, R. (Ed.) (2013). *Carry on Coping: Diary of a Doctor 1942-1945*. Bradford on Avon: Ex Libris Press, pp. 126. [WSHC CHP.611 Original diaries are also available at WSA 4236/1-5].

171 WSA F1/100/10/7.

172 WSA F2/250/95.

173 Bemerton Local History Society (2006). *Memories of Bemerton in Wartime*. Bemerton Local History Society with support of the Big Lottery Fund, pp. 79-80. [WSHC BEM.949].

174 WSA 2309/175/4.

175 Street, A. G. (1943) *Hitler's Whistle*. London: Eyre & Spottiswoode, pp. 15. [WSHC XST.630].

176 Calder, A. (1992). *The People's War: Britain 1939-45*. London: Pimlico (Original work published 1969), pp. 428. [WSHC 941.084].

177 Street, A. G. (1950). *In His Own Country*. London: Eyre & Spottiswoode, pp. 325. [WSHC XST.824].

178 Wiltshire Federation of Women's Institutes (1993). *Wiltshire Within Living Memory*. Newbury: Countryside Books, pp. 212. [WSHC AAA.949].

179 Cantwell, J. (1993). *The Second World*

War: A Guide to Documents in the Public Record Office. London: HMSO (Original work published 1972), pp. 30. [WSHC 16.94053].

180 Calder, A. (1992). *The People's War: Britain 1939-45*. London: Pimlico (Original work published 1969), pp. 428. [WSHC 941.084].

181 Cantwell, J. (1993). *The Second World War: A Guide to Documents in the Public Record Office*. London: HMSO (Original work published 1972), pp. 30. [WSHC 16.94053].

182 Tyrer, N. (1996). *They Fought in the Fields*. London: Sinclair-Stevenson, pp. 4. [WSHC 331.4830941].

183 Dawkins, B. (1989). *When Warm Milk Was Fresh Milk*. Bert Dawkins, pp. 96. [WSHC WAR.949].

184 Gartner, N. (2012). *Operation Pied Piper: The Wartime Evacuation of Schoolchildren from London and Berlin 1938-1946*. Charlotte (USA): ISA (Information Age Publishing), pp. 143.

185 Street, A. G. (1950). *In His Own Country*. London: Eyre & Spottiswoode, pp. 232-233. [WSHC XST.824].

186 WSA F8/100/12.

187 Ibid., F8/933/EA39.

188 Ibid., F8/100/12.

189 Ibid.

190 Ibid., F8/500/258/2/2.

191 Ibid., F8/500/157/1/2.

192 Ibid., F8/500/8/1/2.

193 Ibid., F8/500/173/1/2.

194 Ibid., F1/100/34/3.

194 Ibid., F8/500/157/1/2.

194 Ginn, P., Goodman, R. and Langlands, A. (2012). *Wartime Farm*. London: Mitchell Beazley, pp. 75.

195 WSA F8/100/12.

196 Wiltshire National Farmer's Union (1942). *Wiltshire NFU Record*, 10(8). [WSA 2309/120/9].

197 National Farmer's Union (1942). *The NFU Record*, 20(241). [WSA 2309/120/9].

198 Whatley, C. (1955). *Farm, Fox and Fireside*. Swindon: The Swindon Press Limited, distributed by the National

Farmers Union Offices, Devizes, pp. 28. [WSHC AAA.630].

199 Ginn, P., Goodman, R. and Langlands, A. (2012). *Wartime Farm*. London: Mitchell Beazley, pp. 74.

200 Day, R. (2007). *Savernake at War: A Wartime History of Savernake Forest 1940-1949*. Hungerford: Roger Day, pp. 18. [WSHC SAV.949].

201 Ibid., pp. 30.

202 WSA F5/540/7.

203 Wiltshire National Farmer's Union (1942). *Wiltshire NFU Record*, 10(10). [WSA 2309/120/9].

204 WSA F5/540/7.

205 Vernon, C. (2011). *Malmesbury versus Hitler: The Town's role in the Second World War*. Malmesbury: Malmesbury Civic Trust, pp. 154. [WSHC MAL.949].

206 WSA G24/719/4.

207 Calder, A. (1992). *The People's War: Britain 1939-45*. London: Pimlico (Original work published 1969), pp. 430. [WSHC 941.084].

208 Hall, A. (1993). *Land Girl*. Bradford on Avon: Ex Libris Press, pp. 90. [WSHC AAA.949].

209 Ginn, P., Goodman, R. and Langlands, A. (2012). *Wartime Farm*. London: Mitchell Beazley, pp. 74.

210 Price, W. (1944). War-time Farming. *Ministry of Agriculture Journal*, pp. 3. [WSHC AAA.630 (BL)].

211 Ibid.

212 Hall, A. (1993). *Land Girl*. Bradford on Avon: Ex Libris Press, pp. 99-103. [WSHC AAA.949].

213 Ibid., pp. 104-107.

214 Ibid., pp. 110-115.

215 Price, W. (1944). War-time Farming. *Ministry of Agriculture Journal*, pp. 5. [WSHC AAA.630 (BL)].

216 Hall, A. (1993). *Land Girl*. Bradford on Avon: Ex Libris Press, pp. 117. [WSHC AAA.949].

217 *Lend a Hand on the Land at a Farming Holiday Camp*. (2015). Retrieved February 12, 2015 from the Imperial War Museum website

objer (/s 769)

218 *The Art of War: Learn About the Art.* (2015). Retrieved September 7, 2015 from The National Archives website http://www.nationalarchives.gov.uk theartofwar/inf3.htm

219 Tyrer, N. (1996). *They Fought in the Fields.* London: Sinclair-Stevenson, pp. 5. [WSHC 331.4830941].

220 Ibid., pp. 15-21.

221 Ibid., pp. 22-23.

222 Ibid., pp. 27.

223 Ibid., pp. 24.

224 Ibid., pp. 29.

225 Ibid., pp. 69-70.

226 Calder, A. (1992). *The People's War: Britain 1939-45.* London: Pimlico (Original work published 1969), pp. 428. [WSHC 941.084].

227 Tyrer, N. (1996). *They Fought in the Fields.* London: Sinclair-Stevenson, pp. 118. [WSHC 331.4830941].

228 Ibid., pp. 188.

229 Ibid., pp. 219.

230 Hopkins, H. (1964). *New Look: A Social History of the Forties and Fifties.* London: Secker & Warburg Readers Union, pp. 103.

231 Wiltshire Federation of Women's Institutes (1993). *Wiltshire Within Living Memory.* Newbury: Countryside Books, pp. 211-212. [WSHC AAA.949].

232 Ibid., pp. 214.

233 Tyrer, N. (1996). *They Fought in the Fields.* London: Sinclair-Stevenson, pp. 90. [WSHC 331.4830941].

234 The National Federation of Young Farmers' Clubs (1942). *Annual Report.* National Federation of Young Farmers' Clubs, pp. 3.

235 Tyrer, N. (1996). *They Fought in the Fields.* London: Sinclair-Stevenson, pp. 93-96. [WSHC 331.4830941].

236 Hall, A. (1993). *Land Girl.* Bradford on Avon: Ex Libris Press, pp. 71-72. [WSHC AAA.949].

237 Ibid., pp.

238 Ibid., pp. 76.

239 Ibid., pp. 80-86.

240 Ibid., pp. 88-89.

241 Tyrer, N. (1996). *They Fought in the Fields.* London: Sinclair-Stevenson, pp. 103. [WSHC 331.4830941].

242 Wyeth, R. (1995). *Sterner Days: Codford during the Second World War.* Warminster: Bedeguar Books, pp. 13. [WSHC COD.949].

243 Tyrer, N. (1996). *They Fought in the Fields.* London: Sinclair-Stevenson, pp. 82. [WSHC 331.4830941].

244 Parsons, M. (2005). *Cricklade Revealed: Part 5- Social Life during the Second World War*, Marion Parsons, pp. 15-16. [WSHC CRI.949].

245 Tyrer, N. (1996). *They Fought in the Fields.* London: Sinclair-Stevenson, pp. 78. [WSHC 331.4830941].

246 Ibid., pp. 108.

247 Wiltshire Federation of Women's Institutes (1993). *Wiltshire Within Living Memory.* Newbury: Countryside Books, pp. 212. [WSHC AAA.949].

248 Ibid., pp. 209.

249 Longmate, N. (2002). *How we Lived then: History of Everyday Life during the Second World War.* London: Pimlico, pp. 242.

250 Tyrer, N. (1996). *They Fought in the Fields.* London: Sinclair-Stevenson, pp. 80. [WSHC 331.4830941].

251 Ibid., pp. 108-109.

252 Hall, A. (1993). *Land Girl.* Bradford on Avon: Ex Libris Press, pp. 81-82. [WSHC AAA.949].

253 WSA G17/132/27.

254 Calder, A. (1992). *The People's War: Britain 1939-45.* London: Pimlico (Original work published 1969), pp. 428. [WSHC 941.084].

255 *British Summer Time (BST).* (2015). Retrieved August 13, 2015 from the National Maritime website http:// www.rmg.co.uk/explore/astronomy- and-time/time-facts/british-summer- time

256 Tyrer, N. (1996). *They Fought in the Fields.* London: Sinclair-Stevenson, pp. 61. [WSHC 331.4830941].

257 Hall, A. (1993). *Land Girl.* Bradford on Avon: Ex Libris Press, pp. 77. [WSHC AAA.949].

258 Wiltshire Federation of Women's Institutes (1993). *Wiltshire Within Living Memory*. Newbury: Countryside Books, pp. 212. [WSHC AAA.949].

259 Hickson, J. and Skrine, R. (Ed.) (2013). *Carry on Coping: Diary of a Doctor 1942-1945*. Bradford on Avon: Ex Libris Press, pp. 197. [WSHC CHP.611 Original diaries are also available at WSA 4236/1-5].

260 Pickford, P. and Pickford, R. (Ed.). (1995). *Letters to Liz*. Newnham, Tasmania: Attic Press, pp. 60. [WSHC WAR.949].

261 Agricultural Wages Board (1943). *The Agricultural Wages (Regulation) Acts 1924 and 1940, Holidays with Pay Act 1938, and Regulations 23 of the Defence (Agriculture and Fisheries) Regulations 1939 (Wiltshire)*. London: Agricultural Wages Board, pp. 3. [WSHC AAA.630 (BL)].

262 Ibid.

263 Wiltshire Federation of Women's Institutes (1993). *Wiltshire Within Living Memory*. Newbury: Countryside Books, pp. 213. [WSHC AAA.949].

264 Tyrer, N. (1996). *They Fought in the Fields*. London: Sinclair-Stevenson, pp. 66. [WSHC 331.4830941].

265 Wiltshire Federation of Women's Institutes (1993). *Wiltshire Within Living Memory*. Newbury: Countryside Books, pp. 212. [WSHC AAA.949].

266 Day, R. (2007). *Savernake at War: A Wartime History of Savernake Forest 1940-1949*. Hungerford: Roger Day, pp. 19. [WSHC SAV.949].

267 Hall, A. (1993). *Land Girl*. Bradford on Avon: Ex Libris Press, pp. 78. [WSHC AAA.949].

268 Calder, A. (1992). *The People's War: Britain 1939-45*. London: Pimlico (Original work published 1969), pp. 429. [WSHC 941.084].

269 Tyrer, N. (1996). *They Fought in the Fields*. London: Sinclair-Stevenson, pp. 46-47. [WSHC 331.4830941].

270 Calder, A. (1992). *The People's War: Britain 1939-45*. London: Pimlico (Original work published 1969), pp.

429. [WSHC 941.084].

271 Tyrer, N. (1996). *They Fought in the Fields*. London: Sinclair-Stevenson, pp. 46-49. [WSHC 331.4830941].

272 Ibid., pp. 53.

273 Longmate, N. (2002). *How we Lived then: History of Everyday Life during the Second World War*. London: Pimlico, pp. 240.

274 Wiltshire National Farmer's Union (1942). *Wiltshire NFU Record*, 10(10). [WSA 2309/120/9].

275 Ibid., 10(1).

276 Tyrer, N. (1996). *They Fought in the Fields*. London: Sinclair-Stevenson, pp. 119-120. [WSHC 331.4830941].

277 Ibid., pp. 122.

278 Dawkins, B. (1989). *When Warm Milk Was Fresh Milk*. Bert Dawkins, pp. 96. [WSHC WAR.949].

279 Wiltshire Federation of Women's Institutes (1993). *Wiltshire Within Living Memory*. Newbury: Countryside Books, pp. 211. [WSHC AAA.949].

280 Tyrer, N. (1996). *They Fought in the Fields*. London: Sinclair-Stevenson, pp. 119. [WSHC 331.4830941].

281 Ibid., pp. 123.

282 Buchanan-Dunlop, R. (2011). *Ham: the story of a Wiltshire village*. R. Buchanan-Dunlop, pp. 148. [WSHC HAM.940].

283 Hall, A. (1993). *Land Girl*. Bradford on Avon: Ex Libris Press, pp. 78. [WSHC AAA.949].

284 WSA F4/550/12.

285 Ibid.

286 Ginn, P., Goodman, R. and Langlands, A. (2012). *Wartime Farm*. London: Mitchell Beazley, pp. 53.

287 Tyrer, N. (1996). *They Fought in the Fields*. London: Sinclair-Stevenson, pp. 149. [WSHC 331.4830941].

288 Ibid., pp. 151-152.

289 Ibid., pp. 145.

290 Ibid., pp. 153.

291 Ibid., pp. 146.

292 Ibid., pp. 154.

293 Ibid., pp. 158.

294 Day, R. (2007). *Savernake at War: A Wartime History of Savernake Forest*

1940-1949. Hungerford: Roger Day, pp. 21. [WSHC SAV.949].

295 WSA 2576/47. [Burbage WI].

296 Anderson, B. (1994). *We Just Got On With It: British Women in World War II*. Chippenham: Picton Publishing, pp. 89. [WSHC AAA.949].

297 Wiltshire Federation of Women's Institutes (1993). *Wiltshire Within Living Memory*. Newbury: Countryside Books, pp. 212-3. [WSHC AAA.949].

298 Chapman, E. and Howell, A. (Eds.) (2013). *When the War was Over: Memories of 1945: Mere Literary Festival Community Project*. Unpublished, Unpaginated. [WSHC MER.949].

299 Hall, A. (1993). *Land Girl*. Bradford on Avon: Ex Libris Press, pp. 123. [WSHC AAA.949].

300 Tyrer, N. (1996). *They Fought in the Fields*. London: Sinclair-Stevenson, pp. 214-216. [WSHC 331.4830941].

301 Vernon, C. (2011). *Malmesbury versus Hitler: The Town's role in the Second World War*. Malmesbury: Malmesbury Civic Trust, pp. 157. [WSHC MAL.949].

302 Tyrer, N. (1996). *They Fought in the Fields*. London: Sinclair-Stevenson, pp. 69. [WSHC 331.4830941].

303 Ibid., pp. 217-223.

304 Hall, A. (1993). *Land Girl*. Bradford on Avon: Ex Libris Press, pp. 139-142. [WSHC AAA.949].

305 Tyrer, N. (1996). *They Fought in the Fields*. London: Sinclair-Stevenson, pp. 224. [WSHC 331.4830941].

306 Ibid., pp. 219.

307 Ibid., pp. 232-233.

308 *Archive: Women's Land Army* (2011). Retrieved February 12, 2015 from the Department of Food, Environment and Rural Affairs website [unreadable]

309 *The Prince of Wales unveils memorial to Women's Land Army* (2015). Retrieved February 12, 2015 from The Prince of Wales and The Duchess of Cornwall News and Diary website http://[unreadable]

princeofwales.gov.uk/news-and-diar the-prince-of-wales-unveils-memorial womens-land-army

310 Machray, R. (n.d.). *Great Britain's Humane Treatment of German Prisoners of War*. Published in 'The Great War: The Standard History of the Worldwide Conflict', Chapter CCLXXVIL, pp. 403.

311 Calder, A. (1992). *The People's War: Britain 1939-45*. London: Pimlico (Original work published 1969), pp. 430. [WSHC 941.084].

312 Price, W. (1944). War-time Farming. *Ministry of Agriculture Journal*, pp. 3. [WSHC AAA.630 (BL)].

313 WSA F5/530/3.

314 Jackson, S. (2010). *Churchill's Unexpected Guests: POWs in Britain in World War II*. Stroud: The History Press, pp. 18.

315 Cabble, W. (2014). *Royal Wiltshire Yeomanry Prince of Wales own and Royal Army Veterinary Corps : Memories of the travels and war service, 1937-1946*. Unpublished, Unpaginated. [WSHC WEB.949 (BL)].

316 WSA F5/530/3.

317 Jackson, S. (2010). *Churchill's Unexpected Guests: POWs in Britain in World War II*. Stroud: The History Press, pp. 101-102.

318 Tyrer, N. (1996). *They Fought in the Fields*. London: Sinclair-Stevenson, pp. 181. [WSHC 331.4830941].

319 WSA F5/530/3.

320 Jackson, S. (2010). *Churchill's Unexpected Guests: POWs in Britain in World War II*. Stroud: The History Press, pp. 102.

321 WSA F5/530/5.

322 Thomas, R. (2003). *Twentieth Century Military Recording Project: Prisoner of War Camps (1939-1948)*. Swindon: English Heritage, pp. 33. [https://www.english-heritage.org.uk/publications/prisoner-of-war-camps/prisoner-of-war-camps.pdf].

323 Wyeth, R. (1995). *Sterner Days: Codford during the Second World War*. Warminster: Bedeguar Books, pp. 13.

[WSHC COD.949].

324 Wyeth, R. (2007). *Sword and Ploughshares: Codford during the Twentieth Century*. Codford: Gemini, pp. 168. [WSHC COD.949].

325 WSA F5/530/3.

326 Ibid.

327 Meakin, R. (2002). *Minety at War*. Richard Meakin, pp. 89. [WSHC MIN.949].

328 Ibid., pp. 33.

329 Thomas, R. (2003). *Twentieth Century Military Recording Project: Prisoner of War Camps (1939-1948)*. Swindon: English Heritage, pp. 27. [https://www.english-heritage.org.uk/publications/prisoner-of-war-camps/prisoner-of-war-camps.pdf].

330 Meakin, R. (2002). *Minety at War*. Richard Meakin, pp. 89. [WSHC MIN.949].

331 Thomas, R. (2003). *Twentieth Century Military Recording Project: Prisoner of War Camps (1939-1948)*. Swindon: English Heritage, pp. 29. [https://www.english-heritage.org.uk/publications/prisoner-of-war-camps/prisoner-of-war-camps.pdf].

332 Meakin, R. (2002). *Minety at War*. Richard Meakin, pp. 91. [WSHC MIN.949].

333 Parsons, M. (2005). *Cricklade Revealed: Part 5- Social Life during the Second World War*, Marion Parsons, pp. 18. [WSHC CRI.949].

334 WSA F5/530/3.

335 Ibid.

336 Wiltshire Federation of Women's Institutes (1993). *Wiltshire Within Living Memory*. Newbury: Countryside Books, pp. 190. [WSHC AAA.949].

337 WSA 2576/47. [Burbage WI].

338 Parsons, M. (2006). *Cricklade Revealed: Part 6 - Social Life during the Second World - Social Life during the Second World War*, Marion Parsons, pp. 31. [WSHC CRI.949].

339 WSA F4/550/71.

340 Ibid.

341 Jackson, S. (2010). *Churchill's Unexpected Guests: POWs in Britain in World War II*. Stroud: The History Press, pp. 102.

342 WSA F4/550/71.

343 Ibid.

344 Ibid.

345 Ibid.

346 Jackson, S. (2010). *Churchill's Unexpected Guests: POWs in Britain in World War II*. Stroud: The History Press, pp. 102.

347 Hall, A. (1993). *Land Girl*. Bradford on Avon: Ex Libris Press, pp. 90. [WSHC AAA.949].

348 WSA F5/530/3.

349 Meakin, R. (2002). *Minety at War*. Richard Meakin, pp. 91. [WSHC MIN.949].

350 Devizes Local History Group and Haycock, L. (Ed.). (1995). *How Devizes Won the War!* Devizes Local History Group, pp. 89. [WSHC DEV.949].

351 Dawkins, B. (1989). *When Warm Milk Was Fresh Milk*. Bert Dawkins, pp. 96. [WSHC WAR.949].

352 Buchanan-Dunlop, R. (2011). *Ham: the story of a Wiltshire village*. R. Buchanan-Dunlop, pp. 148. [WSHC HAM.940].

353 Dewhurst, R. (2005). *Crosstracks to Hindon*. Salisbury: Hobnob Press, pp. 98. [WSHC HIN.940].

354 Tyrer, N. (1996). *They Fought in the Fields*. London: Sinclair-Stevenson, pp. 180-182. [WSHC 331.4830941].

355 WSA F4/550/71.

356 Devizes Local History Group and Haycock, L. (Ed.). (1995). *How Devizes Won the War!* Devizes Local History Group, pp. 89. [WSHC DEV.949].

357 Hickson, J. and Skrine, R. (Ed.) (2013). *Carry on Coping: Diary of a Doctor 1942-1945*. Bradford on Avon: Ex Libris Press, pp. 210. [WSHC CHP.611 Original diaries are also available at WSA 4236/1-5].

358 WSA F5/530/3.

359 Partridge, F. (1978). *A Pacifist's War*. The Hogarth Press: London, pp. 105. [WSHC HAM.927].

360 WSA F5/530/3.
361 Jackson, S. (2010). *Churchill's Unexpected Guests: POWs in Britain in World War II.* Stroud: The History Press, pp. 104.
362 WSA F5/530/3.
363 Ibid.
364 Longmate, N. (2002). *How we Lived then: History of Everyday Life during the Second World War.* London: Pimlico, pp. 480.
365 Jackson, S. (2010). *Churchill's Unexpected Guests: POWs in Britain in World War II.* Stroud: The History Press, pp. 104.
366 WSA F4/550/71.
367 Ibid.
368 WSA F5/530/3.
369 WSA 2576/47. [Burbage WI].
370 Wiltshire Heritage Museum (2012). *A Prisoner of War in Devizes: A Day in Camp 23/A1.* Devizes: Wiltshire Heritage Museum, pp. 2-4. [WSHC DEV.949].
371 Ibid., pp. 5.
372 Ibid., pp. 8.
373 Calder, A. (1992). *The People's War: Britain 1939-45.* London: Pimlico (Original work published 1969), pp. 277. [WSHC 941.084].
374 Wiltshire Heritage Museum (2012). *A Prisoner of War in Devizes: A Day in Camp 23/A1.* Devizes: Wiltshire Heritage Museum, pp. 8. [WSHC DEV.949].
375 WSA F5/530/3.
376 Jackson, S. (2010). *Churchill's Unexpected Guests: POWs in Britain in World War II.* Stroud: The History Press, pp. 62.
377 Kochan, M. (1980). *Prisoners of England.* London: Palgrave MacMillan, pp. 51-52.
378 Thomas, R. (2003). *Twentieth Century Military Recording Project: Prisoner of War Camps (1939-1948).* Swindon: English Heritage, pp. 21. [https://www.english-heritage.org.uk/publications/prisoner-of-war-camps/prisoner-of-war-camps.pdf].
379 Kochan, M. (1980). *Prisoners of England.* London: Palgrave MacMillan, pp. 51-52.
380 WSA F5/530/3.
381 Berryman, D. (2002). *Wiltshire Airfields in the Second World War.* Newbury: Countryside Books, pp. 228. [WSHC AAA.352].
382 Davis, J. (2013). *To Locate and Evaluate Local Government Archive Material for North Wiltshire held at the Wiltshire and Swindon History Centre, to Discover its use as a Source for Studying Social Change from 1939-55.* (Unpublished master's dissertation). University of Aberystwyth, Aberystwyth, pp. 18.
383 Kochan, M. (1980). *Prisoners of England.* London: Palgrave MacMillan, pp. 71.
384 Ibid., pp. 88.
385 Jackson, S. (2010). *Churchill's Unexpected Guests: POWs in Britain in World War II.* Stroud: The History Press, pp. 111.
386 Davis, J. (2013). *To Locate and Evaluate Local Government Archive Material for North Wiltshire held at the Wiltshire and Swindon History Centre, to Discover its use as a Source for Studying Social Change from 1939-55.* (Unpublished master's dissertation). University of Aberystwyth, Aberystwyth, pp. 18.
387 Jackson, S. (2010). *Churchill's Unexpected Guests: POWs in Britain in World War II.* Stroud: The History Press, pp. 159.
388 Kochan, M. (1980). *Prisoners of England.* London: Palgrave MacMillan, pp. vii.
389 Chapman, E. and Howell, A. (Eds.) (2013). *When the War was Over: Memories of 1945: Mere Literary Festival Community Project.* Unpublished, Unpaginated. [WSHC MER.949].
390 WSA G24/132/333.
391 WSA F5/530/3.
392 Vernon, C. (2011). *Malmesbury versus Hitler: The Town's role in the Second World War.* Malmesbury: Malmesbury

Civic Trust, pp. 157. [WSHC MAL.949].

393 Merrick, P. (2013). Prisoners of War in Britain in the 1940s. *Local Historian*, 13 (4), pp. 317. [WSHC Local Historian Journal].

394 Jackson, S. (2010). *Churchill's Unexpected Guests: POWs in Britain in World War II*. Stroud: The History Press, pp. 159.

395 Ibid., pp. 162.

396 WSA F5/530/3.

397 WSA G2/132/44.

398 Thomas, R. (2003). *Twentieth Century Military Recording Project: Prisoner of War Camps (1939-1948)*. Swindon: English Heritage, pp. 14. [https://www.english-heritage.org.uk/publications/prisoner-of-war-camps/prisoner-of-war-camps.pdf].

399 Meakin, R. (2002). *Minety at War*. Richard Meakin, pp. 93. [WSHC MIN.949].

400 Whatley, C. (1955). *Farm, Fox and Fireside*. Swindon: The Swindon Press Limited, distributed by the National Farmers Union Offices, Devizes, pp. 24-25. [WSHC AAA.630].

401 Jackson, S. (2010). *Churchill's Unexpected Guests: POWs in Britain in World War II*. Stroud: The History Press, pp. 172.

402 Julie Davis, personal communication with the daughter of an Italian POW and English mother at WSHC, 2013.

403 Kochan, M. (1980). *Prisoners of England*. London: Palgrave MacMillan, pp. vii.

404 Ibid., pp. 107.

405 Merrick, P. (2013). Prisoners of War in Britain in the 1940s. *Local Historian*, 13 (4), pp. 320. [WSHC Local Historian Journal].

406 Thomas, R. (2003). *Twentieth Century Military Recording Project: Prisoner of War Camps (1939-1948)*. Swindon: English Heritage, pp. 14. [https://www.english-heritage.org.uk/publications/prisoner-of-war-camps/prisoner-of-war-camps.pdf].

407 WSA F14/001/10.

408 WSA F1/100/40/1.

409 WSA G4/132/60.

410 WSA F2/860/1.

411 Collingham, L. (2011). *The Taste of War: World War Two and the Battle for Food*. London: Penguin Books Ltd., pp. 92.

412 Martin, J. (2000). *The Development of Modern Agriculture: British Farming Since 1931*. Basingstoke: Macmillan Press Ltd, pp. 197.

413 Ginn, P., Goodman, R. and Langlands, A. (2012). *Wartime Farm*. London: Mitchell Beazley, pp. 247.

414 Martin, J. (2000). *The Development of Modern Agriculture: British Farming Since 1931*. Basingstoke: Macmillan Press Ltd, pp. 107.

415 National Farmer's Union (1942). *The NFU Record*, 20(241). [WSA 2309/120/9].

416 WSA 1284/1.

417 Hennessy, P. (1992). *Never Again: Britain 1945-51*. London: Penguin Books Ltd., pp. 180. [WSHC 941.0854].

418 Kynaston, D. (2007). *A World to Build: Austerity Britain*. London: Bloomsbury, pp. 169.

419 Rogers, R. (1957). *Some Aspects of West Country Farming: Wiltshire*. Royal Agricultural Society of England, pp. 20. [WSHC AAA.630 (BL)].

420 Chippenham and District Committee for Festival of Britain (1951). *Chippenham Wilts Festival of Britain*. Chippenham and District Committee for Festival of Britain, pp. 30. [WSHC CHP.394].

421 Davis, J. (2013). *To Locate and Evaluate Local Government Archive Material for North Wiltshire held at the Wiltshire and Swindon History Centre, to Discover its use as a Source for Studying Social Change from 1939-55*. (Unpublished master's dissertation). University of Aberystwyth, Aberystwyth, pp. 16-19.

422 Kynaston, D. (2007). *A World to Build: Austerity Britain*. London: Bloomsbury, pp. 169.

423 WSA G4/132/20.

424 WSA G4/132/23.

425 Ibid.

426 WSA G5/132/27. [Letter written by the County Secretary to the Clerks of Wiltshire's Local Authorities, April 1947].

427 WSA G4/132/23.

428 WSA G3/132/63.

429 WSA G4/132/120.

430 WSA G4/132/12.

431 WSA G4/132/38.

432 WSA G5/132/71.

433 WSA G4/132/60.

434 WSA F2/860/1.

435 WSA G12/132/12.

436 WSA G3/132/3.

437 WSA 1284/1.

438 WSA 1284/1.

439 WSA G4/132/24.

440 WSA G5/132/54.

441 WSA G6/132/63.

442 WSA G4/132/16.

443 Street, A. G. (1950). *In His Own Country*. London: Eyre & Spottiswoode, pp. 325. [WSHC XST.824].

444 Ibid, pp. xvi.

445 Martin, J. (2000). *The Development of Modern Agriculture: British Farming Since 1931*. Basingstoke: Macmillan Press Ltd, pp. 47-48.

446 Ginn, P., Goodman, R. and Langlands, A. (2012). *Wartime Farm*. London: Mitchell Beazley, pp. 19.

447 Martin, J. (2000). *The Development of Modern Agriculture: British Farming Since 1931*. Basingstoke: Macmillan Press Ltd, pp. 49-50.

448 Martin, J. (2000). *The Development of Modern Agriculture: British Farming Since 1931*. Basingstoke: Macmillan Press Ltd, pp. 65.

449 Ginn, P., Goodman, R. and Langlands, A. (2012). *Wartime Farm*. London: Mitchell Beazley, pp. 304.

450 Martin, J. (2000). *The Development of Modern Agriculture: British Farming Since 1931*. Basingstoke: Macmillan Press Ltd, pp. 65.

451 Martin, J. (2007). George Odlum, the Ministry of Agriculture and 'Farmer Hudson'. *Agricultural History Review*, 55(II), pp. 229. [WSHC MAN.630 (BL)].

452 Martin, J. (2000). *The Development of Modern Agriculture: British Farming Since 1931*. Basingstoke: Macmillan Press Ltd, pp. 58.

453 Martin, J. (2007). George Odlum, the Ministry of Agriculture and 'Farmer Hudson'. *Agricultural History Review*, 55(II), pp. 229. [WSHC MAN.630 (BL)].

454 Martin, J. (2000). *The Development of Modern Agriculture: British Farming Since 1931*. Basingstoke: Macmillan Press Ltd, pp. 65.

455 Martin, J. (2007). George Odlum, the Ministry of Agriculture and 'Farmer Hudson'. *Agricultural History Review*, 55(II), pp. 229. [WSHC MAN.630 (BL)].

456 Martin, J. (2000). *The Development of Modern Agriculture: British Farming Since 1931*. Basingstoke: Macmillan Press Ltd, pp. 58.

457 Ibid., pp. 66.

458 Ibid., pp.70.

459 Newby, H. (1985). *Green and Pleasant Land? Social Change in Rural England*. Hounslow: Wildwood House Limited, pp. 265.

460 Champion, T. and Watkins, C. (1991). *Introduction*. In Champion, T. and Watkins, C. (Eds.). People and Countryside: Studies of Social Change in Rural Britain. London: Paul Chapman Publishing Ltd., pp. 9.

461 Kynaston, D. (2007). *A World to Build: Austerity Britain*. London: Bloomsbury, pp. 169.

462 Shucksmith, M. (1991). *Still no Homes for Locals? Affordable Housing and Planning Controls in Rural Areas*. In Champion, T. and Watkins, C. (Eds.). People and Countryside: Studies of Social Change in Rural Britain. London: Paul Chapman Publishing Ltd., pp. 68.

463 Martin, J. (2000). *The Development of Modern Agriculture: British Farming*

Since 1931. Basingstoke: Macmillan Press Ltd, pp. 76.

464 Kynaston, D. (2007). *A World to Build: Austerity Britain.* London: Bloomsbury, pp. 169.

6 Doing Your Bit...

1 Meisel, J. (1994). Air Raid Shelter Policy and its Critics in Britain before the Second World War. *Twentieth Century British History,* 5(3), pp. 301.

2 Burton, N. (2013). The Establishment and Organisation of Civil Defence Operations in Berkshire 1936-1945. *Local Historian,* 13(4), pp. 305.

3 Meisel, J. (1994). Air Raid Shelter Policy and its Critics in Britain before the Second World War. *Twentieth Century British History,* 5(3), pp. 301-304.

4 Brown, M. (1999). *Put that Light out: Britain's Civil Defence Services at War.* Stroud: Sutton Publishing, pp. 1.

5 Vernon, C. (2011). *Malmesbury versus Hitler: The Town's role in the Second World War.* Malmesbury: Malmesbury Civic Trust, pp. 26-27. [WSHC MAL.949].

6 Brown, M. (1999). *Put that Light out: Britain's Civil Defence Services at War.* Stroud: Sutton Publishing, pp. 3.

7 Vernon, C. (2011). *Malmesbury versus Hitler: The Town's role in the Second World War.* Malmesbury: Malmesbury Civic Trust, pp. 27. [WSHC MAL.949].

8 Brown, M. (1999). *Put that Light out: Britain's Civil Defence Services at War.* Stroud: Sutton Publishing, pp. 4.

9 Vernon, C. (2011). *Malmesbury versus Hitler: The Town's role in the Second World War.* Malmesbury: Malmesbury Civic Trust, pp. 29. [WSHC MAL.949].

10 Brown, M. (1999). *Put that Light out: Britain's Civil Defence Services at War.* Stroud: Sutton Publishing, pp. 5.

11 Vernon, C. (2011). *Malmesbury versus Hitler: The Town's role in the Second World War.* Malmesbury: Malmesbury Civic Trust, pp. 31. [WSHC

MAL.949].

12 Devizes Local History Group and Haycock, L. (Ed.). (1995). *How Devizes Won the War!* Devizes Local History Group, pp. 6. [WSHC DEV.949].

13 Vernon, C. (2011). *Malmesbury versus Hitler: The Town's role in the Second World War.* Malmesbury: Malmesbury Civic Trust, pp. 34. [WSHC MAL.949].

14 WSA G11/225/12.

15 MacKay, R. (1999). *The Test of War: Inside Britain 1939-45.* London: UCL Press, pp. 126.

16 Hobbs, S. (2013). *War Books.* Unpublished, Unpaginated. [WSHC AAA.949 (Ephemera)].

17 WSA 1988/24.

19 WSA G23/225/18.

20 WSA F2/851/3/20.

21 WSA F2/851/3/19.

22 WSA F2/851/4/15.

23 Hobbs, S. (2013). *War Books.* Unpublished, Unpaginated. [WSHC AAA.949 (Ephemera)].

24 Cantwell, J. (1993). *The Second World War: A Guide to Documents in the Public Record Office.* London: HMSO (Original work published 1972), pp. 109. [WSHC 16.94053].

25 Brown, M. (1999). *Put that Light out: Britain's Civil Defence Services at War.* Stroud: Sutton Publishing, pp. 14.

26 Cantwell, J. (1993). *The Second World War: A Guide to Documents in the Public Record Office.* London: HMSO (Original work published 1972), pp. 109. [WSHC 16.94053].

27 Brown, M. (1999). *Put that Light out: Britain's Civil Defence Services at War.* Stroud: Sutton Publishing, pp. 28-29.

28 Meisel, J. (1994). Air Raid Shelter Policy and its Critics in Britain before the Second World War. *Twentieth Century British History,* 5(3), pp. 307.

29 Ibid., pp. 316.

30 Ibid., pp. 232.

31 Coleshill, (2008). *Memoirs of World War II in Castle Coombe.* Unpublished, pp. 4. [WSHC CAC.949].

32 Siddall, M. (1995). *Safe as Houses: Childhood Through the Forties.* Christow: Devonshire House, pp. 23. [WSHC PUR.949].

33 WSA F1/100/36.

34 WSA F1/100/34/1.

35 WSA F1/100/35.

36 WSA G24/224/2.

37 Burton, N. (2013). The Establishment and Organisation of Civil Defence Operations in Berkshire 1936-1945. *Local Historian*, 13(4), pp. 305.

38 Anderson, B. (1994). *We Just Got On With It: British Women in World War II.* Chippenham: Picton Publishing, pp. 32. [WSHC AAA.949].

39 Calder, A. (1992). *The People's War: Britain 1939-45.* London: Pimlico (Original work published 1969), pp. 22. [WSHC 941.084].

40 Meisel, J. (1994). Air Raid Shelter Policy and its Critics in Britain before the Second World War. *Twentieth Century British History*, 5(3), pp. 305.

41 Vernon, C. (2011). *Malmesbury versus Hitler: The Town's role in the Second World War.* Malmesbury: Malmesbury Civic Trust, pp. 30. [WSHC MAL.949].

42 Calder, A. (1992). *The People's War: Britain 1939-45.* London: Pimlico (Original work published 1969), pp. 25. [WSHC 941.084].

43 Thomsett, S. (c. 1974). *Trowbridge 1939-45: A Social History.* Unpublished, Unpaginated study for the Weymouth College of Education. [WSHC TRO.949 (BL – Oversize)].

44 Vernon, C. (2011). *Malmesbury versus Hitler: The Town's role in the Second World War.* Malmesbury: Malmesbury Civic Trust, pp. 34. [WSHC MAL.949].

45 Ibid., pp. 36-37.

46 Hennessy, P. (1992). *Never Again: Britain 1945-51.* London: Penguin Books Ltd., pp. 15. [WSHC 941.0854].

47 Calder, A. (1992). *The People's War: Britain 1939-45.* London: Pimlico (Original work published 1969),

pp. 195. [WSHC 941.084].

48 Cantwell, J. (1993). *The Second World War: A Guide to Documents in the Public Record Office.* London: HMSO (Original work published 1972), pp. 110. [WSHC 16.94053].

49 Anderson, B. (1994). *We Just Got On With It: British Women in World War II.* Chippenham: Picton Publishing, pp. 32. [WSHC AAA.949].

50 Calder, A. (1992). *The People's War: Britain 1939-45.* London: Pimlico (Original work published 1969), pp. 67-68. [WSHC 941.084].

51 Cockbill, T. (1989). *Our Swindon in 1939.* Swindon: The Quill Press, pp. 12-13. [WSHC SWI.949].

52 WSA F8/933/EA48.

53 Ibid.

54 Anderson, B. (1994). *We Just Got On With It: British Women in World War II.* Chippenham: Picton Publishing, pp. 32. [WSHC AAA.949].

55 Calder, A. (1992). *The People's War: Britain 1939-45.* London: Pimlico (Original work published 1969), pp. 196. [WSHC 941.084].

56 Anderson, B. (1994). *We Just Got On With It: British Women in World War II.* Chippenham: Picton Publishing, pp. 33. [WSHC AAA.949].

57 Devizes Local History Group and Haycock, L. (Ed.). (1995). *How Devizes Won the War!* Devizes Local History Group, pp. 54. [WSHC DEV.949].

58 Parsons, M. (2004). *Cricklade Revealed: Part 4 - Social Life during the Second World War.* Marion Parsons, pp. 23. [WSHC CRI.949].

59 WSA G24/225/42.

60 Vernon, C. (2011). *Malmesbury versus Hitler: The Town's role in the Second World War.* Malmesbury: Malmesbury Civic Trust, pp. 72. [WSHC MAL.949].

61 Calder, A. (1992). *The People's War: Britain 1939-45.* London: Pimlico (Original work published 1969), pp. 195. [WSHC 941.084].

62 Devizes Local History Group and

Haycock, L. (Ed.). (1995). *How Devizes Won the War!* Devizes Local History Group, pp. 54. [WSHC DEV.949].

63 Anderson, B. (1994). *We Just Got On With It: British Women in World War II.* Chippenham: Picton Publishing, pp. 35. [WSHC AAA.949].

64 Vernon, C. (2011). *Malmesbury versus Hitler: The Town's role in the Second World War.* Malmesbury: Malmesbury Civic Trust, pp. 31. [WSHC MAL.949].

65 WSA G15/225/25.

66 Eccles, D. (1983). *By Safe Hand: Letters of Sybil and David Eccles, 1939-1942.* London: Bodley Head, pp. 109. [WSHC CHU.928].

67 Hickson, J. and Skrine, R. (Ed.) (2013). *Carry on Coping: Diary of a Doctor 1942-1945.* Bradford on Avon: Ex Libris Press, pp. 80. [WSHC CHP.611 Original diaries are also available at WSA 4236/1-5].

68 Vernon, C. (2011). *Malmesbury versus Hitler: The Town's role in the Second World War.* Malmesbury: Malmesbury Civic Trust, pp. 74. [WSHC MAL.949].

69 WSA F8/500/196/1/2.

70 WSA F5/530/48.

71 Brown, M. (1999). *Put that Light out: Britain's Civil Defence Services at War.* Stroud: Sutton Publishing, pp. 28.

72 Ibid., pp. 32-33.

73 WSA F5/162/3.

74 Brown, M. (1999). *Put that Light out: Britain's Civil Defence Services at War.* Stroud: Sutton Publishing, pp. 33-34.

75 Beaton, C. (1949). *Ashcombe: the Story of a Fifteen Year Lease.* London: B.T. Batsford Ltd., pp. 77. [WSHC BJO.727 (BL)].

76 Calder, A. (1992). *The People's War: Britain 1939-45.* London: Pimlico (Original work published 1969), pp. 67. [WSHC 941.084].

77 Devizes Local History Group and Haycock, L. (Ed.). (1995). *How Devizes Won the War!* Devizes Local History Group, pp. 22. [WSHC DEV.949].

78 WSA F1/100/34/1.

79 Brown, M. (1999). *Put that Light out: Britain's Civil Defence Services at War.* Stroud: Sutton Publishing, pp. 31.

80 Anderson, B. (1994). *We Just Got On With It: British Women in World War II.* Chippenham: Picton Publishing, pp. 35. [WSHC AAA.949].

81 WSA G15/224/6.

82 Devizes Local History Group and Haycock, L. (Ed.). (1995). *How Devizes Won the War!* Devizes Local History Group, pp. 56. [WSHC DEV.949].

83 WSA G15/224/6.

84 WSA 1442/1.

85 Devizes Local History Group and Haycock, L. (Ed.). (1995). *How Devizes Won the War!* Devizes Local History Group, pp. 55. [WSHC DEV.949].

86 Vernon, C. (2011). *Malmesbury versus Hitler: The Town's role in the Second World War.* Malmesbury: Malmesbury Civic Trust, pp. 72. [WSHC MAL.949].

87 Brown, M. (1999). *Put that Light out: Britain's Civil Defence Services at War.* Stroud: Sutton Publishing, pp. 90.

88 Vernon, C. (2011). *Malmesbury versus Hitler: The Town's role in the Second World War.* Malmesbury: Malmesbury Civic Trust, pp. 41. [WSHC MAL.949].

89 Brown, M. (1999). *Put that Light out: Britain's Civil Defence Services at War.* Stroud: Sutton Publishing, pp. 90.

90 Vernon, C. (2011). *Malmesbury versus Hitler: The Town's role in the Second World War.* Malmesbury: Malmesbury Civic Trust, pp. 41. [WSHC MAL.949].

91 Brown, M. (1999). *Put that Light out: Britain's Civil Defence Services at War.* Stroud: Sutton Publishing, pp. 90.

92 WSA G11/225/12.

93 WSA G5/132/8.

94 WSA G11/225/12.

95 Randall, B. (2003). *A Patchwork of Memories.* Bob Randall, pp. 22.

[WSHC TRO.949].

96 Devizes Local History Group and Haycock, L. (Ed.). (1995). *How Devizes Won the War!* Devizes Local History Group, pp. 20. [WSHC DEV.949].

97 Anderson, B. (1994). *We Just Got On With It: British Women in World War II*. Chippenham: Picton Publishing, pp. 38. [WSHC AAA.949].

98 Lane, C. and White, P. (1999). *Warminster in the Twentieth Century*. The Warminster History Society: Warminster, pp. 233. [WSHC WAR.949].

99 Anderson, B. (1994). *We Just Got On With It: British Women in World War II*. Chippenham: Picton Publishing, pp. 38. [WSHC AAA.949].

100 Calder, A. (1992). *The People's War: Britain 1939-45*. London: Pimlico (Original work published 1969), pp. 68. [WSHC 941.084].

101 Brown, M. (1999). *Put that Light out: Britain's Civil Defence Services at War*. Stroud: Sutton Publishing, pp. 96.

102 Calder, A. (1992). *The People's War: Britain 1939-45*. London: Pimlico (Original work published 1969), pp. 195. [WSHC 941.084].

103 Ibid., pp. 208.

104 Brown, M. (1999). *Put that Light out: Britain's Civil Defence Services at War*. Stroud: Sutton Publishing, pp. 93.

105 WSA G14/225/10.

106 Calder, A. (1992). *The People's War: Britain 1939-45*. London: Pimlico (Original work published 1969), pp. 68. [WSHC 941.084].

107 Parsons, M. (2004). *Cricklade Revealed: Part 4 - Social Life during the Second World War*. Marion Parsons, pp. 24. [WSHC CRI.949].

108 Calder, A. (1992). *The People's War: Britain 1939-45*. London: Pimlico (Original work published 1969), pp. 68. [WSHC 941.084].

109 WSA G11/225/12.

110 Vernon, C. (2011). *Malmesbury versus Hitler: The Town's role in the Second World War*. Malmesbury: Malmesbury

Civic Trust, pp. 43. [WSHC MAL.949].

111 Ibid., pp. 83-85.

112 Calder, A. (1992). *The People's War: Britain 1939-45*. London: Pimlico (Original work published 1969), pp. 209. [WSHC 941.084].

113 Lane, C. and White, P. (1999). *Warminster in the Twentieth Century*. The Warminster History Society: Warminster, pp. 234. [WSHC WAR.949].

114 Nock, O. (2006). *A Hundred Years of Speed with Safety: Westinghouse Brake & Signal Company Ltd, 1881-1981*. East Knoyle: Hobnob Press, pp. 240. [WSHC CHP.620].

115 Vernon, C. (2011). *Malmesbury versus Hitler: The Town's role in the Second World War*. Malmesbury: Malmesbury Civic Trust, pp. 88. [WSHC MAL.949].

116 WSA G11/225/12.

117 Bemerton Local History Society (2006). *Memories of Bemerton in Wartime*. Bemerton Local History Society with support of the Big Lottery Fund, pp. 34. [WSHC BEM.949].

118 Lane, C. and White, P. (1999). *Warminster in the Twentieth Century*. The Warminster History Society: Warminster, pp. 234. [WSHC WAR.949].

119 Scott, J. (1996). *Reflections*. Swindon: Scodipur Publications, pp. 53. [WSHC PUR.940].

120 Randall, B. (2003). *A Patchwork of Memories*. Bob Randall, pp. 14. [WSHC TRO.949].

121 Lane, C. and White, P. (1999). *Warminster in the Twentieth Century*. The Warminster History Society: Warminster, pp. 234. [WSHC WAR.949].

122 WSA G5/132/8.

123 Ibid.

124 Calder, A. (1992). *The People's War: Britain 1939-45*. London: Pimlico (Original work published 1969), pp. 340. [WSHC 941.084].

125 Brown, M. (1999). *Put that Light out:*

Britain's Civil Defence Services at War.
Stroud: Sutton Publishing, pp. 102.

126 MacKay, R. (1999). *The Test of War:
Inside Britain 1939-45.* London: UCL
Press, pp. 177.

127 How St Paul's Cathedral Survived
the Blitz. (2010). Retrieved July 5,
2014 from the BBC News website
http://www.bbc.co.uk/news/mobile-
magazine-12016916

128 MacKay, R. (1999). *The Test of War:
Inside Britain 1939-45.* London: UCL
Press, pp. 130.

129 How St Paul's Cathedral Survived
the Blitz. (2010). Retrieved July 5,
2014 from the BBC News website
http://www.bbc.co.uk/news/mobile/
magazine-12016916

130 MacKay, R. (1999). *The Test of War:
Inside Britain 1939-45.* London: UCL
Press, pp. 130.

131 Ibid., pp. 177.

132 Ibid., pp. 130.

133 Wiltshire Federation of Women's
Institutes (1993). *Wiltshire Within
Living Memory.* Newbury: Countryside
Books, pp. 186. [WSHC AAA.949].

134 WSA 1442/1.

135 Devizes Local History Group and
Haycock, L. (Ed.). (1995). *How
Devizes Won the War!* Devizes Local
History Group, pp. 55. [WSHC
DEV.949].

136 Calder, A. (1992). *The People's War:
Britain 1939-45.* London: Pimlico
(Original work published 1969), pp.
207. [WSHC 941.084].

137 Brown, M. (1999). *Put that Light out:
Britain's Civil Defence Services at War.*
Stroud: Sutton Publishing, pp. 103.

138 Ibid., pp. 107.

139 Inchfawn, F. (2010). *Salute to the
Village.* Monkton Farleigh: Folly Books
(Original work published 1943), pp.
130. [WSHC XIN.921].

140 Vernon, C. (2011). *Malmesbury versus
Hitler: The Town's role in the Second
World War.* Malmesbury: Malmesbury
Civic Trust, pp. 77. [WSHC
MAL.949].

141 WSA F8/500/65/4/1.

142 Vernon, C. (2011). *Malmesbury versus
Hitler: The Town's role in the Second
World War.* Malmesbury: Malmesbury
Civic Trust, pp. 77. [WSHC
MAL.949].

143 Lane, C. and White, P. (1999).
Warminster in the Twentieth Century.
The Warminster History Society:
Warminster, pp. 234. [WSHC
WAR.949].

144 Inchfawn, F. (2010). *Salute to the
Village.* Monkton Farleigh: Folly Books
(Original work published 1943), pp.
129-130. [WSHC XIN.921].

145 Hickson, J. and Skrine, R. (Ed.)
(2013). *Carry on Coping: Diary of
a Doctor 1942-1945.* Bradford on
Avon: Ex Libris Press, pp. 67. [WSHC
CHP.611 Original diaries are also
available at WSA 4236/1-5].

146 Devizes Local History Group and
Haycock, L. (Ed.). (1995). *How
Devizes Won the War!* Devizes Local
History Group, pp. 77. [WSHC
DEV.949].

147 Calder, A. (1992). *The People's War:
Britain 1939-45.* London: Pimlico
(Original work published 1969), pp.
207. [WSHC 941.084].

148 Vernon, C. (2011). *Malmesbury versus
Hitler: The Town's role in the Second
World War.* Malmesbury: Malmesbury
Civic Trust, pp. 73. [WSHC
MAL.949].

149 WSA G15/225/5.

150 MacKay, R. (1999). *The Test of War:
Inside Britain 1939-45.* London: UCL
Press, pp. 177.

151 Maidment, A. (1993). *Under Salisbury
Spire.* Salisbury: *Salisbury Journal*, pp.
179. [WSHC SAL.949].

152 WSA G14/225/6.

153 Vernon, C. (2011). *Malmesbury versus
Hitler: The Town's role in the Second
World War.* Malmesbury: Malmesbury
Civic Trust, pp. 76. [WSHC
MAL.949].

154 WSA G15/225/5.

155 MacKay, R. (1999). *The Test of War:
Inside Britain 1939-45.* London: UCL
Press, pp. 130.

156 Calder, A. (1992). *The People's War: Britain 1939-45*. London: Pimlico (Original work published 1969), pp. 340. [WSHC 941.084].

157 MacKay, R. (1999). *The Test of War: Inside Britain 1939-45*. London: UCL Press, pp. 130.

158 Calder, A. (1992). *The People's War: Britain 1939-45*. London: Pimlico (Original work published 1969), pp. 340. [WSHC 941.084].

159 Brown, M. (1999). *Put that Light out: Britain's Civil Defence Services at War*. Stroud: Sutton Publishing, pp. 107.

160 Ibid., pp. 80.

161 Calder, A. (1992). *The People's War: Britain 1939-45*. London: Pimlico (Original work published 1969), pp. 195. [WSHC 941.084].

162 Brown, M. (1999). *Put that Light out: Britain's Civil Defence Services at War*. Stroud: Sutton Publishing, pp. 80.

163 Ibid., pp. 84.

164 Ibid., pp. 81.

165 Parsons, M. (2004). *Cricklade Revealed: Part 4 - Social Life during the Second World War*. Marion Parsons, pp. 24. [WSHC CRI.949].

166 Randall, B. (2003). *A Patchwork of Memories*. Bob Randall, pp. 43. [WSHC TRO.949].

167 Do we Need More Policewomen? (1944). *Picture Post*, 7 October 1944. pp. 20-21. [WSHC Local Studies Reminiscence Collection].

168 WSA F5/530/6.

169 WSA F5/530/4; F5/270/2.

170 WSA F5/5/5/29.

171 WSA F5/530/4.

172 WSA 1292/1.

173 Brown, M. (1999). *Put that Light out: Britain's Civil Defence Services at War*. Stroud: Sutton Publishing, pp. 82.

174 WSA G15/225/1.

175 Brown, M. (1999). *Put that Light out: Britain's Civil Defence Services at War*. Stroud: Sutton Publishing, pp. 57.

176 WSA G15/225/1.

177 Ibid.

178 Devizes Local History Group and Haycock, L. (Ed.). (1995). *How Devizes Won the War!* Devizes Local History Group, pp. 14. [WSHC DEV.949].

179 Cantwell, J. (1993). *The Second World War: A Guide to Documents in the Public Record Office*. London: HMSO (Original work published 1972), pp. 110. [WSHC 16.94053].

180 Brown, M. (1999). *Put that Light out: Britain's Civil Defence Services at War*. Stroud: Sutton Publishing, pp. 58.

181 Ibid., pp. 74.

182 Cantwell, J. (1993). *The Second World War: A Guide to Documents in the Public Record Office*. London: HMSO (Original work published 1972), pp. 110. [WSHC 16.94053].

183 WSA G15/225/5.

184 WSA G15/225/1.

185 Brown, M. (1999). *Put that Light out: Britain's Civil Defence Services at War*. Stroud: Sutton Publishing, pp. 68.

186 Ibid., pp. 72.

187 Ibid., pp. 68.

188 Ibid., pp. 69-70.

189 WSA G23/225/20.

190 Brown, M. (1999). *Put that Light out: Britain's Civil Defence Services at War*. Stroud: Sutton Publishing, pp. 72.

191 *Voluntary Aid Detachments*. (2015). Retrieved July 5, 2015 from the British Red Cross and St. John's Ambulance website http://www.redcross.org.uk/About-us/Who-we-are/Museum-and-archives/Historical-factsheets/Voluntary-Aid-Detachments.

192 *Photo gallery: our work in the Second World War*. (2015). Retrieved July 5, 2015 from the British Red Cross and St. John's Ambulance website http://www.redcross.org.uk/About-us/Who-we-are/Museum-and-archives/Online-exhibitions/Second-World-War-photo

193 Vernon, C. (2011). *Malmesbury versus Hitler: The Town's role in the Second World War*. Malmesbury: Malmesbury Civic Trust, pp. 26. [WSHC MAL.949].

194 Ibid., pp. 32.

195 Ibid., pp. 165.

196 Inchfawn, F. (2010). *Salute to the Village*. Monkton Farleigh: Folly Books

(Original work published 1943), pp. 3-5. [WSHC XIN.921].

197 Lane, C. and White, P. (1999). *Warminster in the Twentieth Century.* The Warminster History Society: Warminster, pp. 25. [WSHC WAR.949].

198 Parsons, M. (2005). *Cricklade Revealed: Part 5 - Social Life during the Second World War.* Marion Parsons, pp. 20. [WSHC CRI.949].

199 Parsons, M. (2004). *Cricklade Revealed: Part 4 - Social Life during the Second World War.* Marion Parsons, pp. 7. [WSHC CRI.949].

200 Parsons, M. (2006). *Cricklade Revealed: Part 6 - Social Life during the Second World War.* Marion Parsons, pp. 6. [WSHC CRI.949].

201 WSA G24/225/45.

202 The Civil Nursing Reserve Advisory Council. (1940). *The British Journal of Nursing,* February 1940, pp. 24.

203 WSA G24/225/29.

204 Anderson, B. (1994). *We Just Got On With It: British Women in World War II.* Chippenham: Picton Publishing, pp. 22. [WSHC AAA.949].

205 The Civil Nursing Reserve Advisory Council. (1940). *The British Journal of Nursing,* February 1940, pp. 24.

206 Anderson, B. (1994). *We Just Got On With It: British Women in World War II.* Chippenham: Picton Publishing, pp. 22. [WSHC AAA.949].

207 Devizes Local History Group and Haycock, L. (Ed.). (1995). *How Devizes Won the War!* Devizes Local History Group, pp. 77. [WSHC DEV.949].

208 Adie, K. (2003). *Corsets to Camouflage: Women at War.* London: Hodder & Stoughton, pp. 78. [WSHC 355.22082].

209 Ibid., pp. 77

210 Ibid., pp. 83.

211 Anderson, B. (1994). *We Just Got On With It: British Women in World War II.* Chippenham: Picton Publishing, pp. 36. [WSHC AAA.949].

212 WSA G15/225/1.

213 Anderson, B. (1994). *We Just Got On With It: British Women in World War II.* Chippenham: Picton Publishing, pp. 37. [WSHC AAA.949].

214 WSA G15/225/1.

215 WSA F1/100/34/1. [Wiltshire County Council Emergency Committee Minutes].

216 Anderson, B. (1994). *We Just Got On With It: British Women in World War II.* Chippenham: Picton Publishing, pp. 36-37. [WSHC AAA.949].

217 Dobson, M. (2011). *Bradford Voices: Life in Bradford on Avon 1900-2010.* Bradford on Avon: Ex Libris Press, pp. 144. [WSHC BRD.949].

218 Lane, C. and White, P. (1999). *Warminster in the Twentieth Century.* The Warminster History Society: Warminster, pp. 224. [WSHC WAR.949].

219 Devizes Local History Group and Haycock, L. (Ed.). (1995). *How Devizes Won the War!* Devizes Local History Group, pp. 57-59. [WSHC DEV.949].

220 Ibid., pp. 59.

221 Randall, B. (2003). *A Patchwork of Memories.* Bob Randall, pp. 15. [WSHC TRO.949].

222 Hickson, J. and Skrine, R. (Ed.) (2013). *Carry on Coping: Diary of a Doctor 1942-1945.* Bradford on Avon: Ex Libris Press, pp. 19-20. [WSHC CHP.611 Original diaries are also available at WSA 4236/1-5].

223 Ibid., pp. 24025.

224 Inchfawn, F. (2010). *Salute to the Village.* Monkton Farleigh: Folly Books (Original work published 1943), pp. 140-141. [WSHC XIN.921].

225 Lane, C. and White, P. (1999). *Warminster in the Twentieth Century.* The Warminster History Society: Warminster, pp. 225. [WSHC WAR.949].

226 WSA G23/990/1-10.

227 Hinton, J. (1998). Voluntarism and the Welfare/Warfare State. Women's Voluntary Services in the 1940s. *Twentieth Century British History,* 9(2),

pp. 277.

228 Randall, B. (2003). *A Patchwork of Memories*. Bob Randall, pp. 43. [WSHC TRO.949].

229 WSA F5/530/17.

230 Vernon, C. (2011). *Malmesbury versus Hitler: The Town's role in the Second World War*. Malmesbury: Malmesbury Civic Trust, pp. 32. [WSHC MAL.949].

231 WSA G15/225/2.

232 Anderson, B. (1994). *We Just Got On With It: British Women in World War II*. Chippenham: Picton Publishing, pp. 44. [WSHC AAA.949].

233 Hinton, J. (1998). Voluntarism and the Welfare/Warfare State. Women's Voluntary Services in the 1940s. *Twentieth Century British History*, 9(2), pp. 284.

234 Anderson, B. (1994). *We Just Got On With It: British Women in World War II*. Chippenham: Picton Publishing, pp. 46. [WSHC AAA.949].

235 Hinton, J. (1998). Voluntarism and the Welfare/Warfare State. Women's Voluntary Services in the 1940s. *Twentieth Century British History*, 9(2), pp. 278.

236 WSA F8/500/65/4/1.

237 Ibid.

238 Parsons, M. (2005). *Cricklade Revealed: Part 5 - Social Life during the Second World War*. Marion Parsons, pp. 29. [WSHC CRI.949].

239 WSA F8/500/42/1/2.

240 WSA 4257/30.

241 WSA G24/225/28.

242 Thomsett, S. (c. 1974). *Trowbridge 1939-45: A Social History*. Unpublished, Unpaginated study for the Weymouth College of Education. [WSHC TRO.949 (BL – Oversize)].

243 Lynn, V. (1994). *We'll Meet Again: A Personal and Social History of WWII*. London: MacMillan, pp. 154.

244 WSA 2309/120/9.

245 Hinton, J. (1998). Voluntarism and the Welfare/Warfare State. Women's Voluntary Services in the 1940s. *Twentieth Century British History*, 9(2),

246 Marshall, R. (1999). *Trowbridge Voices*. Stroud: Tempus Publishing Limited, pp. 92. [WSHC TRO.949].

247 WSA G24/225/29.

248 WSA G24/225/28.

249 Hinton, J. (1998). Voluntarism and the Welfare/Warfare State. Women's Voluntary Services in the 1940s. *Twentieth Century British History*, 9(2), pp. 278.

250 Ibid., pp. 274.

251 Ibid., pp. 282.

252 Ibid., pp. 303.

253 Hinton, J. (2002). *Women, Social Leadership and the Second World War: Continuities of Class*. Oxford: Oxford University Press, pp. 137-138.

254 WSA G24/225/4.

255 Hickson, J. and Skrine, R. (Ed.) (2013). *Carry on Coping: Diary of a Doctor 1942-1945*. Bradford on Avon: Ex Libris Press, pp. 25. [WSHC CHP.611 Original diaries are also available at WSA 4236/1-5].

256 WSA G24/225/28.

257 WSA G24/225/5.

258 Hinton, J. (1998). Voluntarism and the Welfare/Warfare State. Women's Voluntary Services in the 1940s. *Twentieth Century British History*, 9(2), pp. 285.

259 Ibid., pp. 285.

260 WSA F5/530/17.

261 Ibid.

262 Ibid.

263 WSA G24/225/28.

264 MacKay, R. (1999). *The Test of War: Inside Britain 1939-45*. London: UCL Press, pp. 134.

265 Hinton, J. (1998). Voluntarism and the Welfare/Warfare State. Women's Voluntary Services in the 1940s. *Twentieth Century British History*, 9(2), pp. 274.

266 Ibid., pp. 279.

267 Trowbridge Urban District Council. (1951). *Festival of Britain: Souvenir Programme - and Handbook*. Trowbridge: *Wiltshire Times*, pp. 39. [WSHC TRO.394].

268 Anderson, B. (1994). *We Just Got On With It: British Women in World War II*. Chippenham: Picton Publishing, pp. 58. [WSHC AAA.949].

269 *About the WI*. (2014). Retrieved August 11, 2014 from The National Federation of Women's Institute website http://www.thewi.org.uk/about-the-wi

270 Anderson, B. (1994). *We Just Got On With It: British Women in World War II*. Chippenham: Picton Publishing, pp. 58. [WSHC AAA.949].

271 Redlynch and District Local History Society. (2009). *The Redlynch Review*, 11, pp. 25. [WSHC RED.940].

272 Anderson, B. (1994). *We Just Got On With It: British Women in World War II*. Chippenham: Picton Publishing, pp. 58. [WSHC AAA.949].

273 Wyeth, R. (1995). *Sterner Days: Codford during the Second World War*. Warminster: Bedeguar Books, pp. 31-32. [WSHC COD.949].

274 Anderson, B. (1994). *We Just Got On With It: British Women in World War II*. Chippenham: Picton Publishing, pp. 59. [WSHC AAA.949].

275 Ginn, P., Goodman, R. and Langlands, A. (2012). *Wartime Farm*. London: Mitchell Beazley, pp. 128-130.

276 Wyeth, R. (1995). *Sterner Days: Codford during the Second World War*. Warminster: Bedeguar Books, pp. 32. [WSHC COD.949].

277 Wiltshire Federation of Women's Institutes (1993). *Wiltshire Within Living Memory*. Newbury: Countryside Books, pp. 188. [WSHC AAA.949].

278 WSA 2893/1.

279 WSA G2/132/14.

280 *History*. (2014). Retrieved September 15, 2014 from the Townswomen's Guild's website http www.townswomen.org.uk/page.asp?node=23&sec=History

281 *About Us*. (2014). Retrieved September 15, 2014 from the Townswomen's Guild's website http www.townswomen.org.uk/page.

282 Anderson, B. (1994). *We Just Got On With It: British Women in World War II*. Chippenham: Picton Publishing, pp. 60. [WSHC AAA.949].

283 Trowbridge Urban District Council. (1951). *Festival of Britain: Souvenir Programme - and Handbook*. Trowbridge: *Wiltshire Times*, pp. 40. [WSHC TRO.394].

284 Ibid.

285 Ibid., pp. 39-40.

286 Anderson, B. (1994). *We Just Got On With It: British Women in World War II*. Chippenham: Picton Publishing, pp. 52-53. [WSHC AAA.949].

287 Hickson, J. and Skrine, R. (Ed.) (2013). *Carry on Coping: Diary of a Doctor 1942-1945*. Bradford on Avon: Ex Libris Press, pp. 163. [WSHC CHP.611 Original diaries are also available at WSA 4236/1-5].

288 Anderson, B. (1994). *We Just Got On With It: British Women in World War II*. Chippenham: Picton Publishing, pp. 53. [WSHC AAA.949].

289 WSA 3560/10/34/1.

290 WSA G11/231/1.

291 Ibid.

292 Anderson, B. (1994). *We Just Got On With It: British Women in World War II*. Chippenham: Picton Publishing, pp. 53. [WSHC AAA.949].

293 Anderson, B. (1994). *We Just Got On With It: British Women in World War II*. Chippenham: Picton Publishing, pp. 147. [WSHC AAA.949].

294 WSA G24/224/1.

295 Anderson, B. (1994). *We Just Got On With It: British Women in World War II*. Chippenham: Picton Publishing, pp. 147. [WSHC AAA.949].

296 Calder, A. (1992). *The People's War: Britain 1939-45*. London: Pimlico (Original work published 1969), pp. 121. [WSHC 941.084].

297 MacKay, Major E.A. (Ed). (1946). *The History of the Wiltshire Home Guard 1940-1944*. Wiltshire Regiment Old Comrades Association, pp. 25. [WSHC AAA.358].

298 Calder, A. (1992). *The People's War: Britain 1939-45*. London: Pimlico (Original work published 1969), pp. 122. [WSHC 941.084].

299 WSA F5/530/28.

300 MacKay, Major E.A. (Ed). (1946). *The History of the Wiltshire Home Guard 1940-1944*. Wiltshire Regiment Old Comrades Association, pp. 13. [WSHC AAA.358].

301 Ibid., pp. 25.

302 Ibid., pp. 13.

303 Pickford, P. and Pickford, R. (Ed.). (1995). *Letters to Liz*. Newnham, Tasmania: Attic Press, pp. 29. [WSHC WAR.949].

304 WSA F5/530/28.

305 Ivan Clark, email communication, July 2, 2014.

306 WSA F5/530/28.

307 MacKay, Major E.A. (Ed). (1946). *The History of the Wiltshire Home Guard 1940-1944*. Wiltshire Regiment Old Comrades Association, pp. 24. [WSHC AAA.358].

308 Ibid., pp. 14.

309 Wyeth, R. (1995). *Sterner Days: Codford during the Second World War*. Warminster: Bedeguar Books, pp. 53. [WSHC COD.949].

310 Day, R. (2007). *Savernake at War: A Wartime History of Savernake Forest 1940-1949*. Hungerford: Roger Day, pp. 23. [WSHC SAV.949].

311 MacKay, Major E.A. (Ed). (1946). *The History of the Wiltshire Home Guard 1940-1944*. Wiltshire Regiment Old Comrades Association, pp. 13-14. [WSHC AAA.358].

312 Ibid., pp. 103.

313 Hennessy, P. (1992). *Never Again: Britain 1945-51*. London: Penguin Books Ltd., pp. 25. [WSHC 941.0854].

314 Calder, A. (1992). *The People's War: Britain 1939-45*. London: Pimlico (Original work published 1969), pp. 134. [WSHC 941.084].

315 WSA 1988/24.

316 WSA 1988/24.

317 MacKay, Major E.A. (Ed). (1946).

The History of the Wiltshire Home Guard 1940-1944. Wiltshire Regiment Old Comrades Association, pp. 116. [WSHC AAA.358].

318 Wiltshire Federation of Women's Institutes (1993). *Wiltshire Within Living Memory*. Newbury: Countryside Books, pp. 196. [WSHC AAA.949].

319 Meakin, R. (2002). *Minety at War*. Richard Meakin, pp. 97. [WSHC MIN.949].

320 Partridge, F. (1978). *A Pacifist's War*. The Hogarth Press: London, pp. 47. [WSHC HAM.927].

321 Ibid., pp. 89.

322 Ibid., pp. 39.

323 Maidment, A. (1993). *Under Salisbury Spire*. Salisbury: *Salisbury Journal*, pp. 178. [WSHC SAL.949].

324 WSA G24/225/29.

325 Bemerton Local History Society (2006). *Memories of Bemerton in Wartime*. Bemerton Local History Society with support of the Big Lottery Fund, pp. 35. [WSHC BEM.949].

326 Tanner, H. & Hanff, D. (1995). *Out of Nazi Germany*. London: Impact Books, pp. 42. [WSHC XTA.921].

327 WSA F5/530/28.

328 Calder, A. (1992). *The People's War: Britain 1939-45*. London: Pimlico (Original work published 1969), pp. 127. [WSHC 941.084].

329 Hunt, D. (2013). *World War 2 Underground Wireless Station at Hare Warren near Wilton*. Unpublished, unpaginated. [WSHC Archaeology Department 2013.033].

330 Calder, A. (1992). *The People's War: Britain 1939-45*. London: Pimlico (Original work published 1969), pp. 127. [WSHC 941.084].

331 Warwicker, J. (2008). *Churchill's Secret Army*. Barnsley: Frontline Books, pp. 55.

332 Warwicker, J. (Ed.). (2002). *With Britain in Mortal Danger: Britain's Most Secret Army of WWII*. Bristol: Cerberus Publishing Ltd, pp. 54. [WSHC AAA.949 (BL)].

333 Warwicker, J. (2008). *Churchill's Secret*

Army. Barnsley: Frontline Books, pp. 85.

334 Warwicker, J. (Ed.). (2002). *With Britain in Mortal Danger: Britain's Most Secret Army of WWII*. Bristol: Cerberus Publishing Ltd, pp. 56. [WSHC AAA.949 (BL)].

335 Ibid., pp. 217.

336 Ibid., pp. 230.

337 Ibid., pp. 220.

338 Ibid., pp. 223.

339 English Heritage. (2014). *Advice Report: Hare Warren Control Station*. Unpublished, pp. 3. [WSHC Archaeology Department].

340 Hunt, D. (2013). *World War 2 Underground Wireless Station at Hare Warren near Wilton*. Unpublished, unpaginated. [WSHC Archaeology Department 2013.033].

341 English Heritage. (2014). *Advice Report: Hare Warren Control Station*. Unpublished, pp. 3. [WSHC Archaeology Department].

342 Hunt, D. (2013). *World War 2 Underground Wireless Station at Hare Warren near Wilton*. Unpublished, unpaginated. [WSHC Archaeology Department 2013.033].

343 Ginn, P., Goodman, R. and Langlands, A. (2012). *Wartime Farm*. London: Mitchell Beazley, pp. 180.

344 Hunt, D. (2013). *World War 2 Underground Wireless Station at Hare Warren near Wilton*. Unpublished, unpaginated. [WSHC Archaeology Department 2013.033].

345 Warwicker, J. (2008). *Churchill's Secret Army*. Barnsley: Frontline Books, pp. 159-160.

346 Inchfawn, F. (2010). *Salute to the Village*. Monkton Farleigh: Folly Books (Original work published 1943), pp. 67. [WSHC XIN.921].

347 Eccles, D. (1983). *By Safe Hand: Letters of Sybil and David Eccles, 1939-1942*. London: Bodley Head, pp. 113. [WSHC CHU.928].

348 WSA G24/225/29.

349 Inchfawn, F. (2010). *Salute to the Village*. Monkton Farleigh: Folly Books

(Original work published 1943), pp. 67. [WSHC XIN.921].

350 WSA 1442/1.

351 Randall, B. (2003). *A Patchwork of Memories*. Bob Randall, pp. 26. [WSHC TRO.949].

352 The People of Fovant. (2005). *Fovant: Pages from our History*. East Knoyle: Hobnob Press, pp. 152. [WSHC FOV.940].

353 WSA F5/530/28.

354 MacKay, Major E.A. (Ed). (1946). *The History of the Wiltshire Home Guard 1940-1944*. Wiltshire Regiment Old Comrades Association, pp. 29. [WSHC AAA.358].

355 Maidment, A. (1993). *Under Salisbury Spire*. Salisbury: *Salisbury Journal*, pp. 176. [WSHC SAL.949].

356 MacKay, Major E.A. (Ed). (1946). *The History of the Wiltshire Home Guard 1940-1944*. Wiltshire Regiment Old Comrades Association, pp. 104. [WSHC AAA.358].

357 Devizes Local History Group and Haycock, L. (Ed.). (1995). *How Devizes Won the War!* Devizes Local History Group, pp. 79. [WSHC DEV.949].

358 MacKay, Major E.A. (Ed). (1946). *The History of the Wiltshire Home Guard 1940-1944*. Wiltshire Regiment Old Comrades Association, pp. 76. [WSHC AAA.358].

359 Ibid., pp. 95.

360 Calder, A. (1992). *The People's War: Britain 1939-45*. London: Pimlico (Original work published 1969), pp. 152. [WSHC 941.084].

361 WSA F5/530/3.

362 The People of Fovant. (2005). *Fovant: Pages from our History*. East Knoyle: Hobnob Press, pp. 159. [WSHC FOV.940].

363 MacKay, Major E.A. (Ed). (1946). *The History of the Wiltshire Home Guard 1940-1944*. Wiltshire Regiment Old Comrades Association, pp. 49. [WSHC AAA.358].

364 Eccles, D. (1983). *By Safe Hand: Letters of Sybil and David Eccles, 1939-*

1942. London: Bodley Head, pp. 113. [WSHC CHU.928].

365 MacKay, Major E.A. (Ed). (1946). *The History of the Wiltshire Home Guard 1940-1944*. Wiltshire Regiment Old Comrades Association, pp. 81. [WSHC AAA.358].

366 Ibid., pp. 118.

367 Ibid., pp. 65.

368 Ibid., pp. 82.

369 Parsons, M. (2004). *Cricklade Revealed: Part 4 - Social Life during the Second World War*. Marion Parsons, pp. 22. [WSHC CRI.949].

370 MacKay, Major E.A. (Ed). (1946). *The History of the Wiltshire Home Guard 1940-1944*. Wiltshire Regiment Old Comrades Association, pp. 25. [WSHC AAA.358].

371 Ibid., pp. 97.

372 Ibid., pp. 65.

373 Devizes Local History Group and Haycock, L. (Ed.). (1995). *How Devizes Won the War!* Devizes Local History Group, pp. 73. [WSHC DEV.949].

374 MacKay, Major E.A. (Ed). (1946). *The History of the Wiltshire Home Guard 1940-1944*. Wiltshire Regiment Old Comrades Association, pp. 13. [WSHC AAA.358].

375 Ibid., pp. 67.

376 Ibid., pp. 18.

377 Ibid., pp. 68.

378 Ibid., pp. 94.

379 Ibid., pp. 99.

380 Ibid., pp. 19.

381 Ibid., pp. 67.

382 Ibid., pp. 17-19.

383 Ibid., pp. 84.

384 Ibid., pp. 19.

385 Parsons, M. (2004). *Cricklade Revealed: Part 4 - Social Life during the Second World War*. Marion Parsons, pp. 22. [WSHC CRI.949].

386 Ibid., pp. 61.

387 Ibid., pp. 104.

388 Ibid., pp. 35.

389 Maidment, A. (1993). *Under Salisbury Spire*. Salisbury: *Salisbury Journal*, pp. 176. [WSHC SAL.949].

390 WSA 1292/1.

391 MacKay, Major E.A. (Ed). (1946). *The History of the Wiltshire Home Guard 1940-1944*. Wiltshire Regiment Old Comrades Association, pp. 54. [WSHC AAA.358].

392 Ibid., pp. 71.

393 Ibid., pp. 17.

394 WSA G19/996/3.

395 MacKay, Major E.A. (Ed). (1946). *The History of the Wiltshire Home Guard 1940-1944*. Wiltshire Regiment Old Comrades Association, pp. 146. [WSHC AAA.358].

396 Ibid., pp. 80.

397 Ibid., pp. 84.

398 Ibid., pp. 91.

399 Ibid., pp. 70.

400 Ibid., pp. 78.

401 Ibid., pp. 50.

402 Calder, A. (1992). *The People's War: Britain 1939-45*. London: Pimlico (Original work published 1969), pp. 124. [WSHC 941.084].

403 MacKay, Major E.A. (Ed). (1946). *The History of the Wiltshire Home Guard 1940-1944*. Wiltshire Regiment Old Comrades Association, pp. 133. [WSHC AAA.358].

404 Ibid., pp. 139.

405 Ibid., pp. 142.

406 Ibid., pp. 98.

407 WSA 1292/1.

408 Hickson, J. and Skrine, R. (Ed.) (2013). *Carry on Coping: Diary of a Doctor 1942-1945*. Bradford on Avon: Ex Libris Press, pp. 194. [WSHC CHP.611 Original diaries are also available at WSA 4236/1-5].

409 Day, R. (2007). *Savernake at War: A Wartime History of Savernake Forest 1940-1949*. Hungerford: Roger Day, pp. 24. [WSHC SAV.949].

410 Vernon, C. (2011). *Malmesbury versus Hitler: The Town's role in the Second World War*. Malmesbury: Malmesbury Civic Trust, pp. 101. [WSHC MAL.949].

411 MacKay, Major E.A. (Ed). (1946). *The History of the Wiltshire Home Guard 1940-1944*. Wiltshire Regiment

Old Comrades Association, pp. 151. [WSHC AAA.358].

412 Dobson, M. (2011). *Bradford Voices: Life in Bradford on Avon 1900-2010.* Bradford on Avon: Ex Libris Press, pp. 147. [WSHC BRD.949].

413 Vernon, C. (2011). *Malmesbury versus Hitler: The Town's role in the Second World War.* Malmesbury: Malmesbury Civic Trust, pp. 77. [WSHC MAL.949].

414 WSA 2641/31.

415 WSA 2812/8.

416 Mackay, Major E.A. (Ed). (1946). *The History of the Wiltshire Home Guard 1940-1944.* Wiltshire Regiment Old Comrades Association, pp. 72. [WSHC AAA.358].

417 Ibid., pp. 83-84.

418 Ibid., pp. 74.

419 Ibid., pp. 51.

420 Ibid., pp. 40.

421 Maidment, A. (1993). *Under Salisbury Spire.* Salisbury: *Salisbury Journal*, pp. 175. [WSHC SAL.949].

422 Mackay, Major E.A. (Ed). (1946). *The History of the Wiltshire Home Guard 1940-1944.* Wiltshire Regiment Old Comrades Association, pp. 50. [WSHC AAA.358].

423 WSA F2/851/3/19.

424 Mackay, Major E.A. (Ed). (1946). *The History of the Wiltshire Home Guard 1940-1944.* Wiltshire Regiment Old Comrades Association, pp. 50. [WSHC AAA.358].

425 Ibid., pp. 72.

426 Summerfield, P and Peniston-Bird, C. (2000). Women in the Firing Line: the Home Guard and the defence of gender boundaries in Britain in the Second World War. *Women's History Review,* 9(2), pp. 232-234.

427 Eccles, D. (1983). *By Safe Hand: Letters of Sybil and David Eccles, 1939-1942.* London: Bodley Head, pp. 127. [WSHC CHU.928].

428 Olivier, E. (1943). *Night Thoughts of a Country Landlady.* London: B.T. Batsford Ltd., pp. 86. [WSHC XOL.824].

429 Summerfield, P and Peniston-Bird, C. (2000). Women in the Firing Line: the Home Guard and the defence of gender boundaries in Britain in the Second World War. *Women's History Review,* 9(2), pp. 236-238.

430 WSA G5/530/28.

431 Mackay, Major E.A. (Ed). (1946). *The History of the Wiltshire Home Guard 1940-1944.* Wiltshire Regiment Old Comrades Association, pp. 78. [WSHC AAA.358].

432 Ibid., pp. 82.

433 Ibid., pp. 91.

434 Ibid., pp. 93.

435 Ibid., pp. 82.

436 Summerfield, P and Peniston-Bird, C. (2000). Women in the Firing Line: the Home Guard and the defence of gender boundaries in Britain in the Second World War. *Women's History Review,* 9(2), pp. 244.

437 Ibid., pp. 249-251.

438 Mackay, Major E.A. (Ed). (1946). *The History of the Wiltshire Home Guard 1940-1944.* Wiltshire Regiment Old Comrades Association, pp. 59. [WSHC AAA.358].

439 Ibid., pp. 24.

440 Ibid., pp. 82.

441 Ibid., pp. 95.

442 Wills, H. (1985). *Pillboxes: A Study of U.K. Defences 1940.* London: Leo Cooper in association with Secker and Warburg, pp. 1-2. [WSHC AAA.354].

443 Ibid., pp. 9.

444 Ibid., pp. 11.

445 Ibid., pp. 40.

446 Dobson, M. (2011). *Bradford Voices: Life in Bradford on Avon 1900-2010.* Bradford on Avon: Ex Libris Press, pp. 136. [WSHC BRD.949].

447 Wills, H. (1985). *Pillboxes: A Study of U.K. Defences 1940.* London: Leo Cooper in association with Secker and Warburg, pp. 44. [WSHC AAA.354].

448 Maidment, A. (1993). *Under Salisbury Spire.* Salisbury: *Salisbury Journal*, pp. 176. [WSHC SAL.949].

449 Wills, H. (1985). *Pillboxes: A Study of U.K. Defences 1940.* London: Leo

Cooper in association with Secker and Warburg, pp. 43. [WSHC AAA.354].

450 Ibid., pp. 11-12.

451 Green, M., Major. (1999). War Walks: Stop Line Green. Leckhampton: Reardon Publishing, pp. 4-6. [WSHC AAA.949].

452 Dobson, M. (2011). *Bradford Voices: Life in Bradford on Avon 1900-2010*. Bradford on Avon: Ex Libris Press, pp. 134. [WSHC BRD.949].

453 Randall, B. (2003). *A Patchwork of Memories*. Bob Randall, pp. 45. [WSHC TRO.949].

454 WSA F14/001/1.

455 *Save our Pillbox Campaign in Devizes Pays Off*. (2010). Retrieved February 5, 2015 from the *Wiltshire Gazette and Herald* website

456 Green, M., Major. (1999). War Walks: Stop Line Green. Leckhampton: Reardon Publishing, pp. 6. [WSHC AAA.949].

457 MacKay, Major E.A. (Ed). (1946). *The History of the Wiltshire Home Guard 1940-1944*. Wiltshire Regiment Old Comrades Association, pp. 73. [WSHC AAA.358].

458 Ibid., pp. 128.

459 Ibid., pp. 15-16.

460 WSA 1292/1.

461 MacKay, Major E.A. (Ed). (1946). *The History of the Wiltshire Home Guard 1940-1944*. Wiltshire Regiment Old Comrades Association, pp. 15-16. [WSHC AAA.358].

462 Ibid., pp. 106.

463 Ibid., pp. 9.

464 Ibid., pp. 85.

465 Ibid., pp. 89.

466 Scott, J. (1996). *Reflections*. Swindon: Scodipur Publications, pp. 54. [WSHC PUR.940].

467 Hook, J. (1998). *The Endurance of my Companions: The Fatal Civilian Casualties due to Air Raids on the Former County of Wiltshire 1939-1945*. J Hook, pp. 14. [WSHC AAA.949

(BL)].

468 MacKay, Major E.A. (Ed). (1946). *The History of the Wiltshire Home Guard 1940-1944*. Wiltshire Regiment Old Comrades Association, pp. 59. [WSHC AAA.358].

469 Lynn, V. (1994). *We'll Meet Again: A Personal and Social History of WWII*. London: MacMillan, pp. 49.

470 Parsons, M. (2005). *Cricklade Revealed: Part 5 - Social Life during the Second World War*. Marion Parsons, pp. 21. [WSHC CRI.949].

471 MacKay, Major E.A. (Ed). (1946). *The History of the Wiltshire Home Guard 1940-1944*. Wiltshire Regiment Old Comrades Association, pp. 154. [WSHC AAA.358].

472 Ibid., pp. 74.

473 WSA G6/132/77.

474 WSA 1292/7.

475 Vernon, C. (2011). *Malmesbury versus Hitler: The Town's role in the Second World War*. Malmesbury: Malmesbury Civic Trust, pp. 81. [WSHC MAL.949].

476 MacKay, Major E.A. (Ed). (1946). *The History of the Wiltshire Home Guard 1940-1944*. Wiltshire Regiment Old Comrades Association, pp. 81. [WSHC AAA.358].

477 Ibid., pp. 84.

478 Dobson, M. (2011). *Bradford Voices: Life in Bradford on Avon 1900-2010*. Bradford on Avon: Ex Libris Press, pp. 139. [WSHC BRD.949].

479 Hammond, P. (2013). *The Royal Observer Corps at Alderbury*. Alderbury: Alderbury & Whaddon Local History Research Group, pp. 5. [WSHC ALD.359].

480 Dobson, M. (2011). *Bradford Voices: Life in Bradford on Avon 1900-2010*. Bradford on Avon: Ex Libris Press, pp. 139. [WSHC BRD.949].

481 Hammond, P. (2013). *The Royal Observer Corps at Alderbury*. Alderbury: Alderbury & Whaddon Local History Research Group, pp. 5. [WSHC ALD.359].

482 Vernon, C. (2011). *Malmesbury versus*

Hitler: *The Town's role in the Second World War*. Malmesbury: Malmesbury Civic Trust, pp. 34. [WSHC MAL.949].

483 Ibid., pp. 112.

484 Dobson, M. (2011). *Bradford Voices: Life in Bradford on Avon 1900-2010*. Bradford on Avon: Ex Libris Press, pp. 139. [WSHC BRD.949].

485 Hammond, P. (2013). *The Royal Observer Corps at Alderbury*. Alderbury: Alderbury & Whaddon Local History Research Group, pp. 5-6. [WSHC ALD.359].

486 Vernon, C. (2011). *Malmesbury versus Hitler: The Town's role in the Second World War*. Malmesbury: Malmesbury Civic Trust, pp. 112. [WSHC MAL.949].

487 Calder, A. (1992). *The People's War: Britain 1939-45*. London: Pimlico (Original work published 1969), pp. 146. [WSHC 941.084].

488 Vernon, C. (2011). *Malmesbury versus Hitler: The Town's role in the Second World War*. Malmesbury: Malmesbury Civic Trust, pp. 112. [WSHC MAL.949].

489 Dobinson, C. (2010). *Building Radar: Forging Britain's Early Warning Chain, 1939-1945*. London: Methuen London Ltd., pp. 64. [WSHC AAA.949 (BL)].

490 *About the Man*. (2014). Retrieved September 6, 2014 from the Watson-Watt Society website

491 Dobinson, C. (2010). *Building Radar: Forging Britain's Early Warning Chain, 1939-1945*. London: Methuen London Ltd., pp. 326. [WSHC AAA.949 (BL)].

492 Ibid., pp. 367.

493 *Gallery*. (2014), Retrieved September 6, 2014 from the Watson-Watt Society website

494 Dobinson, C. (2010). *Building Radar: Forging Britain's Early Warning Chain, 1939-1945*. London: Methuen

London Ltd., pp. 393. [WSHC AAA.949 (BL)].

495 Dobson, M. (2011). *Bradford Voices: Life in Bradford on Avon 1900-2010*. Bradford on Avon: Ex Libris Press, pp. 139. [WSHC BRD.949].

496 Vernon, C. (2011). *Malmesbury versus Hitler: The Town's role in the Second World War*. Malmesbury: Malmesbury Civic Trust, pp. 112. [WSHC MAL.949].

497 Dobson, M. (2011). *Bradford Voices: Life in Bradford on Avon 1900-2010*. Bradford on Avon: Ex Libris Press, pp. 139. [WSHC BRD.949].

498 Vernon, C. (2011). *Malmesbury versus Hitler: The Town's role in the Second World War*. Malmesbury: Malmesbury Civic Trust, pp. 112. [WSHC MAL.949].

499 Anderson, B. (1994). *We Just Got On With It: British Women in World War II*. Chippenham: Picton Publishing, pp. 136. [WSHC AAA.949].

500 Dobson, M. (2011). *Bradford Voices: Life in Bradford on Avon 1900-2010*. Bradford on Avon: Ex Libris Press, pp. 139. [WSHC BRD.949].

501 Vernon, C. (2011). *Malmesbury versus Hitler: The Town's role in the Second World War*. Malmesbury: Malmesbury Civic Trust, pp. 112. [WSHC MAL.949].

502 Anderson, B. (1994). *We Just Got On With It: British Women in World War II*. Chippenham: Picton Publishing, pp. 136. [WSHC AAA.949].

503 Hammond, P. (2013). *The Royal Observer Corps at Alderbury*. Alderbury: Alderbury & Whaddon Local History Research Group, pp. 6. [WSHC ALD.359].

504 Ibid., pp. 9-10.

505 Sanders, H. (1919) *Trowbridge Roll of Honour*. Trowbridge: Trowbridge Town Council, pp. 9. [WSHC TRO.924].

506 *Wiltshire Gazette*, 19/10/1939. [WSHC Microform Collection].

507 Rose, S. (2003). *Which People's War? National Identity and Citizenship in Wartime Britain 1939-45*. Oxford:

Oxford University Press, pp. 89.

508 Devizes Local History Group and Haycock, L. (Ed.). (1995). *How Devizes Won the War!* Devizes Local History Group, pp. 42. [WSHC DEV.949].

509 Vernon, C. (2011). *Malmesbury versus Hitler: The Town's role in the Second World War.* Malmesbury: Malmesbury Civic Trust, pp. 118-121. [WSHC MAL.949].

510 Wyeth, R. (1995). *Sterner Days: Codford during the Second World War.* Warminster: Bedeguar Books, pp. 102. [WSHC COD.949].

511 Vernon, C. (2011). *Malmesbury versus Hitler: The Town's role in the Second World War.* Malmesbury: Malmesbury Civic Trust, pp. 122. [WSHC MAL.949].

512 Brown, M. (1999). *Put that Light out: Britain's Civil Defence Services at War.* Stroud: Sutton Publishing, pp. 36.

513 Trowbridge Urban District Council (1951). *Festival of Britain: Souvenir Programme - and Handbook.* Trowbridge: *Wiltshire Times*, pp. 39. [WSHC.394].

514 *History of Guiding.* (2014). Retrieved August 11, 2014 from the Girlguiding website

515 *Wiltshire Times*, 30/9/1939. [WSHC Microform Collection].

516 Vernon, C. (2011). *Malmesbury versus Hitler: The Town's role in the Second World War.* Malmesbury: Malmesbury Civic Trust, pp. 119-123. [WSHC MAL.949].

517 WSA G15/225/1.

518 Vernon, C. (2011). *Malmesbury versus Hitler: The Town's role in the Second World War.* Malmesbury: Malmesbury Civic Trust, pp. 81. [WSHC MAL.949].

519 WSA G15/225/1.

520 WSA G23/225/20.

521 Grant, M. (2011). 'Civil Defence Gives Meaning to Your Leisure': Citizenship, Participation, and Cultural Change in Cold War

Propaganda, 1949-54. *Twentieth Century British History*, 22(1), pp. 52. [doi:10.1093/tcbh/hwq040].

522 Kynaston, D. (2007). *A World to Build: Austerity Britain.* London: Bloomsbury, pp. 109.

523 Grant, M. (2011). 'Civil Defence Gives Meaning to Your Leisure': Citizenship, Participation, and Cultural Change in Cold War Propaganda, 1949-54. *Twentieth Century British History*, 22(1), pp. 52. [doi:10.1093/tcbh/hwq040].

524 Ibid., pp. 78.

525 Ibid., pp. 75.

526 Ibid., pp. 70-72.

527 WSA G23/231/1.

528 Lane, C. and White, P. (1999). *Warminster in the Twentieth Century.* The Warminster History Society: Warminster, pp. 27-28. [WSHC WAR.949].

529 Trowbridge Urban District Council (1951). *Festival of Britain: Souvenir Programme - and Handbook.* Trowbridge: *Wiltshire Times*, pp. 3. [WSHC.394].

530 WSA G23/231/1.

531 WSA F5/530/28.

532 Ibid.

533 Grant, M. (2011). 'Civil Defence Gives Meaning to Your Leisure': Citizenship, Participation, and Cultural Change in Cold War Propaganda, 1949-54. *Twentieth Century British History*, 22(1), pp. 77. [doi:10.1093/tcbh/hwq040].

534 Randall, B. (2003). *A Patchwork of Memories.* Bob Randall, pp. 21-22. [WSHC TRO.949].

535 Vernon, C. (2011). *Malmesbury versus Hitler: The Town's role in the Second World War.* Malmesbury: Malmesbury Civic Trust, pp. 66. [WSHC MAL.949].

536 Calder, A. (1992). *The People's War: Britain 1939-45.* London: Pimlico (Original work published 1969), pp. 339. [WSHC 941.084].

537 *Message from the Queen.* (1945). Great Western Railway Magazine, 57(1),

pp. 1. [WSHC GWR Magazine (Journals)].

7 Menace from the Sky

1 Meisel, J. (1994). Air Raid Shelter Policy and its Critics in Britain before the Second World War. *Twentieth Century British History*, 5(3), pp. 316.

2 Ibid., pp. 302.

3 Gartner, N. (2012). *Operation Pied Piper: The Wartime Evacuation of Schoolchildren from London and Berlin 1938-1946*. Charlotte (USA): ISA (Information Age Publishing), pp. 12.

4 Meisel, J. (1994). Air Raid Shelter Policy and its Critics in Britain before the Second World War. *Twentieth Century British History*, 5(3), pp. 302.

5 Ibid., pp. 303.

6 Gartner, N. (2012). *Operation Pied Piper: The Wartime Evacuation of Schoolchildren from London and Berlin 1938-1946*. Charlotte (USA): ISA (Information Age Publishing), pp. 12.

7 Berryman, D. (2002). *Wiltshire Airfields in the Second World War*. Newbury: Countryside Books, pp. 277. [WSHC AAA.352].

8 Carter, G. (1992). *Porton Down: 75yrs of Chemical & Biological Research*. London: HMSO, pp. 32-33. [WSHC IDM.354].

9 Meisel, J. (1994). Air Raid Shelter Policy and its Critics in Britain before the Second World War. *Twentieth Century British History*, 5(3), pp. 304-305.

10 Cantwell, J. (1993). *The Second World War: A Guide to Documents in the Public Record Office*. London: HMSO (Original work published 1972), pp. 109-110. [WSHC 16.94053].

11 Meisel, J. (1994). Air Raid Shelter Policy and its Critics in Britain before the Second World War. *Twentieth Century British History*, 5(3), pp. 316.

12 WSHC AAA.949. [Local Studies Ephemera]. [Lord Privy Seal's Office, unpaginated].

13 Hennessy, P. (1992). *Never Again: Britain 1945-51*. London: Penguin

Books Ltd., pp. 6. [WSHC 941.0854].

14 Calder, A. (1992). *The People's War: Britain 1939-45*. London: Pimlico (Original work published 1969), pp. 25-26. [WSHC 941.084].

15 Hennessy, P. (1992). *Never Again: Britain 1945-51*. London: Penguin Books Ltd., pp. 6. [WSHC 941.0854].

16 Calder, A. (1992). *The People's War: Britain 1939-45*. London: Pimlico (Original work published 1969), pp. 55. [WSHC 941.084].

17 Bemerton Local History Society (2006). *Memories of Bemerton in Wartime*. Bemerton Local History Society with support of the Big Lottery Fund, pp. 31. [WSHC BEM.949].

18 Calder, A. (1992). *The People's War: Britain 1939-45*. London: Pimlico (Original work published 1969), pp. 25-26. [WSHC 941.084].

19 Ibid., pp. 55.

20 Bemerton Local History Society (2006). *Memories of Bemerton in Wartime*. Bemerton Local History Society with support of the Big Lottery Fund, pp. 40. [WSHC BEM.949].

21 Partridge, F. (1978). *A Pacifist's War*. The Hogarth Press: London, pp. 62. [WSHC HAM.927].

22 Calder, A. (1992). *The People's War: Britain 1939-45*. London: Pimlico (Original work published 1969), pp. 55. [WSHC 941.084].

23 Devizes Local History Group and Haycock, L. (Ed.). (1995). *How Devizes Won the War!* Devizes Local History Group, pp. 13. [WSHC DEV.949].

24 Calder, A. (1992). *The People's War: Britain 1939-45*. London: Pimlico (Original work published 1969), pp. 67. [WSHC 941.084].

25 Ibid., pp. 112.

26 Ibid.

27 Parsons, M. (2005). *Cricklade Revealed: Part 5 - Social Life during the Second World War*. Marion Parsons, pp. 27. [WSHC CRI.949].

28 WSA F8/600/97/3/27/1.

29 Partridge, F. (1978). *A Pacifist's War*.

The Hogarth Press: London, pp. 79. [WSHC HAM.927].

30 WSA G15/224/6.

31 Meisel, J. (1994). Air Raid Shelter Policy and its Critics in Britain before the Second World War. *Twentieth Century British History*, 5(3), pp. 304-306.

32 Calder, A. (1992). *The People's War: Britain 1939-45*. London: Pimlico (Original work published 1969), pp. 180. [WSHC 941.084].

33 Ibid., pp. 180-181.

34 Maidment, A. (1993). *Under Salisbury Spire*. Salisbury: *Salisbury Journal*, pp. 167. [WSHC SAL.949].

35 G15/225/25.

36 Calder, A. (1992). *The People's War: Britain 1939-45*. London: Pimlico (Original work published 1969), pp. 181. [WSHC 941.084].

37 Eve, M. (2000). From Better Little Books to Baby Puffins: The Phenomenon of Small English Illustrated Children's Books for Use In and Out of Air-Raid Shelters-1939-1948. *Children's Literature in Education*, 31(2), pp. 125-126.

38 Meisel, J. (1994). Air Raid Shelter Policy and its Critics in Britain before the Second World War. *Twentieth Century British History*, 5(3), pp. 309-315.

39 Calder, A. (1992). *The People's War: Britain 1939-45*. London: Pimlico (Original work published 1969), pp. 199. [WSHC 941.084].

40 Hennessy, P. (1992). *Never Again: Britain 1945-51*. London: Penguin Books Ltd., pp. 199. [WSHC 941.0854].

41 Calder, A. (1992). *The People's War: Britain 1939-45*. London: Pimlico (Original work published 1969), pp. 187. [WSHC 941.084].

42 Ibid., pp. 199.

43 WSA 1988/24.

44 Ibid.

45 WSA 1442/1.

46 WSA G23/225/18.

47 Dawkins, B. (1989). *When Warm Milk Was Fresh Milk*. B. Dawkins, pp. 94. [WSHC WAR.949].

48 WSA F4/550/46.

49 Mason, K. (1996). *Charlton Park: A Short History*. Privately Published, pp. 42-43. [WSHC CHN.727].

50 Turner, J. (2010). *Awards of the George Cross 1940-2009*. Barnsley: Pen & Sword Military, pp. 44.

51 Mason, K. (1996). *Charlton Park: A Short History*. Privately Published, pp. 43. [WSHC CHN.727].

52 Ibid.

53 Partridge, F. (1978). *A Pacifist's War*. The Hogarth Press: London, pp. 57. [WSHC HAM.927].

54 Calder, A. (1992). *The People's War: Britain 1939-45*. London: Pimlico (Original work published 1969), pp. 25. [WSHC 941.084].

55 Bemerton Local History Society (2006). *Memories of Bemerton in Wartime*. Bemerton Local History Society with support of the Big Lottery Fund, pp. 34. [WSHC BEM.949].

56 Ibid., pp. 29.

57 WSA F8/500/65/4/1.

58 Inchfawn, F. (2010). *Salute to the Village*. Monkton Farleigh: Folly Books (Original work published 1943), pp. 138-140. [WSHC XIN.921].

59 Meisel, J. (1994). Air Raid Shelter Policy and its Critics in Britain before the Second World War. *Twentieth Century British History*, 5(3), pp. 306.

60 Calder, A. (1992). *The People's War: Britain 1939-45*. London: Pimlico (Original work published 1969), pp. 179-180. [WSHC 941.084].

61 Maidment, A. (1993). *Under Salisbury Spire*. Salisbury: *Salisbury Journal*, pp. 178. [WSHC SAL.949].

62 Meisel, J. (1994). Air Raid Shelter Policy and its Critics in Britain before the Second World War. *Twentieth Century British History*, 5(3), pp. 306-307.

63 Hennessy, P. (1992). *Never Again: Britain 1945-51*. London: Penguin Books Ltd., pp. 8. [WSHC 941.0854].

64 Calder, A. (1992). *The People's War: Britain 1939-45*. London: Pimlico (Original work published 1969), pp. 180. [WSHC 941.084].

65 Meisel, J. (1994). Air Raid Shelter Policy and its Critics in Britain before the Second World War. *Twentieth Century British History*, 5(3), pp. 307.

66 Calder, A. (1992). *The People's War: Britain 1939-45*. London: Pimlico (Original work published 1969), pp. 179. [WSHC 941.084].

67 Bemerton Local History Society (2006). *Memories of Bemerton in Wartime*. Bemerton Local History Society with support of the Big Lottery Fund, pp. 34-35. [WSHC BEM.949].

68 Summers, J. (2015). *Fashion on the Ration*. London: Profile Books in Partnership with the Imperial War Museum, pp. 58-59.

69 Meisel, J. (1994). Air Raid Shelter Policy and its Critics in Britain before the Second World War. *Twentieth Century British History*, 5(3), pp. 307.

70 Cantwell, J. (1993). *The Second World War: A Guide to Documents in the Public Record Office*. London: HMSO (Original work published 1972), pp. 109-101. [WSHC 16.94053].

71 Calder, A. (1992). *The People's War: Britain 1939-45*. London: Pimlico (Original work published 1969), pp. 180. [WSHC 941.084].

72 Meisel, J. (1994). Air Raid Shelter Policy and its Critics in Britain before the Second World War. *Twentieth Century British History*, 5(3), pp. 307.

73 Calder, A. (1992). *The People's War: Britain 1939-45*. London: Pimlico (Original work published 1969), pp. 112-113. [WSHC 941.084].

74 WSA G15/225/25.

75 Calder, A. (1992). *The People's War: Britain 1939-45*. London: Pimlico (Original work published 1969), pp. 180. [WSHC 941.084].

76 WSA G15/225/25.

77 Ibid.

78 Calder, A. (1992). *The People's War: Britain 1939-45*. London: Pimlico

(Original work published 1969), pp. 113. [WSHC 941.084].

79 WSA G23/225/16.

80 WSA F1/100/34/1. [WCC Emergency Committee Minutes, 2.10.1940].

81 WSA F1/100/34/1.

82 WSA G23/225/16.

83 Calder, A. (1992). *The People's War: Britain 1939-45*. London: Pimlico (Original work published 1969), pp. 187. [WSHC 941.084].

84 Bemerton Local History Society (2006). *Memories of Bemerton in Wartime*. Bemerton Local History Society with support of the Big Lottery Fund, pp. 33. [WSHC BEM.949].

85 Ibid., pp. 46.

86 Calder, A. (1992). *The People's War: Britain 1939-45*. London: Pimlico (Original work published 1969), pp. 187. [WSHC 941.084].

87 WSA F8/500/65/4/1.

88 WSA 1442/1.

89 Bemerton Local History Society (2006). *Memories of Bemerton in Wartime*. Bemerton Local History Society with support of the Big Lottery Fund, pp. 29. [WSHC BEM.949].

90 Ibid., pp. 40.

91 Ibid., pp. 33.

92 WSA F8/500/258/2/2.

93 McCoombe, C. (2001). *The Recollections of Charles McCoombe when he served in the Royal Navy during World War II*. Unpublished, pp. 1. [WSHC HOL.921].

94 Parsons, M. (2005). *Cricklade Revealed: Part 5 - Social Life during the Second World War*. Marion Parsons, pp. 1-3. [WSHC CRI.949].

95 WSA F8/500/179/1/2.

96 Cooper, L. (2009). *A Little London Evacuee*. Diss, Norfolk: Data Tech D.T.P., pp. 62. [WSHC WAR.921].

97 WSA F4/550/11.

98 WSHC (Local Studies Reminiscence Collection) [Lord Privy Seal's Office, Unpaginated].

99 WSA 1988/24.

100 WSA F8/500/196/1/2.

101 WSA G14/225/6.

102 Inchfawn, F. (2010). *Salute to the Village*. Monkton Farleigh: Folly Books (Original work published 1943), pp. 115-116. [WSHC XIN.921].

103 WSA G11/225/12. [Circular 112/1940].

104 WSA F5/505/29.

105 WSA G14/225/6.

106 Devizes Local History Group and Haycock, L. (Ed.). (1995). *How Devizes Won the War!* Devizes Local History Group, pp. 77. [WSHC DEV.949].

107 WSA G14/225/6.

108 Devizes Local History Group and Haycock, L. (Ed.). (1995). *How Devizes Won the War!* Devizes Local History Group, pp. 17. [WSHC DEV.949].

109 WSA G15/225/25.

110 WSA G24/225/42.

111 WSA G24/225/28.

112 WSA G24/225/39.

113 WSA G15/225/25.

114 Parsons, M. (2005). *Cricklade Revealed: Part 5 - Social Life during the Second World War*. Marion Parsons, pp. 4. [WSHC CRI.949].

115 WSA 245/7.

116 Eccles, D. (1983). *By Safe Hand: Letters of Sybil and David Eccles, 1939-1942*. London: Bodley Head, pp. 203. [WSHC CHU.928].

117 Day, R. (2007). *Savernake at War: A Wartime History of Savernake Forest 1940-1949*. Hungerford: Roger Day, pp. 13. [WSHC SAV.949].

118 Partridge, F. (1978). *A Pacifist's War*. The Hogarth Press: London, pp. 67. [WSHC HAM.927].

119 WSA F1/100/35. [Civil Defence and Welfare Committee, Emergency Committee Minutes, 20.8.1941].

120 WSA G24/224/4.

121 WSA G17/224/1.

122 WSA G24/224/4.

123 WSA G19/223/1.

124 Wiltshire Federation of Women's Institutes (1993). *Wiltshire Within Living Memory*. Newbury: Countryside Books, pp. 208-209. [WSHC AAA.949].

125 Randall, B. (2003). *A Patchwork of Memories*. Bob Randall, pp. 15-16. [WSHC TRO.949].

126 Marshall, R. (1999). *Trowbridge Voices*. Stroud: Tempus Publishing Limited, pp. 97. [WSHC TRO.949].

127 Randall, B. (2003). *A Patchwork of Memories*. Bob Randall, pp. 15-17. [WSHC TRO.949].

128 Mock, J. (1997). *Bradford on Avon & District: The War Years (1939-1945)*. J. H. Mock, pp. 45. [BRD.949].

129 Randall, B. (2003). *A Patchwork of Memories*. Bob Randall, pp. 7. [WSHC TRO.949].

130 Wiltshire Federation of Women's Institutes (1993). *Wiltshire Within Living Memory*. Newbury: Countryside Books, pp. 186. [WSHC AAA.949].

131 Partridge, F. (1978). *A Pacifist's War*. The Hogarth Press: London, pp. 65-66. [WSHC HAM.927].

132 Wiltshire Federation of Women's Institutes (1993). *Wiltshire Within Living Memory*. Newbury: Countryside Books, pp. 186. [WSHC AAA.949].

133 Bemerton Local History Society (2006). *Memories of Bemerton in Wartime*. Bemerton Local History Society with support of the Big Lottery Fund, pp. 61-64. [WSHC BEM.949].

134 *Recalling End of Wartime Censorship*. (2009). Retrieved July 5, 2015 from *Wiltshire Times* website http://www.wiltshiretimes.co.uk/news/4511544.Recalling_end_of_wartime_censorship/

135 Eccles, D. (1983). *By Safe Hand: Letters of Sybil and David Eccles, 1939-1942*. London: Bodley Head, pp. 154. [WSHC CHU.928].

136 Meakin, R. (2002). *Minety at War*. Richard Meakin, pp. 76. [WSHC MIN.949].

137 Devizes Local History Group and Haycock, L. (Ed.). (1995). *How Devizes Won the War!* Devizes Local History Group, pp. 22. [WSHC DEV.949].

138 Summers, J. (2015). *Fashion on the Ration*. London: Profile Books in Partnership with the Imperial War Museum, pp. 95.

139 Siddall, M. (1995). *Safe as Houses: Childhood Through the Forties*. Christow: Devonshire House, pp. 27. [WSHC PUR.949].

140 WSA 1442/1.

141 Wiltshire Federation of Women's Institutes (1993). *Wiltshire Within Living Memory*. Newbury: Countryside Books, pp. 218-219. [WSHC AAA.949].

142 WSA 1442/1.

143 Pickford, P. and Pickford, R. (Ed.). (1995). *Letters to Liz*. Newnham, Tasmania: Attic Press, pp. 49. [WSHC WAR.949].

144 Siddall, M. (1995). *Safe as Houses: Childhood Through the Forties*. Christow: Devonshire House, pp. 19. [WSHC PUR.949].

145 WSA G23/225/27.

146 Hook, J. (1998). *The Endurance of my Companions: The Fatal Civilian Casualties due to Air Raids on the Former County of Wiltshire 1939-1945*. J Hook, pp. 6-13. [WSHC AAA.949 (BL)].

147 WSA F5/505/29.

148 WSA F1/100/34/3.

149 *Recalling End of Wartime Censorship*. (2009). Retreived July 5, 2015 from *Wiltshire Times* website http://www.wiltshiretimes.co.uk/news/history/Recalling_end_of_wartime_censorship/

150 WSA G15/225/25.

151 WSA G24/132/331.

152 WSA G24/225/59.

153 WSA G15/225/25.

154 *Parliamentary Business at the House of Commons*. (1998). Retrieved July 5, 2015 from Parliament UK website http://www.publications.parliament.uk/pa/cm199798/cmhansrd/vo980422/debtext/80422-57.htm [22 Apr 1998: Column 943].

155 WSA F2/217/7.

156 Whiles, J. (1995). *Calne at War 1939-1945*. John Whiles, pp. 35. [WSHC CAL.949].

157 WSA 1142/1.

158 Marples, M. (1970). *White Horses and Other Hill Figures*. Wakefield: S. R. Publishers, pp. 88. [WSHC AAA.747].

159 Berryman, D. (2002). *Wiltshire Airfields in the Second World War*. Newbury: Countryside Books, pp. 14. [WSHC AAA.352].

160 Calder, A. (1992). *The People's War: Britain 1939-45*. London: Pimlico (Original work published 1969), pp. 32. [WSHC 941.084].

161 Meakin, R. (2002). *Minety at War*. Richard Meakin, pp. 79. [WSHC MIN.949].

162 Devenish, D. (1948). *A Wiltshire Country Home: A Study of Little Durnford*. London: BT Batsford Ltd., pp. 101-102. [WSHC DUN.727].

163 Day, R. (2014). *The Western Kennet Valley in the Great War*. Wellington: Halsgrove, pp. 75. [WSHC ADK.949].

164 WSHC (Local Studies Reminiscence Collection).

165 Calder, A. (1992). *The People's War: Britain 1939-45*. London: Pimlico (Original work published 1969), pp. 56. [WSHC 941.084].

166 Mock, J. (1997). *Bradford on Avon & District: The War Years (1939-1945)*. J. H. Mock, pp. 4. [BRD.949].

167 Cockbill, T. (1989). *Our Swindon in 1939*. Swindon: The Quill Press, pp. 53. [WSHC SWI.949].

168 Burchell, R. (2013). *Saucepans on our Heads: Growing up in Swindon during World War 2*. Bradford on Avon: Ex Libris Press, pp. 13. [WSHC SWI.949].

169 Bemerton Local History Society (2006). *Memories of Bemerton in Wartime*. Bemerton Local History Society with support of the Big Lottery Fund, pp. 70. [WSHC BEM.949].

170 Calder, A. (1992). *The People's War: Britain 1939-45*. London: Pimlico (Original work published 1969), pp. 63. [WSHC 941.084].

171 Inchfawn, F. (2010). *Salute to the Village*. Monkton Farleigh: Folly Books (Original work published 1943), pp. 101. [WSHC XIN.921].

172 Whalley, P. (n.d.). *Corsham Memories 2: The Prefab Years 1930/40*. Patricia Whalley, pp. 57. [WSHC COR.940].

173 Maidment, A. (1993). *Under Salisbury Spire*. Salisbury: *Salisbury Journal*, pp. 180. [WSHC SAL.949].

174 Devizes Local History Group and Haycock, L. (Ed.). (1995). *How Devizes Won the War!* Devizes Local History Group, pp. 16. [WSHC DEV.949].

175 Calder, A. (1992). *The People's War: Britain 1939-45*. London: Pimlico (Original work published 1969), pp. 63. [WSHC 941.084].

176 Ibid., pp. 241.

177 Maidment, A. (1993). *Under Salisbury Spire*. Salisbury: *Salisbury Journal*, pp. 167. [WSHC SAL.949].

178 Calder, A. (1992). *The People's War: Britain 1939-45*. London: Pimlico (Original work published 1969), pp. 63-64. [WSHC 941.084].

179 Devizes Local History Group and Haycock, L. (Ed.). (1995). *How Devizes Won the War!* Devizes Local History Group, pp. 19. [WSHC DEV.949].

180 Calder, A. (1992). *The People's War: Britain 1939-45*. London: Pimlico (Original work published 1969), pp. 64. [WSHC 941.084].

181 WSA G24/132/331.

182 Calder, A. (1992). *The People's War: Britain 1939-45*. London: Pimlico (Original work published 1969), pp. 64. [WSHC 941.084].

183 Ibid., pp. 74.

184 WSA F8/500/141/1/1.

185 WSA F8/500/65/4/1.

186 Inchfawn, F. (2010). *Salute to the Village*. Monkton Farleigh: Folly Books (Original work published 1943), pp. 49. [WSHC XIN.921].

187 Calder, A. (1992). *The People's War: Britain 1939-45*. London: Pimlico (Original work published 1969), pp.

337. [WSHC 941.084].

188 Hickson, J. and Skrine, R. (Ed.) (2013). *Carry on Coping: Diary of a Doctor 1942-1945*. Bradford on Avon: Ex Libris Press, pp. 227. [WSHC CHP.611 Original diaries are also available at WSA 4236/1-5].

189 Calder, A. (1992). *The People's War: Britain 1939-45*. London: Pimlico (Original work published 1969), pp. 563. [WSHC 941.084].

190 WSA G24/225/59.

191 Calder, A. (1992). *The People's War: Britain 1939-45*. London: Pimlico (Original work published 1969), pp. 63. [WSHC 941.084].

192 Meisel, J. (1994). Air Raid Shelter Policy and its Critics in Britain before the Second World War. *Twentieth Century British History*, 5(3), pp. 316.

193 Hennessy, P. (1992). *Never Again: Britain 1945-51*. London: Penguin Books Ltd., pp. 31. [WSHC 941.0854].

194 Calder, A. (1992). *The People's War: Britain 1939-45*. London: Pimlico (Original work published 1969), pp. 219. [WSHC 941.084].

195 Falconer, J. (2009). *Names in Stone: Forgotten Warriors of Bradford on Avon and District 1939-45*. Bradford on Avon: Bed and Bolster Publishing, pp. 89-90. [WSHC BRD.924].

196 Lane, C. and White, P. (1999). *Warminster in the Twentieth Century*. The Warminster History Society: Warminster, pp. 180. [WSHC WAR.949].

197 Vernon, C. (2011). *Malmesbury versus Hitler: The Town's role in the Second World War*. Malmesbury: Malmesbury Civic Trust, pp. 174. [WSHC MAL.949].

198 Hook, J. (1998). *The Endurance of my Companions: The Fatal Civilian Casualties due to Air Raids on the Former County of Wiltshire 1939-1945*. J Hook, pp. 4. [WSHC AAA.949 (BL)].

199 Wilson, T. (1998). *The Hawthorne Aero-Engine Underground Factory*

1940-1945. Unpublished, pp. 35. [WSHC COR.949 (BL)].

8 Pulling Together

1 Zweiniger-Bargielowska, I. (2000). *Austerity in Britain: Rationing, Controls and Consumption.* Oxford: Oxford University Press, pp. 12-15.

2 Sanders, H. (1919) *Trowbridge Roll of Honour.* Trowbridge: Trowbridge Town Council, pp. 9. [WSHC TRO.924].

3 WSA F8/500/233/10/1.

4 Sanders, H. (1919) *Trowbridge Roll of Honour.* Trowbridge: Trowbridge Town Council, pp. 9. [WSHC TRO.924].

5 Zweiniger-Bargielowska, I. (2000). *Austerity in Britain: Rationing, Controls and Consumption.* Oxford: Oxford University Press, pp. 13.

6 Ibid., pp. 69.

7 Ibid., pp. 13.

8 Ibid., pp. 12-13.

9 Manton, K. (2009). Sir William Beveridge, the British Government and Plans for Food Control in Time of War, c. 1916-1941. *Contemporary British History,* 23(3), pp. 366.

10 Zweiniger-Bargielowska, I. (2000). *Austerity in Britain: Rationing, Controls and Consumption.* Oxford: Oxford University Press, pp. 14.

11 Capie, F. and Wood, G. (2002). Price Controls in War and Peace: A Marshallian Conclusion. *Scottish Journal of Political Economy,* 49(1), pp. 41.

12 Zweiniger-Bargielowska, I. (2000). *Austerity in Britain: Rationing, Controls and Consumption.* Oxford: Oxford University Press, pp. 14-15.

13 Ibid., pp. 16.

14 Manton, K. (2009). Sir William Beveridge, the British Government and Plans for Food Control in Time of War, c. 1916-1941. *Contemporary British History,* 23(3), pp. 372.

15 Zweiniger-Bargielowska, I. (2000). *Austerity in Britain: Rationing, Controls and Consumption.* Oxford: Oxford University Press, pp. 16.

16 Manton, K. (2009). Sir William Beveridge, the British Government and Plans for Food Control in Time of War, c. 1916-1941. *Contemporary British History,* 23(3), pp. 380.

17 Ibid., pp. 364.

18 WSA G18/225/9.

19 WSA G18/225/9.

20 Manton, K. (2009). Sir William Beveridge, the British Government and Plans for Food Control in Time of War, c. 1916-1941. *Contemporary British History,* 23(3), pp. 380.

21 WSHC Local Studies (Ephemera folder AAA.949). [Lord Privy Seal's Office, unpaginated].

22 Zweiniger-Bargielowska, I. (2000). *Austerity in Britain: Rationing, Controls and Consumption.* Oxford: Oxford University Press, pp. 14.

23 Manton, K. (2009). Sir William Beveridge, the British Government and Plans for Food Control in Time of War, c. 1916-1941. *Contemporary British History,* 23(3), pp. 368.

24 WSA F5/530/4.

25 Hennessy, P. (1992). *Never Again: Britain 1945-51.* London: Penguin Books Ltd., pp. 47. [WSHC 941.0854].

26 Pickford, P. and Pickford, R. (Ed.). (1995). *Letters to Liz.* Newnham, Tasmania: Attic Press, pp. 191. [WSHC WAR.949].

27 WSA F5/530/4.

28 Partridge, F. (1978). *A Pacifist's War.* The Hogarth Press: London, pp. 134. [WSHC HAM.927].

29 WSA F5/530/4.

30 Zweiniger-Bargielowska, I. (2000). *Austerity in Britain: Rationing, Controls and Consumption.* Oxford: Oxford University Press, pp. 18.

31 Manton, K. (2009). Sir William Beveridge, the British Government and Plans for Food Control in Time of War, c. 1916-1941. *Contemporary British History,* 23(3), pp. 379.

32 Capie, F. and Wood, G. (2002). Price Controls in War and Peace: A Marshallian Conclusion. *Scottish*

Journal of Political Economy, 49(1), pp. 47.

33 Zweiniger-Bargielowska, I. (2000). *Austerity in Britain: Rationing, Controls and Consumption.* Oxford: Oxford University Press, pp. 16-18.

34 Eccles, D. (1983). *By Safe Hand: Letters of Sybil and David Eccles, 1939-1942.* London: Bodley Head, pp. 30. [WSHC CHU.928].

35 Zweiniger-Bargielowska, I. (2000). *Austerity in Britain: Rationing, Controls and Consumption.* Oxford: Oxford University Press, pp. 19.

36 Cooper, L. (2009). *A Little London Evacuee.* Diss, Norfolk: Data Tech D.T.P., pp. 57. [WSHC WAR.921].

37 Zweiniger-Bargielowska, I. (2000). *Austerity in Britain: Rationing, Controls and Consumption.* Oxford: Oxford University Press, pp. 19.

38 Ibid., pp. 33.

39 Street, A. G. (1950). *In His Own Country.* London: Eyre & Spottiswoode, pp. 319. [WSHC XST.824].

40 Zweiniger-Bargielowska, I. (2000). *Austerity in Britain: Rationing, Controls and Consumption.* Oxford: Oxford University Press, pp. 69.

41 Ibid., pp. 19.

42 Capie, F. and Wood, G. (2002). Price Controls in War and Peace: A Marshallian Conclusion. *Scottish Journal of Political Economy*, 49(1), pp. 47.

43 Calder, A. (1992). *The People's War: Britain 1939-45.* London: Pimlico (Original work published 1969), pp. 276. [WSHC 941.084].

44 Ibid., pp. 355.

45 Mock, J. (1997). *Bradford on Avon & District: The War Years (1939-1945).* J. H. Mock, pp. 29. [BRD.949].

46 Meakin, R. (2002). *Minety at War.* Richard Meakin, pp. 20. [WSHC MIN.949].

47 Devizes Local History Group and Haycock, L. (Ed.). (1995). *How Devizes Won the War!* Devizes Local History Group, pp. 33. [WSHC

DEV.949].

48 Ibid., pp. 36.

49 Ginn, P., Goodman, R. and Langlands, A. (2012). *Wartime Farm.* London: Mitchell Beazley, pp. 195.

50 Zweiniger-Bargielowska, I. (2000). *Austerity in Britain: Rationing, Controls and Consumption.* Oxford: Oxford University Press, pp. 19.

51 Summers, J. (2015). *Fashion on the Ration.* London: Profile Books in Partnership with the Imperial War Museum, pp. 19.

52 Ibid., pp. 67.

53 Zweiniger-Bargielowska, I. (2000). *Austerity in Britain: Rationing, Controls and Consumption.* Oxford: Oxford University Press, pp. 19.

54 Ibid., pp. 48.

55 Summers, J. (2015). *Fashion on the Ration.* London: Profile Books in Partnership with the Imperial War Museum, pp. 75.

56 Zweiniger-Bargielowska, I. (2000). *Austerity in Britain: Rationing, Controls and Consumption.* Oxford: Oxford University Press, pp. 49.

57 Ibid., pp. 20.

58 Summers, J. (2015). *Fashion on the Ration.* London: Profile Books in Partnership with the Imperial War Museum, pp. 77.

59 Ibid., pp. 80.

60 Ibid., pp. 88.

61 Ibid., pp. 88.

62 Ibid., pp. 90-92.

63 Ibid., pp. 139.

64 Ibid., pp. 73.

65 Olivier, E. (1943). *Night Thoughts of a Country Landlady.* London: B.T. Batsford Ltd., pp. 54-55. [WSHC XOL.824].

66 Summers, J. (2015). *Fashion on the Ration.* London: Profile Books in Partnership with the Imperial War Museum, pp. 95.

67 Summers, J. (2015). *Fashion on the Ration.* London: Profile Books in Partnership with the Imperial War Museum, pp. 106.

68 Ibid., pp. 87.

69 Ibid., pp. 109-111.
70 Devizes Local History Group and Haycock, L. (Ed.). (1995). *How Devizes Won the War!* Devizes Local History Group, pp. 37. [WSHC DEV.949].
71 Summers, J. (2015). *Fashion on the Ration*. London: Profile Books in Partnership with the Imperial War Museum, pp. 137.
72 Olivier, E. (1943). *Night Thoughts of a Country Landlady*. London: B.T. Batsford Ltd., pp. 54-55. [WSHC XOL.824].
73 Browning, B. (2005). *EKCO's of Cowbridge*. Malmesbury: Cowbridge Publishing, pp. 60. [WSHC MAL.620].
74 Parsons, M. (2005). *Cricklade Revealed: Part 5 - Social Life during the Second World War*. Marion Parsons, pp. 34. [WSHC CRI.949].
75 Hickson, J. and Skrine, R. (Ed.) (2013). *Carry on Coping: Diary of a Doctor 1942-1945*. Bradford on Avon: Ex Libris Press, pp. 144. [WSHC CHP.611 Original diaries are also available at WSA 4236/1-5].
76 Summers, J. (2015). *Fashion on the Ration*. London: Profile Books in Partnership with the Imperial War Museum, pp. 20.
77 Ibid., pp. 57-58.
78 Ibid., pp. 74.
79 Ibid., pp. 129-130.
80 Pickford, P. and Pickford, R. (Ed.). (1995). *Letters to Liz*. Newnham, Tasmania: Attic Press, pp. 107. [WSHC WAR.949].
81 Summers, J. (2015). *Fashion on the Ration*. London: Profile Books in Partnership with the Imperial War Museum, pp. 146.
82 Summers, J. (2015). *Fashion on the Ration*. London: Profile Books in Partnership with the Imperial War Museum, pp. 136.
83 Parsons, M. (2005). *Cricklade Revealed: Part 5 - Social Life during the Second World War*. Marion Parsons, pp. 34. [WSHC CRI.949].
84 *Vogue Knit Series No. 9: Warm Jumpers and Woolies for War Workers from Vogue*. (1940s). London: The Condé Naste Publications Ltd, Unpaginated. [WSHC Local Studies Reminiscence Collection].
85 Calder, A. (1992). *The People's War: Britain 1939-45*. London: Pimlico (Original work published 1969), pp. 379. [WSHC 941.084].
86 Summers, J. (2015). *Fashion on the Ration*. London: Profile Books in Partnership with the Imperial War Museum, pp. 131.
87 Pickford, P. and Pickford, R. (Ed.). (1995). *Letters to Liz*. Newnham, Tasmania: Attic Press, pp. 126. [WSHC WAR.949].
88 Summers, J. (2015). *Fashion on the Ration*. London: Profile Books in Partnership with the Imperial War Museum, pp. 134.
89 Ibid., pp. 151.
90 Zweiniger-Bargielowska, I. (2000). *Austerity in Britain: Rationing, Controls and Consumption*. Oxford: Oxford University Press, pp. 21.
91 Ibid., pp. 71.
92 Ibid., pp. 20.
93 Ibid., pp. 49.
94 Ibid., pp. 88.
95 Ibid., pp. 21.
96 Ibid., pp. 45.
97 Ibid., pp. 20.
98 WSA G18/225/9.
99 Zweiniger-Bargielowska, I. (2000). *Austerity in Britain: Rationing, Controls and Consumption*. Oxford: Oxford University Press, pp. 47-51.
100 Summers, J. (2015). *Fashion on the Ration*. London: Profile Books in Partnership with the Imperial War Museum, pp. 95-97.
101 Ibid., pp. 10.
102 Ibid., pp. 5.
103 Ibid., pp. 106.
104 Zweiniger-Bargielowska, I. (2000). *Austerity in Britain: Rationing, Controls and Consumption*. Oxford: Oxford University Press, pp. 94.
105 Summers, J. (2015). *Fashion on the*

Ration. London: Profile Books in Partnership with the Imperial War Museum, pp. 140-141.

106 Zweiniger-Bargielowska, I. (2000). *Austerity in Britain: Rationing, Controls and Consumption.* Oxford: Oxford University Press, pp. 95.

107 Ibid., pp. 31.

108 Ibid., pp. 21-23.

109 WSA F8/500/65/4/1.

110 Zweiniger-Bargielowska, I. (2000). *Austerity in Britain: Rationing, Controls and Consumption.* Oxford: Oxford University Press, pp. 10.

111 Ibid., pp. 73.

112 Ibid., pp. 36.

113 Ibid., pp. 74.

114 Collingham, L. (2011). *The Taste of War: World War Two and the Battle for Food.* London: Penguin Books Ltd., pp. 389.

115 Calder, A. (1992). *The People's War: Britain 1939-45.* London: Pimlico (Original work published 1969), pp. 277. [WSHC 941.084].

116 Zweiniger-Bargielowska, I. (2000). *Austerity in Britain: Rationing, Controls and Consumption.* Oxford: Oxford University Press, pp. 71.

117 Ibid., pp. 23.

118 Collingham, L. (2011). *The Taste of War: World War Two and the Battle for Food.* London: Penguin Books Ltd., pp. 393.

119 Zweiniger-Bargielowska, I. (2000). *Austerity in Britain: Rationing, Controls and Consumption.* Oxford: Oxford University Press, pp. 36.

120 Calder, A. (1992). *The People's War: Britain 1939-45.* London: Pimlico (Original work published 1969), pp. 277. [WSHC 941.084].

121 Zweiniger-Bargielowska, I. (2000). *Austerity in Britain: Rationing, Controls and Consumption.* Oxford: Oxford University Press, pp. 37.

122 Collingham, L. (2011). *The Taste of War: World War Two and the Battle for Food.* London: Penguin Books Ltd., pp. 116.

123 Ibid., pp. 98.

124 Ibid., pp. 116.

125 Zweiniger-Bargielowska, I. (2000). *Austerity in Britain: Rationing, Controls and Consumption.* Oxford: Oxford University Press, pp. 37.

126 Collingham, L. (2011). *The Taste of War: World War Two and the Battle for Food.* London: Penguin Books Ltd., pp. 390.

127 Ginn, P., Goodman, R. and Langlands, A. (2012). *Wartime Farm.* London: Mitchell Beazley, pp. 109-110.

128 Zweiniger-Bargielowska, I. (2000). *Austerity in Britain: Rationing, Controls and Consumption.* Oxford: Oxford University Press, pp. 70.

129 WSA G18/225/9.

130 Parsons, M. (2004). *Cricklade Revealed: Part 4 - Social Life during the Second World War.* Marion Parsons, pp. 28. [WSHC CRI.949].

131 Zweiniger-Bargielowska, I. (2000). *Austerity in Britain: Rationing, Controls and Consumption.* Oxford: Oxford University Press, pp. 71.

132 Ibid., pp. 60-65.

133 Ibid., pp. 71.

134 Ginn, P., Goodman, R. and Langlands, A. (2012). *Wartime Farm.* London: Mitchell Beazley, pp. 228.

135 Waley, M. H. (c. 1965). *Great Cheverell: A retrospect.* Unpublished, pp. 192. [WSHC GRC.940].

136 Eccles, D. (1983). *By Safe Hand: Letters of Sybil and David Eccles, 1939-1942.* London: Bodley Head, pp. 160. [WSHC CHU.928].

137 Parsons, M. (2005). *Cricklade Revealed: Part 5 - Social Life during the Second World War.* Marion Parsons, pp. 33. [WSHC CRI.949].

138 Wyeth, R. (1995). *Sterner Days: Codford during the Second World War.* Warminster: Bedeguar Books, pp. 31. [WSHC COD.949].

139 Parsons, M. (2005). *Cricklade Revealed: Part 5 - Social Life during the Second World War.* Marion Parsons, pp. 32-33. [WSHC CRI.949].

140 Adie, K. (2003). *Corsets to Camouflage:*

Women at War. London: Hodder & Stoughton, pp. 148. [WSHC 355.22082].

141 WSA F5/530/25.

142 Summers, J. (2015). *Fashion on the Ration*. London: Profile Books in Partnership with the Imperial War Museum, pp. 45.

143 Zweiniger-Bargielowska, I. (2000). *Austerity in Britain: Rationing, Controls and Consumption*. Oxford: Oxford University Press, pp. 90.

144 WSA F5/520/25.

145 Zweiniger-Bargielowska, I. (2000). *Austerity in Britain: Rationing, Controls and Consumption*. Oxford: Oxford University Press, pp. 88.

146 Ibid., pp. 78-79.

147 Hickson, J. and Skrine, R. (Ed.) (2013). *Carry on Coping: Diary of a Doctor 1942-1945*. Bradford on Avon: Ex Libris Press, pp. 56. [WSHC CHP.611 Original diaries are also available at WSA 4236/1-5].

148 Zweiniger-Bargielowska, I. (2000). *Austerity in Britain: Rationing, Controls and Consumption*. Oxford: Oxford University Press, pp. 91.

149 Calder, A. (1992). *The People's War: Britain 1939-45*. London: Pimlico (Original work published 1969), pp. 378. [WSHC 941.084].

150 Browning, B. (2005). *EKCO's of Cowbridge*. Malmesbury: Cowbridge Publishing, pp. 64. [WSHC MAL.620].

151 Mock, J. (1997). *Bradford on Avon & District: The War Years (1939-1945)*. J. H. Mock, pp. 29. [BRD.949].

152 Zweiniger-Bargielowska, I. (2000). *Austerity in Britain: Rationing, Controls and Consumption*. Oxford: Oxford University Press, pp. 91.

153 Calder, A. (1992). *The People's War: Britain 1939-45*. London: Pimlico (Original work published 1969), pp. 378. [WSHC 941.084].

154 Summers, J. (2015). *Fashion on the Ration*. London: Profile Books in Partnership with the Imperial War Museum, pp. 4-5.

155 Ibid., pp. 166.

156 Inchfawn, F. (2010). *Salute to the Village*. Monkton Farleigh: Folly Books (Original work published 1943), pp. 122. [WSHC XIN.921].

157 Adie, K. (2003). *Corsets to Camouflage: Women at War*. London: Hodder & Stoughton, pp. 148. [WSHC 355.22082].

158 Waller, M. (2005). *London 1945*. London: John Murray, pp. 207.

159 Burchell, R. (2013). *Saucepans on our Heads: Growing up in Swindon during World War 2*. Bradford on Avon: Ex Libris Press, pp. 39. [WSHC SWI.949].

160 Summers, J. (2015). *Fashion on the Ration*. London: Profile Books in Partnership with the Imperial War Museum, pp. 145.

161 Zweiniger-Bargielowska, I. (2000). *Austerity in Britain: Rationing, Controls and Consumption*. Oxford: Oxford University Press, pp. 147.

162 Eccles, D. (1983). *By Safe Hand: Letters of Sybil and David Eccles, 1939-1942*. London: Bodley Head, pp. 211. [WSHC CHU.928].

163 Zweiniger-Bargielowska, I. (2000). *Austerity in Britain: Rationing, Controls and Consumption*. Oxford: Oxford University Press, pp. 148.

164 Burchell, R. (2013). *Saucepans on our Heads: Growing up in Swindon during World War 2*. Bradford on Avon: Ex Libris Press, pp. 95. [WSHC SWI.949].

165 Zweiniger-Bargielowska, I. (2000). *Austerity in Britain: Rationing, Controls and Consumption*. Oxford: Oxford University Press, pp. 148.

166 Hickson, J. and Skrine, R. (Ed.) (2013). *Carry on Coping: Diary of a Doctor 1942-1945*. Bradford on Avon: Ex Libris Press, pp. 185. [WSHC CHP.611 Original diaries are also available at WSA 4236/1-5].

167 Ginn, P., Goodman, R. and Langlands, A. (2012). *Wartime Farm*. London: Mitchell Beazley, pp. 228-230.

168 Cockbill, T. (1989). *Our Swindon in 1939*. Swindon: The Quill Press, pp. 22. [WSHC SWI.949].

169 WSA 1442/1.

170 Zweiniger-Bargielowska, I. (2000). *Austerity in Britain: Rationing, Controls and Consumption*. Oxford: Oxford University Press, pp. 148-149.

171 Collingham, L. (2011). *The Taste of War: World War Two and the Battle for Food*. London: Penguin Books Ltd., pp. 392.

172 Zweiniger-Bargielowska, I. (2000). *Austerity in Britain: Rationing, Controls and Consumption*. Oxford: Oxford University Press, pp. 80.

173 Calder, A. (1992). *The People's War: Britain 1939-45*. London: Pimlico (Original work published 1969), pp. 383. [WSHC 941.084].

174 Zweiniger-Bargielowska, I. (2000). *Austerity in Britain: Rationing, Controls and Consumption*. Oxford: Oxford University Press, pp. 66.

175 Ibid., pp. 77.

176 Moran, J. (2005). Queuing up in Post-War Britain. *Twentieth Century British History*, 16(3), pp. 286.

177 Inchfawn, F. (2010). *Salute to the Village*. Monkton Farleigh: Folly Books (Original work published 1943), pp. 109. [WSHC XIN.921].

178 Moran, J. (2005). Queuing up in Post-War Britain. *Twentieth Century British History*, 16(3), pp. 286.

179 Parsons, M. (2005). *Cricklade Revealed: Part 5 - Social Life during the Second World War*. Marion Parsons, pp. 34-35. [WSHC CRI.949].

180 Olivier, E. (1943). *Night Thoughts of a Country Landlady*. London: B.T. Batsford Ltd., pp. 55. [WSHC XOL.824].

181 Kynaston, D. (2007). *A World to Build: Austerity Britain*. London: Bloomsbury, pp. 87.

182 Olivier, E. (1943). *Night Thoughts of a Country Landlady*. London: B.T. Batsford Ltd., pp. 53-54. [WSHC XOL.824].

183 WSA G22/130/40.

184 Zweiniger-Bargielowska, I. (2000). *Austerity in Britain: Rationing, Controls and Consumption*. Oxford: Oxford University Press, pp. 201.

185 Ibid., pp. 88.

186 Ibid., pp. 166.

187 *Wiltshire Gazette*, 27.8.1942. [WSHC Microform Collection].

188 *Wiltshire Times*, 24.7.1943. [WSHC Microform Collection].

189 Manners, L. (1973). *A Countryman Looks Back*. Minety: Taylor & Sons, pp. 124. [WSHC MIN.921].

190 Dawkins, B. (1989). *When Warm Milk Was Fresh Milk*. Bert Dawkins, pp. 96. [WSHC WAR.949].

191 Parsons, M. (2005). *Cricklade Revealed: Part 5 - Social Life during the Second World War*. Marion Parsons, pp. 32. [WSHC CRI.949].

192 Day, R. (2007). *Savernake at War: A Wartime History of Savernake Forest 1940-1949*. Hungerford: Roger Day, pp. 28. [WSHC SAV.949].

193 WSA F5/540/7.

194 Meakin, R. (2002). *Minety at War*. Richard Meakin, pp. 15. [WSHC MIN.949].

195 Parsons, M. (2004). *Cricklade Revealed: Part 4 - Social Life during the Second World War*. Marion Parsons, pp. 10. [WSHC CRI.949].

196 Hickson, J. and Skrine, R. (Ed.) (2013). *Carry on Coping: Diary of a Doctor 1942-1945*. Bradford on Avon: Ex Libris Press, pp. 36-37. [WSHC CHP.611 Original diaries are also available at WSA 4236/1-5].

197 Mock, J. (1997). *Bradford on Avon & District: The War Years (1939-1945)*. J. H. Mock, pp. 6. [BRD.949].

198 WSA F5/525/5.

199 WSA G18/225/7.

200 Zweiniger-Bargielowska, I. (2000). *Austerity in Britain: Rationing, Controls and Consumption*. Oxford: Oxford University Press, pp. 168-170.

201 WSA F5/530/4.

202 Ibid.

203 Hickson, J. and Skrine, R. (Ed.) (2013). *Carry on Coping: Diary of a*

Doctor 1942-1945. Bradford on Avon: Ex Libris Press, pp. 125. [WSHC CHP.611 Original diaries are also available at WSA 4236/1-5].

204 Zweiniger-Bargielowska, I. (2000). *Austerity in Britain: Rationing, Controls and Consumption*. Oxford: Oxford University Press, pp. 171-173.

205 Ginn, P., Goodman, R. and Langlands, A. (2012). *Wartime Farm*. London: Mitchell Beazley, pp. 112.

206 Zweiniger-Bargielowska, I. (2000). *Austerity in Britain: Rationing, Controls and Consumption*. Oxford: Oxford University Press, pp. 160-161.

207 Dawkins, B. (1989). *When Warm Milk Was Fresh Milk*. Bert Dawkins, pp. 96. [WSHC WAR.949].

208 Zweiniger-Bargielowska, I. (2000). *Austerity in Britain: Rationing, Controls and Consumption*. Oxford: Oxford University Press, pp. 202.

209 Ibid., pp. 201.

210 Kynaston, D. (2007). *A World to Build: Austerity Britain*. London: Bloomsbury, pp. 111.

211 Zweiniger-Bargielowska, I. (2000). *Austerity in Britain: Rationing, Controls and Consumption*. Oxford: Oxford University Press, pp. 161-163.

212 WSA F8/933/EA48.

213 Pickford, P. and Pickford, R. (Ed.). (1995). *Letters to Liz*. Newnham, Tasmania: Attic Press, pp. 61. [WSHC WAR.949].

214 Capie, F. and Wood, G. (2002). Price Controls in War and Peace: A Marshallian Conclusion. *Scottish Journal of Political Economy*, 49(1), pp. 47.

215 WSA G18/225/7.

216 Ibid.

217 Hickson, J. and Skrine, R. (Ed.) (2013). *Carry on Coping: Diary of a Doctor 1942-1945*. Bradford on Avon: Ex Libris Press, pp. 109. [WSHC CHP.611 Original diaries are also available at WSA 4236/1-5].

218 WSA G18/225/7.

219 WSA F8/500/8/1/1.

220 WSA F8/500/65/4/1.

221 Bemerton Local History Society (2006). *Memories of Bemerton in Wartime*. Bemerton Local History Society with support of the Big Lottery Fund, pp. 33. [WSHC BEM.949].

222 WSA G24/225/12.

223 Lynn, V. (1994). *We'll Meet Again: A Personal and Social History of WWII*. London: MacMillan, pp. 104.

224 Acton, L. (2011). *Allotment Gardens: A Reflection of History, Heritage, Community and Self*. (PIA - Papers from the Institute of Archaeology). London: University College, 21, pp. 49. [doi:].

225 Sanders, H. (1919) *Trowbridge Roll of Honour*. Trowbridge: Trowbridge Town Council, pp. 17-18. [WSHC TRO.924].

226 Acton, L. (2011). *Allotment Gardens: A Reflection of History, Heritage, Community and Self*. (PIA - Papers from the Institute of Archaeology). London: University College, 21, pp. 50. [doi:].

227 Ginn, P., Goodman, R. and Langlands, A. (2012). *Wartime Farm*. London: Mitchell Beazley, pp. 296.

228 Calder, A. (1992). *The People's War: Britain 1939-45*. London: Pimlico (Original work published 1969), pp. 430. [WSHC 941.084].

229 Ginn, P., Goodman, R. and Langlands, A. (2012). *Wartime Farm*. London: Mitchell Beazley, pp. 296.

230 Calder, A. (1992). *The People's War: Britain 1939-45*. London: Pimlico (Original work published 1969), pp. 430. [WSHC 941.084].

231 WSA 2625/19.

232 WSA G13/132/61.

233 Ibid.

234 WSA G18/225/19.

235 WSA 2625/19.

236 WSA 1815/39.

237 Meakin, R. (2002). *Minety at War*. Richard Meakin, pp. 8. [WSHC MIN.949].

238 WSA G18/225/19.

239 WSA G24/225/50.
240 MacKay, R. (1999). *The Test of War: Inside Britain 1939-45*. London: UCL Press, pp. 181.
241 Ginn, P., Goodman, R. and Langlands, A. (2012). *Wartime Farm*. London: Mitchell Beazley, pp. 98.
242 Wiltshire Federation of Women's Institutes (1993). *Wiltshire Within Living Memory*. Newbury: Countryside Books, pp. 215. [WSHC AAA.949].
243 WSA F8/760/17/10.
244 WSA G13/132/61.
245 Ibid.
246 Ibid.
247 Ginn, P., Goodman, R. and Langlands, A. (2012). *Wartime Farm*. London: Mitchell Beazley, pp. 301.
248 WSA G13/132/61.
249 Ibid.
250 Ibid.
251 Ibid.
252 Ibid.
253 Ginn, P., Goodman, R. and Langlands, A. (2012). *Wartime Farm*. London: Mitchell Beazley, pp. 94.
254 Devizes Local History Group and Haycock, L. (Ed.). (1995). *How Devizes Won the War!* Devizes Local History Group, pp. 85. [WSHC DEV.949].
255 WSA F8/500/65/4/1.
256 WSA F8/500/80/1/2.
257 Bemerton Local History Society (2006). *Memories of Bemerton in Wartime*. Bemerton Local History Society with support of the Big Lottery Fund, pp. 29. [WSHC BEM.949].
258 Brierley, J. (2002). *Stapleford: The Story of a Wiltshire Village*. Unpublished, pp. 21. [WSHC STP.940].
259 Parsons, M. (2005). *Cricklade Revealed: Part 5 - Social Life during the Second World War*. Marion Parsons, pp. 28. [WSHC CRI.949].
260 WSA F8/933/EA39.
261 Acton, L. (2011). *Allotment Gardens: A Reflection of History, Heritage, Community and Self*. (PIA - Papers from the Institute of Archaeology). London: University College, 21, pp.

53. [doi:].
262 Hickson, J. and Skrine, R. (Ed.) (2013). *Carry on Coping: Diary of a Doctor 1942-1945*. Bradford on Avon: Ex Libris Press, pp. 199. [WSHC CHP.611 Original diaries are also available at WSA 4236/1-5].
263 Ginn, P., Goodman, R. and Langlands, A. (2012). *Wartime Farm*. London: Mitchell Beazley, pp. 102-103.
264 WSA 1815/39.
265 WSA 4257/30.
266 WSA F8/760/17/10.
267 Hickson, J. and Skrine, R. (Ed.) (2013). *Carry on Coping: Diary of a Doctor 1942-1945*. Bradford on Avon: Ex Libris Press, pp. 51. [WSHC CHP.611 Original diaries are also available at WSA 4236/1-5].
268 WSA 4257/30.
269 Heath, N. (1999). *Life and Herbing in Sutton Benger: Memories of a Wiltshire Village*. Nesta Heath, pp. 26-31. [WSHC SUB.949].
270 WSA G18/225/9.
271 WSA 1815/39.
272 WSA G18/225/9.
273 Waley, M. H. (c. 1965). *Great Cheverell: A retrospect*. Unpublished, pp. 192. [WSHC GRC.940].
274 WSA F8/500/42/1/2.
275 WSA F8/500/196/1/2.
276 WSA G13/132/61.
277 Ginn, F. (2012). Dig for Victory! New Histories of Wartime Gardening in Britain. *Journal of Historical Geography*, 38, pp. 298. [doi:10.1016/j.jhg.2012.02.001].
278 Ginn, P., Goodman, R. and Langlands, A. (2012). *Wartime Farm*. London: Mitchell Beazley, pp. 94.
279 Ginn, F. (2012). Dig for Victory! New Histories of Wartime Gardening in Britain. *Journal of Historical Geography*, 38, pp. 298. [doi:10.1016/j.jhg.2012.02.001].
280 Ibid., pp. 302.
281 Ibid., pp. 297-303.
282 WSA G13/132/61.

283 WSA G13/132/61.

284 Lane, C. and White, P. (1999). *Warminster in the Twentieth Century.* The Warminster History Society: Warminster, pp. 26. [WSHC WAR.949].

285 WSA G13/132/61.

286 WSA F8/760/17/10.

287 *Parish Councils Advisory Handbook No. 9: Allotments.* (1951). The National Council of Social Service (Incorporated), pp. 2.

288 Acton, L. (2011). *Allotment Gardens: A Reflection of History, Heritage, Community and Self.* (PIA - Papers from the Institute of Archaeology). London: University College, 21, pp. 51. [doi: http://dx.doi.org/10.5334/pia.379].

289 Ginn, P., Goodman, R. and Langlands, A. (2012). *Wartime Farm.* London: Mitchell Beazley, pp. 158-160.

290 Calder, A. (1992). *The People's War: Britain 1939-45.* London: Pimlico (Original work published 1969), pp. 430. [WSHC 941.084].

291 Ginn, P., Goodman, R. and Langlands, A. (2012). *Wartime Farm.* London: Mitchell Beazley, pp. 161.

292 Mock, J. (1997). *Bradford on Avon & District: The War Years (1939-1945).* J. H. Mock, pp. 22. [BRD.949].

293 Collingham, L. (2011). *The Taste of War: World War Two and the Battle for Food.* London: Penguin Books Ltd., pp. 99-100.

294 Ginn, P., Goodman, R. and Langlands, A. (2012). *Wartime Farm.* London: Mitchell Beazley, pp. 118.

295 Martin, J. (2000). *The Development of Modern Agriculture: British Farming Since 1931.* Basingstoke: Macmillan Press Ltd, pp. 40.

296 Ginn, P., Goodman, R. and Langlands, A. (2012). *Wartime Farm.* London: Mitchell Beazley, pp. 118.

297 Ibid., pp. 218.

298 Devizes Local History Group and Haycock, L. (Ed.). (1995). *How Devizes Won the War!* Devizes Local History Group, pp. 85. [WSHC DEV.949].

299 WSA G18/225/9.

300 Ginn, P., Goodman, R. and Langlands, A. (2012). *Wartime Farm.* London: Mitchell Beazley, pp. 119.

301 Ibid.

302 Calder, A. (1992). *The People's War: Britain 1939-45.* London: Pimlico (Original work published 1969), pp. 430. [WSHC 941.084].

303 Eccles, D. (1983). *By Safe Hand: Letters of Sybil and David Eccles, 1939-1942.* London: Bodley Head, pp. 165. [WSHC CHU.928].

304 Ibid., pp. 231-232.

305 Meakin, R. (2002). *Minety at War.* Richard Meakin, pp. 9. [WSHC MIN.949].

306 Martin, J. (2000). *The Development of Modern Agriculture: British Farming Since 1931.* Basingstoke: Macmillan Press Ltd, pp. 50.

307 Meakin, R. (2002). *Minety at War.* Richard Meakin, pp. 9. [WSHC MIN.949].

308 Dawkins, B. (1989). *When Warm Milk Was Fresh Milk.* Bert Dawkins, pp. 94. [WSHC WAR.949].

309 Baker, E. (n.d.). Enfield Precision Enginering. Unpublished, unpaginated. [WSHC WEW.629].

310 Browning, B. (2005). *EKCO's of Cowbridge.* Malmesbury: Cowbridge Publishing, pp. 57. [WSHC MAL.620].

311 Hickson, J. and Skrine, R. (Ed.) (2013). *Carry on Coping: Diary of a Doctor 1942-1945.* Bradford on Avon: Ex Libris Press, pp. 144. [WSHC CHP.611 Original diaries are also available at WSA 4236/1-5].

312 WSA G24/225/29.

313 WSA G24/225/29.

314 Meakin, R. (2002). *Minety at War.* Richard Meakin, pp. 8. [WSHC MIN.949].

315 Martin, J. (2000). *The Development of Modern Agriculture: British Farming Since 1931.* Basingstoke: Macmillan Press Ltd, pp. 40.

316 Daniels, p. (1990). *Around Amesbury in Old Photographs*. Stroud: Sutton Publishing, pp. 117. [WSHC AME.771].

317 Meakin, R. (2002). *Minety at War*. Richard Meakin, pp. 8. [WSHC MIN.949].

318 Parsons, M. (2005). *Cricklade Revealed: Part 5 - Social Life during the Second World War*. Marion Parsons, pp. 32-33. [WSHC CRI.949].

319 Devizes Local History Group and Haycock, L. (Ed.). (1995). *How Devizes Won the War!* Devizes Local History Group, pp. 79. [WSHC DEV.949].

320 Martin, J. (2000). *The Development of Modern Agriculture: British Farming Since 1931*. Basingstoke: Macmillan Press Ltd, pp. 54.

321 Ginn, P., Goodman, R. and Langlands, A. (2012). *Wartime Farm*. London: Mitchell Beazley, pp. 162.

322 Meakin, R. (2002). *Minety at War*. Richard Meakin, pp. 8-10. [WSHC MIN.949].

323 Ginn, P., Goodman, R. and Langlands, A. (2012). *Wartime Farm*. London: Mitchell Beazley, pp. 218.

324 WSA F8/933/EA48.

325 Mock, J. (1997). *Bradford on Avon & District: The War Years (1939-1945)*. J. H. Mock, pp. 26. [BRD.949].

326 Eccles, D. (1983). *By Safe Hand: Letters of Sybil and David Eccles, 1939-1942*. London: Bodley Head, pp. 133. [WSHC CHU.928].

327 Inchfawn, F. (2010). *Salute to the Village*. Monkton Farleigh: Folly Books (Original work published 1943), pp. 110. [WSHC XIN.921].

328 WSA F8/933/EA48.

329 WSA F8/500/65/4/1.

330 Calder, A. (1992). *The People's War: Britain 1939-45*. London: Pimlico (Original work published 1969), pp. 149. [WSHC 941.084].

331 Ginn, P., Goodman, R. and Langlands, A. (2012). *Wartime Farm*. London: Mitchell Beazley, pp. 219.

332 Lane, C. and White, P. (1999).

Warminster in the Twentieth Century. The Warminster History Society: Warminster, pp. 25. [WSHC WAR.949].

333 WSA F8/500/65/4/1.

334 Calder, A. (1992). *The People's War: Britain 1939-45*. London: Pimlico (Original work published 1969), pp. 149. [WSHC 941.084].

335 WSA F8/500/65/4/1.

336 Siddall, M. (1995). *Safe as Houses: Childhood Through the Forties*. Christow: Devonshire House, pp. 26-27. [WSHC PUR.949].

337 Lynn, V. (1994). *We'll Meet Again: A Personal and Social History of WWII*. London: MacMillan, pp. 161.

338 Vernon, C. (2011). *Malmesbury versus Hitler: The Town's role in the Second World War*. Malmesbury: Malmesbury Civic Trust, pp. 165. [WSHC MAL.949].

339 Ibid., pp. 162-163.

340 WSA F8/933/EA48.

341 Calder, A. (1992). *The People's War: Britain 1939-45*. London: Pimlico (Original work published 1969), pp. 504. [WSHC 941.084].

342 WSHC, Local Studies Reminiscence Collection.

343 Pickford, P. and Pickford, R. (Ed.). (1995). *Letters to Liz*. Newnham, Tasmania: Attic Press, pp. 165. [WSHC WAR.949].

344 WSA G4/132/20.

345 WSA 4257/14 and 4257/15.

346 WSA F8/500/141/1/1.

347 WSA 4257/14 and 4257/15.

348 WSA F8/500/65/4/1.

349 WSA F8/500/141/1/1.

350 WSA F8/500/157/1/2.

351 WSA F8/500/179/1/2.

352 WSA F8/500/258/2/2.

353 WSA G14/225/9.

354 Ibid.

355 Ibid.

356 Vernon, C. (2011). *Malmesbury versus Hitler: The Town's role in the Second World War*. Malmesbury: Malmesbury Civic Trust, pp. 163-164. [WSHC MAL.949].

357 Dobson, M. (2011). *Bradford Voices: Life in Bradford on Avon 1900-2010.* Bradford on Avon: Ex Libris Press, pp. 146. [WSHC BRD.949].

358 Devizes Local History Group and Haycock, L. (Ed.). (1995). *How Devizes Won the War!* Devizes Local History Group, pp. 85. [WSHC DEV.949].

359 Cockbill, T. (1989). *Our Swindon in 1939.* Swindon: The Quill Press, pp. 41. [WSHC SWI.949].

360 Dobson, M. (2011). *Bradford Voices: Life in Bradford on Avon 1900-2010.* Bradford on Avon: Ex Libris Press, pp. 146. [WSHC BRD.949].

361 Parsons, M. (2004). *Cricklade Revealed: Part 4 - Social Life during the Second World War.* Marion Parsons, pp. 30. [WSHC CRI.949].

362 Vernon, C. (2011). *Malmesbury versus Hitler: The Town's role in the Second World War.* Malmesbury: Malmesbury Civic Trust, pp. 161. [WSHC MAL.949].

363 Sanders, H. (1919) *Trowbridge Roll of Honour.* Trowbridge: Trowbridge Town Council, pp. 16. [WSHC TRO.924].

364 Calder, A. (1992). *The People's War: Britain 1939-45.* London: Pimlico (Original work published 1969), pp. 356. [WSHC 941.084].

365 WSA G14/225/1.

366 Ibid.

367 WSA F8/600/106/1/27/1.

368 WSA G14/225/3.

369 Eccles, D. (1983). *By Safe Hand: Letters of Sybil and David Eccles, 1939-1942.* London: Bodley Head, pp. 275. [WSHC CHU.928].

370 Vernon, C. (2011). *Malmesbury versus Hitler: The Town's role in the Second World War.* Malmesbury: Malmesbury Civic Trust, pp. 171. [WSHC MAL.949].

371 WSA G24/225/45.

372 *Wiltshire Times,* 8.7.1944. [WSHC Microform Collection].

373 Sanders, H. (1919) *Trowbridge Roll of Honour.* Trowbridge: Trowbridge Town Council, pp. 8. [WSHC TRO.924].

374 Parsons, M. (2005). *Cricklade Revealed: Part 5 - Social Life during the Second World War.* Marion Parsons, pp. 36. [WSHC CRI.949].

375 WSA G14/225/2.

376 WSA G14/225/3.

377 WSA G14/225/1.

378 Vernon, C. (2011). *Malmesbury versus Hitler: The Town's role in the Second World War.* Malmesbury: Malmesbury Civic Trust, pp. 171. [WSHC MAL.949].

379 WSA G10/132/41.

380 Calder, A. (1992). *The People's War: Britain 1939-45.* London: Pimlico (Original work published 1969), pp. 347-349. [WSHC 941.084].

381 WSA G14/225/3.

382 WSA G14/225/2.

383 Ibid.

384 WSA G14/225/2.

385 Ibid.

385 WSA F8/500/307/1/3.

386 WSA F8/500/65/4/1.

387 Capie, F. and Wood, G. (2002). Price Controls in War and Peace: A Marshallian Conclusion. *Scottish Journal of Political Economy,* 49(1), pp. 45.

388 Calder, A. (1992). *The People's War: Britain 1939-45.* London: Pimlico (Original work published 1969), pp. 357-357. [WSHC 941.084].

389 Vernon, C. (2011). *Malmesbury versus Hitler: The Town's role in the Second World War.* Malmesbury: Malmesbury Civic Trust, pp. 166. [WSHC MAL.949].

390 WSA 1815/40.

391 WSA 1442/1.

392 Summers, J. (2015). *Fashion on the Ration.* London: Profile Books in Partnership with the Imperial War Museum, pp. 139.

393 WSA 1815/40.

394 MacKay, Major E.A. (Ed.). (1946). *The History of the Wiltshire Home Guard 1940-1944.* Wiltshire Regiment Old Comrades Association, pp. 130. [WSHC AAA.358].

395 WSA F8/933/EA48.

396 Zweiniger-Bargielowska, I. (2000). *Austerity in Britain: Rationing, Controls and Consumption.* Oxford: Oxford University Press, pp. 37.

397 Kynaston, D. (2007). *A World to Build: Austerity Britain.* London: Bloomsbury, pp. 227.

398 Collingham, L. (2011). *The Taste of War: World War Two and the Battle for Food.* London: Penguin Books Ltd., pp. 392.

399 Zweiniger-Bargielowska, I. (2000). *Austerity in Britain: Rationing, Controls and Consumption.* Oxford: Oxford University Press, pp. 256.

400 Ibid., pp. 54.

401 Ibid., pp. 82.

402 Ibid., pp. 24.

403 Laslett, S. (2013). *Brylcreem and Broken Biscuits: A Street Trail History of Bradford on Avon's Shops in the 1950s.* Bradford on Avon: Ex Libris Press, pp. 17-18, 98. [WSHC BRD.655].

404 Ibid., pp. 98.

405 Hennessy, P. (1992). *Never Again: Britain 1945-51.* London: Penguin Books Ltd., pp. 306. [WSHC 941.0854].

406 Zweiniger-Bargielowska, I. (2000). *Austerity in Britain: Rationing, Controls and Consumption.* Oxford: Oxford University Press, pp. 60.

407 Ibid., pp. 66.

408 Hennessy, P. (1992). *Never Again: Britain 1945-51.* London: Penguin Books Ltd., pp. 47. [WSHC 941.0854].

409 Capie, F. and Wood, G. (2002). Price Controls in War and Peace: A Marshallian Conclusion. *Scottish Journal of Political Economy*, 49(1), pp. 48-49.

410 Collingham, L. (2011). *The Taste of War: World War Two and the Battle for Food.* London: Penguin Books Ltd., pp. 101.

411 Summers, J. (2015). *Fashion on the Ration.* London: Profile Books in Partnership with the Imperial War Museum, pp. 8.

412 Ibid., pp. 177.

413 Ibid., pp. 141.

414 Zweiniger-Bargielowska, I. (2000). *Austerity in Britain: Rationing, Controls and Consumption.* Oxford: Oxford University Press, pp. 256.

415 Ibid., pp. 149.

416 Ibid., pp. 39.

417 Ibid., pp. 97.

418 Ibid., pp. 10.

9 Home Front Health

1 Huxley, R, Lloyd, B., Goldacre, M. and Neil, H. (2000). Nutritional Research in World War 2: The Oxford Nutrition Survey and its research potential 50 years later. *British Journal of Nutrition*, 84, pp. 247.

2 Cantwell, J. (1993). *The Second World War: A guide to documents in the Public Record Office.* London: HMSO (Original work published 1972), pp. 29. [WSHC 16.94053].

3 Collingham, L. (2011). *The Taste of War: World War Two and the Battle for Food.* London: Penguin Books Ltd., pp. 350-353.

4 Welshman, J. (1998). Evacuation and Social Policy During the Second World War: Myth and Reality. *Twentieth Century British History*, 9(1), pp. 44.

5 Huxley, R, Lloyd, B., Goldacre, M. and Neil, H. (2000). Nutritional Research in World War 2: The Oxford Nutrition Survey and its research potential 50 years later. *British Journal of Nutrition*, 84, pp. 247.

6 WSA 2893/1.

7 Welshman, J. (1998). Evacuation and Social Policy During the Second World War: Myth and Reality. *Twentieth Century British History*, 9(1), pp. 48.

8 Collingham, L. (2011). *The Taste of War: World War Two and the Battle for Food.* London: Penguin Books Ltd., pp. 386-389.

9 Zweiniger-Bargielowska, I. (2000). *Austerity in Britain: Rationing, Controls and Consumption.* Oxford: Oxford University Press, pp. 32-33.

10 Briggs, A. (2000). *Go to It: Working for*

Victory on the Home Front 1939-1945. London: Octopus Publishing Group Ltd., pp. 90.

11 Zweiniger-Bargielowska, I. (2000). *Austerity in Britain: Rationing, Controls and Consumption*. Oxford: Oxford University Press, pp. 134-135.

12 Cooper, L. 2009). A Little London Evacuee. Diss: Data Tech D.T.P., pp. 66. [WSHC WAR.921].

13 Bemerton Local History Society (2006). *Memories of Bemerton in Wartime*. Bemerton Local History Society with support of the Big Lottery Fund, pp. 29. [WSHC BEM.949].

14 Collingham, L. (2011). *The Taste of War: World War Two and the Battle for Food*. London: Penguin Books Ltd., pp. 396.

15 Cooper, L. 2009). A Little London Evacuee. Diss: Data Tech D.T.P., pp. 44. [WSHC WAR.921].

16 Parsons, M. (2005). *Cricklade Revealed: Part 5 - Social Life during the Second World War*. Marion Parsons, pp. 28. [WSHC CRI.949].

17 Huxley, R, Lloyd, B., Goldacre, M. and Neil, H. (2000). Nutritional Research in World War 2: The Oxford Nutrition Survey and its research potential 50 years later. *British Journal of Nutrition*, 84, pp. 247.

18 Chapman, E. and Howell, A. (Eds.) (2005). When the War was Over: Mere Literary Festival Community Project. Unpublished, unpaginated. [WSHC MER.949].

19 Calder, A. (1992). *The People's War: Britain 1939-45*. London: Pimlico (Original work published 1969), pp. 421. [WSHC 941.084].

20 WSA F8/500/42/1/2.

21 Calder, A. (1992). *The People's War: Britain 1939-45*. London: Pimlico (Original work published 1969), pp. 384-385. [WSHC 941.084].

22 Zweiniger-Bargielowska, I. (2000). *Austerity in Britain: Rationing, Controls and Consumption*. Oxford: Oxford University Press, pp. 134-135.

23 WSA F8/500/80/1/2.

24 WSA F8/500/65/4/1.

25 MacKay, R. (1999). *The Test of War: Inside Britain 1939-45*. London: UCL Press, pp. 215.

26 Welshman, J. (1998). Evacuation and Social Policy During the Second World War: Myth and Reality. *Twentieth Century British History*, 9(1), pp. 46.

27 Hickson, J. and Skrine, R. (Ed.) (2013). *Carry on Coping: Diary of a Doctor 1942-1945*. Bradford on Avon: Ex Libris Press, pp. 29. [WSHC CHP.611 Original diaries are also available at WSA 4236/1-5].

28 Ibid., pp. 234.

29 Zweiniger-Bargielowska, I. (2000). *Austerity in Britain: Rationing, Controls and Consumption*. Oxford: Oxford University Press, pp. 139.

30 Gartner, N. (2012). *Operation Pied Piper: The Wartime Evacuation of Schoolchildren from London and Berlin 1938-1946*. Charlotte (USA): ISA (Information Age Publishing), pp. 6.

31 Ginn, P., Goodman, R. and Langlands, A. (2012). *Wartime Farm*. London: Mitchell Beazley, pp. 111.

32 Phillips, J. and French, M. (1999). State Regulation and the Hazards of Milk. *The Society for the Social History of Medicine*, 12(3), pp. 371.

33 Ginn, P., Goodman, R. and Langlands, A. (2012). *Wartime Farm*. London: Mitchell Beazley, pp. 111.

34 Calder, A. (1992). *The People's War: Britain 1939-45*. London: Pimlico (Original work published 1969), pp. 384. [WSHC 941.084].

35 Collingham, L. (2011). *The Taste of War: World War Two and the Battle for Food*. London: Penguin Books Ltd., pp. 384.

36 Martin, J. (2000). *The Development of Modern Agriculture: British Farming Since 1931*. Basingstoke: Macmillan Press Ltd, pp. 31-32.

37 Zweiniger-Bargielowska, I. (2000). *Austerity in Britain: Rationing, Controls and Consumption*. Oxford: Oxford University Press, pp. 44.

38 Calder, A. (1992). *The People's War:*

Britain 1939-45. London: Pimlico (Original work published 1969), pp. 383. [WSHC 941.084].

39 Burchell, R. (2013). *Saucepans on our Heads: Growing up in Swindon during World War 2*. Bradford on Avon: Ex Libris Press, pp. 102. [WSHC SWI.949].

40 Zweiniger-Bargielowska, I. (2000). *Austerity in Britain: Rationing, Controls and Consumption*. Oxford: Oxford University Press, pp. 89.

41 Ibid., pp. 142-144.

42 WSA F8/933/EA48.

43 Summers, J. (2015). *Fashion on the Ration*. London: Profile Books in Partnership with the Imperial War Museum, pp. 148.

44 Kynaston, D. (2007). *A World to Build: Austerity Britain*. London: Bloomsbury, pp. 121.

45 WSA F8/500/141/1/1.

46 WSA F8/500/38/1/2.

47 Zweiniger-Bargielowska, I. (2000). *Austerity in Britain: Rationing, Controls and Consumption*. Oxford: Oxford University Press, pp. 143.

48 WSA 1815/39.

49 Devizes Local History Group and Haycock, L. (Ed.). (1995). *How Devizes Won the War!* Devizes Local History Group, pp. 73. [WSHC DEV.949].

50 WSA F8/500/141/1/1.

51 WSA G13/132/61.

52 Ginn, P., Goodman, R. and Langlands, A. (2012). *Wartime Farm*. London: Mitchell Beazley, pp. 94.

53 Welshman, J. (1998). Evacuation and Social Policy During the Second World War: Myth and Reality. *Twentieth Century British History*, 9(1), pp. 47.

54 Zweiniger-Bargielowska, I. (2000). *Austerity in Britain: Rationing, Controls and Consumption*. Oxford: Oxford University Press, pp. 33.

55 Ibid., pp. 135.

56 Welshman, J. (1998). Evacuation and Social Policy During the Second World War: Myth and Reality. *Twentieth Century British History*, 9(1), pp. 47.

57 Calder, A. (1992). *The People's War: Britain 1939-45*. London: Pimlico (Original work published 1969), pp. 385. [WSHC 941.084].

58 Lynn, V. (1994). *We'll Meet Again: A Personal and Social History of WWII*. London: MacMillan, pp. 107.

59 Hennessy, P. (1992). *Never Again: Britain 1945-51*. London: Penguin Books Ltd., pp. 50. [WSHC 941.0854].

60 Fussel, P. (1989). *Wartime: Understanding and Behaviour in the Second World War*. Oxford: Oxford University Press, pp. 204.

61 MacKay, R. (1999). *The Test of War: Inside Britain 1939-45*. London: UCL Press, pp. 135.

62 WSA G22/225/4.

63 Zweiniger-Bargielowska, I. (2000). *Austerity in Britain: Rationing, Controls and Consumption*. Oxford: Oxford University Press, pp. 76.

64 Calder, A. (1992). *The People's War: Britain 1939-45*. London: Pimlico (Original work published 1969), pp. 385. [WSHC 941.084].

65 Zweiniger-Bargielowska, I. (2000). *Austerity in Britain: Rationing, Controls and Consumption*. Oxford: Oxford University Press, pp. 76.

66 Calder, A. (1992). *The People's War: Britain 1939-45*. London: Pimlico (Original work published 1969), pp. 385-386. [WSHC 941.084].

67 Mass Observation (1987). *War Factory*. London: The Cresset Library (Original work published 1943), pp. 105. [WSHC SAI.684].

68 Calder, A. (1992). *The People's War: Britain 1939-45*. London: Pimlico (Original work published 1969), pp. 386. [WSHC 941.084].

69 Randall, B. (2003). *A Patchwork of Memories*. Bob Randall, pp. 12-13. [WSHC TRO.949].

70 Calder, A. (1992). *The People's War: Britain 1939-45*. London: Pimlico (Original work published 1969), pp. 387. [WSHC 941.084].

71 WSA F2/850/10.

72 WSA G22/225/4.
73 WSA F1/100/34/3.
74 Ibid., [31.3.1943].
75 WSA F1/100/34/3.
76 Ibid., [1.7.1943].
77 WSA F8/500/141/1/1.
78 WSA F8/500/173/1/2.
79 WSA F8/500/38/1/2.
80 WSA F8/500/258/2/2.
81 WSA F8/500/38/1/2.
82 WSA G24/225/36.
83 WSA G22/225/4.
84 WSA G15/225/22.
85 Mernick, P. (2015). Substitution of Paper Meal Tickets by Tokens of Plastic Material. Transcription of 1942 Ministry of Food Circular WT/CMF/62. Retrieved July 19, 2015 from the British Restaurant Tokens Website http://mernick.org.uk/br/notices.pdf
86 The Numismatic Bibliomania Society. (2012). Featured Website: British Restaurant Tokens. Retrieved July 19, 2015 from The E-Sylum electronic publication of the Numismatic Bibliomania Society website http://www.coinbooks.org/esylum_v16n04a24.html
87 Mernick, P. (2015). British Restaurant Tokens. Retrieved July 19, 2015 from the British Restaurant Tokens website http://www.mernick.org.uk/br/issuers.htm#marlborough
88 WSA G15/225/22.
89 WSA G22/225/4.
90 WSA F1/100/34/3. [26.8.1943].
91 WSA G22/225/4.
92 WSA G18/225/6.
93 Chippenham and District Committee for Festival of Britain. (1951). *Chippenham Wilts Festival of Britain.* Chippenham: Chippenham and District Committee for Festival of Britain, pp. 32-33. [WSHC CHP.394].
94 Zweiniger-Bargielowska, I. (2000). *Austerity in Britain: Rationing, Controls and Consumption.* Oxford: Oxford University Press, pp. 33.
95 Calder, A. (1992). *The People's War: Britain 1939-45.* London: Pimlico (Original work published 1969), pp.

461. [WSHC 941.084].
96 George, A. (c. 1993). 130th Station Hospital History. In Harman (ed.). 130th Station Hospital Reunion Dayton, Ohio, October 15-18, 1993. Unpublished, pp. 9. [WSHC AAA.949 (BL)].
97 Mackay, R. (1999). *The Test of War: Inside Britain 1939-45.* London: UCL Press, pp. 156.
98 WSA F8/500/42/1/2.
99 Reynolds, D. (1996). *Rich Relations.* London: Harper Collins, pp. 203. [WSHC AAA.949].
100 Ibid., pp. 208.
101 Ibid., pp. 205.
102 Ibid., pp. 207.
103 *Wiltshire Times*, 22.4.1944. [WSHC Microform Collection].
104 WSA G24/225/4.
105 Glynn, S. and Booth, A. (1996). *Modern Britain: An Economic and Social History.* London: Routledge, pp. 162.
106 Hennessy, P. (1992). *Never Again: Britain 1945-51.* London: Penguin Books Ltd., pp. 133. [WSHC 941.0854].
107 Glynn, S. and Booth, A. (1996). *Modern Britain: An Economic and Social History.* London: Routledge, pp. 156.
108 Lane, C. and White, P. (1999). *Warminster in the Twentieth Century.* The Warminster History Society: Warminster, pp. 241. [WSHC WAR.949].
109 Mackay, R. (1999). *The Test of War: Inside Britain 1939-45.* London: UCL Press, pp. 64.
110 Hennessy, P. (1992). *Never Again: Britain 1945-51.* London: Penguin Books Ltd., pp. 133-134. [WSHC 941.0854].
111 Ibid., pp. 139.
112 Ministry of Health (1939). *Emergency Hospital Organisation.* London: HMSO, pp. 1. [WSHC AAA.949 (Ephemera folder)].
113 Ibid., pp. 3-5.
114 Ibid., pp. 17.

115 Hennessy, P. (1992). *Never Again: Britain 1945-51*. London: Penguin Books Ltd., pp. 134. [WSHC 941.0854].

116 Mackay, R. (1999). *The Test of War: Inside Britain 1939-45*. London: UCL Press, pp. 156.

117 Ibid., pp 64.

118 Ibid., pp. 156.

119 Hennessy, P. (1992). *Never Again: Britain 1945-51*. London: Penguin Books Ltd., pp. 134. [WSHC 941.0854].

120 Darwin, B. (1947). *A Century of Medical Service: The Story of the Great Western Railway Medical Fund Society 1847 to 1947*. Swindon: GWR Medical Fund Society, pp. 29. [WSA J6/163/3].

121 Ibid., pp. 41-44.

122 Marshall, R. (1999). *Trowbridge Voices*. Stroud: Tempus Publishing Limited, pp. 105. [WSHC TRO.949].

123 Utting, J. & J. (Eds.). (1995). *The Village on the Hill: Aspects of Colerne History* Volume 2. Chippenham: Colerne History Group, pp. 290. [WSHC COL.940].

124 Ibid., pp. 284.

125 Ibid., pp. 201.

126 Lane, C. and White, P. (1999). *Warminster in the Twentieth Century*. The Warminster History Society: Warminster, pp. 254. [WSHC WAR.949].

127 Hickson, J. and Skrine, R. (Ed.) (2013). *Carry on Coping: Diary of a Doctor 1942-1945*. Bradford on Avon: Ex Libris Press, pp. 110-111. [WSHC CHP.611 Original diaries are also available at WSA 4236/1-5].

128 WSA F1/100/34/3.

129 Hickson, J. and Skrine, R. (Ed.) (2013). *Carry on Coping: Diary of a Doctor 1942-1945*. Bradford on Avon: Ex Libris Press, pp. 116. [WSHC CHP.611 Original diaries are also available at WSA 4236/1-5].

130 Ibid., pp. 215.

131 Mackay, R. (1999). *The Test of War: Inside Britain 1939-45*. London: UCL

Press, pp. 176-177.

132 Ibid., pp. 214.

133 Calder, A. (1992). *The People's War: Britain 1939-45*. London: Pimlico (Original work published 1969), pp. 357. [WSHC 941.084].

134 Gartner, N. (2012). *Operation Pied Piper: The Wartime Evacuation of Schoolchildren from London and Berlin 1938-1946*. Charlotte (USA): ISA (Information Age Publishing), pp. 139.

135 Wheeler, L. C. (1993). 1939-1945: As I Remember. Unpublished, pp. 164-165. [WSHC WEB.921].

136 Tilney, R. (1999). The Second World War Memorial: Malmesbury, Wiltshire. Unpublished, pp. 21. [WSHC MAL.949].

137 Vernon, C. (2011). *Malmesbury versus Hitler: The Town's role in the Second World War*. Malmesbury: Malmesbury Civic Trust, pp. 130. [WSHC MAL.949].

138 WSA F8/500/65/4/1.

139 WSA F8/500/80/1/2.

140 Mackay, R. (1999). *The Test of War: Inside Britain 1939-45*. London: UCL Press, pp. 156.

141 Bemerton Local History Society (2006). *Memories of Bemerton in Wartime*. Bemerton Local History Society with support of the Big Lottery Fund, pp. 11. [WSHC BEM.949].

142 Ibid.

143 Salisbury NHS Foundation Trust. (2014). History of the Hospital. Retrieved September 7, 2015 from the Salisbury NHS Foundation Trust website http://www.salisbury.nhs.uk/ABOUTUS/WHOANDWHAT/Pages/Hospital-History.aspx

144 Lane, C. and White, P. (1999). *Warminster in the Twentieth Century*. The Warminster History Society: Warminster, pp. 254. [WSHC WAR.949].

145 Kynaston, D. (2007). *A World to Build: Austerity Britain*. London: Bloomsbury, pp. 146.

146 Hennessy, P. (1992). *Never Again: Britain 1945-51*. London: Penguin

Books Ltd., pp. 135. [WSHC 941.0854].

147 Briggs, A. (2000). *Go To It! Working for Victory on the Home Front 1939-1945*. London: Octopus Publishing Group Ltd., pp. 90.

148 Browning, B. (2005). *EKCO's of Cowbridge*. Malmesbury: Cowbridge Publishing, pp. 67. [WSHC MAL.620].

149 Mass Observation (1987). *War Factory*. London: The Cresset Library (Original work published 1943). [WSHC SAI.684].

150 Michael Marshman, personal communication, 20.7.2015.

151 Pickford, P. and Pickford, R. (Ed.). (1995). *Letters to Liz*. Newnham, Tasmania: Attic Press, pp. 110-111. [WSHC WAR.949].

152 WSA G12/225/1.

153 WSA G12/335/1.

154 *Wiltshire Times*, 5.8.1944. [WSHC Microform Collection].

155 Whalley, P. (2013).*Corsham Memories 2: The Prefab Years 1930/40*. Patricia Whalley, pp. 41. [WSHC COR.940].

156 WSA G2/132/12.

157 WSA G7/132/13.

158 WSA G5/225/1.

159 Henderson, P. (1995). *100 Years in Corsham Parish*. Corsham: Corsham Parish Council, pp. 71-72. [WSHC COR.940].

160 Parsons, M. (2005). *Cricklade Revealed: Part 5 - Social Life during the Second World War*. Marion Parsons, pp. 32. [WSHC CRI.949].

161 WSA G7/132/13.

162 WSA G5/225/1.

163 Collier, C. (1992). *Southern Electric: A History*. Maidenhead: Southern Electric, pp. 83. [WSHC AAA.625].

164 Zweiniger-Bargielowska, I. (2000). *Austerity in Britain: Rationing, Controls and Consumption*. Oxford: Oxford University Press, pp. 80.

165 Ibid., pp. 37.

166 Prynne, C., Paul, A., Mishra, G., Hardy, R., Bolton-Smith, C. and Wadsworth, M. (2002).

Sociodemographic Inequalities in the Diet of Young Children in the 1946 British Birth Cohort. *Public Health Nutrition*, 5(6), pp. 737-739. [DOI: 10.1079/PHN2002342].

167 Ibid., pp. 741-744.

168 Ginn, P., Goodman, R. and Langlands, A. (2012). *Wartime Farm*. London: Mitchell Beazley, pp. 111.

169 Zweiniger-Bargielowska, I. (2000). *Austerity in Britain: Rationing, Controls and Consumption*. Oxford: Oxford University Press, pp. 139.

170 Hennessy, P. (1992). *Never Again: Britain 1945-51*. London: Penguin Books Ltd., pp. 277. [WSHC 941.0854].

171 Kynaston, D. (2007). *A World to Build: Austerity Britain*. London: Bloomsbury, pp. 107.

172 Zweiniger-Bargielowska, I. (2000). *Austerity in Britain: Rationing, Controls and Consumption*. Oxford: Oxford University Press, pp. 139.

173 Ibid., pp. 81.

174 Ibid., pp. 44.

175 Collingham, L. (2011). *The Taste of War: World War Two and the Battle for Food*. London: Penguin Books Ltd., pp. 175.

176 Ibid., pp. 385.

10 Morale of the Masses

1 *Oxford Dictionary of National Biography*. (2015). Aitkin, William Maxwell. Retrieved November 9, 2015 from the Oxford University Press website http://www.oxforddnb.com/view/article/30358?docPos=2

2 MacKay, R. (1999). *The Test of War: Inside Britain 1939-45*. London: UCL Press, pp. 138-141.

3 Briggs, A. (1994). *A Social History of England*: New Edition. London: Weidenfield & Nicholson (First published 1983), pp. 291.

4 MacKay, R. (1999). *The Test of War: Inside Britain 1939-45*. London: UCL Press, pp. 141.

5 Cantwell, J. (1993). *The Second World*

War: *A guide to documents in the Public Record Office*. London: HMSO (Original work published 1972), pp. 116. [WSHC 16.94053].

6 MacKay, R. (1999). *The Test of War: Inside Britain 1939-45*. London: UCL Press, pp. 161.

7 Calder, A. (1992). *The People's War: Britain 1939-45*. London: Pimlico (Original work published 1969), pp. 502-503. [WSHC 941.084].

8 MacKay, R. (1999). *The Test of War: Inside Britain 1939-45*. London: UCL Press, pp. 149-150.

9 Calder, A. (1992). *The People's War: Britain 1939-45*. London: Pimlico (Original work published 1969), pp. 503. [WSHC 941.084].

10 Ginn, P., Goodman, R. and Langlands, A. (2012). *Wartime Farm*. London: Mitchell Beazley, pp. 190.

11 Calder, A. (1992). *The People's War: Britain 1939-45*. London: Pimlico (Original work published 1969), pp. 503. [WSHC 941.084].

12 MacKay, R. (1999). *The Test of War: Inside Britain 1939-45*. London: UCL Press, pp. 150.

13 Hennessy, P. (1992). *Never Again: Britain 1945-51*. London: Penguin Books Ltd., pp. 40. [WSHC 941.0854].

14 WSA G24/225/29.

15 Hickson, J. and Skrine, R. (Ed.) (2013). *Carry on Coping: Diary of a Doctor 1942-1945*. Bradford on Avon: Ex Libris Press, pp. 232-233. [WSHC CHP.611 Original diaries are also available at WSA 4236/1-5].

16 Irving, H. (2015). The Publishing History of the Ministry of Information. Retrieved August 24, 2015 from the MOI Digital website http://www.moidigital.ac.uk/blog/publishing-history-ministry-information/

17 MacKay, R. (1999). *The Test of War: Inside Britain 1939-45*. London: UCL Press, pp. 147-150.

18 Ibid., pp. 153-154.

19 Ibid., pp. 154.

20 Aulich, J. (2012). Stealing the Thunder: The Soviet Union and Graphic Propaganda on the Hone Front during the Second World War. Visual Culture in Britain, 13(3), pp. 361. [doi: http://dx.doi.org/10.1080/14714787.2012.717214].

21 MacKay, R. (1999). *The Test of War: Inside Britain 1939-45*. London: UCL Press, pp. 154.

22 Aulich, J. (2012). Stealing the Thunder: The Soviet Union and Graphic Propaganda on the Hone Front during the Second World War. Visual Culture in Britain, 13(3), pp. 361. [doi: http://dx.doi.org/10.1080/14714787.2012.717214].

23 MacKay, R. (1999). *The Test of War: Inside Britain 1939-45*. London: UCL Press, pp. 155.

24 Ibid., pp. 161.

25 Ibid., pp. 155.

26 Aulich, J. (2012). Stealing the Thunder: The Soviet Union and Graphic Propaganda on the Hone Front during the Second World War. Visual Culture in Britain, 13(3), pp. 356-357. [doi: http://dx.doi.org/10.1080/14714787.2012.717214].

27 MacKay, R. (1999). *The Test of War: Inside Britain 1939-45*. London: UCL Press, pp. 157.

28 Partridge, F. (1978). *A Pacifist's War*. The Hogarth Press: London, pp. 179. [WSHC HAM.927].

29 Laslett, S. (2013). *Brylcreen and Broken Biscuits: A Street Trail History of Bradford on Avon's Shops in the 1950s*. Bradford on Avon: Ex Libris Press, pp. 37. [WSHC BRD.655].

30 Smith, J. (J. Currie et. al. Eds.). (1981). *Wiltshire Lives*. Salisbury: St. Edmunds Arts Centre, unpaginated. [WSHC AAA.924].

31 Maidment, A. (1993). *Under Salisbury Spire*. Salisbury: Salisbury Journal, pp. 170. [WSHC SAL.949].

32 MacKay, R. (1999). *The Test of War: Inside Britain 1939-45*. London: UCL Press, pp. 158.

33 Parsons, M. (2006). *Cricklade Revealed:*

Part 6 - Social Life during the Second
World War, Marion Parsons, pp. 21.
[WSHC CRI.949].

34 Hennessy, P. (1992). *Never Again:
Britain 1945-51*. London: Penguin
Books Ltd., pp. 26. [WSHC
941.0854].

35 WSHC P54134. [Wiltshire Historic
Print and Photograph Collection].

36 British Library of Information. (2015).
Prime Minister Winston Churchill's
Speech to the Allied Delegates, June
12, 1941. Retrieved July 21, 2015 from
the ibiblio website http://www.ibiblio.
org/pha/policy/1941/410612b.html

37 Parsons, M. (2006). *Cricklade Revealed:
Part 6 - Social Life during the Second
World War*, Marion Parsons, pp. 21.
[WSHC CRI.949].

38 Hickson, J. and Skrine, R. (Ed.)
(2013). *Carry on Coping: Diary of
a Doctor 1942-1945*. Bradford on
Avon: Ex Libris Press, pp. 36. [WSHC
CHP.611 Original diaries are also
available at WSA 4236/1-5].

39 MacKay, R. (1999). *The Test of War:
Inside Britain 1939-45*. London: UCL
Press, pp. 183.

40 Ibid., pp. 143.

41 Dobson, M. (2011). *Bradford Voices:
Life in Bradford on Avon 1900-2010*.
Bradford on Avon: Ex Libris Press, pp.
146. [WSHC BRD.949].

42 Lewis, P. (1984). *A People's War*.
London: Methuen London Ltd, pp.
178.

43 Calder, A. (1992). *The People's War:
Britain 1939-45*. London: Pimlico
(Original work published 1969), pp.
65. [WSHC 941.084].

44 Ginn, P., Goodman, R. and Langlands,
A. (2012). *Wartime Farm*. London:
Mitchell Beazley, pp. 188.

45 Cantwell, J. (1993). *The Second World
War: A guide to documents in the
Public Record Office*. London: HMSO
(Original work published 1972), pp.
115. [WSHC 16.94053].

46 The National Archives. (2015). Political
Warfare Executive and Foreign Office,
Political Intelligence Department:

Papers. Retrived November 9, 2015
from The National Archives website
http://discovery.nationalarchives.gov.
uk/details/r/C8197

47 Calder, A. (1992). *The People's War:
Britain 1939-45*. London: Pimlico
(Original work published 1969), pp.
503. [WSHC 941.084].

48 Ginn, P., Goodman, R. and Langlands,
A. (2012). *Wartime Farm*. London:
Mitchell Beazley, pp. 191.

49 Cantwell, J. (1993). *The Second World
War: A guide to documents in the
Public Record Office*. London: HMSO
(Original work published 1972), pp.
115. [WSHC 16.94053].

50 Lynn, V. (1994). *We'll Meet Again: A
Personal and Social History of WWII*.
London: MacMillan, pp. 132.

51 Lewis, P. (1984). *A People's War*.
London: Methuen London Ltd, pp.
180.

52 Calder, A. (1992). *The People's War:
Britain 1939-45*. London: Pimlico
(Original work published 1969), pp.
364-365. [WSHC 941.084].

53 Lewis, P. (1984). *A People's War*.
London: Methuen London Ltd, pp.
181.

54 Burchell, R. (2013). *Saucepans on our
Heads: Growing up in Swindon during
World War 2*. Bradford on Avon:
Ex Libris Press, pp. 51. [WSHC
SWI.949].

55 Lewis, P. (1984). *A People's War*.
London: Methuen London Ltd, pp.
181.

56 WSA 2893/1.

57 Kynaston, D. (2007). *A World to Build:
Austerity Britain*. London: Bloomsbury,
pp. 44.

58 *Wiltshire Gazette*, 20.8.1942. [WSHC
Microform Collection].

59 Siddall, M. (1995). *Safe as Houses:
Childhood Through the Forties*.
Christow: Devonshire House, pp. 21-
22. [WSHC PUR.949].

60 Ibid., pp. 26.

61 Meakin, R. (2002). *Minety at War*.
Richard Meakin, pp. 12. [WSHC
MIN.949].

62 Ibid., pp. 23.

63 Calder, A. (1992). *The People's War: Britain 1939-45*. London: Pimlico (Original work published 1969), pp. 504. [WSHC 941.084].

64 Cockbill, T. (1991). *Our Swindon, When Summer Suns were Glowing, Still: 1941-1943*. Swindon: The Quill Press, pp. 25. [WSHC SWI.949].

65 Randall, B. (2003). *A Patchwork of Memories*. Bob Randall, pp. 34. [WSI IC TRO.949].

66 Cockbill, T. (1989). *Our Swindon in 1939*. Swindon: The Quill Press, pp. 29. [WSHC SWI.949].

67 Ibid., pp. 55-57.

68 Hickson, J. and Skrine, R. (Ed.) (2013). *Carry on Coping: Diary of a Doctor 1942-1945*. Bradford on Avon: Ex Libris Press, pp. 234. [WSHC CHP.611 Original diaries are also available at WSA 4236/1-5].

69 Calder, A. (1992). *The People's War: Britain 1939-45*. London: Pimlico (Original work published 1969), pp. 367. [WSHC 941.084].

70 Ibid., pp. 64.

71 MacKay, R. (1999). *The Test of War: Inside Britain 1939-45*. London: UCL Press, pp. 152.

72 Ibid., pp. 186.

73 Ibid., pp. 152.

74 Randall, B. (2003). *A Patchwork of Memories*. Bob Randall, pp. 33. [WSHC TRO.949].

75 Maidment, A. (1993). *Under Salisbury Spire*. Salisbury: *Salisbury Journal*, pp. 168. [WSHC SAL.949].

76 Mass Observation (1987). *War Factory*. London: The Cresset Library (Original work published 1943), pp. 81. [WSHC SAI.684].

77 Reynolds, D. (1996). *Rich Relations*. London: Harper Collins, pp. 263. [WSHC AAA.949].

78 Randall, B. (2003). *A Patchwork of Memories*. Bob Randall, pp. 33. [WSHC TRO.949].

79 Crowman, D. (1991). *A History of Tidworth and Tedworth House*. Chichester: Phillimore & Co Ltd., pp.

54. [WSHC NOT.940].

80 Kynaston, D. (2007). *A World to Build: Austerity Britain*. London: Bloomsbury, pp. 56.

81 Ginn, P., Goodman, R. and Langlands, A. (2012). *Wartime Farm*. London: Mitchell Beazley, pp. 190.

82 WSA F8/760/17/10/11.

83 WSA F8/500/196/1/2. [1.1940].

84 Federation of Women's Institutes (1993). *Wiltshire Within Living Memory*. Newbury: Countryside Books, pp. 192. [WSHC AAA.949].

85 Duffy, M. (1983). *That's How it Was*. London: Virago (Original work published 1962), pp. 122-125. [WSHC AAA.823].

86 WSA G3/760/1164.

87 Calder, A. (1992). *The People's War: Britain 1939-45*. London: Pimlico (Original work published 1969), pp. 366-367. [WSHC 941.084].

88 Langhammer, C. (2003). A Public House is for all Classes, Men and Women Alike': Women, Leisure and Drink in Second World War England. *Women's History Review*, 12(3), pp. 424. [doi: http://dx.doi.org/10.1080/09612020300200367].

89 Ibid., pp. 428.

90 Ibid. pp. 429.

91 Ibid., pp. 430-431.

92 Langhammer, C. (2003). A Public House is for all Classes, Men and Women Alike': Women, Leisure and Drink in Second World War England. *Women's History Review*, 12(3), pp. 432-435. [doi: http://dx.doi.org/10.1080/09612020300200367].

93 Ibid., pp. 437.

94 Calder, A. (1992). *The People's War: Britain 1939-45*. London: Pimlico (Original work published 1969), pp. 64. [WSHC 941.084].

95 Ibid., pp. 374-376.

96 Ibid., pp. 64.

97 Maidment, A. (1993). *Under Salisbury Spire*. Salisbury: *Salisbury Journal*, pp. 168. [WSHC SAL.949].

98 WSA G24/225/4.

99 Williams, D. (2004). *Gwendolin*.

Lifestory, pp. 19-22. [WSHC COR.922].

100 Baker, E. (n.d.). Enfield Precision Enginering. Unpublished, unpaginated. [WSHC WEW.629].

101 Parsons, M. (2006). *Cricklade Revealed: Part 6 - Social Life during the Second World War*, Marion Parsons, pp. 21-23. [WSHC CRI.949].

102 Vernon, C. (2011). *Malmesbury versus Hitler: The Town's role in the Second World War*. Malmesbury: Malmesbury Civic Trust, pp. 175. [WSHC MAL.949].

103 Lewis, P. (1984). *A People's War*. London: Methuen London Ltd, pp. 187.

104 Leventhal, F. M. (1990). 'The Best for the Most': CEMA and State Sponsorship of the Arts in Wartime, 1939-1945. *Twentieth Century British History*, 1(3), pp. 289-290.

105 Ibid., pp. 291-292.

106 Calder, A. (1992). *The People's War: Britain 1939-45*. London: Pimlico (Original work published 1969), pp. 509. [WSHC 941.084].

107 Leventhal, F. M. (1990). 'The Best for the Most': CEMA and State Sponsorship of the Arts in Wartime, 1939-1945. *Twentieth Century British History*, 1(3), pp. 292.

108 MacKay, R. (1999). *The Test of War: Inside Britain 1939-45*. London: UCL Press, pp. 158.

109 Adie, K. (2003). *Corsets to Camouflage: Women at War*. London: Hodder & Stoughton, pp. 159. [WSHC 355.22082].

110 Calder, A. (1992). *The People's War: Britain 1939-45*. London: Pimlico (Original work published 1969), pp. 373. [WSHC 941.084].

111 Leventhal, F. M. (1990). 'The Best for the Most': CEMA and State Sponsorship of the Arts in Wartime, 1939-1945. *Twentieth Century British History*, 1(3), pp. 294.

112 Weingartner, J. (2006). *The Arts as a Weapon of War*. London: Tauris & Co. Ltd., pp. 9.

113 Ibid., pp. 62-63.

114 Anderson, B. (1994). *We Just Got On With It: British Women in World War II*. Chippenham: Picton Publishing, pp. 98. [WSHC AAA.949].

115 Vernon, C. (2011). *Malmesbury versus Hitler: The Town's role in the Second World War*. Malmesbury: Malmesbury Civic Trust, pp. 176-178. [WSHC MAL.949].

116 Leventhal, F. M. (1990). 'The Best for the Most': CEMA and State Sponsorship of the Arts in Wartime, 1939-1945. *Twentieth Century British History*, 1(3), pp. 295.

117 Ibid., pp. 298-299.

118 Ibid., pp. 302.

119 Ibid., pp. 305-306.

120 MacKay, R. (1999). *The Test of War: Inside Britain 1939-45*. London: UCL Press, pp. 158.

121 Anderson, B. (1994). *We Just Got On With It: British Women in World War II*. Chippenham: Picton Publishing, pp. 98. [WSHC AAA.949].

122 Millie, A. and Ware, K. (2015). A Brief History of the Theatre. Retrieved July 19, 2015 from the Salisbury Playhouse website http://www.salisburyplayhouse.com/page/a-brief-history-of-the-theatre

123 Bailey, D. (2005). *The Story of Chiseldon Camp: Part Two*. Chiseldon: Chiseldon Local History Group, pp. 60. [WSHC CHS.949].

124 Wyeth, R. (1995). *Sterner Days: Codford during the Second World War*. Warminster: Bedeguar Books, pp. 12. [WSHC COD.949].

125 Ibid., pp. 58-59.

126 Parsons, M. (2006). *Cricklade Revealed: Part 6 - Social Life during the Second World War*, Marion Parsons, pp. 21. [WSHC CRI.949].

127 Burchell, R. (2013). *Saucepans on our Heads: Growing up in Swindon during World War 2*. Bradford on Avon: Ex Libris Press, pp. 51. [WSHC SWI.949].

128 The People of Fovant (2005). *Fovant: Pages from our History*. East Knoyle:

Hobnob Press, pp. 87.

129 DCSA (2006). *Corsham Tunnels: A Brief History.* Corsham: Corporate Communications (Crown Copyright), unpaginated. [WSHC COR.949].

130 Calder, A. (1992). *The People's War: Britain 1939-45.* London: Pimlico (Original work published 1969), pp. 510. [WSHC 941.084].

131 Wyeth, R. (1995). *Sterner Days: Codford during the Second World War.* Warminster: Bedeguar Books, pp. 12. [WSHC COD.949].

132 Tate (2014). Artist Biography: Rex Whistler. Retrieved July 6, 2015 from the Tate website http://www.tate.org. uk/art/artists/rex-whistler-2140

133 Calder, A. (1992). *The People's War: Britain 1939-45.* London: Pimlico (Original work published 1969), pp. 510. [WSHC 941.084].

134 The National Archives (2015). The Art of War: Learn About the Art. Retrieved September 7, 2015 from The National Archives website http://www. nationalarchives.gov.uk/theartofwar/ inf3.htm

135 Leventhal, F. M. (1990). 'The Best for the Most': CEMA and State Sponsorship of the Arts in Wartime, 1939-1945. *Twentieth Century British History*, 1(3), pp. 299-301.

146 MacKay, R. (1999). *The Test of War: Inside Britain 1939-45.* London: UCL Press, pp. 186-188.

147 Leventhal, F. M. (1990). 'The Best for the Most': CEMA and State Sponsorship of the Arts in Wartime, 1939-1945. *Twentieth Century British History*, 1(3), pp. 316.

148 Hennessy, P. (1992). *Never Again: Britain 1945-51.* London: Penguin Books Ltd., pp. 40. [WSHC 941.0854].

149 Calder, A. (1992). *The People's War: Britain 1939-45.* London: Pimlico (Original work published 1969), pp. 373. [WSHC 941.084].

150 McCamley, N. (2010). *Subterranean Britain: 2WW Secret Bunkers.* Monkton Farleigh: Folly Books, pp. 202. [WSA

AAA.354].

151 Kynaston, D. (2007). *A World to Build: Austerity Britain.* London: Bloomsbury, pp. 37.

152 Leventhal, F. M. (1990). 'The Best for the Most': CEMA and State Sponsorship of the Arts in Wartime, 1939-1945. *Twentieth Century British History*, 1(3), pp. 314.

153 Ibid., pp. 290.

154 Waring, C. (2013). Our First Christmas Issue. *Wiltshire Life*, December Issue, pp. 26.

155 Willis, E. (2005). English Detective Fiction and the "People's War". *Forum for Modern Language Studies*, 42(1), pp. 13. [doi: 10.1093/fmls/cqi033].

156 Kynaston, D. (2007). *A World to Build: Austerity Britain.* London: Bloomsbury, pp. 44.

157 Aulich, J. (2012). Stealing the Thunder: The Soviet Union and Graphic Propaganda on the Hone Front during the Second World War. *Visual Culture in Britain*, 13(3), pp. 351. [doi: http://dx.doi.org/10.1080/1 4714787.2012.717214].

158 Willis, E. (2005). English Detective Fiction and the "People's War". *Forum for Modern Language Studies*, 42(1), pp. 20. [doi: 10.1093/fmls/cqi033].

159 Waller, M. (2005). *London 1945.* London: John Murray, pp. 96.

160 Aulich, J. (2012). Stealing the Thunder: The Soviet Union and Graphic Propaganda on the Hone Front during the Second World War. *Visual Culture in Britain*, 13(3), pp. 356. [doi: http://dx.doi.org/10.1080/1 4714787.2012.717214].

161 Ibid., pp. 351.

162 Ibid., pp. 360.

163 MacKay, R. (1999). *The Test of War: Inside Britain 1939-45.* London: UCL Press, pp. 151.

164 Randall, B. (2003). *A Patchwork of Memories.* Bob Randall, pp. 11-12. [WSHC TRO.949].

165 Ross, M. (1996). *Planning and the Heritage: Policy and Procedures* Second Edition. London: E & FN Spon, pp.

20. [WSHC 344.094].

166 Martin, J. (2000). *The Development of Modern Agriculture: British Farming Since 1931*. Basingstoke: Macmillan Press Ltd, pp. 23.

167 Pickford, P. and Pickford, R. (Ed.). (1995). *Letters to Liz*. Newnham, Tasmania: Attic Press, pp. 14. [WSHC WAR.949].

168 Calder, A. (1992). *The People's War: Britain 1939-45*. London: Pimlico (Original work published 1969), pp. 517-518. [WSHC 941.084].

169 Ibid., pp. 519-522.

170 Ibid., pp. 515-516.

171 Ibid., pp. 504.

172 Picture Post, 1939-1945. [WSHC Local Studies Reminiscence Collection].

173 Hodgson, G. (2015). Propaganda Sheets? *History Today*, 65(2), pp. 4-5.

174 Calder, A. (1992). *The People's War: Britain 1939-45*. London: Pimlico (Original work published 1969), pp. 511-512. [WSHC 941.084].

175 Willis, E. (2005). English Detective Fiction and the "People's War". *Forum for Modern Language Studies*, 42(1), pp. 15. [doi: 10.1093/fmls/cqi033].

176 Hennessy, P. (1992). *Never Again: Britain 1945-51*. London: Penguin Books Ltd., pp. 318. [WSHC 941.0854].

177 Kynaston, D. (2007). *A World to Build: Austerity Britain*. London: Bloomsbury, pp. 56.

178 Waring, C. (2013). Our First Christmas Issue. *Wiltshire Life*, December Issue, pp. 26.

179 Ginn, P., Goodman, R. and Langlands, A. (2012). *Wartime Farm*. London: Mitchell Beazley, pp. 190.

180 Calder, A. (1992). *The People's War: Britain 1939-45*. London: Pimlico (Original work published 1969), pp. 357. [WSHC 941.084].

181 University of London (2014). On This Day 1939. Retrieved July 8, 2014 from the School of Advance Study, University of London's Facebook site https://www.facebook. com/schoolofadvancedstudy/ posts/10152249230285922

182 Zweiniger-Bargielowska, I. (2000). *Austerity in Britain: Rationing, Controls and Consumption*. Oxford: Oxford University Press, pp. 65.

183 WSA F1/100/35.

184 Hickson, J. and Skrine, R. (Ed.) (2013). *Carry on Coping: Diary of a Doctor 1942-1945*. Bradford on Avon: Ex Libris Press, pp. 208. [WSHC CHP.611 Original diaries are also available at WSA 4236/1-5].

185 Smithsonian National Postal Museum (2015). Microfilm Models: Precursors of V-Mail. Retrieved July 19, 2015 from the Smithsonian National Postal Museum website http://postalmuseum. si.edu/victorymail/introducing/ microfilm.html

186 MacKay, R. (1999). *The Test of War: Inside Britain 1939-45*. London: UCL Press, pp. 168.

187 Hickson, J. and Skrine, R. (Ed.) (2013). *Carry on Coping: Diary of a Doctor 1942-1945*. Bradford on Avon: Ex Libris Press, pp. 25. [WSHC CHP.611 Original diaries are also available at WSA 4236/1-5].

188 Machin, G. (1996). British Churches and Social Issues, 1945-1960. *Twentieth Century British History*, 7(3), pp. 346.

189 Calder, A. (1992). *The People's War: Britain 1939-45*. London: Pimlico (Original work published 1969), pp. 487-488. [WSHC 941.084].

190 WSA G14/225/2.

191 Randall, B. (2003). *A Patchwork of Memories*. Bob Randall, pp. 12-13. [WSHC TRO.949].

192 Kynaston, D. (2007). *A World to Build: Austerity Britain*. London: Bloomsbury, pp. 94-96.

193 Ibid., pp. 124.

194 Hennessy, P. (1992). *Never Again: Britain 1945-51*. London: Penguin Books Ltd., pp. 311. [WSHC 941.0854].

195 Kynaston, D. (2007). *A World to Build: Austerity Britain*. London:

Bloomsbury, pp. 214.

196 Hennessy, P. (1992). *Never Again: Britain 1945-51*. London: Penguin Books Ltd., pp. 448. [WSHC 941.0854].

197 Ibid., pp. 176.

198 Kynaston, D. (2007). *A World to Build: Austerity Britain*. London: Bloomsbury, pp. 192.

199 Ibid., pp. 210-211.

200 Hennessy, P. (1992). *Never Again: Britain 1945-51*. London: Penguin Books Ltd., pp. 319. [WSHC 941.0854].

201 Ibid., pp. 177.

202 Ibid., pp. 316.

203 Hunting, D. (2014). Cycle Speedway Teams Down the Ages. Retrieved July 7, 2014 from the Cycle Speedway Teams website http://www.cyclespeedwayhistory.org.uk/

204 WSA G6/132/63.

205 Kynaston, D. (2007). *A World to Build: Austerity Britain*. London: Bloomsbury, pp. 175-177.

206 Hennessy, P. (1992). *Never Again: Britain 1945-51*. London: Penguin Books Ltd., pp. 326. [WSHC 941.0854].

207 Kynaston, D. (2007). *A World to Build: Austerity Britain*. London: Bloomsbury, pp. 235.

208 Hennessy, P. (1992). *Never Again: Britain 1945-51*. London: Penguin Books Ltd., pp. 311. [WSHC 941.0854].

209 Kynaston, D. (2007). *A World to Build: Austerity Britain*. London: Bloomsbury, pp. 266.

210 Laslett, S. (2013). *Brylcreen and Broken Biscuits: A Street Trail History of Bradford on Avon's Shops in the 1950s*. Bradford on Avon: Ex Libris Press, pp. 18. [WSHC BRD.655].

211 MacKay, R. (1999). *The Test of War: Inside Britain 1939-45*. London: UCL Press, pp. 159-162.

212 Ibid., pp. 232.

213 Briggs, A. (1994). *A Social History of England*: New Edition. London: Weidenfeld & Nicholson (First

published 1983), pp. 290.

214 Kynaston, D. (2007). *A World to Build: Austerity Britain*. London: Bloomsbury, pp. 39-40.

11 Victory is Here!

1 WSA F5/530/16.

2 WSA F5/530/16.

3 WSA F5/530/16.

4 Hennessy, P. (1992). *Never Again: Britain 1945-51*. London: Penguin Books Ltd., pp. 56-61. [WSHC 941.0854].

5 Partridge, F. (1978). *A Pacifist's War*. The Hogarth Press: London, pp. 212-213. [WSHC HAM.927].

6 Hickson, J. and Skrine, R. (Ed.) (2013). *Carry on Coping: Diary of a Doctor 1942-1945*. Bradford on Avon: Ex Libris Press, pp. 240. [WSHC CHP.611 Original diaries are also available at WSA 4236/1-5].

7 Kynaston, D. (2007). *A World to Build: Austerity Britain*. London: Bloomsbury, pp. 8.

8 Summers, J. (2015). *Fashion on the Ration*. London: Profile Books in Partnership with the Imperial War Museum, pp. 111.

9 Hennessy, P. (1992). *Never Again: Britain 1945-51*. London: Penguin Books Ltd., pp. 59. [WSHC 941.0854].

10 Chapman, E. and Howell, A. (2005). *When the War was Over: Memories of 1945*. Liz Fricker (Community Printer) (Mere Literary Festival Community Project), unpaginated. [WSHC MER.949].

11 Ibid.

12 White, J. and Russell, D. (2008). Longbridge Deverill Parish Memoirs. Longbridge Deverill Local History Group, pp. 93. [WSHC LOD.949].

13 Mock, J. (1997). *Bradford on Avon & District: The War Years (1939-1945)*. J. H. Mock, pp. 51. [BRD.949].

14 Devizes Local History Group and Haycock, L. (Ed.). (1995). *How Devizes Won the War!* Devizes Local History Group, pp. 47-48. [WSHC DEV.949].

15 Daniels, P. (1995). *The Archive Photographs Series: Salisbury.* Chalford: The Chalford Publishing Company, pp. 120-121. [WSHC SAL.771].

16 WSA F8/500/157/1/2.

17 Hickson, J. and Skrine, R. (Ed.) (2013). *Carry on Coping: Diary of a Doctor 1942-1945.* Bradford on Avon: Ex Libris Press, pp. 240. [WSHC CHP.611 Original diaries are also available at WSA 4236/1-5].

18 WSA F5/530/16.

19 Hennessy, P. (1992). *Never Again: Britain 1945-51.* London: Penguin Books Ltd., pp. 86-88. [WSHC 941.0854].

20 Henderson, P. (1995). *100 Years in Corsham Parish.* Corsham Parish Council, pp. 77. [WSHC COR.940].

21 Devizes Local History Group and Haycock, L. (Ed.). (1995). *How Devizes Won the War!* Devizes Local History Group, pp. 48. [WSHC DEV.949].

22 Mock, J. (1997). *Bradford on Avon & District: The War Years (1939-1945).* J. H. Mock, pp. 55. [BRD.949].

23 Lynn, V. (1994). *We'll Meet Again: A Personal and Social History of WWII.* London: MacMillan, pp. 188.

24 WSA F5/530/16.

25 Ibid.

26 Royal Air Force Museum (2013). Polish Air Force Casualties. Retrieved September 7, 2015 from the RAF Museum website http://www.rafmuseum.org.uk/research/online-exhibitions/the-polish-air-force-in-world-war-2/polish-air-force-casualties.aspx

12 The Post War World

1 Chapman, E. and Howell, A. (2005). *When the War was Over: Memories of 1945*: Mere Literary Festival Community Project. Unpublished, unpaginated. [WSHC MER.949].

2 Morgan, K. (1990). *The People's Peace: British History 1945-1989.* Oxford: Oxford University Press, pp. 3.

3 Rose, S. (2003). Which People's War? National Identity and Citizenship in Wartime Britain 1939-45. Oxford: Oxford University Press, pp. 64.

4 Kynaston, D. (2007). *A World to Build: Austerity Britain.* London: Bloomsbury, pp. 45.

5 Inchfawn, F. (2010). *Salute to the Village.* Monkton Farleigh: Folly Books (Original work published 1943), pp. 124. [WSHC XIN.921].

6 Briggs, A. (1994). *A Social History of England*: New Edition. London: Weidenfield & Nicholson (First published 1983), pp. 291.

7 Kynaston, D. (2007). *A World to Build: Austerity Britain.* London: Bloomsbury, pp. 63.

8 *The Times,* 26.7.1945. [WSHC Microform Collection].

9 Ibid., 21.7.1945. [WSHC Microform Collection].

9a WSA 2893/1.

10 Pickford, P. and Pickford, R. (Ed.). (1995). *Letters to Liz.* Newnham, Tasmania: Attic Press, pp. 178. [WSHC WAR.949].

11 Morgan, K. (1990). *The People's Peace: British History 1945-1989.* Oxford: Oxford University Press, pp. 27.

12 *The Times,* 27.7.1945. [WSHC Microform Collection].

13 Lewis, P. (1984). *A People's War.* London: Methuen London Ltd, pp. 240.

14 Hennessy, P. (1992). *Never Again: Britain 1945-51.* London: Penguin Books Ltd., pp. 84. [WSHC 941.0854].

15 Lewis, P. (1984). *A People's War.* London: Methuen London Ltd, pp. 242.

16 Hennessy, P. (1992). *Never Again: Britain 1945-51.* London: Penguin Books Ltd., pp. 327. [WSHC 941.0854].

17 Harris, J. (1992). Society and the State in 20th Century Britain. In Thompson, F. M. L. (Ed.). *The Cambridge History of Britain 1759-1950* (Vol. 3, Social Agencies and

Institutions, pp. 92). Cambridge: Cambridge University Press.

18 Morgan, K. (1990). *The People's Peace: British History 1945-1989.* Oxford: Oxford University Press, pp. 21.

19 Kynaston, D. (2007). *A World to Build: Austerity Britain.* London: Bloomsbury, pp. 79.

20 Waring, C. (2013). Our First Christmas Issue. *Wiltshire Life,* December Issue, pp. 26.

21 Ibid.

22 Kynaston, D. (2007). *A World to Build: Austerity Britain.* London: Bloomsbury, pp. 115.

23 WSA 1247/3.

24 Whiles, J. (1995). *Calne at War 1939-1945.* John Whiles, pp. 52. [WSHC CAL.949].

25 WSA 2142/26.

26 Ibid.

27 WSA G13/225/10.

28 Corsham Welcome Home Committee. (c. 1947). *War Records of Corsham 1939-1945.* Corsham: Corsham Parish Council, Foreward. [WSHC COR.949 (BL)].

29 WSA G23/132/76.

30 Calder, A. (1992). *The People's War: Britain 1939-45.* London: Pimlico (Original work published 1969), pp. 570. [WSHC 941.084].

31 MacKay, R. (1999). *The Test of War: Inside Britain 1939-45.* London: UCL Press, pp. 220.

32 Calder, A. (1992). *The People's War: Britain 1939-45.* London: Pimlico (Original work published 1969), pp. 570. [WSHC 941.084].

33 MacKay, R. (1999). *The Test of War: Inside Britain 1939-45.* London: UCL Press, pp. 220.

34 Hennessy, P. (1992). *Never Again: Britain 1945-51.* London: Penguin Books Ltd., pp. 321. [WSHC 941.0854].

35 Ibid., pp. 89.

36 McCoombe, C. (2001). The Recollections of Charles McCoombe when he served in the Royal Navy during World War II. Unpublished,

pp. 23. [WSHC HOL.921].

37 Kynaston, D. (2007). *A World to Build: Austerity Britain.* London: Bloomsbury, pp. 97.

38 Summers, J. (2015). *Fashion on the Ration.* London: Profile Books in Partnership with the Imperial War Museum, pp. 179.

39 Hinton, J. (1998). Voluntarism and the Welfare/Warfare State. Women's Voluntary Services in the 1940s. *Twentieth Century British History,* 9(2), pp. 280.

40 Mock, J. (1997). *Bradford on Avon & District: The War Years (1939-1945).* J. H. Mock, pp. 51. [BRD.949].

41 Wheeler, L. C. (1993). 1939-1945: As I Remember. Unpublished, pp.227. [WSHC WEB.921].

42 Hillier, J. (1995). *The Long Road to Victory: War Diary of an Infantry Despatch Rider 1940-1946.* John Hillier, pp. 171-172. [WSHC TRO.921].

43 McCoombe, C. (2001). The Recollections of Charles McCoombe when he served in the Royal Navy during World War II. Unpublished, pp. 23. [WSHC HOL.921].

44 Adie, K. (2003). *Corsets to Camouflage: Women at War.* London: Hodder & Stoughton, pp. 205. [WSHC 355.22082].

45 Waller, M. (2005). *London 1945.* London: John Murray, pp. 381-382.

46 Calder, A. (1992). *The People's War: Britain 1939-45.* London: Pimlico (Original work published 1969), pp. 314. [WSHC 941.084].

47 Marwick, A. (2000). *A History of the Modern British Isles 1914-1999.* Oxford: Blackwell Publishing Ltd., pp. 192.

48 Cantwell, J. (1993). *The Second World War: A guide to documents in the Public Record Office.* London: HMSO (Original work published 1972), pp. 120. [WSHC 16.94053].

49 Kynaston, D. (2007). *A World to Build: Austerity Britain.* London: Bloomsbury, pp. 102.

50 WSA G24/132/355.
51 WSA G4/132/20.
52 WSA G5/132/12.
53 WSA G24/132/369.
54 WSA 2495/11.
55 Robertson, A. (1987). *The Bleak Midwinter 1947*. Manchester: Manchester University Press, pp. 7-9.
56 Ibid., pp. 14-15.
57 Margaret Monk, personal communication, 3.6.2014.
58 Hennessy, P. (1992). *Never Again: Britain 1945-51*. London: Penguin Books Ltd., pp. 214. [WSHC 941.0854].
59 WSA 2857/3.
60 Robertson, A. (1987). *The Bleak Midwinter 1947*. Manchester: Manchester University Press, pp. 146.
61 Kynaston, D. (2007). *A World to Build: Austerity Britain*. London: Bloomsbury, pp. 194.
62 Martin, J. (2000). *The Development of Modern Agriculture: British Farming Since 1931*. Basingstoke: Macmillan Press Ltd, pp. 75.
63 WSA G24/132/355.
64 Kynaston, D. (2007). *A World to Build: Austerity Britain*. London: Bloomsbury, pp. 188-191.
65 Ibid., pp. 193.
66 Hennessy, P. (1992). *Never Again: Britain 1945-51*. London: Penguin Books Ltd., pp. 277. [WSHC 941.0854].
67 Ibid., pp. 273.
68 Kynaston, D. (2007). *A World to Build: Austerity Britain*. London: Bloomsbury, pp. 194.
69 Hennessy, P. (1992). *Never Again: Britain 1945-51*. London: Penguin Books Ltd., pp. 282-284. [WSHC 941.0854].
70 Kynaston, D. (2007). *A World to Build: Austerity Britain*. London: Bloomsbury, pp. 194.
71 Ibid., pp. 200.
72 Hennessy, P. (1992). *Never Again: Britain 1945-51*. London: Penguin Books Ltd., pp. 277. [WSHC 941.0854].
73 Robertson, A. (1987). *The Bleak Midwinter 1947*. Manchester: Manchester University Press, pp. 158-159.
74 Kynaston, D. (2007). *A World to Build: Austerity Britain*. London: Bloomsbury, pp. 104.
75 Zweiniger-Bargielowska, I. (2000). *Austerity in Britain: Rationing, Controls and Consumption*. Oxford: Oxford University Press, pp. 64.
76 Hennessy, P. (1992). *Never Again: Britain 1945-51*. London: Penguin Books Ltd., pp. 274. [WSHC 941.0854].
77 Zweiniger-Bargielowska, I. (2000). *Austerity in Britain: Rationing, Controls and Consumption*. Oxford: Oxford University Press, pp. 37.
78 Robertson, A. (1987). *The Bleak Midwinter 1947*. Manchester: Manchester University Press, pp. 4-6.
79 Kynaston, D. (2007). *A World to Build: Austerity Britain*. London: Bloomsbury, pp. 124.
80 Robertson, A. (1987). *The Bleak Midwinter 1947*. Manchester: Manchester University Press, pp. 6-7.
81 Kynaston, D. (2007). *A World to Build: Austerity Britain*. London: Bloomsbury, pp. 106-108.
82 Zweiniger-Bargielowska, I. (2000). *Austerity in Britain: Rationing, Controls and Consumption*. Oxford: Oxford University Press, pp. 24.
83 Ibid.
84 Ibid., pp. 64.
85 Hennessy, P. (1992). *Never Again: Britain 1945-51*. London: Penguin Books Ltd., pp. 308. [WSHC 941.0854].
86 Kynaston, D. (2007). *A World to Build: Austerity Britain*. London: Bloomsbury, pp. 255.
87 Zweiniger-Bargielowska, I. (1994). Rationing, Austerity and the Conservative Party Recovery after 1945. *The Historical Journal*, 37(1), pp. 174.
88 Pynchon, P. (2003). Introduction. In Orwell, G. *Nineteen Eighty Four*, pp.

ix. London: Penguin Group.

89 Kynaston, D. (2007). *A World to Build: Austerity Britain*. London: Bloomsbury, pp. 227-228.

90 Ibid., pp. 247.

91 Ibid., pp. 227-228.

92 Fell, J. and Carrott, P. (1988).*Memoirs of a Countryman*. Devizes: Devizes Instant Print, pp. 62. [WSHC COM.949].

93 WSA F3/530/25.

94 Zweiniger-Bargielowska, I. (2000). *Austerity in Britain: Rationing, Controls and Consumption*. Oxford: Oxford University Press, pp. 29.

95 Ibid., pp. 51.

96 Ibid., pp. 28.

97 Ibid., pp. 64.

98 Ibid., pp. 29.

99 Hennessy, P. (1992). *Never Again: Britain 1945-51*. London: Penguin Books Ltd., pp. 46. [WSHC 941.0854].

100 Kynaston, D. (2007). *A World to Build: Austerity Britain*. London: Bloomsbury, pp. 258.

101 Zweiniger-Bargielowska, I. (2000). *Austerity in Britain: Rationing, Controls and Consumption*. Oxford: Oxford University Press, pp. 95.

102 Kynaston, D. (2007). *A World to Build: Austerity Britain*. London: Bloomsbury, pp. 273-274.

103 Hennessy, P. (1992). *Never Again: Britain 1945-51*. London: Penguin Books Ltd., pp. 317. [WSHC 941.0854].

104 Zweiniger-Bargielowska, I. (2000). *Austerity in Britain: Rationing, Controls and Consumption*. Oxford: Oxford University Press, pp. 95.

105 Moran, J. (2005). Queuing up in Post-War Britain. *Twentieth Century British History*, 16(3), pp. 285-290.

106 Kynaston, D. (2007). *A World to Build: Austerity Britain*. London: Bloomsbury, pp. 252.

107 Zweiniger-Bargielowska, I. (2000). *Austerity in Britain: Rationing, Controls and Consumption*. Oxford: Oxford University Press, pp. 66.

108 Moran, J. (2005). Queuing up in Post-War Britain. *Twentieth Century British History*, 16(3), 289

109 Kynaston, D. (2007). *A World to Build: Austerity Britain*. London: Bloomsbury, pp. 255.

110 Hennessy, P. (1992). *Never Again: Britain 1945-51*. London: Penguin Books Ltd., pp. 326. [WSHC 941.0854].

111 Ibid., pp. 306.

112 Ibid., pp. 139.

113 Marwick, A. (2000). *A History of the Modern British Isles 1914-1999*. Oxford: Blackwell Publishing Ltd., pp. 155.

114 Lewis, P. (1984). *A People's War*. London: Methuen London Ltd, pp. 227.

115 Harris, J. (1992). Society and the State in 20th Century Britain. In Thompson, F. M. L. (Ed.). *The Cambridge History of Britain 1759-1950* (Vol. 3, Social Agencies and Institutions, pp. 92). Cambridge: Cambridge University Press.

116 Glynn, S. and Booth, A. (1996). *Modern Britain: An Economic and Social History*. London: Routledge, pp. 160.

117 Malpass, P. (2003). The Wobbly Pillar? Housing and the British Postwar Welfare State. *Journal of Social Policy*, 32(4), pp. 593.

118 Kynaston, D. (2007). *A World to Build: Austerity Britain*. London: Bloomsbury, pp. 25.

119 Ibid., pp. 41.

120 Lewis, P. (1984). *A People's War*. London: Methuen London Ltd, pp. 228.

121 Hopkins, H. (1964). *New Look: A Social History of the Forties and Fifties*. London: Secker & Warburg Readers Union, pp. 22.

122 Lewis, P. (1984). *A People's War*. London: Methuen London Ltd, pp. 228-229.

123 Harris, J. (1992). Society and the State in 20th Century Britain. In Thompson, F. M. L. (Ed.). *The*

Cambridge History of Britain 1759-1950 (Vol. 3, Social Agencies and Institutions, pp. 89). Cambridge: Cambridge University Press.

124 Hopkins, H. (1964). *New Look: A Social History of the Forties and Fifties.* London: Secker & Warburg Readers Union, pp. 24.

125 Kynaston, D. (2007). *A World to Build: Austerity Britain.* London: Bloomsbury, pp. 45.

126 Morgan, K. (1990). *The People's Peace: British History 1945-1989.* Oxford: Oxford University Press, pp. 20.

127 Kynaston, D. (2007). *A World to Build: Austerity Britain.* London: Bloomsbury, pp. 143.

128 Collingham, L. (2011). *The Taste of War: World War Two and the Battle for Food.* London: Penguin Books Ltd., pp. 399.

129 Kynaston, D. (2007). *A World to Build: Austerity Britain.* London: Bloomsbury, pp. 145.

130 Collingham, L. (2011). *The Taste of War: World War Two and the Battle for Food.* London: Penguin Books Ltd., pp. 399.

131 Hickson, J. and Skrine, R. (Ed.) (2013). *Carry on Coping: Diary of a Doctor 1942-1945.* Bradford on Avon: Ex Libris Press, pp. 126. [WSHC CHP.611 Original diaries are also available at WSA 4236/1-5].

132 Ibid., pp. 192-193.

133 Ibid., pp. 196.

134 Glynn, S. and Booth, A. (1996). *Modern Britain: An Economic and Social History.* London: Routledge, pp. 162.

135 Hennessy, P. (1992). *Never Again: Britain 1945-51.* London: Penguin Books Ltd., pp. 141-142. [WSHC 941.0854].

136 Kynaston, D. (2007). *A World to Build: Austerity Britain.* London: Bloomsbury, pp. 147.

137 Hennessy, P. (1992). *Never Again: Britain 1945-51.* London: Penguin Books Ltd., pp. 129. [WSHC 941.0854].

138 Harris, J. (1992). Society and the State in 20th Century Britain. In Thompson, F. M. L. (Ed.). *The Cambridge History of Britain 1759-1950* (Vol. 3, Social Agencies and Institutions, pp. 98). Cambridge: Cambridge University Press.

139 Kynaston, D. (2007). *A World to Build: Austerity Britain.* London: Bloomsbury, pp. 278.

140 Hennessy, P. (1992). *Never Again: Britain 1945-51.* London: Penguin Books Ltd., pp. 130. [WSHC 941.0854].

141 Kynaston, D. (2007). *A World to Build: Austerity Britain.* London: Bloomsbury, pp. 281-282.

142 Hennessy, P. (1992). *Never Again: Britain 1945-51.* London: Penguin Books Ltd., pp. 123. [WSHC 941.0854].

143 Ibid., pp. 132.

144 Glynn, S. and Booth, A. (1996). *Modern Britain: An Economic and Social History.* London: Routledge, pp. 160.

145 Hennessy, P. (1992). *Never Again: Britain 1945-51.* London: Penguin Books Ltd., pp. 135. [WSHC 941.0854].

146 Glynn, S. and Booth, A. (1996). *Modern Britain: An Economic and Social History.* London: Routledge, pp. 160.

147 Lane, C. and White, P. (1999). *Warminster in the Twentieth Century.* The Warminster History Society: Warminster, pp. 243. [WSHC WAR.949].

148 Ibid., pp. 248.

149 Ibid., pp. 254.

150 Ibid., pp. 251.

151 WSA G24/225/66.

152 Lane, C. and White, P. (1999). *Warminster in the Twentieth Century.* The Warminster History Society: Warminster, pp. 248. [WSHC WAR.949].

153 Briggs, A. (1994). *A Social History of England*: New Edition. London: Weidenfeld & Nicholson (First

published 1983), pp. 309.

154 Glynn, S. and Booth, A. (1996). *Modern Britain: An Economic and Social History*. London: Routledge, pp. 162.

155 Hennessy, P. (1992). *Never Again: Britain 1945-51*. London: Penguin Books Ltd., pp. 155. [WSHC 941.0854].

156 The Cabinet Papers 1915-1986: Attempts at Reform. (2015). Retrieved May 14, 2015 from The National Archives website http://www. nationalarchives.gov.uk/cabinetpapers/ themes/attempt-at-reform.htm

157 Calder, A. (1992). *The People's War: Britain 1939-45*. London: Pimlico (Original work published 1969), pp. 541. [WSHC 941.084].

158 Marwick, A. (2000). *A History of the Modern British Isles 1914-1999*. Oxford: Blackwell Publishing Ltd., pp. 155.

159 Kynaston, D. (2007). *A World to Build: Austerity Britain*. London: Bloomsbury, pp. 26.

160 Glynn, S. and Booth, A. (1996). *Modern Britain: An Economic and Social History*. London: Routledge, pp. 162.

161 Marwick, A. (2000). *A History of the Modern British Isles 1914-1999*. Oxford: Blackwell Publishing Ltd., pp. 155.

162 Hennessy, P. (1992). *Never Again: Britain 1945-51*. London: Penguin Books Ltd., pp. 160. [WSHC 941.0854].

163 Morgan, K. (1990). *The People's Peace: British History 1945-1989*. Oxford: Oxford University Press, pp. 19.

164 Hopkins, H. (1964). *New Look: A Social History of the Forties and Fifties*. London: Secker & Warburg Readers Union, pp. 163.

165 Calder, A. (1992). *The People's War: Britain 1939-45*. London: Pimlico (Original work published 1969), pp. 585. [WSHC 941.084].

166 Morgan, K. (1990). *The People's Peace: British History 1945-1989*. Oxford:

167 MacKay, R. (1999). *The Test of War: Inside Britain 1939-45*. London: UCL Press, pp. 217.

268 Ibid., pp. 219.

169 Briggs, A. (1994). *A Social History of England*: New Edition. London: Weidenfield & Nicholson (First published 1983), pp. 119.

170 WSA F1/001/1.

171 WSA F8/116/1.

172 Hennessy, P. (1992). *Never Again: Britain 1945-51*. London: Penguin Books Ltd., pp. 160. [WSHC 941.0854].

173 WSA G3/760/1178.

174 WSA G2/132/14.

175 WSA G4/132/15.

176 Tomlinson, J. (1998). Why so Austere? The British Welfare State of the 1940s. *Journal of Social Policy*, 27(1), pp. 65-66.

177 Parsons, M. (2011). *Cricklade Revealed: Part 8 - Social Life during the Second World War*. Marion Parsons, pp. 22. [WSHC CRI.949].

178 WSA F8/110/87/2/1.

179 WSA G4/132/15.

180 WSA F1/100/17/17 and WSA F14/001/1.

182 WSA F14/001/1.

183 WSA G4/132/4.

184 WSA F100/17/17.

185 WSA F8/100/32.

186 WSA G3/132/63.

187 WSA F8/100/32.

188 Smith, B. (1989). *Our Wiltshire Village: Steeple Ashton*. Gloucester: Alan Sutton, pp. 82-83. [WSHC STE.940].

189 WSA G24/132/351.

190 WSA G4/122/32.

191 WSA G3/132/63.

192 WSA G4/132/14.

193 Henderson, P. (1995). *100 Years in Corsham Parish*. Corsham: Corsham Parish Council, pp. 81. [WSHC COR.940].

194 WSA F8/300/185.

195 MacKay, R. (1999). *The Test of War: Inside Britain 1939-45*. London: UCL

Press, pp. 151.

196 Kynaston, D. (2007). *A World to Build: Austerity Britain*. London: Bloomsbury, pp. 152.

197 Ibid., pp. 221.

198 MacKay, R. (1999). *The Test of War: Inside Britain 1939-45*. London: UCL Press, pp. 217.

199 Glynn, S. and Booth, A. (1996). *Modern Britain: An Economic and Social History*. London: Routledge, pp. 153.

200 Marwick, A. (2000). *A History of the Modern British Isles 1914-1999*. Oxford: Blackwell Publishing Ltd., pp. 163.

201 Glynn, S. and Booth, A. (1996). *Modern Britain: An Economic and Social History*. London: Routledge, pp. 155.

202 Waller, M. (2005). *London 1945*. London: John Murray, pp. 348.

203 MacKay, R. (1999). *The Test of War: Inside Britain 1939-45*. London: UCL Press, pp. 204.

204 Hennessy, P. (1992). *Never Again: Britain 1945-51*. London: Penguin Books Ltd., pp. 94. [WSHC 941.0854].

205 Robertson, A. (1987). *The Bleak Midwinter 1947*. Manchester: Manchester University Press, pp. 3.

206 Hennessy, P. (1992). *Never Again: Britain 1945-51*. London: Penguin Books Ltd., pp. 97. [WSHC 941.0854].

207 Kynaston, D. (2007). *A World to Build: Austerity Britain*. London: Bloomsbury, pp. 226.

208 Hennessy, P. (1992). *Never Again: Britain 1945-51*. London: Penguin Books Ltd., pp. 305. [WSHC 941.0854].

209 Kynaston, D. (2007). *A World to Build: Austerity Britain*. London: Bloomsbury, pp. 226.

210 Ibid., pp. 230.

211 Hennessy, P. (1992). *Never Again: Britain 1945-51*. London: Penguin Books Ltd., pp. 174. [WSHC 941.0854].

212 Ibid., pp. 292.

213 Ibid., pp. 296.

214 Ibid., pp. 339.

215 Zweiniger-Bargielowska, I. (2000). *Austerity in Britain: Rationing, Controls and Consumption*. Oxford: Oxford University Press, pp. 52-54.

216 Ibid., pp. 58.

217 Tomlinson, J. (1998). Why so Austere? The British Welfare State of the 1940s. *Journal of Social Policy*, 27(1), pp. 63.

218 Ibid., pp. 64.

219 Ibid., pp. 74.

220 Martin, J. (2000). *The Development of Modern Agriculture: British Farming Since 1931*. Basingstoke: Macmillan Press Ltd, pp. 75.

221 Hennessy, P. (1992). *Never Again: Britain 1945-51*. London: Penguin Books Ltd., pp. 191. [WSHC 941.0854].

222 Kynaston, D. (2007). *A World to Build: Austerity Britain*. London: Bloomsbury, pp. 137-138.

223 Ritschel, D. (1995). The Making of Consensus: The Nuffield College Conferences During the Second World War. *Twentieth Century History*, 6(3), pp. 271.

224 Ibid., pp. 276.

225 Ibid., pp. 283.

226 Ibid., pp. 301.

227 Ibid., pp. 271.

228 Tomlinson, J. (1992). Planning: Debate and Policy in the 1940s. *Twentieth Century British History*, 3(2), pp. 172.

229 Davis, J. (2013). To Locate and Evaluate Local Government Archive Material for North Wiltshire held at the Wiltshire and Swindon History Centre, to Discover its use as a Source for Studying Social Change from 1939-55. (Unpublished master's dissertation). University of Aberystwyth, Aberystwyth, pp. 12.

230 Ritschel, D. (1995). The Making of Consensus: The Nuffield College Conferences During the Second World War. *Twentieth Century History*, 6(3), pp. 285-287.

231 Ibid., pp. 298.
232 Glynn, S. and Booth, A. (1996). *Modern Britain: An Economic and Social History.* London: Routledge, pp. 259.
233 WSA F5/530/25.
234 Hennessy, P. (1992). *Never Again: Britain 1945-51.* London: Penguin Books Ltd., pp. 207. [WSHC 941.0854].
235 Glynn, S. and Booth, A. (1996). *Modern Britain: An Economic and Social History.* London: Routledge, pp. 260.
236 The Oldest Motorway. (2010). Retrieved May 14, 2015 from The Motorway Archive website http://www.ukmotorwayarchive.org/
237 Morgan, K. (1990). *The People's Peace: British History 1945-1989.* Oxford: Oxford University Press, pp. 6.
238 Ibid., pp. 10.
239 Hennessy, P. (1992). *Never Again: Britain 1945-51.* London: Penguin Books Ltd., pp. 196-197. [WSHC 941.0854].
240 Ibid., pp. 343-344.
241 Ibid., pp. 356.
242 Eccles, D. (1983). *By Safe Hand: Letters of Sybil and David Eccles, 1939-1942.* London: Bodley Head, pp. 299. [WSHC CHU.928].
243 Barnett, C. (1986). *The Audit of War: The Illusion and Reality of Britain as a Great Nation.* London: Papermac, pp. 11.
244 Malpass, P. (2003). The Wobbly Pillar? Housing and the British Postwar Welfare State. *Journal of Social Policy,* 32(4), pp. 592.
245 Lewis, P. (1984). *A People's War.* London: Methuen London Ltd, pp. 221.
246 Harris, J. (1992). Society and the State in 20th Century Britain. In Thompson, F. M. L. (Ed.). *The Cambridge History of Britain 1759-1950* (Vol. 3, Social Agencies and Institutions, pp. 92). Cambridge: Cambridge University Press.
247 Morgan, K. (1990). *The People's Peace:*

248 Calder, A. (1992). *The People's War: Britain 1939-45.* London: Pimlico (Original work published 1969), pp. 534. [WSHC 941.084].
249 Morgan, K. (1990). *The People's Peace: British History 1945-1989.* Oxford: Oxford University Press, pp. 15.
250 Rose, S. (2003). *Which People's War? National Identity and Citizenship in Wartime Britain 1939-45.* Oxford: Oxford University Press, pp. 218.
251 Hennessy, P. (1992). *Never Again: Britain 1945-51.* London: Penguin Books Ltd., pp. 180-181. [WSHC 941.0854].
252 Ibid., pp. 434.
253 Ibid., pp. 209-210.
254 WSA G24/132/306.
255 WSA F14/001/10.
256 WSA F14/001/10.
257 Ibid.
258 McCamley, N. (2007). *Secret Underground Cities.* Barnsley: Pen & Sword, pp. 196-197. [WSHC COR.949].
259 WSA G6/132/12.
260 WSA G24/132/357.
261 WSA G6/132/12.
262 WSA G6/132/21.
263 WSA G24/132/357.
264 WSA F14/001/1.
265 WSA G24/132/355.
266 Ibid.
267 F1/100/40/1.
268 Crittall, E. (Ed.). (1959). *The Victoria History of Wiltshire:* Volume IV. London: Oxford University Press, pp. 360-361. [WSHC AAA.940].
269 Census Search Results. (2011). Retrieved July 7, 2015 from the Wiltshire Community History website http://history.wiltshire.gov.uk/community/getcensus.php?id=84
270 WSA F14/001/10.
271 WSA G24/132/57.
272 WSA F14/001/5.
273 WSA G3/132/43.
274 WSA G4/132/21.
275 WSA 2857/3.

276 Kynaston, D. (2007). *A World to Build: Austerity Britain*. London: Bloomsbury, pp. 31.

277 Ibid., pp. 159.

278 Ibid., pp. 167.

279 Ross, M. (1996). Planning and the Heritage: Policy and Procedures Second Edition. London: E & FN Spon, pp. 19-22. [WSHC 344.094].

280 Kynaston, D. (2007). *A World to Build: Austerity Britain*. London: Bloomsbury, pp. 165.

281 Ross, M. (1996). Planning and the Heritage: Policy and Procedures Second Edition. London: E & FN Spon, pp. 27. [WSHC 344.094].

282 Ibid., pp. 30.

283 WSA G5/132/12.

284 WSA F1/001/1.

285 Little, J. (1991). Women in the Rural Labour Market: A Policy Evaluation. In Champion, T. and Watkins, C. (Eds.). *People in the Countryside: Studies of Social Change in Rural Britain* (pp. 143). London: Paul Chapman Publishing Ltd.

286 Lowe, P., Bradley, T. and Wright, S. (Eds.). (1986). *Deprivation and Welfare in Rural Areas*. Norwich: Geo Books, pp. 29.

287 Shucksmith M. (2011, August). Inequity, Power and Injustice in Rural Areas: Beyond Social Exclusion? Paper presented at the XXIV Congress of the European Society for Rural Sociology, 13-14.

288 Little, J. (1991). Women in the Rural Labour Market: A Policy Evaluation. In Champion, T. and Watkins, C. (Eds.). *People in the Countryside: Studies of Social Change in Rural Britain* (pp. 136). London: Paul Chapman Publishing Ltd.

289 Briggs, A. (1994). *A Social History of England*: New Edition. London: Weidenfield & Nicholson (First published 1983), pp. 318.

290 Newby, H. (1985). *Green and Pleasant Land? Social Change in Rural England*. Hounslow: Wildwood House Limited, pp. 32.

291 Ambrose, P. (1974). *The Quiet Revolution: Social Change in a Sussex Village 1871- 1971*. London: Sussex University Press by Clarke, Irwin and Co., pp. 97-99.

292 Champion, T. and Watkins, C. (1991). Introduction. In Champion, T. and Watkins, C. (Eds.). *People in the Countryside: Studies of Social Change in Rural Britain*. London: Paul Chapman Publishing Ltd., pp. 4-6.

293 Briggs, A. (1994). *A Social History of England*: New Edition. London: Weidenfield & Nicholson (First published 1983), pp. 318.

294 WSA G24/225/34.

295 WSA G24/132/57.

296 Cattell, J. and Falconer, K. (1995). *Swindon: Legacy of a Railway Town*. London: HMSO, pp. x. [WSHC SWI.385].

297 Pugh, P. (1988). *The History of Blue Circle*. Cambridge: Cambridge Business Publishing, pp. 150-151. [WSHC WEB.666].

298 WSA G17/132/3.

299 Ibid.

300 Pugh, P. (1988). *The History of Blue Circle*. Cambridge: Cambridge Business Publishing, pp. 151. [WSHC WEB.666].

301 Calder, A. (1992). *The People's War: Britain 1939-45*. London: Pimlico (Original work published 1969), pp. 315-316. [WSHC 941.084].

302 Hennessy, P. (1992). *Never Again: Britain 1945-51*. London: Penguin Books Ltd., pp. 163. [WSHC 941.0854].

303 Malpass, P. (2003). The Wobbly Pillar? Housing and the British Postwar Welfare State. *Journal of Social Policy*, 32(4), pp. 594. [PRO CAB 87/9, R(44)153].

304 Ibid., pp. 593-594.

305 MacKay, R. (1999). *The Test of War: Inside Britain 1939-45*. London: UCL Press, pp. 216.

306 Malpass, P. (2003). The Wobbly Pillar? Housing and the British Postwar Welfare State. *Journal of Social Policy*,

32(4), pp. 597-600.

307 Ibid., pp. 601-602.

308 Ibid., pp. 595. [PRO CAB 117/125 Post War Housing Policy, appendix iv, para. 3].

309 Ibid., pp. 594-596.

310 Tomlinson, J. (1998). Why so Austere? The British Welfare State of the 1940s. *Journal of Social Policy*, 27(1), pp. 66.

311 Malpass, P. (2003). The Wobbly Pillar? Housing and the British Postwar Welfare State. *Journal of Social Policy*, 32(4), pp. 596.

312 WSA G4/132/20.

313 Calder, A. (1992). *The People's War: Britain 1939-45*. London: Pimlico (Original work published 1969), pp. 316. [WSHC 941.084].

314 WSA G5/132/27.

315 WSA G7/132/31.

316 MacKay, R. (1999). *The Test of War: Inside Britain 1939-45*. London: UCL Press, pp. 216.

317 Calder, A. (1992). *The People's War: Britain 1939-45*. London: Pimlico (Original work published 1969), pp. 585. [WSHC 941.084].

318 Briggs, A. (1994). *A Social History of England*: New Edition. London: Weidenfield & Nicholson (First published 1983), pp. 314.

319 Hopkins, H. (1964). *New Look: A Social History of the Forties and Fifties*. London: Secker & Warburg Readers Union, pp. 45.

320 Kynaston, D. (2007). *A World to Build: Austerity Britain*. London: Bloomsbury, pp. 52-53.

321 WSA G4/132/32.

322 WSA G4/132/20.

323 Hennessy, P. (1992). *Never Again: Britain 1945-51*. London: Penguin Books Ltd., pp. 174. [WSHC 941.0854].

324 Kynaston, D. (2007). *A World to Build: Austerity Britain*. London: Bloomsbury, pp. 72.

325 WSA G4/132/4.

326 Dinton Historical Society. (2003). *Days of Cowslips and Skylarks: Dinton Looks Back*. Salisbury: A & D Media

Ltd., pp. 15. [WSHC DIN.940].

327 Parsons, M. (2009). *Cricklade Revealed: Part 7 - Social Life during the Second World War*. Marion Parsons, pp. 22. [WSHC CRI.949].

328 Summers, J. (2015). *Fashion on the Ration*. London: Profile Books in Partnership with the Imperial War Museum, pp. 170.

329 Hopkins, H. (1964). *New Look: A Social History of the Forties and Fifties*. London: Secker & Warburg Readers Union, pp. 48.

330 Hennessy, P. (1992). *Never Again: Britain 1945-51*. London: Penguin Books Ltd., pp. 174. [WSHC 941.0854].

331 WSA G3/132/3.

332 WSA G3/132/63.

333 WSA G1/132/15.

334 WSA G3/132/64.

335 WSA G3/132/40.

336 WSA G12/225/1.

337 WSA G5/132/27.

338 Hennessy, P. (1992). *Never Again: Britain 1945-51*. London: Penguin Books Ltd., pp. 174. [WSHC 941.0854].

339 WSA G3/132/3.

340 WSA G4/132/4.

341 Parsons, M. (2009). *Cricklade Revealed: Part 7 - Social Life during the Second World War*. Marion Parsons, pp. 21-22. [WSHC CRI.949].

342 WSA G3/132/3.

343 WSA G5/225/5.

344 WSA G3/132/2.

345 WSA G6/132/16.

346 Ivan Clark, personal communication, 5/4/2014.

347 WSA G24/132/332.

348 WSA G24/132/356.

349 WSA G6/132/22.

350 WSA G3/132/41.

351 Ibid.

352 WSA G3/132/3.

353 Parsons, M. (2011). *Cricklade Revealed: Part 8 - Social Life during the Second World War*. Marion Parsons, pp. 16. [WSHC CRI.949].

354 WSA G4/132/4.

355 WSA 2857/3. [Written in minute book as November 1946 in error; should read 1945].
356 WSA G24/132/961.
357 Malpass, P. (2003). The Wobbly Pillar? Housing and the British Postwar Welfare State. *Journal of Social Policy*, 32(4), pp. 589-592.
358 Ibid., pp. 603-604.
359 Cole, I. and Goodchild, B. (2001). Social Mix and the 'Balanced Community' in British Housing Policy - a Tale of Two Epochs. *GeoJournal*, 51, pp. 353.
360 Malpass, P. (2003). The Wobbly Pillar? Housing and the British Postwar Welfare State. *Journal of Social Policy*, 32(4), pp. 601.
361 Cole, I. and Goodchild, B. (2001). Social Mix and the 'Balanced Community' in British Housing Policy - a Tale of Two Epochs. *GeoJournal*, 51, pp. 353.
362 Jackson, B. (2005). Revisionism Reconsidered: 'Property-owning Democracy' and Egalitarian Strategy in Post-War Britain. *Twentieth Century British History*, 16(4), pp. 419-424.
363 WSA G24/225/11.
364 WSA G6/132/110.
365 WSA G5/132/73.
366 Ibid.
367 WSA G5/132/27.
368 WSA G4/132/60.
369 WSA F14/001/1.
370 WSA G5/132/73.
371 WSA G18/132/16.
372 WSA G7/132/13.
373 WSA G3/132/8.
374 Chippenham and District Committee for Festival of Britain. (1951). *Chippenham Wilts Festival of Britain*. Chippenham: Chippenham and District Committee for Festival of Britain, pp. 10. [WSHC CHP.394].
375 WSA G7/132/11.
376 Collier, C. (1992). *Southern Electric: A History*. Maidenhead: Southern Electric, pp. 78-84. [WSHC AAA.625].
377 WSA F14/001/1.

378 Collier, C. (1992). *Southern Electric: A History*. Maidenhead: Southern Electric, pp. 85-86. [WSHC AAA.625].
379 WSA F1/001/1.
380 Hopkins, H. (1964). *New Look: A Social History of the Forties and Fifties*. London: Secker & Warburg Readers Union, pp. 103.
381 WSA F5/530/27.
382 Tanner, H. & Hanff, D. (1995). *Out of Nazi Germany*. London: Impact Books, pp. 45-46. [WSHC XTA.921].
383 Hopkins, H. (1964). *New Look: A Social History of the Forties and Fifties*. London: Secker & Warburg Readers Union, pp. 464.
384 WSA G24/132/371.
385 Swindon. (2015). Retrieved July 2, 2015 from the Oxford Dictionaries website http://www.oxforddictionaries.com/definition/english/Swindon?q=swindon
386 WSA G24/132/371.
387 Hopkins, H. (1964). *New Look: A Social History of the Forties and Fifties*. London: Secker & Warburg Readers Union, pp. 465.
388 Hennessy, P. (1992). *Never Again: Britain 1945-51*. London: Penguin Books Ltd., pp. 441. [WSHC 941.0854].
389 Kynaston, D. (2007). *A World to Build: Austerity Britain*. London: Bloomsbury, pp. 275.
390 Hennessy, P. (1992). *Never Again: Britain 1945-51*. London: Penguin Books Ltd., pp. 441. [WSHC 941.0854].
391 Kynaston, D. (2007). *A World to Build: Austerity Britain*. London: Bloomsbury, pp. 274-275.
392 Hennessy, P. (1992). *Never Again: Britain 1945-51*. London: Penguin Books Ltd., pp. 440-442. [WSHC 941.0854].
393 Experience of Work. (2015). Retrieved July 2, 2015 from the Wiltshire & Swindon History Centre website http://www.wshc.eu/sound-clips/16-wshc/education/183-experiences-of-

work.html

394 Reactions and Racism. (2013). Retrieved July 2, 2015 from the Wiltshire & Swindon History Centre website http://www.wshc.eu/sound-clips/16-wshc/education/186-reactions-and-racism.html

395 Leaving Home. (2013). Retrieved July 2, 2015 from the Wiltshire & Swindon History Centre website http://www.wshc.eu/sound-clips/16-wshc/education/184-leaving-home.html

396 Browning, B. (2005). *EKCO's of Cowbridge*. Malmesbury: Cowbridge Publishing, pp. 61. [WSHC MAL.620].

397 WSA G4/132/21.

398 WSA G4/132/4.

399 WSA G24/132/351.

400 Ibid., [Circular 176/45].

401 Ibid.

401a WSA G6/132/12.

401b Ibid.

401c Defective Properties/Concrete Properties. (2015). Retrieved July 2, 2015 from the Taylor Made Solutions website http://prchouserepairs.co.uk/prefab-houses.html

402 BISF Steel Framed Houses are not Classed as Defective Housing. (2015). Retrieved July 2, 2015 from the Taylor Made Solutions website http://prchouserepairs.co.uk/blog/viewpost/215.html

403 WSA G3/132/63.

404 WSA G24/132/360.

405 Kynaston, D. (2007). *A World to Build: Austerity Britain*. London: Bloomsbury, pp. 102.

406 WSA F1/100/1.

407 Kynaston, D. (2007). *A World to Build: Austerity Britain*. London: Bloomsbury, pp. 102-103.

408 Parsons, M. (2009). *Cricklade Revealed: Part 7 - Social Life during the Second World War*. Marion Parsons, pp. 24. [WSHC CRI.949].

409 Margaret Monk, personal communication, 3.6.2014.

410 Kynaston, D. (2007). *A World to Build: Austerity Britain*. London:

Bloomsbury, pp. 155.

411 Hennessy, P. (1992). *Never Again: Britain 1945-51*. London: Penguin Books Ltd., pp. 182. [WSHC 941.0854].

412 WSA G5/132/27.

413 WSA G4/132/20.

414 Hennessy, P. (1992). *Never Again: Britain 1945-51*. London: Penguin Books Ltd., pp. 173. [WSHC 941.0854].

415 WSA G4/132/20.

416 Ibid.

417 Briggs, A. (1994). *A Social History of England*: New Edition. London: Weidenfield & Nicholson (First published 1983), pp. 318.

418 WSA G4/132/20.

419 WSA G5/132/27.

420 Harris, J. (1992). Society and the State in 20th Century Britain. In Thompson, F. M. L. (Ed.). *The Cambridge History of Britain 1759-1950* (Vol. 3, Social Agencies and Institutions, pp. 98). Cambridge: Cambridge University Press.

421 Hennessy, P. (1992). *Never Again: Britain 1945-51*. London: Penguin Books Ltd., pp. 169. [WSHC 941.0854].

422 WSA G24/132/357.

423 Richards, J. (2011). Life in Britain for German Prisoners of War. Retrieved June 11, 2015 from BBC website http://www.bbc.co.uk/history/british/britain_wwtwo/german_pows_01.shtml

424 Thomas, R. (2003). *Twentieth Century Military Recording Project: Prisoner of War Camps (1939-1948)*. Swindon: English Heritage, pp. 14. [https://www.english-heritage.org.uk/publications/prisoner-of-war-camps/prisoner-of-war-camps.pdf].

425 Hennessy, P. (1992). *Never Again: Britain 1945-51*. London: Penguin Books Ltd., pp. 173. [WSHC 941.0854].

426 Ibid., pp. 210.

427 Tomlinson, J. (1992). Planning: Debate and Policy in the 1940s.

Twentieth Century British History, 3(2), pp. 161.

428 WSA G24/132/333.

429 WSA G4/132/20.

430 WSA G4/132/24.

431 WSA G4/132/21.

432 WSA G4/132/20.

433 WSA G24/132/319.

434 WSA G24/225/66.

435 WSA G24/132/333.

436 WSA G4/132/32.

437 WSA G4/132/20.

438 WSA G24/225/35.

439 WSA G4/132/40.

440 WSA G4/132/27.

441 WSA G4/132/15.

442 WSA G4/132/21.

443 WSA G4/132/20.

444 Hennessy, P. (1992). *Never Again: Britain 1945-51*. London: Penguin Books Ltd., pp. 17. [WSHC 941.0854].

445 Ibid., pp. 170.

446 WSA G24/132/357.

447 Hennessy, P. (1992). *Never Again: Britain 1945-51*. London: Penguin Books Ltd., pp. 209. [WSHC 941.0854].

448 WSA G24/132/355.

449 WSA G4/132/20.

450 WSA G24/132/351.

451 WSA G4/132/32.

452 WSA G4/132/13.

453 WSA G4/132/14.

454 WSA G3/132/64.

455 WSA G3/132/3.

456 WSA G7/132/31.

457 WSA G8/132/31.

458 Wiltshire Federation of Women's Institutes (1993). *Wiltshire Within Living Memory*. Newbury: Countryside Books, pp. 227-228. [WSHC AAA.949].

459 Parsons, M. (2009). *Cricklade Revealed: Part 7 - Social Life during the Second World War*. Marion Parsons, pp. 2. [WSHC CRI.949].

460 Ibid., pp. 25.

461 WSA. G24/132/305.

462 WSA G6/132/14.

463 WSA G4/132/1.

464 WSA G11/132/21.

465 WSA G4/132/20.

466 WSA G3/132/10.

467 WSA G6/132/20.

468 WSA 981/27.

469 Hopkins, H. (1964). *New Look: A Social History of the Forties and Fifties*. London: Secker & Warburg Readers Union, pp. 91.

470 Kynaston, D. (2007). *A World to Build: Austerity Britain*. London: Bloomsbury, pp. 249.

471 Ibid., pp. 42-43.

472 Kynaston, D. (2007). *A World to Build: Austerity Britain*. London: Bloomsbury, pp. 42-43.

473 Smith, H. (1986). *War and Social Change: British Society in the Second World War*. Manchester: Manchester University Press, pp. 153.

474 Kynaston, D. (2007). *A World to Build: Austerity Britain*. London: Bloomsbury, pp. 109-113.

475 Hennessy, P. (1992). *Never Again: Britain 1945-51*. London: Penguin Books Ltd., pp. 445. [WSHC 941.0854].

476 Kynaston, D. (2007). *A World to Build: Austerity Britain*. London: Bloomsbury, pp. 268.

477 Hennessy, P. (1992). *Never Again: Britain 1945-51*. London: Penguin Books Ltd., pp. 445. [WSHC 941.0854].

478 Kynaston, D. (2007). *A World to Build: Austerity Britain*. London: Bloomsbury, pp. 202.

479 Ibid., pp. 217.

480 Ibid., pp. 224.

481 Parsons, M. (2011). *Cricklade Revealed: Part 8 - Social Life during the Second World War*. Marion Parsons, pp. 26. [WSHC CRI.949].

482 Ibid., pp. 29-30.

483 Hennessy, P. (1992). *Never Again: Britain 1945-51*. London: Penguin Books Ltd., pp. 425-426. [WSHC 941.0854].

484 Henderson. P. (1995). 100 Years in Corsham Parish. Corsham: Corsham

Parish Council, pp. 86. [WSHC COR.940].

485 WSA F14/427/9.

486 Kynaston, D. (2007). *A World to Build: Austerity Britain*. London: Bloomsbury, pp. 35.

487 Ibid., pp. 174.

488 Hennessy, P. (1992). *Never Again: Britain 1945-51*. London: Penguin Books Ltd., pp. 436. [WSHC 941.0854].

489 Kynaston, D. (2007). *A World to Build: Austerity Britain*. London: Bloomsbury, pp. 244-245.

490 Henderson. P. (1995). *100 Years in Corsham Parish*. Corsham: Corsham Parish Council, pp. 82. [WSHC COR.940].

491 *Wiltshire Times*, 6.6.1953.

492 The People of Fovant. (2005). *Fovant: Pages from our History*. East Knoyle: Hobnob Press, pp. 83. [WSHC FOV.940].

493 Henderson. P. (1995). *100 Years in Corsham Parish*. Corsham: Corsham Parish Council, pp. 88. [WSHC COR.940].

494 Lane, C. and White, P. (1999). *Warminster in the Twentieth Century*. The Warminster History Society: Warminster, pp. 27. [WSHC WAR.949].

495 Borough of Chippenham. (1953). *Souvenir Programme of the Coronation of Her Majesty Queen Elizabeth II*. Chippenham: Chippenham Coronation Executive Committee, unpaginated. [WSHC CHP.394].

496 *Salisbury Journal*, 5.6.1953. [WSHC Microform Collection].

497 *Wiltshire Times*, 6.6.1953. [WSHC Microform Collection].

498 Wiltshire News, 6.6.1953. [WSHC Microform Collection].

499 *Wiltshire Times*, 6.6.1953. [WSHC Microform Collection].

500 Ibid.

501 Morgan, K. (1990). *The People's Peace: British History 1945-1989*. Oxford: Oxford University Press, pp. 28.

502 Davis, J. (2013). To Locate and Evaluate Local Government Archive Material for North Wiltshire held at the Wiltshire and Swindon History Centre, to Discover its use as a Source for Studying Social Change from 1939-55. (Unpublished master's dissertation). University of Aberystwyth, Aberystwyth, pp. 11.

503 Ibid., pp. 13.

504 Hennessy, P. (1992). *Never Again: Britain 1945-51*. London: Penguin Books Ltd., pp. 424-425. [WSHC 941.0854].

505 Ibid., pp. 449-450.

506 Mock, J. (1997). *Bradford on Avon & District: The War Years (1939-1945)*. J. H. Mock, pp. 58. [BRD.949].

507 Hennessy, P. (1992). *Never Again: Britain 1945-51*. London: Penguin Books Ltd., pp. 309. [WSHC 941.0854].

Postscript

1 Davis, J. (2013). To Locate and Evaluate Local Government Archive Material for North Wiltshire held at the Wiltshire and Swindon History Centre, to Discover its use as a Source for Studying Social Change from 1939-55. (Unpublished master's dissertation). University of Aberystwyth, Aberystwyth, pp. 10.

2 Zweiniger-Bargielowska, I. (2000). *Austerity in Britain: Rationing, Controls and Consumption*. Oxford: Oxford University Press, pp. 645.

3 Davis, J. (2013). To Locate and Evaluate Local Government Archive Material for North Wiltshire held at the Wiltshire and Swindon History Centre, to Discover its use as a Source for Studying Social Change from 1939-55. (Unpublished master's dissertation). University of Aberystwyth, Aberystwyth, pp. 13.

4 Hopkins, H. (1964). *New Look: A Social History of the Forties and Fifties*.

London: Secker & Warburg Readers Union.

5 Calder, A. (1992). *The People's War: Britain 1939-45*. London: Pimlico (Original work published 1969), pp. 17. [WSHC 941.084].

6 Davis, J. (2013). To Locate and Evaluate Local Government Archive Material for North Wiltshire held at the Wiltshire and Swindon History Centre, to Discover its use as a Source for Studying Social Change from 1939-55. (Unpublished master's dissertation). University of Aberystwyth, Aberystwyth, pp. 11.

7 Hopkins, H. (1964). *New Look: A Social History of the Forties and Fifties*. London: Secker & Warburg Readers Union, pp. 161.

8 Jackson, B. (2005). Revisionism Reconsidered: 'Property-owning Democracy' and Egalitarian Strategy in Post-War Britain. *Twentieth Century British History*, 16(4), pp. 419-424.

9 Davis, J. (2013). To Locate and Evaluate Local Government Archive Material for North Wiltshire held at the Wiltshire and Swindon History Centre, to Discover its use as a Source for Studying Social Change from 1939-55. (Unpublished master's dissertation). University of Aberystwyth, Aberystwyth, pp. 17.

10 Orwin, C. (Ed.) (1944). *Country Planning. A Study of Rural Problems*. National Institute of Agricultural Engineering.

11 Davis, J. (2013). To Locate and Evaluate Local Government Archive Material for North Wiltshire held at the Wiltshire and Swindon History Centre, to Discover its use as a Source for Studying Social Change from 1939-55. (Unpublished master's dissertation). University of Aberystwyth, Aberystwyth, pp. 19-20. sociationparishcouncilsallotments1951. pdf/.

Index

This is an index of persons, places and subjects. Principal references to subjects are printed in **bold** text. Names of RAF bases are listed together under RAF; Town halls are listed together under Town halls. Places are in Wiltshire unless otherwise stated.

Printed in May 2023
by Rotomail Italia S.p.A., Vignate (MI) - Italy